BROAD
are the
BRANCHES
AN AMERICAN SAGA

⹝ *Part I* ⹝
DRIVEN

BROOKIE CONDIE SWALLOW

BookWise Publishing
3138 Matterhorn Drive
West Jordan, UT 84084

www.bookwise.com

Cover paintings: *Wagons in the Shallows* and *Eventide* by artist Carl Seyboldt
Cover and book design by Eden Graphics, LLC
Photographs on pages 87 – 94 by Hyrum P. Haynes and Grover Swallow

Library of Congress Cataloging-in-Publication Data
Swallow, Brookie Condie
Driven /Brookie Condie Swallow
LCN 2012918399
ISBN 978-1-60645-105-2

10 9 8 7 6 5 4 3 2 1

First Printing

This true narrative is dedicated to
all of our Early American Ancestors
and their millions of descendants
and foreign additions
who have braved the elements,
ever struggling,
and with the help of God,
worked to create, build, and expand
this great country of
the United States of America
and the individual freedoms
of all mankind
that it represents.

Contents

~ Broad are the Branches ~

Part I: DRIVEN begins with JOHN's parents and grandparents in frontier Ralls County, Missouri. These great-grandparents and their histories have been researched extensively and recorded as accurately as presently available. Not all accounts are in total agreement, but differences are indicated. Part I moves these "driven" people, chased by armies and Indians, across the west to the shores of the Pacific during the Mexican War and ends in the early 1860s in Utah Territory, then back to Missouri during the United States Civil War.

Part II: STANDING FIRM begins with another U. S. Army moving into Salt Lake City and Northern Utah, and tells of many depredations during the Black Hawk Indian War in central Utah. The LDS Church expands into Nevada and Idaho, and Utah finally gains statehood. The story moves through some eventful politics and amazing spiritual experiences within the three states, including some more current events. Early American ancestry and their relations are discovered beginning in 1607 in Virginia and then expanded throughout the original colonies.

Part III: REBELLION tells about the thirteen original colonies in 1744 and the "Broad Branches" during the French and Indian War, followed by events and battles that unite these separate colonies with the signing of the Declaration of Independence, forming the United States of America. It ends with the first major victory at Saratoga and the hope it brings.

Part IV: UNITED STATES? proceeds through the discouragement of Valley Forge and other devastating winters, extending into the war in the Southern states with the final victory. The fragmented, poverty-stricken states unite again under a new constitution, but differences persist, and another war erupts with England, aided by their loyal Indian allies. Still seeking unity, the book ends with the death of President ABRAHAM LINCOLN.

☙ FOREWORD ☙

Brookie Condie Swallow is as ambitious as she is eloquent in describing the intertwining branches of the Ivie and Allred family histories with the unfolding history of The Church of Jesus Christ of Latter-day Saints (the Mormons) and the tapestry of American history.

Though not all readers will have ancestors mentioned in the fascinating saga, nearly everyone will have ancestors who were contemporary to the times described in detail. Brookie Swallow has conducted thorough background research for *Broad are the Branches* so the reader is confident in the historical facts forming the foundation of the work, but she stops short of telling us more than we ever wanted to know about a given topic.

The cast of characters is animated by well-selected narratives which truly bring the subjects to life because we are hearing of events by witnesses in their own words. This is the first volume of a four volume series and readers will be anxiously awaiting the arrival of Volume II.

—SPENCER J. CONDIE

~ Introduction ~

TRENTON WOLFGANG RUSHTON

When my grandson, TRENTON, approached the age of five, his greatest desire was to be an Admiral-Captain Pirate when he grew older. While visiting, I was told that pirates must have swords and pistols, and it is good if they know karate. After a fierce demonstration of sword play and karate kicks, he explained that, of course, he would be a good pirate and perhaps a fake sword and pistol would do.

Trenton drew treasure maps and explained we must follow them to find the treasure. His favorite shirt was a worn-out black one with a white skull and cross bones on the front. The Jolly Roger flew defiantly over his cabin and sailor ropes hung from its entrance in his backyard playground. Living near Boston, we explored the U.S.S. Constitution in the harbor. After many previous visits, he still carefully examined the cannons on both decks and stood proudly when chosen to be the "powder monkey," who brings the ammunition to fire the cannon.

Compiling and writing this book, *Broad are the Branches,* has been like a long treasure hunt. There have been clues in libraries, courthouses, old treasure trunks, museums, maps, church records, cemeteries, computers, and trails that go north, south, east, and west in this saga of American ancestors, distant cousins, and more distant relations-in-law, and friends. Their daily struggles helped create and preserve our liberties, though some were agents of their destruction.

To really understand who we are and what we have been given, we must go back into the past and actually become acquainted with these individuals, rather than just spinning the facts as we look back from the present. Identifying and empathizing with their truthful difficulties and challenges in establishing our nation and its freedoms brings new appreciation of what we have and hopefully inspires us to greater personal heights to preserve them, rather than selfishly desecrate and destroy. I have focused on my own relations, whose names I have capitalized for quick identification, because I know more about them, not to be exclusive, but rather inclusive of everyday people everywhere. We are all more closely related than we realize—we all have known and unknown broad branches that intermingle in innumerable ways.

I did find a pirate, a distant fourth-cousin, SAMUEL MASON, who didn't measure up as a good pirate, but he never robbed the churchmen. I found ship captains, shipbuilders, and a distant first-cousin, ESEK HOPKINS, a descendant of the *Mayflower* pilgrims, who was given the honor of being the first "Commander in Chief" or Commodore of the United States Continental Navy. Distant sixth-cousin J.P. MORGAN should be mentioned. He had the money and worldly treasure chests. Some consider him top of the list of robber barons; however, maybe he was sometimes a good robber with a fake sword and pistol, for this financial genius had sufficient integrity to stabilize our nation and the international financial world at troubled times of panic and left us one of his treasure chests, The Metropolitan Museum of Fine Arts in New York City. But if his personal desire was to gain wealth and power, and enslave and walk upon humanity for his own secret purposes, destroying their right to think and act for themselves, he is certainly among the worst of villains. Another distant sixth cousin was ABRAHAM LINCOLN, whose moral character has stood strong through the ages.

My oldest son, TOM, when two and a half years old, aspired to the great career of cowboy. His grandmother CONDIE bought him the whole wardrobe including boots, shirt, Levis, hat, and his two toy six-shooters. He was honored that year in the centerfold of the "Preston Rodeo Program" riding his homemade rocking horse as "Preston's Youngest Cowboy." Preston, Idaho, prided itself in its clean streets and would run water down the gutters of their paved main street to help with debris. One day our son pulled away from my hand and with his tummy on the sidewalk, tried to drink from the gutter—because cowboys drink that way from streams. Shortly after, we took him to see Disney's *Peter Pan*. The cowboy lost out. He then became, in turn, Michael, John, Mr. Smee or Captain Hook.

I have not hesitated to report the disturbing court records or disagreeable stories about some relations, and there are some colorful ones. The closets have been searched as well as the headlines. Unfortunately, court records are not usually designed to flatter the accused, but hiding the truth usually distorts events. In reading, remember our Savior's words, *"He that is without sin among you, let him first cast a stone"* [John 8:7] and *"For with what judgment ye judge, ye shall be judged: and with what measure ye mete, it shall be measured to you again."* [Matthew 7:2] My husband, GROVER SWALLOW, memorized this poem in his youth and has used it many times since.

THE MAN IN THE GLASS
(AUTHOR UNKNOWN)

When you get what you want in your struggle for self

And the world makes you King for a day,

Then step to the mirror and look at yourself,

To see what that guy has to say.

For it isn't your husband or brother or wife

whose judgment upon you must pass;

But the one who counts most in your life

Is the one staring back from the glass.

He's the one you must please—

Never mind all the rest

For he's with you clear up to the end;

And you've passed your most difficult, dangerous test,

If the man in the glass is your friend.

You can be like Jack Horner and chisel a plum

And get pats on the back as you pass;

But your final reward will be heartache and tears

If you've cheated the man in the glass.

⸺ A NOTE FROM THE AUTHOR ⸺

In attempting to organize these "Broad Branches," I have limited this broad expansion mostly to the area of the United States of America and added only the stories from the various countries and ships that brought my ancestors and their relations to these shores. It has thus become an "American Saga," beginning around 1607 on the Norfolk peninsula of Virginia and the Jamestown settlement.

If there are two central characters in this drama, it would have to be JOHN LEHI IVIE, born in Missouri in 1833, and MARY CATHERINE BARTON, born in Pennsylvania in 1837. They traveled as young children on their journey west across the great plains of the mid-west from Winter Quarters [Florence, Nebraska], and Council Bluffs, Iowa, to Salt Lake City in Brigham Young's first company of 9 June 1848. Their union in marriage on 16 May 1852 was sealed in the President's Office in Salt Lake City on 28 July 1852—uniting my progenitors of the North with those of the South a decade before the American Civil War began.

Whenever possible, I have tried to quote the actual words of the historical characters, and these quotations have been given without changing their spelling or grammar. Some of the connections might be questionable for records were scarce in those early colonizing days. I wanted to tell this story through the eyes of the common people, and let my numerous relations tell their stories in their own words, if available, but much of this book contains the related histories of their more diligent peers who took the time to write them down. I give my sincere thanks to all the multitude of authors whose work has contributed to this collection; *some are unknown and I apologize to those whose names have been forgotten.*

—BROOKIE CONDIE SWALLOW

⌐ Cast of Characters ⌐

All passed on to a happier world, but not forgotten!

JOHN LEHI IVIE, known as the colonel in the Utah militia in his later life. Born in Florida, Missouri, 11 June 1833. He was my great-grandfather, and the husband of

MARY CATHERINE BARTON, who was born in Pennsylvania, 30 June 1837. My great-grandmother, and daughter of

JOHN BARTON and **SUSANNAH WILKINSON,** also of Pennsylvania. His parents were NOAH BARTON and MARY COOLEY of Hunterdon County, New Jersey.

AARON WILKINSON, father of SUSANNAH WILKINSON, who married MARY SUSANNAH POYER, both of Pennsylvania.

JAMES RUSSELL IVIE, who was born in Georgia in 1803, father of JOHN LEHI IVIE, married to **ELIZA McKEE FAUSETT** in Tennessee. She was the daughter of RICHARD FAUSETT and MARY McKEE. His father and mother were

ANDERSON IVIE, born in Virginia in 1774, and **SARAH ALLRED** of North Carolina. They are the parents of JAMES RUSSELL IVIE. SARAH ALLRED, is a sister of

JAMES ALLRED, the father of **ISAAC ALLRED,** who was killed by

THOMAS C. [or K.] **IVIE,** whose trial is in the final chapters. He is a brother of JAMES RUSSELL IVIE.

JAMES ALEXANDER (JIM) IVIE, older brother of JOHN LEHI IVIE. Accused of starting the (Utah) Walker Indian War.

JAMES OSCAR IVIE, born in Mount Pleasant, Utah, in 1863, son of JOHN LEHI IVIE. Married **ANNIE CATHERINE MORTENSEN,** of Salina, Utah, whose parents came from Denmark.

~ 1 ~

DELAY THE CURFEW
INDIAN STORIES AND GRANDPARENTS
(ABOUT 1933)

The blizzard was blowing the snow into six-foot drifts on the north of the two-story log house on our ranch, near Carey, Idaho. It would make good slides tomorrow when the crust had formed. I fought for my place on my grandfather's knee. There were three others that I had to contend with. Our grandparents were visiting from Salina, located in central Utah.

"Tell us a story!" we sang out in unison.

"What kind of a story?" he asked us with a twinkle in his eye.

"An Indian story!" It was always an Indian story with Grandfather JAMES OSCAR IVIE. He was thin, a little stooped, and walked with a cane. He was proud of his canes, most of which were hand carved and had a history that could be told with warmth and humor. He wore a black suit and a white shirt with blue pinstripes, and always a vest with his gold watch that we listened to and tried to discover how it opened.

"Well," he began, "one day when I was five years old, my father was taking us to Thistle in the wagon, when some Indians started to chase us. Father told me to get down under some boxes. Mother drove the team, and he got his rifle. I kept real low. The arrows were whizzing past, and I was scared." I watched his hand. It shook constantly in the "pill rolling" fashion. Earlier in his life he had been thrown from a horse and injured his wrist. He had told the family that maybe this was part of the reason for the shaking palsy he was then suffering from. (Parkinson's Disease was not part of our vocabulary at that time.)

"Going up a little hill," he continued, "the wagon slowed down, and I poked my head up just a little and saw that the Indians were closer. I snuggled down again and waited; waited to see the head of an Indian leering over the wagon at me. Mother was whipping the team and they were running with all the strength they had. Downhill the wagon rolled faster and jogged over the rocks making the boxes jolt and change positions."

"Father (JOHN LEHI IVIE) called to Mother, 'Turn off at this next fork.' The wagon slid around the corner. Father took the reins and brought the team to a halt in some thick trees and shrubbery. Then we peered carefully over the sideboard of the wagon and watched as the Indians came over the top of the hill and continued on the other road."

"Did they come back?" I asked.

"No, not that time, but once . . ."

"Father, I think we better let the children get to bed now," my mother called from the kitchen.

"Please, one more story?"

"Not tonight."

"Let Grandmother tell us a poem then." We bargained for every minute. It was cold upstairs with no heat. We could wrap a flatiron in a newspaper. There were hot-water bottles, but not enough for all of us. The six flatirons were kept on the back of the black, coal-burning cook stove in the kitchen, and were very warm. Then, if we put our flannel pajamas on in front of the open oven and dashed upstairs quickly, sliding the wrapped flatirons down between the blanket sheets and cuddling close to our bed partner, with our feet on the wrapped flatirons, we were able to stay somewhat warm until our bodies warmed the ice-cold bedding.

"Please?"

Relenting, Mother consented to one poem. Grandmother (ANNIE CATHERINE MORTENSEN IVIE) had many long poems she had learned from memory. Our favorite was "Curfew Must Not Ring To-night," and it was very long. We tried for an encore, but patience was getting thin, so after family prayer with our pajamas on, we rolled our flatirons in the old newspaper and hurried upstairs.

50TH GOLDEN WEDDING ANNIVERSARY OF GRANDFATHER JAMES OSCAR IVIE
AND GRANDMOTHER ANNIE CATHERINE MORTENSEN IVIE

Grandmother ANNIE CATHERINE MORTENSEN IVIE, in all my memories, was quite deaf. She would cup her hand behind her best ear and look at us wistfully if she thought we were speaking to her. Dutifully, we would approach her and speak loudly into that ear. She would nod her head and answer in her kind, soft voice. I never actually heard what caused her deafness, but I suppose this weakness was created by one of the many communicable diseases that she had contracted earlier in her life.

When I was in the fourth grade, I had bragged to one of my friends that my grandmother had survived all the diseases. She looked at me skeptically and started naming all the diseases she could think of: red measles, German measles, chickenpox, scarlet fever, mumps, whooping cough, diphtheria, smallpox, and typhoid fever. These were the diseases we were very familiar with and, if contracted, our families would be quarantined by the Public Health Department and a big warning sign would be displayed on our door. I answered yes to all of them. My friend then asked if grandmother had survived malaria. Disappointed, I had to say no to this question, and she gave me that superior look.

My grandmother IVIE, of course, was not always deaf; but that was before I was born. On one occasion, however, her hearing was better than I appreciated. I was thirteen years old, and we had just moved to Twin Falls, Idaho, about three years after my father died of cancer 13 Jun 1939. Twin Falls had only two LDS (Latter-day Saint) wards at that time. We lived in the Second Ward and Grandmother IVIE was visiting with us from Salina for a few months. There was a boy in our ward that sat in the front with the deacons to pass the sacrament. He was probably a little older than I was and quite good-looking. Unfortunately, whenever I looked in his direction, he would have his head turned around looking at me. This made me feel uncomfortable.

One Sunday a dance was announced, and when the meeting ended, he approached me and asked me to go with him. I don't believe I said yes. I was highly embarrassed and very naïve. Some of the girls in my class encouraged me to go with him, but I remember feeling very hesitant. The evening of the dance, I happened to glance out the window and saw him coming in his best suit to pick me up. I was quite shocked, as nothing more had been said about it, so naturally, I was not ready. Grandmother, my brother JAMES, and I were the only ones home. I asked JAMES if he would go to the door and tell him I wasn't home. He refused. We were in our mother's bedroom. The doorbell rang. I was horrified when I heard Grandmother call out, "There's someone at the door." She had heard! I hid in my mother's walk-in clothes closet. JAMES quickly joined me. Grandmother called again when the doorbell rang the second time. Then we heard her footsteps. She went to the door and invited him in while she came to look for us. Eventually, she returned to the door and politely informed him she couldn't find anyone home. When we became brave enough to emerge from the closet, she informed us that a nice young man had just come by to see one of us.

In those days, she had a hearing aid that hung around her neck, but it was rare that she turned it on. It would usually squeal and make awful sounds if she tried to use it. Mother would help her adjust it. She spent many hours reading, crocheting, and looking for her glasses.

When she was a young woman, her mother sent her to Salt Lake City to learn the art of dressmaking. She became very skilled at it. She made her dress in the accompanying photograph of their wedding day.

At one Stake Conference in Sevier County with Brigham Young as the presiding authority and main speaker, President Young asked a wife of one of the Stake Presidency to stand up. He then requested that the audience look at her and explained that everything she was wearing was homemade: her hat, her handbag, her dress, and accessories. He complimented her and proceeded to exhort all of them to be as independent in their own clothing. Grandmother said she felt a little hurt. The dress, the hat, the handbag and accessories were homemade all right, but not by the wife of the Stake Presidency member who had taken the honors. Teenager "TREENY," as grandmother was called by those close to her, had done all the work—from sheep to completion.

One day when she was in her nineties, she told us that she believed she and one other woman were the only women in the state of Utah that could shear a sheep, clean the wool, card it, spin it, dye it, and weave it into cloth. One of my brothers-in-law was to later comment that at her age, he felt she might have some difficulty catching and holding the sheep while she sheared it.

Grandmother and Grandfather IVIE were involved in the local dramatics. On one occasion when Grandfather was being attacked by the villain of the melodrama with a fake club, my mother, a small child at the time, cried out from the audience, "Don't you hurt my Papa!"

"Curfew Must Not Ring Tonight" by Rose Hartwick Thorpe (1850-1939) was scanned from the page of one of Grandmother's old 1880 books. The title, cover, and author's name had worn off with much use.

CURFEW MUST NOT RING TO-NIGHT

by Rose Hartwick Thorpe (1850-1939)

ENGLAND's sun was setting
 Oe'r the hilltops far away,
Filling all the land with beauty
 At the close of one sad day;
 And its last rays kissed the forehead
Of a man and maiden fair,
He with step so slow and weakened,
 She with sunny, floating hair;
He with sad bowed head, and thoughtful,
 She, with lips so cold and white,
Struggling to keep back the murmur,
 "Curfew must not ring to-night!"

"Sexton," Bessie's white lips faltered,
 Pointing to the prison old,
With its walls so dark and gloomy,
 Walls so dark, and damp and cold,—
"I've a lover in the prison,
 Doomed this very night to die,
At the ringing of the Curfew,
 And no earthly help is nigh.
Cromwell will not come till sunset,"
 And her face grew strangely white,
As she spoke in husky whispers,
 "Curfew must not ring to-night!"

"Bessie," calmly spoke the sexton—
 Every word pierced her young heart
Like a thousand gleaming arrows,
 Like a deadly poisoned dart;
"Long, long years I've rung the Curfew
 From that gloomy, shadowed tower;
Every evening, just at sunset,
 It has tolled the twilight hour.
I have done my duty ever,
 Tried to do it just and right,
Now I'm old, I will not miss it;
 Girl, the Curfew rings to-night!"

Wild her eyes and pale her features,
 Stern and white her thoughtful brow,
As within her heart's deep centre,
 Bessie made a solemn vow.
She had listened while the judges
 Read, without a tear or sigh,
"At the ringing of the Curfew,
 Basil Underwood *must die.*"
And her breath came fast and faster,
 And her eyes grew large and bright—
One low murmur scarcely spoken—
 "Curfew *must not* ring to-night!"

She with light step bounded forward,
 Sprang within the old church-door,
Left the old man coming slowly,
 Paths he'd often trod before,
Not one moment paused the maiden,
 But with cheek and brow aglow,
Staggered up the gloomy tower,
 Where the bell swung to and fro;
Then she climbed the slimy ladder,
 Dark, without one ray of light,
Upward still, her pale lips saying,
 "Curfew shall not ring to-night."

She has reached the topmost ladder,
 O'er her hangs the great dark bell;
And the awful gloom beneath her,
 Like the pathway down to hell;
See, the ponderous tongue is swinging,
 'Tis the hour of Curfew now—
And the sight has chilled her bosom,
 Stopped her breath, and paled her brow.
Shall she let it ring? No, never!
 Her eyes flash with sudden light,
As she springs, and grasps it firmly—
 "Curfew shall not ring to-night!"

Out she swung, far out, the city
 Seemed a tiny speck below;
There, twixt heaven and earth suspended,
 As the bell swung to and fro.
And the half-deaf Sexton ringing,
 (Years he had not heard the bell,)
And he thought the twilight Curfew
 Rang young Basil's funeral knell;
Still the maiden, clinging firmly,
 Cheek and brow so pale and white,
Still her frightened heart's wild beating—
 "Curfew shall not ring tonight!"

It was o'er—the bell ceased swaying,
 And the maiden stepped once more
Firmly on the damp old ladder,
 Where for hundred years before
Human foot had not been planted:
 And whar she this night had done,
Should be told in long years after—
 As the rays of setting sun
Light the sky with mellow beauty,
 Aged sires with heads of white,
Tell the children why the Curfew
 Did not ring that one sad night.

O'er the distant hills comes Cromwell;
 Bessie saw him, and her brow,
Lately white with sickening terror,
 Glows with sudden beauty now.
At his feet she tells her story,
 Showed her hands all bruised and torn;
And her sweet young face so hagggard,
 With a look so sad and worn,
Touched his heart with sudden pity,
 Lit his eyes with misty light;
"Go! your lover lives," cried Cromwell;
 "Curfew shall not ring to-night."

Wide they flung the massive portals,
 Led the prisoner forth to die,
All his bright young life before him.
 Neath the darkening English sky,
Bessie came, with flying footsteps,
 Eyes aglow with lovelight sweet;
Kneeling on the turf beside him,
 Laid his pardon at his feet.
In his brave, strong arms he clasped her,
 Kissed the face upturned and white.
Whispered, "Darling, you have saved me.
 Curfew will not ring to-night."

~ 2 ~

WEST OF THE MISSISSIPPI IN
"MARK TWAIN" COUNTRY
ABOUT 1830

JOHN LEHI IVIE was born 11 June 1833 in Florida, Monroe County, Missouri. He was the fifth child of JAMES RUSSELL and ELIZA McKEE FAUSETT IVIE. His middle name, LEHI (from the *Book of Mormon*), is evidence that they belonged to the LDS Church when he was born. Florida, Missouri was also the birthplace of Samuel Langhorne Clemens, later known as *Mark Twain*, born 30 November 1835, also a fifth child. He described their common birthplace as "the almost invisible village of Florida."

During Thomas Jefferson's presidency in 1803, the nation was able to purchase the vast lands beyond the Mississippi River from Napoleon Bonaparte of France—land that had been given to France by Spain to avoid conflict with this ambitious and aggressive leader. The treaty forbad Napoleon to sell the land to the United States, but he did it anyway; he needed the money to transport his troops by sea to conquer England—a plan that never materialized because of the sagacity of the British. This territory, known as the Louisiana Purchase, had only Indians and the small early Spanish settlements along the Mississippi with the French mostly in New Orleans. Slavery was dividing the nation. Congress finally accepted the Missouri Compromise, and Missouri became an additional slave state in February 1821. Ralls County was established and then divided to create Monroe County where the sparsely settled Florida, Missouri, came into existence. Uncle WILLIAM SHELTON IVIE, young and unmarried, was the taxed owner of one of the lots.

The IVIEs came to Missouri in 1829. The third child of JAMES RUSSELL and SARAH ALLRED IVIE, tiny SARAH, was born 23 April 1829 en route from Tennessee, and their fourth child, JAMES A., was born 17 March 1830 in Florida, Missouri. They are listed in the 1830 Census. Monroe County's first deed sold and recorded was on the

> "second day of May in the year of our Lord, one thousand eight hundred and thirty-one, between ANDERSON IVIE and SARAH IVIE, his wife, of the one part, and John T. Grigsby of the other part, witnesseth, that the said ANDERSON IVIE and SARAH IVIE, his wife, for and in consideration of the sum of five hundred dollars, to them in hand paid in good and lawful money of the United States, by the said John T. Grigsby."

> John T. Grigsby and others placed a real estate advertisement in the Columbia *Missouri Intelligencer*. It read: "LOTS FOR SALE in the town of *FLORIDA*. The Proprietors will offer for sale at public auction, on the first day of June next, a quantity of lots, in the town of *FLORIDA*, on credit of six and twelve months; (purchasers giving bond with approved security.)

> "FLORIDA is situated on a ridge, half a mile from the junction, and immediately between, the North and South Forks of Salt River, Monroe County, Missouri, in the centre of an extensive and fertile region of country, which at present embraces several good settlements, and from the tide of emigration, will, in a very short time be densely populated. From the local situation of *Florida*, few places in the interior of Missouri possess equal advantages: Salt River is navigable for Keel, Batteaux, and Flat Boats, several months in the year, at the Forks; and arrangements have been made by the Legislature, for the opening of said river to the junction, which will make *Florida* the principal place of deposit for all the surplus produce raised within thirty or forty miles of said place. There are, at present, two good Grist, and one Saw Mill, (now in operation,) on each side and within half a mile of the Cite; and yet enough water power to put in operation an immense quantity of machinery.

> "*Florida* being situated about 30 miles from Hannibal, Palmyra, and New-London, and no probability of any Village being established between it and those places must cause an extensive business to concentrate at said place.

> "Persons wishing to purchase Town property will do well to call and examine for themselves. William Keenan, William N. Penn, H.A. Hickman, J. T. Grigsby, Robert Donaldson, John Witt.

> *Monroe County, April 1, 1831.*"

Mark Twain tells us that his parents came in the early 1830s, in answer to this ad, and that when he was born, there were a hundred people in the town, and he increased the population one per cent, 30 November 1835. He recalled,

"The village had two streets, each a couple of hundred yards long; the rest of the avenues mere lanes, with rail fences and cornfields on either side. Both the streets and the lanes were paved with the same material—tough black mud in wet times, deep dust in dry. Most of the houses were of logs—all of them, indeed, except three or four; these latter were frame ones. There were none of brick and none of stone."

By 1835 some relatives had left the area. Cousin ISAAC ALLRED, son of uncle JAMES ALLRED, tells us that: "In the year 1835, in the fall, I in company with my father and brothers with our families moved from Monroe to Clay County . . . bought land and made one crop."

They had joined their fellow *"Mormons"* who had been forcefully driven from Jackson County in November 1833. The IVIE families stayed in Monroe County that year. Some would go later to Caldwell County, but some never left. There were at least forty in ANDERSON and SARAH ALLRED IVIE's immediate family, counting spouses and their children.

Trying to locate ANDERSON IVIE's grave, my mother corresponded with Mary Janes of Stoutsville, Missouri, in October 1968. The following are excerpts from one of Mrs. Janes' letters:

"Florida doesn't have a post office just now. The cemetery has no sexton . . . We retired in 1952 and have been able to take care of the cemetery . . . There will be no charge; but a donation for 'Florida Cemetery Association' would sure be appreciated. There are so few people left who have relatives buried there. We get it mowed for $28.00 each time, it takes 4 times a year depending on the weather, and sometimes five times . . . You will hear they are building a Cannon Dam and Lake. They are working five miles east of Florida, it will flood many acres, but it will not bother Florida Cemetery. They plan to move 20 graves into the northwest corner."

There is a Mark Twain State Park in Florida, Missouri now. It includes Tom Sawyer Lake and Huckleberry Hill, the Buzzard's Roost Area that views the South Fork of the Salt River, the Mark Twain Birthplace Memorial Shrine, the Ulysses S. Grant's Headquarters in Florida, the picnic grounds, and an organized group area. There is a motel on part of the old ANDERSON IVIE farm land.

ANDERSON IVIE's tombstone was there, but no additional relatives' graves were found. The lake and dam are beautiful. Obviously few of the forecasts made by the early developers of Florida in their advertisement have materialized.

Mark Twain visited his uncle John Quarles' farm near Florida every summer after they moved to Hannibal until he was around thirteen years old. From *A Heavenly Place for a Boy,* his description includes:

"the solemn twilight and mystery of the deep woods . . . the far-off hammering of woodpeckers and the muffled drumming of wood pheasants in the remoteness of the forest . . . the prairie, and its loneliness and peace, and a vast hawk hanging motionless in the sky, with his wings spread wide . . . I can see the woods in their autumn dress, the oaks purple, the hickories washed with gold, the maples and the sumacs luminous with crimson fires . . . the blue clusters of wild grapes hanging among the foliage of the saplings, and I remember the taste of them and the smell . . . I know the taste of maple sap, and when to gather it, and how to arrange the troughs and the delivery tubes, and how to boil down the juice . . . I know how a prize watermelon looks when it is sunning its fat rotundity among pumpkin vines and 'siblins'; I know how to tell when it is ripe without 'plugging' it . . . I know the cracking sound it makes when the carving knife enters its end . . . I know how a boy looks behind a yard-long slice of that melon, and I know how he feels; for I have been there . . . I know how the nuts, taken in conjunction with winter apples, cider and doughnuts, make old people's old tales and old jokes sound fresh and crisp and enchanting, and juggle an evening away before you know what went with the time . . . I can see the white and black children grouped on the hearth, with the firelights playing on their faces and the shadows flickering upon the walls, clear back toward the cavernous gloom of the rear, and I can hear Uncle Dan'l telling the immortal tales which Uncle Remus Harris was to gather into his books and charm the world with, by and by . . . I can remember the howling of the wind and the quaking of the house on stormy nights, and how shut and cozy one felt, under the blankets, listening; and how the powdery snow used to sift in, around the sashes, and lie in little ridges on the floor and make the place look chilly in the morning and curb the wild desire to get up—in case there was any . . . I can remember how dismal the hoo-hooing of the owl and the wailing of the wolf, sent mourning by on the night wind. I remember the raging of the rain on that roof, summer nights, and how pleasant it was to lie and listen to it, and enjoy the white splendor of the lightning and the majestic booming and crashing of the thunder . . .

I remember the 'coon and 'possum hunts, nights with the Negroes, and the long marches through the black gloom of the woods, and the excitement which fired everybody when the distant bay of an experienced dog announced that the game was treed; then the wild scramblings and stumblings through briers and bushes and over roots to get to the spot; then the lighting of a fire and the felling of the tree . . . and weird picture it all made in the red glare—I remember it all well, and the delight that everyone got out of it, except the 'coon. I remember the pigeon seasons, when the birds would come in millions and cover the trees and by their weight break down the branches. They were clubbed to death with sticks; guns were not necessary . . . I remember the squirrel hunts, and the prairie-chicken hunts, and wild-turkey hunts, and all that; and how we turned out, mornings, while it was still dark, to go on these expeditions, and how chilly and dismal it was, and how often I regretted that I was well enough to go. A toot on a tin horn brought twice as many dogs as were needed, and in their happiness they raced and scampered about, and knocked small people down, and made no end of unnecessary noise. At the word, they vanished away toward the woods, and we drifted silently after them in the melancholy gloom. But presently the gray dawn stole over the world, the birds piped up, then the sun rose and poured light and comfort all around, everything was fresh and dewy and fragrant, and life was a boon again. After three hours of tramping we arrived back wholesomely tired, over laden with game, very hungry, and just in time for breakfast."

Third-great-grandfather ANDERSON IVIE's tombstone in the Florida Cemetery reads: "DIED—May 29, 1852—aged 78 yrs—2 mo's." His wife, SARAH, survived him.

ANDERSON IVIE's grandson, my great-grandfather, JOHN LEHI IVIE, was in Provo in 1852 and was married that same month and year in Great Salt Lake City, Utah Territory, to great-grandmother MARY CATHERINE BAR-TON of Bountiful, 16 May 1852. That year, young Samuel Clemens [Mark Twain] was working as a "rarely paid journeyman in his brother Orion's unprofitable print shop" in Hannibal, Missouri. Across the Mississippi River in Illinois, lawyer ABRAHAM LINCOLN was called upon to deliver a fifty-minute eulogy at the funeral of the great Henry Clay, foremost of Whigs—born in 1777. Further east, in 1852, a young mother of six wrote her chapters, and the eight power presses rapidly spit out the 800,000 copies of her new book, *Uncle Tom's Cabin, or Life Among the Lowly.* An instant success, it spread throughout the nation and across the Atlantic. It was dramatized in theaters in many languages. Four months after the publication, the author, Harriet Beecher Stowe, received a check for $10,000.00. With her husband, she made her first sea voyage to Europe. Living much of her life in Cincinnati on the Ohio River, she had witnessed many events. The storm clouds of division in America were rapidly forming. ABE LINCOLN wrote,

> "As labor is the common burden of our race, so the effort of some to shift their share of the burden onto the shoulders of others is the great durable curse of the race."

~ 3 ~

"Wheat Fields Ready to Harvest," if You are Brave Enough

In the spring of the year of 1820, an event of great magnitude quietly occurred in the state of New York near its western Canadian border. It was the bare beginning of the events that would draw together the "Broad Branches" of my ancestry. Both the biblical *Old Testament* and *New Testament* had predicted it and many astute students of the *Bible*, rich and poor, were discussing and speculating on these predictions. With the discovery of the printing press, the *Bible* was available to all who were able to read. The historical Reformation movement of Christianity, with its various sects and factions, had created such opinionated discord among the people that the "Peace I Leave with You," that should have come with following Christ's teachings, had become more and more confusing and obscure. It was a day of large tent revival meetings where the instigators would travel from village to village proclaiming their own interpretations of Biblical passages as, in their opinion, God no longer communicated with men.

Confused with all this discord, young fourteen year-old Joseph Smith Jr., while reading the book of *James* in the *New Testament*, Chapter 1, pondered upon verses three through eight.

"If any of you lack wisdom, let him ask of God, that giveth to all men liberally, and upbraideth not; and it shall be given him. But let him ask in faith, nothing wavering. For he that wavereth is like a wave of the sea driven with the wind and tossed. For let not that man think that he shall receive any thing of the Lord. A double minded man is unstable in all his ways."

Young Joseph knew he lacked wisdom in regards to the confusion presented by the various religious creeds. If God would give to *all* men and not upbraid those that asked, why not try asking him? So finding a quiet, secluded spot in the grove of trees near his home, he knelt in prayer. That morning the young man was introduced to two very powerful forces: the power of evil and darkness that nearly destroyed him, until the second power of light overpowered this destructive force and two glorious personages appeared.

One spoke, *"Joseph, this is my beloved Son. Hear Him."* With sufficient faith, the youth asked which of the multitude of churches he should join. He was told, *"None of them."* Additional instructions were given to help him prepare for his participation in the events that would transpire when he was sufficiently mature.

He wanted to shout it to the world that all might rejoice; but he soon found that many in the world loved their own ideas and creations much more. He spoke with a minister of the Methodist Church, who explained to Joseph how his immaturity had tricked his mind into believing impossible things. The persecutions began.

> Joseph Smith recorded: "I was led to say in my heart: Why persecute me for telling the truth? I have actually seen a vision; and who am I that I can withstand God, or why does the world think to make me deny what I have actually seen? For I had seen a vision: I knew it, and I knew that God knew it, and I could not deny it, neither dared I do it; at least I knew that by so doing I would offend God, and come under condemnation." [Pearl of Great Price, Joseph Smith–History 1:25]

Four years later, he had another vision. This time it was an angel who came to him, who called himself Moroni. In life, he had lived four hundred years after the birth of Jesus Christ on the American continent. He spoke of golden plates on which his father, Mormon, had written the early history of his people, who had journeyed to this continent six hundred years B.C.; then, through their wickedness, this Nephite nation was destroyed by their Lamanite brethren one thousand years later. The angel gave him instructions and quoted scriptures, including the last two verses of the Old Testament, Malachi 4:5-6, regarding the sending of Elijah, the prophet, stating that this prophesy would soon be fulfilled. Moroni returned with the same message two more times.

At daybreak, the exhausted young man joined his father and brothers in their daily labors. His father, who was laboring with him, felt something was wrong and told him to go home. In attempting to cross the fence, his strength entirely failed him and he fell helpless on the ground. The vision of the previous night was again repeated. Joseph was shown in the vision the place where the golden plates were deposited in a nearby hill.

> "I knew the place the instant that I arrived there." He was allowed by the angel to dig and view the contents of the box in which the golden plates had lain hidden for fourteen hundred years. He was not allowed to touch them and was instructed, he "should come to that place precisely in one year from that time, and that" the angel Moroni would there meet with him, and would continue to do so every year "until the time should come for obtaining the plates."

In 1828, eight years after his first vision, the persecuted, unschooled Joseph Smith was allowed to remove the plates and commence his efforts towards their protection and translation into English. After much more persecution, a lost manuscript and numerous attempts to steal the golden plates, Joseph Smith, with the help of his clerk, Oliver Cowdery, was able to complete the whole 531 pages of the translation in sixty-five days of concerted effort in 1829. Three witnesses were allowed to see the angel, view the golden plates and the other items that were returned back into Angel Moroni's hands. Their witness is printed at the beginning of the book.

Eight additional witnesses were allowed to hold the golden plates and turn the precious pages. Their testimony is printed below that of the *Three Witnesses*. Many of these witnesses later left the LDS Church. Some returned again into the fold; but none of the eleven, even on their death beds, denied their witness. *The Book of Mormon, Another Testament of Jesus Christ* was first printed early in 1830. After its publication and the restoration of the priesthood, on 6 April 1830, The Church of Jesus Christ of Latter-day Saints was officially organized with six members. This restored church and book have survived the test of time—about 180 years. From the six members of 1830, its membership has grown to more than 13.5 million (2009) extending around the world.

The *Book of Mormon* was not the only revelation given to the Church. Joseph Smith continued to have revelations from the Lord throughout his life. *The Doctrine and Covenants of The Church of Jesus Christ of Latter-day Saints*, [D&C] contains official revelations from our Lord beginning 1823 until the death of Joseph Smith, with some additions by later prophets.

From NETTIE M. ROBINS' "The History of JAMES RUSSELL IVIE &
ELIZA McKEE FAUCETT" we read, "It was in the early 1830s in Missouri
that the Mormon Missionaries came to the parts of Missouri where the
IVIEs lived. Parley P. Pratt was one of the Elders who came so often to their
home. It was he who brought the *Book of Mormon* to them and taught the
Gospel and converted them. He also helped to baptize them as members
of the church of Jesus Christ of Latter Day Saints. Their homes were always
the homes of the traveling missionaries."

In October 1830 Joseph Smith had become concerned about the Indians,
the descendants of the ancient people told about in the *Book of Mormon*. He
prayed and received D&C 32 in which Parley P. Pratt and Ziba Peterson were to
accompany Oliver Cowdery and Peter Whitmer Jr. into the wilderness among
the Lamanites (or Indian tribes). The gateway west was Independence, Jackson
County, Missouri. The four men were the first missionaries to go to Missouri.

According to *Parley P. Pratt's Autobiography,* on "December the 20th we
took passage on a steamer for St. Louis. In a few days we arrived at the
mouth of the Ohio, and finding the [Mississippi] river blocked with ice,
the boat did not proceed further. We therefore landed and proceeded on
foot [north] for two hundred miles to the neighborhood of St. Louis... Although in the midst of strangers, we were kindly entertained, found many
friends, and *preached to large congregations in several neighborhoods...* After
much fatigue and some suffering we all arrived in Independence, in the
county of Jackson, on the extreme western frontiers of Missouri, and of
the United States ... about 1500 miles from where we started ... most of
the journey on foot, through wilderness country, in the worst season of the
year, occupying about four months, during which *we had preached the gospel to tens of thousands of Gentiles and two nations of Indians; baptizing, con-
firming and organizing many hundreds of people into churches of Latter-day
Saints* ... This was the first mission performed by the elders of the Church
in any of the States west of New York and we were the first members of the
same which were ever on this frontier."

In the spring, Parley was chosen by the four men to return to New York and
report. He traveled by foot across Missouri, arriving in St. Louis in nine days.
From there, he went down the Mississippi and up the Ohio River by steamboat.
If Parley P. Pratt converted them to the LDS Church, it was probably on the
way *to* Jackson County. His second missionary journey into Missouri came after
other missionaries had arrived in the settlement with a *Book of Mormon.*

On 7 Jun 1831, in Kirtland, Ohio, a revelation was received that opened the door further, quoting D&C 52:3-10, *"Wherefore, verily I say unto you, let my servants Joseph Smith, Jun., and Sidney Rigdon take their journey as soon as preparations can be made to leave their homes, and journey to the land of Missouri. And inasmuch as they are faithful unto me, it shall be made known unto them what they shall do; And it shall also, inasmuch as they are faithful, be made known unto them the land of your inheritance . . . And again, verily I say unto you, let my servant Lyman Wight and my servant John Corrill take their journey speedily; and also my servant John Murdock, and my servant Hyrum Smith* [Joseph Smith's older beloved brother] *take their journey unto the same place by the way of Detroit. And let them journey from thence preaching the word by the way, saying none other things than that which the prophets and apostles have written, and that which is taught them by the Comforter through the prayer of faith. Let them go two by two, and thus let them preach by the way in every congregation, baptizing by water, and the laying on of the hands by the water's side."*

John Murdock was a faithful Latter-day Saint who joined the church when he was living in Ohio. He kept a journal which explained his own conversion and told of this early journey with the prophet's brother Hyrum into the Salt River settlement (Florida, Monroe County, Missouri) where our ancestors and relations were living.

He wrote: "I, finding the people called the Campbellites, so well agreeing with my feelings, and they professed to be in search of truth as I was, therefore I united with them. I think it was in the year A.D. 1827 . . . I continued a member with them, about 3 years, I think; but at length finding their principal leader, Alex Campbell, with many others, denying the gift and power of the Holy Ghost . . . I had firmly became convinced that all the sects were out of the way . . . Where is the man to commence the work of baptizing? Or where shall he get his authority? . . . About one month [later], word came to me that four men had arrived at Kirtland from the state of New York, who were preaching, baptizing, and building up the church after the ancient order . . . I was also told that Elder Rigdon, with many others of the Campbellite Church, were baptized by them. I replied to my informer that it was an insinuation of the devil but I was immediately checked in my feelings, and I made no more harsh expressions respecting them.

"I . . . went to see for myself, a distance of about twenty miles. I heard the sayings of many people by the way, some for the new preachers, and some against, but I observed the Spirit that stimulated those for, and those against. I met Squire Waldo, who was a Campbellite [and] bitterly opposed. He tried to have me take another road, and not go to Kirtland, but I told him I was of age, and the case was an important one, of life and death, existing between me and my God, and I must act for myself, for no one can act for me. I rode about three miles further and met another man of the same order; I . . . tarried at father ISAAC MORLEY's about dark, and was soon introduced to those four men from New York, and presented with the Book of Mormon; I now said within myself, I have items placed before me that will prove to me whether it be of God or not, viz: four men professing to be servants of the most high God, authorized to preach the gospel, and practice the ordinances thereof, and build up the Church after the ancient order; and having a book professing to have come forth by the power of God, containing the fullness of the gospel; I said if it be so their walk will agree with their profession, and the Holy Ghost will attend their ministration of the ordinances, and the Book of Mormon will contain the same plan of salvation as the Bible. I was sensible that such a work must come forth; but the question with me was, are these [the] men that are to commence the work? I did not ask a sign of them by working a miracle . . . only I desired to know whether the Spirit would attend their ministration." There was a confirmation meeting till about ten o'clock at night. "They went and I stayed alone, and read the "Book of Mormon." I read till it was late and went into Father MORLEY's chamber to bed and had not been long in bed, before they returned . . . although I was in bed up [in the] chamber, the spirit of the Lord rested on me, witnessing to me the truth of the work. I could no longer rest in bed but got up and went down and sat in a chair and conversed with them, and I found they appeared very tender in their feelings. I could not help secretly rejoicing on the occasion. The next morning I conversed with about half a dozen men separately who had been confirmed in the meetinghouse the night before. I found their testimony agreed on the subject that there was a manifestation of the spirit attended the ministration of the ordinance of laying on hands, and I found the items [*The Book of Mormon* and the four Elders] placed before me . . . testified that it was of God.

"About ten o'clock that morning, being November 5th, 1830, I told the servants of the Lord that I was ready to walk with them into the water of baptism. Accordingly, Elder P. [Parley] P. Pratt baptized me in the Chagrin river and the spirit of the Lord sensibly attended . . . and I came out of the water rejoicing and singing praises to God, and the Lamb. An impression sensibly rested on my mind that cannot, by me be forgotten . . . This was the third time I had been immersed, but I never before felt the authority of the ordinance, but I felt it this time and felt as though my sins were forgiven . . . on Sunday evening they confirmed about thirty. I was one of the number. Elder Oliver Cowdery was administrator. I was also ordained an elder [in the priesthood]; and it was truly a time of the out pouring of the spirit. I know the spirit rested on me as it never did before and others said they saw the Lord and had visions.

"I continued to labor in the ministry, preaching and building up the Church in that region from November 1830, till June 1831. On the 6th of June 1831, a conference of the Elders of the Church was held in Kirtland and myself was advanced to the High Priesthood, under the hand of Joseph Smith, Junior, the Prophet, and so were others. Soon after, a number of us received a revelation to travel to Missouri." [Mentioned earlier]

John Murdock with Hyrum Smith continued as commanded, first to Detroit, Michigan, and then south—teaching and preaching as they went. They crossed the Illinois River on 1 August 1831, the next day the Mississippi River on the Louisiana Ferry.

Murdock complained: "I got my feet wet by which I took a violent cold by which I suffered near unto death . . . Traveled 25 miles to New London, found it a very wicked place. As we slept in a tavern, in the night Brother Hyrum lay on the far side of the bed with his hand out on our clothes, which hung on a chair by the bedside, and a person seized his wrist. Brother H. [Hyrum] cried out, 'Who is there,' and at the same time broke his hold, which awoke me. We heard the bedstead in the other room creak which notified us that he had gone to bed.

"Thursday 4th, arrived at *Salt River (Florida, Missouri)* where *we preached next day*, but I was sick and went to bed, and we continued there near one week and then I gave my watch in pay to WM. IVY to carry me in a wagon to Chariton 70 miles. We stayed there 2 days. Met Brother J. [Joseph] Smith Jr., S. [Sidney] Rigdon and others, and received the revelation recorded in the 'Book of Covenants,' which instructs Hyrum Smith and John Murdock, and other missionaries, to continue on their journey to Zion (Independence, Missouri.) They are to hold a meeting, after which they may return, preaching as they go two by two."

Murdock met Harvey Whitlock and David Whitmer, but was still very weak. At Lexington, "they took me into a house and left me there . . . After which I was carried in a wagon [to Jackson County], where I lay sick two or three months . . . yet my belief was so firm that it could not be moved. I believe that I could not die because my work was not yet done."

Harvey Whitlock and David Whitmer went south on their journey and among their contacts was William E. McLellin (1803–1886). His first journal of six encompasses the time period of 18 July 1831–20 November 1831. His journals were thought to be lost for over one hundred years. Then in the 1980s, the notorious expert forger, Mark Hoffmann of Salt Lake City, Utah, claimed he had located them and wanted to sell his fantasies to the highest bidder. His lies were uncovered, but not before he had murdered in an attempt to cover his own criminal acts. After he was imprisoned, the original journals were found among the holdings of The Church of Jesus Christ of Latter-day Saints in Salt Lake City. They had acquired the journals in 1908 along with many other papers that had been lost in the shuffle. Because of the great interest created by Hoffmann in these journals, they were given to two highly qualified professors to be edited and printed in book form: Jan Shipps, a professor of religious studies and history at Indiana University, Purdue University, at Indianapolis, and John W. Welch, a Brigham Young University (BYU) professor of law and editor-in-chief of BYU Studies.

McLellin's first paragraphs describe his first acquaintance with the two missionaries. "At this time I was living in Paris, Illinois. Teaching school—This morning I heard very early that two men (who said they were traveling to Zion which they said was in upper Missouri. They had also a book with them which they sd was a Revelation from God. Calling it the book of Mormon) were to preach 2 ½ miles below Paris. I taught school until 12 o'clock. I saddled Tom and rode there with speed. Anxious to see and hear those quear beings. Their names were Harvy Whitlock & David Whitmer. . . I invited them to go and preach in Paris, which they did next day."

Describing Harvey Whitlock, "I never heard such preaching in all my life. The glory of God seemed to encircle the man and the wisdom of God to be displayed in his discourse . . . On Friday I closed my school and on Saturday the 30th . . . I left Paris . . . about 6 o'clock P.M. & started for Jackson Co. Mo."

On the twelfth and thirteenth, he crossed the Mississippi River: "I crossed in a horse boat, pd 50 cts and landed . . . in Louisiana a little town on the bank. Thence 12 ms through a dreary region all alone and it dark, to esqr McCune's & staid all night . . . rode on (though yet weak) 31 ms to Mr. Rogerses, staid all night.

"August 14. I rose early paid 50 cts and rode on 3 ms to a Mr. IVEY's and fed my horse and took breakfast. Here two Elders had staid about a week (viz) Hiram Smith and John Moredock though they were gone. They had no book with them and when Mrs. IVY found out that I had a book, she said she must see it and when she saw it she said I must sell it to her which I did and then pursued my course toward the western horizon 32 ms to Mr. Milligin's and took dinner in Monroe Co." I do not know which of the three Mrs. IVIEs got the *Book of Mormon.*

On 18 August he arrived in "Independence—Jackson Co... I conversed with a number in the villagers about those people that they called Mormonites. They thought they were generally a very honest people but very much deluded by Smith and others. Notwithstanding all I felt anxious to see them and examine for myself... I then started but before I got out of the village I met with David Whitmer & Martin Harris who accompanied me about 10 miles further westward where I found: The bishop E. Partridge and his council ISAAC MORLEY and John Corrill with several other Elders and a number of private members both male and female. I spent the evening with them and had very agreeable conversation... Saw Love, Peace, Harmony and Humility abounding among them. A rare circumstance occurred while attending family prayr which convinced me that the Elders had the power of deserning spirits. It affected me so that my weakness was manifest. I took Hiram the brother of Joseph and we went into the woods and set down and talked together about 4 hours. I inquired into the particulars of the coming forth of the record, of the rise of the church and of its progress and upon the testimonies given to him & c. This evening I went to one of their prayr meetings. Here I saw the manner of their worship, heard them converse freely upon the things of religion ...

"Saturday the 20th I rose early and betook myself to earnest prayr to God to direct me into truth, and from all the light that I could gain by examinations searches and researches I was bound as an honest man to acknowledge the truth and Validity of the book of Mormon and also that I had found the people of the Lord—The Living Church of Jesus Christ."

William E. McLellin joined the Church in Jackson County. With Hyrum Smith, they retraced their steps though Missouri; 3 Sepember 1831, his journal continues:

"Saturday eve we called at Esqr Davis' on the head water of Salt River he wished us to hold a meeting and agreed to next day. He went and sent out and informed the people.

"Sunday 4th Bro. Hiram had obtained relief of his Diorhoea. The people collected, and he arose and addressed them a few minutes—I then got up and warned them of the judgements of God which would fall on them unless they would repent. But there seemed to be an impenetrable gloom hanging over their minds. They seemed to be willingly and willfully wicked. Therefore we dismissed them and got our horse and traveled on about 8 ms and staid all night.

"Monday 5th In the afternoon we reached Mr. IVEY's. Their friends gathered in, in the eve and we had much social conversation with them. They seemed to be somewhat believing. I arose to address them and was filled with the spirit to that degree that I spoke with much warmth . . . but none seemed willing to go forward in obedience.

Tuesday 6th We bid our friends Fare-well and pursued our course Eastward."

McLellin would become one of the Twelve Apostles, but later apostatize. He died in 1883 in Independence, Missouri—still firm in his testimony of *The Book of Mormon*.

[Note: The three IVIE families in the U. S. Census of 1830 were my third-great-grandparents ANDERSON and SARAH ALLRED IVIE; second-great-grandparents JAMES RUSSELL and ELIZA McKEE FAUSETT IVIE, and James Russell Ivie's brother and his wife—JOHN ANDERSON and ANNE ROBINSON IVIE.]

When the Salt River Branch (of Florida, Missouri) was organized about one year later, uncle JOHN ANDERSON IVIE was called as the Branch President. At that time many relations were baptized. ISAAC ALLRED, son of JAMES ALLRED, states in his autobiography,

"We lived in Monro County four years [1831–fall of 1835] in which time I with the rest of my father's family joined the Church of Jesus Christ of Latter-Day-Saints in the year 1832 on the tenth of September . . . We were baptized by George M. Hinkle and Daniel Cathcart . . . In 1833, I was or-dained a teacher under the hand of JOHN IVIE, President of the branch at Salt River."

Parley P. Pratt's second journey into Missouri with Orson Pratt was much slower than the others. He arrived after Hyrum Smith and John Murdock had left the Salt River settlement.

He explained: "We traveled through the States of Ohio, Indiana, Illinois and Missouri, in the midst of the heat of summer on foot, and faithfully preached the gospel in many parts of all these States. We suffered the hardships incident to a new and, in many places, unsettled country, such as hunger, thirst, fatigue, etc. We arrived in Upper Missouri [Jackson County] in September, having baptized many people and organized branches of the Church in several parts of Ohio, Illinois and Indiana. I felt somewhat disappointed in not meeting with the brethren; but was consoled with the reflection that I had been diligent in preaching the gospel on my journey, while others had hurried through the country, perhaps, without tarrying to do much good.

"On our arrival we found a considerable settlement of the brethren from Ohio, who had immigrated during the summer and taken up residence in Jackson County. President Smith, and many of the Elders, had been there and held a conference, and, having organized a Stake of Zion, pointed out and consecrated certain grounds for a city and temple, they had again returned to the East. With them, the brethren whom I had left there the previous winter had also returned."

In Jackson County, Parley P. Pratt was "sick with the fever and ague," owing to the exposures of the climate. He suffered for several months. In February, 1832, a Conference was held and he was determined to go. Though almost unable to sit on a horse, he rode twelve miles. At the close, several Elders were returning to Ohio. He wanted to go with them and requested that they "lay their hands on me and pray. They did so." He was instantly healed, and the next morning started a journey of twelve hundred miles on foot. He wrote: "I gained strength at every step, and the second evening, after wading through the snow about six inches deep for some ten miles, I was enabled to address a congregation for the first time in several months." They arrived in Kirtland in May, where he determined to "take his wife and remove to Western Missouri." The Pratt family went by boat and arrived at the Colesville Branch, on the western boundaries of Missouri 1 August 1832, and commenced cutting hay, building, purchasing, and planting land. He stayed in Colesville until winter. During the winter of 1832-3, Parley P. Pratt took a mission with William E. McLellin through the State of Missouri and into Illinois, crossing the Mississippi at Clarksville.

He writes, "As we approached Clarksville, we were told by several . . . inhabitants not to attempt a meeting or any religious instruction there, for they were a hardened and irreclaimable set of blasphemers and infidels, given to gambling, drinking and cursing, etc.; and that many . . . had attempted in vain to reclaim them. After praying mightily, we entered the town and called at a hotel. We told the landlord that we had come in the name of Jesus Christ to preach the gospel to the people, being sent by him without purse or scrip. 'Well,' said he, 'you are welcome to my house and such fare as we have; and we will meet together and hear your religion, and if it proves to be better than ours we will embrace it; for we confess that our religion is to fiddle and dance, and eat and drink, and be merry, and gamble and swear a little; and we believe this is better than priestcraft.' We replied that we would try them anyhow. So a meeting was convened; we preached, had good attention, and much of a candid spirit of inquiry was manifest, and we were treated with hospitality and friendship, and even ferried over the river free; and this was more than those religious sectaries would do, who had warned us against them."

The Journal of William E. McLellin gives a more detailed account of this missionary journey.

"Wednesday 20th. . . at eve we attended a meeting at Br ISAAC ALLRED's. [uncle Isaac, father of the twins, or cousin Isaac?] Br Parley opened the meeting and spoke about 1 ½ hours & I spoke about one hour with Zeal and warmth, the brethren seemed encouraged and rejoiced . . . praying and blessing the name of the Lord for his goodness . . . After meeting was dismissed I felt somewhat unwell . . . I felt so bad that I asked Br Parley to lay his hands upon me which he did and I dropped to sleep, but in the night when I awaked I was shaking most tremendiously hard . . . as much as 2 hours— then a very violent fever ensued, my stomach became very sour, my bowels also were much affected, which caused severe vomiting & purging . . . Thursday I was confined to my bed and I think I never was much sicker in my life, in the evening I called for the Elders—Friday I was some better . . . Saturday I am still some better—Br Parley on Friday night attended another meeting among the brethren where he . . . unfolded to them the dealings of the Lord from the creation down until John said 'It is done.'

"Sunday 24th The brethren and sisters collected at Br. I. ALLRED's and I took the lead of the meeting . . . I spoke on the Covenants & Articles on the officer's duty and the beauty of such regulations & c. I spoke about 1 hour and 20 mts. Br Parley spoke a few minutes—then the meeting was conducted by various ones speaking. I gave a lecture on the operation of the Spirit—Br Parley gave a testimony of the Lord Jesus that he is, that he lives and will come & c. In which he says, he does not recollect to have ever had more of the Spirit and Power of God upon him—in truth we had a great meeting. It was dismissed about sun set.

"Monday 25th The Elders, Priests, Teachers & c met with us (by the request of Br. G. Hinkle) at Br Hinkle's to hear our instructions—We found by examination that the Elders were young and inexperienced, yet sound in faith and good works . . . We unitedly advised them that the time of their mission in the world had not come and that they remain a season at home and search the scriptures and lay up rich treasures in their minds till the time come—They seemed willing to take our advice . . . Dismissed thence to Br JAMES ALLRED's and staid all night." They left on Tuesday the 26th, as he was "able though weak, to travel."

Parley P. Pratt returned to Jackson County and was there when the Saints were ruthlessly driven by mobs across the Missouri River, on Thursday, 7 November 1833, he records:

"The shore began to be lined on both sides of the ferry with men, women and children; goods, wagons, boxes, provisions, etc., while the ferry was constantly employed; and when night again closed upon us the cottonwood bottom had much the appearance of a camp meeting. Hundreds of people were seen in every direction, some in tents and some in the open air around their fires, while the rain descended in torrents. Husbands were inquiring for their wives, wives for their husbands; parents for children, and children for parents . . . The scene was indescribable . . . Next day our company still increased, and we were principally engaged in felling cottonwood trees and erecting them into small cabins. The next night being clear, we began to enjoy some degree of comfort . . . About two o'clock the next morning we were called up by the cry of signs in the heavens. We arose, and to our great astonishment all the firmament seemed enveloped in splendid fireworks, as if every star in the broad expanse had been hurled from its course, and sent lawless through the wilds of ether. Thousands of bright meteors were shooting through space in every direction, with long trains of light following in their course. This lasted for several hours, and was only closed by the dawn of the rising sun. Every heart was filled with joy at this majestic display of signs and wonders, showing the near approach of the coming of the Son of God . . . The Saints who fled took refuge in the adjoining counties, mostly in Clay County, which received them with some degree of kindness."

They were not accepted into the counties of Van Buren and Lafayette, Missouri. The excuses they offered, according to Parley P. Pratt were:

"First: The society were guilty principally of being eastern or northern people.

"Secondly: They were guilty of some slight variations in manners and language from the other citizens of the State, who were mostly from the South.

"Thirdly: Their religious principles differed in important particulars from other societies.

"Fourthly: They were guilty of immigrating rapidly . . . and of purchasing large quantities of land, and of being more enterprising and industrious than their neighbors.

"Fifthly: Some of them were guilty of poverty—especially those who had been driven, from time to time, and robbed of their all. And,

"Lastly: They were said to be guilty of believing in the present Government administration of Indian affairs, viz: that the land west of the Mississippi, which the Government had deeded in fee simple to the immigrating tribes, was destined by Providence for their permanent homes.

"All these crimes were charged upon our society, in the public proceedings of the several counties, and were deemed sufficient to justify their unlawful proceedings against us.

"After making our escape in the county of Clay—being reduced to the lowest poverty—I made a living by day labor, jobbing, building, or wood cutting, till some time in the winter . . . it was decided that two of the Elders should be sent to Ohio, in order to counsel with President Smith and the Church at Kirtland."

Parley P. Pratt reluctantly volunteered and "at length" Lyman Wight volunteered to accompany him. Pratt explained, "I was at this time entirely destitute of proper clothing for the journey; and I had neither horse, saddle, bridle, money nor provisions to take with me; or to leave with my wife, who lay sick and helpless most of the time." With faith and the blessings of God, the way was cleared and the journey commenced on 1 Feb 1834. "We mounted our horses, and started in good cheer to ride one thousand or 1500 miles through a wilderness country. We had not one cent of money in our pockets on starting. We traveled every day, whether through storm or sunshine, mud, rain or snow; except when our public duties called us to tarry. We arrived in Kirtland early in the spring, all safe and sound; we had lacked for nothing on the road, and now had plenty of funds in hand."

Probably that journey took him through the Allred Settlement and the homes of the IVIEs and ALLREDs, where provisions and funds were undoubtedly given.

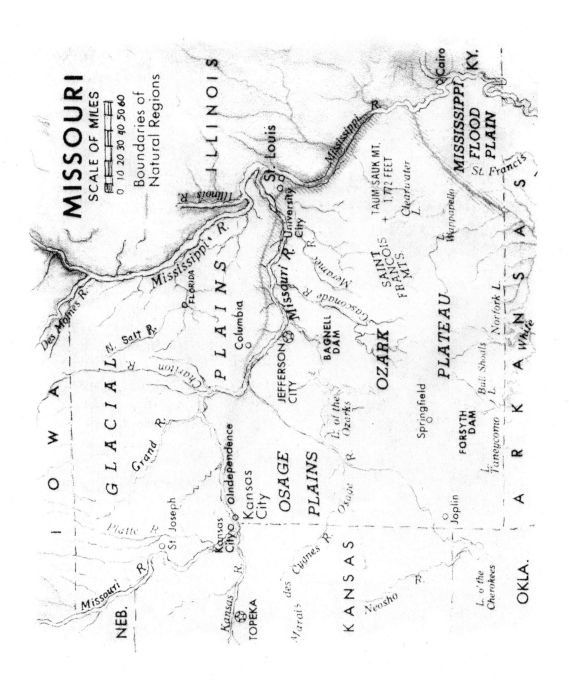

~ 4 ~

ZION'S CAMP, THE SALT RIVER, AND INTO TORRENTS OF RAIN AND DISEASE

After Parley P. Pratt returned to Kirtland, Ohio, with the news of the disaster in Jackson County, Missouri, Joseph Smith Jr. prayed for instructions and his answer came by revelation. He was to organize a small army and proceed to Jackson County to help their members. This group was called *Zion's Camp.* He had wanted 500 men, but was disappointed. His brother, Hyrum, was sent to Michigan to enlist additional members and bring them to Missouri. The two groups were to meet in Missouri at the Salt River Settlement (*Florida, Missouri*). On 7 June 1834, Joseph Smith's group "camped in a piece of woods, near a spring of water, at Salt River." [HC p. 87] A note in the *Addenda* states:

> "[Men] had previously followed us passed us several times during the day, and were in search of us this evening. The guard heard them say, 'They have turned aside, damn 'em, we can't find 'em.' Elders Seth Johnson and Almon W. Babbitt, who had been sent to the Bowling Green branch to gather recruits, returned to the camp on the morning of the 7th with a small company, two wagons and several horses."

A second note adds:

> "One of the camp walked on ahead to procure some milk. A number of men armed with guns met him and said: 'Here's one damn Mormon alone— let's kill him.' But at the same instant they discovered a number of others just coming over the hill, when they immediately rode off in great haste. A branch of the church, known as the Salt River branch, but frequently called the Allred Settlement, was located here. We remained at this place several days, washing our clothes, and preparing to pursue our journey."

Parley P. Pratt had recruited in the East, joining with Joseph Smith's small army from time to time, bringing additional recruits and provisions. He reports:

"Arriving in the Allred settlement, near Salt River, Missouri . . . the camp rested a little, and despatched Elder Orson Hyde and myself to Jefferson City." Their journey to Jefferson City to "request a sufficient military force, with orders to reinstate the exiles, and protect them in the possession of their homes in Jackson County" was a disappointment. During their interview, Governor Daniel Dunklin "acknowledged the justice of the demand, but frankly told us he dare not attempt the execution of the laws in that given respect, for fear of deluging the whole country in civil war and bloodshed. He advised us to relinquish our rights, for the sake of peace, and to sell our lands from which we had been driven. To this we replied with firmness, that we would hold no terms with land pirates and murderers."

On 7 June from the Church Historical Records of the Michigan group they "crossed the bottom lands and forded the north and south Fabius Rivers and passed through the village of Palmyra, Marion County, Mo., a thriving place of one hundred houses, a goodly number of stores; many of the houses were of brick. Passing on we went to the nine mile prairie on the road to Salt River and camped within four miles of the branch of the Church . . .

"June 8 Sunday. Prayer by Brother Rich. We went on and forded West and South Salt Rivers in a tremendous rain with thunder and lightning and arrived at Brother JAMES [R] IVEY'S in Monroe County, Mo., where we found that the brethren had arrived the night before and that we had camped about twenty-three miles apart after starting from different places through different counties and with different hindrances by the way, this being the place of meeting agreed upon without any time specified to meet in."

From the *History of the Church* Joseph Smith writes: "Soon after the arrival of Brother Hyrum and his company . . . JAMES ALLRED, Sen., and TEN others of this branch joined our camp, which now numbered two hundred and five men, all armed and equipped as the law directs. It was delightful to see the company, for they were all young men, except one company whom we called the Silver Greys, and who ate at my table. We were all in good spirits, and were taught the sword practice by Brother William Cherry (who was a native of Ireland), and expert drill master, who had been in the British dragoon service for upwards of twenty years, and deserves much credit for his unwearied exertions in imparting all he knew to the brethren. This was our first attempt at learning the sword exercise. Brothers Hiram Stratton and Nelson Tubbs procured a shop of Myres

Mobley and repaired every firelock that was out of order, and David Elliott shod our horses. Here Brother James Foster was taken sick. I proposed to him to remain behind. He said, 'Brother Joseph, let me go with you if I die on the road.' I told him in the name of the Lord, that if that was his faith, to go on his bed in the wagon, and he should get better every day until he recovered, which was literally fulfilled."

[Note: Listed with the members of Zions Camp in the "History of the Church" are seven relatives: JAMES ALLRED, age 50, the father of ISAAC ALLRED, age 20, and MARTIN C. ALLRED, age 27; JOHN FOS-SETT was probably ELIZA M. FAUSETT IVIE's brother, age 29; JAMES RUSSELL IVIE age 34 and his brothers WILLIAM SHELTON IVIE, age 22, and JOHN ANDERSON IVIE, age 29. There is an Edward Ivie listed; this was really Edward Ives who was later listed as dying of cholera.]

June 10, Elijah Fordham writes: "This day we (the Michigan Saints) con-secrated all of our money and lead for Zion's cause to the Commissary-General Doctor Brown."

Moses Martin's journal recalls: "We were organized into companies. Joseph Smith chose twenty swordsmen for a life guard. These were divided into ten, with Hyrum Smith as captain of the first ten and Roger Orton as captain of the second ten. Then twenty of the best rifle men were chosen out of the whole camp for rangers, I being one of the first companies. Col. Fred G. Williams was chosen captain of the first company of rifle rangers and Hazen Aldrich captain of the second company."

L. O. Littlefield, a young man from the Michigan group wrote when he was older: "Zion's Camp was halted at Brother ALLRED's place, at Salt River . . . it was no very great distance from the city of Quincy, across the Mississippi River, west . . . The camping ground presented a city of tents and covered wagons. These were arranged in an order which made them quite convenient for all purposes of passing to and fro for horsemen, carriages or footmen. Visitors were struck with this feature of order, and seemed to look upon the camp as quite a novelty, and the people as being a class used to good order and thriftiness. The visiting resident citizens at this point . . . were by no means unfriendly, but were quite civil and courteous . . . Brother ALLRED and family were especially kind and active in making comfortable as many as possible of our large number . . . As I was then so very young I was, naturally enough, not made acquainted with the intricate or minute order in which the camp was organized for traveling; but I remember that they were classed into messes of tens for purposes of cooking, washing our clothing, eating, sleeping, etc. While there, the men were paraded outside of the camp for exercise and instruction. This was an unpleasant feature for me, as I was too young and too small of stature to act with the men. This created within me . . . some lonesome reflections. I sat down upon a rock where the men were passing, the better to observe their movements. While thus seated, the Prophet Joseph Smith, who happened to be passing by in quite a hurry, noticed me. He stepped to where I sat alone. It might have been my isolated position that attracted him. I knew not the motive; but that man, who to me appeared so good and so godlike, really halted in his hurry to notice me—only a little boy. Placing one of his hands upon my head, he said: 'Well, bub, is there no place for you?'

"This recognition from the man whom I then knew was a Prophet of God created within me a tumult of emotions. I could make him no reply. My young heart was filled with joy to me unspeakable. He passed on and left me in my lonely attitude, for he was then in quite a hurry to accomplish something pertaining to the movements of the men which could not be delayed.

"I mention this circumstance as it illustrates a trait of his character, which in after years he has often been seen to exemplify. He was naturally fond of the young—especially little children. He did not like to pass a child, however small, without speaking . . . He was not only kind and gentle to the youth, but the aged he treated with the respect due their whitened locks; and their tottering limbs could ever find ready and willing support on his strong arm, ever prompt to lead them to the place where inclination or duty called for their presence."

On 12 June, Zions Camp left the Salt River and traveled about fourteen miles. The *History of the Church* recorded, "The inhabitants of Salt River manifested a great respect for us, and many of them accompanied us some distance on our journey." JAMES ALLRED Sr. was one of the *Silver Greys* that ate at Joseph Smith's table.

Young L. O. Littlefield recorded the journey:

"We had still to travel a long and weary road which lay, portions of it at least, through a country thickly settled by people who we had reasons to believe were much prejudiced against us and who according to rumor, would oppose our advance when we should reach their settlements. We had but one alternative which was to trust in God and go ahead.

"The bugle sounded for prayers night and morning . . . This sacred duty was generally performed in the various tents and wagons according as the brethren were associated together in messes of tens, when some one of that little family would offer prayer for their respective number. In connection with these seasons of devotion . . . the sweet singers would sing with the spirit and the understanding, some of the hymns which had been inspired in connection with the great latter-day work . . . Even the unbelieving strangers who happened to be passing were attracted by these exercises; but the hearts of some were hardened and filled with the spirit of rage and bitterness.

"Frequently the leading men of the camp would speak to us and encourage us by their words and testimony concerning the truthfulness of the strange work which God had just brought to light. The Prophet himself frequently spoke to us in a collective capacity, and often with a power and force of utterance that exceeded anything that the members of the camp had ever before heard or seen manifested by mortal man . . . Hyrum Smith was much beloved by all the members of the camp for zeal, faithfulness and a straightforward, even course from day to day. His daily deportment was exemplary and whatever he said privately to the brethren or when he talked to them in a collective body, was received with approval and had great influence with them in stimulating them to endure the fatigues of travel with patience. He was a strong support to the Prophet and rendered every service in his power to carry out his counsels.

"Men were detailed to stand guard every night to watch our animals and to see that the threats of molestation made occasionally by some of the inhabitants were not carried into effect. The camp moved forward day after day and the routine of labors that were necessary to be performed was kept up in general good order and punctuality. Nearly every person in the camp had specific duties and labors assigned him. Some were cooks, some drove and took care of the teams; others acted as commissary agents for the various messes, by visiting farm houses and places to purchase provisions. Persons also were charged with the duty of procuring water for drinking and cooking purposes, while others procured fuel, all to be obtained as speedily as possible when the wagons were halted. We had no drones, and what was very agreeable, none performed these several duties with reluctance; but all were accomplished orderly, with willing hands and cheerful hearts.

"The labors and duties that necessarily had to be performed by the members of Zion's Camp, day after day and night after night, were very fatiguing. The large majority of them walked the most of the way. The Prophet was relieved of this task. His duties were such that he had provided himself—extra from his baggage wagons—with a light, open carriage. Frequently he was under the necessity of driving several miles . . . to transact business or hold an interview with some of the leading men, in order to allay excitement which here and there existed in opposition to our passing through the country with so large and well-disciplined a force . . . [which] seemed to become more frequent as we traveled to the west . . . At times the possibility of reaching the western counties of Missouri seemed dark and forbidding, and had it not been for the firm trust the Prophet and all in camp had in the overruling hand of God, we certainly would have been inclined to abandon all idea . . . But night after night the prayers of the faithful ascended into the ears of Jehovah to soften the hearts of the people toward us, as we had no design of violence or evil against them or their country. We traveled by faith and the Lord heard our importunities."

Zion's Camp reached Fishing River, Missouri, Thursday, 19 June 1834, L. O. Littlefield continues:

"It was about 4 o'clock in the afternoon . . . the day was warm and very pleasant. I think there was not a cloud to be seen in the sky. We found the river in fine condition for fording. The water was reported, by the brethren who went down to it where the road crossed, to be not over knee-deep. Of course, we had plenty of time and might easily have crossed and made our encampment on the opposite shore long before dark; but the brethren felt impressed not to cross the stream at that time. We were soon busy pitching our tents and placing the wagons in position, as was our custom.

"While we were building fires and commencing to prepare supper, two or three men rode hastily into camp and commenced a blasphemous tirade about 'Jo Smith and the G-d d--d Mormons.' They wanted to know what the h--l so many of us were traveling through the county for. They swore that we had got to our journey's end. They declared also that a large force, consisting of several hundred armed men, would be at the ford on the opposite side of the river in a short time, and that our company would all be slaughtered before morning. The Prophet remonstrated firmly but quietly with them. He tried to calm their excited minds by assuring them that we had nothing but peaceable intentions toward the inhabitants.

"I thought the men were intoxicated; but whether this was their condition or not they certainly were very earnest and loud-spoken in their denunciations of the Mormons and 'Jo Smith,' as they called him. During this parley—entirely unexpected on our part—the entire camp naturally gathered around them. Their position was on the main traveled road, on both sides of which our tents had been pitched. Joseph and a few of the leading men happened to be near the spot where they halted and commenced their angry declamation. I was at the outskirts of the brethren, who were quite densely massed around the rude intruders; but still near enough to note the contrast manifested between Joseph and the brethren and that of the rough, demoniacal appearance of these men as they sat upon their horses and swung their arms uncouthly around to give emphasis to their wicked threats of slaughter.

"Joseph maintained his usual dignity of demeanor. They failed to draw from him any angry resentment of words. He firmly and kindly assured them, however, that the remaining portion of our journey would be characterized by the same moderation and justice towards the inhabitants as had been the case all along our route of travel; that we had not asked any aid from the people except we had paid the price asked for what we had obtained; and he intended to pay a just equivalent for all supplies furnished us until our journey was ended. He only asked to travel peaceably through the country as an American citizen, with no intention other than to fully respect the rights of the citizens. He did not quail before them a particle, but took all the pains possible in the short time the men tarried to correctly inform them as to the honesty and justice of our motives. The men finally reined up their horses and spurred away, still shouting their anathemas to the effect that our company were all to be massacred during that night.

"These men were gone just long enough for us to look around a little, when we observed the sky was being rapidly overcast with densely dark and angry clouds. I think we had not all finished eating our suppers, when the rain began to fall in torrents, accompanied with a terribly fierce wind. So violent was the wind and torrents of rain that neither our wagons nor tents afforded us protection, and we were quickly drenched and almost unable to stand against the fierceness of the blast . . . Close by where we were encamped was a large log meeting-house. We had no alternative but to seek shelter within the strong walls of this building. The door was found locked, but the windows were easily raised and we hastily found ingress thereby. Had it not been for that shelter our suffering must have been great—the effects from which might have been fatal to some of us at least.

"I have witnessed rain storms in various portions of the earth, but nothing I have ever experienced has equaled that storm in point or the terrible fierceness of the wind and the immensity of the water that fell. What added to the destructiveness of the storm were the missiles of hail that were hurled in vast quantities by the currents of wind that rushed and roared through the woods which surrounded our place of shelter, causing the sound of falling trees and massive limbs to add additional terrors to the general clang of the storm.

"The vast electric artillery of the expansive firmament seemed to be in a state of rapid combustion, so that night, which otherwise would have been as dark as night could possible become, was at times rendered so light that we could look far out beyond the swaying trees, and falling splintered branches hurled along the air and striking the earth with a fury that made us truly thankful for the protecting walls of the strong blockhouse that rendered us secure from the perils of that exciting hour . . . The voice of thunder uttered anathemas against the enemies of truth and righteousness, who were massed with arms across the river, ready at that hour to fall upon us and spill our blood. And that thunder shook the very earth with terrible force, as if threatening to open its caverns and engulf whatever existed upon its surface within the range of that perilous storm. But our trust was in Jehovah, and we looked confidently for His preservation, for we knew, by the faith that the gospel had implanted in our hearts, that the arm of the Eternal Father was stretched out for our preservation.

"I cannot relate how our animals fared outside; but the peltings of the rain and hail hurled against them by such fierce wind as blew through that night must have tortured them unmercifully. I understood, however, that they, as much as possible, were placed at the lee side of the wagons and the large building that sheltered us. Nearly everything in our wagons was wet and unfit for use until overhauled and dried.

"At length the terrible night was passed and a glorious morning's sun chased away the darkness and revealed for our inspection the fragmentary condition of the woods and fields. A visible change had been wrought by the warring elements. The work of havoc and devastation met the eye in every direction. Trees were uprooted and limbs hurled in great quantities to the earth. But the brightness of the new-born day and the reviving warmth of the June sun reassured all nature . . . The brethren also partook of the genial influence. They rejoiced in the morning's effulgence and thanked God that He had preserved them and revived within them an increase of faith in His overruling providence. They took hasty excursions here and there and found the storm had left its destructive mark to an extent that surpassed expectation. From the place of our encampment we heard the roar of water in the river and in a short time some of our men returned and declared that the water in Fishing River was forty feet deep! When we made our encampment there it was no more than knee deep. What did we understand by this? We understood that the Almighty had sent that storm for the special preservation of Zion's Camp. This was a great truth that was plain to our comprehension and the gratitude we felt to our Heavenly Father was such that melted our hearts with thankfulness.

"As soon as we well could, we prepared for starting . . . We found the road in many places strewn with limbs and a few trees, some of which we had to remove before we could proceed . . . the roads were muddy and our progress . . . anything but rapid. After we had traveled a few miles we came to a friendly family who received us with feelings of humane sympathy. We camped at that place and took time to rest . . . The Prophet there made a speech to the members of the camp, and, if I remember correctly, a few strangers were present. Joseph spoke almost with superhuman force and clearness. He told us that the storm had been sent by the God of Israel to place a barrier between us and our enemies, to prevent them from falling upon us during the night to massacre us, as the men who rode into our camp the evening before had declared was the intention. We soon learned from the inhabitants that this was certainly in the program of a few hundred men to do, who were posted not far from the ford on the opposite shore.

"Could we now have the prophetic declarations made by the Prophet Joseph in his speech at that place they would be far above the value of gold . . . I can see him to this day, in memory, as his tall, manly form stood erect and commanding. His face shone with the light of the Holy Spirit, his mild blue eyes fairly sparkled with the fire of the divinity that possessed his being . . .

"He declared the storm of that night was to be numbered among the manifestations which were to follow in the last days in defense of the house of Israel, scattered among the nations of the earth. He said the fury of elements would yet waste away the wicked, and floods would overflow the river banks and sweep the precious fruits of soil from the possession of those who had labored to mature them. The sea would sweep beyond its bounds and work havoc, and that earthquakes would shake the earth and cast down the dwellings of those whose hearts rebelled against the everlasting gospel. God would visit the wicked nations with just retribution, for many of them would harden their hearts against the testimony of the humble ambassadors of truth; that the time was nigh when He would have a controversy with the people of the earth, for they would yet shed the blood of His prophets and cast out His people from their borders. These sayings were not uttered in the exact words here written, but this will convey to the reader a portion of the substance of his declarations. He said also that Jehovah had commanded that journey to be taken and He would protect the members of the camp to their place of destination; that no hand should prosper that should be lifted against them, if they would continue to be united and faithful in walking by the counsel that should be imparted to them from time to time by the influence of the Spirit of the Great Jehovah."

The *History of the Church, Vol. II* states that warnings had been given by some of the Missourians to the members of the Camp that sixty men were coming from Ray County and seventy more from Clay County to join the Jackson County mob, who had sworn their utter destruction. Samuel C. Owens and James Campbell had been in Independence to raise the army.

"Campbell swore, as he adjusted his pistols in his holsters, 'The eagles and turkey buzzards shall eat my flesh if I do not fix Joe Smith and his army so that their skins will not hold shucks, before two days are passed.' They went to the ferry and undertook to cross the Missouri river after dusk, and the angel of God saw fit to sink the boat about the middle of the river, and seven out of twelve that attempted to cross, were drowned . . . Campbell was among the missing. He floated down river some four or five miles, and lodged upon a pile of drift wood, where the eagles, buzzards, ravens, crows, and wild animals ate his flesh from his bones, to fulfill his own words. He was discovered about three weeks after . . . Owens saved his life only after floating four miles down the stream, where he lodged upon an island, 'swam off naked about day light, borrowed a mantle to hide his shame, and slipped home rather shy of the vengeance of God.'"

The five men on horseback in their camp, swearing vengeance, had crossed Fishing River before the wind, thunder, and rising cloud indicated an approaching storm, but after a short time the rain and hail began to fall.

"The storm was tremendous; wind and rain, hail and thunder met them in great wrath, and soon softened their direful courage, and frustrated all their designs to 'kill Joe Smith and his army.' Instead of continuing a cannonading which they commenced when the sun was about one hour high, they crawled under wagons, into hollow trees, and filled one old shanty, till the storm was over, when their ammunition was soaked, and the forty in Clay County were extremely anxious in the morning to return to Jackson . . . fully satisfied, as were those survivors of the company who were drowned, that when Jehovah fights they would rather be absent."

Zion's Camp moved on to "procure food for ourselves and horses, and defend ourselves from the rage of our enemies . . . on Saturday the 21st, Colonel Sconce, with two other leading men from Ray County, came to see us, desiring to know what our intentions were; 'for,' said he, 'I see that there is an Almighty power that protects this people, for I started from Richmond, Ray County, with a company of armed men, having a fixed determination to destroy you, but was kept back by the storm, and was not able to reach you.' When he entered our camp, he was seized with such a trembling that he was obliged to sit down to compose himself; and when he had made known the object of their visit, I [Joseph Smith Jr.] arose, and, addressing them, gave a relation of the sufferings of the Saints in Jackson County, and also our persecutions generally, and what we had suffered by our enemies for our religion; and that we had come one thousand miles to assist our brethren, to bring them clothing, etc., and to reinstate them upon their own lands; and that we had no intention to molest or injure any people, but only to administer to the wants of our afflicted friends; and that the evil reports circulated about us were false, and got up by our enemies to procure our destruction. When I had closed a lengthy speech, the spirit of which melted them into compassion, they arose and offered me their hands, and said they would use their influence to allay the excitement which everywhere prevailed against us; and they wept when they heard of our afflictions and persecutions, and learned that our intentions were good. Accordingly they went forth among the people, and made unwearied exertions to allay the excitement.

"Brother Ezra Thayre and Joseph Hancock were sick with the cholera. Previous to crossing the Mississippi River I had called the camp together and told them that in consequence of the disobedience of some who had been unwilling to listen to my words, but had rebelled, God had decreed that sickness should come upon the camp, and if they did not repent and humble themselves before God they should die like sheep with the rot; that I was sorry, but could not help it. The scourge must come; repentance and humility may mitigate the chastisement, but cannot altogether avert it. But there were some who would not give heed to my words . . .

"June 23—We resumed our march for Liberty, Clay County, taking a circuitous course around the heads of Fishing River, to avoid the deep water . . . and encamped on the bank of Rush Creek, in Brother Burket's field . . . [Negotiations continued. Church callings were given.]

"June 24— This night the cholera burst forth among us, and about midnight it was manifested in its most virulent form. Our ears were saluted with cries and moanings, and lamentations on every hand; even those on guard fell to the earth with their guns in their hands, so sudden and powerful was the attack of this terrible disease . . . The moment I attempted to rebuke the disease I was attacked, and had I not desisted in my attempt to save the life of a brother, I would have sacrificed my own. The disease seized upon me like the talons of a hawk, and I said to the brethren; 'If my work were done, you would have to put me in the ground without a coffin."

HC page 116 quotes from Heber C. Kimball's journal:

"This was our situation, the enemies around us, and the destroyer in our midst . . . It was truly affecting to see the love manifested among the brethren for one another, during the affliction . . . All that kept our enemies from us was the fear of the destroyer which the Lord so sent among us."

Joseph Smith sent letters to the Missourians, telling of the persecutions of the Lord's people. He recovered sufficiently that on the 1st of July, "I [Joseph] crossed the Missouri River, in company with a few friends, into Jackson County, to set my feet once more on the 'goodly land'; and on the 2nd I went down near Liberty, and visited the brethren. A considerable number of the Camp met me at Lyman Wight's. I told them if they would humble themselves before the Lord and covenant to keep His commandments and obey my counsel, the plague should be stayed from that hour, and there should not be another case of cholera among them. The brethren covenanted to that effect with uplifted hands, and the plague was stayed. [About 68 of the Saints suffered from this disease, of which 14 died.]

"On the third of July, the High Priests of Zion assembled in the yard of Col. Arthurs, where Lyman Wight lived, in Clay County, and I proceeded to organize a High Council . . . for the purpose of settling important business that might come before them, which could not be settled by the Bishop and his council. David Whitmer was elected president, and William W. Phelps and John Whitmer, assistant presidents . . . I authorized General Lyman Wight to give a discharge to every man of the Camp who had proved himself faithful, certifying that fact and giving him leave to return home."

We have no record that any of the IVIEs or ALLREDs was afflicted with cholera. They, of course, were not numbered with the dead. In cousin ISAAC ALLRED's autobiography, he says:

"After the church was driven from Jackson County in the spring in company with the Prophet and two hundred brethren, we marched to Clay County to liberate the Brethren from their bondage; but it was all in vain of all human endeavor."

— 5 —

"I AM NOT ASHAMED," MISSIONARIES AND DISSENTERS

When Zion's Camp disbanded, the Prophet Joseph Smith suggested that some should stay in Clay County, especially the young unmarried men. Wilford Woodruff, Milton Holmes, Joseph Holbrook, his wife and two children, and his brother, Chandler, and his wife Eunice were among those who stayed. Wilford Woodruff was soon called to go on a mission to Arkansas, Tennessee, and Kentucky with a senior companion, Harry Brown. They started in frontier Arkansas with little success, and Harry Brown became anxious to return to his family in Kirtland. They took a poorly marked, uncleared route that was obstructed by swamps, rivers, and creeks, hoping to speed up their arrival in Tennessee. Unfortunately, by 24 Mar 1835, perhaps sixty miles west of the Mississippi, the cold swampy conditions had inflicted one of Woodruff's knees with severe rheumatic pain, and he could not walk.

Wilford Woodruff wrote:

"Instead of staying to help his companion, Brown decided to press on alone to Memphis where he could catch a steamer for an Ohio River port. Left alone on a stump, Woodruff commented with perhaps a bit of understatement that although he did not object to the proposition . . . he thought he would not be willing to leave a lame companion in the ministry in an open swamp without knowing whether he would ever be able to walk far enough to again meet with any company more acceptable than the wolves, bears, and alligators with which he was surrounded. Woodruff sat on the log until Brown passed from sight, then knelt down and prayed to be healed." He writes, "The Lord heard my prayer and the Spirit of God descended upon me and I was healed and I arose and went my way rejoicing."

He went to Tennessee, and joining with more diligent companions, he was more successful. Woodruff labored along both sides of the northern Tennessee River and into Kentucky. Joseph Holbrook and Milton Holmes went eastward across Missouri and into Tennessee on their mission. In his autobiography Joseph Holbrook writes:

"On the 23rd of December, 1834, I . . . started in company with Amasas Lyman, Heman T. Hyde and Milton Holmes. We preached on our way whenever we could get a privilege, sometimes going a day and night without food in the winter season across the prairies with houses 25 miles apart which made it very severe upon me until we came to the Salt River church where there was a conference held. On account of being lame, it was counseled that Milton Holmes, my former partner, should take WILLIAM IVIE and go to Tennessee and that I remain a few days with the church and MARTIN ALLRED and go on a . . . mission in [that] part of Missouri and Illinois."

Milton Holmes sent his report:

"I journeyed with Elder W. IVY, we journeyed as far as Montgomery co.–Ill. preached by the way and baptized two. From thence we journeyed to Bedford Co. Tennessee; we tarried in this State about two months. [The IVIEs and ALLREDs lived in Bedford County before they moved to Missouri.] The people flocked from every quarter, to hear preaching, many were convinced of the truth, but few obeyed the gospel. We baptized five in this State; we left Bedford Co. the first day of June; arrived at Hamilton co. Ill. [about 30 miles north of the Ohio River], the 8th day of the same month, here we tarried, and labored in company with elders E.H. Groves and I. Higbee about three weeks, and baptized 33. After this Elder IVY and myself baptized seven . . . Elder IVY left here the 29 of September, since he left, I baptized two more, I expect to baptize a number more in this place, who believe the work of the Lord. The Lord is blessing his children here with some of the gifts of the gospel. I remain your brother in the new covenant, Milton Holmes." Milton Holmes was called back to Kirtland.

One of these converts from Illinois, George Averett, wrote, "about April A.D. 1835, Elisha Graves and Isaac Higbee, Latter-day Saints, come through our parts of the country and stopped at my father's house and preached to me and to my father's family all of them that was at home at that time, baptizing some of them; my father and mother and three sisters and two brothers . . . There come into the settlement WILLIAM IVY and

Milton Homes and assisted them in their labors in that part of the country.

"The power of the Lord was made manifest to the believers. Mostly they spoke with new tongues and gave the interpretation of the same. The sick was healed and the hearts of all the believers had cause to rejoice in the goodness of God and the writer of this biography had as a testimony given to him from his Heavenly Father of the truth of the Latter-day work. Although he was only a child about nine years old the Lord answered his humble prayer and made manifest his power by healing him instantly of disease. For the first time he ever had faith to ask the Lord for such a blessing, seeing and hearing my mother and sister and many other spake with new tongues and give interpretation of the same. And many other manifestations of his power made manifest to his Saints in them days when they loved one another and sought the interests of each other, and the Lord blessed them that loved and worshipped him the true and living God.

"About April in the spring of A.D. 1836, my [sister and brothers and others] emigrated to the Caldwell County, Missouri [followed by parents and others in 1837] . . . This country seemed to teem with all of the blessings that mortals had or to wish for . . . honey, deer, turkeys, hens, quails, and the streams teeming with their furry tribes by the thousands and easy to obtain many beautiful groves of . . . timber and convenient wild fruit and nuts too numerous to mention."

[Note: According to family records, WILLIAM SHELTON IVIE married JULIA LOUISE VAN DYNE on the 2 August 1835 in Hamilton, Illinois. WILLIAM was age 23, and his young bride was 18 years old. He returned from his mission the end of September, 1835. Their first child, a boy, was born 11 Aug 1837. They gave him the name of my second-great-grandfather, JAMES RUSSELL IVIE. JULIA's parents were JOHN and SARAH BROWN VAN DYNE. The young couple would have eight children.]

According to cousin ISAAC ALLRED's history, he states: "In the year 1835, in the fall, I in company with my father and brothers with our families moved from Monroe to Clay County and stayed one year, bought land and made one crop. And in this year the people were as reckless as ever as were some members of the church living with them. After awhile, it was thought best for our people to live more to themselves, [so] In the fall of the year 1836, there was a location sought out by some delegates from both sides for the Church to settle . . . in Ray County . . . we moved to a new location, which afterwards was organized into a county and called Caldwell. I bought of the Government and made a farm."

In the spring of 1836, cousin ISAAC ALLRED responded to another mission call. He wrote: "Myself in company with Elder Benjamin L. Clapp started on the 13th day of December . . . We travelled 1100 miles and preached 41 times and baptized 5. I left Brother Clapp for home and ordained one Elder and got home on the 18th of March. After I got home I was sick with the measles. I went to a general Conference at Far West, on the 6th of April [1837]."

During the fall of 1837 and until April of 1838, there were many internal problems within The Church of Jesus Christ of Latter-Day Saints. When Joseph Smith was in Missouri with Zion's Camp in 1834, he established, through revelation, a presidency and high council to direct and help the church in Missouri, consisting of President David Whitmer, Counselors, John Whitmer and W. W. Phelps, with Oliver Cowdery, the assistant and clerk. Thomas B. Marsh and David Patten of the Council of the Twelve Apostles remained in Missouri, and Bishop Partridge remained in his position.

The Missouri stake presidency was accused of the misuse for their own benefit of *temple funds* in the purchase of the land for the temple site and the city of Far West. The situation totally deteriorated, with the presidency in Missouri and Oliver Cowdery on one side and the high council, the two Apostles, Bishop Partridge and most of the church membership on the other. This contention climaxed before Joseph Smith arrived for their 7 April 1878 conference, when with the vote of the people, the stake presidency was not sustained.

On 12 and 13 April 1838, in Missouri, Oliver Cowdery and David Whitmer were called separately before the high council on a variety of charges; Joseph Smith was present. Neither was willing to appear and asked that their names be withdrawn from church membership. They were then excommunicated. John Whitmer and W. W. Phelps also left the church. A new Missouri presidency was installed with the funds placed under the care of Bishop Partridge.

Oliver Cowdery and David Whitmer were two of the *Three Witnesses to the Book of Mormon*. John Whitmer was one of the *Eight Witnesses*. It would be later that year in Kirtland that Martin Harris, the last of the *Three Witnesses*, would also leave the church. Not one of them, however, ever denied their witness to the *Book of Mormon*. Oliver Cowdery and Martin Harris returned to the Church later; but David and John Whitmer never did. David Whitmer moved to Richmond, Missouri, and John Whitmer stayed in Far West

Kirtland's problems were also bad because of the bank problems that had spread throughout the nation in 1837. Warren Parrish was accused of skimming money from the Kirtland bank, while speculation in land and homes by many of the Saints created additional problems. An attempt was made by Warren Parrish to displace Joseph Smith as President and Prophet of the Church, and replace him with David Whitmer, who had not consented. Parrish and his followers had taken over the sacred Kirtland Temple, which the Saints had struggled so hard to build and where Moses, Elias, and Elijah had appeared in 1836 to open this new dispensation. Warren's group moved into the temple and defended their position with guns.

> Alexander H. Stephens' *History of the United States* describes the nation's problems. "Soon after Mr. Van Buren became president occurred a great commercial crisis. This was in April, 1837, and was occasioned by a reckless speculation, which had, for two or three preceding years, been fostered and encouraged by excessive banking, and the consequent expansion of paper currency beyond all the legitimate wants of the country. During the months of March and April of this year the failures in New York City alone amounted to $100,000,000."

Bankruptcies were occurring in Kirtland and Joseph Smith Jr. was blamed by many and accused by many dissenters as being a *fallen prophet*—partially because he hadn't saved them from their own speculations.

[Note: We have no exact date from the family histories, when the IVIEs left Monroe County, Missouri, and moved to Far West, Caldwell County. Second-great-grandparents JAMES RUSSELL and ELIZA IVIE's sixth child, POLLY ANN, was born in Florida, Missouri, on 24 Aug 1835, and they were in Caldwell County when their seventh child, ELIZABETH CAROLINE, was born 1 Nov 1837. So it would seem that this family moved west sometime between these two dates. By the time their eighth child, JOSEPH ORSON, was born, 1 Jan 1840, the family had been driven back across the state and was in Monroe County again. In 1837, JAMES RUSSELL IVIE would be 35 years old, his oldest child, RICHARD ANDERSON IVIE (named after his two grandfathers), would be 12 years old and great-grandfather JOHN LEHI IVIE was only 4 years old.

In *The Mormon Battalion* by Kate B. Carter, a brief history of REDDICK NEWTON ALLRED states, "He and his twin brother REDDIN, were baptized into the Latter-day Saints Church in the spring of 1833 by JOHN IVIE." These twins were sons of *uncle* ISAAC ALLRED, a brother of SARAH ALLRED IVIE, therefore, they were first cousins of JAMES RUSSELL IVIE—but younger. The JOHN IVIE mentioned would be JOHN ANDERSON IVIE, the brother of second-great-grandfather JAMES RUSSELL IVIE. He is the JOHN A. IVIE of Zion's Camp. REDDICK NEWTON ALLRED is the Colonel ALLRED of the Utah Indian Wars, and great-grandfather Colonel JOHN LEHI IVIE's commanding officer in Sanpete County, Utah. REDDICK N. ALLRED's history says, "On the 25th of April, 1838, the family moved to Far West."]

Cousin ISAAC ALLRED went on another mission.

"On the 29th of April, I preached at Brother Crides and baptized and confirmed them. I put a crop in the spring of the year, 1838, and then on the

11th day of June, I started in company with Clapp . . . Lay . . . Alexander and Petty to preach again on my second mission. I took passage on the steamer Kansas at Jack Ferry in Ray County. I went to St. Louis, then down the [Mississippi] river and up the Ohio to Prode Ferry and then commenced our labours. I left Petty and Alexander at the mouth of the Tennessee River. We landed on the Kentucky side and went up into Warren County and Clapp and Lay left me. [ISAAC's mother, a WARREN, had been born there.]

"I laboured in that County for four weeks and then I left and came back to Missouri and laboured where I had travelled before in my first mission. I returned home after traveling 2100 miles, preached 35 times and baptized 4 souls. I got home on the 29th of September, 1838."

Back in Kirtland, Ohio, Milton Holmes, WILLIAM IVIE's former missionary companion, was called to be Wilford Woodruff's missionary companion, and they were called to go to England. Woodruff would serve as the president of the branch in Manchester, England. In Kirtland, Wilford Woodruff had married PHEBE W. CARTER, and she accompanied him on his mission, although she was pregnant. Their child was born in Scarborough, Maine, where her parents lived. They did a great deal of missionary work in this area before they left for England. PHEBE W. CARTER, was probably related to JOHN and DOMINICUS CARTER, as their father lived in Scarborough, also.

— 6 —

EXTERMINATION ORDERS OF THE WORST KIND — FAR WEST, CALDWELL, MISSOURI

On 6 March 1838 there was a meeting in the Kirtland Temple to discuss the moving of the Saints in Kirtland to the land of Missouri, in accordance with the commandments and revelations of God, and on Saturday, 17 March, a Constitution was drawn up and subscribed to. Among the signers were: NATHAN STAKER, a second-great-grandfather of my sister ADELIA's husband, JOSEPH RILE, and JOHN and DOMINICUS CARTER. The CARTER brothers had arrived in Kirtland just shortly before. This "Kirtland Camp" arrived in Far West on Tuesday, 2 October 1838, having traveled eight hundred and thirty miles. Some were still living in their wagons when the terrible extermination order was signed by Governor Boggs of Missouri, who was a former member of the Jackson County mobbers. A few of these Ohio saints had remained at Haun's Mill, and they were there on that fateful massacre day.

In Far West, the saints had experienced calm in their daily living until the 4th of July celebration of 1838 when war clouds began to gather and threaten as the fall elections approached. Parley P. Pratt wrote, "Those who had combined against the laws in the adjoining counties had long watched our increasing power and prosperity with jealousy, and with greedy and avaricious eyes. It was a common boast that, as soon as we had completed our extensive improvements, and made a plentiful crop, they would drive us from the State, and once more enrich themselves with the spoils."

George Averett, the young convert from Hamilton County, Illinois, described events in Far West as follows:

"About the months of July and August the mobbers of the neighbor-hood and joining counties of Ray, Clinton and La Fayette, Jackson and Daviess began to howl like so many bloodthirsty wolves, appealing to their neighbors for help and declaring that the Mormons and Joe Smith would overrun the country, and at the same time making all manners of lying, slandering reproaches against the Latter-day Saints and especially against Joseph Smith, the prophet of the Lord, having driven the Saints from time to time from Jackson County and Ray, Clay, and Clinton, robbing them of their homes and property.

"In August . . . at the election polls in [Gallatin,] Daviess County, Missouri, some of the mobbers decided that the d--d Mormons shouldn't vote and in consequence of their undertaking to enforce the same, one of the Saints by the name of Butler and some several of the mob got into a fight . . . Butler coming out victorious in the skirmish by being an expert in wielding his cudgel. This affair still enraged the mobbers still more in Daviess and the adjoining counties."

The Far West militia was ordered to help the Saints in Daviess County. Their defense was so efficient that the mobs that were collecting dispersed, realizing that other tactics would be needed. They took their belongings out of some of their log cabins and then set fire to the cabin, blaming the Mormons for destroying their homes, in an effort to gain the support of the government, for they knew that the Mormons always obeyed the laws of the country.

The following incident occurred during the time the militia was defending their families and their lands, and the law was on the side of the Mormons. The WILLIAM ALLRED mentioned was a brother of third-great-grandmother SARAH ALLRED IVIE.

[see *HC Vol. III, p. 74*] It was Sunday, September 9 that "Captain WILLIAM ALLRED took a company of ten mounted men and went to intercept a team with guns and ammunition, sent from Richmond to the mob in Daviess County. They found the wagon broken down, and the boxes of guns drawn into the high grass near by the wagon; there was no one present that could be discovered. In a short time two men on horseback came . . . and immediately behind them was a man with a wagon; they . . . were taken by virtue of a writ on the supposition that they were abetting the mob, by carrying guns and ammunition to them. The men were taken, together with the guns, to Far West; the guns were distributed among the brethren, for their defense, and the prisoners were held in custody . . . Captain ALLRED acted under the civil authorities in Caldwell, who issued the writ for securing the arms and arresting the carriers . . . The "spoils of war" were delivered to the Colonel of the regiment, who delivered them to the higher State authorities."

From George Averett's journal, "Sometimes during that fall a portion of the Saints who lived at DeWitt on or near the Missouri River [southeast Carroll County] was driven from their homes and full grown fields of corn, and would have been murdered if it had not of been that the hand of the Lord was over his people for good and his prophet Joseph was awake to his duties and went to their welfare with some of his brethren of the Saints and assisted them and guarded them to the city of Far West . . . One of the mobbers, before the Saints left DeWitt, approaching the night guard (a man by the name of Alexander Williams) while on duty and firing their guns at him without effect and breaking to run he, Williams, fired his gun at one of them striking him near the mouth, and to use the language of Williams he made the mobber call on his God he thought for the first time in his whole lifetime, and it was stated that Williams shot his chew of tobacco out of his mouth."

Butler's and William's victories for their rights and self-preservation were used as a pretext for a general rising of the insurrectionists in all the adjoining counties. They were alarmed for fear the *Mormons,* as they called them, should become so formidable as to maintain their rights and liberties, insomuch that they could no more drive and plunder them. Public meetings were held in Carroll, Saline, and other counties in which resolutions were passed and published, openly declaring the treasonable and murderous intention of driving the citizens belonging to the Church from their counties, and, if possible, from the State.

Averett's journal continues: "Resolutions to this effect were published in the journals of Upper Missouri, and this without a single remark of disapprobation. Nay, more: this murderous gang, when assembled in arms and painted like Indian warriors, and when openly committing murder, robbery, house burning and every crime known to the laws, were denominated citizens . . . in most of the journals of the State. While those who stood firm to the laws of the land, and only defended themselves, and their homes and country, were denominated 'Mormons,' as if we had been some savage tribe of foreigners . . . They commenced firing upon our citizens, plundering, and taking peaceable citizens prisoners. The people of the Church made no resistance, except to assemble on their own ground for defence . . . Hundreds were thus compelled to flee to the cities . . . Many women and children came in at the dead hours of the night, and in the midst of dreadful storms of rain and snow, in which they came near perishing . . . land and crops were abandoned to the enemy. Men slept in their clothes, with arms by their sides, and ready to muster at a given signal at any hour of the night."

Parley P. Pratt described the Battle at Crooked River:

"The night was dark, the distant plains far and wide were illuminated by blazing fires, immense columns of smoke were seen rising in awful majesty, as if the world was on fire . . . This scene, added to the silence of midnight, the rumbling sound of the tramping steeds over the hard and dried surface of the plain, the clanking of swords in their scabbards . . . and the unknown destiny of the expedition, or even of the people who sent it forth . . . In this solemn procession we moved on for some two hours . . . We were then ordered to dismount and leave our horses with a guard. This done, we proceeded on foot for a mile or two in search of the enemy. We had not proceeded far when, as we entered the wilderness, we were suddenly fired upon by an unknown enemy in ambush. One of our little number fell at the first fire, being mortally wounded . . . At a short distance we could now behold the camp fires of the enemy. It was now dawn of day in the eastern horizon, but darkness still hovered over the scenes of conflict. Orders were issued to form in the brush, and under cover of the trees, which was instantly done. The fire now became general on both sides, and the whole wilderness seemed one continued echo of the report of the deadly rifle. After a few rounds of discharges, orders were given to charge the enemy in the camp. As we rushed upon them the strife became deadly, and several fell on both sides. At this instant a ball pierced the brave Colonel, David Patten, who was then at my side, and I saw him fall. Being on the eve of victory, I dared not stop to look after his fate, or that of others, but rushed into the enemy's camp. This was located on the immediate banks of Crooked River, which was several rods wide, and not fordable. The enemy being hard pushed, flung themselves into the stream, and struggled for the other shore. Those who reached it soon disappeared . . . Our little band, which had been thrown into some disorder, were instantly formed, and their pieces reloaded. This done, a detachment surveyed the field, to look after the wounded . . . Many . . . were wounded, and some dangerously. The enemy had left their horses, saddles, camp and baggage, in the confusion of their flight. We harnessed some of their horses and placed them before a wagon, arranged blankets therein, on which we laid those who were not able to mount a horse; this done, our whole troop mounted the horses we had taken . . . We then moved slowly back to the guard and horses we had left. Here we halted and readjusted the wounded. It was an awful sight to see them pale and helpless, and hear their groans. There were about six of our men wounded, and one dead . . . The enemy suffered a similar loss, besides their camp, and many of their arms and military stores.

"We ascertained from the prisoners whom we rescued, that the enemy consisted of about sixty marauders, headed by a Methodist preacher, named Bogart. Our 'posse' who were actually engaged, could not have been more than fifty. At the commencement of the engagement there were three of our fellow citizens held prisoners in their camp; they had been kidnaped from their peaceful homes the day previous. Two of these made their escape at the commencement of the engagement; the third was shot through the body in attempting to run to our lines, but fortunately recovered."

After returning to Far West, David Patten, a member of the Twelve Apostles, died that night. Possibly JAMES RUSSELL IVIE and other relations belonged to this Caldwell County Militia, a requirement for all unassigned able-bodied men, ordered to defend the county against these bandits, or the self-appointed mobs at Crooked River.

Parley P. Pratt writes:

"These several defeats of the insurrectionists in Daviess County, as well as in Caldwell County, checked for a time their ruinous ravages. They saw that it was impossible to conquer a people who were fighting for their homes, their wives and children, as well as for their country and conscience, unless they could come against them with some show of authority; for it had become an established fact that the people of the Saints never resisted authority, however abused. The next exertion of the enemy was to spread lies and falsehoods of the most alarming character. All our acts of defence were construed into insurrection, treason, murder and plunder. In short, the public were deceived by bigotry, priestcraft, and a corrupt press. Murderous gangs were construed [as] peaceable militia in the State service, and to resist them was, on the part of the Saints, murder, treason and robbery . . . And, as if this were not enough, parties set fire to their own houses, or that of their neighbors, and then laid it to the Saints . . . This flame was greatly assisted by several dissenters from the Church through fear, or for love of power and gain. These dissenters became even more false, hardened, and blood-thirsty than those who had never known the way of righteousness. Many of them joined the enemy, and were the leaders in all manner of lying, murder and plunder. The Governor and ex-mobber, Lilburn W. Boggs, who had long sought some opportunity to destroy us, and drive us from the State, now issued an order for some ten thousand troops to be mustered into service and marched to the field against the 'Mormons.' He gave the command of this formidable force to General Clark, who lived, perhaps, a hundred and fifty miles or more from the scene of trouble. The order was expressly to exterminate the 'Mormons,' or drive them from the State.

"It said nothing of criminals; it made no allusion to punishing crime and protecting innocence; it was sufficient to be called a 'Mormon.' A peaceable family just emigrating, or passing through the country; a missionary going or coming on his peaceable errand of mercy; an aged soldier of the American revolution on his death bed, or leaning on his staff in the chimney corner; a widow with her babes; the tender wife or helpless orphan; all were included in this order of wholesale extermination . . . On the other hand, all the bandits, murderers, robbers, thieves, and house burners who had mobbed our people for the five years previous, were now converted into orderly, loyal, patriotic State militia, and mustered into service under pay, or suffered to murder people of every age and sex, and plunder them on their own hook wherever they chose, provided they were considered 'Mormons.'

"While General Clark was mustering his forces for this wholesale murder and treason, Major General D. Lucas and Brigadier General Moses Wilson, who were well known as the old leaders of the former outrages in Jackson County, under this same Boggs—being nearer the scene of action, and wishing to share the plunder and immortalize their names—put themselves at the head of all the old mobbers of Jackson County they could muster, and all those bandits who had more lately infested the counties of Carroll, Davies and Caldwell, and marched directly for the City of Far West, where they arrived while General Clark and his forces were several days' journey from the scene of action. The army of Lucas, thus mustered and marched, consisted of some three or four thousand men."

George Averett writes:

"Difficulty occurred betwixt the Saints and the mob in the neighborhood of Haun's Mill and the two parties met together and held a treaty of peace, [but when the extermination order was signed], the mobbers, contrary to their solemn agreement, returned and commenced some 200 hundred of them to fire on the unsuspecting Saints, men, women and children, massacring them in a most brutal manner so much so that my ability is inadequate to describe the extent of the same after satisfying their hellish desires by the shedding of blood. And some of them mangling the bodies of the slain after death; one man, by the name of McBride whose body was horribly mangled by being cut to pieces with a mowing scythe. It was also told that some of the mobbers fired at some of the women of that place, shutting them in their place after they had done all the meanness by killing all the men they could find alive. They murdered two small boys to satisfy their hellish disposition. All of this shouting happening at or near the Haun's Mill where there was a small [number] of houses and amongst the worst, one blacksmith's shop in which the most part, as I am informed of the murder, was committed and after the affair was all over 17 of the slain was buried in an old well near the shop by the few men that was left and the women of the place."

Parley P. Pratt stated:

"In the meantime the Governor's orders and these military movements were kept an entire secret from the citizens of Caldwell and Davies, who were suffering all this oppression from lawless outrages; even the mail was withheld from Far West. We had only heard that large bodies of armed men were approaching from the south, and we had sent a hundred and fifty men with a flag of truce to make inquiries. While they were absent on this mission an alarm came to town that the whole county to the south was filled with armed men, who were murdering, plundering, and taking peaceful citizens prisoners in their own houses. On the receipt of this intelligence every man flew to arms for the protection of our city.

"It was now towards evening, and we had heard nothing from the reconnoitering company who went south in the morning. While we stood in our armor, gazing to the south in anxious suspense, we beheld an army of cavalry, with a long train of baggage wagons advancing over the hills, at two miles distance. At first we conjectured it might be our little troop with the flag of truce; but we soon saw that there were thousands of them. Our next thought was that it might be some friendly troops sent for our protection; and then again we thought it might be a concentration of all the bandit forces combined for our destruction.

"At all events, there was no time to be lost; for, although our force then present did not exceed five hundred men, yet we did not intend that they should enter the town without giving some account of themselves. We accordingly marched out upon the plains on the south of the city and formed in order of battle. Our line of infantry extended near half a mile. A small company of horses was posted on our right wing on a commanding

53

eminence, and another small company in the rear of our main body, intended as a kind of reserve. [The land surrounding Far West is very flat.] By this time the sun was near setting, and the advance of the unknown army had come within plain view, at less than one mile distant. On seeing our forces presenting a small but formidable front, they came to a halt, and formed along the borders of . . . Goose Creek.

"Both parties sent out a white flag, which met between the armies. Our messenger demanded to know who they were, and their intentions? The reply was: 'We want three persons out of the city before we massacre the rest!' This was a very alarming and unexpected answer. But they were soon prevailed on to suspend hostilities till morning . . . The enemy, under the command of Major General D. Lucas, of Jackson County mob memory, then commenced their encampment for the night. Our troops continued under arms during the night. The company of a hundred and fifty soon returned from the south, informing us that they had been hemmed in by the enemy during the day, and only escaped by their superior knowledge of the ground.

"We also sent an express to Davies County, and by morning were reinforced by quite a number of troops . . . In the meantime a noted company of Banditti . . . who had long infested our borders, and been notorious for their murders and daring robberies, and who painted themselves as Indian warriors, came pouring in from the West to strengthen the camp of the enemy.

"Another company of murderers came in from Carroll County, and were taken into the ranks of Lucas, after murdering some eighteen or twenty of our citizens (men, women and children) at Haun's Mill . . . The citizens of Far West being determined, if attacked, to defend their homes, wives and children to the last, spent the night in throwing up temporary breastwork of building timber, logs rails, floor plank, etc . . . In the morning the south side of the city was thus fortified, and also a considerable portion of the east and west sides—the whole line extending a mile and a half. October 31, 1838.—In the afternoon we were informed that the Governor had ordered this force against us, with orders to exterminate or drive every 'Mormon' from the State."

The following is from the journal of Mosiah Hannock:

"There was a mob of 1600 camped in the vicinity of Far West. Judas Iscariot [George M.] Hinkle came in and reported the state of affairs in the camp of the mobbers . . . A few days later, Hinkle formed a brotherhood in a hollow square, and made them cast their arms of defense on the ground. He then delivered the Prophet over to the mob! After they had taken the arms from the brethren, they kept the brethren in the square for three days and two nights without food. The mob became very brave after they had taken the brethren's arms. One of their officers complimented the men on their bravery, and said, 'Now you can go and do as you please with their women.' Many of them left with the intention of committing rapine. When the terrified women ran out to escape those brutal fiends, it was more than the men in the square could stand! They ran out to protect their loved ones; then the mobbers turned loose and shot down men, women, and children! They shot the children because they said that 'Nits Make Lice.'

"I saw C. C. Richardson going from Far West with a white flag of truce. As he and his companions approached the camp, they were fired upon by the mobbers. Luckily, none of the brethren were hit, and a truce was patched up. But the mobbers were not to be trusted. After the brethren had delivered up their arms, father mounted his horse Turk, and rode off to Adam-ondi-Ahman. A party of forty-two of the mobs cavalry started in pursuit of father. A whisper came to him, 'Go through the Hale thicket, then turn to the left.' This he did, and it brought him in the rear of the gang that was pursuing him. He said to one of the men in the rear, 'Where has that fellow gone?' 'I don't know' was the answer, 'but we will soon catch him.' Father stopped his horse and pretended to tighten his saddle-girth and then he escaped from his pursuants.'"

From Joseph Fielding Smith's *Gospel Doctrine. p. 526* we read,

"Governor Boggs had issued his order to exterminate the 'Mormons' . . . through the heartless treachery of Colonel Hinkle, Joseph and Hyrum and several other leaders of the people were betrayed into the hands of an armed mob under General Clark." Some of our ALLRED relations were baptized into the Church by this "heartless" neighbor of Monroe County, Colonel George M. Hinkle.

Joseph Smih Jr. stated,

"After we were bartered away by Hinkle, and were taken into the militia camp, we had all the evidence we could have asked for that the world hated us. If there were priests among them of all the different sects, they hated us, and that most cordially too. If there were generals, they hated us; if there were colonels, they hated us; and the soldiers, and officers of every kind, hated us, most cordially. And now what did they hate us for? Purely because of *the testimony of Jesus Christ.*" [Teachings of the Prophet Joseph Smith" p. 125]

Parley P. Pratt with Joseph and Hyrum Smith, and others were taken to the enemy camp. Pratt described the situation:

"[W]ith thousands of malicious fiends, all clamoring, exulting, deriding, blaspheming, mocking, railing, raging and foaming like a troubled sea . . . placed under strong guard . . . without shelter during the night, lying on the ground in the open air, in the midst of a great rain . . . [They were informed that they would be shot in the morning at 8 o'clock. General Doniphan refused to carry out this order of "*cold-blooded murder*."] The next morning Gen. Lucas demanded that the Caldwell militia give up their arms, which was done. As soon as the troops who had defended the city were disarmed, it was surrounded by the enemy and all the men detained as prisoners. None were permitted to pass out of the city—although their families were starving for want of sustenance; the mills and provisions being some distance from the city. The brutal mob was now turned loose to ravage, steal, plunder and murder without restraint. Houses were rifled, women ravished, and goods taken as they pleased. The whole troop, together with their horses, lived on the grain and provisions. While cattle were shot down for mere sport, and sometimes men, women and children fared no better."

The prisoners, saved by Brigadier General Doniphan's refusal to shoot them, were loaded in a wagon and returned to Far West for a change of clothing and to say farewell to their families.

Parley P. Pratt continues:

"[H]undreds of the brethren crowded around us, anxious to take a parting look, or a silent shake of the hand; for feelings were too intense to allow of speech . . . A march of twelve miles brought us [the prisoners] to Crooked River, where we camped for the night. Here Gen. Wilson began to treat us more kindly; he became very sociable; conversing very freely on the subject of his former murders and robberies committed against us in Jackson. He did not pretend to deny anything . . . Said he: 'We Jackson County boys know how it is; and, therefore, have not the extremes of hatred and prejudice which characterize the rest of the troops. We know perfectly that from the beginning the Mormons have not been the aggressors at all. As it began in '33 in Jackson County, so it has been ever since. You Mormons were crowded to the last extreme and compelled to self-defence; and this has been construed into treason, murder and plunder. We mob you without law; the authorities refuse to protect you according to law; you then are compelled to protect yourselves, and we act upon the prejudices of the public, who join our forces, and the whole is legalized, for your destruction and our gain. Is not this a shrewd and cunning policy? When we drove you from Jackson County, we burned two hundred and three of your houses; plundered your goods; destroyed your press, type, paper, books, office and all—tarred and feathered old Bishop Partridge, as exemplary an old man as you can find anywhere. We shot down some of your men, and, if any of you returned the fire, we imprisoned you, on your trial for murder . . . D---'d shrewdly done, gentlemen; and I came d---'d near kicking the bucket myself; for, on one occasion, while we were tearing down houses, driving families, and destroying and plundering goods, some of you good folks put a ball through my son's body, another through the arm of my clerk, and a third pierced my shirt collar and marked my neck. No blame, gentlemen; we deserved it. And let a set of men serve me as your community have been served, and I'll be d---'d if I would not fight till I died. It was repeatedly insinuated, by the other officers and troops, that we should hang you prisoners on the first tree we came to on the way to Independence. But I'll be d----d if anybody shall hurt you. We just intend to exhibit you in Independence, let the people look at you, and see what a d----d set of fine fellows you are. And, more particularly, to keep you from the G--d d----d old bigot of a Gen. Clark and his troops, from down country, who are so stuffed with lies and prejudice that they would shoot you down in a moment.'"

George Averett remembered events in Far West—1838:

"[A]s soon as the mob and militia got possession of the city, they commenced to plunder the Saints' property in every quarter taking goods and chattels in every direction pretending that they was their goods and said that the d----d Mormons had stolen them from them, often claiming mens' horses that they never had seen before and taking them straightway with them biding defiance to all opposition. The writer of this sketch being a witness of some of their thefts in the following manner: he and his younger brother, being in a corn field gathering corn that they and their father and brothers had raised for their own use to make them bread and to feed their stock, the unprincipled mob came into their field of corn in great numbers, sweeping the corn as they went, asking no odds of the owner. And making their way up to the writer of the same and making a proposition to the affect that they would make these boys haul their corn to their camp, and no doubt would have carried their hellish plans into effect had not there have been one among them that had more human principle than the rest of his kind, riding up right in the nick of time and telling them to leave the boys alone. As soon as this opening presented itself, myself and my brother hastily left for home taking with us what corn that we had gathered without waiting to gather a full load. Things moved on in about this manner more or less until the Saints left the county of Caldwell, Missouri for the state of Illinois in cold weather thinly clad and poorly furnished with provisions in cold weather. In the winter and spring . . . leaving their homes in Caldwell, Daviess, and Clinton County to their enemies without asking for any remuneration whatever, my father leaving quite an improvement some two miles from Far West . . . my brothers left similar ones near Far West. The foregoing brothers names were Elijah and Elisha Averett who endured many hardships during the persecutions of the Saints in Missouri and also in Illinois."

Wilford Woodruff, on a mission to the South, stated:

"I left the sword and knife with Lyman Wight. When he was taken prisoner at Far West, with Joseph and Hyrum, he had both the sword and the knife with him. All their weapons were taken from them, so were the arms of many of the Saints at Far West, under promise that they should be returned to them when they were prepared to leave the State. When the brethren went to get their arms, Father JAMES ALLRED saw my sword, which Lyman Wight had laid down, and took it and left his own, and afterwards gave it to me and I still have it. I prize it because the Prophet Joseph carried it in Zion's Camp. The knife I never regained." [*Wilford Woodruff, Leaves From My Journal*]

Brigham Young, 18 February 1855, gave us this explanation:

"The starting point of our persecutions there [Caldwell County] arose by our enemies setting fire to their own houses, and swearing that they were burnt out and driven by the 'Mormons.' This I know, for it came under my own observation. When General Clark came into Far West with his army, he sent George M. Hinkle, the apostate, to call out the remainder of the brethren on to the public square, and when they were assembled he surrounded them with his men and said, 'Gentlemen, I have discretionary power in my hands, and I will now tell you what we desire. We wish one to go home with this man, and another with that man, and take your wives and children with you, and distribute yourselves through the State. You are the best mechanics and the most industrious people we have; and you have accomplished more here in two years, than our old settlers have in twelve. We wish you to live with us. Why cannot you associate with us? I want you to scatter among our people, and *give up your religion, and the prophet,* for I will tell you now, in the beginning, you will never see your Prophet, Joseph Smith, again.' (Said I to myself, 'That is a falsehood.') 'Only mingle with us, and give up your Prophet, your Apostles, and your assembling yourselves together, and we wish you to stay with us, *for you are the best citizens in the state.* I thought that these expressions did not correspond well with many of his remarks, and being determined not to give up my religion, I at once concluded that he might go to hell, and I would leave the State; and so I did, with the balance of the Latter-day Saints, as they had previously killed many."

On Saturday, 3 November 1838, Joseph and Hyrum Smith, Parley P. Pratt, and the other prisoners were hurried across the Missouri River by ferry and marched into Independence for exhibition as General Lucas had desired. Shortly after they crossed the river, a woman inquired of Joseph whether he professed to be the Lord and Savior. He replied:

> "I profess to be nothing but a man, and a minister of salvation, sent by Jesus Christ to preach the Gospel." This answer so surprised the woman that she inquired into the doctrine and Joseph Smith preached a discourse to her and her companions and the soldiers who listened *"with almost breathless attention."* The woman was satisfied, and praised God in the hearing of the soldiers, and went away, praying that God would protect and deliver them. They were marched into Independence, "past noon, in the midst of a great rain, and a multitude of spectators who had assembled to see [them]."

On Monday, 5 November 1838, in Far West, General Clark ordered the brethren to form a line and the names of fifty-six present were called and made prisoners to await their trial "for something they knew not what," and were kept under a close guard. Included in this list of "most wanted men" was cousin MARTIN C. ALLRED and uncle WILLIAM ALLRED, brother of SARAH ALLRED IVIE; also ANDREW WHITLOCK, who married a daughter of JAMES ALLRED, and HENRY ZABRISKIE, whose son later married a daughter of JAMES RUSSELL IVIE. Uncles JAMES and ISAAC ALLRED, were not listed, but were mentioned later as prisoners. On Tuesday, 6 November 1838, these prisoners at Far West were marched off for Richmond, under a strong guard. There was a severe snow storm. [*HC Vol. III pp. 202-9*]

General Clark exhaustively searched the statutes in an attempt to try the prisoners under a military court marshal, hoping to fulfill his desire to execute the prisoners, but finally unable to find any legal way, he turned the prisoners over to the civil authorities to be tried. Joseph Smith and the other prisoners with him were brought to Richmond to be tried with the 56 new prisoners by Judge Austin A. King on charges of high treason against the state, murder, burglary, arson, robbery, and larceny. The prisoners were asked to name their witnesses for their defense. As a witness was named, they were not brought as witnesses, but were imprisoned and charged with the same offenses as the other prisoners, which led to the observation and advice of the defense lawyers, Messrs. Doniphan and Reese, "that no other witnesses be named as there would not be one of them left for final trial." One man who was called as a witness was James Rollins. His journal records:

> "The Lightner brothers came up with a wagon, a prairie schooner, and they took . . . my sister . . . into this wagon. I was assisting . . . and they plead with me to go with them, and take my young wife along . . . They . . . secreted me in the bottom of the wagon lying with my face downward, and they threw bedding on top of me . . . We camped some 15 miles distance from Far West that night in the open prairie, and made our beds on the ground, and when we awoke . . . there was 2 or 3 inches of snow above us." They passed through Richmond and "arrived at Pomeroy ferry about 4 o'clock in the afternoon. The women and children were taken in the yowl, and the wagon and team were taken in the ferry boat. The ice being very bad, float-ing down in great chunks." The ferry-man didn't want to take him across but "Mr. Lightner said to him, 'Mr. Harwood, I want you to understand that when I go, he goes, and if he stays, I stay also.'"
>
> The ferryman took him across, but after they had been at Abner Lightner's house near Lancaster, Missouri, "some 5 days . . . there came a knock on the door. I bid them come in. A man stepped in the room and asked if Mr. Rollins was there. I told him I was the man. His name was Raglin, whom I knew very well in Daviess County. He said to me, 'Can you pay me for a horse that you bought of me?' I told him that he knew very well that I had nothing; that my partner, Slade, in Far West, had all my property and he (Slade) would pay it. At this time, two other men rapped at the door inquiring for me . . . I asked them what they wanted me for, and if they had any papers. They said, 'No, they were under martial law,' and I was wanted for a witness against others . . . They then ordered me to get onto one of the horses behind one of them. It was snowing very hard at the time. We went to the river where the ferry boats were lying awaiting their return.

We crossed the river among the flowing ice. The ferryman, Mr. Harwood, grinning at me, by whose means I was traced to Lightner's house."

He was then taken to the Richmond court house, where "General Clark appeared at the door, the men saying, 'Here is the man you sent us for.'

"He said, 'You get down off the horse, and go to the bull pen,' where sure enough there I found some 40 or 50 of our brethren, such as Bishop Partridge, Isaac Morley, JAMES and ISAAC ALLRED, and many others that I will not mention here, that were old men, and many of my former 10.

"I was called the next morning when court had convened and the state prosecutor read the charges which were treason, murder, arson, larceny, burglary. He asked me if I was guilty of any of these. I told him, 'No, sir, I am not guilty of none of them.' About 11 o'clock the Prophet Joseph and Hyrum were brought into the court department which was situated on the same floor where we were kept. A pole was stretched across to keep us back from Judge King and his court. I stood, close to the pole, at the back of Joseph and Hyrum, and the lawyers Donaphan and Atchison. A man was brought in as witness against me, by the name of Odell, who testified that I had burned his house. I spoke openly, as I stood behind Joseph and Hyrum, that he was a curly headed liar. Joseph turned his head toward me and said, 'Shaw, Henry, don't say anything.' This saying caused some consternation in the court room. What was done about it, I don't remember. We were kept prisoners for several weeks. At last it was agreed that we could bail each other out, one of the brethren bailing another. Sometimes one would go bail for three or four of the brethren until they were all bailed out but myself. ISAAC ALLRED having agreed to bail me out previous to this, but did not. I got one of the guards to go with me to find him. I asked him about it and he said he couldn't as he had already bailed out four or five of the men. I was then taken back and put under guard until evening."

He was told his beautiful young wife had come to see him.

"Donaphan and Atchison, the lawyers, took me to Gudgels Hotel to see her. They said I should stay there with my wife that night. They put us in a room 6 by 8 with 2 guards inside the room with their heads against the door. I was taken very sick in the night and my wife [wanted to get something] to relieve my pain. The guard was determined to not let her go out, when my brother-in-law, Mr. Carr, said, 'O let her go.' He was one of the mob.

"The next morning . . . about 10 o'clock in the day I succeeded in obtaining bail. My bail was fixed for all these crimes and I was signed by the notorious Beaugard Methodist preacher, Nathaniel Carr, my brother-in-law. Soon after this was settled, I obtained a horse, saddle and bridle, and started with my wife on the same horse for Far West, 36 miles distance. It was quite cold, and we had to ride and run alternately to get warm until we arrived, wearied, at Far West in the night safely. We had not been home long, [when] Beaugard appeared in Far West and exacted my step-father's hotel, my father-in-laws's hundred acres of land, and 40 acres of my own land, at least a thousand dollars worth of other property for security for the five hundred dollars for my bail, or he would take me back to prison. Some of the land that he wanted lay 3 miles from Haun's Mill. I had not heard whether my wife's father would consent to Beaugard's requirements or not."

After organizing the exodus, Brigham Young and others had to escape, or they would have been added to the "bull pit." From the History of the Church Joseph Smith recorded his imprisonment:

"About 30 of the brethren have been killed, many wounded, about a hundred are missing, and about sixty at Richmond awaiting their trial—for what they know not.

"Sunday, 11.—[November, 1838]—While in Richmond we were under the charge of Colonel [Sterling] Price from Chariton county [later General Price of Missouri in the Civil War], who allowed all manner of abuses to be heaped upon us. During this time my afflictions were great, and our situation was truly painful. [It was here he rebuked the 'vileness of the guards.'] General Clark informed us that he would turn us over to the civil authorities for trial . . .

"Monday, 12.—The first act of the court was to send out a body of armed men, without a civil process, to obtain witnesses.

"Tuesday, 13.—We were placed at the bar, Austin A. King presiding, and Thomas C. Burch, the state's attorney. Witnesses were called and sworn at the point of the bayonet.

"Dr. Sampson Avard was the first brought before the court. He had previously told Mr. Oliver Olney that if he [Olney] wished to save himself, he must swear hard against the heads of the Church, as they were the ones the court wanted to criminate; and if he could swear hard against them, they would not (that is, neither court nor mob) disturb him. 'I intend to do it,' said he, 'in order to escape, for if I do not, they will take my life.'

"This introduction is sufficient to show the character of his testimony, and he swore just according to the statement he had made, doubtless thinking it a wise course to ingratiate himself into the good graces of the mob."

In his *Comprehensive History of the Church*, B. H. Roberts states:

"The testimony taken before Judge King is published by the legislature of Missouri . . . and makes altogether sixty-five pages of matter. The 'evidence' is made up almost exclusively of the statements of apostates, and the saint's bitterest enemies among the 'old settlers;' and of the sixty-five pages which it fills, less than four is occupied with testimony for the defense. The court found sufficient cause for holding most of the prisoners on one or the other of the offenses charged . . . Joseph Smith [and 5 others] were committed to prison without bail in Liberty, Clay County, for want of a suitable jail in Caldwell county. Parley P. Pratt [and 4 others], charged with murder, and hence not bailable, were confined in Richmond prison . . . About twenty of the other prisoners were held on various charges, and were either admitted to bail or allowed to go upon their own recognizance. Before the time set for the trial of their cases, they and their bondsmen were compelled to leave the state. The testimony which was most effective in holding these men to investigation before grand juries was the sworn statements of apostates— Dr. Sampson Avard, John Corrill, Reed Peck, W. W. Phelps, George M. Hinkle, John Whitmer, Burr Riggs, and others less prominent [Nathaniel Carr, Thomas B. Marsh.] It is in this testimony and principally in the statement of Dr. Avard, that the existence of the 'Danites' in the 'Mormon' church is affirmed . . . A lie once hatched, how long it lives! How easy it is for people to believe what they desire established as fact!"

In *HC Vol. III, p. 211*, it records:

"Defendants against whom nothing is proven, viz. [included in this list are ANDREW WHITLOCK, HENRY ZOBRISKIE, MARTIN C. ALLRED, WILLIAM ALLRED]. The above defendants have been discharged by me, there being no evidence against them.

Austin A. King, Judge, etc.
November 24, 1838"

Parley P. Pratt was eventually imprisoned in Columbia, Missouri, located on the Missouri River about midway between Independence and St. Louis.

Meanwhile, in the city of Far West, the Saints prepared to leave the State, amidst much terror, persecution, and crossing the Mississippi into Illinois with much suffering in this cold, icy weather. JAMES RUSSELL IVIE, his immediate family, and his brother, THOMAS C. IVIE, returned to Monroe County, Missouri, still faithful to their beliefs. They still had some land and were accepted in the community. Their parents, ANDERSON and SARAH ALLRED IVIE, and some of their brothers and sisters and their families were there. Some had not originally joined the Church, and some had left it. Former branch president, uncle JOHN ANDERSON IVIE, was no longer a member, but it is unlikely the families joined in the persecution of their relatives.

Cousin ISAAC ALLRED stated:

"The Church was mobbed and drove out from Missouri in the fall of the year 1838 and Spring of 1839. After being mobbed and plundered and murdered, the Prophet and others of the brethren were cast into prison. In the spring of 1838-39, I left the State and went to Illinois with the Church taking my family with me. We settled on Military land and took a lease for five years and made an improvement. We stayed one year and preached in the Church and to the world and baptized some. Then in the spring of year, 1840, I moved to the city of Nauvoo and built a house and did the best I could for a living."

[Note: Uncle JAMES ALLRED went to Pittsfield, Illinois, and then to Nauvoo. Uncle ISAAC ALLRED with his family went to Illinois, including his sons WILLIAM MOORE ALLRED and the twins, REDDICK N. and REDDIN A. ALLRED and the rest of his family. Uncle WILLIAM ALLRED with his large family also went to Illinois and settled near Quincy.

In the *HC, Vol. III, pp. 251-254*, there is a list of the names of Saints who had signed their names to stand by and assist one another in helping all families, including the worthy poor and destitute, to remove from Missouri. Included in this list of about 250 assistants are the names of WILLIAM M. FOSSETT (William McKee Faucett); WILLIAM ALLRED; MARTIN C. ALLRED; and SHADRACH ROUNDY. President Brigham Young got eighty subscribers to the covenant the first day, and three hundred the second day.

The Missouri affidavits of claims include: "Of Damage sustained By Mr. Wm. ALLRED by the Mob of the State of Missouri and the Exterminating Order of Governor Bogs it is 4 Four thousand Dollars at a moderate rate." MARTIN C. ALLRED also filed a claim.]

Regarding the trial, Joseph Smith Jr. wrote a letter to the Church from Liberty Jail, 16 December 1838, in which he stated [referring to the *Bible, Book of Isaiah*]:

"We have reproved in the gate, and men have laid snares for us. We have spoken words, and men have made us offenders. [But] our minds are not yet darkened, but feel strong in the Lord. But behold the words of the Savior: 'If the *light* which is in you become *darkness*, behold how great is that darkness.' Look at Mr. Hinkle—a wolf in sheep's clothing. Look at his brother John Corrill. Look at the beloved brother Reed Peck, who aided him in leading us, as the Savior was led, into the camp of his enemies, as a lamb prepared for the slaughter, as a sheep dumb before his shearers; so we opened not our mouths."

~ 7 ~

ESCAPE FROM PRISON

From Parley P. Pratt's autobiography:

"On the 20th of April, 1839, the last of the Society departed from Far West. Thus had a whole people, variously estimated at from ten to fifteen thousand souls, had been driven from houses and lands and reduced to poverty, and had removed to another State during one short winter and part of a spring. The sacrifice of property was immense—including houses, lands, cattle, sheep, hogs, agricultural implements, furniture, household utensils, clothing, money and grain. One of the most flourishing counties of the State and part of several others were reduced to desolation, or inhabited only by marauding gangs of murderers and robbers."

It was on Monday evening, 15 April 1839, that Joseph Smith and the other prisoners in his company escaped as they were being taken to Boone County. On 4 July 1839, then in the Colombia prison, a plan had been devised for the escape of Parley P. Pratt and his two prison companions, Mr. Follett and Mr. Phelps. With three horses waiting for them in the nearby thicket, Pratt wrote:

"Mr. Follett was to give the door a sudden pull, and fling it wide open the moment the key was turned. Mr. Phelps being well skilled in wrestling was to press out foremost, and come in contact with the jailer; I (Mr. Pratt) was to follow in the centre, and Mr. Follett, who held the door, was to bring up the rear, while sister Phelps was to pray . . . We found ourselves in the open air, in front of the prison and full view of the citizens . . . in another instant . . . we were all three scampering off through the fields towards the thicket.

"By this time the town was all in motion. The quietness of the evening was suddenly changed into noise and bustle . . . The streets on both sides of the fields where we were running were soon thronged with soldiers in uniform, mounted riflemen, footmen with fence stakes, clubs, or with whatever came to hand, and with boys, dogs, etc., all running, rushing, screaming, swearing, shouting, bawling and looking, while clouds of dust rose behind them. The cattle also partook of the general panic and ran bellowing away, as if to hide from the scene. The fields behind us also presented a similar scene. Fences were leaped or broken down with a crash; men, boys and horses came tumbling over hedge and ditch, rushing with the fury of a whirlwind in the chase; but we kept our course for the thicket, our toes barely touching the ground, while we seemed to leap with the fleetness of a deer . . . Our friends who had stood waiting in the thicket, had watched the last rays of the sun as they faded away, and had observed the quiet stillness of the evening as it began to steal over the distant village where we were confined; and had listened with almost breathless anxiety for the first sound which was to set all things in commotion, and which would say to them in language not to be misunderstood, that the struggle had commenced . . . As soon as the prisoners drew near, they were hailed by their friends, and conducted to the horses . . . breathless and nearly ready to faint, they were assisted to mount, and a whip and the reins placed in their hands . . . 'Fly quickly, they are upon you!' 'Which way shall we go?' 'Where you can; you are already nearly surrounded.' 'But what will you do? They will kill you if they cannot catch us.' 'We will take care of ourselves; fly, fly, I say, instantly.' These words were exchanged with the quickness of thought, while we were mounting and reining our horses; in another instant we were all separated from each other, and each one was making the best shift he could for his own individual safety.

"I had taken about the third jump with my horse when I encountered a man rushing upon me with a rifle, and, taking aim at my head, he said, 'G-d d--n you, stop, or I'll shoot you.' He was then only a few paces from me, and others were rushing close in his rear, but I turned my horse quickly in another direction, and rushed with all speed into the thickest of the forest, followed for some minutes by him and his dog; but I soon found myself alone, while I could only hear the sound of distant voices, the rushing of horsemen in every direction, with the barking of dogs. What had become of my companions or our friends, I knew not."

Parley tied his horse and climbed a tree, braced himself well and watched and waited until dark. He fainted, and upon recovery found it very dark and his horse gone. After wandering and finally asking directions on two occasions, he entered upon a vast prairie or untimbered plain without inhabitants. Through this plain there was a direct road to Paris, Missouri, which was twenty miles distant and directly on his way. It was nearly evening, and the rain was still pouring in torrents, while the wind blew almost to a tempest. Weary and exhausted with fatigue and hunger, and chilled and benumbed with the rain and wind, he found a stranger who let him stay the night.

"On the third or fourth day after my escape from prison I found myself in the neighborhood of a settlement where I had formed some acquaintances years before, and where once lived a small branch of the Church, but they had all moved West, and, as I supposed, were driven out of the State with the others. But I recollected a family by the name of IVY, [JOHN A.] who would still be living on the road, and who had been members, but were now dissenters. I was now very hungry and wanted a friend, but was in doubt whether they would befriend or betray me, as they had once been my friends, and not only so, but their *near kindred* had suffered in the general persecution, and had shared the common banishment. I hesitated, prayed, and at length came to the conclusion that I would venture past their door in open day, and if no one discovered or recognized me I would take it as a Providence, and conclude it was wisdom in God, as I would not be safe with them; but if, on the other hand, I was saluted by them, then I would think it a sign which Providence had given me as a witness that I could trust them. I accordingly walked past their dwelling on Sunday evening, about two hours before sundown. As I got nearly past, the little children who were playing in the front door yard discovered me and cried out with surprise and joy, 'There is brother Pratt!' At this a young man [THOMAS C. IVIE] came running out to me, who proved to be one of my acquaintances, who was still a member of the Church, and who had been driven from the upper country; but, instead of going to Illinois with the rest, he had come back and settled in his old neighborhood. I asked him where Mr. IVY, the man of the house, was. He replied that he and his wife had gone to a neighbor's, two or three miles distant, on a visit; and,' continued he, 'I also am here on a visit at the same time, and by this means I have very unexpectedly met with you; and I am very glad, for the news has just reached here that the prisoners had escaped, and that they burst a cap at one, and took another and carried him back to prison. The other two have not been found.' This was the first news I had heard either of myself or the others. I then requested him to go and charge the children strictly not to mention that they had seen me, and then come with me into the woods.

"He did so. I then told him I was very hungry, faint and weary; and not only so, but so lame I could hardly move; besides, my feet were blistered, skinned and bloody. He said that his brother [JAMES RUSSELL IVIE], who was also a member, and had been driven with him from the upper country, lived in an obscure place in the woods, some two miles distant, and that his brother's wife and children were as true and genuine Mormons as ever lived. He then took me on his horse and conducted me through a pathless wild for two miles, and, coming in sight of his brother's house, I dismounted and hid myself in a deep valley, whose sides were nearly perpendicular and formed of craggy rock, while he went to reconnoiter the house, and to get something ready for me to eat. He soon returned, informing me that his brother was out, and would not be in till dark; but the family wished very much that I would come in, as the children would hold their tongues, and it was thought to be perfectly safe. I declined, however, for the present, and he brought me out some bread, milk and cream, on which I refreshed myself till they prepared a more substantial supper.

"As evening came on, being pressed to come in, I finally consented. On entering, I was received with joy by the family and sat down to supper. One of their neighbors, a young man, soon came in and seemed determined to tarry till the arrival of the man of the house, as he had some errand with him. This embarrassed me very much, for I was fearful that he would arrive and salute me as an old acquaintance, and call my name in the presence of the young man. But the little children (bless their souls) [JIM & JOHN LEHI] took good care for that matter, they watched very narrowly for the arrival of their papa, and when they saw him they whispered to him that brother P. was there, and being just out of prison, he must not know him till Mr.___ had gone. The man [JAMES RUSSELL IVIE] came in, and I looked up with a vacant stare, or rather with a strange and distant air, and inquired if he was the man of the house? He nodded coolly in the affirmative. I then inquired of him if he had seen any stray "nags" in his neighborhood? I then went on to describe my horse which had strayed from me, and observed that I was out in search of him, and being weary and hungry, I had stopped to get some refreshment with him. He said I was welcome to his house, and such fare as he had; but he had not seen any nags, except what was owned in the neighborhood.

"The young man soon did his errand and withdrew. We then shook each other by the hand most heartily, and, with a burst of joy and smiles, inquired after each other's welfare. I told him I was well nigh exhausted and worn out, and, withal, very lame, but still I had some hopes of making my escape out of the State, and of living to see my friends once more in a land of liberty. I then begged of him to exchange with me, and take my fur cap and give me a hat in its stead, which he did, and then saddled his horse with a side saddle, as the young man . . . just borrowed the other saddle, and, placing me on horseback, he ran before me and by my side on foot, to take me on my journey . . . We travelled till twelve o'clock at night, when I dismounted, and he bid me farewell, in order to reach his home again before the neighbors would arise and find him missing.

He had given me directions which would lead to the Mississippi River much nearer than the Louisiana ferry, and also more in the direct course towards my family, who resided at Quincy, and, besides all these advantages, the route was more obscure, and therefore, safer for me."

Parley P. Pratt escaped across the Mississippi and joined his family at Quincy, Illinois. Quoting from the history of cousin NETTIE M. ROBINS, "I had heard the story many times from great grandma and her son, my Grandpa IVIE. Only as I remembered it, the side saddle and his horse got him well on his way but the horse never found his way back." Uncle LLOYD O. IVIE says it was his uncle JIM's (age 9) brand new, home-made straw hat that was given to Elder Pratt.

PRINCIPAL SQUARE IN SUNBURY

⚊ 8 ⚊

DISINHERITED WHERE THE SUSQUEHANNA RIVER CONVERGES IN PENNSYLVANIA

The Northern Branch of the Susquehanna River wiggles its way from New York into the northeastern border of Pennsylvania, curves by the township of Harmony, [home of Isaac and Elizabeth Hale and their nine children, including Emma, the wife of the Prophet Joseph Smith,] then snakes its way back into New York—then westerly for about fifty miles before it turns southeast to Wilkes-Barre where it turns southwest until it meets and joins its western branch and flows south to Harrisburg—where it turns southeast to the northern tip of the Chesapeake Bay. At the junction of its two branches in the central eastern half of Pennsylvania is the present day city of Sunbury, Northumberland County. Sunbury was first laid out about the year of 1775; but not incorporated as a borough until 14 April 1828. The original name of this previous Indian settlement was Shamokin.

Shikellamy, the great Oneida chieftain, sent by the mighty Six Nations in 1728 to assert the right of the Iroquois over the conquered remnants of the native Pennsylvania Indians, lived at Shamokin. For some twenty years he was the chief negotiator between the Indians and the British Provincial government—one of the truly outstanding Indian statesmen of early American history. A Moravian mission was established in 1742. This marked the beginnings of white civilization in the county. Some early French settled with the Indians and adopted their way of life. The struggle and border disputes for the extension of lands westward increased between the French and English, and the British governor decided to build a fort at this outpost. Fort Augusta was established, using the Pennsylvania militia to garrison and maintain it.

With the outbreak of the Seven Year War in Europe [French and Indian War in America], the fort became more important. The Indian occupants of the valley were friendly to the British and remained so. The fort's strategic location concerned the French, who tried unsuccessfully to destroy it. As the war continued, the Indians felt threatened and sold their land, moving westward. Some white settlers came in; but when the problems of the Revolutionary War increased and the British and Indians massacred the settlers in the adjoining northern Wyoming valley, these white settlers virtually abandoned the region. Other forts fell to the British; but the Pennsylvania militia was able to hold Fort Augusta.

This wild and beautiful country with its waterway, timber, lush fertile valley, iron, and anthracite coal was a dream area for the recluse. It had sufficient sustenance, but the rugged mountainous surroundings limited its expansion. Dr. Joseph Priestley, discoverer of oxygen, built his home in Sunbury, where it is preserved as an historic shrine. It was into this picturesque valley that great-grandmother MARY CATHERINE BARTON was born on 30 June 1837—a charmer even at that very early age. She was the first child of JOHN BARTON and SUSANNAH WILKINSON, who had both grown up in this area—their young parents having arrived soon after the Revolutionary War had ended, or maybe during the war in the case of AARON WILKINSON, the father of SUSANNAH.

One history of the valley reads:

"WILKISON or WILKINSON. Both forms of this name are in use among the descendants of AARON WILKISON, a pioneer of Northumberland county, Pa., who was a native of New Jersey and came to this section at an early day, settling in Augusta township, along Shamokin creek, where he lived for some years. He then moved to the Irish Valley, in Shamokin township, this county, settling on the property now owned by Francis Wynn, a tract of 120 acres. By occupation he was a farmer. He died while yet a young man, and is buried at the Presbyterian Church near Snydertown, though he was a Methodist. His wife, whose maiden name was POYER, long survived him. They had children as follows: JOSEPH; JOHN, who located near his father's place in the Irish Valley; and SAMUEL, who succeeded to the ownership of his brother JOHN's farm when the latter died."

The history tells more about the other children and adds that AARON's daughter, "SUSANNA married JOHN BARTON and they live at Salt Lake City, Utah; ELIZABETH married HIRAM ROCKEFELLER, of Irish Valley." ELIZABETH and HIRAM had no children.

According to one family record, AARON WILKINSON, was born 23 May 1781 in Shamokin, Northumberland, Pennsylvania, and was the son of JOHN WILKINSON and SUSANNAH of Bucks County, Pennsylvania, born about 1754 [and in another history 1758]. If this family record of AARON's birth is correct, then his parents were in Shamokin during the Revolutionary War; but since all settlers had moved to the fort, perhaps JOHN WILKINSON was a member of the Pennsylvania army or militia defending the fort. We have no death dates for AARON's parents, or any record of additional children. No record of his military service has been found, as yet. AARON died 14 Jan 1837, which would make him 55 years old. AARON's daughter SUSANNAH appears to be the only member of this WILKINSON family to go to Nauvoo and then hence to Utah.

[Note: There is a JOHN WILKINSON, son of JOHN and MARY LACY WILKINSON of Bucks County, Pennsylvania, who died of his wounds at his father's home during the Revolutionary War. My ancestor, third-great-grandfather JOHN WILKINSON, is believed to be his first cousin, and the son of JOSEPH WILKINSON, the brother who stayed and managed their family estate in Hunterdon County, New Jersey, when his older brother JOHN moved with their father, also JOHN WILKINSON, to the Philadelphia country side. JOSEPH married BARBARA LACY, a young aunt of MARY LACY. The recorded county history quoted earlier in this chapter states that AARON came from New Jersey, not Bucks County.]

In the middle of the 1930s, at a gathering of IVIE relations, one of my cousins whispered to me that the *adults* said that Grandma IVIE was related to the Rockefellers. Still a small child, I wondered how my Danish grandmother could be related to this very rich man. I had seen the elderly John D. Rockefeller in the newsreels at the movies in his expensive touring car giving dimes to many of the children of America. He died in 1937, but his wealth and political influence has magnified through his posterity and is currently a major force nationally and internationally. I was a few years older when I realized the *adult* Grandma IVIE would be MARY CATHERINE BARTON, whose mother's sister had married HIRAM ROCKEFELLER. The Northumberland history reads:

"ROCKEFELLER. The Rockefeller family has long been well represented among the best class of citizens in Northumberland county, and one of the townships of the county bears the name. The family was founded here by Godfrey Rockefeller . . . The Rockefeller family traces its beginning in America to one Peter Rockefeller, who was born in Europe in 1710 and on emigrating to America settled at Amwell, Hunterdon Co., N. J. [Also the home of our BARTON, COOLEY, and JOSEPH WILKINSON ancestors.] He died there about 1740, leaving to his son, who was also named Peter, 763 acres of land in the county mentioned.

"Godfrey Rockefeller, born in 1747, was a son of Peter Rockefeller (2). He came to Northumberland county, Pa., in 1789, and took up land in the vicinity of Snydertown . . . they had a family of eleven children, three sons and eight daughters. One of the sons was the grandfather of John D. Rockefeller, of Standard Oil fame."

This history was written in 1910. It gives several pages on the Rockefeller descendants who were living there at the time. John D. Rockefeller, however, was born 8 July 1839, in Tioga County, New York, a Pennsylvania border county where the Susquehanna enters Pennsylvania—he was two years younger than MARY CATHERINE BARTON. His family moved on to Cleveland, Ohio, where he was educated and became a clerk in a mercantile establishment. In 1870, Standard Oil was incorporated, with John D. as president. By 1892 it was estimated that he was the only billionaire in the world. There was nothing additional on HIRAM ROCKEFELLER of Irish Valley in this history. Some of the Rockefellers evidently remained in Hunterdon County, New Jersey, since we find that MARY COOLEY (Barton), originally of New Jersey, had a sister whose marriage is recorded as follows: "ELIZABETH COOLEY married WILLIAM VANDERBELT, January 5, 1797. Rockefellar, J. P." The J. P. (Justice of the Peace).

JOHN BARTON's father, NOAH BARTON, was not mentioned in this history of Northumberland County. We find him as a taxpayer in Amwell Township, Hunterdon County, New Jersey, as late as 1786. In the New Jersey Militia Records, we find him listed as "exempt" in the Alexandria township list of 1792, when his brothers and cousins joined the militia that was formed by George Washington and ALEXANDER HAMILTON to squash the "Whiskey Rebellion." Although family records show him marrying MARY COOLEY in Shamokin in 1791, this seems a little unrealistic as her father JOHN COOLEY and NOAH's family were still in New Jersey at that time.

[Note: Although most family records show Shamokin instead of Sunbury, it is obvious from the history that the family lived in the valley and not the present Shamokin, which was later incorporated in the mountainous area and is an Indian and coal mining settlement.]

NOAH BARTON was born 23 November 1764 in Hunterdon County, New Jersey. He was 11 years old when the Revolution began. His father, ELISHA BARTON, was a captain and was probably also the young private ELISHA BARTON of Westchester, New York, in the French and Indian War. NOAH was 28 years old in 1792. Perhaps he was "exempt" for his Quaker beliefs, age, injury, or because he was going to Pennsylvania and would serve there. His oldest child was born in Shamokin, 21 June 1793, according to family records. NOAH died 26 June 1829 in Shamokin. His wife, MARY COOLEY BARTON survived him until 22 October 1847.

At least four of the NOAH BARTON children went to Nauvoo in 1841: ELIZABETH—who would marry ISRAEL BARLOW—was then 37; CATHERINE, age 35—would marry THOMAS MENDENHALL; JOHN (my ancestor) was 32 and had already married SUSANNAH WILKINSON. His younger sister MARY ANN, age 27, would marry DAVID CANDLAND, an Englishman, who joined the LDS Church in England and then came to Nauvoo. Tradition says that the prominent Pennsylvania families of BARTON and WILKINSON disinherited these relatives when they joined the *Mormon Church.*

I do not know the dates of their baptisms, how long they stayed in Pennsylvania before their journey to Nauvoo, Illinois, of over 800 miles, friends or relations that came with them, but four year old MARY CATHERINE BARTON and her younger brother WILLIAM GILBERT BARTON came with their three maiden aunts and their parents. I would guess that they were very well cared for.

I do not know which missionaries brought them into the LDS Church, but in charts showing early church missionary assignments, this area is part of the larger area that the first missionary, Samuel H. Smith, the brother of the Prophet Joseph Smith, was assigned.

In the Methodist Church records, which seems to be the favorite church of the WILKINSON family, we find that the

> *"Rev.[George] Lane* was appointed Presiding Elder of the Susquehanna District at the Conference" [110 ministers and their bishop in western New York]. He was so named because he was one "who incessantly travels his

extensive territory, preaching, counseling the traveling . . . meeting the official members of the circuit Societies, and promoting the interest of the Church in every possible way.' The circuits which comprised the Susquehanna District in 1819 were the Bald Eagle, Lycoming, *Shamokin*, Northumberland, Wyoming, Canaan, Bridgewater, Wyalusing, Tioga, and Wayne." In 1820 the Broome circuit was added.

Oliver Cowdery, the scribe of Joseph Smith Jr., writes in the *Messenger and Advocate* in December 1834:

> "It is necessary to premise this account by relating the situation of the public mind relative to religion at this time: One *Mr. Lane*, a presiding Elder of the Methodist church, visited Palmyra and vicinity. Elder Lane was a talented man possessing a good share of literary endowments, and apparent humility. There was a great awakening, or excitement raised on the subject of religion, and much inquiry for the word of life. Large additions were made to the Methodist, Presbyterian, and Baptist churches.—*Mr. Lane's* manner of communication was peculiarly calculated to awaken the intellect of the hearer, and arouse the sinner to look about him for safety— much good instruction was always drawn from his discourses on the scriptures, and in common with others, our brother's [Joseph Smith's] mind became awakened."

Since Shamokin was part of the Reverend Lane's Susquehanna District, Sunbury, which became incorporated on 14 April 1828, with four recognized churches—Old and New School Presbyterian, German Reformed, and Methodist, it would have had a similar public spirit to that which occurred in Palmyra, New York. Certainly the circuitous preachers would bring to them all the same ugly rumors of the Prophet Joseph Smith and his Gold Plates that they had heard in the northern part of this district and would try to prejudice and confuse their members against this new religion throughout their whole district. So when the four BARTON children, with JOHN's wife, SUSANNAH, and their two children, left the Shamokin Valley to go to Nauvoo, it was not with the goodwill of those they left behind—but it was remembered by them in 1910 that "SUSANNA married JOHN BARTON, and they live at Salt Lake City, Utah."

⇁ 9 ⇀

APOSTATES AND MARTYRS

When a lying spirit is abroad,
it is difficult for truth to be understood.

– JOSEPH SMITH –

W. W. Phelps, after lying in his testimony against the prisoners, repented and was forgiven. W. W. Phelps had written the words to *The Spirit of God Like a Fire is Burning* that was sung at the Kirtland Temple dedication. He also authored an additional fourteen hymns in the current LDS [1985] hymn book, including *O God, the Eternal Father* and *Praise to the Man.*

We do not know the reason JOHN ANDERSON IVIE [brother of JAMES RUSSELL IVIE], who had been the branch president of the Allred Settlement and a member of Zion's Camp, became a dissenter; but Parley P. Pratt knew he had left the church and returned to Monroe County before Pratt went to prison [Nov. 1838], which suggests that uncle JOHN may have been disillusioned or close to some of those leaders who left the church earlier that year.

[Note: The 1840 U.S. Census records of Monroe County, Missouri, lists the names of "JAMES IVI," with a wife and 8 children; "ANDERSON IVI" with a wife, 4 older children and a 80-90 year old female [probably SARAH's mother, ELIZABETH THRASHER ALLRED]; "M. J. IVI" with a wife and 2 very young children; "W. S. IVI" and a wife and 2 very young children; "Jn IVY" with a wife and 9 children, and "W. H. ALLRED" with a wife, and 8 children.

We know that WILLIAM HACKLEY ALLRED and his wife, ELIZABETH (or Betsy) IVIE [J.R.'s older sister] moved to Caldwell County, since one of their children was born there. Cousin ISAAC ALLRED, said in 1848, that his brother WILLIAM had left the church. His wife (and also his first cousin) ELIZABETH IVIE ALLRED was with him when years later they came to Utah from Texas. She was unhappy in Spring City and they returned to Grayson, Texas, where she died. In 1876, WILLIAM H. ALLRED received his endowments in Utah. He died in 1890 in Spring City, Utah.]

The Captain WILLIAM ALLRED, referred to in the defense of Far West and who was the WILLIAM ALLRED imprisoned in Richmond, was a brother of third-great-grandmother SARAH ALLRED IVIE. WILLIAM became ill from his terrible exposure to the elements and died near Quincy, Illinois—leaving a large family. SARAH's other brothers ISAAC and JAMES remained very active in the church. There is not, as yet, any record that SARAH and her husband ANDERSON IVIE ever joined the LDS Church. They are both buried in Monroe County, Missouri. Their daughter, SARAH, married WILLIAM LONG and they remained in Monroe County; also, their son ISAAC who married MELISSA LONG.

It is very doubtful that any of the family who broke away from the Church was involved in its persecution, since they were in eastern Missouri and had welcomed back the members of their family who had gone into Clay and Caldwell Counties. It is also obvious from Parley P. Pratt's account that he, as an escaped prisoner, would not have been welcomed by the majority of their friends and neighbors had they discovered him in their midst.

NETTIE M. ROBINS [in her short history] remembered her great-grandmother, ELIZA McKEE FAUSETT IVIE, telling her of this time in Missouri, "I would go through the timber to a small spring for a pail of water. I was so frightened; I could often hear the plaintive cry of the panther (or `panter' as Grandmother called it)." ELIZA had two brothers and three sisters and their families that remained active in the Church and moved into Nauvoo and then came west.

> HC, Vol II: "While the great body of the church made its exit from Missouri via Quincy, all did not do so. Some went northward into the then territory of Iowa. Among these was a brother ISRAEL BARLOW, who, taking a northeasterly course from Far West, struck the Des Moines River a short distance above its mouth. He was without food and destitute of clothing. Making his wants known to the people living in that locality, they kindly supplied him with food and raiment. To them he related the story of the persecution of the Latter-day Saints in Missouri, and how his people, poor and destitute as himself, were fleeing from the state 'en masse'. His relation of the sufferings of the saints, and the cruelties heaped upon them by their heartless persecutors, enlisted the sympathies of his hearers, and they gave him letters of introduction to . . . Isaac Galland, a gentleman of some influence, living at Commerce [later Nauvoo] . . . During this time the toils and privations of life, the afflictions and sickness and the death of

friends, brothers and sisters, my pen cannot paint neither can my tongue tell; but those that experienced it know for themselves."

This incident began the series of events and letters to the Prophet in Liberty Jail that ended with the purchase by the Church of the lands in Illinois and Iowa that would become Nauvoo in Illinois and Zarahemla in Iowa. ISRAEL BARLOW later married, among others, ELIZABETH BARTON, sister of second-great-grandfather JOHN BARTON.

My Uncle LLOYD O. IVIE, a great-grandchild, stated, "JAMES RUSSELL IVIE and family went to Nauvoo. JAMES RUSSELL served, as did others, as a bodyguard to the Prophet during those hectic days preceding the tragedy at Carthage. Those two boys of Elder Pratt's escape days were then thirteen [JIM] and eleven years of age [JOHN L. IVIE]. The Prophet had been in their home. They sat on his lap, and at his feet listening to his sacred voice—and witness of God. They knew, and nothing could daunt them. Nothing ever did. So it is no wonder that when word of the martyrdom reached their ears, they too, like Isaiah of old, shed 'rivers of tears.' They, too, were pierced to the very center with a wound that never healed."

{Note: The Prophet and his brother, Hyrum, were killed on 27 Jun 1844. Sometime before this event, JAMES RUSSELL IVIE and his family, and his brother THOMAS CELTON IVIE moved to Nauvoo. We find in the Nauvoo Records that "THOMAS C. IVIE and JANE MOORE [were married], 24 August 1844, at Nauvoo, by ISAAC ALLRED—[his uncle]." The Marriage Record Index recorded 30 marriages in September 1844. Most family records show the twins [of J. R. and ELIZA IVIE], ELIZA MARIE IVIE and MARI BETSY IVIE, born 29 Mar 1842 in Monroe County, MARI died at birth; then ISAAC THOMAS IVIE was born 24 May 1844 in Monroe County. Other records question this birth place, believing they were born in Nauvoo.]

Cousin ISAAC ALLRED's autobiography of this time reads:

"Then in the spring of the year, 1840, I moved to the city of Nauvoo and built a house and did the best I could for a living . . . then I let the Church have my improvement and I got another lot and built upon it and stayed one year. Then I let Lyman [Wight] have it. I bought a place of Lyman [Wight], moved on and built and then went to Missouri with Brother Solomon Hancock to preach to the Missourians after they had [driven] us out of the State. I baptized some and organized a branch of 13 members. Then I went home and went to work for Mr. [William] Law [a counselor to Joseph Smith who later became a bitter apostate and led the enemies of the Church toward the martyrdom of Joseph and Hyrum Smith]. I cut 100 cord of wood and then made a contract with Law and went on his farm for two years . . . The mob raised up against the church and killed the Prophet

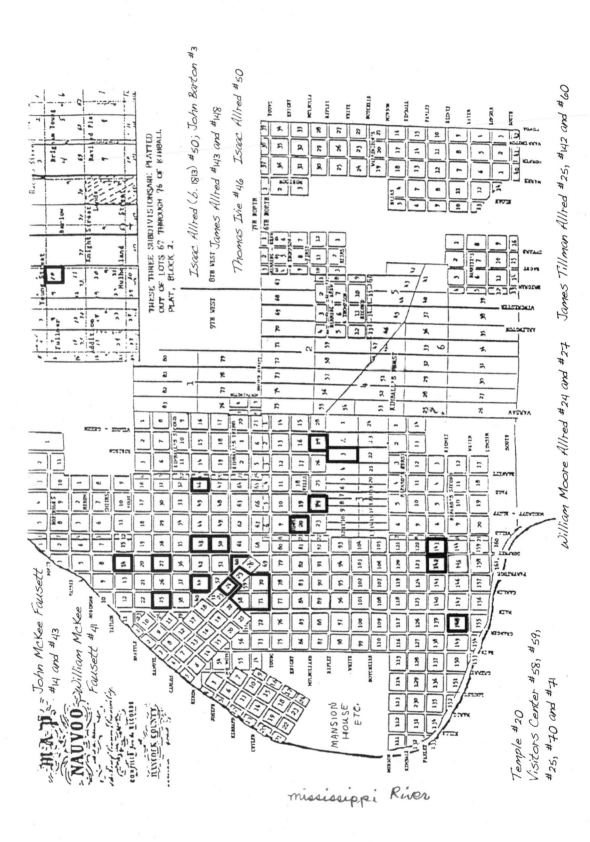

and Patriarch. And at this time the Nauvoo Legion was organized and the City was incorporated and I received a commission in the Legion and was Colonel of the 5th Regiment at the time of slaughter of the Prophet and his brother Hyrum. The Laws left the church and disposed me of my place. I moved back to my house and went to work on the temple and worked until it was finished. I took an active part with the Brethren in quelling the mob in the time of the burning [of homes in Hancock County] in which time some of the devils was killed. I was thrown off my horse and hauled home in a baggage wagon. At this time, Backenstos had his posse out. I went to Peoria with Backenstos to attend his trials for killing one of the devils [Frank C. Worrell] . . . I came home and went into the temple and labored during the endowments . . . I with my wife was blessed with all the privileges of the endowment as also did Mary Henderson [a second wife] with us."

[Note: ISAAC's brother MARTIN died 2 May 1840, his sister ELIZA died 10 Jul 1842 and his sister NANCY also died in 1842.]

JAMES ALLRED went into Illinois after being expelled from Missouri. On 7 July 1840, within the limits of Hancock County, Noah Rogers and he were "peaceably pursuing their own lawful business" when a group of Missourians "forcibly arrested" and kidnapped them, taking them into the State of Missouri. In his Statement to the State of Illinois, Hancock County, uncle JAMES ALLRED disclosed [HC, Vol IV]:

"[I]n a short time after he had been so taken into the state of Missouri, he was put into a room with said Rogers, and there kept until some time during the following night, when they were taken out of the room where they were confined, into the woods near by, and [he] was bound by the persons conducting him, to a tree, he having been forcibly stripped by them of every particle of clothing. Those having him in charge then told [him] that they would whip him; one of them . . . saying, 'G-d D---n you, I'll cut you to the hollow.' They, however, at last unbound [him] without whipping him . . . Rogers was taken just beyond the place where [ALLRED] was bound with a rope around his neck, and he heard a great number of blows, which he then supposed, and has since learned were inflicted upon said Rogers, and heard him cry out several times as if in great agony; after which [ALLRED and Rogers] were taken back to the former room . . . and detained until [the next] Monday . . . at which time he received from one of the company, who had imprisoned him, a passport, of which the following is a copy— 'Tully, [Lewis County] Missouri, July 12 1840.

The people of Tully, having taken up Mr. ALLRED, with some others, and having examined into the offenses committed, find nothing to justify his detention any longer, and have released him. By order of the committee. H.M. Woodward.' And then [ALLRED] was permitted to return home into the state of Illinois."

In a Memorial to Governor Carlin from some of the saints we read:

"That feeling ourselves so happy and secure, and beginning again to enjoy the comforts of life, we are sorry to say that our quiet has been disturbed, our fears alarmed, and our families annoyed by the citizens of Missouri; who, with malice and hatred, which is characteristic of them, have un-constitutionally sent an armed force and abducted some of our friends, namely, JAMES ALLRED . . . and carried them into the state of Missouri, and treated them with the greatest barbarity and cruelty; even now their wives and children, as well as their friends, are alarmed for the safety of their lives." [Ibid]

"Brown and ALLRED, by some means, were liberated, but we [Rogers and Benjamin Boyce] were put in jail and put in irons until the 21st of August, when through the kindness of God we made our escape and returned to Nauvoo."

I wonder if the difference in the treatment of the prisoners might have been because ALLRED was Southern and had lived in Missouri, but the others had not.

[Note: JAMES ALLRED's name continues to show up in the history: 4 Feb 1841—Nauvoo Legion organized, JAMES ALLRED, guards & assistant aids-de-camp. 27 Feb 1841—incorporating the Nauvoo Agricultural and Manufacturing Association--including JAMES ALLRED and ISRAEL BARLOW. On 8 Mar 1841—supervisor of streets, JAMES ALLRED; then high constables, JAMES ALLRED and others. 7 Apr 1841, "Resolved: That JAMES ALLRED be appointed to the office of High Councilor, in the place of Charles C. Rich, who had been chosen a counselor to the president of this [Nauvoo] stake." As one of the High Council members of the Nauvoo Stake, his name appears with others of that body on several church documents, until the Saints are driven from Nauvoo. On 10 Apr 1843 he was appointed as one of the elders "to administer baptism for the dead in the river while the font could not be used."

In the "Minutes of conference at Commerce [later Nauvoo], Illinois, 6, 7 and 8 Oct 1839, we find listed the names of . . . REDDIN A. ALLRED . . . REDDICK N. ALLRED . . . and WILLIAM (probably MOORE) ALLRED . . . who "were appointed Elders of the Church, who all accepted of their appointment . . . ." [HC, Vol IV pp. 12-13] All three were the sons of ISAAC ALLRED, brother of SARAH ALLRED IVIE.

On 20 March 1841, "An Inquiry" was made of the Prophet Joseph Smith, City of Nauvoo, as follows:

"Brother WILLIAM ALLRED, Bishop of the stake at Pleasant Vale, and also Brother Henry W. Miller, president of the stake at Freedom, desire President Joseph Smith to inquire of the Lord His will concerning them. I

(Joseph Smith) inquired of the Lord concerning the foregoing question, and received the following answer—'Revelation. Let my servants, WILLIAM ALLRED and Henry W. Miller, have an agency for the selling of stock for the Nauvoo House, and assist my servants Lyman Wight, Peter Haws, George Miller, and John Snider, in building said house; and let my servants WILLIAM ALLRED and Henry W. Miller take stock in the house, that the poor of my people may have employment, and that accommodations may be made for the strangers who shall come to visit this place, and for this purpose let them devote all their properties, saith the Lord.'"

After the fellowship of the Church was withdrawn from the adulterous traitor, John C. Bennett, on 25 May 1842, President Joseph Smith gave a short address to the Relief Society—the women of the Church. LILLIE CONDIE marked these passages in the "History of the Church":

"As females possess refined feelings and sensitiveness, they are also subject to overmuch zeal . . . Notwithstanding the unworthy are among us, the virtuous should not, from self importance, grieve and oppress needlessly, those unfortunate ones . . . [He] recommended . . . [1] to put a double watch over the tongue: no organized body can exist without this at all. [2] . . . help those not so good reform and return to the path of virtue . . . which will influence to virtue and goodness . . . I do not want to cloak iniquity—I want the innocent to go free—rather spare ten iniquitous among you, than condemn one innocent one. 'Fret not thyself because of evil doers. God will see to it.'"

After his excommunication, John C. Bennett sought forgiveness, which he was granted. In a few days, he left Nauvoo and commenced circulating black falsehoods against the Church in articles he signed "Joab, General in Israel." He later published a book against the Church, quoting these articles as his source, hoping to give credence to his lies and creating mischief for a short period, especially in Missouri. Unrenowned, he died a miserable lonely death in 1868.

"28 Jun 1844—News arrived in Nauvoo at daylight, that Joseph and Hyrum were murdered yesterday while in jail. At 7:30 a.m., General Dunham [Illinois Militia] issued orders for the whole of the Nauvoo Legion to meet on the parade ground, east of the Temple, at 10 a.m. They met accordingly, where addresses were delivered, and exhortations given to the saints to keep quiet, and not let their violently outraged feelings get the better of them. About noon a council of officers of the Legion was held, and from thence they went to meet the sad procession that accompanied the bodies of the murdered Prophet and Patriarch.

"At 2:30 p.m., the corpses arrived at Mulholland Street, on two wagons, guarded by a few men from Carthage, and nearly all the citizens collected together and followed the bodies to the Mansion, where the multitude were addressed by Dr. Richards, W. W. Phelps, and Messrs. Woods and Reid, who exhorted the people to be peaceable and calm and use no threats.

"The names of the prophet's bodyguard that day were: Alpheus Cutler, capt., John Snyder, Amos C. Hodge, Christian Kreymer, JAMES ALLRED, Lewis D. Wilson, Thomas Grover, William Marks, Reynolds Cahoon, James Emmet, SHADRACH ROUNDY, John S. Butler, Samuel H. Smith. Edward Hunter, herald and armor bearer.

Saturday, 29— The Legion was out all last night, expecting a mob to come."

The Prophet Joseph Smith gave his sword to JAMES ALLRED when he was jailed at Carthage. Joseph, who could not keep it, told him that he would need it more on his journey home. The sword, which was kept by the ALLRED family, is presently on display in the Museum of Church History and Art by Temple Square in Salt Lake City, Utah.

John Taylor, who was with Joseph and Hyrum at Carthage Jail, was severely wounded. After Joseph jumped from the window to save the lives of the others, the frightened mob soon dispersed, some calling, "The Mormons are coming!" The uninjured Dr. Willard Richards, fearing the mob might return, moved John Taylor from under the bed to the prison room on the same floor, which was barred, but unlocked. There was straw and a small mattress, so he hid his companion under it, while he sought help. His fear was unnecessary, for fear now raged in the hearts of the dispersed mob. The bodies of the two martyrs were placed in wagons and returned with their "body guards" to the arms of their family and the multitude of friends waiting for them in Nauvoo. Taylor was taken to a nearby hotel in Carthage to recover.

Writing about this event, Taylor recalled:

"I do not remember the time that I stayed at Carthage, but I think three or four days after the murder, when Brother Marks with a carriage, Brother JAMES ALLRED with a wagon, Dr. Ells, and a number of others on horseback, came for the purpose of taking me to Nauvoo. I was very weak at the time, occasioned by the loss of blood and the great discharge of my wounds, so when my wife asked me if I could talk I could barely whisper no. Quite a discussion arose as to the propriety of my removal, the physicians and people of Carthage protesting that it would be my death, while my friends were anxious for my removal if possible.

"I suppose the former were actuated by the above-named desire to keep me. Colonel Jones was, I believe, sincere: he had acted as a friend all the time, and told Mrs. Taylor she ought to persuade me not to go, for he did not believe I had strength enough to reach Nauvoo. It was finally agreed, however, that I should go; but as it was thought that I could not stand riding in a wagon or carriage, they prepared a litter for me; I was carried downstairs and put upon it. A number of men assisted to carry me, some of whom had been engaged in the mob. As soon as I got downstairs, I felt much better and strengthened, so that I could talk; I suppose the effect of the fresh air.

"When we had got near the outside of the town I remembered some woods that we had to go through, and telling a person near to call for Dr. Ells, who was riding a very good horse, I said, 'Doctor, I perceive that the people are getting fatigued with carrying me; a number of Mormons live about two or three miles from here, near our route; will you ride to their settlement as quick as possible, and have them come and meet us?' He started off on a gallop immediately. My object in this was to obtain protection in case of an attack, rather than to obtain help to carry me. Very soon after, the men from Carthage made one excuse after another, until they had all left, and I felt glad to get rid of them. I found that the tramping of those carrying me produced violent pain, and a sleigh was produced and attached to the hind end of Brother JAMES ALLRED's wagon, a bed placed upon it, and I was propped up on the bed. Mrs. Taylor rode with me, applying ice water to my wounds. As the sleigh was dragged over the grass on the prairie, which was quite tall, it moved very easily and gave me very little pain.

"When I got within five or six miles of Nauvoo the brethren commenced to meet me from the city, and they increased in number as we drew nearer, until there was a very large company of people of all ages and both sexes, principally, however, men.

"For some time there had been almost incessant rain, so that in many low places on the prairie it was from one to three feet deep in water, and at such places the brethren whom we met took hold of the sleigh, lifted it, and carried it over the water; and when we arrived in the neighborhood of the city, where the roads were excessively muddy and bad, the brethren tore down the fences, and we passed through the fields.

"Never shall I forget the differences of feeling that I experienced between the place that I had left and the one that I had now arrived at. I had left a lot of reckless, bloodthirsty murderers, and had come to the City of the Saints, the people of the living God; friends of truth and righteousness, thousands of whom stood there with warm, true hearts to offer their friendship and services, and to welcome my return. It is true it was a painful scene, and brought sorrowful remembrance to my mind, but to me it caused a thrill of joy to find myself once more in the bosom of my friends, and to meet with the cordial welcome of true honest hearts. What was very remarkable, I found myself very much better after my arrival at Nauvoo than I was when I started on my journey, although I had traveled eighteen miles.

"The next day, as some change was wanting, I told Mrs. Taylor that if she could send to Dr. Richards, he had my purse and watch, and they would find money in my purse.

"Previous to the doctor leaving Carthage, I told him that he had better take my purse and watch, for I was afraid the people would steal them. The doctor had taken my pantaloons pocket, and put the watch in it with the purse, cut off the pocket, and tied a string around the top; it was in this position when brought home. My family, however, were not a little startled to find that my watch had been struck with a ball. I sent for my vest, and upon examination, it was found that there was a cut as if with a knife, in the vest pocket which had contained my watch. In the pocket the fragments of the glass were found literally ground to powder. It then occurred to me that a ball had struck me at the time I felt myself falling out of the window, and that it was this force that threw me inside. I had often remarked to Mrs. Taylor the singular fact of finding myself inside the room, when I felt a moment before after being shot, that I was falling out, and I never fully elucidated, and was rendered plain to my mind. I was indeed falling out, when some villain aimed at my heart. The ball struck my watch, and forced me back; if I had fallen out I should assuredly have been killed, if not by the fall, by those around, and this ball, intended to dispatch me, was turned by an overruling Providence into a messenger of mercy, and saved my life. I shall never forget the feelings of gratitude that I then experienced towards my heavenly Father; the whole scene was vividly portrayed before me, and my heart melted before the Lord. I felt that the Lord had preserved me by a special act of mercy; that my time had not yet come, and that I had still a work to perform upon the earth.

[Signed] John Taylor." [HC pp. 117-120]

THE SCHOOL OF THE PROPHETS

The School of the Prophets met in this room above the Newel K. Whitney General Store. Adjoining this room was a suite of rooms used by Joseph and Emma Smith and their family while they were living in Kirtland, Ohio. Many of the revelations included in the Doctrine and Covenants were given in this room during this early period of LDS Church history.

One of these Revelations was Section 89, given February 27, 1833, known as the *Word of Wisdom,* and given as a consequence of the early brethren using tobacco in their meetings— Emma was not very happy cleaning spittoons. After praying to the Lord, Joseph Smith Jr. received the revelation. It begins:

"A Word of Wisdom, for the benefit of the council of high priests, assembled in Kirtland, and the church, and also the saints in Zion—To be sent greeting, not by commandment or constraint, but by revelation and the word of wisdom, showing forth the order and the will of God in the temporal salvation of all saints in the last days—Given for a principle with promise, adapted to the capacity of the weak and the weakest of all saints . . . In consequence of evils and designs which do and will exist in the hearts of conspiring men in the last days, I have warned you . . . by giving unto you this word of wisdom . . . That inasmuch as any man drinketh wine or strong drink among you, Behold it is not good . . . and again, tobacco is not for the body . . . and again hot drinks are not for the body." More instructions were given regarding herbs and proper nutrition. The section ends with a promise that by keeping this commandment they would "find wisdom and great treasures of knowledge . . . run and not be weary, walk and not faint."

Driving home from an eastern journey on I-80, GROVER and I decided to visit some LDS Church sites and complete our homeward trek on I-70. Without a map of Missouri, we drove south on the freeway from Des Moines, Iowa, along I-35 and stopped at one of those wonderful Iowa Traveler's Information Rest Areas. They regretted that they had no maps of Missouri, nor did Missouri have similar information centers. However, if we took the first freeway exit after arriving in Missouri and stopped at a certain gas station, in that parking lot there was a small trailer with wooden steps leading up to its door that could give us some local information about the state.

We arrived, and while GROVER filled the car with gas, I climbed the steps up to the narrow reception room with limited displays. Asking the smiling relaxed, perhaps sixty year old man for maps or travel information on northern Missouri, he shook his head, then his eyes lit up and he warmly told us, "There is a spot nearby that you really must go to. I go there quite often, especially every spring. It's really a wonderful place—some church owns it, I think."

"Would it be Adam-ondi-Ahman?"

"Yes! That's right. That's its name."

GROVER had arrived, and he directed us to get back on the freeway and take the next exit—about one mile away, then into the country roads, until the small sign he believed would direct us to the turnoff. There would be rest rooms.

Arriving that September morning, we found the parking lot empty and no one around. A metal plaque gave directions to Galantin, Far West, and Liberty Jail. We viewed the large flat amphitheater surrounded by slow rising hills. The quiet peace and serenity was wonderful.

Returning to the parking lot, a family with quite a few children in hiking clothes was emerging from their station wagon with excitement. They told us they came every year as a family and hiked to the old Nephite alter that still remained across the arena—a yearly family tradition they really enjoyed.

From the *Teachings of Joseph Smith* p. 122 (19 May 1838): "by the mouth of the Lord it was named Adam-ondi-Ahman, because . . . it is the place where Adam shall come to visit his people, or the Ancient of Days shall sit, as spoken of by Daniel the Prophet.

ADAM ONDI AHMAN

In Galantin, they have a large sign in front of their courthouse. One side tells about their former residents' first fight against the *Mormons* after they had refused to allow them to vote in the election. The other side tells about their trial of the prisoner, Frank James. From there we drove to the corner stones that were laid for a future temple in Far West, where the twelve apostles met in 1839 [see D&C 118], before their missions to England—in spite of the oaths proclaimed by the Missourians that they would kill them, for the exact date was given in the revelation.

FAR WEST TEMPLE SITE — DEDICATED IN 1839

The City of Far West is no longer there. Across the road from the Temple site is a small church belonging to the Community of Christ—formerly the Reorganized LDS Church. It is the only edifice within miles in this fertile flat farm land. Arriving, we found the gate was closed, but two *LDS Service Missionaries* were scraping and painting the black iron fence. They had locked the entrance gate to plant new grass. With over 100,000 visitors throughout the summer, it had worn thin. After taking a few pictures and using their immaculately cleaned rest rooms, which they claimed were the cleanest in the Church, we returned to our car to find that we had both left our keys inside the car. We were locked out. Our cell phone, of course, was inside the car. There wasn't a phone of any kind outside. Eventually another visitor arrived, who had a cell phone. The closest service was over twenty miles away. The locksmith finally arrived and we were soon on our way to Independence and their visitor's center, where we spent the night in a nearby motel. To our further embarrassment, the next day, at a gas station half-way across Kansas, we once more locked our keys in the car; but help was much closer. The charge in both cases was $35.00. It never happened before, or after—so far.

RESTORATION OF LIBERTY JAIL ON ITS ORIGINAL SITE IN MISSOURI

After the trials at Richmond, Missouri, Joseph and Hyrum Smith and several other prisoners were moved to the jail at Liberty, Missouri. Many attempts at petitions and appeals to the executive and judicial governments had failed. Reports arrived, telling Joseph of the atrocities that were happening to his people. Section 121 of the Doctrine and Covenants, 20 Mar 1839, is his appeal to the Lord, followed by the comforting answer he received.

"O God, where art thou? . . . how long will thy hand be stayed, and thine eye . . . behold from the eternal heavens the wrongs of thy people . . . and thine ears be penetrated by their cries?" . . .

"My son, Peace be unto thy soul; thine adversities and thine afflictions shall be but a small moment; And then, if thou endure it well, God shall exalt thee on high; thou shalt triumph over all thy foes . . . How long can rolling waters remain impure? What power can stay the heavens? As well might man stretch forth his puny arm to stop the Missouri river in its decreed course . . . as to hinder the Almighty from pouring down knowledge from heaven upon the heads of the Latter-day Saints . . . know that thy faithfulness is stronger than the cords of death. Let thy bowels also be full of charity towards all men, and to the household of faith, and let virtue garnish thy thoughts unceasingly; then shall thy confidence wax strong in the presence of God."

CARTHAGE JAIL

The above is the window with the wide sill at the Carthage, Illinois, jail that Joseph Smith jumped from into the midst of the armed mob of over 150 assassins waiting beneath and crying for his death, 27 June 1844. By jumping, he preserved the lives of two of the remaining prisoners and sealed his testimony with his blood.

I sat on the window sill while the guide told the story and showed us the hole in the door made by the bullet that had killed Joseph's brother Hyrum when he had attempted to hold the unlockable door closed with the force of his body. He fell to the floor exclaiming, "I am a dead man." Willard Richards was at the door with a rod trying to knock the barrels of the pistols and rifles that protruded through the door opening at the top of the numerous narrow steps that rose to this high second-story room. John Taylor had been shot four times and was under the bed, barely surviving. I looked out the window to the ground below—much too far to be a means of escape. Joseph cried, "O Lord my God," as he jumped for the ground. His limp body was grabbed and set against a well-curb close to the jail. Four men shot him simultaneously, and one grabbed his hair and raised his long bowie knife to claim the $1000 reward for his head. Some described it as lightning from heaven in a cloudless sky that enveloped the whole wicked scene in an instant. The raised arm was paralyzed, as were the men that fired the shots. The mob with their blackened faces dispersed quickly. Orders were given and some returned for their stiffened comrades—still unable to move—placing them in the waiting wagons.

PALMYRA VISITOR'S CENTER

Our Lord Jesus Christ welcomed Joseph Smith Jr. into exaltation after his "small" moment of mortality. Christ has opened his arms and led the way, that all mankind who are heavy laden can answer his call, "Come follow Me!" Near Palmyra, New York, Jenni and Jonathan, like two babes lost in the woods, find love and peace at the feet of the sculpture of our Savior, Jesus Christ, in the Visitor's Center by the Hill Cumorah and the Sacred Grove, where God, The Father, and His Son, Jesus Christ, first appeared [1820] to young Joseph Smith in answer to his prayer, "Which of the many Christian Churches should he join?"

The Nauvoo Temple was only completed through the first floor when Joseph Smith Jr. and his brother Hyrum were "murdered in cold blood" in Carthage, Illinois, 27 June 1844. Through the determination of the saints, the capstone was laid on Saturday, 24 May 1845, about six o'clock in the morning amid the general rejoicing and shouts of "Hosanna" from the thousands of assembled saints. John Taylor's journal states, "Although there were several officers watching for us [the apostles] . . . yet we escaped . . . when the singing commenced . . ."

The completion of the temple sent a strong message to the anti-Mormons that the death of Joseph Smith was not the death of Mormonism. In his "History of Illinois," Governor Ford wrote, "In the fall of 1845, the anti-Mormons of Lima . . . held a meeting to devise means for the expulsion of the Mormons . . . They appointed some persons of their own number to fire a few shots at the house where they were assembled . . . [then] suddenly breaking up their meeting, rode all over the country spreading the dire alarm, that the Mormons had commenced the work of massacre and death." An attack was made upon the MORLEY settlement, and on 11 Sep 1845 twenty-nine houses were burned down, while their families were driven into the bushes, where men, women, and children laid drenched with rain through the night. Among them was young MARY ETT CARTER, born 11 December 1841 in Lima. She would become the second wife of great-grandfather JOHN LEHI IVIE on 23 January 1857.

ONE OF THE ORIGINAL NAUVOO TEMPLE "SUN STONES"

In the 1990s, we visited the temple site that had been purchased by the Church. The corner stones were there and two of the large original Sun Stones were displayed—another was in the Smithsonian in Washington D.C. The basement of the baptistery and the site were covered with grass and cared for beautifully.

Hancock County's Sheriff Jacob Backenstos defended the Mormons and called for a militia—only the Mormons volunteered. The anti-Mormons responded by calling for executive interference, and Governor Ford sent a detachment of four hundred state militia into Hancock County under the command of General John J. Hardin, who was accompanied by J. A. McDougal, attorney general, and also by Judge Stephen L. Douglas and Major W. B. Warren as advisors. Sheriff Backenstos left the county, and would join the U.S. Army in their war with Mexico.

After the saints had been driven out of Nauvoo, the mob took possession of the Nauvoo Temple and desecrated many of their sacred rooms. Colonel Thomas L. Kane befriended the saints; he visited Nauvoo and the temple and wrote: "In and around the splendid temple, which had been the chief object of my admiration, armed men were barracked, surrounded by their stacks of musketry, and pieces of heavy ordinance . . . They particularly pointed out to me certain features . . . sedulously defiled and defaced . . . " At nightfall Colonel Kane crossed the river to the camps of the exiles. Here he could hear the sounds "of a revel of a party of the guard within the city [Nauvoo] . . . every now and then, when their boisterous orgies strove to attain a sort of ecstatic climax, a cruel spirt of insulting frolic carried some of them into a high belfry of the temple steeple, and there, with the wicked childishness of inebriates, they whooped and shrieked, and beat the drum that I had seen, and rang in charivaric unison their loud-tongued steamboat bell."

Fearing the saints might want to return, on 10 November 1848, an incendiary was hired to set the temple on fire. The tower was destroyed, and the whole building shattered; then, on 27 May, 1850, a tornado blew down the north wall. Finally all the walls were torn down for building purposes—not one stone stood upon another.

THE BEAUTIFUL RESTORED NAUVOO TEMPLE TODAY, AUGUST 2004

The Nauvoo Temple was rebuilt as originally drawn by architect William Weeks and dedicated on international satellite with 2,983 sites in 68 countries participating, while the Mormon Tabernacle Choir provided the music on 27 June 2002, the 158th anniversary of the martyrdom of the Prophet Joseph Smith Jr.

— 10 —

"WE NEED CASH!"
THE NAUVOO TEMPLE—
A CASE OF MISTAKEN IDENTITY

It was dusk when the young Italian emigrant arrived in Nauvoo by steamboat. He had seen the beautiful white temple as they docked. All alone he trudged down the street wondering what to do next. He patted his money-belt; it contained $2500 in gold coin from the sale of his tug boat in New York harbor. He had worked hard to buy that tug boat when he came to America. But he had discovered the Church—bringing converts from the ships when they had landed after their journey from the British Isles and European countries. They had invited him to their meetings in New York City. He had joined the Church, sold his boat and had come to Nauvoo. Well, he must find a place to stay tonight. A carriage stopped. The man questioned him a little, then introduced himself as Brigham Young and invited him to stay at his home—but first, he was going to a meeting. Would he mind accompanying him? "That would be fine."

It was a meeting of the Twelve Apostles in Nauvoo. The purpose centered on a discussion of how to complete the building of the Nauvoo Temple. Brigham Young conducted. They only needed $2500; but where were they to get it? All funds had been exhausted. They needed cash. Without hesitation the young Italian, Joseph Toronto, unbuckled his money-belt and placed it on the table. It was just what they needed. They could have it all; but he would need a place to stay and food, until he could get work. With tears in his eyes, Brigham Young announced to the others present that the Lord had provided. [This had been his promise to the men working on the temple, after they had distributed the last of the rations.] Embracing the young man, Brigham Young stated, "You shall be my son and live with my family." Then he made him this promise, "Because you have done this for the Lord, you and all your posterity will be blessed. You will always have food. None of you will ever know real hunger." [7 July 1845]

The young man stayed with Brigham Young as his son, joining in the work and helping his family on the trek west and in Salt Lake City. He married, and one of his great-grandsons, Joseph Toronto, tall and still handsome in his seventies and a former member of the first Provo Temple Presidency, told us [in 1987] that this promise through the years has been fulfilled. Through depressions and hard times, his descendants have always had food in abundance and have been able to help others less fortunate. Every Sunday during the depression, various guests were invited to share their wonderful meals.

Part of the Nauvoo temple had been dedicated before its total completion and baptisms for the dead were being performed; the *Capstone Dedication* was on 24 May 1845, at about six o'clock in the morning to avoid the officers who sought to serve writs upon members of the Twelve Apostles on trumped-up charges against the law.

Still, the Lord would not allow them to do the endowments and sealings for time and eternity until more of the temple was completed and dedicated. About a year and a half after the deaths of Joseph and Hyrum [when the temple was only about one story high], this was accomplished with much dedication, hard work and sacrifice by the members. It was a glorious day on 10 December 1845 when the washing and anointing began, and, again, on the 11th when the first couples received their endowments; and all was recorded. There were two sessions on that first day. In the second session, my second-great-grandfather JOHN BARTON's youngest sister, MARY ANN BARTON was endowed along with her husband, DAVID CANDLAND. They had originally married 27 March 1844. Also, in this second group were Brigham Young, John Taylor, Parley P. Pratt, W. W. Phelps, Amasa Lyman, ISAAC MORLEY, William Clayton, John D. Lee, and many others.

DAVID CANDLAND was an early English convert, born 15 October 1819 in Highgate, Middlesex, England. The *History of the Church Vol. VII p. 554 records:*

> "Lewis Robbins is cleaning and putting in order the washing rooms and furniture, Peter Hanson is translating the Book of Mormon into the Danish language, Elisha Averett is doorkeeper, John L. Butler, fireman, DAVID

CANDLAND and L.R. Foster, clerks."

On page 562, Brigham Young reports, 4 Jan 1846:

"I attended a council of the Twelve in the Temple. DAVID CANDLAND was appointed *a mission to England.*"

In Hosea Stout's Diary we read:

"The Second Cohort (militia) was under my command. Previous to taking command, I appointed DAVID CANDLAND to be my clerk, who took his place as such . . . (18 September 1845) . . . DAVID CANDLAND, my clerk, came and wrote the address of Lieutenant General Brigham Young. At half past three General Rich came from thence. I went with him to see Charles Shumway, who is still very sick. From there we went to the temple to meet the police at five o'clock. Captain Hunter and McRae of the Fur Company were dispatched on an expedition to reconnoiter the enemy lines near Carthage. (10 Oct 1845) This morning heard that troops were coming here from Quincy and that the people there were trying to shoot [Jacob] Backenstos [the sheriff of Hancock County, Illinois, living at Carthage, who was trying to keep the mobs from destroying Nauvoo and surroundings] and swear that he shall not get away alive . . . Received orders from the Lieutenant General by A. P. Rockwood to have the Second Cohort ready to be called out at a moment's warning, for them not to be far from home and to rally as usual at the hoisting of the flag at the [Nauvoo] temple, for them not to give up their gains to our enemies but first to shoot. [This order was later changed.] I then went home very sick with the headache and went to bed and lay till Brother James Pace came after me in a buggy to take me to the police, which he did, though I was hardly able to sit up. From there I came home about dark still very sick. Brother D. CANDLAND, my clerk, came here to write out my journal for me, which he did until about eleven o'clock p. m. I was some better after taking some nourishments. (13 Dec 1845) Went to Dustin Amy's for some tin ware and there saw D. CANDLAND about the endowment as he had been through and went from there to the temple."

[Note: Other relatives receiving their endowments in the Nauvoo temple were:

1845–December 12:	James Allred	hp	and Elizabeth Warren Allred
	19:	Isaac Allred	sev	and Julia Ann Taylor Allred
	20:	Rueben W. Allred	sev	and Lucy Ann Butler Allred
		Andrew Whitlock	sev	and Hannah C. Allred Whitlock
	23:	William Fausett	hp	and Matilda Butcher Fausett
				Rebecca Faucett

1846–January	3:	Moses M. Sanders	sev	and Amanda Armstrong Fausett Sanders
		Reddin A. Allred	sev	and Julia Ann Bates Allred
		William M. Allred	sev	and Orissa A. Bates Allred
		John Fausett	sev	and Margaret Smith Fausett
	9:	James T.S. Allred	sev	and Eliza Bridget Manwaring Allred
		Wiley P. Allred	sev	and Sally Zabrisky Allred
	17:	Isaac Allred	hp	and Mary Calvert
		Allen Taylor	sev	and Sarah Louisa Allred Taylor
	20:	Joseph Egbert	sev	and Mary C. Allred
	21:			Elizabeth Barton
	23:	Reddick N. Allred	sev	and Lucy Hoyt Allred
	24:			Catherine Barton
		Thomas C. Ivie		and Amanda Jane Moore Ivie
	28:	Mary Ann Fausett		
	29:	George Edwards	sev	and
		Levi Allred		and Abigail McMurtrey Allred
	31:	JOHN BARTON	sev	and SUSANNA WILKINSON Barton
February	6:	James R. Allred	sev	and

It is of interest that ISRAEL BARLOW, sev, b. 13 Sep 1806 in Granville, Hampton, Massachusetts, was endowed and sealed to Elizabeth Haven Barlow of Massachusetts on 16 Dec 1845. On 28 Jan 1846 he married ELIZABETH BARTON, endowed the 21 Jan 1846—another wife. She was a sister to second-great-grandfather JOHN BARTON and would have been 42 years old.]

On Tuesday, 23 December 1845 [the day WILLIAM and MATILDA FAUSETT received their endowments] some interesting events occurred [*HC Vol VII p. 549*]:

"Early this morning the drying house of Captain Charles C. Rich's Emigrating Co. No. 13 was burned to the ground, consuming $300.00 worth of wagon timber. The high council met in the Temple for prayer.

"One-five p. m., Almon W. Babbitt came into the Temple and informed me [Brigham Young] that there were some federal officers from Springfield accompanied by several of the state troops in the city for the purpose of arresting some of the Twelve, especially Amasa Lyman and myself. It was soon reported that they were at the door of the Temple and were intending to search it. George D. Grant, my coachman, went below and drove my carriage up to the door as if he was waiting for me to come down.

"William Miller [president of the high priests] put on my cap and Brother Kimball's cloak and went downstairs meeting the marshal and his assistants at the door, as he was getting into my carriage the marshall arrested him, on a writ from the United States court, charging him with counterfeiting the coin of the United States. Miller told him there must be some mistake about it, as he was not guilty of anything of the kind, but the marshal insisted it was right. Miller desired the marshal to go down to the Mansion where he could get counsel and ascertain if the proceedings were legal. On reaching the Mansion they went into a private room where Esq. Edmonds examined the writ and pronounced it legal. Miller gave Edmonds the name of four witnesses for subpoena for him, and asked the marshal to remain until morning; he consented, but soon got uneasy and said he must go to Carthage. Miller then inquired if he would wait three quarters of an hour until he could get his witnesses, but in fifteen minutes he said he must go, and would wait no longer. Miller got into his carriage; Esq. Edmonds rode with the marshal's guard and they started for Carthage, Miller protesting there was some mistake about it, for he certainly was not guilty of any such things as were charged in the writ. On the way to Carthage the marshal was very social, and remarked that the people had got quite a joke upon him for letting Turley give him the dodge. As they approached Carthage, the troops began to whoop and holler and went into town in high glee, performing the journey which was eighteen miles in two hours.

"The marshal put up at Hamilton's Tavern, and the rumor soon spread through the town that Brigham Young was in the custody of the marshal at Hamilton's. Among others, George W. Thatcher, the county commissioner's clerk, who was well acquainted with Miller came into the tavern to see me. The marshal at his request took Miller into a private room. After a little conversation one of the guards came in and the marshal went out. The marshall soon returned and said to Mr. Miller, 'I am informed you are not Mr. Young.' 'Ah!' exclaimed Miller, 'then if I should prove not to be Mr. Young, it would be a worse joke on you than the Turley affair.'

"He replied, 'I'll be d----d if it won't.'

"The marshal asked Miller if his name was Young. He answered, 'I never told you my name was Young, did I?' 'No,' replied the marshal, 'but one of my men professed to be acquainted with Mr. Young, and pointed you out to me to be him.' William Backenstos was called in and he told them William Miller was not Brigham Young. Another man came, and said [he could swear] Miller was not Brigham Young. The marshal said he was sorry, and asked Miller his name. He replied, 'It is William Miller.' The marshal left the room and soon returned accompanied by Edmonds who was laughing heartily at him. Edmonds inquired if he had anything more to do with 'Mr. Young.' The marshal replied that he did not know that he had anything further to do with Mr. Miller.

"Eighty-seven persons received the ordinances. Seven-thirty p. m., I met with the Twelve in prayer, and thanked the Lord for deliverance from the snares of our enemies. Eight-twenty, I left the Temple disguised and shortly after Brothers Heber C. Kimball, Parley P. Pratt, George A. Smith and Amasa Lyman left, to elude the vexatious writs of our persecutors.

"Wednesday 24.—William Miller remained last night at Carthage at Jacob B. Backenstos'. Miller said he could not sleep being interrupted by Edmonds' continued roars of laughter at the marshal's discomfiture. Miller saw two of the marshal's guards, one of whom threatened his life. Miller came in with the stage; the driver told him that the officers said it would be like searching for a needle in a hay mow now, to undertake to find Brigham Young in Nauvoo.

"Friday 26.—I [Brigham Young] said we will have no more anointing at present, and if the brethren do not get anything more than they have already received, they have got all they have worked for in building this house; and if there is any more to be received it is because the Lord is merciful and gracious . . . Sheriff Backenstos informed me that the United States deputy marshal was in town with writs for the Twelve and Brother George Miller. Eight p. m., Elder Kimball and I left the Temple.

"Saturday, 27.—This morning was a very pleasant one—moderately cold, the sun shining clear and bright in the heavens. Orson Pratt was the only one of the Twelve present in the Temple. Ten-fifteen a.m., the United States Deputy Marshal Roberts, went to the Temple in company with Almon W. Babbitt and searched for the Twelve and others. He was freely admitted to every part of the Temple, to which he desired access; he went into the tower, on to the roof, into the attic story and while viewing the city from the tower he expressed his astonishment at its magnificence and extent and said considering the unfavorable circumstances with which the people had been surrounded it seemed almost impossible that so much should have been accomplished. He passed through the various departments into the east room where he very intently examined the portraits, and made inquiries as to whose they were. On entering the attic hall he was requested to take off his boots and uncover his head, to which he complied; after remaining about half an hour he departed. About two p. m., the marshal returned accompanied by a gentleman whom he introduced as from New Orleans, and Sheriff Backenstos. They visited the middle room and the tower and departed after about half an hour . . . Lewis Robbins is cleaning and putting in order the washing rooms and furniture, Peter Hanson is translating the 'Book of Mormon' into the Danish language. DAVID CANDLAND and L. R. Foster, clerks. Orson Pratt has been engaged in making astronomical calculation.

"Friday, January 2, 1846.—Sixty-four persons received ordinances . . . This morning elder Heber C. Kimball related the following dream: Last evening, before retiring to bed he asked God to enlighten his mind with regard to the work of the endowment; while sleeping he beheld a large field of corn that was fully ripe, he and a number of others were commanded to take baskets and pick off the corn with all possible speed, for there would soon be a storm that would hinder the gathering of the harvest. The hands engaged in gathering the harvest were heedless and unconcerned and did not haste, as they were commanded; but he and the man he assisted had a much larger basket than the rest, and picked with all their might of the largest ears of the field, they once in a while would pick an ear that had a long tail on each end and but a few grains scattering over the center of the cob, which were very light.

"The interpretation of the dream is, that the field represented the church, the good corn represented good saints, the light corn represented the light and indifferent saints, the laborers are those appointed to officiate in the Temple, the storm is trouble that is near upon us, and requires an immediate united exertion of all engaged in giving the endowments to the saints, or else we will not get through before we will be obliged to flee for our lives . . .

"Wednesday, 7.—The supply of provisions brought in today has been very abundant, and much has been sent away to those families that are destitute . . . This afternoon, the new altar was used for the first time, and four individuals and their wives were sealed . . . .

"Monday, 12.—One hundred and forty-three persons received their endowments in the Temple. I [Brigham Young] officiated . . . Such has been the anxiety manifested by the saints to receive the ordinances [of the Temple], and such the anxiety on our part to administer to them, that I have given myself up entirely to the work of the Lord in the Temple night and day, not taking more than four hours sleep, upon an average, per day, and going home but once a week . . .

"Tuesday, 13.—A council was held in the Temple. The captains of fifties and tens made reports of the number in their respective companies, who were prepared to start west immediately, should the persecutions of our enemies compel us to do so: one hundred and forty horses and seventy wagons were reported ready for immediate service . . .

"Tuesday, 20.—One hundred and ninety-five persons received ordinances in the Temple. Public prejudice being so strong against us, and the excitement becoming alarming we determined to continue the administration of the ordinances of endowment night and day . . . The high council published the following . . . 'Beloved Brethren and Friends:

We the members of the high council of the church by the voice of all her authorities, have unitedly and unanimously agreed . . . that we intend to send out into the western country from this place, sometime in March, a Company of Pioneers, consisting mostly of young, hardy men, with some families. These are destined to be furnished with an ample outfit; taking with them a printing press, farming utensils of all kinds, with mill irons and bolting cloths, seeds of kinds, grain, etc. The object of this early move is to put in a spring crop, to build houses, and to prepare for the reception of families who will start so soon as grass shall be sufficiently grown to sustain teams and stock. Our Pioneers are instructed to proceed west until they find a good place to make a crop, in some good valley in the neighborhood of the Rocky Mountains, where they will infringe upon no one, and not be likely to be infringed upon . . . We also further declare for the satisfaction of some who have concluded that our grievances have alienated us from our country, that our patriotism has not been overcome by fire—by sword— by daylight, nor by midnight assassinations, which we have endured; neither have they alienated us from the institutions of our country . . . men who wish to buy property very cheap, to benefit themselves and are willing to benefit us, are invited to call and look; and our prayer shall ever be that justice and judgment—mercy and truth may be exalted, not only in our own land, but throughout the world . . . Done in council [stake high council] at the city of Nauvoo, on the 20th day of January, 1846.

[Signed] Samuel Bent, JAMES ALLRED (and 10 others).

"Tuesday, 27.—One hundred and twenty-six persons received ordinances . . . Sheriff Backenstos has returned from Springfield, and says that Governor Ford has turned against us, and that Major Warren is making calculations to prevent our going away . . . and placing the county under martial law . . . remained in the Temple all night.

"Thursday, 29—I continued giving endowments . . . One hundred and thirty-three persons received ordinances. Quite a number of the governor's troops are prowling around our city; I am informed that they are seeking to arrest some of the leading men of the church.

"February, Monday, 2.—Two hundred and thirty-four persons received ordinances. Ten a.m., the Twelve, Trustees and a few others met in council, to ascertain the feelings of the brethren that were expecting to start westward. We agreed that it was imperatively necessary to start as soon as possible. I counseled the brethren to procure boats and have them in readiness to convey our wagons and teams over the river, and let everything for the journey be in readiness, that when a family is called to go, everything necessary may be put into the wagon within four hours, at least, for if we are here many days, our way will be hedged up. Our enemies have resolved to intercept us whenever we start. I should like to push on as far as possible before they are aware of our movements. In order to have this counsel circulated, I sent messengers to notify the captains of hundreds and fifties to meet at 4 p. m. at Father Cutlers'. At four o'clock, I met with the captains of hundreds and fifties, and laid my counsel before them, to which they all consented, and dispersed to carry it into execution.

"Tuesday, 3.—Notwithstanding that I had announced that we would not attend to the administration of the ordinances, the House of the Lord was thronged all day, the anxiety being so great to receive, as if the brethren would have us stay here and continue the endowments until our way would be hedged up, and our enemies would intercept us. But I informed the brethren that this was not wise, and that we should build more Temples, and have further opportunities to receive the blessings of the Lord, as soon as the saints were prepared to receive them. In this Temple we have been abundantly rewarded, if we receive no more. I also informed the brethren that I was going to get my wagons started and be off. I walked some distance from the Temple supposing the crowd would disperse, but on returning I found the house filled to overflowing. Looking upon the multitude and knowing their anxiety, as they were thirsting and hungering for the word, we continued at work diligently in the House of the Lord. Two hundred and ninety-five persons received ordinances.

"Wednesday, 4.—I continued loading up my wagons, preparatory to starting west.

"Friday, 6.—Five hundred and twelve persons received the first ordinances and endowment in the Temple. Bishop George Miller and family crossed the Mississippi river. They had six wagons.

"Saturday, 7.—According to G.A. Smith's Journal upwards of six hundred received the ordinances [i.e. of the Temple]: One hundred and twenty-six of which were reported in the Seventies Record.

"Sunday, 8.—I met with the Council of the Twelve in the southeast corner room of the attic of the Temple. We knelt around the altar, and dedicated the building to the Most High. We asked his blessing upon our intended move to the west; also asked him to enable us some day to finish the Temple, and dedicate it to him, and we would leave it in his hands to do as he pleased; and to preserve the building as a monument to Joseph Smith. We asked the Lord to accept the labor of his servants in this land. We then left the Temple. I addressed the saints in the grove and informed them that the company going to the west would start this week across the river.

"Monday, 9.—A detachment of the governor's troops came into the city . . . Elder George A. Smith sent his family across the river. Three-thirty p. m., the roof of the Temple was discovered to be on fire. An alarm was immediately given, when the brethren marched steadily to its rescue . . . Willard Richards called on the brethren to bring out all their buckets, to fill them with water, and pass them on. Lines inside were formed, and the buckets passed in quick succession. The fire raged near half an hour. It was caused by the stovepipe being overheated, drying the clothing in the upper room . . . several of the troops went to the Temple and attempted to enter, but were prevented by the brethren at the door . . . The crossing of the river was superintended by the police, under the direction of Hosea Stout. They gathered several flatboats, some old lighters, and a number of skiffs, forming altogether quite a fleet, and were at work night and day, crossing the saints.

"Sunday, 15.—[February 1846] I [Brigham Young] crossed the river with my family accompanied by W. Richards and family and George A. Smith. We traveled on four miles, when we came to the bluff. I would not go on until I saw all the teams up. I helped them up the hill with my own hands. At dusk started on, and reached Sugar Creek about 8 p. m., having traveled nine miles. The roads were very bad."

[Note: Cousin ISAAC ALLRED writes: "In February, 1846, I left the city with the Church, perfectly destitute of anything to help myself."

It is likely that the majority of my relations who received their endowments left Nauvoo in February. JAMES RUSSELL IVIE and his wife are not recorded as receiving their endowments at this time. There is not a record that they owned property in Nauvoo at that time, either, although THOMAS C. IVIE and his wife AMANDA had property. Second-great-grandparents JAMES R. IVIE and their family had probably sold their Nauvoo land and returned to their land in Missouri to arrange their affairs in that state, prepare for the journey west, and try once more to persuade their other family members to accompany them to the Rocky Mountains. They appear to have been more successful financially in this quest than some of the others. They joined with the early Mormon wagon trains crossing Iowa that spring.]

~ 11 ~

FORCED EVACUATION INTO THE WESTERN INDIAN TERRITORY

While JOHN BARTON waited in his covered wagon with his family for his turn to cross the wide Mississippi River on that cold February morning, he glanced up at the beautiful white temple. He had worked hard to help with its completion. He glanced at his wife, SUSANNAH. She was sitting straight with a determined look on her face. They were leaving behind the small grave of ELIZABETH JANE, who had died 17 September 1843 of diarrhea. She was five months and seven days old. They had another little girl now, born 23 June 1845—PHEBE ELEN. She was asleep, wrapped tightly in her blanket and shawl to protect her from the bitter wind. MARY CATHERINE, who was named after his two sisters, was lively and impatient. Friends were important to her and she held her own with the best of them, always in the middle of their childhood games. She was eight years old and he had baptized her last September. Five-year-old WILLIAM pushed his way forward and sat on his father's lap, the only other male in this wagon full of women. However, blue-eyed father JOHN was 37 years old, quiet and very capable.

Two of his sisters were with them. His youngest sister, MARY ANN BARTON CANDLAND, had a brand new baby, SARAH EMILY CANDLAND, born 18 January 1846. Her husband, DAVID CANDLAND had been called on a mission to England two weeks before the baby was born, 4 January 1846. She had been given a more protected place back in the wagon. The baby was so tiny. His older sister CATHERINE was helping her. He had checked on his forty-two-year-old sister, ELIZABETH, who had just married ISRAEL BARLOW, as a plural wife. She would travel with her husband's family, and seemed quite delighted with them.

It was hard to leave their home. JOHN took pride in having the best kept yard in the city. His grain stacks were absolute perfection. His wife and two sisters kept the house in perfect order. They had been remarkably happy here—especially the children.

JOHN remembered the Prophet Joseph Smith. His family group had been in the audience at the funeral when the prophet gave his public address called the "King Follet Sermon." Tears of gratitude collected in his eyes as he remembered the comfort they felt when he explained to them that the little children who die before they are baptized at eight years old are taken into the arms of their Heavenly Father and will still be their own children, if they live worthy of them. All his sisters, his wife, and he had their endowments and were sealed in the Nauvoo Temple—a gift that gave them courage for what they knew would be a long, hard journey ahead into the distant Rocky Mountains, an unsettled land of savage Indians and wild animals. They had come over eight hundred miles to get to Nauvoo. They had felt the persecution and seen Governor Ford's soldiers beginning to arrive on their streets. The journey would be hard, but a new city of peace was in the distance. Their team was being helped onto the ferry. It was time to move on.

[Note: Of the 14 children of RICHARD and MARY McKEE FAUSETT of Tennessee, five of them came west at this time; REBECCA STONE FAUSETT TURNER, who lived in Macoupin, Illinois, came later. JOHN McKEE FAUSETT, WILLIAM McKEE FAUSETT, and AMANDA ARMSTRONG FAUSETT SANDERS each had large families of their own, and had been driven from Caldwell County arriving early in Nauvoo. AMANDA's husband, MOSES MARTIN SANDERS, had been one of the 40 policemen chosen by Captain Jonathan Dunham the 29 Dec 1843, with Charles C. Rich, 1st Lieut.; Hosea Stout, 2nd Lieut.; and SHADRACH ROUNDY, 3rd Lieut. These FAUSETTs were endowed and sealed in the Nauvoo Temple. WILLIAM was a high priest and JOHN and MOSES were seventies.

MARTHA SPENCER FAUSETT married JOHN BRUSH, 9 Jan 1845, in Nauvoo. This was evidently her second husband. JOHN FAUSETT's daughter, AMANDA CAROLINE FAUSETT married GEORGE W. CLIFT in Nauvoo on 9 Jul 1840. According to family records, WILLIAM and MATILDA FAUSETT had their ninth child, WILLIAM CALVIN FAUSETT, born in Nauvoo, 6 Oct 1844. Their oldest daughter married WILLIAM ALEXANDER FOLLETT 29 Sep 1845, and were sealed on 28 Jan 1846 in the Nauvoo Temple. Family records show another daughter, NARICISSA REBECCA FAUSETT, being married and sealed in the Nauvoo temple on 22 Jan 1846 to CORNELIUS PETER LOTT.

MOSES and AMANDA FAUSETT SANDERS had a set of twins in Nauvoo, EMILY and EMMA; then they had ELIZA JANE, and if records are correct they had another set of twins, HYRUM SMITH SANDERS and MOSES MARTIN SANDERS, born 10 Oct 1845. If this is correct, then twin MOSES must have died as they later named another child MOSES MARTIN. This would give them 12 or 13 children when they left Nauvoo. It would appear that the FAUSETT family, as they left Nauvoo and journeyed westward, included around 38 people and they would be joined very soon on the trail by their sister ELIZA McKEE FAUSETT IVIE, the wife of JAMES RUSSELL IVIE, whose family would add 13 more—bringing the total in this first group going through Iowa with Brigham Young to around 50 descendants of our third-great-grandparents, RICHARD and MARY McKEE FAUSETT (including their spouses.)

There were three ALLRED brothers in Far West: JAMES, ISAAC and WILLIAM. All three had large families. WILLIAM, the Captain and prisoner in our previous chapter, died of exposure while he was in Quincy, Illinois, in 1841. He left a family of eleven children. He had married SARAH WARREN; his brother JAMES had married ELIZABETH WARREN, and their youngest brother, JOHN, had married NANCY WARREN. JOHN and NANCY were in Monroe County, Missouri, in the 1840 census, as was their oldest sister, SARAH ALLRED IVIE—wife of ANDERSON IVIE. Before leaving Nauvoo, JAMES ALLRED had married, as a second wife, his brother's widow, SARAH WARREN, and had taken on the responsibility of her large family as they journeyed west. Both JAMES and ISAAC had six married children at this time that had been endowed and sealed in the Nauvoo Temple; but they still had unmarried children and had left behind children and grandchildren that had died during these troubled times. Counting this ALLRED group with their spouses that left Nauvoo and vicinity, they probably numbered around 70 people. Of course, they were related also to the IVIEs and SANDERS listed above, as their second oldest sister, MARY, had married DAVID SANDERS (who was killed in New Orleans, during the War of 1812). She was the mother of MOSES MARTIN SANDERS. Listed in the endowments were LEVI ALLRED and his wife, ABIGAIL McMURTREY. LEVI was a first cousin to the three brothers; his father was MOSES ALLRED, a younger brother to their father, fourth-great-grandfather WILLIAM ALLRED.

If we combine the ALLREDs, BARTONs, FAUSETTs and IVIEs, it comes to about 140 people. We could also add to this their future relatives, such as MARY ETT CARTER and her large family; ELIZABETH DOBSON, who married RICHARD IVIE; WILLIAM DAYTON; WARREN FOOTE; JEROME ZABRISKIE; ELIZABETH PORTER; the YOUNG sisters; HANNAH SMITH; HENRY McARTHUR; WILLIAM SEELEY; the MEMMOTTs; the ROBINS; the SWEATS and the list increases the further down the posterity line it goes, into the JOHNSONs; the ROUNDYs; the DUKEs; the TAYLORs; the HESSes; the STAKERs; and into the thousands of unknown and future "relatives-in-laws"—the "branches" appear to be "broadening" very rapidly.]

This group that left Nauvoo in the desperately cold month of February were a united people. They struggled and helped each other as brothers and sisters and moved across the wild, untamed and uncharted trails through southern Iowa, building bridges, homes, orchards, farms and in every way trying to ease the burdens of those who would follow. They were a new kind of pioneer—concerned for others, perhaps more than themselves.

NETTIE ROBINS claimed that JAMES RUSSELL IVIE's father— ANDERSON IVIE "owned a large track of land or plantation with seventy-five Negros slaves." This has to be an exaggeration. Their last will mentions only nine slaves, and no large plantation. It was probably true, however, that when JAMES R. left their home in Missouri to come west, his father gave him a "little negro boy. He was old enough to help grandma [ELIZA] with the smaller children. When they reached Omaha and were getting ready to start west, they were told not to burden themselves with an extra mouth to feed; so grandpa, JAMES RUSSELL, gave the little boy his freedom and told him either to find his way back to his family or to live with another family. As they left the little fellow cried and said, 'Who will take care of Missy BETSY and MARIE? I do love you Mama IVIE.' Both Grandfather and Grandmother loved the little boy and hated leaving him behind."

Mark Twain tells us a little about slavery in Missouri at that time: "In my schoolboy days I had no aversion to slavery. I was not aware that there was anything wrong about it. No one arraigned it in my hearing; the local papers said nothing against it; the local pulpit taught us that God approved it, that it was a holy thing and that the doubter need only look in the Bible if he wished to settle his mind . . . if the slaves themselves had an aversion to slavery they were wise and said nothing. In Hannibal we seldom saw a slave misused; on the farm never . . . there was nothing about the slavery of the Hannibal region to rouse one's dozing humane instincts to activity. It was the mild domestic slavery, not the brutal plantation article. Cruelties were very rare and exceedingly and wholesomely unpopular . . . for to our whites and blacks alike the Southern plantation was simply hell; no milder name could describe it. If the threat to sell an incorrigible slave 'down the river' would not reform him, nothing would—his case was past cure . . . All of the Negroes were friends of ours, and with those of our own age we were in effect comrades. I say in effect, using the phrase as a modification . . . It was on the farm that I got my strong liking for [this] race and my appreciation of certain of [their] fine qualities. This feeling and this estimate have stood the test of sixty years and . . . the black face is as welcome to me now as it was then."

NETTIE M. ROBINS history continues:

"Besides JAMES RUSSELL [IVIE] and family, two of his brothers, THOMAS KELTON and WILLIAM SHELTON families journeyed as far as Morrion, Missouri, on their way to join the wagon train which would soon be headed west toward Utah. It was here that WILLIAM SHELTON's wife decided she did not want to go on, so they dropped out of the company. There was some trouble over one of WILLIAM's daughters marrying as a plural wife to a man by the name of Long. Both parents strongly opposed the marriage."

There are problems with this paragraph, also. THOMAS [C. or K.] IVIE owned a lot in Nauvoo and was married to AMANDA JANE MOORE in Nauvoo. They received their temple ordinances on 24 January 1846—very close to the February departure date of the others. It seems more likely that his brother JAMES R., who had already sold his lot and is not listed in the temple records, had left earlier and brought his two wayward brothers, JOHN A. IVIE and WILLIAM SHELTON IVIE and their families with him when he came north. WILLIAM's daughters were SARAH FRANCIS IVIE, age 4; and MARY ELIZABETH, age 2—not marriageable ages. This would not be true of their brother JOHN ANDERSON IVIE's family. He had a daughter, ELIZABETH, who was 18 years old and married to TICE CAIN and another daughter, SARAH, who was 16 years old. In the 1850 census we find that both JOHN and WILLIAM and their families are living in Kirksville, Adair, Missouri. Also with them in Kirksville are the families of JOHN ALLRED, their mother's youngest brother, and TICE and ELIZABETH CAIN. There are many LONG families in Missouri. Their brother ISAAC IVIE married MELISSA LONG and their younger sister SARAH married WILLIAM LONG. Both families remained in Monroe County.

Dr. WILLIAM HORACE IVIE of Berkeley, California, who believed he was the last living descendant of WILLIAM SHELTON IVIE reported (1955) that his ancestor "had a farm on Big Farm Creek. In 1857 they moved into Kirksville, Missouri, and built a hotel, which he ran until his death, 30 Aug 1858, after which his wife ran it until her death, 22 Dec 1889, and that WILLIAM became a Campbellite minister."

The Journey across Iowa

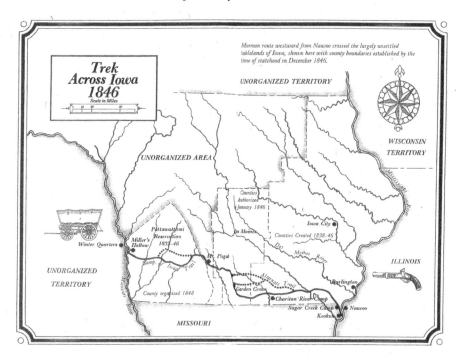

From the *Diary of Aroet Lucious Hale,* son of Jonathan H. Hale and Olive Boynton, who were baptized in New Hampshire in June, 1834:

"My father was a bishop and stayed in Nauvoo until every Latter-day Saint was out of Nauvoo, across the Mississippi River . . . Sugar Creek [was] organized into the great camp of Israel, bound for the Rocky Mountains. The camp stayed here until the first of March, Sunday morning . . . President Brigham Young called the people together . . . The orders were for every man to be ready to roll out and start his journey at 10 o'clock the next morning . . . Our travels were very slow, not averaging more than four miles a day . . . The whole camp had to cut browse and herd their cattle and horses. They were very poor. Some died. We arrived at the east fork of Grand River on the 25th of April. Sunday, President Young spoke on the principle of stopping here and opening up a farm, putting in gardens and crops, building houses for the poor that was left behind that could not get any further. [On Monday] the men were all called together and organized into different companies, some to splitting rails, some to cutting house logs, and some to digging, every man to work at the best advantage. I was organized into the company to cut house logs and build log cabins . . . the 1st of May, we raised the first log house on the farm. We continued working on the farm until the 16th of May, then left Garden Grove. The Twelve and a large portion traveled on until the 23rd of May and camped on Grand River. Here a part of the camp was called upon to stop and put in another farm crop . . . It was considered best for all that could not make a good outfit to stop on the farm. I continued working on the farm until the 16th of June. I then was counseled to return to Nauvoo to meet my father. I met my father on Soap Creek, 50 miles from Mount Pisgah, that being the name of the farm that we built on Grand River. We arrived at Mount Pisgah the first day of July, father being counseled not to stop but to proceed on to the bluffs of the Missouri River . . . We arrived at the bluffs on the 16th of July . . . Father camped on Mosquito Creek about nine miles from the trading post on the Missouri River.

"July 16 [1846] in obedience to a call of the authorities of the camps of the Saints, the men all met at headquarters on Mosquito Creek. Colonel Thomas L. Kane who had arrived in camp, and Captain Allen, were present. President Brigham Young, Captain Allen and others addressed the Saints in regard to furnishing the battalion. Four companies were raised on that day and the day following. I had a desire to go with the battalion as a drummer boy, being a member of the martial band in Nauvoo . . . President Heber C. Kimball talked to me. Said he, 'Aroet, you have been away from your father and mother five months in the camp of Israel, as a teamster. Your dear father is on crutches with a broken leg and no help but your mother and her little ones.' I took President Kimball's counsel and well that I did. Father was called as one of the high council to preside on the east side of the Missouri River. The council picked for their winter quarters Council Point, near the Missouri River . . . The weather was very warm, the river water very bad and in a few weeks nearly all the camp was taken down with the chills and fever. A great many died. My dear father died September 4, 1846, and my mother September 8, 1846; only four days between their deaths. Mother was confined about ten or twelve days before father died and having the chills and fever, being very sick, she gave up all hopes . . . Mother was kneeling beside the bed when father drew his last breath. I led her to the wagon which was in the rear of the tent. She called Sister ALLRED and Sister MORLEY, wives of two of the counselors, into the wagon and told them . . . she wanted her sister Clarisa Harriman to have her infant baby and Clarisa never had any children. Uncle Henry Harriman had crossed the Missouri River and was at Winter Quarters. Sister ALLRED and Sister MORLEY started after mother died, with the infant. They came to the ferry boat on the river. The wind blew so hard for two days that the boat could not cross the river . . . the infant died and [was] buried with its father and mother.

"I will here relate a prophecy of President Kimball upon my head. I was taken sick before my father, with the ague and fever shock about two hours in the forenoon and a burning fever in the afternoon. I was not able to take care of myself. Brother Kimball came into the tent where I was laying on the bed. He said, 'Aroet, where are your cattle that your father moved into this camp with?' . . . 'if you will get up tomorrow morning and go and hunt cattle enough to move your wagons out of this camp, up to Winter Quarters, you never shall have another ague shake as long as you live.' I tried to make some excuse but no good. Some of the brethren and sisters had gathered around the tent door, hearing him talk to me. Said he, 'Will you go?' I said, 'I will try to go.' Brother Kimball then spoke to Uncle JAMES ALLRED [written above line: then administered to me.] Said he, 'Brother ALLRED, you have a horse, saddle and bridle here tomorrow by eight o'clock. Brother Hale is going to get cattle enough to take his wagons up to Winter Quarters, at my camp, a distance of twelve miles.'

"In the morning, Brother ALLRED was there with the riding animals which were little white mules which belonged to some of the brethren that had come from Texas that year. I started according to agreement.

They watched me as far as they could see me. Some of the women said that I would never return alive. Some found fault with Brother Kimball to sending a boy as sick as I was alone to hunt cattle. I rode to Mosquito Creek, five miles. I was nearly chocked for water. I corralled my mule to the creek and had a good drink of water, laid back on the bank to rest me, and fell asleep. I did not wake up until after dark. I found my mules a short distance below on the creek. I caught the mules and was thinking what to do. I had not seen any camps as yet on the creek. While thinking what course to pursue, I heard a dog bark up the creek. I crawled onto the mule and started up the creek. I soon found a camp and told them who I was and what I was after. The man was a little acquainted with father. They took me in and took care of me and in the morning sent a boy with me. The third day I found three oxen and one cow. I returned to camp. Some were surprised to see me . . . told them I had not had an ague shake once I left them . . . if there ever was a prophet of God on this earth . . . Heber C. Kimball was one.

"The next morning, the brethren helped me hitch up my teams. My sister Rachel drove the light wagon, and I the other wagon. We arrived at the boat landing all right. Brother Heber C. Kimball was there and soon I was told to drive my wagon onto the boat. I will here say that others had to pay one dollar a wagon, but I was told to drive off.

"Brother Kimball walked ahead of the wagons and piloted me to where Uncle Henry Harriman was building his cabin. They were pleased to see us children. Uncle Harriman had his cabin three rounds high. I went to work with oxen and wagon and we put a room onto the end of his house. My sister Rachel was old enough to keep house for [us], and we were soon comfortable for the winter. Brother Kimball made me promise that I never would make any general move without counseling him. I always kept that counsel or promise as long as he lived. And I was always blessed and prospered in doing so.

"Winter Quarters was soon a city of log and sod houses, divided into 22 wards, each presided over by a bishop. The first of December, Winter Quarters inhabitants numbered 3,483 souls. Many Saints suffered and died on the banks of the Missouri River. The Saints on the east side of the river were divided into wards and presided over by bishops."

Before his mother died "she said to me, 'Aroet, promise me one thing, that you will take good care of my darling children and go to the mountains with President Brigham Young and Heber C. Kimball. There is where your dear father started to go with them. Don't be persuaded to turn back by any of our relations that are writing to us. Do as I have counseled you and I bless you and the Lord will bless you.' . . . I never have forgotten those words. I promised her that I would do as she had requested me to do. I kept my promise good."

[*CHC Vol. III*] "At first the city [Winter Quarters] was divided into thirteen wards with a bishopric appointed to preside over each . . . Following is a list of the bishops of these wards: First ward, Levi E. Riter; second, WILLIAM FOSSETT; third and fourth, Benjamin Brown; fifth and sixth, John Vance; seventh, Edward Hunter; eighth, David Fairbanks; ninth, Daniel Spencer; tenth, Joseph Mathews; eleventh, Abraham Hoagland; twelfth, David D. Yearsley; thirteenth, Joseph B. Noble . . . Before the winter set in the number increased to twenty-two. A high council was also authorized to exercise the functions both of an ecclesiastical high council, and also a municipal council. Such a council was given also to the camps at Pisgah, Garden Grove, Kanesville (Council Bluffs), Council Point, and also Bishop Miller's camp—about one hundred and fifty miles northwest of Winter Quarters."

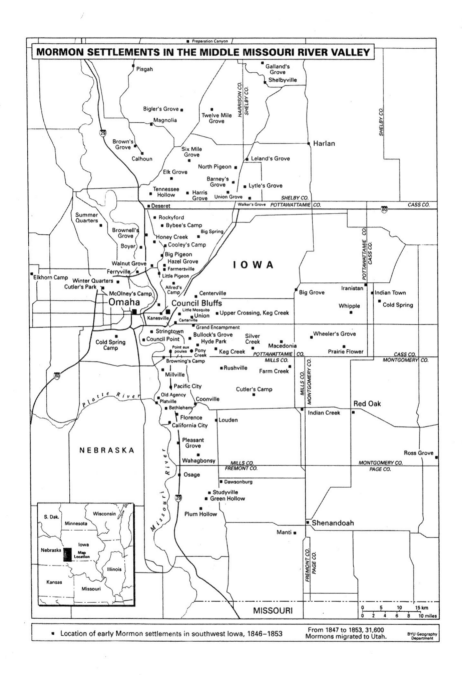

MORMON SETTLEMENTS IN THE MIDDLE MISSOURI RIVER VALLEY

■ Location of early Mormon settlements in southwest Iowa, 1846–1853

From 1847 to 1853, 31,600 Mormons migrated to Utah.

BYU Geography Department

~ 12 ~

GATHERING ON THE FRINGES OF CIVILIZATION— MISSOURI RIVER
1846-1847

The following was taken from a letter to Elders Hyde, Pratt, and Taylor, who were in England on a Special Mission: from the Camp of Israel, Omaha Nation, Winter Quarters, near Council Bluffs, 6 January 1847 (to wit, one o'clock next morning). [Brigham Young and W. Richards]

"Dearly beloved brethren,—Four days since, a letter was received by sister Taylor from brother Taylor, dated Liverpool, October 3rd, 1846, giving an account of his and Elder Hyde's arrival at their destination, which made our hearts to rejoice, and also to mourn at the calamities of our fellow beings upon the mighty ocean . . . we have heard nothing since the report by the New York Herald, of their sailing . . . Your families are all in usual health . . .

"Our last letter shewed the prospects of a city which we now realize and feel the benefit of . . . we have upwards of 700 houses in our miniature city, composed mostly of logs in the body, covered with puncheon, straw and dirt, which are warm and wholesome; a few are composed of turf, willows, straw, &c., which are very comfortable this winter, but will not endure the thaws, rain, and sunshine of spring like stone, burnt clay, or even hickory . . . so many houses having been built in so short a time is a proof of the general industry of the people . . .

"The Twelve, Municipal High Council, Bishops and Counsellors, have commenced building a Council house, 32 by 24 inclusive; the rafters, that is to say the puncheons are nearly ready to receive the dirt on the roof. Hitherto the Council has met at various places, mostly at Dr. Richard's Octagon, a queer looking thing, six rods east of President Young's, and very much resembling a New England Potatoe heap in the time of frost . . .

"On or about the 10th of December, Big Head, the second chief of the Omaha nation, with his family and friends were encamped near us, in their Wika ups; between one and two in the morning [they] were fired upon by a band of the Iowas. Big Head was severely hurt, and two or three others—one arm was amputated by our surgeons and their whole camp was taken care of by us, and in our midst until about the 18th, when another encampment of their tribe passed through our city on their way south, having lost about 73 of their number while asleep, about sixty miles north of this, on the morning of the 12th, by a band of the Sioux . . . those who were here went with them . . . Almost all their warriors and hunters still being on a buffalo hunt; those who were here have lived mostly on our cattle, either by gift or theft . . .

"On the 9th of October, while our teams were waiting on the banks of the Mississippi for the Saints who had been driven out of Nauvoo by an infuriated mob, and left without houses, beds, bed clothes, coats, frocks, tents, stoves, beef, pork, potatoes, or any of the necessaries of life, and there was nothing but starvation and death staring them in the face, with the fever and ague, and all other complaints incident to that climate preying upon them, and they had nothing to start their journey with—the Lord sent FLOCKS OF QUAILS, which lit upon their wagons, and on their beds, and upon their empty tables, and upon the ground within their reach, which the Saints, and even the sick, caught with their hands, until they were satisfied, and their breakfast and their dinner was full; not only the Saints saw this but the world—a steam boat was passing during part of the time, within six rods, and passengers marvelled at the sight—others in the camp, not of us, wondered also; this occurrence continued through the day, and followed the camp when they started from the river . . .

"Bishop Whitney returned from St. Louis several weeks since with a large lot of merchandize, which he has been dealing out to the sisters and friends of the battalion, and others who sent money by him, which has added much to the comfort of many souls in camp, indeed, to the camp generally. The water was very low and navigation difficult, which made freight and cartage from St. Louis very high . . .

"Since our buildings were completed many of the Saints have turned their attention to the manufacture of willow baskets, hundred of dollars worth have already been completed, and there is a prospect of quite an income from this source in the spring—other articles are also commencing, such as wash boards, half bushels, &c.

"January 8th—. At eight yesterday morning, mercury fell to 8 degrees below zero, and it has been pretty cold since.

"We have no very late news from Nauvoo. Some time after the Saints were driven out, Governor Ford took courage and gathered a troop, variously estimated from 80 to 150, and marched down to the devoted city, for the purpose of reinstating the new citizens in their rights. On his arrival he appears to have found but little or no opposition: quartered his troops in the Temple—locked arms with the ringleaders of the mob— patrolled the streets—visited the grog shops, not forgetting to take a drop of the aqua vitae—ate splendid suppers—attended fancy balls, and was hail fellow, well met, with his Black Majesty's Princes, while they were swearing behind his back, that as soon as little Tom was gone, the New Citizens should leave with far less ceremony or mercy that had been shown the Mormons . . .

"The Temple and public property have not been sold . . . Rigdonism is unknown, and the probability is, that Rigdon himself is about ready to deny the faith. Strang is very little better off, indeed not so well, for he had already denied his faith, or changed and altered it so many times that no man can tell what he does believe . . .

"President Kimball wishes Elder DAVID CANDLAND [MARY ANN BARTON's husband, serving a mission in England] to return to camp . . .

"Since writing the foregoing, report has reached us from the public print, that Gens. Santa Anna and Taylor have had an interview, agreed upon articles of peace between the United States and Mexico, giving the Californians the privilege of religious toleration and choice of government for the time being; and further intelligence, that the 200 dragoons marching with the Mormon Battalion had received orders for countermarch, and were on their return; while the battalion was pursuing their course to their destination, and the United States Paymasters were on their way to settle up with their troops; of the truth of which every man must judge for himself . . . We remember all the dear Saints upon the Islands in kindness, love, faith, and prayer, and blessing them and yourselves.

"We subscribe ourselves, your brethren, in behalf of the Council of the Twelve Apostles,

Brigham Young, President; W. Richards, Clerk."

[James R. Clark, *Messages of the First Presidency, Vol. 1, pp. 308-314*]

Cousin ISAAC ALLRED wrote:

"In February, 1846, I left the city with the church, perfectly destitute of anything to help myself. The Church helped me to Garden Grove . . . I stayed at Garden Grove 2 years in which time I travelled to and from place to place after the entire loss of my property. I rented a little property in Garden Grove. President Young finding out my condition sent for me to leave the Grove. By the help of my father [JAMES ALLRED], I left in the spring of 1848 and moved to Council Bluff . . . I was elected constable at the August election and I went to Monro County to be sworn into office with others of the brethren. I returned home and was re-elected and sworn in when the county was organized."

[Note: Family vital statistics in Council Bluffs, Pottawattamie, Iowa, unless otherwise noted:

Married: RICHARD ANDERSON IVIE to ELIZABETH DOBSON, 16 Jun 1846

Born: BENJAMIN MARTIN IVIE to JAMES RUSSELL and ELIZA IVIE, 15 Sep 1846

Died: PHEBE ELLEN BARTON, 4 Dec 1846, age–one-and-one-half-years[place not shown]

Born: JOHN OSCAR BARTON to JOHN and SUSANNAH BARTON, 29 Oct 1847

Born: MARY CATHERINE CANDLAND to DAVID and MARY CANDLAND, 29 May 1848 [in Winter Quarters, Nebraska]

Born: WILLIAM HARVEY IVIE to THOMAS C. and AMANDA J. IVIE, 8 Dec 1848

Married: JOHN F. L. ALLRED to MARINDA MELVINA KNAPP, 11 Jun 1847, Council Point

Married: PAULINUS HARVEY ALLRED to MELISSA ISABELL NORTON, 3 Feb 1848

Born: NANCY ELVINA TAYLOR to ALLEN and SARAH L. ALLRED TAYLOR, 30 May 1846

Born: MARVIN ADELBERT ALLRED to WILLIAM M. and ORISSA ALLRED, Aug 1849

Born: SARINDA JANETTE ALLRED to REDIN and JULIA ALLRED, 29 Mar 1848, Allred Settlement, Pottawattamie, Iowa

Died: JULIA LAVETTE ALLRED, 26 Apr 1847, age–one year, dau of REDIN & JULIA

Born: ELVIRA AUGUSTA EGBERT to JOSEPH and MARY ALLRED EGBERT, 9 Aug 1846 and twin, ELIZA ANGELINA EGBERT.

Born: JOSEPH ORSON EGBERT to JOSEPH and MARY ALLRED EGBERT, 28 Dec 1848 Died as a child, no date given.

Married: MARY ANN FAUSETT and JOHN SMYLIE or LOTT, 5 Apr 1846, no place given

Died: HYRUM SMITH SANDERS, 27 Sep 1846, age 1 year, no place given

Died: ELIZA JANE SANDERS, 4 Apr 1847, age 6 years, no place given

Died: WILLIAM CALVIN FAUSETT, 5 Oct 1847, age 3 years, no place given]

— 13 —

THE BATTALION!
FIGHTING THE ELEMENTS THROUGH
DESERTS TO THE PACIFIC OCEAN

16 July 1846, Council Bluffs, Iowa, until 16 July 1847,
Los Angles, California

"Brother Brigham . . . arose and said . . . Our fathers and ourselves fought for the liberties of this country . . . if we go and help take the country we will at least have that equal right, and I do not want anybody to be in those wildernesses . . . before we are. I think the president has done us a great favor by calling upon us. It is the first call that has been made upon us that ever seemed likely to benefit us. Now I want you men to go and all that can go, young or married. [The requirement was that they be healthy, able-bodied men of from eighteen to forty-five-years-of-age.] I will see that their families are taken care of . . ." [CHC Vol. III, p. 87]

[Note: Daniel Tyler"s "A Concise History of the Mormon Battalion in the Mexican War, 1846-1848", from which all the quotes in this chapter, unless designated otherwise, are taken, has a list of those who enlisted. Sixteen were relations at that time, or in the near future.

COMPANY A	age	relationship to James Russell & Eliza Ivie
Officers: Reddick N. Allred, 3rd Sergt.	24	1st cousin, son of uncle Isaac Allred
Privates: Allred, James R.	19	1st cousin, son of uncle Isaac Allred
Allred, James T. S.	21	1st cousin,son of uncle James Allred
Allred, Reuben W.	18	1c1r, son of Martin C. Allred
Ivy, Richard A.	21	son
COMPANY B		
Officers: William Hyde, 2nd Orderly Sgt.	27	*hus of 1c1r Sally, dau of M.C.Allred
Privates: Dayton, William J. (A.)	22	husband of daughter Sarah, md. 1845
Follett, William A.	abt 20	nephew-in-law, husband of Nancy Fausett
Zabriskie, Jerome	18	*son-in-law, md. Polly Ann Ivie, 1851
COMPANY C		
Privates: Ivie, Thomas C.	25	brother

COMPANY D

Privates: Hirons, James	abt 19	*hus #2 of daughter Sarah, md 1850
McArthur, Henry	26	*hus #3 of daughter Sarah, md 1860
Sanderson, Henry W.	abt 18	*nephew-in-law—md—Rebecca Sanders

COMPANY E

| Privates: Sanders, Richard T. | 18 | nephew, son of Amanda Fausett Sanders |

LIST OF FAMILIES WHO ACCOMPANIED —Mrs. J. T. S. Allred and Mrs. Reuben Allred]

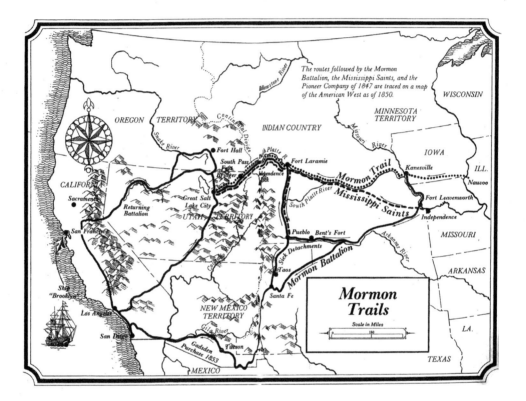

In 1836, Texas had won its independence from Mexico. In December 1845, it was annexed by the United States. California, New Mexico, Arizona, Utah, Nevada, and parts of Wyoming and Colorado still belonged to Mexico; but there were border disputes in Texas, and Mexico still hoped they could regain Texas. With the 1846 declaration of war by Congress against Mexico, thousands of Americans volunteered. Volunteers from North Carolina, Virginia, and Mississippi went south with General Zachary Taylor, his disciplined army, and his Texas volunteers to Corpus Christi, Texas, and into the disputed territory between it and the Rio Grande River. The Mormon Battalion was to go first to Fort Leavenworth for fitting then west and south to discourage Mexican armies from advancing north.

Their first destination was Santa Fe—still part of Mexico at that time. From there they were to go to California and help with the conquest of that state. They were to be joined by volunteers from Arkansas and Missouri. This war was the first time the U. S. had sent troops into foreign territory (excluding Canada in the War of 1812 and the Revolutionary War). Its laws, designed for peace at home, had not been prepared for the discipline problems that would face the generals with the undisciplined volunteers, camp followers, and Mexican settlers. In addition, the climate, living conditions, and other hardships in the camps and on the march south of the Rio Grande claimed the lives of more than 12,000 Americans; eight times the number who died in battle.

The inhabitants of Corpus Christi at that time were characterized as those who had committed crimes in the United States and escaped to Texas, then committing another crime in Texas had fled south to the disputed border area to avoid prosecution. As problems increased in this lawless situation, the generals were finally forced to make many of their own military laws, which could involve the volunteers and private citizens of the territory: importation of "spirituous liquors" up the Rio Grande to the cities along its banks was forbidden; camp followers (gamblers, prostitutes, and adventurers) were forbidden in certain areas; the army was restricted from entering Monterrey without an assignment or a pass. Peaceful citizens were caught in the cross fire. Any rancho in this disputed area failing to supply Mexican guerrilla bands was burned by Mexicans; any supplying Mexican guerrillas was burned by Americans.

[Note: WILLIAM HYDE was born 11 Sep 1818, in York, Livingston County, New York. His father, Heman Hyde with his wife and oldest son, also Heman Hyde, had moved from Vermont around 1813. Their family joined the Church early and is mentioned quite often in the early Church history. Orson Hyde, whose family came from Connecticut, was not a close relation. WILLIAM HYDE had married Elizabeth Bullard in Nauvoo in 1842 and they had two children born in Nauvoo. They would have three more children, before he married SALLY ALLRED, daughter of MARTIN CARRELL ALLRED, who died in Illinois. WILLIAM HYDE married SALLY 1 Sep 1850, in Salt Lake City. He and SALLY had 13 children. Their home was Hyde Park, Cache County, Utah, near Logan. Since REDICK N. ALLRED and WILLIAM HYDE were officers that kept journals, they are referred to quite often in Sgt. Daniel Tyler's Battalion history.]

WILLIAM HYDE, wrote:

"The thoughts of leaving my family at this critical time are indescribable. They were far from the land of their nativity, situated upon a lonely prairie with no dwelling but a wagon, the scorching sun beating upon them, with the prospect of the cold winds of December finding them in the same bleak, dreary place. My family consisted of a wife and two small children, who were left in company with an aged father and mother and a brother. The most of the Battalion left families, some in care of the Church and some in the care of relatives, with some in their own care. When we were to meet with them again, God only knew. Nevertheless, we did not feel to murmur."

On Saturday, 18 July 1846, President B. Young, H. C. Kimball, P. P. Pratt, W. Richards, John Taylor and Wilford Woodruff met in private council with the commissioned and non-commissioned officers, on the bank of the Missouri river, and there gave their last charge and blessing, "with a firm promise that, on condition of faithfulness on our part, our lives should be spared, our expedition should result in great good and our names should be held in honorable remembrance to all generations."

They instructed the officers to be as fathers to the privates, to remember their prayers, to see that the name of the Deity was revered, and that virtue and cleanliness were strictly observed. They were also instructed to treat all men with kindness and never to take that which did not belong to them, even from their worst enemies, not even in time of war if they could possibly prevent it; and in case they should come in contact with the enemies and be successful, they should treat prisoners with kindness and never take life when it could be avoided. On the 20th of July, the men of each company subscribed liberally of their wages to be sent back for the support of their families and to aid in gathering the poor from Nauvoo.

Sergeant Daniel Tyler writes:

"On the [24th] we crossed the Nishnabotany River at Hunsaker's Ferry, and camped near Lindon, Missouri. The weather being excessively warm, Colonel Allen was in favor of moderate marches; but Adjutant Dykes, being himself a great walker, and having the advantage of a horse to ride, urged long marches. Colonel Allen consented to this, presuming, probably, that the men wished it. They, however, desired only reasonable, healthful marches. Thus many began to fail at almost the beginning of a journey of over two thousand miles. Several parties, about this time, were taken sick, and were healed by anointing with oil and the laying on of hands."

Sergeants WM. HYDE and Wm Coray, finding the long marches in the broiling sun too hard for them, each purchased an Indian pony, paying twenty-five dollars apiece for them.

When they had crossed the Nodaway River and camped at the town of Oregon, a Missourian, probably a mobocrat that had been hired to deliver a load of flour, refused to deliver it to the Quartermaster because he was a Mormon. He would deliver it to no one but the Colonel. That noble officer, however, was highly insulted, and ordered him to deliver the flour immediately upon pain of being arrested and put under guard. Delivery was made immediately.

"Good for the Colonel!" and "God bless the Colonel!" were repeated from one end of the camp to the other.

They found the country poor and broken, the road bad and the inhabitants very miserable. A great many of these settlers were old mobocrats, as several of them admitted. They said that they had been misled by false rumors, and very much regretted having persecuted the Saints. They would have been glad to take their old *Mormon* neighbors back. They had not prospered since the Saints were banished from the State, and the men they then hired to labor for them accomplished only about one half the amount of work in a day that the *Mormons* did.

On the 29th, they passed St. Joseph, Missouri, then a town of some importance. While there, Luke Johnson, formerly one of the Twelve Apostles, but at that time out of the Church, met Sergeant WM. HYDE and informed him that the Missourians were perfectly astonished at the course the "Mormons" were taking. The Missourians had supposed, when they heard of the President's requisition, that the Saints would only spurn it. But when they saw the Battalion march through with civility and in good order, they were really dumbfounded.

On the 30th, they passed through Bloomington and camped on a small creek, where, about 9 o'clock p. m., the wind commenced to blow a gale and continued until the trees fell in all directions around the camp. The men were aroused from their slumbers, and hurried out of their rude brush shelters or 'wigwams,' looking every moment for the trees in camp to fall. About eighty smoldering fires were revived by the gale, while the howling of the wind, the crashing of the trees, the vivid lightning and the roar of thunder made the scene one of terror. Yet not one tree fell in their camp. The only harm done was the killing of one ox. The owner of the field afterwards remarked that it was a marvel that they were not all killed. He had been quite alarmed lest his house should blow down.

They marched to the ferry on the Missouri river, opposite Fort Leavenworth, and were nearly five hours in crossing. They found companies of Missouri volunteers there, and received their tents the same day which added much to their comfort, but the hot sun beating upon them "made it warm for us" in the middle of the day. They camped on the public square of the Fort. They had come two hundred miles, directly down the Missouri river.

On the 3rd of August, companies A, B and C drew their arms, which consisted of U. W. flint-lock muskets, with a few cap-lock yaugers (or yagers) for sharpshooting and hunting purposes. The usual accoutrements were also drawn, as well as camp equipage and provisions, the want of which had been seriously felt on the way. Volunteers from different parts of the country arrived at the garrison daily to get their outfits. Many of them were rough, desperate-looking characters. Quarreling and fighting were not unusual among those from Upper Missouri. While they remained at the Fort, one of the Missouri volunteers from Platte County struck a comrade with a hatchet, inflicting a dangerous, perhaps mortal, wound. The members of the Mormon Battalion were more submissive and obedient to their commanding officers. The weather at this time was extremely warm, the thermometer indicating 101 degrees in the shade and 135 degrees in the sun. Some of those who had taken sick on the road were much improved, but a number of new cases of sickness from ague and fever were developed while in garrison. Sergeant WM. HYDE was among the number.

On the 12th, companies A, B and C, took up the line of march for Santa Fe, followed on the 14th by companies D and E. They crossed the Kansas or Kaw river, which at the ferry was about three hundred yards in width, in flat boats by some Delaware and Shawnee Indians who were living there and cultivating the soil. They advanced about four miles to Stone Coal Creek.

> "After our encampment, a furious hurricane, accompanied by rain, hail, vivid lightning and peals of thunder, like the constant roar of heavy artillery, met us from the west . . . When the storm reached us only five or six out of over one hundred tents were left standing, and it took six men to each tent to hold it . . . The storm lasted about twenty minutes. Colonel Sterling Price and his command of cavalry, who left the garrison two days

in advance of us, were encamped at Stone Coal Creek when we arrived there. During the storm his animals were scattered in all directions, and several days were spent in searching before they could be recovered. The result was a portion of Price's cavalry did not overtake the Battalion until after we arrived at Santa Fe."

In Ferguson's journal he states that the Battalion had wanted the right to appoint their own officers from their own people, but Colonel James Allen of the regular dragoons was commissioned by United States' President Polk to command them. He treated them very well, but while they were at Fort Leavenworth, he became very ill, so the lesser officers marched on, leaving him behind. Word was sent near the end of August that he had died.

Ferguson wrote:

"At Council Grove, [Kansas] we were halted to deliberate how to proceed. The command of the Battalion was here given to Lieutenant Smith, of the First Dragoons. Letters were dispatched to President Polk, praying for the privilege due to us, of electing our commander . . . Our commander was not of himself cruel and wicked, but he was weak, and became, to a great extent, the creature of Doctor Sanderson, a rotten-hearted quack, that was imposed upon us as our surgeon. The hospital wagons, designed for our use by Colonel Allen, were left behind." The Battalion moved on.

On 5 September, they saw a few buffalo, "the first that most of us had ever seen. Several carcasses of these animals that had been killed by Missouri Volunteers lay by the wayside, no portion of them having been used except the tongues. On the following day we not only saw plenty of buffalo, but one of the soldiers killed one. We thought the meat very good. It was, however, like most of the male 'sentinels,' rather tough. We learned in time to select for our eating younger and more tender animals, instead of shooting the oldest, which were generally found singly, at some distance from the herd."

About noon on the 11th, they reached the Arkansas River. The men dug holes about two or three feet deep in the sand, thereby obtaining a sufficiency of water for all needful purposes. The afternoon was a general time of washing clothes and spearing fish in the shallow water with swords and bayonets.

"After crossing the river we overtook five companies of Colonel Sterling Price's regiment from western Missouri. We found them a profane, wicked and vulgar set of men. Price will be remembered as the commander of a portion of the mob militia at Far West in 1838, when a few officers and about seventeen ministers of different denominations sat as a court martial and condemned Joseph Smith and others to be shot on the public square in view of their families." Fortunately General Doniphan refused to obey the order.

"At this point, Captain Higgins, with a guard of ten men, was detailed to take a number of the families that accompanied the Battalion, to Pueblo, a Mexican town located farther up the Arkansas, to winter. Many of the Battalion were dissatisfied with this move, as President Young had counseled the officers not to allow the Battalion to be divided on any account . . . but Adjutant Dykes objected, saying . . . that President Young did not know our circumstances. The families, therefore, were forced to leave us on the 16th of September, notwithstanding the fears and protests of their relatives and friends.

"While we remained at that point Alva Phelps, of Company E, died, a martyr to his country and religion. It is understood that he begged Dr. Sanderson not to give him any strong medicine, as he needed only a little rest and then would return to duty; but the Doctor prepared his dose and ordered him to take it, which he declined doing, whereupon the Doctor, with some horrid oaths, forced it down him with the rusty spoon. A few hours later he died, and the general feeling was that the Doctor had killed him. Many broadly expressed the opinion that it was a case of premeditated murder. When we consider the many murderous threats previously made, this conclusion is by no means far-fetched. Brother Phelps was buried on the south side of the Arkansas river, in a grave only about four feet deep, its shallowness being due to the fact that the water was very near the surface of the soil. He was the husband of Margaret Phelps."

It was 30 April 1878, that Margaret wrote the following to Sergeant Tyler's inquiries:

"We were traveling [to Winter Quarters] when the call came for him to leave us [16 Jul 1846]. It was midnight when we were awakened from our slumbers with the painful news that we were to be left homeless, without a protector. I was very ill at the time, my children all small, my babe also extremely sick; but the call was pressing; there was no time for any provision to be made for wife or children; no time for tears; regret was unavailing. He started in the morning. I watched him from my wagon-bed till his loved form was lost in the distance; it was my last sight of him. Two months from the day of his enlistment, the sad news of my bereavement arrived. This blow entirely prostrated me. But I had just embarked upon my sea of troubles; winter found me bed-ridden, destitute, in a wretched hovel which was built upon a hill-side; the season was one of constant rain; the situation of the hovel and its openness, gave free access to piercing winds, and water flowed over the dirt floor, converting it into mud two or three inches deep; no wood but what my little ones picked up around the fences, so green it filled the room with smoke; the rain dropping and wetting the bed which I was powerless to leave; no relative to cheer or comfort me, a stranger away from all who ever loved me; my neighbors could do but little, their own troubles and destitution engrossing their time; my little daughter of seven my only help; no eye to witness my sufferings but the pitying one of God—He did not desert me. Spring brought some alleviation from my sufferings, yet one pan of meal was my all, my earthly store of provisions. I found sale for the leaders of my team. The long, dreary winter had passed, and, although it was many months before health and comparative comfort were my portion, still I thank the Lord this was the darkest part of my life."

Back to the Battalion as they continued on across a dreary desert suffering intensely from excessive heat and want of water, as did their teams.

"We passed one lone pond full of insects of all sizes and shapes. Out of this pond we drove several thousand Buffalo . . . Whether Colonel Smith had had no experience in traveling with teams, or whether he desired to use up the teams and leave the Battalion on the plains helpless, does not appear. It is true, however, that, for the last two hundred miles, where there had been but little feed, he had shown no wisdom or care in preserving either man or beast; but on the contrary, no matter whether our drives were to be long or short, he had driven on forced marches, on which account many, in fact nearly all, of the teams as well as men, failed very fast." On the 21st they camped on the Cimmeron, and had to dig in the sand in the bed of the river for water for both man and beast."

Samuel H. Rogers' journal of this date has the following:

"Last night I stood Horse-guard. When I went to report myself to the Adjutant I found the five orderlies and the Colonel talking about the sick. It appears that the Colonel and Surgeon are determined to kill us, first by force marches to make us sick, then by compelling us to take calomel or to walk and do duty.

"On the 27th we marched over rough sand hills and encamped by a pond of stagnant water. There were a few buffalo chips, which were soon gathered, when some who had none of this kind of fuel, traveled two miles to timber and brought wood on their shoulders. A few antelope added to our short rations were quite a treat. The monotony of the barren plains in our rear was considerably relieved by the view of numerous mountain peaks in front, the first many of us ever saw . . . A number of antelope were killed and some bears and wild turkeys were seen, but no buffalo were visible, as we were quite out of the country over which they ranged."

They reached Red River on the 2nd of October, and "a council of officers was called. The commander informed the council that he had received orders from General Kearny that unless the command reached Santa Fe by the 10th we would be discharged. He suggested selecting fifty able-bodied men from each company, taking the best teams and traveling on a double forced march, leaving the sick and the weak teams to follow as best they could." Some of the Battalion objected including Sergeant WM. HYDE "[o]n the ground that Colonel Allen had pledged himself that the Battalion would not be divided."

However, the Battalion was divided. The able-bodied soldiers and most of the commissioned officers, including Colonel Smith and Dr. Sanderson, hastened to Santa Fe, leaving the sick and feeble men and the worn out teams to follow.

"The fact of Dr. Sanderson leaving the sick behind while he proceeded on with those who were healthy, is a fair indication of the interest he took in attending to the duties of his office. But the sick did not complain on that score. The sorrow which they felt at the loss of friends through having the Battalion divided, was in a great measure compensated by the relief they experienced at being rid of the Doctor's drugs and cursing for a few days. There was a noticeable improvement, too, in most of those who were sick after the Doctor left, so that when they arrived in Santa Fe many of them were convalescent . . . No unnecessary time was spent on the road. [All] were anxious to reach Santa Fe . . . lest their friends of the advance division should be attached to some other corps and they be left to serve under their old religious persecutor, of Missouri memory, Colonel Sterling Price."

The first division of the Battalion arrived at Santa Fe on the evening of October 9th, 1846. On their approach, General Doniphan, the commander of the post, ordered a salute of one hundred guns to be fired from the roofs of houses, in honor of the Mormon Battalion. The second division arrived on the 12th of October. When Colonel Sterling Price with his cavalry command arrived at Santa Fe, he was received without any public demonstration, and when he learned of the salute which had been fired in honor to the *Mormons,* he was enraged.

[Note: "This same General Doniphan, who had been an eminent lawyer of Clay County, Missouri, was present when Joseph Smith and others were tried by a court-martial of the mob at Far West, in 1838. When the prisoners were sentenced upon that occasion to be shot, General Doniphan denounced the decision as 'cold-blooded murder.'"]

Their new commander, Colonel P. St. George Cooke, wrote:

"Everything conspired to discourage the extraordinary undertaking of marching this Battalion eleven hundred miles, for the much greater part through an unknown wilderness, without road or trail, and with a wagon train. It was enlisted too much by families; some were too old, some feeble, and some too young; it was embarrassed by many women; it was undisciplined; it was much worn by traveling on foot, and marching from Nauvoo, Illinois; their clothing was very scant; there was no money to pay them, or clothing to issue; their mules were utterly broken down; the quartermaster department was without funds, and its credit bad; and animals were scarce. Those procured were very inferior, and were deteriorating every hour for lack of forage or grazing. So every preparation must be pushed—hurried."

Eighty-seven weak and sick men with all the women (except five, who would be expected to furnish their own transportation), were sent to Pueblo to join Higgins' earlier group. These were under the command of Captain James Brown. Among this departing group from Company A were JAMES T. S. ALLRED, REUBEN W. ALLRED, their wives, and JAMES HIRONS from Company D. The detachment started north on the eighteenth. Very good time was made in traveling, considering the miserable plight of the teams and the feeble condition of most of the men. Owing to the weak condition of the teams, the sick were obliged to walk when ascending steep hills and where the roads were unusually bad, which was a great hardship to them. They crossed the Arkansas River, and on entering Pueblo on 17 November 1846, selected a camping place near the quarters of Captain Higgins' detachment and a company of Saints from Mississippi, who had stopped there to winter.

It was immediately agreed that eighteen rooms, fourteen feet square, should be erected for the winter quarters, and the men who were able to chop were dispatched to the woods to procure timbers for the houses, with the understanding that the first rooms finished should be allotted to the sick. The work was pushed with all possible rapidity, but before they were finished sufficiently to shelter the sick from the piercing winds and cold mountain storms, some had already died.

Back in Santa Fe, the quartermaster could only undertake to furnish rations for sixty days; and, in fact, full rations of only flour, sugar, coffee and salt; salt pork only for thirty days, and soap for twenty, and to venture without pack-saddles would be grossly imprudent. REDICK N. ALLRED, Quartermaster Sergeant of Company A, made the purchases mentioned.

Under the date of 19 November, the commander adds:

"I have brought road tools and have determined to take through my wagons; but the experiment is not a fair one, as the mules are nearly broken down at the outset. The only good ones, about twenty, which I bought near Albuquerque, were taken for the express for Fremont's mail—the General's order requiring the twenty-one best in Santa Fe."

With few exceptions, the mule and ox teams used from Santa Fe to California were the same worn-out and broken down animals that had been driven all the way from Council Bluffs and Fort Leavenworth—some of them had been driven all the way from Nauvoo the same season. On the 22nd, the Assistant Quartermaster tried to obtain fresh mules and oxen from some small Mexican towns, but the prejudice of the natives was so strong against the Government of the United States, that they refused to assist beyond selling a little feed and perishable vegetables. On the 23rd, however, he succeeded in exchanging thirty of worthless mules for half the number of fresh, though, as a rule, the small mules owned by the Mexicans. The Colonel also purchased eight mules from officers of Captain Burgwin's command, and exchanged about as many for better ones, and ten yoke of oxen.

"Two of our poorest heavy wagons were also exchanged for lighter and better ones. The hand of an all-wise providence was certainly in these things, as, without something of the kind, we must inevitably have been left without means of conveyance on the great desert, in an enemy's country, surrounded by the most ferocious savages.

On the 25th they received (Order No. 12) with strict rules of conduct. It began with camp rules and the last sentence reminded them:

"When the guard is stationed, death is the punishment awarded by law to a sentinel who sleeps on his post in a time of war, which now exists."

The next day they passed several Mexican villages. They tried to purchase pack-saddles, blankets and mules, but the prices demanded were unreasonable. Otero, the owner, had five of six thousand sheep driven off the previous evening by Indians, and two shepherds were killed.

Their course was now down the Rio Del Norte. The men were carrying heavy loads of ammunition and muskets on their backs, and living on short rations. At times they still had to pull at long ropes to aid the teams. The deep sand alone, without any load, was enough to wear out both man and beast. Upon one occasion, several wild geese were killed by some of the hunters, which proved a treat to them and their immediate comrades or messmates. If any of their cattle were slaughtered for food, they had strict orders it must be only those that were unable from sheer weakness and exhaustion to work. Nor was any portion of the animal thrown away that could possibly be utilized for food. Even to the hides, tripe and entrails. All were eagerly devoured, and that, too, in many cases without water to wash them in. The marrow bones were considered a luxury and issued in turns to the various messes.

On the 27th, they encountered cold rain in the valley of the Rio Del Norte. Heavy snow also fell upon the mountains. On the 30th they left the river for a time and had twenty men to each wagon with long ropes to help the teams pull the wagons over the sand hills. They found the judgment of Colonel Cooke in traveling much better than that of Smith. In fact, it was first-class. He never crowded the men unnecessarily, but as they advanced, the roads grew so much worse that both men and teams failed fast—"our only hope of success lay in our faith in God and on pulling at the ropes."

Far into Mexican territory, about the 4th of November, a rumor was spread that the Mexicans in the region were planning to revolt against the American rule. Their guides were fearful and quite downcast at learning the news, but their commander took the matter very coolly and maintained an air of indifference. On the 6th of November, they arrived at the place where General Kearny had left his wagons, and from which point he had preceded with pack-animals.

General Kearny, having learned while he was at Santa Fe that the Mexicans in California had surrendered to Commodore Stockton, resolved to push on through as hastily as possible and assume control of the country as governor and commander in chief of California, in accordance with his commission from the President of the United States. He accordingly disbanded most of his soldiers at Santa Fe, and, with one hundred picked men, set out for the coast some time previous to their arrival at that post. Previous to starting, however, he gave orders for Colonel Cooke to follow on with the Mormon Battalion, and open a wagon road to the coast.

"The prospect before us from this point was anything but encouraging. Besides what we had previously endured from hunger and having to help our worn-out animals pull the overloaded wagons, we now had before us the additional task of having to construct a wagon road over a wild, desert and unexplored country, where wagons had never been before.

"On the 10th, it was decided that a detachment of fifty-five sick men, under command of Lieutenant W. W. Willis, be sent back to Pueblo, by way of Santa Fe, to winter. The Colonel ordered that they be furnished with twenty-six days' rations, allowing ten ounces of flour per day— eighteen ounces being the usual soldier's ration. It appears though, that through some mistake, probably an oversight in loading the wagon, this amount was not taken . . . [Lieutenant Willis recalled,] 'we had collected of invalids—fifty-six, one big government wagon, four yoke of poor cattle, five days' rations and two dressed sheep, as food for the sick. Our loading for the one wagon consisted of the clothing, blankets, cooking utensils, tents and tent poles, muskets, equipage, and provisions, and all invalids who were unable to walk. With some difficulty I obtained a spade or two and a shovel, but was provided with no medicines or other necessaries for the sick except the mutton before referred to, and only five days' rations, to travel near three hundred miles. Thus armed and equipped we commenced our lonesome march, retracing our steps to Santa Fe . . . One yoke of our oxen got mired in the mud. We took off the yoke when one got out. The other we undertook to pull out with a rope and unfortunately broke his neck. Our team was now too weak for our load. In the night Brother John Green died . . . What to do for a team we did not know. This was a dark time, and many were the earnest petitions that went up to our God and Father for Divine aid. The next morning we found with our oxen a pair of splendid young steers, which was really cheering to us. We looked upon it as one of the providences of our Father in heaven. Thus provided for, we pursued our march [some died].

"We continued our march to Albuquerque, where we presented our orders for assistance to Captain Burgwin, of Kearny's brigade. He gave me five dollars, cash, and the privilege of exchanging our heavy wagon for a lighter one. I had fuel and everything to buy, and spent $66 of my own private money before reaching Santa Fe, which was as near as I can recollect, about the 25th of November.

"On my arrival at that place, General Price, commander of the post, ordered me to Pueblo, on the Arkansas river. He also ordered Quartermaster McKissock to furnish us with the necessary provisions, mules, etc. to perform a journey of about three hundred miles, over the mountains, and in the winter . . . We arrived [in Pueblo] on the 24th of December."

On the 15 Jan 1847 "nine wagons, loaded with sixty days' rations for the command at Pueblo arrived from Bent's Fort, and the convalescent soldiers and their families were thereby enabled to experience the contrast between short food and hard labor and full rations and no labor. On the 18th of May, Captains Brown and Higgins and others, returned from Santa Fe with the soldiers' money and orders to march to California." They loaded their wagons and marched north by way of Fort Laramie, on the Platte river, towards California 24 May 1847, at noon.

On the afternoon of 11 June, "while on Pole Creek, to the great joy of the detachments, they were met by Elder Amasa M. Lyman [and others] . . . from Winter Quarters, bringing letters from the families and friends of the soldiers, as well as counsel from President Brigham Young; also news of the travels and probable destination of the Church."

President Young, with a company of pioneers, making their way westward, had passed Laramie twelve days previously, and with a view of overtaking them, the command made an early start and followed up their trail. The command failed to overtake the pioneers, but arrived 27 July 1847, three days after the company of pioneers entered the valley. Word had arrived from Los Angeles that the Mexican War was over, and they were formally discharged in the Great Salt Lake Valley, having served in the United States army for a little over one year.

Our narrative, however, returns to the main army of the Battalion on the Rio Grande del Norte, on 10 November 1846, journeying under command of Colonel Cooke, and building a new road through to the Pacific Ocean. Realizing the difficulty that was facing them, Colonel Cooke issued an order to leave the remaining ox wagons there—the teams were necessary for the further march of the Battalion. He reduced their number of tents to one for nine instead of six men, and left all the upright poles and extra camp kettles.

They did some packing on both oxen and mules. The frightened oxen kicked up before and reared up behind; they bellowed and snorted, pawed and plowed the ground with their horns, whirling and jumping in every direction, creating much merriment among the soldiers.

On the 11th, they marched about fifteen miles. Colonel Cooke, seeing a patch of willows and cane grass followed it down to where he found water and grass plentiful. "We camped on the bluff. Here, for the first time, we tried our commander's new invention of using our muskets for tent poles . . . We saw for the first time during our journey, some Indian wigwams, although we were traveling through a country where Indians were numerous. Their hostility to the whites led them to keep their families secluded."

On 13 November, they left the Rio Grande, which flows southeast at this place and soon forms the boundary of Texas and Mexico, emptying into the Gulf of Mexico. To the west were the distant southern peaks of the Sierra Nevada Mountain range. They traveled in a south-westerly direction, camping the following night near a natural reservoir in the rocks in a deep ravine. This well was about thirteen feet in diameter and probably a hundred feet deep. The route which they were taking was new to the guides, as they had never traveled in this direction. On 16 November, they passed through the gap in the mountains, and came to a place where mining for precious metals had evidently been carried on in the distant past. On 20 November, the guides returned disheartened, declaring that they did not think any more water would be found short of the Gila River, a distance of about one hundred miles. To turn back was starvation, to go forward seemed rashness, and to follow the road to Yanos would take them to Old Mexico and General Wool. The commander called his staff and the captains of companies together in council.

"The decision was to follow the road . . . A gloom was cast over the entire command . . . In this critical moment, Father Pettegrew . . . and Brother Hancock, went from tent to tent, in a low tone of voice counseled the men to 'pray to the Lord to change the Colonel's mind.' . . . That night over three hundred fervent prayers ascended to the throne of grace for that one favor.

"On the morning of the 21st, the command resumed its journey marching in southern direction for about two miles, when it was found that the road began to bear south-east instead of south-west . . . The colonel looked in the direction of the road, then to the south-west, then west, saying, 'I don't want to get under General Wool, and lose my trip to California.' He arose in his saddle and ordered a halt. He then said with firmness: 'This is not my course. I was ordered to California'; and, he added with an oath, 'I will go there or die in the attempt!' Then, turning to the bugler, he said, 'Blow the right.'

"At this juncture, Father Pettegrew involuntarily exclaimed, 'God bless the Colonel!' The Colonel's head turned and his keen, penetrating eyes glanced around to discern whence the voice came, and then his grave, stern face for once softened and showed signs of satisfaction.

"The next day we traveled about eighteen miles and camped without water. Here it was decided and ordered that the men walk in double file in front of the wagons, just far enough apart to make trails for the wheels, and that at the end of an hour's march the leading companies and teams halt and allow the others to precede them and take their turn at breaking the road. This gave all an equal share of the burden. This plan was followed subsequently in traveling over all the heavy, sandy road until we reached the coast. It was much like tramping snow—very hard on the men, especially those who took the lead, as we had no road or trail to follow . . .

"On the 28th we reached the backbone of North America—the summit of the Rocky Mountains. Here we found plenty of deer, bear, antelope and small game.

"On the 29th, preparations were made for descending the mountain to the valley below. Most all of the animals were packed and sent down the mountain a distance of about six miles, into the valley, where a guard was left in charge of the baggage while the men and animals returned. The next day this process was repeated, and then the work of taking the wagons down was commenced . . . Long ropes were attached to the wagons, upon which the men pulled, and in this manner the wagons were all lowered. One of them, by some accident, got loose, and ran down with such force that it became badly damaged, and was abandoned as worthless."

They reached the ruins of the rancho, San Bernardino, on 2 December.

"The spring and dwelling had been surrounded by a wall with two bastions (adobe, if my memory serves me right), but which were now much dilapidated. The country seemed to be mostly mezquit flats or tables. The first wild cattle were found here. They were . . . brought here by a Mexican, who was driven out by the Apache Indians and forced to leave his stock behind."

Sergeant Major James Fergeson recorded:

"Surprised, and some of them wounded by our hunters, a herd of wild cattle made their appearance on all sides of us. Some, more furious than the rest, made a dash at our train. One pitched a poor fellow into the air, severely wounding him. Another tossed a mule on its horns, and tore his entrails, while another lifted a wagon out of its track . . . Wild cattle abounded in that region. It is asserted that 80,000 head were driven to this ranch before it was abandoned . . . We jerked beef until about 2 p.m., when we were ordered to take up the line of march. This order gave much dissatisfaction, as another day would have enabled them to dry much more meat without increasing the weight of our loads."

The next day they cut their way through mesquite brush. A cold rain and some snow fell. During the day's journey, the author, Daniel Tyler was quite sick, but hid in the tall grass until the command had all passed by, and then slowly and painfully made his way to camp. He had not forgotten, nor entirely recovered from the effects of his previous drugging and dreaded having to take another dose of Dr. Sanderson's arsenic. The fact that the doctor's calomel had given out and arsenic was substituted was no secret. Sanderson had openly stated the fact long before.

"On the 14th, the Battalion ascended the bluff and traveled up hill for eight or nine miles before joining a trail leading to Tucson, [in Arizona]. The commander selected fifty men with whom he pushed forward. Passing the front guard, he soon reached water, where he found four or five Mexican soldiers cutting grass. Their arms and saddles were on their horses near by, easily accessible. The Mexicans paid but little attention to them. The Colonel learned from a Mexican sergeant that a rumor of a large force of American soldiers had reached the town and great excitement prevailed. Indians who had seen us in the distance had largely over-estimated our numbers, and this served to impress the people of Sonora with the truth of the statement.

"The Colonel also learned from the Mexican sergeant that the commander of the garrison had orders from the governor not to allow an armed force to pass through the town without resistance . . . The Battalion marched in front of the wagons to protect the provisions. They were now ordered to load their muskets and be ready for an engagement; but had not traveled far before two other Mexicans met them, stating that their soldiers had fled and forced most of the inhabitants to leave the town. They had also taken two brass pieces of artillery with them. About a dozen well-armed men, probably soldiers in citizen's dress, met and accompanied the Battalion to the town. Before passing through the gate, a halt was ordered, and Colonel Cooke made a short speech stating 'that the soldiers and citizens had fled, leaving their property behind and in our power; that we had not come to make war on Sonora, and that there must not be any interference with the private property of the citizens.'"

As they marched through the town, a few aged men and women, as well as some children, brought them water and other little tokens of respect. A quantity of public wheat, however, was found, perhaps about 2,000 bushels, and Colonel Cooke ordered that they take all the teams could haul, for feeding the animals.

"On arriving at Tucson, the Battalion had been some time without salt, but could only purchase three bushels there. As our passage through Tucson was on Sunday, it was rumored that the inhabitants, being Catholics, had marched to the little village higher up the stream before our arrival and held mass, that their commander could report to the Governor, as an excuse, that we surprised the town while they were at worship."

Resuming their journey, the mules were watered—the last water for a considerable distance. The main portion of the road was baked clay, but in places they had sand beds to pull through. At sundown the advance of the command reached a small pool of water, enough to give the most of those present a drink by lying down to it, which was the only method allowed. Dipping was forbidden, in order that as many as possible might have a chance for a drink. The main portion of the army, however, had no water during the entire day, save a few drops which the men managed to suck from the mud in small puddle holes found by the wayside.

"The advance struck water and camped about noon on the 20th and several parties took mules and canteens and went back and relieved the suffering of their comrades, or doubtless some would have perished. The stragglers continued to arrive the whole of the afternoon."

On the 21st, a march of ten miles brought them to the Gila River, where they were visited by from 1,500 to 2,000 Pima Indians.

"Although all our property was exposed and might have easily been stolen, one of the guides assured them that these Indians were so scrupulous that they had been known to follow travelers half a day to restore lost property to the owner. They arrived on the 22nd at the Pima village of about 4,000 inhabitants. They were quite a large-sized, fine-looking race of people and very industrious and peaceable. They engaged in agriculture, and manufactured blankets and other fabrics by hand ... The Colonel presented their chief with three ewe sheep with a fair prospect of increase."

Traveling the next day about fifteen miles, they were met by three pilots who had been through to San Diego with General Kearny, informing them that they were at least one month in advance of the General's expectations, but that the Mexicans had again revolted, and the safety and conquest of California depended upon the prompt and energetic action of the General and command. Their march was now through rich, cultivated grounds with a beautiful plain of from fifteen to twenty miles in all directions. On the night of 23 December, and during the 24th, they camped at a village of the Maricopa Indians, who were estimated to number about ten thousand. As an evidence of their honesty, General Kearny had left bales of goods and a number of broken down mules to be called for by Colonel Cooke on his arrival, and they were delivered promptly.

Christmas day they marched eighteen miles up hill, over sand, and camped without water.

"Our route from this point lay down the river, over heavy sandy bottoms, in some places quicksand. It was so difficult traveling that we only made sixty miles in six days, and even then the men had to work very hard at helping the mules to pull the loads. Of course, all our beef secured in the wild bull region was exhausted, and the famished sheep and oxen that were slaughtered had so little flesh on their bones that very little could be got from them to appease our hunger . . . When an animal was slaughtered the entire carcass was rationed out."

Traveling down the river, they found rocks covered with ancient hieroglyphics, including profiles of men, beasts and reptiles. Grass was very scant. Concerned for his teams and their heavy loads, Colonel Cooke prepared a boat of two pontoon wagon-bodies lashed together, end to end, between two dry cottonwood logs, and placed all the baggage he could risk in it.

"This move cast a gloom over the men generally,[feeling] no further risk of loss ought to be taken . . . Finally, on the 5th . . . one of our guides and interpreters, brought the sad news that . . . much of the provisions had been . . . left on the sandbars and on the river bank . . . Men were immediately detailed to go back and aid the boat. On the 7th of January, the quartermaster ordered the remaining provisions weighed, and found that we had only four days allowance of our short rations left . . . When we camped our mules had to swim the river to obtain feed."

The following day they traveled over a rich alluvial bottom, where they found wild hemp growing, and reached the mouth of the Gila River, which flowed into the Colorado River. They ferried across the Colorado River in the pontoon wagon-boxes commencing on the tenth and continuing all night and until late the next morning. The crossing ranged down the river, which was over half a mile wide, hence the ford was nearly a mile long, including two channels, in the middle of which it was difficult to reach the bottom with our tent poles. Planks from wagon boxes left on the road were laid on top of the wagon-beds and a portion of the provisions placed upon them, and hauled over by the mules, which had to swim in the deepest portions of the river. Two mules were drowned while being driven across. After the baggage was all over, the loose animals were driven across. One hundred and thirty of their sheep were still alive.

On 15 January, "[t]he march of the last five days was the most trying of any we had made, on both men and animals. We here found the heaviest sand, hottest days and coldest nights, with no water and but little food. Language fails to provide adjectives strong enough to describe our situation . . . At this time the men were nearly barefooted; some used, instead of shoes, rawhide wrapped around their feet, while others improvised a novel style of boots by stripping the skin from the leg of an ox. To do this, a ring was cut around the hide above and below the gambrel joint, and then the skin taken off without cutting it lengthwise. After this, the lower end was sewed up with sinews, when it was ready for the wearer, the natural crook of the hide adapting it somewhat to the shape of the foot. Others wrapped cast-off clothing around their feet, to shield them from the burning sand during the day and the cold at night. Before we arrived at the Cariza, many of the men were so nearly used up from thirst, hunger and fatigue, that they were unable to speak until they reached the water or had it brought to them. Those who were strongest reported, when they arrived, that they had passed many lying exhausted by the way-side."

All but five of their government wagons had been abandoned at this time. They traveled fifteen miles over very heavy sand and encamped between two mountains. Colonel Cooke remarked that "this fifteen miles of very bad road was accomplished, under the circumstances, by mules or men, is extraordinary. The men arrived here completely worn down; they staggered as they marched, as they did yesterday." And he might have added, many other days.

"During this day, the Indian magistrate of the town of San Philipi, and a companion, brought a letter to the Colonel from the Governor of San Diego, announcing the arrival of their men, who had been sent for supplies, and he promised assistance and welcomed them. We did not advance any on the 18th, but spent the day in cleaning up our arms, and in the evening the men were paraded and inspected. The Colonel expressed great surprise at seeing the half starved, worn-out men who, only the night previous, had staggered into camp, like so many inebriates, from sheer exhaustion and hunger, now playing the fiddle and singing merry songs.

"On the 19th . . . We had a rugged mountain ridge some two hundred or more feet high to surmount. Owing to rumors that we would probably meet an army of Californians, the Colonel ordered the baggage to the rear. We surmounted all difficulties and succeeded in getting over the ridge inside of two hours. Other and seemingly more formidable barriers now presented themselves. Our route lay up a dry ravine, through openings in the solid rocks. Our guides, who had always traveled either north or south of this route, were as ignorant of its practicability as ourselves. As we traveled up the dry bed, the chasm became more contracted until we found ourselves in a passage at least a foot narrower than our wagons. Nearly all of our road tools, such as picks, shovels, spades, etc., had been lost in the boat disaster. The principal ones remaining were a few axes, which the pioneers were using at the time the boat was launched, a small crow-bar, and perhaps a spade or two. These were brought into requisition, the commander taking an ax and assisting the pioneers. Considerable was done before the wagons arrived. One wagon was taken to pieces and carried over about an hour before sunset. The passage was hewn out and the remaining wagons got through about sundown, by unloading and lifting through all but two light ones, which were hauled by the mules.

"Both men and teams were now exhausted and the water we had expected to reach early in the afternoon was at least seven or eight miles farther on. We traveled until dark and camped without water, but with good grass for the animals. That night was very cold, and we had only a little brush for fuel . . . At this point we met Charbonaux, returning from San Diego . . . Orders were . . . received for the Battalion to march to San Diego instead of Los Angeles.

"On the 21st, we traveled about ten or twelve miles to Warner's rancho. Warner's was the first house we saw in California, although we had been in that State since crossing the Colorado . . . Here we had the first full meal, except at Tucson and the wild bull country, since the reduction of our rations on the Rio Del Norte . . . Cattle and horses were very cheap, the country being overrun with them; some ranchmen owned several thousand head, and there was no general market for livestock. We remained at Warner's and rested during the 22nd, and our rations were raised to four pounds of beef per day. We had no other food nor even salt to season our meat."

On 25 January 1847, they received a dispatch from General Kearny, ordering the march to San Diego. They reached Temecula Valley that day, where they found some of the San Luis Rey Indians burying their dead. Both the Indians and the Battalion mistook each other for Californians, and both lines were in battle array before the mistake was discovered. The Indians were pleased to see them, and the leading men shook hands with many. Traveling down the river, on the 27th, they arrived at San Luis Rey, a deserted Catholic mission, about noon. One mile below the mission, they ascended a bluff, and the long-looked for view of the great Pacific Ocean appeared about three miles away.

They arrived in San Diego on 29 January 1847, and located their camp four or five miles from the seaport town of San Diego, where General Kearny was quartered. He asked Major Cloud if he thought Cooke could rely on these *Mormons* in case of an attack. The Major unhesitatingly replied, "The Battalion will follow where you dare to lead."

"HEADQUARTERS MORMON BATTALION, MISSION OF SAN DIEGO. January 30, 1847 (Orders No. 1)

"The Lieutenant-Colonel commanding congratulates the Battalion on their safe arrival on the shore of the Pacific Ocean and the conclusion of their march of over two thousand miles.

"History may be searched in vain for an equal march of infantry. Half of it has been through a wilderness where nothing but savages and wild beasts are found, or deserts where, for want of water, there is no living creature. There, with almost hopeless labor we have dug deep wells, which the future traveler will enjoy. Without a guide who had traversed them, we have ventured into trackless table-lands where water was not found for several marches. With crowbar and pick and axe in hand, we have worked our way over mountains, which seemed to defy aught save the wild goat, and hewed a passage through a chasm of living rock more narrow than our wagons. To bring these first wagons to the Pacific, we have preserved the strength of our mules by herding them over large tracts, which you have laboriously guarded without loss. The garrison of four presidios of Sonora concentrated within the walls of Tucson gave us no pause. We drove them out, with their artillery, but our intercourse with the citizens was unmarked by a single act of injustice. Thus, marching half naked and half fed, and living upon wild animals, we have discovered and made a road of great value to our country.

"Arrived at the first settlement of California, after a single day's rest, you cheerfully turned off from the route to this point of promised repose, to enter upon a campaign, and meet, as we supposed, the approach of an enemy; and this too, without even salt to season your sole subsistence of fresh meat.

"Lieutenants A. J. Smith and George Stoneman, of the First Dragoons, have shared and given valuable aid in all these labors.

"Thus, volunteers, you have exhibited some high and essential qualities of veterans. But much remains undone. Soon, you will turn your attention to the drill, to system and order, to forms also, which are all necessary to the soldier.

"By order

Lieut. Colonel P. St. George Cooke.

P. C. Merrill, Adjutant."

On the 31st, of January 1847, they received orders to return to San Luis Rey and maintain the mission as a military post ready to meet whatever emergency might arise, while holding an important position between Pueblo de Los Angeles and San Diego out of the enemy's hands in case hostilities were again resumed, which, at the time seemed quite probable.

"Accordingly, on the 1st of February, 1847, the Battalion marched back to San Luis Rey. On the 4th, about eighty men were detailed as police to clear up the square and quarters and make necessary repairs, which were done in good order, making everything look as cheerful and respectable as the dirt floors would permit. Many of the men were almost naked, without a change of underclothing to keep off dust or the worst of vermin, with which the country abounded and which even many of the 'elite' of the native Californians were said to be never free from."

On the 5th, an order was read relating to the duties of the soldiers when in garrison, such as times of parade, cleaning arms and clothes, shaving, cutting hair, saluting officers, etc. It prescribed that no beard be allowed to grow below the tip of the ear; hence the moustache only could be saved. The hair also must be clipped even with the tip of the ear.

From the diary of Henry Standage, a member of the Battalion:

"February 6.—Went into the garden and washed my shirt and a pair of pants, which I had made out of an old wagon cover—all the clothing I had."

"After arriving at San Luis Rey, the very able and worthy quartermaster sergeant of Company A, REDICK N. ALLRED, was appointed quartermaster sergeant in Colonel Cooke's noncommissioned staff, in which he remained until our final discharge.

"During the first Sunday we spent in our new quarters, the Battalion was called out on dress parade. This practice was followed up nearly if not every Sunday until we were discharged. While we were in garrison, we made it a rule, when possible, to hold religious services on Sunday, which were frequently presided over by Captain Hunt, but sometimes by Father Pettegrew or Levi W. Hancock. On the 15th of February, Company B was ordered to the port of San Diego to garrison that place."

On the 14th of March, Major H. S. Turner arrived at San Luis Rey, bearing documents to Colonel Cooke, announcing General Kearny as "Brigadier General and Governor of California." As Governor, General Kearny made a proclamation; it "absolved all the inhabitants of California from any further allegiance to the Republic of Mexico, and announced that they might consider themselves as citizens of the United States, as henceforth Americans and Californians would be one people."

Orders were sent at the same time by General Kearny to Lieutenant Colonel Fremont, ordering him to disband his battalion, with the understanding that those desiring to might re-enlist under Colonel Cooke. Fremont refused to obey orders at first, but then agreed to submit to his commands. The Colonel's order of the 18th required a few men, under Lieutenant Oman, to remain to garrison San Luis Rey, and the balance of Companies A, C, D and E was required to go to Pueblo de Los Angeles, to hold that place, which had formerly been the Mexican capital.

"On the 24th, Colonel Cooke rode to the San Gabriel Mission, about eight miles from Los Angeles, where Fremont's battalion was stationed. He found Captain Owens in command in the absence of Fremont, and both he and the other officers there disclaimed any knowledge of orders having been received for their disbandment. They regarded Colonel Fremont as the highest authority in the land, and refused to let Colonel Cooke have possession of any of the cannon."

Sergeant Major Ferguson adds this additional information about Fremont:

"Arriving in the Sacramento area at the beginning of the insurrection, he took over and organized the various American groups, fueling the war with Mexico. His army had pushed down to Los Angeles before General Kearny arrived. He had attempted to retain the governorship of California, against General Kearny, when our arrival put a stop to his insubordination.

"When he came into our midst at a subsequent period [returning to the East, his party arrived at Winter Quarters before any of the Battalion,] how different his reception. He was starved, dismounted, and weary. His party sick and dying daily. We gave him shelter, fed him, furnished him with horses, and healed his sick. A dog will show gratitude to the hand that feeds him. But HE is silent, or snaps like a wolf."

Fremont was found guilty of the charges Kearny made against him in Washington D. C., but President Polk did not care to pursue the matter. Fremont would later run for President of the United States against Buchanan.

General Kearny, having sent word to his superiors in office in the east that he was anxious to be relieved of his charge in California as soon as peace was established, Colonel R. B. Mason was sent to succeed him in command; and he, being superior in rank to Fremont, was sent by Kearny to Los Angeles to enforce the discharge of Fremont's battalion and obedience to other orders. After some difficulty, he finally succeeded in discharging Fremont's men, taking ten pieces of cannon held by them to Colonel Cooke.

"For some reason unknown to us, and certainly without a just cause, the men who composed Fremont's command manifested a great deal of animosity towards the Mormon Battalion. It was currently reported, and was probably true, that Fremont himself did all he could to arouse this ill-feeling, not only among his own men but also among the native population. We were assured by some of the Mexicans that he had told them the *Mormons* were cannibals, and especially fond of eating children. It seemed, too, that the story gained some credence among the natives, for their shyness about approaching near our camp for some time was attributed by them to this cause.

"After Colonel Cooke made the demand upon Fremont's men for ordnance stores, which Captain Owens refused to comply with, and especially after their subsequent discharge, their bitterness towards us seemed to increase. We frequently heard of their threatening to make a raid upon our camp and wipe us out of existence. However, they never attempted to put any such threat into execution, and it was probably as well for them that they did not, as they would have met with a warm reception. A few of the most belligerent of them sought quarrels with some of our men on meeting them in Los Angeles, but beyond this we were not molested by them."

On 11 Apr 1847, Company C of the Mormon Battalion, "will march tomorrow and take post in the canyon pass of the mountains, about forty-five miles eastward of this town. Lieutenant Rosecrans, its commander, will select a spot for his camp as near to the narrowest and most defensible part as the convenience of water, feed and grass will admit of, and, if necessary, effectually to prevent a passage of hostile Indians with or without horses, he will erect a sufficient cover of logs or earth. It will be his duty to guard the pass effectually, and if necessary to send out armed parties, either on foot or mounted, to defend the ranchos in the vicinity, or to attack wandering parties of wild Indians."

In Los Angeles, most of the officers and men became very proficient in military tactics. Colonel Mason, of the First Dragoons, an experienced officer, gave the Battalion the credit of excelling any volunteers he had ever seen in going through the manual arms. The few dragoons that remained there were, true to their country and to the Battalion, if they were insulted in their hearing.

"When bullies came into the town and began to impose upon the 'Mormon boys,' the dragoons would not allow them to take their own part if they could avoid it, but would say: 'Stand back; you are religious men, and we are not; we will take all of your fights into our hands,' and with an oath would say: 'You shall not be imposed upon by them.'"

On 5 May, news arrived of the death of the wife of Captain Jesse D. Hunter, at San Diego. "The funeral discourse was preached by Elder WM. HYDE. She was a very estimable lady and faithful Latter-day Saint. She left a male child about two weeks old.

"On the 9th, General Kearny arrived at Los Angeles from Monterey. A salute of twenty-one guns was fired. The General came to our camp . . . He remarked to an officer, that history might be searched in vain for an infantry march equal to that performed by the Battalion, all circumstances considered, and added: 'Bonaparte crossed the Alps, but these men have crossed a continent.'"

On 10 May, General Kearny gave his farewell address to the Battalion and concluded by stating:

"[H]e would take pleasure in representing our patriotism to the President and in the halls of Congress, and give us the justice our praiseworthy conduct had merited. Three men were detailed from each company as an escort, to accompany the General to Fort Leavenworth. The General and party started on their return trip on the 13th." A niece of Amos Cox, one of the selected Battalion members, wrote that the men selected for Kearny were to be "the very best all around men: men who could ride the longest and hardest, load pack-mules and most expeditiously; do double guard duty which meant do without half enough sleep."

Some lists record only twelve escorts, but there were five companies [3 x 5 = 15] and Turner claimed fifteen Mormon guards accompanied Kearny, "for the Iowa adjutant-general's office muster-out role indicated that Bidman Gordon, THOMAS C. IVIE, and Samuel G. Clark were discharged on Bear River, Oregon, on 16 July 1847, which suggests they were part of Kearny's escort."

Kearny took the coastal journey north to Monterey; then crossed the mountains to the San Joaquin valley; hence north to Sutter's Fort; north to Donner's Pass; along the California Trail by the Humboldt River; through Wells, (Nevada); to Fort Hall (by Blackfoot, Idaho); to (Soda Springs, Idaho) on the Bear River, the place of their discharge, which was part of the Oregon Territory at that time.

This group was among the first to reach the dead bodies of the starved, infamous Donner Party, when they crossed the Sierra Nevada Mountains at Donner's Pass—going east. They buried the remains of their bodies and cleaned-up the campsite as best they could. Matthew Caldwell remembered: "This was the most awful sight that my eyes were ever to behold. There was not a whole person that we could find." One witness described burying the former Mormon Levinah Murphy, whose body was found "lying near one of the huts, with her thigh cut away for food, and the saw used to dismember the body lying along side of her."

Kearny left the Bear River and continued across Wyoming, and then near the north and south division of the Platt River, they crossed to the south side and thence back to Fort Leavenworth. The escort then followed the Missouri River back to Winter Quarters.

[Note: THOMAS C. IVIE with his two companions from Company C may have left General Kearny and the group sometime after they were discharged in Soda Springs, Idaho, and took a southern route back to Winter Quarters. There was a short unsigned history, written by one of his descendents, among my mother's records that stated that he, with two other men, returned by way of Taos, New Mexico, and suffered great hardships. Gold was mentioned, but this was before it was discovered in California. Perhaps this is why they are not listed with the others.]

Company B, who left the Battalion at San Luis Rey for San Diego on the 15 March 1847, replaced the dragoons that garrisoned San Diego. Sergeant WILLIAM HYDE was appointed to take eighteen men and quarter in the fort built by the marines, on an eminence about one-fourth of a mile from the town. This fort was constructed by digging a trench on the summit of a hill and placing a row of large logs around the same. Against these, gravel and rock were thrown up, thus forming a barricade, which was thought to be invulnerable. Seventeen pieces of artillery were so arranged as to command the town and surrounding country.

"Religious services were held by the detachment every Sunday, which were generally well attended by strangers, and Lieutenant WM. HYDE, and others, delivered a number of excellent discourses and lectures, which gave general satisfaction to all parties. A society was also organized, entitled the Young Men's Club, for the purpose of lecturing, reciting, declaiming, debating, etc., a kind of Young Men's Mutual Improvement Association.

"On the 4th of May, the company received six months' pay, the most of which was expended, by each individual, in purchasing animals, clothing, etc., as an outfit for the return trip. It was exceedingly fortunate for the Battalion that horses and mules were so very cheap. Wild mares were from three to four dollars each, those broken, to ride, from six to twelve dollars. Gentle mares, however, seldom brought more than seven or eight dollars. Horses, unbroken, were from six to eight dollars, horses broken to ride, from ten to twenty dollars. Good herding stallions were worth about fifty dollars each, and mules were worth about double the price of common horses.

"The Indians, who were located about San Diego, occasionally stole each other's wives. When caught, they were put in the stocks for a few days, and sometimes weeks, as a punishment. The stocks consisted of two hewn logs, one above the other, with semicircles cut in each so as to form a round hole, when joined together, large enough to go around the neck, and another smaller on each side in which to place the legs. To put culprits in, the top log had to be raised, and, after the head and feet had been put in place, it was again lowered and secured, leaving the head and feet on one side and the body on the other, resting on the ground. Sometimes only the head, and at others, only the feet, were put in the stocks.

"Many of the Californian ladies dressed in silks and satins, and were exceedingly fair. As a rule, however, their reputation for morality and virtue was not the best . . .

"A letter from San Francisco to Sergeant HYDE, received on the 30th, stated . . . the Saints who sailed from New York, on the ship 'Brooklyn,' had arrived and sown 145 acres of wheat, and Samuel Brannan had gone to meet the Saints at . . . the Great Salt Lake.

"On the 14th of June, news of General [Zachary] Taylor's victory in Mexico arrived, and twenty rounds of artillery were fired, and the General cheered long and loud.

"H. W. Bigler and others cleared the first yard for moulding brick in San Diego, and indeed, the first in California. The labor was performed for a Californian, named Bandena. Philander Colton and Rufus Stoddard laid up and burnt the kiln. About this time, G. W. Taggart made a quantity of pack-saddles for the return trip.

"On the 4th of July, the roar of cannon at daybreak announced the seventieth anniversary of our nation's birth . . . In the evening, Captain Jesse D. Hunter, and Colonel Stevenson, with Sergeant HYDE and Corporal Horace M. Alexander, who had been to Los Angeles, arrived and were heartily cheered. The prominent citizens of the town were also enthusiastically greeted, which pleased them much. They sincerely regretted that the company was going to leave them. Mrs. Bandena, one of the most prominent ladies of the town, in an address, requested that the company take the American flag with them, as there would be no one left to defend it.

"Orders were immediately given for the company to be in readiness to march to Los Angeles and join the remainder of the Battalion, preparatory to being discharged on the 16th. It is proper to state here that the company, having greatly improved the town, as well as being peaceful, honest, industrious and virtuous, the citizens plead with them in the strongest terms not to leave. They had dug from fifteen to twenty good wells—the only ones in town, several of which were walled with brick, besides building brick houses, including a court-house, to be used for courts, schools, etc. They had paved some of the sidewalks with brick, while some, being house carpenters, had done the finishing work on the inside.

"On the 6th, the citizens of San Diego sent an express to P. St. George Cooke, commander of the southern military district, requesting that another company of 'Mormons' be immediately sent to take the place of Company B, stating that they did not wish any other soldiers quartered there.

"Up to the time of the company leaving San Diego, Philander Colton, Henry Wilcox, Rufus Stoddard and William Garner had burnt forty thousand brick. Sidney Willis had also made several log pumps and put them into wells, which gave universal satisfaction. On the 9th [July 1847], Company B took up the line of march for Los Angeles, at which place they arrived on the 15th, and took position in line."

Returning to the main army, who were left on the hill at Los Angeles on 13 May. On the 4th and 5th of June, a number of the soldiers stationed at Los Angeles, by order of the Colonel, engaged in killing dogs, with which the town was overrun. The 6th being Sunday, the Californians spent it, as they usually did the Sabbath, in horse racing. On the 28th, Colonel Stevenson returned from San Diego, accompanied by Captain Hunter, Sergeant HYDE and Corporal Alexander. On the 29th, at 8:30 a.m., the assembly call was beaten and the Battalion responded. An address was then delivered by Colonel Stevenson, in substance as follows:

"The Spaniards are whipped but not conquered. Your term of service will soon close. It is of the utmost importance that troops be kept here until others can be transported. I have the right to press you into the service for six months longer, if deemed necessary . . . but believing, as I do, that enough, if not all, will re-enlist without, I have decided not to press you to serve longer. I am required to make a strong effort to raise at least one company, and the entire Battalion if possible. If the whole Battalion, or even four companies, enlists, you shall have the privilege of electing your own Lieutenant Colonel, Major and all subordinate officers. Your commander will be the third in rank in California . . . your patriotism and obedience to your officers have done much towards removing the prejudice of the government . . . I am satisfied that another year's service would place you on a level with other communities." Sergeant Daniel Tyler compared this last remark "to the heifer that gave a good bucketful of milk and then kicked it over. It was looked upon as an insult added to the injuries we had received without cause. We could challenge comparison with the world for patriotism and every other virtue, and did not care to give further sacrifice to please pampering demagogues.

"At the close of the Colonel's remarks, we were dismissed into the hands of our officers . . . We met at ten a.m., on a barren point, a quarter of a mile west of the fort. [Some of the Captains and Lieutenants spoke in favor of re-enlistment; but] Father Pettegrew . . . thought it our duty to return and look after our outcast families; others could do as they thought best; but he believed we had done all we set out to do, and that our offering was accepted and our return would be sanctioned by our Church leaders."

Sergeant HYDE, in a mild yet forcible manner agreed with Father Pettegrew. "He thought we should now return and be ready for any sacrifice which might be necessary to make in the future. All, so far as we had any knowledge, were satisfied with our past year's service, and he believed God was satisfied." After a few other remarks, the meeting adjourned.

On the 4th, the entire command of the place assembled under Colonel Stevenson in the fort at sunrise. The *Star-Spangled Banner* was played by the New York volunteer band, while the colors were being raised. Nine cheers were given for the stars and stripes, and *Hail Columbia* was played by the band, after which thirteen guns were fired by the First Dragoons.

"On the evening of the 9th of July, the town was illuminated in honor of Roman Catholic festivities, and the next day a Mexican bull fight occurred on the flat near the town. It was supposed to be a ruse on the part of the Californians to draw the Battalion from the fort, that they might obtain possession, secure the arms and ammunition and gain control of the country. The Battalion, accordingly, remained in the fort, from which point the men could view the sports below the hill, almost as well as if they had been present . . . Besides the bull fight, a grand ball was gotten up and the Battalion especially invited to attend. The best music and seemingly every other attraction was offered to induce us to leave the fort, but we did not take the bait."

On the 15th, Company B arrived from San Diego, preparatory to being discharged, and the next day at 3:00 p. m., the five companies of the Battalion were formed according to the letter of the company, with A in front and E in the rear, leaving a few feet of space between.

"The notorious Lieutenant, A. J. Smith, then marched down between the lines in one direction and back between the next lines, then in a low tone of voice said: 'You are discharged.' This was all there was of the ceremony of mustering out of the service this veteran corps of living martyrs to the cause of their country and religion. None of the men regretted the Lieutenant's brevity; in fact, it rather pleased them."

On the 17th and 18th, some of the companies drew their pay and, on the 20th, one company made up from the discharged Battalion, re-enlisted for six months and elected Captain Daniel C. Davis, former Captain of Company E, to command them. The object of their enlistment was to garrison the post of San Diego. Of our group of relatives and relatives-in-law only JEROME ZABRISKIE, formerly of Company B, re-enlisted for six more months. Ferguson ended his journal by saying:

> "Many who had once been our enemies became our friends. But none of our friends have ever become enemies. The most warlike of the many tribes of the red men that we passed, met us in kindness and parted from us in peace, because we did not abuse their hospitality."

— 14 —

RETURNING TO FRIENDS AND FAMILIES
THROUGH THE UNYIELDING HIGH SIERRAS

On 16 July 1848, the "discharged Battalion" was in the "center of sedition and profligacy—Los Angeles, a town which could boast, perhaps, of more lewdness than any other upon the coast." The former Battalion sergeant Daniel Tyler stated that they, as a group, maintained their sobriety and virtue. He offered "as proof that the men did not partake of the immorality of the place . . . that a hospital surgeon was heard to say that among over seventy soldiers which he treated at Los Angeles for a loathsome disease, only one was a 'Mormon.' And if it be any palliation of the sin in the case of that one, it may be said that he was led to pollute himself while intoxicated. That same surgeon gave it as his opinion that, for virtue, the Mormon Battalion were without a parallel among soldiers."

On 20 July 1847 the majority of those who did not re-enlist were organized into companies for traveling wiith captains of hundreds, fifties and tens, as follows: Lieutenants Andrew Lytle and James Pace, captains of hundreds; Sergeants WILLIAM HYDE, Daniel Tyler [the author], and REDICK N. ALLRED, captains of fifties.

Daniel Tyler's book continues:

"On the 21st, the pioneers advanced, scarcely knowing whither they went, only that they had been told that by traveling northward, mainly under the base of the mountains, Sutter's Fort, on the Sacramento river, might be reached in about 600 miles, while the seashore route would be 700 miles."

CAPTAIN ALLRED'S fifty left on the 23rd, and traveled twenty miles to General Pico's rancho, which appeared to have been an old deserted Catholic Mission. There were two large gardens, including vine-yards, no grain, but fruit in abundance: grapes, figs, pears, apricots, cherries, plums, peaches, apples, olives, and dates. The next day they were in the rugged, steep and high mountain, where two pack-animals lost their footing and rolled twenty or thirty feet before they regained it. They arrived at Francisco's rancho, and remained four days, awaiting the arrival of the other two fifties, who were completing their outfit of animals and provisions.

When Daniel Tyler arrived with his fifty, he recognized the place. He had seen it in a dream before they were discharged. Their intention at that time was to take the southern route through Cajon Pass, and reach the Great Salt Lake from the South.

In his dream, Tyler "saw that we traveled northward and subsequently eastward." On arriving at this rancho, they had passed all of the wild animals (past temptations and troubles) that had sought to destroy or impede their progress, the last being a lion, which the company passed without halting or seeming to notice. He drank from the creek, as he had done in his dream, and received strength.

> "I was then caught away in the spirit to the valley of the Great Salt Lake, and saw myself with many others in a holy Temple, where the Twelve Apostles presided. The house was filled with the glory of God, and in a room adjoining the main one in which I sat was Jesus, the Redeemer of the world. I did not see Him, but knew He was there. Lucifer also appeared, claiming to be the Christ, and offering free salvation to all who would accept him as their ruler without any church obligations. He was finely dressed, in black, and very genteel, until he discovered that no one paid any attention to his sophistry, when he became enraged and threatened to 'tear down the Temple and destroy the kingdom of God,' when, as commanded, he left the house. All was calm as a summer's morning and no one seemed to fear any of the threats made or to believe he would have power to do any harm."

He awoke and parts of his dream were repeated in open vision. From that time he knew that the Salt Lake Valley would be the final destination of the outcast Saints.

On 11 August they journeyed north across a dry plain. The pleasant day became excessively hot and suffocating in the afternoon. Two men gave out and could not ride or travel; others made but little progress, and it almost seemed that all must perish. Those who reached camp first, drank, filled their canteens and returned to revive their thirsting comrades. They had no thermometer, but all agreed that this was the hottest day they ever experienced in any country.

Having no guide, one of the men had procured an old map at Los Angeles, in the hope of defining the different localities, but "it proved of no avail to us, as we could not even tell the names of the streams of water we were traveling on." Unable to find Walker's Pass over the Sierra Nevada Mountains, they decided to seek no farther, but continue northward to Sutter's Fort, situated about one-and-a-half miles from the lone military post in a wilderness that would soon become the city of Sacramento. On the 20th, they arrived at the Sacramento River and encamped. There were several small farms in this region, mostly planted in corn, and cultivated by Indians. On the 22nd, after crossing a beautiful valley and camping on a fine mountain stream, three men were sent ahead to Sutter's Fort for provisions.

On 24 August, they were overjoyed at reaching a settlement of white people—the first since leaving Fort Leavenworth. But best was the news brought by a man named Smith, who had accompanied Samuel Brannan to meet the Church, and who informed them that the Saints were settling in the Great Salt Lake Valley, and that five hundred more wagons were on the way—the first news of the movements of the Church since crossing the Arkansas River. Some having a poor fit-out, wished to remain and labor until spring; wages were good and labor in demand; besides, a settlement of Brannan's New York Saints was within a few miles. The rest traveled twenty miles and encamped on American Fork, two miles from Sutter's Fort. Here the animals that had become tender-footed were shod at a cost of one dollar per shoe.

While the bulk of the company remained to get their horses shod, an advance group continued northward about eighteen miles to the point where their course changed eastward, and arrived on 28 August at Captain Johnson's mill on Bear Creek. Captain Johnson was said to have been one of Fremont's battalion, and his young wife was one of the survivors of the ill-fated Donner party. Her mother was Mrs. Murray, who perished in that horrible scene of death.

She told how her widowed mother with several children had resided in Nauvoo, but had found employment at Warsaw, an *anti-Mormon* town, thirty miles down the Mississippi. In the spring of 1846, an emigrating party offered to furnish passage for her and her children on the condition that she would cook and do the washing for the party. Believing California would be the final destination of the Saints, she accepted. They crossed the plains during the summer of 1846, under the guidance of Captain Hastings. They passed through Salt Lake Valley, around the south end of the lake, and proceeded westward. Lacking the union which has characterized companies of Saints, they split up into factions, each party determined to take its own course. The few who remained with the persevering Captain pushed through to California, while the others were caught in the snows of the Sierra Nevada Mountains.

> "After their food was exhausted, and several had succumbed to death through hunger and others were subsisting upon their flesh, a few of them, one of whom was Mrs. Murray's eldest daughter (afterwards Mrs. Johnson), in desperation, resolved to make an attempt to cross the mountains and obtain relief. Fitting themselves out with snow shoes they started, and, after proceeding some distance, they met Captain Hastings and a party from the Sacramento Valley, coming with provisions to relieve them. On reaching the camp of the starving emigrants, the relief party found Mrs. Murray dead and others perfectly ravenous from starvation. Children were actually crying for the flesh of their parents while it was being cooked. There was good reason to suspect that Sister Murray had been foully dealt with, as she was in good health when her daughter left her, and could scarcely have perished from hunger during the brief period of her absence."

Leaving Captain Johnson's mill, they moved on, following the trail of General Kearny. On 3 September, they passed the place where General Kearny's party had buried the remains of the famished emigrants, and at night reached the place where part of the rear wagons of the unfortunate Hastings company were blocked by the snow, and were horrified at the sight which met their view—a skull covered with hair lying here, a mangled arm or leg yonder, with bones broken as one would break a beef shank to obtain the marrow from it; a whole body in another place, covered with a blanket, and portions of other bodies scattered around in different directions. It had not only been the scene of intense human suffering, but also of some of the most fiendish acts that man made desperate by hunger could conceive. When relief came, one man had even acquired such a mania for that kind of food, that after he had been in the Sacramento Valley some months, where food was plentiful, he admitted to having a longing for another such meal.

On the morning of 6 September, they resumed their journey, and in a short time met Samuel Brannan returning from his trip to meet the Saints. They learned from him that the pioneers had reached Salt Lake Valley in safety, but his description of the valley and its facilities was anything but encouraging. Among other things, Brannan said the Saints could not possibly subsist in the Great Salt Lake Valley, as, according to the testimony of mountaineers, it froze there every month in the year, and the ground was too dry to sprout seeds without irrigation, and if irrigated with the cold mountain streams, the seeds planted would be chilled and prevented from growing, or, if they did grow, they would be sickly and fail to mature. He was confident the Saints would emigrate to California the next spring.

Asked if he had given his views to President Brigham Young, Brannan answered that he had and that the President laughed and made some rather insignificant remark, "but when he has fairly tried it, he will find that I was right and he was wrong, and will come to California."

> "They camped over night with Brannan, and after he had left them the following morning, Captain James Brown, of the Pueblo detachment, came up with a small party. He brought letters from their families, also a letter from the Twelve Apostles advising those who had not means of subsistence to remain in California and labor and bring their earnings with them in the spring."

Henry W. Bigler's letter from Elder George A. Smith stated that Brigham Young, with one hundred and forty-three pioneers, arrived in Salt Lake Valley on the 24th day of July. Some were busy putting in garden and field crops, while others were making adobes to build a fort as a safeguard against Indians. It also said that President Young and the pioneers would return to Council Bluffs, and Father John Smith, Patriarch, would preside until they returned.

> Over half of the discharged Battalion returned, as instructed in the letter of the Twelve Apostles, to spend the winter in California. They were joined "by a portion of the company left at Sutter's Fort and a few others who had remained behind . . . to travel slowly with Brother Henry Hoyt, who was sick. Brother Hoyt had gradually failed since our separation, and finally died on the 3 Sep 1847." He had several times received strength

through the ordinance of laying on of hands, and again continued his journey. Just before his death, he was asked if he did not wish to stop and rest. He answered, "No, go on." These were the last words. Growing faint, "he was aided by Sergeant R. N. ALLRED and other companions from his horse, and laid upon the ground under the shade of a tree, where, in a few moments, he expired without a struggle or a groan. He was buried in the best manner the company could afford, although in absence of proper utensils his grave was rather shallow. He died as he had lived, a faithful Latter-day Saint."

They travelled on to Fort Hall, on the Snake River, then to the Salt Lake Valley, where they arrived 16 October, and were overjoyed to meet so many friends and relatives. They found them living in a fort consisting of a row of buildings running at right angles around a ten acre block. The rooms all opened into the enclosure, and had small windows or port holes looking outward, for purposes of defense and ventilation. The entrance was through a large gate in the center of the east side.

"The gate was locked at night. The site of that first structure, which is in the Sixth Ward of Salt Lake City, is known still as 'the old fort.' The walls, however, have long since been removed; hence the temporary fortification now exists only in name."

Many men from the Battalion were extremely destitute of clothing, but their necessities were somewhat relieved by a collection among the families of the settlers of such articles of wearing apparel as they could spare. Anything that would cover the nakedness of the men or help to keep them warm was acceptable. Comfort was the first consideration, and they were thankful to get anything. Different members brought various kinds of garden and fruit seeds, as well as grain, from California—very useful in this valley a thousand miles from any source of supply.

A few of the members of the Battalion found their families in Salt Lake Valley; some others were so worn down with fatigue and sickness that they were unable to go further, and still others preferred to remain in the valley and prepare a home for their families. Thirty-two, eager to meet their wives and children, continued their journey another thousand miles. They expected to obtain flour in the valley for the remainder of the journey, but found that the people had not enough to subsist upon until they could harvest a crop. They were told that plenty of flour could be obtained at Fort Bridger, only 115 miles further, so they started eastward on 18 October 1847.

They arrived at Fort Bridger during a rather severe snow storm, the first of the season, and found the stock of flour had all been bought up by emigrants to California and Oregon. Bridger informed them those located at the post were then living solely upon meat. He thought, however, they could get all we wanted at Laramie. They traveled on, killing two buffalo bulls before reaching Laramie, and jerked the best of the meat. They baked their last cake on 4 November, but they had eaten considerable buffalo, beef, elk, and small game. It was 10 November that they reached Fort Laramie—again disappointed about getting flour. The only bread-stuff purchased was one pound of crackers by Captain Andrew Lytle. The post trader advised them not to kill any buffalo when they reached the Indian range, as it would offend the Indians. He considered it safer to employ the Indians to kill some buffalo for them.

Those who had a little money purchased what meat they could afford and divided with the company. Twelve miles below Laramie they found an Indian trader on the south side of the Platte river, where they purchased 100 pounds of flour, or about three pounds each—only enough for making gravy, or for thickening soup. They still had about 500 miles to travel. Then about sixty miles below the fort, their meat was exhausted. There were a few scattered buffalo, but they worried about killing any that were claimed by the Indians.

As their hunger increased, however, they decided that:

"[h]e who owned 'cattle upon a thousand hills' had a claim on these, and, being His offspring, we would venture to take one. Besides, there had been no Indians in sight for several days, and, last but not least, we might as well die in battle as of hunger, as in the former case our sufferings would be of shorter duration."

They killed one bull and a calf. While skinning the bull, they saw a smoke and discovered Indians on the south side of the river, opposite to where they were. Some considered leaving the animals, but Captain R. N. ALLRED suggested that with their worn-down animals, this would be useless. If the Indians chose to fight, they could soon overtake them.

"We dressed our beef and reached camp on the river some time after dark. We were not molested. Near that point, Captain R. N. ALLRED traded a small worn-out mule to an Indian for a pony . . . About fifteen miles below we passed, perhaps, 300 lodges of the Sioux tribe. There a stalwart Indian came out and seized the pony by the bridle bit." Captain Lytle and Daniel Tyler, leading, returned to help Brother ALLRED. Many other Indians, squaws and papooses had gathered around.

Tyler "wore a broad-brimmed Panama hat, having undressed elk-skin descending from the under side of it, with the hairy side inward, to shield his ears and face from the cold. His body was covered with a large dressing gown, which had been donated to the company by our venerable Presiding Bishop, Edward Hunter. The reader can imagine how a man weighing not more than 135 pounds would appear attired in the capacious folds of such a garment, made to fit a person several inches taller and upward of one hundred pounds heavier than himself. His unique appearance, when mounted upon a mule, was not very inviting to a white man, and it actually seemed to strike terror to the hearts of the 'reds,' so that, at his approach, all scattered and left Brother ALLRED, except the stalwart fellow who held the horse by the bit. He maintained his grip and stood firm as a statue, evidently determined on having the pony at all hazards."

The mystery was soon solved when another brave lead out the decrepit mule which Brother ALLRED had recently traded for the pony—proving the Indian regretted his bargain. The Indian also indicated by gestures that he felt cheated. With no interpreter, there seemed no other way but for Brother ALLRED to yield up the pony and take back the mule that only needed rest to become the more valuable of the two. The exchange was made, and all disputes settled.

About 150 miles below Laramie, they awoke one morning to find them-selves under about twelve inches of snow. From this point to Winter Quarters, about 350 miles, they had to travel and break the trail through snow from one to two feet in depth. Near the crossing of the Loup Fork River, the head of a donkey was found. Captain ALLRED took an ax and opened the skull, and he and his messmates had a fine supper made of the brains.

"The day we reached the Loup Fork, we divided and ate the last of our food, which in the main consisted of rawhide *saddle-bags* we had used from California to pack our provisions in. This was during a cold storm which lasted several days. Our next food was one of Captain Lytle's young mules, which had given out. This was the first domestic animal our little company had killed since our beef cattle in California, although we had several times looked with a wistful eye upon a small female canine belonging to Jos. Thorne, who, with his wife and one or two children . . . had accompanied us from Fort Bridger. Friend Joseph, however, removed the temptation by trading her to the Pawnee Indians for a small piece of dried buffalo meat." The Indians had a rare treat, their greatest feasts being composed mainly of dog meat.

"Owing to floating ice, we were unable to cross the Loup Fork for five days, in which time we traveled a few miles down the river and found Captain Pace's company just in time to save them from the danger of being robbed by Pawnee Indians who came over in considerable numbers. The remnants of the two companies afterwards remained together."

The cold became so intense that the river froze entirely over, and on the morning of the sixth day "we commenced to cross upon the ice. The ice bent and cracked, and holes were soon broken in it, but we persevered until everything was over . . . But a short time had elapsed after we had safely gained the other shore before the ice broke away and the river was again covered with floating fragments. A kind providence had made the congealed water bridge for our special benefit, and removed it as soon as it had fulfilled its mission."

With ten day's travel, subsisting upon mule meat alone, without salt, they arrived at the Elk Horn River, thirty miles from Winter Quarters, and found a ferry-boat with ropes stretched across, ready to step into and pullover. This boat was built by the pioneers, and was first used by them. It afterwards served the companies who followed on their trail. They crossed on 17 December 1847. The next morning, they arose early and arrived in Winter Quarter about sundown.

At Winter Quarters, now Florence, Nebraska, all the soldiers, although respectable,

"were unavoidably dirty and ragged; yet they found only warm-hearted, sympathetic brethren, sisters and friends among the people, from President Young and the Twelve Apostles to the least child who knew what the words *Mormon Battalion* meant. They had been taught to know that valiant corps had been offered like Isaac, a living sacrifice for the Church as well as the nation."

Cousin ISAAC ALLRED wrote:

"[On] the 9th of December, 184[7], the church made a feast for these soldiers that had returned to the place of their enlistment; at which time, I had the privilege of waiting on them . . . Three of the twelve were there and blessed them and we had a good time and I thank the Lord that I yet live and have a standing with the saints."

⥋ 15 ⥋

MORE PRECIOUS THAN GOLD

Upon the advice of the Twelve Apostles, nearly half of the company had returned to the isolated Sutter's Fort, near present day Sacramento, to obtain
work and bring cash and supplies to the Saints in the Salt Lake Valley the following
spring. They arrived on 14 September 1747. RICHARD A. IVIE, son of JAMES
RUSSELL IVIE, and cousin JAMES R. ALLRED, son of third-great-grandmother
SARAH IVIE's younger brother ISAAC ALLRED, were among them.

Captain John A. Sutter, a Swiss-German emigrant who had purchased large
land holdings from the Mexicans and doing well in land development, while running a trading post, quickly hired all of them. The Mexican and Indian workers
were unreliable and he was desirous of improving the area with a flouring mill,
some six miles from the fort, and a sawmill about forty-five miles away. The frame
of the flouring mill was raised the latter part of December and the sawmill a little
later. About 24 January 1848, the water was turned into the race above the sawmill.

The race was fine; but as the water left the flume and reached the head of the
tail race, having a considerable fall, it washed a hole near the base of the building. Superintendent James Marshall had turned off the water, and early the next
morning, while the men were filling their stomachs with a breakfast of flapjacks,
he examined the hole. Something glittered in the sun. He picked it up. It was
about the size of a large pea with some gravel attached. Gold? He wondered. He
showed it to the men who were still eating.

"Fool's gold."
"Yeh, just some iron pyrite."
They continued their breakfast. Mr. Marshall ambled into the house
and showed it to Mrs. Wimmer, who was making soap. She looked at it and
promptly plopped it into the soap mixture.

"If it's gold, it won't hurt it. If it isn't, this lye will eat it up," she stated matter of fact and resumed her work. Marshall returned to his men and his own breakfast.

That night, with the tail race deepened, as James sat smoking his pipe and perhaps thinking of the lumber from the tall redwoods and the profits that could be gained in the sleepy town of San Francisco—down the river, he was suddenly interrupted by Mrs. Wimmer. She had a satisfied look and plunked the small stone on his pine table.

"It's *gold*, all right, Mr. Marshall!"

He pounded it with a stone. It didn't break. Early the next morning, he searched for more gold and collected a fair amount in a small buckskin bag. Then he headed to Sutter's Fort, presumably for supplies. He took it to Captain Sutter and together they weighed it and determined it was the pure product. Together they determined to keep it quiet. Mr. Marshall wanted to collect more, and Captain Sutter worried about his already prosperous property. But, the former Mormon leader, Sam Brannan, had a store at Sutter's Fort and rumors were quietly being passed with great rapidity. Sam Brannan was not one to keep his mouth shut. He quickly told it to the newspapers and authorities in San Francisco— great advertising for his business.

Of course, the Mormon Battalion workers soon found out. At first there was skepticism; but within a few weeks, there were fabulous reports.

Daniel Tyler wrote that in the "settlements along the coast and on the rivers, lawyers closed their offices, doctors forsook their patients, schools were dismissed, farmers allowed their grain to fall to the ground uncared for, and almost everybody came in every conceivable way and manner, in one grand, wild rush to the *gold diggings*; on horses, mules, with wheelbarrows, with packs on their own backs, and some with nothing but the dirty rags they stood up in, and in a few weeks, the mountain wilderness was turned into busy mining camps, and the whole face of the country seemed to change as if by magic. It may also be . . . stated here that the excitement of the late war with Mexico now subsided and the malcontent Californians, who had sought a favorable opportunity to re-take the country, relinquished all idea of another conquest, and, true to the Spanish instinct, turned their attention to mining, thus closing and healing the bloody chasm . . . To the patriotism and unflinching industry of the Mormon Battalion is due the honor of closing the Mexican war in California."

Anxious to return to their families, a company of eight *Mormons* started on 1 May 1848 to pioneer a wagon road over the Sierra Nevada Mountains eastward, the Truckee route being impracticable at that season of the year. This company consisted of David Browett, Captain, Ira J. Willis, J. C. Sly, Israel Evans, Jacob G. Truman, Daniel Allen, J. R. ALLRED, Henderson Cox, and Robert Pixton.

"Three days' travel brought this company to Iron Hill, where they found the snow so deep they could travel no farther. A donkey belonging to one of the men was completely buried in the snow, except his ears. On this occasion, these appendages were not to be despised, ugly and unique as they usually appear, for one or two of the men got hold of them and dragged Mr. Donkey on to terra firma and saved his life. None of that company will be very likely to wonder why those animals are made with large ears."

They ascended to the summit of a mountain and seeing nothing but snow-capped mountains, decided to postpone the enterprise until a later period, judging a wagon road would at least be possible and perhaps a success.

"One day's travel in descending took them back from winter's cold, snowy regions to a warm, spring atmosphere, where flowers bloomed and vegetation was far advanced. The balance of May and the month of June were spent in digging gold, buying wagons and a full outfit for a wagon train, and making a rendezvous in Pleasant Valley, a beautiful place, about fifty miles east of Sutter's Fort."

On 24 June 1848, "Captain Browett, Daniel Allen and Henderson Cox, desired to cross the mountains on a second exploring tour, but their friends, or at least a portion of them, thought the undertaking risky, owing to the wild Indians. They, however, being fearless and anxious to be moving, decided to brave all dangers and make the effort."

The three men started and by the 2nd of July the remainder began their assent into the high Sierras. In two days they were in Sly's Park, a small valley or mountain dell named for Captain James C. Sly, who first discovered it. Here they stopped, while ten men marched on to pioneer the way over the summit of the mountains. Four days' travel over rough and rugged mountains took them across, and they found themselves safely landed at the head of Carson Valley, Nevada. Returning, they spent six days trying to find a better route, but failed.

On 16 July, the company of thirty-seven individuals followed their route with sixteen wagons and two small Russian cannon, which they had purchased before leaving Sutter's Fort, one a four, and the other a six-pounder. The cost of these guns was four hundred dollars.

"This little band, like most of the Battalion, had great confidence in Divine interposition in their behalf, believing that a kind Providence would second their efforts to return to their families and friends . . . They had no guide, nor, so far as known, had the foot of white man ever trod upon the ground over which they were then constructing, what subsequently proved to be a great national highway for the overland travel."

In around five miles they arrived at a place they named Tragedy Springs.

"After turning out their stock and gathering around the spring to quench their thirst, some one picked up a blood-stained arrow, and after a little search other bloody arrows were also found, and near the spring the remains of a camp fire, and a place where two men had slept together and one alone. Blood on rocks was also discovered, and a leather purse with gold dust in it was picked up and recognized as having belonged to Brother Daniel Allen. The worst fears of the company: that the three missing pioneers had been murdered, were soon confirmed. A short distance from the spring was found a place about eight feet square, where the earth had lately been removed, and upon digging therein they found the dead bodies of their beloved brothers, Browett, Allen and Cox, who left them twenty days before. These brethren had been surprised and killed by Indians. Their bodies were stripped naked, terribly mutilated and all buried in one shallow grave.

"The company covered them again, and built over their grave a square monument of rocks to mark their last resting place, and shield them from the wolves. They also cut upon a large pine tree nearby their names, ages, and manner of death. After the darkness of night had gathered around them and they were sadly conversing by the camp-fire, Indians or wild animals came within smelling or hearing distance of their stock, which became so frightened that they rushed to within a few rods of the camp-fire, forming a circle around it with their eyes shining like balls of fire in the darkness. As quick as possible, a cannon was loaded and fired. The belching forth of fire in the darkness, accompanied by the terrific report, echoing many times across the little valley, so terrified their animals that they scattered in every direction, and it was not until late the second day that all were recovered, some having been overtaken at a distance of twenty-five miles on their back track. If, as was thought, Indians were in the vicinity, intending to make a raid upon the camp, the report of the cannon so frightened them that they fled, as nothing was seen of them. The Digger Indians, at that time, were almost entirely unacquainted with the use of fire arms, and the roaring of a cannon, in the stillness of the night, may easily be imagined.

"At Rock Springs the company halted two or three days, and with the entire force were only able to work the road for a distance of three miles to another opening, after which the camp marched only five miles to the top of the highest mountains, though not over the main dividing ridge. This was about the first of August, and yet their wagons had to be hauled over various bands of the beautiful snow, in some places from ten to fifteen feet deep. On this short day's march, two wagons were upset and two broken. New spokes were, however, soon made from a dry pine tree near at hand with such expertise that the wheel required no further repairs."

Other work was required upon the road, and then with a journey of about five miles they reached the summit of the dividing ridge of the Sierra Nevada Mountains. The next morning, the wagons were lightened by placing the heaviest freight on pack mules that carried it over the ridge and down the steep descent of the mountain. The next day's travel, took them to the lower end of the valley. Then with four more days spent working the road, they traveled another five miles down the canyon to the head of Carson Valley.

"Here, like the Puritan fathers upon landing at Plymouth Rock, they tendered thanks to God who had delivered them, not from the dangers of the sea, but the far more dreaded merciless savages, the ferocious wild beasts that abounded in that region, and from being dashed to pieces while traveling over and around the steep precipices of the everlasting snow-capped mountains. They had no idea of the magnitude of the work they had performed."

Within twelve months many thousands of their fellow countrymen would gladly avail themselves of this road to reach a land they had so cheerfully and recently left.

After a few days of travel down the Carson River, "they were almost overjoyed to find themselves in the emigrant road, near the lower crossing of the Truckee River." They soon met a few trains of California emigrants, who, on learning that they were fresh from a new Eldorado, were anxious to learn what the prospects were. One of the returning soldiers took his purse from his pocket, poured into his hand perhaps an ounce of gold dust and began stirring it with his finger. One aged man of probably over seventy years, who had listened with intense interest while his expressive eyes fairly glistened, could remain silent no longer; he sprang to his feet, threw his old wool hat upon the ground, and jumped upon it with both feet, then kicked it high in the air, and exclaimed, "Glory, hallelujah, thank God, I shall die a rich man yet!" Many very interesting and somewhat similar scenes occurred as the tidings were communicated to other trains. This company had brought over the snow-capped Sierra Nevada Mountains, the first news of the discovery of gold in California.

This enterprising little company, instead of following the old emigrant road via Fort Hall, on the Snake River, some two hundred miles out of their way, struck out across the country crossing the Malad and Bear rivers a few miles above their junction. They arrived in Salt Lake Valley 1 October 1848, feeling thankful that they had exchanged the land of gold for wives, children and friends—the home of the Latter-day Saints.

~ 16 ~

EXODUS
"THE LAND NOT EVEN THE INDIANS WANT"
SALT LAKE VALLEY IN 1848

The IVIEs' old friend, Parley P. Pratt, arrived in the Salt Lake Valley in 1847. He remembered:

"January 1st 1848. The opening of the year found us and the community generally in good comfortable, temporary log or adobe cabins, which were built in a way to enclose the square commenced by the pioneers, and a portion of two other blocks of the city plot. Here life was as sweet and the holidays as merry as in the Christian palaces and mansions of those who had driven us to the mountains. In February we again commenced to plough for spring crops, while I had the happiness to behold the tender blade of my wheat and rye, clothing a few acres with a beautiful green, pleasingly contrasted with the gray, wild, wormwood and other traits of our dreary solitude; while similar pleasing sights stretched away in the distance, marking the bounds of agriculture as possessed by my neighbors.

"March 25th—My oldest son Parley celebrated his birthday with a family party—being then eleven years of age . . . I exhorted him to prepare to walk in my footsteps, and to do good and serve God and his fellow men by a well ordered life, and by laying hold of knowledge and a good education. I rehearsed to him my own sufferings, and the sufferings of my family, and of the Church while in the States—telling him of the murder of our prophets and Saints, and how we had been driven to the mountains, robbed and plundered of a very large amount of property and possessions . . .

"I continued my farming operations, and also attended to my ministry in the Church. Devoting my Sabbaths and leisure hours to comforting and encouraging the Saints, and urging them to faith and persevering industry in trying to produce a first harvest in a desert one thousand miles from the nearest place which had matured a crop in modern times. We had to struggle against great difficulties in trying to mature a first crop. We had not only the difficulties and inexperience incidental to an unknown and untried climate, but also swarms of insects equal to the locusts of Egypt, and also a terrible drought, while we were entirely inexperienced in the art of irrigation; still we struggled on, trusting in God.

"During this spring and summer my family and I, in common with many of the camp, suffered much for want of food. This was the more severe on me and my family because we had lost nearly all our cows, and the few which were spared to us were dry, and, therefore, we had no milk to help out our provisions. I had ploughed and subdued land to the amount of near forty acres, and had cultivated the same in grain and vegetables. In this labor every woman and child in my family, so far as they were of sufficient age and strength, had joined to help me, and toiled incessantly in the field, suffering every hardship which human nature could well endure. Myself and some of them were compelled to go with bare feet for several months, reserving our Indian moccasins for extra occasions. We toiled hard and lived on a few greens and on thistle and other roots. We had sometimes a little flour and some cheese, and sometimes we were able to procure from our neighbors a little sour skimmed milk or buttermilk. In this way we lived and raised our first crop in these valleys. And how great was our joy in partaking of the first fruits of our industry. On the 10th of August we held a public feast under a bowery in the center of our fort."

Aunt PEARL IVIE STANFORD and ROZELLA JORDAN claim that JAMES RUSSELL IVIE wanted to be in the first group to enter the Salt Lake Valley, but his family was large—10 children (besides RICHARD), and he was appointed by Brigham Young to assist in looking after the health of the Saints at Council Bluffs. His cousin, [no first name given] ALLRED, had been set apart by the Prophet to heal with herbs. They worked together and were able to make many more comfortable. It was said, "The JAMES R. IVIE family had two Indians to help in their household, from whom the family learned many things." When Brigham Young returned to Winter Quarters prepared to lead the first company of 1848, the IVIEs were ready and waiting.

It is reported in other histories that JAMES's wife ELIZA was very skilled in the use of the available medicines and delivered many babies. With their survival skills, equipment, and livestock, the family were better prepared than most of the refugees from Nauvoo. They were frontier people. In an early newspaper article in Monroe County, Missouri, J. R. IVIE was appointed to appraise the value of a horse, placing its value at $25, which shows that his knowledge of animals was trusted in that area. These second-great-grandparents had three sons who were also very skilled in both hunting and farming: WILLIAM FRANKLIN IVIE was 20 years old in 1848; JAMES ALEXANDER IVIE, 17 years; and great-grandfather JOHN LEHI IVIE, 15 years. They had with them their daughter SARAH, whose husband, WILLIAM A. DAYTON, was with the Mormon Battalion and their Mormon Battalion son RICHARD's wife, ELIZABETH DOBSON IVIE. In addition to these there were three younger daughters and three younger sons, the youngest was born in Council Bluffs, 15 September 1846.

Grandfather JAMES OSCAR IVIE writes of his father, JOHN LEHI IVIE:

"Father told me there were many hardships and shortages of food while traveling but the buffalo supplied the Saints with food and he had a riding horse that they could ride upon the buffalo or by his side and kill them, and at one time he rode on to a black bear and killed it—the only horse in the company that could catch the buffalo and bear and other wild game."

Second-great-grandparents JOHN BARTON and his wife, SUSANNAH WILKINSON BARTON, were also in this First Company of saints going west in 1848. They had lost two daughters: one was buried in Nauvoo, the other in Council Bluffs. A new son was born in the fall of 1847, JOHN OSCAR BARTON. Young great-grandmother, MARY CATHERINE BARTON, even then beautiful and charming, was eleven years old. Although too young for marriage, it is very likely that JOHN LEHI IVIE and MARY CATHERINE BARTON were attracted to each other as they crossed the plains, and perhaps, even before.

THOMAS C. IVIE, one of the members of the Mormon Battalion, with his wife and family remained in Council Bluffs a little longer. Their family records show WILLIAM HARVEY IVIE being born 8 December 1848, in Council Bluffs. JAMES ALLRED's biography states that he waited and came west in 1850, as did many of the ALLRED relatives.

[Note: From the Church Historian's Archives reports on the Emigration of 1848, we read: "The emigration across the plains and mountains from the Missouri River to the Great Salt Lake City in 1848 was divided into three divisions, [which were] in [the] charge of the First Presidency of the Church, namely,

A BUFFALO HUNT

(This is the way the pioneers secured meat for the camp)

Young JOHN LEHI IVIE had a very fast horse. It had been given to him by his Pottawattamie Indian friend. It could outrun the buffalo. He learned to spear them like the Indians did.

(Illustration taken from *Autobiography of Parley P. Pratt*) the First Division in [the] charge of President Brigham Young; the Second Division in [the] charge of President Heber C. Kimball, and the Third Division in [the] charge of President Willard Richards.

"The First Division was composed of 1229 souls and had with them 397 wagons, 74 horses, 19 mules, 1275 oxen, 699 cows, 184 loose cattle, 411 sheep, 141 pigs, 605 chickens, 37 cats, 82 dogs, 3 goats, 10 geese, 2 hives of bees, 8 doves and one crow. (J.H. June 16, 1848) This division left the Elkhorn River June 1st and arrived in G.S.L. City Sept. 20, 1848 and on the few following days."

The following is the roster of the First Division:
FIRST DIVISION, Brigham Young, General Superintendent and Leader of First Division.
Daniel H. Wells, Aide-de-camp to President Brigham Young
    Officers of the First Company. (Also called President Young's Company)
        ISAAC MORLEY, Captain of Hundred
        Wm. W. Major, Capt. of Fifty
        Chauncey G. Webb, Capt. of Fifty
        ALEXANDER NEIBAUR, Capt. of Ten
        Amos R. Neff, Capt. of Ten
        Jasper Twitchell, Capt. of Ten
        Horace S. Eldredge, Marshall
        Hosea Stout, Capt. of night guard
        Thomas Bullock, scribe
    The officers of the Second, Third, Fourth and Fifth Companies (names that I recognized):
    Second Company—Zera Pulsipher, Capt. of Hundred
    Third Company—Lorenzo Snow, Capt. of Hundred
    Fourth Company—John D. Lee, Capt. of Fifty
    Fifth Company—ANSON CALL, Capt. of Ten
        TIMOTHY B. FOOTE, Capt. of Ten
        David Redfield, Capt. of Ten
        Erastus Snow, Capt. of Ten

Following the list of officers is an alphabetical partial list of the [mostly heads of households] in the First Division, which included many of the members of Brigham Young's family.

Recognized names included in this long list are:
    WM. FRANKLIN IVIE, JAMES IVY, [JOHN BARTON not found]
    Gardner Snow, Joseph Toronto

The Second Division with Heber C. Kimball as Leader "was composed of 602 souls, 226 wagons, 57 horses, 25 mules, 737 oxen, 284 cows, 150 loose cattle, 243 sheep, 96 pigs, 209 chickens, 17 cats, 52 dogs, 3 hives of bees, 8 doves, 5 ducks and 1 squirrel. (J.H. 16 Jun 1848 p. 2) This division left the Elkhorn River June 7th 1848 and arrived in G.S.L. Valley Sept. 24, 1848."

Included as officers were:
    Second Company—Isaac Higbee, Capt. of Hundred
        JEHU COX, Capt. of 4th Ten
        William Clayton, Clerk of Company.
    Third Company—John Pack, Capt. of Hundred
        SHADRACH ROUNDY, Capt. of Ten
    Fourth Company—Peter Conover, Capt. of 4th Ten
        Howard Egan, Capt. of the Mississippi Company.
The partial alphabetical listing of the Second Division includes:
        Aroet Lucius Hale; Rachel Hale, sister; Alma Helamen Hale, Solomon Hale, brothers,
        Daniel S. McKay
        Mary Fielding Smith, widow of the martyred Patriarch, Hyrum Smith
        Also 5 of their children, including Joseph F. (10 years old)

The Third Division with Willard Richards as leader was composed of "502 whites, 24 negroes, 169 wagons, 50 horses, 20 mules, 515 oxen, 426 cows and loose cattle, 369 sheep, 63 pigs, 5 cats, 170 chickens, 4 turkeys, 7 ducks, 5 doves and 3 goats." (Contributor Vol. 13 pp. 12,13) The Third Division left the Elkhorn River 10 July and arrived in G.S.L. City 19 October 1848.

    Included as officers were:
        First Company—Franklin D. Richards, Capt. of Hundred
           Wm. McBride, Capt. of Ten
           Robert L. Campbell, Historian
        Second Company—Amasa M. Lyman, Capt. of Hundred.
           Chapman Duncan, Capt. of 1st Ten (not a close Duncan relative)
        The partial alphabetical listing of the Third Division includes:
           ISRAEL BARLOW (ELIZABETH BARTON was his second wife)
           Samuel Dewey, MILLIE McKEE Dewey, wife
           JAMES DUKE, ELLIS M. SANDERS]

The following is from Thomas Bullock's camp journal, who was the scribe of Brigham Young's First Division, First Company, which included the IVIE and BARTON ancestors. This is only a small part of the journal, but it helps us understand a little of the camp activities.

"30 Jun 1848—The cattle were unloosed at 3 a.m., but the feed was poor, the morning was cloudy and cool; the camp started at 7:45 a.m. for the bluffs, the wagons dragged heavily. We had to stop for Pulsipher's camp who had killed a buffalo last night. After they started, we followed over the hill, which was hard work for the cattle. At 9:15, after getting over the hill, we took a bee line for timber. On arriving at the timber we turned to the right and traveled up the banks of Skunk creek. At 12:15 we halted to water and graze our teams. An hour and half later, we resumed our journey and traveled up the banks of the creek, which we finally crossed. Afterwards we passed three small lakes on the south, going over a sandy road in some places. We saw three buffaloes in a ravine. We continued our journey until we arrived at a good spring of cold water, passed Pulsipher's camp and formed our corral under a high bluff, near a spring of splendid water that rises out of one hole making a stream, about 3 feet wide and 1 foot deep with a very rapid current. John A. Mikesell killed a buffalo which he brought in and distributed among the brethren, while JAMES IVY killed two. Samuel Mecham killed one and wounded one, Duff Potter and Seth Dodge wounded three and Alexander Williams killed and wounded four—all a dead loss, except about 20 lbs., and a cruel waste of life."

"Thursday, July 6 [Thomas Bullock clerk]: The cattle were unloosed at 3:30 a.m. The morning was pleasant after the rain. The camp started about 7 a.m. and crossed Goose Creek, then traveled over a heavy, sand road for some distance, also crossed two small creeks, one making a perfect pool of muddy water. We had to go down a steep pitch in order to cross Duck Weed creek. After crossing this stream, the road was excellent . . . we traveled by the bank of the river and passed Cedar Bluffs, which looked very pretty. Two of the camps ahead had, through carelessness or negligence, set fire to the prairie and left it burning, one of the fires being within ten rods of our road . . . A buffalo, which had previously been wounded, came towards our camp on a gallop; several dogs ran at it, but it still came. When within distance of the camp Isaac Morley, Jr., gave it a fatal ball; it immediately reeled, received three other balls and fell. Another company of ten drew it to camp and claimed it. About 5 o'clock the corral was formed on the banks of the Platte. This was a delightful day's travel; a northeast breeze was blowing. After prayers, TIMOTHY B. FOOT was brought before ISAAC MORLEY and counsellors for not crying the time, while on guard and being in his wagon. He was cautioned and discharged. JAMES IVIE was also admonished for having slept while on guard." [Father or son?]

Our young orphaned Aroet Hale, whose parents died in Council Bluffs and who called JAMES ALLRED his uncle, was in the Second Company with Heber C. Kimball. He wrote:

"Tuesday, the 9th of May, 1848, 22 wagons, the first of the season, left Winter Quarters for the valley. The first week in June, President Young broke camp at Elkhorn and started for the Great Salt Lake valley . . . I was organized into Heber C. Kimball's company, first fifty, Henry Harrison, captain of first fifty. My outfit consisted of . . . one yoke of oxen on one light wagon and one yoke of oxen and one yoke of cows on the heavy wagon . . . I was appointed one of the hunters for the first 50 hours . . . Buffalo and antelope were very plentiful and common up the Platte River. We had good luck and supplied our division with what buffalo meat they needed while we were in the buffalo country.

"Our travels across the plains was a long, tiresome trip over one thousand miles with ox teams. It was hard on old people and women with children. The young folks had enjoyment. Presidents Young and Kimball were very kind and indulgent to the young. They frequently stopped within a mile or so apart. The young would visit from one camp to the other and frequently would get music and have a good dance on the ground. Sometimes the older folks would join with us. On one occasion, President Young took part in the enjoyment. I formed an acquaintance with a young lady crossing the plains that I afterwards married . . . So I did my sparking

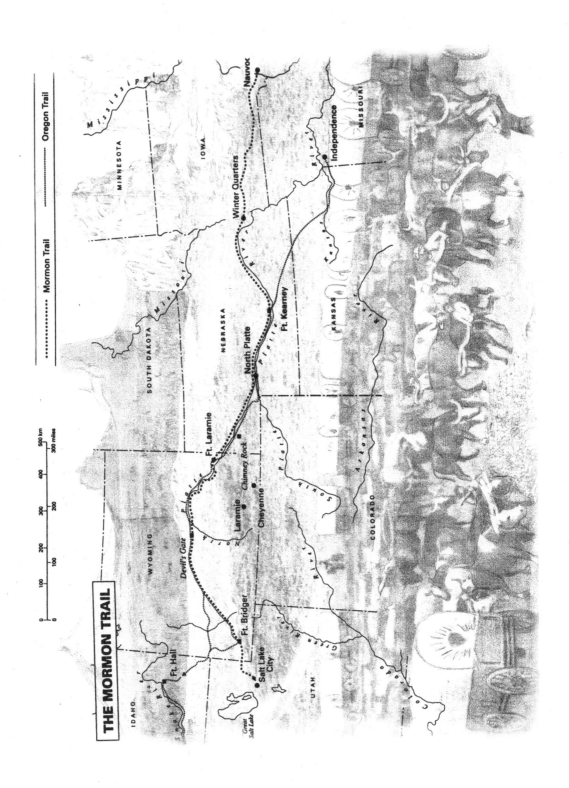

THE MORMON TRAIL

•••••••••• Mormon Trail   ———— Oregon Trail

along the road. So I did not have so much to do after I got into the valley.

"On our travels, as we neared the valley, we met Saints of 1847 on their way back to the Missouri River after their families that were left, also quite a number of Battalion boys. My dear old friend, Lucus Hoagland was one of the number. He found what he was looking for, my dear sister Rachel Hale. They commenced keeping company before they left Nauvoo. Of course, he turned about and came into the valley with us.

"We arrived in the valley of Great Salt Lake in the fall of 1848. We camped around the Old Fort that the pioneers of 1847 had built. In the fall of 1848 all the Saints had liberty to scatter out and farm nearby settlements, and settle on their city lots. President Kimball, my good advisor, sent for me to come and see him. Said he, 'Aroet, you are naturally ingenious. Go to the adobe yard and make you 7 or 8 hundred large Spanish adobes. While they are drying, enclose one of your wagons. Go to the canyon and get a load of logs. Take them to the saw pit. Have them sawed for your doors, frames and window frames, and by . . . I will show you your city lot.'

"I did as my advisor counseled me to do. I took one of the end gates out of the wagon and went to the carpenter shop. I found there [an] old Nauvoo acquaintance. He was glad to see me and soon had a pair of adobe molds made. The adobes that were first made for our small houses were 18 x 9 x 4, what were called Spanish adobe. I unloaded one wagon and went to the North Canyon in company with other teams, got a small load of logs, and took them to the saw pit . . . For my share, I got lumber enough to make us one door frame, two window 6 liter frames and two plates for the wall.

"I was now ready to report to President Kimball . . . Said he, 'Aroet, come up onto the city town site tomorrow afternoon and I will show you your city lot.' I . . . found quite a number of the brethren and the surveyor, surveying ten acre blocks. [These were divided into lots.] I soon had my wagons on my lot. One was loaded and I commenced hauling stone, sand and clay. By the time the foundation was laid, the adobes were ready to haul . . . The wards were soon laid off. My city lot was in the [17th] ward . . . I was called and acted as teacher in the ward and was ordained a seventy . . . In the spring of 1849, I drew or received five acres of land . . . now situated in what is known as the Sugarhouse Ward. Here my first experience in irrigation commenced . . . I watered my wheat from Mill Creek. It came up and looked well . . . About the middle of June, I went to water my wheat and to my surprise it was covered with crickets. Myriads of big black crickets came down from the mountains and began to sweep away fields of grain. I lost most of my little crop of wheat. The most of the barley grain near the city was saved by immense flocks of seagulls which came and devoured the crickets. This was considered a God send and many escaped what might have been a severe famine. A fine of five dollars was placed upon the head of anyone that killed a seagull. One thing singular, the oldest mountaineers and trappers said that they never saw a seagull until after the Mormons settled this country.

"In consequence of the scanty harvest of 1848, bread stuff and other provisions became very scarce. Many had to eat raw hides, dig segos and thistle roots for months. I was one of that number. The last of June, just before harvest, was the hardest time of 1849 . . .

"We had two cows, luckily both giving milk. When I went to the field to water the wheat and fight the crickets, I used to drive one cow to the field with me at night, milk the cow, and strain the milk. As soon as it was cool, I would stir in two or three spoonsful of moldy corn meals, set it over the campfire make my porridge and go to bed. I did the same in the morning. This was better with the blessing of the Lord on it than boiled rawhide and thistle roots. For dinner, I would take my shovel and go out on the bench land and dig segos which were plentiful, thank the Lord.

"While I was tending the wheat, Lucas was working around where he could get a little provisions for the family. He used to go to the Provo River with fishing parties, catch fish, salt and dry them. They were very good and considered a rarity.

"My wheat was heading out and commenced turning a little yellow. I thought I could glean a little out that would do to thresh and grind in a hand mill, which many did. I saw several going to Neff's Mill with small grists of corn that were rare in 1848. The thought struck me that I might be able to trade for some. I had a fine little saddle horse that Lucas Hoagland had told me to trade for bread stuff or edibles of any kind. I saddled up, went to the mill, and saw several there begging or trying to (some widows with families). I spoke to Neff and told him my situation. I offered him the horse, saddle and bridle . . . for three pecks of corn meal, one peck to take home with me, one peck the next week, the third peck, the third week. Now for the answer. Said he, 'You great booby, here trying to get three pecks of meal. There are women here begging for two quarts to take home with them to feed their little children.' This anger hurt my feelings very badly. I thought of the situation I had left the family in in the morning, without a spoonful of anything to eat of bread stuff kind. Then I cried like a baby to be called a booby for trying to make an honest trade with the miller.

"I continued fighting crickets until nearly night, when I heard a noise towards the mouth of Emigration Canyon, a little north of me. I looked and to my surprise, I saw a train of four-and six-horse wagons coming out of Emigration Canyon. This proved to be a company of the gold emigration, the first that arrived in the valley. I sprung to my horse and went across the bench into their camp. I was the first Mormon boy in their camp. They appeared to be very much excited over gold and the mines and asked many questions. What news from the gold mines? Is there any more of the battalion boys come in? What news do they bring? Have you seen any? Have you got any gold? I had a very little that Hoagland had given me to try and get a little bread stuff with. I let them see what gold I had. They were all excited in a minute and all had to see the gold dust. While they were looking at the gold dust, an old gentleman touched me on the shoulder and beckoned me to one side. Said he, 'I have a span of young American colts, four years old. They have been worked on lead, and have pulled themselves down very poor.' Said he, 'I will give you that span of young horses, their harness and lead bars for your pony, saddle and bridle.' I told him that I would go with him and see the horses. We went, and he showed me the horses. They were as he reckoned them to me. I thought of the trade I had offered the Miller Neff a few hours before. I thought of my sister and the little boys at home without anything to eat but a little milk and segos for supper.

"Said I, Could you spare me a few pounds of flour, a small piece of bacon, a quart of beans or any kind of vegetables?' 'Come to the wagon and I will see what I can find.' He got into the wagon, threw out a sack with eight or ten pounds of flour, ten pounds of bacon and by that time the boys had gotten supper. They invited me into the tent. There I ate the best supper that I ever ate, or relished the best. I had not tasted nice white bread and fried bacon for months. I led my horses to the city. When my sister Rachel saw the flour and bacon, she wept for joy.

"Gold emigration continued to come and they were willing to trade their poor stock for those that were in better condition. The gray horses that I got for the saddle pony brought me two yoke of oxen and wagons and a nice suit of clothes. This reminds me of a prophecy of President Heber C. Kimball two months before the gold emigration came into the valley. He prophesied that clothing would be cheaper in Salt Lake City than it was in New York City. We saw this prophecy come to pass. They were loaded too heavy to continue their journey and all had something to sell or trade, horses, harnesses or wagons, clothing, provisions, cooking utensils, stoves, tents, guns and ammunition. This was considered a God send."

Cousin NETTIE ROBIN's wrote:

"It was in the spring of 1848 in the month of May that JAMES RUSSELL [IVIE], his wife and nine of their eleven children began making plans to move westward . . . It was on the first of June 1848, that the IVIE's left Elkhorn in the company of the Saints . . . Grandfather's outfit was equipped with a good wagon and teams. His son RICHARD's wife, ELIZABETH DOBSON IVIE, was with them. [The history mentions ELIZABETH had watched when the bodies of Joseph and Hyrum Smith were brought back from Carthage.] The trip across the plains and mountains was about the same as most of them in the company. Great Grandmother helped in cases of sickness and births as well as others where ever they were needed while on their trek to Utah. The pioneers reached Great Salt Lake Valley about September 20, 1848. They must have spent the winter in Salt Lake for on February 25, 1849, Grandmother gave birth to a son . . . HYRUM LEWIS IVIE [in Salt Lake] . . . From Salt Lake City they went to what was then called 'Rhodes' or Roads Valley and later called Provo Valley."

Our IVIE and BARTON ancestors, who arrived in the valley in September 1848, were soon joined by their son RICHARD and some other relations of the Mormon Battalion.

ELISHA KEMBER BARTON writes of his parents (my second-great-grandparents) JOHN and SUSANNAH BARTON:

"Under the leadership and direction of Brigham Young, the family journeyed westward with other families of Latter-day Saints . . . They knew fully the hardships, lack of food, Indian troubles and privations of the pioneers who crossed the plains at that time. They had been in Salt Lake City only a short time when they were asked to go to Bountiful, Davis County, Utah, and with the other Saints settle that territory. They lived in Bountiful about ten years. Three children were born there. They were EMILY ALICE, SYLVESTER AARON and ELISHA KEMBER [BARTON]." Barton Creek was named after this family. Presently, 1997, there is a street and subdivision named Barton Creek, located in the hills just southwest of the Bountiful LDS Temple.

Grandfather JAMES OSCAR IVIE told of his father and grandfather:

"After arriving in Salt Lake they were advised to go and settle Bountiful, which they [did], but were soon called to settle Provo and remained there until later orders."

From the Church Historical Collection:

"Sunday, Dec. 24, G.S.L. City was visited by a severe snow storm the previous night. The day was dull. Thomas Bullock and John D. Lee wrote out articles of agreements for extermination of birds and beasts and made out a list of 180 names . . . to carry on a war of extermination against all the ravens, hawks, owls, wolves, foxes, etc., now alive in the valley of the Great Salt Lake. Firstly, it is agreed that the two companies shall participate in a social dinner with their ladies . . . paid for by the company that produces the least number of game. Secondly, the game shall count as follows: the right wing of a raven counting one, a hawk or owl two, the wings of an eagle five, the skin of a minx or pole cat five, the skin of a wolf, fox, wild cat, or catamount ten, the pelt of a bear or panther fifty. No game shall be counted that has been killed previous to this date. Thirdly, the skins of the animals, and the wings of the birds, shall be produced by each hunter at the recorder's office, on the 1st day of February, 1849, at 10 a.m. for examination. Fourthly, ISAAC MORLEY and Reynolds Cahoon shall be the judges . . . Thomas Bullock be the clerk, to keep a record of each man's skill . . . Fifthly: The man who produces the most proofs of his success shall receive a public vote of thanks on the day of the feast."

[Note: This listing includes only the names of those people I know something about. The lists are much longer:

John D. Lee's company: Heber C Kimball, Willard Richards, Parley P. Pratt, John Young . . . JAMES R. ALLRED, Peter Conover . . . James Orr, Hosea Stout . . . Levi Stewart . . . Isaac Morley Jr. . . . . Jedediah M. Grant . . . Robert L. Campbell, GEORGE BEAN, JAMES IVIE, Justin Stoddard, FRANKLIN IVIE, John Higbee . . . William Matthews . . . CORNELIUS P. LOTT, SHADRACH ROUNDY(?) . . . William Pace . . . Lorenzo Snow . . . Levi Hancock . . . Daniel D. McArthur . . . and Zera Pulsipher.

John Pack's company: Brigham Young, Amasa M. Lyman, John Taylor, John Smith, Edward Hunter . . . Charles C. Rich, Daniel Garn, Daniel H. Wells . . . SHADRACH ROUNDY(?) . . . O. Porter Rockwell . . . Robins (from Jersey) . . . Erastus Snow . . . Dimick Huntington . . . Isaac Higbee . . . Abraham Conover . . . William M. Lemon . . . Joseph Fielding . . . Newel K. Whitney . . . Daniel Miller . . . Wm. Burgess." Check the original records for the complete list.]

~ 17 ~

"INTO THE LANDS THE INDIANS WANT THE MOST"
FORT UTAH—PROVO—UTE WAR

The mountaineers had told Brigham Young that the area east of the fresh water lake in the valley south of the Great Salt Lake was the best agricultural land, and in their opinion the best area to settle. They also told him that the Indians in that area were the most vicious and warlike in the whole territory. But Brigham Young knew where the Saints were to settle. He also said, "We'll settle that valley, too." But after talking to them at Fort Bridger, he changed his intended southern route, and his first company searched for the best northern route into the Salt Lake Valley. The wagon train of 1847 didn't need Indian troubles.

Not long after they arrived, scouting parties explored this southern beautiful valley and clear blue lake. Parley P. Pratt and John Higbee took a boat to check out the west side. The east side was the best. The grass was tall. The trout were huge. Wild life abounded. The lake was like the Sea of Galilee and they quickly named the river that flowed from it to the Great Salt Lake the Jordan River. There were Indians—actually, all the Ute bands of the valleys for 200 miles, east and south, would gather there because of the wonderful supply of fish moving up the stream from the lake to their spawning grounds every spring. GEORGE W. BEAN reported, "The river would be full from bank to bank as thick as they could swim for hours and sometimes days." Those who were called to settle this area would need to be fearless and capable, when the time came; but first the Saints would solidify in the more peaceful and less inhabitable Salt Lake Valley. With the arrival of the Saints in September 1848—increasing their population to about 5000, the need to expand the colonization to other areas became necessary for survival.

From the journal of GEORGE W. BEAN:

"Early in the spring of 1849 a move was made to commence a settlement at Provo, among the powerful tribe of Timpanodes, (Timpanogos). John S. and Isaac Higbee and Alex Williams gathered up a company of about thirty families, JAMES BEAN among the rest. They reached the river Provo the 1st of April."

[Note: Counting all members of these families, there were about 150 people. Numbered in this group, as given by Jensen in his 1924, *History of Provo*, were JAMES R. IVIE; ELIZA M. IVIE; WILLIAM F. IVIE; JOHN L. IVIE; POLLY ANN IVIE; ELIZABETH C. IVIE; JOSEPH O. IVIE; ELIZA IVIE; ISAAC T. IVIE; BENJAMIN M. IVIE; HYRUM S. IVIE; RICHARD A. IVIE; ELIZABETH IVIE; LUCENDA M. IVIE [maybe this was WILLIAM F. IVIE's new wife, MALINDA ?]; WILLIAM A. DAYTON; SARAH IVIE DAYTON; NANCY M. DAYTON; JAMES P. HIRAN; HENRY ZABRISKIE is named, but not his family, which were probably with him. JEROME ZABRISKIE was with RICHARD IVIE in the shirt incident which will be told later. JAMES (Jim) A. IVIE was not mentioned, but he was there. GEORGE W. and JAMES WILLIAM BEAN, from Illinois, would be related to us later, through marriage, when great-uncle WILLIAM FAUSETT joined this group and his daughter, HARRIET CATHERINE FAUSETT married JAMES ADDISON BEAN, a son of JAMES W. BEAN, 10 February 1853—additionally, MARY BEAN is shown in their genealogy as the wife of our fourth-great-grandfather ALEXANDER McKEE (North Carolina and Tennessee.)]

GEORGE BEAN's journal continues:

"About three miles out they were met, by a young brave, Angatewats by name, who placed himself on horseback across the trail in front of the foremost wagon and forbade them from proceeding further. Interpreter Dimie B. Huntington, who was with the Company pleaded with them to try the emigrants a while and see if they could not live in peace together, and after about an hour's delay, they were allowed to proceed in peace. They located on the south side of the [Provo] river, near the lower crossing.

"At the time of their arrival at Provo, the Timpanodes were governed by a chief called by the whites, Little Chief, but in about a month after this, he led a party of warriors to attack Wanship's band, north of Salt Lake City, and was killed in a battle up at Ogden hole, or north Ogden. [He was succeeded by] Opecary (Stick in the Head). There was also Old Elk, (Pareyarts), Old Battiste, (Tintic, his brother, Portsovic, Angatewats and other noted ones here, Old Sawiet, old Petnich, Walker and his brother, and old Uinta and his sons, Tabby, Graspero, and Niquia, old Antero, and some times Kanosh. These with their bands were accustomed to meet at Provo, and have a great good time, horse racing, trading, gambling and eating fish, for several weeks every year. There were some additions made to the [white] population at Provo during the summer, and in the fall when Indian troubles broke out, they were situated in the fort."

According to the *LDS Historian Office* records, a short time before the settlers arrived in Provo (on 28 February 1849) a company of 30 men, led by John Scott, had come into the valley in search of their cattle and the thieving Indians who had taken them. Finding the Utes on the Provo River, with Little Chief's son as a guide, they were led to a creek—present day Pleasant Grove. Here a battle ensued for three or four hours. The squaws and children were captured and the four bucks were killed. The skins of the fifteen cattle that they had killed were found nearby. This area became known as "Battle Creek." Jensen's History (1924) places this battle in September. He also adds:

> "The Provo Branch of the Latter-day Saints was organized on the 18th of March, 1849, with John S. Higbee as president and Isaac Higbee and Dimick Huntington as his counselors."

Jenson in 1924 describes the fort:

"On the third of April settlers commenced building 'Fort Utah,' located about 40 rods north of Center street, and twenty rods east of the Lake View or lower county road, approximately forty-five rods to the southeast of the wagon bridge across Provo River. It consisted of a stockade, fourteen feet high, with log houses inside, and an elevation in the center called a bastion, on which was placed a cannon commanding the surrounding country. The fort ran east and west, its dimensions being about twenty by forty rods. There were two windows for each room, one to the front, and the other to the rear. As the settlers had no glass, course cloth was used as a substitute in the windows."

Fort Utah at Provo

"There were gateways at the east and west ends of the fort; and at the southeast corner was a large stockade corral, in which the cattle were kept at night. Within the corral was a guard house. The logs for the fort were obtained from Box Elder Island, a forty acre tract lying between two channels of Provo River, about a mile west of the fort. Boxelder was preferred to cotton-wood as building material on account of its greater durability . . . By the middle of May the settlers had 225 acres of land laid out and apportioned to forty families, the colony having increased in number by the arrival of other settlers from Great Salt Lake Valley. The small grain had been sowed, and the principal part of the corn had been planted, but on the 23rd of May there was a severe snow storm, lasting nearly three hours, and on the night following, the frost was so severe that it destroyed the greater part of the vegetation . . . Independence day was celebrated by organizing a company of militia, this act being deemed necessary as a means of protection against the Indians. The company was placed under the command of Major Jefferson Hunt of the Mormon Battalion, and consisted of sixty men, including stalwart youths.

"On 30 August, a deplorable accident occurred. A hatful of powder having been secured from some emigrants, WILLIAM DAYTON [a former member of the Mormon Battalion and married to J. R. IVIE's daughter SARAH], who had some knowledge of cannons, assisted by GEORGE W. BEAN, gave a demonstration of the use of the cannon on the bastion. The gun had been fired and was being reloaded, but the gunners had failed to swab out the bore and insure against danger from remaining sparks. Suddenly as the charge was being rammed home, there was an explosion and the men were hurled from the bastion nearly half way to the gate. DAYTON was killed and BEAN seriously wounded. As there was no physician or surgeon in the colony, it became necessary to send for one. 'Hout' Conover started out at eight o'clock in the evening, soon after the accident occurred, and by hard riding and changing horses on the way, succeeded in bringing Dr. Blake from Centerville to the fort by four o'clock the next day. He had ridden 120 miles over rough roads in twenty hours . . . BEAN's wounds were dressed and his left forearm amputated [below] the elbow."

Captain Conover's first harvest of grain was remarkable. He describes it:

"We stayed at Millcreek [Salt Lake Valley], until 1849, when I was called to go and help settle Provo. The boys and I came up in March and built a house; then I went back and got my [motherless] family . . . I had only about two and one-half bushels of wheat, but I sowed that and raised one hundred and forty seven bushels. I had not had a morsel of bread in my house since the first of April until my crop was raised and thrashed. It was the first grain out, in Utah County.

"I cut it on the sixteenth of July. About an hour after, it rained as hard for an hour as I ever saw rain. It then cleared up and the sun came out as bright as if it had not rained. I had to let it lay out days before it was dry enough to thresh. I threshed it on the twentieth with a flail, cleaning it with the wind. Then my sons Abram and Charles took it to Neff's mill on Millcreek, forty miles away. It took them two days. When they got home my family had a feast of bread, and it was a feast. We had not tasted bread for about five months.

"Immediately after getting my wheat off the ground, a heavy rain came causing the wheat to sprout from stubble. It grew until it was taller than the first crop. It ripened and was a good heavy crop. Making two crops in one season, from one planting. It was the first crop raised in Utah Valley." [The event has probably not recurred in the county or state since that time.]

Conover's journal continues:

"In July was organized a Military Company. Jefferson Hunt, was elected Captain and I was first Lieutenant. In the fall of 1849, Captain Hunt was called to pilot a company of Emigrants to San Bernadino on the Southern Route. I was then chosen Captain and remained commander of the Company until after the Indian War in 1860.

"In the summer of 1849, P. P. Pratt and others took a company and went down south exploring the country as far down as the Colorado River. They started back in November. The snow was up to their saddle girths. When they got to Buttermilk Fort, they were snow bound.

"They left their wagons and cattle and twenty-five men, and the rest came on. Before they got to Provo their horses gave out; their provisions were gone and they were starving. Parley took the best animal and came for relief. Soon we had two bushel sacks of biscuits and other food. Two of us started back for the perishing men and met them at what we now call Payson. Nearly all of them were starving and perishing with the cold."

Family tradition tells us that young JOHN LEHI IVIE went with this expedition. Jensen writes:

"For some time after the settlement of Provo the Indians were quite friendly. They sometimes visited the fort in large numbers, but made no hostile demonstrations. They were inveterate beggars, however, and often made themselves nuisances.

"In September [1849] . . . a company of emigrants on their way to the California gold fields camped near Provo. Needing horses, they traded guns and ammunition to the Indians for them, and so supplied the savages with the means of hostilities.

"The Indians grew less friendly in their behavior, and became bold in their thievery and other depredations. They stole grain from the fields, drove off cattle, and shot arrows at the boys getting wood in the river bottoms. Pitch pine knots were sometimes tied to their arrows, ignited and shot into the fort. They did no damage, however, as the houses were covered with dirt, and could not be fired. But when these blazing arrows were shot into the corral and chanced to light on the back of cattle, there was trouble enough. The piece of sinew holding the knot would burn, letting the arrow fall to the ground but leaving the flaming knot on the animal's back. A fierce bellowing would ensue, greatly frightening the women and children in the fort.

"The settlers endeavored to frighten the Indians by firing the fort cannon, but the savages were not to be awed by sound and smoke . . . Whenever the settlers came outside the fort, the Indians would fire on them; the stockade was virtually in a state of siege."

Gottfredson's *Indian Depredation"* records:

"The first serious outbreak was occasioned by three of our people, namely: RICHARD A. IVIE, Rufus Stoddard and JEROME ZABRISKIE, who met an Indian called Bishop Whitney, in the field and claimed a shirt [a hickory shirt of special value] the Indian had on. The Indian refused to give it up. IVIE claimed it as his and tried to take it, was resisted . . ."

John Clark, another early settler said, "The Indian had stolen the shirt from a clothesline. When the owner attempted to take the shirt from the Indian, the red man made an attempt to shoot him with a bow and arrow; but another white man quickly raised his gun and fired, killing the Indian."

Gottfredson stated, "His body weighted with rock, was sunk in the river. So reported by the Indians, who found the body after a 24 hours search. This killing of the Old Bishop, so called, occurred about the 1st of August, 1849, and immediately caused great excitement amongst the Indians . . . They first demanded the murderers, which, of course, was refused by the whites. They then required compensation in cattle and horses, but nothing was ever given, and shortly after this cattle and horses were found with arrows sticking in them, several persons were shot at while in the woods and other places . . . The leading Indians ordered the people off their lands. They made serious threats in case of failure to leave and stock was stolen from time to time . . . Our militia company continued to practice almost daily . . . towards Christmas, open war seemed inevitable. The measles got among our people and from there to the natives . . . from them the disease spread through the tribe."

Conover wrote:

"In the winter of 1849, the Indians became very troublesome. They would not let us go after our stock, or after wood, without shooting at us. We put up with it until February, trying to keep peace with them, but all in vain. They called us old women and cowards, and that we were afraid to fight them. The Bishop appointed Miles Weaver and myself to go and see President Young, to see what was best to do. We rode the fifty miles in four hours and laid the case before Brigham. He ordered out fifty men, to come back with us. One hundred and fifty (150)."

Jensen explained it this way:

"Governor Young on receiving the message, found himself in a somewhat peculiar position . . . The thought of more fighting and bloodshed was most repugnant to him . . . 'Feed them and not fight them,' was his life-long motto and policy toward the red men . . . Fortunately, there was a government officer on the grounds, a brave and honorable man, Captain Howard Stansbury. It being evident—all conciliatory efforts having failed—that force must be employed to put an end to the aggressions of the savages, the Captain was asked by Governor Young and other officials for an expression of opinion as to what view the Government would probably take of it. 'I did not hesitate to say to them,' says Stansbury, 'that in my judgment the contemplated expedition against these savage marauders was a measure not only of good policy, but one of absolute necessity and self-preservation.'

"He therefore warmly approved of it, and not only that, but at Governor Young's request permitted Lieutenant Howland to accompany the expedition as its adjutant, and contributed arms, ammunition, tents and camp equipage for the soldiers. Dr. Blake, of the Stansbury party, acted as surgeon for the expedition.

"A company of fifty minute men under Captain George D. Grant started from Salt Lake City, Feb. 7, 1850, followed by fifty others, commanded by Major Andrew Lytle. Colonel Scott had been ordered to go, but declined, for which he was afterwards court-martialed. Major Lytle went in his stead. [It seems that Scott felt reprimanded and perhaps ostracized by many because of his previous encounter with the Indians at Battle Creek. Many of the early settlers came from areas of peace and calm and had little conception of the life-threatening danger of an angry Indian.] The expedition set out early in February, 1850. The weather was extremely cold, and the snow, frozen and hard-crusted, was over a foot deep in the valleys. Progress was therefore rendered very difficult. Captain Grant's cavalry, after marching all night, on the morning of the 8th, arrived at

Provo River. Such a march was deemed necessary in order to take the Indians unaware and secure an advantageous position."

JOHN LEHI IVIE's federal pension paper reads:

"Enrolled on or about the 15th day of January, 1850, as a private in Company Infantry, commanded by George Grant . . . commanded by Andrew Lytle . . . in the war with the Indians, known as the Timpanoga and the Walker Tribe . . ."

JAMES RUSSELL IVIE is recorded in an old handwritten book of *Commissioned Officers* as a lieutenant. All his older sons fought in this battle, as would all the able-bodied men.

"The militia found the settlers in their fort on the south side of the stream, and the Indians strongly entrenched in the willows and timber of the river-bottom, a mile or two above. They were protected not only by the river-bank, but by a breastwork of cotton-wood trees which they felled. Near by their strong-hold stood a double log house facing the river. This house, built by JAMES A. BEAN [maybe this should read JAMES W. BEAN, his father?] and sons . . . had been deserted . . . taking refuge at the fort. The house was now held by the savages who, during the battle, kept up a continuous fire from its windows and crevices . . . Captain Conover, commander at the fort, united his men with Captain Grant's, and the main forces then proceeded to occupy a position near the deserted building, about a half a mile south-west of the log house mentioned. The Indians were led by Chiefs Elk and Ope-Carry—surnamed 'Stick-in-the-Head'—the latter, like Sowiette, rather friendly with the whites, while Elk . . . was more like the warlike Walker. Ope-Carry, it seems, desired peace, and had come out of the redoubt to talk with Dimick B. Huntington, the interpreter, when Elk and his warriors opened fire, and the battle was thus begun."

Conover's journal further explains:

"The night we were in the City, the Indians came down and stole four head of Captain Hunt's cows out of his corral, near the fort and killed them. The one-hundred and fifty men got into Provo the next night, so the Indians did not know that reinforcements had arrived. The next day we started after them. A little after sunrise, I with my company crossed the river, right by the fort and up on the west side of the river, and came above their camp with sixty men.

"Alex. Williams, Lieutenant, took thirty men and went up on the east side of the river. When we got to their camp, I ordered the Company to face to the right and march right down to the river. They were camped on the east side of the river. When we got to the river we saw that their horses were all between the camp and the river. I called for some of the men to go with me to get their horses. The Indians began to shoot at us. One old Indian climbed up a tree to see where we were, but he forgot how to climb and fell down head first. Jumping up and knowing that I was Captain, he tried hard to shoot me. He fired six shots at me. One ball came so near me that it blistered my cheek. But through the protection of a kind Providence I did not receive a scratch.

"We fought until sundown. The wounded and dead we sent down to the fort. Colonel Grant ordered us to go to the Fort to get our supper, as we had had nothing to eat since morning. When we started down, the Indians followed us shooting at us all the way. There were eight wounded that day.

"Old Ankatowats and family were on the west side of the river, even with the Fort. They said they would not fight the Mormons, so we thought we had better bring them into the fort so they could not telegraph movements to the other Indians. The next morning I took ten men and went over before sunrise and brought them into the Fort . . . The snow was three feet deep on the level all over the country."

Jensen continues:

"The engagement lasted two days, during which time an almost incessant fusillade was kept up between the white assailants and the dusky defenders of the river redoubt. Artillery was also employed against the savages, but with little effect, as they were right under the bank, and most of the balls passed harmlessly over . . . The Indians would make frequent sorties, and after delivering their fire, return to cover. Again, they would thrust their gun barrels through the snow lying deep upon the banks above them, and momentarily raising their heads high enough to take aim, discharge their broad-side at the besiegers. They fought so stubbornly that all efforts to dislodge them for a time proved futile. They killed Joseph Higbee, son of Isaac Higbee—then president of the settlement—and wounded several others of the attacking force.

"Finally, in the afternoon of the second day, (Feb. 9th) Captain Grant, whose care had been to expose his men as little as possible, determined to capture the log-house at all hazards. He therefore ordered Lieutenant William H. Kimball, with fifteen picked men, to charge upon the house and take it . . . Kimball and his men proceeded up the river until directly opposite the log-house, which now intervened between them and the stream. They turned to the left, facing the rear of the house, and the leader gave the word of charge. Dashing forward through a ravine that for some moments hid them from view, the horsemen emerged upon the flat and were within a few rods of the house, in the act of crossing a small slough, when a roaring volley from the log citadel met them. Isham Flyn was wounded and the charge was momentarily checked. Several swept on, however, and the Indians hastily vacating the house, fled to their entrenchments.

"The first two troopers to gain the house were Lot Smith and Robert T. Burton, who, riding around to the front of the building, entered the passage between the two compartments. Bullets whizzed past them, splintering the wood-work all around, but both they and their horses were soon under shelter. Their companions, a moment later, gathered to the rear of the house, and none too soon, for the Indians, recovering from their surprise, began pouring their volleys into the ranks of cavalry and upon the captured building. Half the horses were instantly killed and their riders escaped by miracle. Lieutenant Kimball . . . and others, darting around the corner of the house, gained the inside, while others waited until an opening had been made in the rear.

"To support the cavalry charge, Captain Grant ordered forward a small detachment of infantry. These men, ten in number, were a portion of Captain Conover's command, and were led by Jabez B. Nowlin. On reaching the log-house, with saw and ax they effected an entrance at the rear. Some, however, went around the corner into the passage, and were fired upon by the savages; Nowlin being wounded in the nose. The services of a surgeon was now in demand. Seeing that something was wrong, Captain Grant requested Hiram B. Clawson, General Wells' aide, who had accompanied the expedition, to ride to the house and ascertain what was needed. He did so, performing the hazardous feat successfully, though bullets sung past him as he rode. His friends at the house, seeing him coming, redoubled their volleys and drew most of the Indians fire in their direction. Returning, Colonel Clawson reported that surgical aid was at once required for the wounded. He and his cousin, Steven Kinsey, a surgeon, then rode back to the building. Returning, the two were again fired upon, one bullet just missing Clawson's head and piercing Kinsey's hat. Later another ball came nigh hitting Clawson and went through Kensey's trousers. Both, however, escaped unhurt. Meantime, Lieutenant Howland had conceived the idea of a movable battery, to operate against the Indian redoubt."

Conover states:

"We had a lot of sleds made of two inch planks. We fastened them together and made breastworks of them, fastening blankets on the side next to us. [The outside was covered with brush and boughs.] We pushed it ahead of us and when the Indians would shoot, the balls would go through the two inch planks and strike the blankets and fall to the ground. The Indians did not understand this kind of work and began to get scared, and try to run away. A few of the men stayed and fought until night. When we started down for our supper again, they followed us, yelling, like demons. Then about half way to the fort we turned and gave them a volley, and they scampered back in a hurry."

Jensen continues:

"Accordingly, that evening, they opened a furious fire upon the position held by the troops, and under cover of the darkness withdrew . . . General Wells, who had been sent for to take charge of further operations, arrived next morning, Feb. 10th, but on preparing to attack the Indians it was discovered that they had gone. One party, the smaller band, had retreated in the direction of Rock Canyon, a rough and difficult gorge a little north-east of Provo, [the beautiful, craggy, boxed, canyon just north of "Y" mountain behind BYU's extended campus and the LDS Provo Temple] while the main party had fled southward in the direction of Spanish Fork. A dead squaw—the one killed by a cannon shot—was found in the Indian encampment; also two or three warriors, dead or dying. Elk, the chief, subsequently died of wounds received during the siege. His being wounded had probably disheartened the savages and caused the retreat quite as much as Lieutenant Howland's battery . . . Some of the Indians, more friendly than their fellows, had deserted their ranks, before the fighting began, taking refuge with the white families in the fort.

"Detailing certain men to garrison the stockade, and others to pursue the Rock Canyon refugees, Gen. Wells, with the main body of the cavalry, set out upon the trail of the Indians who had gone southward. At Spanish Fork and Pe-teet-neet [now Payson]—short skirmishes occurred, and eventually, on Feb. 11th, the Indians were overtaken near Table Mountain, at the south end of Utah Lake. Another battle ensued, and the Indians were practically annihilated. Most of the fighting took place on the ice, which was very slippery, making it extremely difficult for the horses to keep their feet. The Indians, being shot at, would fall, as if dead, and then, as their pursuers drew near, rise up and fire. They killed several horses in this manner, but none of the cavalrymen were hurt.

"Night came down, and a bitter night it was. The soldiers were forced to take refuge in the wickiups vacated by the Indians on the bleak mountainside . . . these primitive shelters swarmed with vermin . . . On returning to Fort Utah, General Wells found that Major Lytle [JOHN LEHI IVIE was a private under Major Andrew Lytle, the former lieutenant in the Mormon Battalion] and Captain Lamereus, joining their forces, had pursued the other band of Indians up Rock Canyon. The fate of these savages was similar to that of their fellows at Table Mountain. The total

Indian loss was about forty, more than half the number of warriors engaged. Efforts were made to civilize the squaws and papooses who were captured, but as a rule without avail. They lived with the whites during the winter, but in the spring again sought their native mountains. A treaty of peace was entered into between the settlers and the Indians, and the latter now agreed to be friendly and molest their white neighbors no more."

JOHN LEHI IVIE was honorably discharged 5 April 1850. Conover adds:

"The second day of the fight, Black Hawk (a boy then), shot at me twice, with a bow and arrows. One struck my buckle and cut half way through. The other one struck my scabbard; but my time had not come. I don't think I was born to be killed by an Indian."

In Peter Conover's handwritten record, he spelled his name as Cownover. Although his spelling of his own name should be correct, all other records leave out the "w." I have used the other spelling to avoid confusion.

This narrative is told in the book *The CARTERS of Provo, Utah:*

"The Indians were camped just at the bottom of the Provo dugway. There was a young brave died and the Indians had a big bonfire and danced around it all night. The white people didn't dare go to bed because they didn't know what the Indians were planning. Just after daylight a young squaw came running into Provo and ran into Sister Elmore's house and went under her bed. Her head was bleeding a stream. Mrs. Elmore got her to come out from under the bed and she bandaged the wound. In a little while the Indians came hunting her. They told the white people her mate had died and they must kill her and put her in with him. They hunted and couldn't find her so they went back to their camp. In a little while they came back again. By this time Edset Elmore had got home. He could talk the Indian language. He talked to them and finally they promised they wouldn't hurt her if she would come back to the wigwam. So in a few days she went back home but she came every morning for Mrs. Elmore to doctor her head. The wound in her head was where they had tried to kill her by hitting her in the head with a tomahawk, but she ran just as they hit her and her life was spared."

JOHN H. CARTER and his two wives and children arrived in Provo, Utah, 3 October 1850. He was a blacksmith and had a shop in downtown Provo. He bought eighty acres of land, including Carterville on the Provo River bottom with the Orem and Provo sagebrush bench above.

~ 18 ~

SLEEPING WITH THE RATTLESNAKES, SANPETE COUNTY SETTLED 1849

Chief Walker had invited Brigham Young to send settlers to *Sandpeetch* to teach his people to farm; so during the fall LDS General Conference of 1849, church leaders called those who were to go, and the action was sustained by the general church membership. With ISAAC MORLEY, a band of 224 colonists and 240 cattle set out for their new home going south past Fort Utah, west of Mount Nebo, then southeast down Salt Creek Canyon, east of present-day Nephi, 28 October 1849. Although winter travel was difficult, it was common for the early settlers to journey in the winter so they would be established in time to plant their early crops. This would be the fifth area settled, being proceeded by the Salt Lake Valley, Bountiful, Ogden, and Provo.

Unfortunately, the winter of 1849-50 was severe, the worst in memory, according to Indians of that area. They arrived on the present hill-site of the Manti Temple 19 November 1849.

> "This is a long, narrow canyon and not even a jack rabbit could exist on its desert soil," complained counselor Seth Taft. But stubborn MORLEY countered, "This is our God-appointed place and stay I will, though but 10 men remain with me."

But the rabbits proved a blessing to these hungry settlers. The group dug into the hillside making shallow shelters and living in these and in their wagons—turned end to end. It was a miserable winter with snow ten to twenty feet deep in Salt Creek Canyon. Unable to get further supplies they devoured the rabbits. The saying went:

Rabbits young and rabbits old;
Rabbits hot and rabbits cold;
Rabbits tender and rabbits tough;
Thank the Lord, we've had rabbits enough.

Keeping the cattle alive through the winter became a great challenge. Spiteful Indians had burned off the grasses. The herd was taken two miles south and daily the men and boys shoveled snow to get down to the vegetation. Regardless, the animals began to die and their carcasses were given to the Indians, who smiled at these foolish white people who seemed to prefer biscuits. These were the people who were supposed to help them learn to survive? By spring they had only 113 cattle that must be fed and prepared to pull the plows for the spring planting.

As welcome as spring was, it brought an unexpected terror. A slithering, rattling sound alarmed the colony when they discovered the source to be an invasion of great, gaunt, spotted-back rattlesnakes that were hibernating in nearby caves and were attracted to the warmth of their campfires. With torches the men searched them out and in one night claimed they had killed three hundred snakes. The invasion continued several weeks and they considered it a miracle that no one was bitten. It was a bit unsettling to find a rattlesnake as your bed partner when you awoke.

The Indians proved to be poor students at land cultivation. It seemed wiser and more satisfying for them to fish and hunt. And Chief Walker was unpredictable. On one occasion, Walker and five hundred to seven hundred warriors returned from a raid on the Shoshones. They set up their wickiups in a semicircle around the Manti campsite and celebrated their victory for two weeks. Captive squaws were forced to sing and dance with the heads of their family members stuck on poles—a reminder to the new colonizers that Chief Walker and his braves should not be taken lightly.

Among these early settlers with ISAAC MORLEY was JAMES T. S. ALLRED. At Council Bluffs, JAMES enlisted in the Mormon battalion in company A, and was discharged in Salt Lake City 29 July 1847 with the Pueblo, Colorado, group. His wife had accompanied him. At first he made adobes in Great Salt Lake City, but in May 1849, he was sent with ten others, by President Young, to construct a bridge across the Platte River. They ferried teams at $4 each wagon, at the rate of seventy per day. He cleared $1000 and returned to Salt Lake City with an outfit of two wagons, four yoke of oxen, four cows and a heifer, with all kinds of merchandise picked up on the river, having been left by emigrants. He brought a good supply of seed wheat, which was taken to Manti in Captain ISAAC MORLEY's company of thirty. He also took a whip-saw and sawed lumber there and in other settlements. The first winter was severe, and he lost nine head of stock and fed most of his seed wheat.

On 22 March 1852, he and his father, with their families, went north to an area with many springs of clear, pure water at the foot of Horseshoe Mountain. At first it was called Springtown, or the Allred Settlement—today Spring City. Arriving first, he brought a log house ready to put up and cover with boards. He erected it the first day. The company consisted of JAMES, his wife and two children, his father, wife and son ANDREW J., their three grandchildren, and CHARLES WHITLOCK, GEORGE M. ALLRED and JAMES F. ALLRED, with an Indian boy and girl he had bought from the Utes. Others came in the fall. On 29 July 1853, they lost all their stock to the Indians and returned to Manti, but in October they were back in Springtown.

ISAAC MORLEY's close friends, the CARTER family, who had been with his company of Saints from Maine to Kirtland, to Far West, and then back to Lima, Hancock County, Illinois, joined him in Sanpete County. From the book *The CARTERS of Provo, Utah*:

> "JOHN H. CARTER and family moved from Provo to Manti for a short time, then to Nephi." The 1850 Census of Utah for the City of Manti, County of San Pete, State of Deseret lists "JOHN CARTER age 33 born in Maine; ELIZABETH age 32, SOPHIA age 23 also born in Maine; MARRIETTE age 9—Illinois; JOHN age 4—Iowa; HARRISON and LIBBA age 2—Iowa."

[Note: The CARTER's had moved to Nephi [called Salt Creek] by 1852. The bishop's ward report of that year includes them among their ward members as follows: JOHN CARTER. Their children: SAMUEL CARTER b. 8 Sept 1840 [died on the plains coming to Utah]; MARY ETT CARTER b 11 Dec 1842; LORENZO CARTER b 9 April 1844 [died on plains coming to Utah]; JOHN HIRUM CARTER b 17 Aug 1847; HARRISON MARTIN 'Haas' CARTER b. 4 April 1849; DOMINICUS 'Mink' CARTER b 20 Apr 1852.]

Uncle THOMAS C. IVIE has not been mentioned since he joined with General Kearny as one of the fifteen body guards on his journey from Los Angles to

Fort Leavenworth. Kearny left his guard there and continued onward to report to the President in Washington, D.C. The battalion guard followed the Missouri River northward to Winter Quarters. We know that TOM was in Winter Quarters or Council Bluffs 20 January 1848 for his name appears on a petition with over a thousand other names:

"To the Honorable Postmaster General of the United States."

It was a request that "there being no Post Office within forty or fifty miles of said Tabernacle, and the public good requires a convenient office." The names appear to be listed in the order that the petition was signed with close households signing together.

[Note: On page 2, the name of M. M. SANDERS is followed by JOHN SANDERS, DAVID SANDERS and JOSEPH SANDERS. On page 6 we find the names THOMAS K IVIE, George D. Grant, Robert Campbell, George A. Smith, JOHN BARTON, Edward Johnson, and WM. F. IVY. Later on this page are the names of WARREN FOOTE, R. N. ALLRED and THOMAS DOBSON. On page 10 are the names of JOHN STAKER, ANDREW J. ALLRED, Tailor Bird, JAMES ALLRED, W. E. Wilson, John C. L. Smith, Heman Hyde, William Draper jur., Robert Waltz, JOHN F. ALLRED and, further down on the page, WM. HYDE and REUBEN ? ALLRED. Page 11 lists WILLIAM FAUSETT, JOSEPH FAUSETT and WILLIAM FOLLETT. On page 13 is Hyrum Dayton, WILLIAM DAYTON, Lysander Dayton, Meroura Dayton, Almon F. Dayton, Alma T. Dayton.]

According to family records, THOMAS CELTON (or KELTON) and his wife AMANDA MOORE IVIE had a child born in Council Bluffs, 8 December 1848. RICHARD IVIE, another member of the *Mormon Battalion,* who was at Sutter's mill when gold was discovered in California, and his wife ELIZABETH DOBSON IVIE, are listed with the first Provo settlers in the spring of 1849. THOMAS C. IVIE's name was not included, nor any of his family.

The first record I found of him in Provo was on 19 May 1852 when THOS. C. IVIE signed a petition with many others in Provo. In George A. Smith's report of his trip to Utah County, 23 November 1854, he reports:

"Horace Roberts has erected quite a large dwelling house, also THOMAS IVIE; a number of others are in progress."

Earlier records show THOMAS' child, AMOS E. IVIE, was born in Nevada; then the following child was born in Provo, 9 August 1852. This suggests, that THOMAS was part of a very early settlement in Douglas County, Nevada, at the foot of the Sierra Nevada Mountains—the valley below the southern shore of Lake Tahoe which was settled in 1851. It was first called Mormon Station; then later named Genoa—the first town in Nevada. Perhaps he visited the

California gold fields through this period of time. It was not until 1855 that the Lytle family was called to help colonize the Carson Valley.

The last mention of the BARTON family was their arrival in Bountiful. Quoting from my mother's first cousin, neighbor, and close friend, IDA BELLE GLEDHILL (Christensen, Buchanan,) she tells us:

"My father, THOMAS GLEDHILL, used to say Grandmother MARY CATHERINE [his mother-in-law] was the most beautiful woman he'd ever seen. She was refined, kind spoken, thrifty and made a fine home. She had black curly hair, and laughing eyes. Aunt IDA told me she had met an old friend of her mother's in Bountiful, who said, 'She was the prettiest, and most popular girl in their crowd. She was loved by everyone who knew her. When she married we all hated to have her leave Bountiful.'"

JOHN LEHI IVIE, the energetic, capable fifteen year-old handsome youth, who could hunt buffalo and ride with such dexterity, was also greatly admired, not only by his peers, but by his older brothers and leaders within the company. The attraction between the two young people was so strong that the distance between Bountiful and Provo could not separate them. Both needed to grow up—at least, a little more. On 16 May 1852, the two were married. MARY CATHERINE was nearly fifteen years old, and JOHN was eighteen. Their son, my grandfather, JAMES OSCAR IVIE, said they were called with the early settlers to settle Sanpete County, in Springtown. His great-uncle JAMES ALLRED's group was called to strengthen the Manti settlement and proceeded south in the spring of 1852, which may have hastened this young marriage.

As the Indians became more treacherous, JOHN LEHI IVIE, brought his wife, MARY CATHERINE, to Provo for the birth of their first child, JOSEPH ALMA IVIE, who was born 21 May 1853. The young son died the same day. Indian troubles became worse that summer and JOHN LEHI IVIE enlisted in the Provo militia in July [Chief Walker's War], defending their home and fort at Springtown, as well as Utah Valley and the Fillmore area, which was then being settled.

In the book, *Mount Pleasant* compiled by Longsdorf in 1939, we get a little different perspective of the events than in the usual accounts of this war, which focus on Utah County. In 1853, the Springtown residents used a sawmill that was located on Pleasant Creek. They called this settlement *Hambleton* [the later settlement was named Mount Pleasant].

"In the early summer of 1853, while most of the able bodied men were away . . . in Salt Lake City for supplies, Chief Walker and a band of painted warriors, demanded that Charles Shumway and others, against whom Walker had grievances, be delivered to them that they might be tortured and put to death. When this demand naturally was not granted, Walker threatened to massacre all the people then in camp, mostly women and children and old men. Preparations were made to resist the attack. However, the aged Chief Sowiette pleaded with his people to let the white man alone, and his policy of peace again prevailed.

"On July 9th, a band of blood thirsty Indians fired upon guards at the Hambleton and Potter sawmill, but were forced back. Before this they had made many attempts to take the stock belonging to the Hambleton settlement. Once they tried to take them out of the corral, which, however, was well guarded. On this occasion they had crawled in the bed of the creek until they were opposite the corral which stood on the bend of the creek. They then jumped in and attempted to stampede the cattle, but the guards discovered them in time and the Indians fled.

"Chief Walker, humiliated at what he termed cowardice of his tribe, mounted his pony and rode off to the mountains to hide, no doubt thinking Sowiette's followers would come to him. He and his followers remained surly, and frequent pow wows were held in the mountains. On the 18th day of July [1853], Arropine, a brother of Chief Walker, enraged at being caught stealing cattle, killed Alexander Keel, a guard at Payson. This act, it is said, was the beginning of the noted Walker Indian War which lasted three years." [The "Mormons" never declared war, only defended themselves. The Indians had already been on the warpath, but at this point the militia organized and helped to defend their communities. This may be why this incident has been called the beginning of the war. Peace treaties were signed, but depredations didn't always stop. The Indians were not a united nation.]

"During the night of July 19th, they again made an attempt to make a raid on the corralled cattle but they were fired upon by guards, and two of the Indians were killed. The other Indians made their retreat, carrying with them their dead comrades and leaving behind them a gun and a blood-covered blanket.

"On July 20th, in a raid made upon the cattle at Manti, several head were stolen. An attack was also made on the range near Nephi. At Springville, after the Indians had wounded William Jolly, the people became alarmed and in order to protect their homes and families, they were at once organized. Captain P. W. Conover, with a company of fifty men, was sent from Provo to assist the settlers at Hambleton, and on July

23rd, the troops met the savages at Hambleton's and Potter's mill, where a fierce and bloody battle followed, resulting in the death of six warriors, while the others fled to the mountains. [According to Conover's journal, his command followed the Indians and tried to collect the stolen animals, while Manti's Higgins and his men protected the homeland. A day later, word came from Brigham Young that Conover and his men were to return back to Provo, which they did.]

"The few settlers at Hambleton were not considered strong enough to protect themselves against the savages, and the following morning the veterans and their families, cattle, and provisions were moved to Allred's Settlement [Springtown], about six miles south, where about fifteen families had settled and built a fort in 1852. While the settlers were rushing to Allred's Settlement for shelter, their wagons, homes, saw mill, and lumber at the mouth of the canyon were burned and destroyed by the raging Indians who were on the war path.

"The Indians did not wait long before making another attack, and on Sunday, August the 2nd, they attacked Allred's Settlement; they rounded up all the cattle, leaving only a few calves which had been corralled, and drove them towards the mountains. The herders were fired upon and forced to flee to the fort for protection, while the Indians with loud shrieks and yells, waving their arms and red blankets, rode away in defiance. For the purpose of recovering their cattle and horses, a posse was at once organized and was soon upon the trail of the Indians. When they neared the herd, a number of Indians rushed with Indian strategy back toward the fort as if to attack the wives and children left there, and the posse was compelled to return to protect their families. When they neared the fort, the Indians fled towards the mountains, joining those of their tribe who were rushing on with the cattle. Two of the herding ponies escaped from the band and returned to the fort. This gave the settlers means of communication with Manti, the only point from which they could hope to obtain help.

"A messenger was immediately dispatched and by riding west and then south across the valley, succeeded in evading the Indian scouts. The messenger reached Manti at three o'clock in the afternoon, having made one of the quickest trips so far recorded. When the news reached Manti, drums were beat and the cattle were rounded up at once. Sentries were posted at all important points, while hasty preparations were made to send relief to Allred's Settlement. A number of good wagons, drawn by ox teams, accompanied by teamsters and twelve mounted guards left as soon as it was possible, arriving at the little settlement at daylight the following morning.

The settlers were then taken to Manti and given quarters in the fort, which had been erected there that year. From here, with the aid of the militia, some of the settlers returned to their farms at Hambleton, to irrigate their lands and harvest their crops which turned out quite well considering the circumstances."

~ 19 ~

DISCONTENT WITH FORT UTAH AND CHIEF WALKER'S WARPATH EXPANDS

Going back to the spring of 1850, the Provo River overflowed. Members of the Church Presidency arrived and observed pools of water extending to and beyond the Fort. They rode out approximately two miles east and southward and found an area they said was a very eligible place to build a new larger fort as a residence. But the people had additional concerns. They had crops to plant—building another fort required a lot of time, some people were not living in the Fort, and they wanted more freedom to live close to their land with individual lots of their own.

Partially following the admonition of their religious leaders to establish a new fort, the original fort was soon rapidly vacated as a place of residence; but they were slow in building or moving into a new fort at the new location. However, there was still the continuing danger of Chief Walker and his Indians, and the Church leadership urged the people to protect themselves and complete the new fort.

In the summer of 1850, Peter Conover's journal reads:

"Walker, the war chief of all the Ute Nation, came down to Provo, with a very large force, with the full intention of massacreing all the Mormons and clearing them out of the Country. Old Soweette, another chief, but a friend of the Mormons, came right after Walker did, with a large force of friendly Indians. He . . . told us what Walker was going to do, and told me, Walker should not come into the fort as long as he (Sowiette) lived, for he and his men were going to fight for us. He came in the night. I immediately waked every man in the fort that had a gun and had [them] stand guard . . . Sowiette, would not allow them to fight. At last they all went away together . . . We stood guard night and day until they went away."

This stopped his plan in Utah County, but other areas were molested and cattle and horses continued to disappear.

A charter was granted to Provo by the Legislative Assembly and a city council came into existence on 28 April 1851. They met at the school house in Fort Utah at four o'clock and at once established their rules of procedure. Ellis Eames was selected as Provo's first mayor. Three of the elected aldermen and ten of the councilors were present at the original city officers' meeting. The councilors who were present included JAMES R. IVIE, JONATHAN O. DUKE, DAVID CLUFF, George A. Smith, DOMINICUS CARTER (in place of William Pace who had moved to Salt Lake City), and others.

[Note: The first ordinance passed by the council required every able bodied male citizen over the age of 18 years residing within the limits of the City Corporation to work one day on the public road when called on by the supervisor. If they refused they paid a two dollar fine.

The second ordinance passed stated that timber that was cut and not hauled within 30 days should become the property of any citizen.

The third ordinance required all persons who owned land to make a good substantial fence—acceptable to the 'fence viewer.'

The fourth ordinance on 3 May 1851 prohibited the erection of fences, hedges or ditches that prohibit entrance into timber areas.

Ordinance 5 prohibited persons leaving open any gate, bars, or fences. Punishment was the paying of all damages that might result.

Ordinance 6 was regarding the proper use of water and the cleaning and repair of the ditches.

On 13 June 1851, a 1% sales tax was imposed, with a $100.00 fine as a penalty for not complying.

On 27 June 1851, an ordinance was passed with a penalty against citizens who violated the peace on the Sabbath day by horse racing and other rude behavior.

On 14 May 1853, the assessor was given directions for assessing property taxes.

6 August 1853, the city council passed an ordinance stating "that any person or persons that are found guilty of willful stealing or destroying any melons, corn, potatoes, or other property of any description shall be fined or publicly whipped and pay four fold at the discretion of those having jurisdiction."]

People continued to move away from the fort. A petition from 126 persons was sent to Brigham Young asking for a new organization of that stake 31 May 1852. As a result George A. Smith was appointed to preside and "a portion of his family are about to locate themselves at Provo." On 22 August 1852, President Smith made the choice of DOMINICUS CARTER (MARY ETT CARTER's uncle) and Isaac Higbee as his counselors. A high council of the stake was organized, consisting of the following members: Asahel Perry, Thomas Guyman, James A. Smith, Samuel Clark, JAMES R. IVIE, Harlow Redfield, Aaron Johnson, William Pace, John Banks, Peter W. Conover, David Canfield, and William Miller.

During August, 1852, Provo was divided into five ecclesiastical wards, and the following men were selected as bishops: First Ward, JONATHAN OLD-HAM DUKE; Second Ward, James Bird; Third Ward, Elias H. Blackburn; Fourth Ward, William Madison Wall; Fifth Ward, WILLIAM FAUSETT. The boundaries were probably as follows: First Ward, that part of the city south of Center Street and east of Fourth West Street; Second Ward, south of Center Street and west of Fourth West Street; Third Ward, north of Center Street and west of Fourth West Street; Fourth Ward, east of Fourth West Street, and lying between Center Street and Eleventh North; and the Fifth Ward was north of Provo Fourth Ward.

The log school house had been moved from the fort to a block north of the public square and an additional two wings in the center were added. It continued to be used as a meeting house during the winter months. In the summer time the people met for worship, celebrations, and other purposes in a large *bowery*, which had been erected on the public square [now Pioneer Park].

In the spring of 1853, Peter W. Conover was appointed colonel. Early in 1854 the militia of Utah County was reorganized into seven battalions of infantry and one of cavalry and in 1855 into a brigade with Colonel Peter W. Conover unanimously elected brigadier-general. On 6 July 1857, the following officers were unanimously elected: William Byron Pace, colonel; JONATHAN O. DUKE, 1st major, 1st Battalion; Lyman L. Woods, 2nd major, 2nd Battalion; WILLIAM A. FOLLETT, 3rd major, 3rd Battalion; JOHN L. IVIE, 4th major, 4th Battalion, and DOMINICUS CARTER, chief of music.

From Andrew Jensen's *History of Provo*:

"It appears that the smoldering ill-will of Walker and his braves was fanned to a flame by one Pedro Leon and a party of Spanish-

Mexicans who come to the Territory and engaged in trading with the Indians in Sanpete Valley and elsewhere, exchanging horses for Indian children and firearms, etc." Although they supposedly had licenses granted by the Governor of New Mexico, Brigham Young strongly opposed the practice of selling Indian children into slavery. "Warnings to the Mexicans to desist from their traffic were treated with impudence and contempt.

"Finally in the winter of 1851-52 Pedro Leon and a number of his associates were arrested and tried before a justice of the peace at Manti and subsequently brought before Judge Zerubbabel Snow of the First District Court. Judge Snow decided against the eight defendants, and the Indian slaves in their possession, a squaw and eight children, were liberated, and the Mexicans sent away; however, some of the slave-traders began stirring up the Indians against the Utah settlers. By April 1853, the situation had become so serious that Governor Young on arriving at Provo . . . felt impelled to issue a proclamation warning the people against the acts of the Mexicans, and to be on their guard against Indian attack."

Captain Wall of the Provo militia, with a detachment of thirty men, was sent through the southern settlements of Utah to reconnoiter and "direct the inhabitants to be on their guard against any sudden surprise." They were cautioned to avoid being taken in ambush, and to warn all militia groups to be in readiness to march, if called. All Mexicans in the Territory were required to remain quiet in the settlements and not attempt to leave, until further advised. The officers were directed to treat them with kindness and supply their needs.

"Two incidents occurred in the summer of 1853, which were instrumental in bringing about hostilities. The first took place at the Provo fort. Several Indians were engaged in the common custom of going from cabin to cabin begging for food. When they came to the home of Alfred Young they were met at the door by Mrs. Young, a strong, fearless woman, who would not allow them to enter. One of the Indians in the rear had a gun in his hand, the stock resting on the ground. He raised his foot and with his toe pulled the hammer. The gun was discharged and an Indian in front was shot and killed. The purpose of firing the gun had probably been to kill or frighten Mrs. Young, and the slaying of the Indian was entirely unanticipated. Hyrum Cluff . . . was a boy in the fort at the time, and witnessed the tragedy.

"The Indians would not believe the story of the killing, but ascribed the deed to the whites. There was much excitement among the red men when they learned of the happening, and they made the night hideous with their yells and the firing of guns. The two Indians who had been with the man killed left for the south, and were never seen in the vicinity of Provo again."

Peter Conover in his journal explains the second incident this way:

"Arrapene and several other chiefs came down to Provo to fish and were very friendly. In going back to Payson, where the rest of the band were camped; they had a row with JIM IVIE, at Porter's, between Provo and Springville, over trading a gun. IVIE knocked the Indian down and that is the first start of the Walker War."

This account has many problems; but it shows one of the local citizen's idea of how it happened. The incident involved uncle JIM A. IVIE, and the following was written by his brothers:

"It seemed to young JIM IVIE that he was fated to run-in after run-in with the local Indians. He reflected on this as he sipped his 'Mormon tea' out of a tin cup. Sitting cross-legged on the ground, staring into his small campfire, he remembered the incident in Springville like it happened yesterday.

"JIM was blamed with starting the 'Chief Walker Indian War.' Everyone knew relations with the Indians that spring had been more than strained as a result of Brigham Young's official decree and the enforcement of his anti-slavery law. [This was about a decade before the U.S. Civil War. Slavery was still allowed in the Slave States.]

"The practice of this ancient form of trade and commerce, being the only honorable 'career' left for the proud warriors after smoking the peace pipe with their ancient tribal enemies, the Shoshones, Crow, Paites, Navajo, all had [touched the pen] in the Salt Lake Valley along with the rites. But, all the tribe 'warrior societies' believed fervently in their hereditary right to plunder and enslave the lesser 'Digger' Indian tribe. These slaves would be traded for horses with the Mexican traders who came up once a year just for this trade.

"This particular year, acting Indian Agent and Territorial Governor Brigham Young had sent 'Mormon Militia' troopers to intercept and incarcerate these traffickers in human flesh. After being held in Parowan Jail for two weeks, they were solemnly escorted south, out of the territory. After this incident the Ute warriors that were seen around the Mormon forts were openly hostile, arrogant beyond belief. It was during this tense period that it happened.

"JIM was digging a well behind his cabin at Springville. As he wiped the sweat off his face with a worn kerchief, he noticed four Indians on horseback approaching his small cabin from the foothill side. This was really nothing unusual because Indians were always around, either trading fish or game for flour and sugar, or just sitting out of the way somewhere passing the time of day—amusing themselves by watching the endless and seemingly endless labors of the Saints.

"As they approached, JIM made them out to be three 'bucks' and one squaw. They stopped a little bit away from the cabin. The woman dismounted, unstrung three large fish from the saddlehorn and walked to the cabin door. The next thing JIM heard was his wife calling him to ask his advice on the trade. JIM walked through the door. He said, 'Hello' to the squaw and looked over the fish. They had plenty of fish, while flour was scarce; but they agreed that one cup of flour for each fish would be a fair trade.

"Leaving his wife to pay out the flour, JIM gave the squaw the Ute hand sign for farewell and went back to his work on the well.

"As JIM resumed his digging, he watched one of the Indian bucks dismount and enter the cabin, after first leaning his musket against the door frame. Within minutes JIM heard a clatter and a man's voice hollering something in Ute. He then heard his wife's strained cry, 'JIM, come quick.' JIM was there in seconds, and when he entered the cabin utter chaos ruled. The haughty warrior was displeased with the trade made by his woman, and had began screaming at her in Ute, while kicking and beating her about the body with a piece of cordwood. In her attempt to escape the blows, the squaw fell against the baby crib, knocking it and JIM's baby son to the dirt floor.

"When JIM entered the cabin, on the run, he saw his baby screaming on the floor, his wife backed into a corner almost hysterical with fear, and the Indian continuing to attack his squaw and upset the cabin. In an instant JIM had reached the Indian, grabbed him roughly around the waist and pinned his arms to his sides. He swung them both around and pushed the Indian out of the cabin door. As the Indian fell to the porch, he reached out and grabbed his musket. JIM saw the barrel being leveled at him and barely had time to dive at the Indian and grab the gun. The two wrestled over the gun for a brief moment before it broke apart in their hands with the Indian getting the stock and JIM getting the barrel. In that instant JIM brought the shining barrel down on the head of Shower-osho-scats. He was one of Chief Walker's most revered lieutenants.

"Before the Indian had hit the ground, JIM heard a hoarse war cry behind him. He spun around just in time to take a Ute arrow in his right shoulder. The arrow's owner stood only five feet away and was rapidly refitting an arrow to his bow. JIM took two quick steps toward him swinging the gun barrel up from the side. The barrel connected with the Indians head and jaw—knocking him unconscious. With his back to the cabin door, JIM then heard an inhuman shriek behind him. As he spun around, the squaw came flying at him off the porch. She struck JIM's left cheekbone, using the same piece of cordwood used on her just moments before, while tearing at his eyes with her free hand. Again, JIM brought the gun barrel down on an Indian head and the squaw went down. The remaining Indian had stayed on his horse. JIM yelled at him to get to the fort for help; but the Indian pony wheeled in its tracks and headed towards the skyline.

"The Bishop and a young Mormon interpreter had loaded the two Indians in a wagon and carted them up Spanish Fork Canyon to Chief Walker's camp, and en route the warrior, Shower-osho-scats did not survive. Chief Walker demanded JIM IVIE's scalp immediately. After refusing to comply, the two white men were lucky to leave that camp with their own hair intact. It was only their good relationships with Chief Walker that ensured their safe departure. This incident caused every 'Saint' in Utah Valley to have to fort up. Before news was sent of the incident, Chief Walker's brother 'Arapeen' shot a sentry off the wall of Fort Nephi [actually Fort Payson] and the Walker War had begun.

"JIM had been tried in 'Fort Utah' (Provo) and found guilty of using poor judgment in a tense situation, but not guilty of murder on the grounds of self-defense. [signed by]
    (RICHARD ANDERSON IVIE)
    (WILLIAM FRANKLIN IVIE)
    (ISAAC THOMAS IVIE)"

Jensen's history reads:

"The next morning, July 18, with a number of warriors, he [Arapeen] rode down to Fort Payson, whose inhabitants, anticipating no trouble, received the Indians kindly and gave them food as usual. The Indians showed no signs of hostility until they started back to camp in the evening when they shot and killed Alexander Keel, who was standing guard near the fort. Arapeen hastened to join Walker; and together, with their followers, they retreated up Payson Canyon."

Arapeen, Chief Walker's half-brother, struck the first blow. Colonel P. W. Conover, of the Provo militia, quietly collected a hundred and fifty men, and proceeded at once to Payson, arriving there on 20 July. They were joined by additional men from Springville and Spanish Fork. A council of war was held and they decided to follow the Indians, believing that they were headed for Sanpete County. They went to Salt Creek [Nephi] that night, arose the next morning, and were in Manti the following day by 4 o'clock. They were joined by Colonel William H. Kimball from Great Salt Lake City with 100 mounted men.

Meanwhile the Indians had shot and wounded William Jolly at Springville. At Nephi, Juab County, they had stolen cattle and fired upon the guard. On the afternoon of 23 July, two men returning with dispatches for General Wells in Great Salt Lake City were fired upon by Indians concealed in a deserted Santaquin home. One of the dispatchers was shot through the shoulder, and the other his wrist. They spurred their horses to full-speed. The Indians were in hot pursuit, but they were out-distanced, and the two wounded men reached Fort Payson.

Colonel George A. Smith, commanding all the militia south of GSLC, sent the following orders throughout the territory:

> "To all we wish to say, that it is evident that the Indians intend to prey and subsist upon our stock, and will shoot and kill whenever they can. It is therefore expected that these orders will be rigidly enforced and complied with, and the small settlements . . . must be evacuated, and the inhabitants of all weak settlements and stronger ones upon their borders should not be permitted to wander out any distance from the fort alone, or after dark, but keep themselves secure, and not permit any sense of security to lull them into a spirit of carelessness or indifference to their safety . . . look out that you are not surprised in harvesting and haying in the fields, or in hauling between the fields and the stack yards; and as soon as may be, thresh the wheat and safely store it, and be careful that you save hay sufficient for the winter if you should have to keep up stock, or in case any emergency should arise."

Jensen continues:

> "The Indians continued stealing cattle, burning outlying houses and mills, and occasionally wounding or killing some lone settler . . . Travel from place to place was unsafe and usually not attempted except in groups large

enough for self protection. The trouble was at first confined to the Utes, but other tribes were brought into the struggle by the murder of two Pawvante Indians and the wounding of several others by a company of Missourians on their way to California and by the excitement and unrest incident to the war.

"Indians are quick to retaliate, but the retaliation does not always fall on the responsible persons. The Missourians who had murdered the Pawvantes having gone on their way, the vengeance of the Indians fell upon a party of twelve surveyors working in the Sevier Valley under Captain J. W. Gunnison. The Indians fired from ambush killing eight of the party, Captain Gunnison being one of the first to fall. The other four managed to escape. (Three of the Indian murderers were tried before Judge Kinney at Nephi, in March, 1855, found guilty of man slaughter, and sentenced to three years' imprisonment in the Penitentiary.)"

At the Tabernacle in Salt Lake City, 31 July 1853, *Journal of Discourses Vol. I*, Brigham Young addresses the Saints regarding Chief Walker, the Saints, and Indian troubles.

"There seems to be some excitement among the people, and fears are arising . . . as to the general safety. Some people have been shot at by the Indians, or some Indians were seen in an hostile condition. And away go messengers to report to headquarters, saying, 'What shall we do! for we cannot tell, but we shall all be killed by them . . . when, perhaps, tomorrow, the very Indians who have committed these depredations will come and say, 'How do you do! We are friendly; cannot you give us some Chitcup?' They will shake hands, and appear as though it were impossible for them to be guilty of hostility. And what is the next move? Why, our wise men, the Elders of Israel, are either so fluctuating in their feelings, so unstable in their ways, or so ignorant of the Indian character, that the least mark of friendship manifested by these treacherous red men, will lull all their fears, throw them entirely off their guard, saying, 'It is all right; wife, take care of the stock, for I am going to the canyon for a load of wood.'

"Away he goes without a gun or a pistol to defend himself, in case of an attack from some Indian or Indians, to rob him of his cattle, and perhaps his life. Herds of cattle are driven upon the range, the feelings of the people are divested of all fear by this little show of Indian friendship, and their hearts are at peace with all mankind. They lie down to sleep at night with the doors of their houses open, and in many instances with no way to close them . . . only by means of hanging up a blanket. Thus they go to sleep with their guns unloaded, and entirely without any means of defence, in case they should be attacked in the night . . . Today all are in arms, war is on hand . . . Tomorrow all is peace, and every man turns to his own way . . . No concern is felt as to protection in the future, but 'all is right, all is safety' and they lie down to sleep in a false security, to be murdered in the night by their enemies . . . I can tell you one thing . . . those wild Indians are actually wiser . . . in the art of war than this people are. They lay better plans, display greater skill, and are steadier in their feelings. They are not so easily excited, and when excited are not so easily allayed, as the men who have come to inhabit these mountains, from where they have been trained and educated in the civilization of modern nations . . . Your determination was . . . formed to go up to the Valleys of the mountains, where you could enjoy peace and quiet . . . When the people arrive here, many of them come to me and say, 'Brother Brigham, can we go here, or there, to get us farms? Shall we enter into this or that speculation? We have been very poor, and we want to make some money, or we want the privilege of taking with us a few families to make a settlement in this or that distant valley.' If I inquire why they cannot stay here, their answer is, 'because there is no room . . . We have a considerable stock of cattle, we want to go where we can . . . ride over the prairies, and say, I am Lord of all I survey. We do not wish to be disturbed, in any way, nor to be asked to pay tithing, to work upon the roads, nor pay territorial tax; but we wish all the time to ourselves.' I have not given you the language of their lips, but the language of their hearts.

"Elders of Israel are greedy after the things of this world. If you ask them if they are ready to build up the kingdom of God, their answer is prompt—'Why to be sure we are, with our whole souls; but we want first to get rich, and then we can help the Church considerably . . . We do not believe in the necessity of doing military duty, in giving over our surplus property for tithing; we never could see into it; but we want to go and get rich.' If that is not the spirit of this people, then I do not know what the truth is concerning the matter.

"Now I wish to say to you who are fearing and trembling, do not be afraid at all, for it is certain if we should be killed off by the Indians, we could not die any younger . . . If we all go together, the dark valley of the shadow of death will be lighted up for us, so do not be scared. But there will not be enough slain by the Indians at this time to make the company very conspicuous in that dark valley . . . I have no fault to find with the Latter-day Saints [in regards to their courage], for they love to fight a little too well. I . . . have more fear in the consequence of the ignorant and foolish audacity of the Elders, than in their being afraid . . . On that point I am a coward myself, and if people would do as I tell them, I would not only save my own life, but theirs likewise . . . If the people in San Pete County had done as they were told, from the beginning of that settlement, they would have been safe at this time, and would not have lost their cattle. The day before yesterday, Friday, July 29th, the Indians came from the mountains, to FATHER ALLRED's settlement, and drove off all the stock, amounting to two hundred head. If the people had done as they were told, they would not have suffered this severe loss, which is a just chastisement.

"I recollect when we were down at FATHER ALLRED's settlement last April, they had previously been to me not only to know if they might settle in San Pete, but if they might separate widely from each other, over a piece of land about two miles square, each having a five acre lot for their garden, near their farms. They were told to build a good substantial fort, until the settlement became sufficiently strong, and not live so far apart and expose themselves and their property to danger. FATHER ALLRED told me they were then so nigh together, they did not know how to live! I told him they had better make up their minds to be baptized into the Church again, and get the Spirit of God, that each one might be able to live at peace with his neighbor in close quarters, and not think himself infringed upon.

"They wanted to know if they were to build a fort. 'Why, yes,' I said, 'build a strong fort, and a corral, to put your cattle in, that the Indians cannot get them away from you.' 'Do you think, brother Brigham, the Indians will trouble us here?' they inquired. I said, 'It is none of your business whether they will or not; but you will see the time that you will need such preparations.' But I did not think it would come so quickly . . . I said also to the brethren at Utah [Provo—second fort], 'make a fort and let it be strong enough, that Indians cannot break into it.' They commenced, and did not make even the shadow of a fort, for in some places there was nothing more than a line to mark where the approaching shadow would be. They began to settle round upon the various creeks and streamlets and the part of the fort that existed was finally pulled up, and carried away somewhere else.

"I told the settlement in San Pete, at the first, to build a fort. They did not do it, but huddled together beside a stone quarry . . . They did after a while, build a temporary fort at San Pete, which now shields them in a time of trouble.

"When the brethren went to Salt Creek [Nephi], they wanted to make a settlement there, and inquired of me if they might do so. I told them, no, unless they first built an efficient fort. I forbade them taking their women and children there, until that preparatory work was fully accomplished. Has it ever been done? No, but families went there and lived in wagons and brush houses, perfectly exposed to be killed. If they have faith enough to keep the Indian off, it is all right. From the time these distant valleys began to be settled, until now, there has scarcely been a day but what I have felt twenty-five ton weight, as it were, upon me, in exercising faith to keep this people from destroying themselves; but if any of them can exercise faith enough for themselves, and wish to excuse me, I will take my faith back.

"The word has gone out now, to the different settlements, in the time of harvest, requiring them to build forts. Could it not have been done last winter, better than now? . . . Now the harvest is upon us . . . go to work, men, women, and children, and gather in your grain, and gather it clean, leave none to waste, and put it where the Indians cannot destroy it . . . Let every man and woman who has a house make that house a fort, from which you can kill ten where you can now only kill one, if Indians come upon you . . . From the day I lived where brother Joseph Smith lived, I have been fortified all the time so as to resist twenty men, if they should come to my house in the night, with an intent to molest my family, assault my person or destroy my property; and I have always been in the habit of sleeping with one eye open, and if I cannot then sufficiently watch, I will get my wife to help me. Let a hostile band of Indians come round my house, and I am good for quite a number of them . . .

"But instead of the people taking this course, almost every good rifle in the territory has been traded away to the Indians, with quantities of powder and lead, though they waste it in various ways when they have got it. The whites would sell the title to their lives, for the sake of trading with the Indians. You will be whipped until you have the Spirit of the Lord Jesus Christ sufficiently to love your brethren and sisters freely, man, women, and children; until you can live at peace with yourselves, and with every family around you; until you can treat every child as though it were the tender offspring of your own body, every man as your brother, and every woman as your sister; and until the young persons treat the old with that respect due to parents, and all learn to shake hands, with a warm heart, and a friendly grip, and say, 'God bless you,' from morning till evening; until each person can say, 'I love you all, I have no evil in my heart to any individual, I can send my children to school with yours, and can correct your children when they do wrong, as though they were my own, and I am willing you should correct mine, and let us live together until we are a holy and sanctified society.' There will always be Indians or somebody else to chastise you, until you come to that spot . . . When FATHER ALLRED was advised to adopt measures to secure themselves and their property, he replied, 'O, I do not think there is the least danger in the world; we are perfectly able to take care of our stock and protect ourselves against the Indians.' All right, I thought, let circumstances prove that. Now as difficulties surround them, they say to me, 'Why, brother Brigham, if you had only told us what to do, we would have done it. Were we not always willing to take your counsel?' Yes, you are a great deal more willing to take it, than to obey it. If people are willing to carry out good counsel, they will secure themselves accordingly.

"I will relate one action of (Chief) Walker's life, which will serve to illustrate his character. He, with his band, about last Feb., fell in with a small band of Piedes, and killed off the whole of the men, took the squaws prisoner, and sold the children to the Mexicans, and some few were disposed of in this territory . . . The Indians in these mountains are continually on the decrease; bands that numbered 150 warriors when we first came here, number not more than 35 now; and some of the little tribes in the southern parts of this territory, towards New Mexico, have not a single squaw amongst them, for they have traded them off for horses, &c. This practice will soon make the race extinct. Besides, Walker is continually, whenever an opportunity presents itself, killing and stealing children from the wandering bands that he has any power over, which also has its tendency to extinguish the race . . . From all appearance, there will not be an Indian left, in a short time, to steal a horse. Are they not fools . . . to make war with their best friends.

"Do you want to run after them to kill them? I say, let them alone . . . But they will come to us and try to kill us, and we shall be under the necessity of killing them to save our own lives . . . We must be so prepared that they dare not come to us in a hostile manner without being assured they will meet a vigorous resistance . . . The Lord will suffer no more trouble to come upon us than is necessary to bring this people to their senses. You need not go to sleep under the impression that it is the north and south only that is in danger, and we are safe here . . . Be ready at any moment to kill twenty of your enemies at least. Let every house be a fort.

"After the cattle were stolen at San Pete, a messenger arrived here in about thirty hours to report the affair, and obtain advice. I told brother Wells, you can write to them, and say, 'Inasmuch as you have no cows and oxen to trouble you, you can go to harvesting, and take care of yourselves . . . 'God helps them that help themselves.'

"I am my own policeman, and have slept, scores of nights, with my gun and sword by my side, that is, if I slept at all . . . It is as important for me to watch now, as well as pray, as it ever has been since I came into this kingdom. It requires watching, as well as praying men; take turns at it . . . never let any time pass without a watcher, lest you be overtaken in an hour when you think not; it will come as a thief in the night. Look out for your enemies, for we know not how they will come, and what enemy it will be. Take care of yourselves . . . Let me reiterate to the sisters, do not be afraid of going into the harvest field. If you are found there helping your sons, your husbands, and your brethren, to gather in the harvest, I say, God bless you, and I will also."

On 30 September 1853, four ox-drawn wagons loaded with grain left Manti for Great Salt Lake City. A few hours later, under the leadership of ISAAC MOR-LEY, they were followed with twelve wagons drawn by horses. These wagons were loaded with provisions and feed, as well as a number of Saints en route to attend the semi-annual conference. Both groups were to camp at Shum-way (Duck) Springs, near Moroni and then travel together through Salt Creek Canyon. For some reason, the first teams kept going until they reached Uinta Springs (Fountain Green) where they camped overnight and the horse teams did not overtake them as planned.

Early on the morning of 1 October, the Indians made an attack and all four drivers were killed and their bodies badly mutilated. The grain was emptied from the sacks, which the savages took possibly for clothing. When MORLEY's company came along, they found three bodies—later Clark's body was found in the bottom of a wagon box, covered with the emptied wheat. He had been scalped, his head crushed, his body cut open and his heart taken out. The bodies were taken to Salt Creek (Nephi) for interment. Several Indians were seen watching from among the trees and bushes making gestures of joy over the massacre. When the wagons bearing the bodies reached Nephi, seven Indians who had followed at a safe distance were captured and shot.

Although guards had been kept at the little grist mill at the mouth of the canyon, east of Manti, until sufficient flour could be ground for the winter, on 1 October, the Indians killed the miller, John F. Warner, and the guard, William Mills, whose bodies were found a short distance from the mill. Their clothing had been removed; their faces badly disfigured. The mill was left undisturbed;

however, the Indians returned and burned it. Indians were later seen wearing the clothing that had been taken from the bodies of the two men. The Indians claimed these acts had been committed because of the shooting of five Indians, alleged to have been killed by a company of immigrants en route to California.

Great-grandfather JOHN L. IVIE's pension papers read:

"That he also served from July 1853 to November 1853 in the Walker War, being enlisted at Provo, Utah, and discharged at the same place . . . "

The Indian, Squash-head, in May 1851, found a child who had wandered from his parents; he later bragged how he had tortured the little one by taking off its toes and fingers, and finally finished his brutal work by taking him by the heels and smashing the back of his head on a rock. The child was twenty months and six days old at the time of his death—the parents lived in the Alpine area. Of course, parents worried even more about their children. As the Saints moved to the safety of their forts and guarded their families and livestock, the brutal killing of the *white* men and their families continued to occur in the more isolated places, while in the more fortified places (to paraphrase Mark Twain) they had many worries, most of which never happened.

~ 20 ~

"Freezing Cold" Wyoming,
Fort Supply Mission to the Indians

Another problem came to the attention of Brigham Young at this time. It seemed the *Mountain Men* who often wintered at Fort Bridger and used the fort as their center for trading with the Indians, were deliberately trying to increase the Saints problems with the Indians by telling lies and exaggerations about them to the Indians. They were also sending totally false reports of the Mormons back east—unhappy with the Mormons, because they were taking some of the trade and river ferrying that they felt rightfully belonged to them. Fort Bridger sold the Indians guns, ammunition, and liquor—illegal in Utah Territory.

In October General Conference in Salt Lake City, 1853, Orson Hyde read off the names of thirty-nine young men who were to participate in the Green River Mission. On the list were JOHN L. IVIE (now twenty years-old), MOSES SANDERS, John M. Lytle, and thirty-six others. Their captain was John Nebeker. They were to be ready by October the 18th. Winter was coming to this high mountain region. They accepted the call and left for this forlorn area in high spirits, according to organizer Orson Hyde on 2 November 1853.

James S. Brown, an elected second lieutenant reported:

"Elder Orson Hyde was chosen to lead the company to somewhere in the region of the Green River, select a place and there build an outpost from which to operate as peace makers among the Indians. To preach civilization to them, to try to teach them to cultivate the soil, to instruct them in the arts and sciences, if possible, and by that means prevent trouble for the frontier settlements and emigrant companies. We were to identify our interests with theirs and even to marrying among them if we would be permitted to take the young women of the chief and leading men, and have them dress like civilized people and be educated. It was thought that [so doing] . . . we would have more power to do them good and keep peace among the . . . tribes and also with our own people. It was known that there were wicked and cruel white men among the Indians working up the spirit of robbery and murder among the savage tribes and against our Mormon people. Our missionary call was to take our lives in our hands as true patriots and head off and operate as far as possible against the wicked plots of the white man, who were trying to carry out their plans to success through the Indians, and possibly, set the savages on the warpath that the government might send troops out and thus, make a better market for the schemers herds of cattle and horses."

Although the men accepted the call gladly, some had very strong reservations about accepting Indian wives. Chief Washakie shook his head and said,

"No, for we have not got daughters enough for our own men; and we cannot afford to give our daughters to the white men; but we are willing to give him an Indian girl for a white girl. I cannot see why a white man wants an Indian girl. They are dirty, ugly, stubborn, and cross, and it is a strange idea for white men to want such wives. The white men may look around though and if any of you could find a girl that would go with him, it would be all right; but the Indian must have the same privilege among the white man." This ended any further concern of the missionaries about marrying an Indian girl.

Aging Washakie poses for famed Western photographer W.H. Jackson.

When the first company arrived at Fort Bridger, probably on 12 November 1853, they found twelve to fifteen rough mountain men there who "seemed to be very surly and suspicious of us and the spirit of murder and death appeared to be lurking in their minds. Many of our party could feel the terrible influence and made remarks about it. They were informed that two of the mountain men had fought a duel the night before with butcher knives and both had been killed and thrown into a common grave. Thus the gloom and cloud of death that we had felt plainly was partially explained."

They left Fort Bridger and camped on Black's Fork. That night it snowed about six inches. They had planned to camp at Henry's Fork, but were told that fifteen or twenty mountain men had moved there, and the Ute Indians were coming there to winter. They were also told that a well-organized band of from seventy to a hundred desperados were "in the vicinity of the Green River at the very point that we had hoped to occupy with our little company. The situation was serious and with snow on the ground, to decide what to do was a most important matter."

Leaving this decision to the missionaries, Orson Hyde returned to Salt Lake City for support and "in less than two weeks time, I had fifty-three young, hardy men well fitted out with large supplies of everything necessary, twenty-six wagons, from two to five yoke of oxen as many milk cows, mechanics of all sorts and kinds necessary, tools and implements in abundance besides much clothing, blankets, leather, nails, and so on. Much of the outfits for these men was raised in the Session settlement (present day Ogden) by voluntary donations ... It is not always those who are most able and the most anxious to be thought forward and liberal that really do the most. This I found to be true in raising and fitting out this company. It is one thing to wear the name of a Mormon, another thing to do the works of a Mormon."

According to the *Deseret News*, JAMES (JIM) IVIE (23 yrs.); JOHN FAW-CETT; LORIN H. ROUNDY; ISAAC BULLOCK (Capt.); C. Billingsley; Or-rin Hatch; Ransome Hatch; and forty-two others arrived in the Fort Bridger area on November 25th. Meanwhile, the first company had left Black's Fork on the 14th of November and gone southeasterly toward Smith's Fork, when "the spirit seemed to forbid them from going any further." They stopped and sent a committee of six men to pick a spot. The committee followed up the creek to a point where the water came through the foothills and there, between the forks of the stream, they selected the place which they called Fort Supply. Joined soon by the second company, the ninety-two men built the blockhouse in two weeks time. "This was not an hour too soon for the weather was very cold and threatening," Orson Hyde reported. He and his party arrived on December 8 with letters and more provisions. But around December 23, they were lacking sufficient flour, so Orson Hyde with seven others took four wagons toward Salt Lake for an additional supply. W. W. Sterrett reported this journey:

"The winter set in early, and when we got within a half mile of the top of the big mountain, the snow became so deep that we had to camp, the oxen not being able to pull the wagons. We counseled what was best to do. Some was for returning but some of us was for pushing ahead. The snow was about five feet deep and snowing still. Six of us concluded to try and tramp a trail to the top of the mountain. We started about eight o'clock p.m. and took it single file. One kept the lead as long as he could stand it, then fell back to the rear and waited until he again came into the lead. By this means we worked our way by Sunrise the next morning to the top, and went back and drove our oxen along our trail. When we got them to the Summit, the crust bore them up. We left our wagons there that winter. We sent a man to the city on horse back for help and by two o'clock plenty of help came, and we got to the city that night. Spent winter in the city. Next spring went back. Bro. Orson Hyde going with us."

Back at the blockhouse, James S. Brown explains:

"This blockhouse had four wings or rooms of equal size united at the corners, thus forming a center room. This room was built two stories high, the lower one being used for storage and the upper for a guard house from which position the surrounding country could be surveyed. All of the rooms in the blockhouse were provided with portholes. The work of building was continued until all were comfortably housed in log cabins, and a heavy log corral was constructed for stock in case of emergency."

Wolves and the cold weather were their biggest problems. They reported that they partially resolved the wolf problem with rifles, traps and strychnine; but the cold weather just had to be endured, in January at times it would be 30 degrees below zero. In the later part of February, a heavy storm accompanied by winds buried some of their cabins; "but the wind, which had piled the snow high on the cabins, had cleared other areas of the land and the grass was bare for the cattle to eat and the animals saved."

The first company had with them a former mountain man who had joined the church, Elijah B. Ward and his Shoshone Indian wife, Sally, and their children. Ward and his wife agreed to teach the missionaries the Shoshone language and conducted learning sessions during the winter of 1853-54. In addition to Ward's wife, six other Indians wandered into the camp and aided in these training sessions. By spring the first attempts at missionary work were begun, and the men most skilled in the language were sent to the surrounding Indian camps. At times they were fortunate to escape with their lives. Others of the camp, when the weather broke, proceeded to plant crops; but this was discouraging—on 30 May the thermometer registered ten degrees above zero. In July 1854, Fort Supply was abandoned; but others were called back at later dates.

While JOHN L. IVIE spent the winter at Fort Supply, Wyoming, his wife MARY CATHERINE returned to Bountiful to be with her parents. Their second child, PHOEBE ELLEN IVIE was born in Bountiful 25 July 1854, about the time JOHN's mission ended. Meanwhile, Springtown was burned by the Indians on 6 January 1854. It would not be rebuilt for five years. The entire population of Sanpete County (765) fortified themselves at Manti.

Isaac Behunin was the first settler of a site called Pine Creek—so called because of a few scattered pines growing on the bank of the stream. He made a dugout in the bank of the creek, where he, with his wife and nine children, spent the winter of 1852. Because of Indian troubles, he moved to Manti during the fall of 1853. He later sold to Caleb G. Edwards.

In the early part of 1854, a group of men came from Manti and started the construction of a fort to afford protection for the settlers who would follow. Their fort enclosed about one and a half acres of ground. The walls were seven feet high and there was only one gate, which was on the west side. It was called the Little Fort when the larger one commenced soon after.

[Note: Among these first settlers were JAMES ALLRED, REUBEN W. ALLRED, WILEY P. ALLRED, JAMES T. S. ALLRED, Isaac Behunin, GEORGE MARTIN ALLRED, and JACK ALLRED. The first dwelling cabin completed in the fort was built by JAMES T. S. ALLRED. The first presiding elder at Fort Ephraim was REUBEN WARREN ALLRED. He had formerly acted as Bishop in Springtown. His counselors were WILEY PAYNE ALLRED and JAMES T. S. ALLRED, but late in the summer of 1854 these two counselors resigned.]

When trying to decide on a name for their new settlement, the name "Ephraim" was suggested, and it was quickly adopted. The Little Fort was completed rather quickly, but a great number of Scandinavian converts had arrived from Europe, and most of them only spoke Danish. In an effort to keep them together, Brigham Young sent them south, hoping also to strengthen the area against the Indians. The need for a larger fort was imperative. Some veteran fort builders were required, and many from the IVIE families were enlisted to help build the second, including JOHN LEHI and MARY CATHERINE IVIE.

The larger fort enclosed an area of 60 x 44½ rods, or about seventeen acres. This embraced the block on which the little fort was built, and most of the block lying immediately north of it. The walls around the fort were 14 feet high and 4 feet thick at the top; but it was only completed to the full height on the north. In many places it was only seven feet high. It had two gates, one on the east, and one on the west. In building the wall, the brethren would take turns in working on the wall, hauling wood and timber, and working on the canyon road. This fort was completed in 1855 at a cost of $13,000, and with its construction came other settlers.

"On August 5, 1854, after Ephraim precinct was organized, Henry Beal was appointed Magistrate, thus relieving Elder ALLRED of a few of his worries . . . With so many saints unable to understand English, it became necessary for the Danish saints to hold prayer meetings on Thursday night; the English speaking saints on Friday night . . . All immigrants from other countries and all American-born people were obliged to learn the Danish language, if they wished to converse conveniently and freely with their neighbors. And they did live close to their neighbors in those days. Many a family of the original settlers took an immigrant family into their small one-room dwelling until a house could be built for the newcomers. The saints shared their meager food supplies not only with the new saints, they also fed the Indians . . . and many of the red men became friendly. James Farmer wrote in a letter to friends in England under the date of January 15, 1855: 'Our red friends are very friendly—often visit us. We feed and clothe them—a number of the chiefs and braves have been baptized into the Church and ordained Elders.'" [Millennial Star, 17:477]

Life was hard these first years. In addition to the necessity of preparing a defense, there were crops to be planted and cared for, canals to be dug, and roads and bridges to be made. All the while there were arrivals of immigrants to swell the numbers to be fed and housed. Some crops were said to have been harvested in the year of 1854, but in 1855 the grasshoppers came and only a few potatoes were harvested, as all other crops were destroyed. The women took turns gathering and preparing food, helping in the field, caring for the sick, and many other tasks.

The largest Danish company arrived at Fort Ephraim 22 October 1854, with twenty-eight wagons, some of these contained several families in each wagon. They were under the leadership of Christian J. Larsen and Hans P. Olsen. The settlers from Denmark were in predominance in those early days, and although others at first made light of their dress and customs, they learned to live and work together, and the Danish language was used by most people. All the work was under the direction of the Mormon Bishop. When an important work was confronted, the bishop would call for so many men to be on the job, and even more appeared than were asked, ready to work.

The first man to die in Ephraim was Mane Warring. There was no cemetery, so on their way for burial, they were warned by some white men of approaching Indians and were told to dig a grave and bury him immediately—their own cemetery was started. During the years the pioneers lived in the forts they were constantly on guard watching for Indians. In 1860 the people began to build on their own land.

All the first settlers and the immigrants who came later to Ephraim were members of The Church of Jesus Christ of Latter-day Saints. No sacrifice was too great a price to pay for the freedom to worship God as they chose, and to assist in the building of His kingdom on earth. Their faith gave them strength to separate themselves from comfortable homes, family, and friends; to endure bitter persecution; and survive great hardships, if required. Ephraim became the first successful colony in Sanpete County, outside of Manti.

During 1854, the Indians confined themselves mostly to southern Utah. Yet often they invaded the herds of Sanpete County, stealing horses and cattle and making their escape in safety. Conover reported in his journal that Utah County had a small group of Indians at Goshen that were troublesome, but they refused any additional help in controlling them. He then stated that Utah County had no more trouble with the Indians until 1856.

⁓ 21 ⁓

STOTTS, AND SCOTS, PERSECUTION, SHIPS—
CHIEF WALKER DIES

Yorkshire and Lancashire, England

The third-great-grandparents of my husband, GROVER SWALLOW, JOHN and SUSAN STOTT of Rishworth, Yorkshire, England, were baptized along with many members of their family about 1843. "About this time, the FISHER and NIELD families of Lancashire accepted Mormonism, which seems to have brought these families together."

[Note: From the *Life Sketch of WILLIAM H. STOTT* by his son R. EARL STOTT: Leaving England, from Liverpool on the ship Berlin to come to America, during the summer of 1849, were GROVER's second-great-grandfather, WILLIAM STOTT, with two sons and two daughters: WILLIAM HENRY: EDWIN: HANNAH LEES, and EMMA—also, JAMES FISHER who became the husband of HANNAH LEES STOTT before their journey across the plains. Father WILLIAM STOTT's wife had died a few months before.]

This voyage to America, in 1849, was an ill-fated one for many who set sail. For six long weeks and four days they were on the water. Great-uncle EDWIN STOTT remembered:

"When out at sea two weeks, the wind ceased blowing and we were in a dead calm sea. Just at this time a disease struck us which was much like the cholera and in twenty-one days forty-three of the ships passengers died and were cast into the sea. The wind began to blow again and . . . we landed in New Orleans. In three days we were on the move again, going up the Mississippi River to St. Louis where we remained until the next spring. My father obtained work as a mechanic for nine dollars a week and I worked for two dollars a week. The next spring we went up the Missouri to the state of Iowa and located about eight or ten miles south of Kanesville [Council Bluffs]. Father bought two fine cows for twenty dollars each. He also bought a fifteen acre farm from which we cut sufficient wild hay to last until the next spring."

WILLIAM and his son WILLIAM HENRY returned to St. Louis for employment to get enough money to continue west. WILLIAM HENRY was employed as a hotel cook. They worked there until the spring of 1852, and then returned to Iowa, bringing with them two wagons, five yoke of cattle, and one team of horses, also provisions to continue the journey. They sold the farm and crossed the river on a flat boat a few miles below the present city of Omaha, where a company of forty wagons was organized with a captain over each ten wagons. ISAAC BULLOCK was in charge of the group.

Uncle JAMES FISHER related that one day while traveling, one of the wheels struck a chuck in the road which caused his wife HANNAH to be thrown out of the wagon and in front of a wheel. JAMES heard the spirit say, "Grab the wheel." Obeying instantly, he caught it, a spoke in each hand, at the same time bracing his knee against the hub, stopping the two yoke of oxen. He was able to hold the wheel until his wife was able to safely get up.

> "It would appear that Captain ISAAC BULLOCK was at times concerned with matters other than Indians and buffalo. Aunt EMMA STOTT ... then an early teenager seems to have made a vivid and favorable impression on him. Some time later he sought and obtained her hand in marriage as a 'plural' wife and built her an adobe house on West Center Street in Provo."

Isaac Bullock — President of
Fort Supply Mission 1855 - 1857

A few days after the arrival of the company in Salt Lake City, the STOTTs and FISHERs were appointed by Brigham Young to settle in Fillmore. Here WILLIAM STOTT, his son, WILLIAM HENRY STOTT, and JAMES FISHER were selected to work on the Territorial State House. Fillmore was at first chosen as the capital of the state by President Young, because of its more central location.

"The picture was far from rosy as this group arrived at the frontier town of Fillmore in the fall of 1852. After preparing temporary dugouts they began getting out logs to build more permanent dwellings.

During part of the winter of 1852-53, most of the people of Fillmore were out of flour which had to be hauled from Nephi." The following summer Indian trouble began. Great-uncle EDWIN STOTT's wrote: "We now turned our attention to farming; but the Indian troubles grew greater. All were stealing cattle and horses and killing men at every opportunity."

Lanarkshire, Scotland

In the year of 1597, a law was passed in Scotland making it possible to keep the children of vagrants in lifelong bondage, usually in the coal or salt mines. They were confined to one area, and could not move. They and their descendants remained in the same parish, unless they were transferred to another mine or sold to another master. Two hundred years later, in the year 1799, this law was rescinded and all miners were freed from their virtual slavery. They could go to other mines or take other types of employment if they wished.

Three years later, in 1801, large quantities of ironstone were discovered on the land between the rivers Clyde and Forth, in the Central Lowlands of Scotland. Iron works were built, and Englishmen were brought in to show the Scots the best method of developing and using these resources. This discovery caused a movement of miners to this locality. By 1818, canals had been developed and the Scots were flocking to the cities and large towns where coal mines, steel works, and weaving mills were established. Among those arriving in the very early 1800s in the area around Glasgow were the families of JOHN McLAUCHLIN from the Campbelltown peninsula, JAMES DUNCAN from Stirlingshire, and DAVID SNEDDEN from West Lothian [more of GROVER SWALLOW's great-grandparents]. MARY McLAUCHLIN, daughter of JOHN McLAUCHLIN, married JAMES DUNCAN, son of JAMES DUNCAN, in Cambuslang. They had six sons, in Greenend, Dungeonhill, Cambuslang, Barony, and then in Maryston— all in areas around Glasgow. Two sons died as young children. Included in the 1841 census at Maryston are JAMES and MARY DUNCAN with their sons JAMES, JOHN, ADAM, and GEORGE.

In the years of 1846-1851, Ireland had its terrible "potato famine." Thousands of these starving Irishmen left Ireland, a great majority going to America. On one of these "famine" immigrant ships—the *Susan* leaving from Glasgow 19 September 1849—we find on the passenger list:

DUNCAN, Mary	40	F	wife
James	21	M	Miner
John	14	M	Miner [What happened to ADAM?]
George	12	M	Miner
SNEDDIN, Janet	18	F	none

On arriving in America, they went to the Pittsburgh, Pennsylvania area, where father JAMES DUNCAN had come earlier and found work. JANET worked for a lady by the name of Walker as a cook, and (son) JAMES DUNCAN courted her, having already become acquainted with her on the ship. They were married before the 1850 census, when they were found to be living in the Elizabethtown precinct. Mother MARY McLAUGHLIN DUNCAN died in Pittsburgh, where she was buried. Father JAMES DUNCAN, with his sons and daughter-in-law, JANET, decided to move west. There were mines in the St. Louis area, so they worked there for additional money to complete the journey. Here father JAMES DUNCAN died of cholera. In the spring of 1852, the brothers and JANET joined a wagon train going to California.

There were some Latter-day Saints in the group and as they came west, JAMES and JANET were converted to the church. The younger brothers were quite indignant and when JAMES and JANET stayed in Salt Lake City and were baptized, they continued west and refused to have anything more to do with them. JAMES and JANET settled in Sessions (Ogden) and worked for ANSON CALL. When the Legislature met in Fillmore, Legislator ANSON CALL had to go to Fillmore. He took JAMES and JANET DUNCAN with him. When the session ended, JAMES went back with ANSON, and JANET waited for him in Fillmore. GEORGE DUNCAN went on to San Mateo, California, where he later died, a strong member of the community, but unmarried. JOHN DUNCAN went to Rye Patch, Nevada, near Reno. He had a daughter and a grandson, who later contacted us—quite thrilled to find a relation. He was an historian in Carson City. GEORGE and JOHN DUNCAN never joined the LDS Church.

Clackmannon, Scotland, a family history

In 1847, the "gospel" was preached in Clackmannon, Scotland, by Elders William Gibson, John Sharp, and others in a rented hall in the upper part of the Crown Inn, which was operated by THOMAS CONDIE, my second-great-grandfather. Tall with dark hair and blue eyes, THOMAS had worked in the coal mines as a young man and later found work operating the engine used in pulling the coal out of the mine. On 21 August 1830, he married HELEN SHARP, the daughter of LUKE SHARP and JANET WHITE, who was also tall, dark and blue-eyed. By 1835 he had become a grocer—selling groceries, provisions, liquor, and tobacco. He kept a stable in his Crown Inn and was in charge of some buildings in Alloa, two miles away. He had cows and farm land under cultivation. Business was good. They would have twelve children.

"HELEN SHARP CONDIE would slip in and attend the meetings of the missionaries. She was the first in the family to accept the gospel and was baptized; but THOMAS was very bitter when he found out and greatly persecuted his wife, not allowing her to be confirmed for six months. He was a great reader of the Bible, and firm in his Presbyterian beliefs. However, as religious discussions continued, he realized he was in error, and that his faith was built on a weak foundation. He often told how the Lord had given him a testimony in a remarkable way. One night a voice repeated to him 'thrice sundry times' the scripture found in Isaiah, 54th chapter, last three verses. After this manifestation he had a fervent testimony all his life. On 1 Sep 1848, in Dunfermline, Fife, Scotland, he was baptized by Alexander Dow and confirmed by Wm. McMaster, president of the Dunfermline Branch.

"About this time THOMAS was having trouble with his business. He and a partner had leased a coal mine, but through the dishonesty of his partner, THOMAS failed in business and was forced to leave Clackmannan to seek employment. His wife, HELEN, took charge and settled up the indebtedness, with the help of their son GIBSON.

"HELEN and the children, JANET, GIBSON, HELEN, MARGARET, THOMAS, and MARY then packed their belongings and hired a team to take them and their luggage to the train depot seven miles away. At Glasgow, they met THOMAS, and boarded a steamer for Liverpool, arriving on Christmas Day, 1848, after a cold rough, unpleasant journey.

"While waiting in Liverpool for the ship to be made ready to sail, THOMAS was cleaning his shotgun with vitriol. When he was not looking, little MARY took the cup and drank the poison. The two eldest children, JANET and GIBSON, were sent to find some Mormon elders. They found Orson Pratt, then president of the mission, who sent two elders. They administered to MARY, rebuking the poison, and promised that she would live. No sooner had they taken their hands away than she began to vomit and the poison was cast upon the floor. It was so strong that it burned the floor and the skin of her throat and tongue.

"When the ship *Zetland* was ready, over 400 Saints from England and Scotland went aboard. Among them were THOMAS' youngest brother GIBSON and his family. He was born in June 1815 and in 1844 had married CECELIA SHARP, a widow with two children, JOYCE and MARY. Orson Pratt came aboard and organized the company and promised that if all lived right, they would arrive safely in New Orleans. On 29 Jan 1849 the vessel was towed out to sea. The first mate got drunk and neglected his duty, and the ship was nearly dashed on the rocks in the Irish Channel. During the voyage the galley fireplace caught fire and it seemed the vessel was doomed, but again the Lord preserved them. Nine weeks later, on 2 April, they arrived in New Orleans, and thence by steamboat for St. Louis.

"About seven miles from St. Louis were coal mines, Grovi Diggins, where good wages were being paid. Many old friends who had come from Clackmannan the previous year were here, the Sharps, Fifes, and others. They decided to remain here for awhile as THOMAS had obtained work. They bought two cows for $11, and other goods were low in price. MARY died here during an epidemic of cholera. A son ROBERT was born, but died soon after. On 28 Aug 1849, daughter JANET married JOSEPH SHARP. Grovi Diggins was an unhealthful place to live and THOMAS was desirous of moving on to Council Bluffs, Iowa. In St. Louis he did some trading and obtained the money to proceed on their way. JANET and husband, JOSEPH SHARP, and his brother GIBSON CONDIE, remained as they were planning to go to Salt Lake City from Independence, Missouri, in the spring of 1850.

"Leaving St. Louis on 1 Mar 1850, the THOMAS CONDIE family went by steamboat up the Missouri River to St. Joseph. HELEN was very ill with a miscarriage, so they remained there until she was able to travel. The remainder of the journey was made by ox team through mud and in bad weather. Arriving in Council Bluffs (Kanesville), Iowa, THOMAS began looking for a place to live. Purchasing a farm located on Mosquito

Creek from Enos Curtis, he bought a cow and calf and began to plant corn and potatoes.

"There had been no rain for months that spring and crops were failing after three plantings. At a conference held on 10 May 1850, at which Wilford Woodruff, Orson Pratt, and Orson Hyde were the speakers, Elder Hyde predicted good crops if those who could would help the poor. Many handed in their names declaring they would give employment to the poor. Soon small black spots appeared in the sky, then increased in size and the sky became very black. It began to rain, and from then on there were regular rains.

"While living at Council Bluffs, THOMAS CONDIE and his family did not have sufficient to eat; but with the aid of Elder Orson Hyde, they obtained some cornmeal on which to subsist until the crop was harvested. Nuts were plentiful and the family gathered sacks of them, also wild plums. When they went to the mill, which was three miles away, they packed the corn in sacks on their shoulders and heads. The father and his four children would each take a sack of corn and return with the flour or meal. They also went to the woods and carried all of their firewood the same way. THOMAS then made a trade for a yearling calf to mate the one they had. They made a yoke and small wagon and used this team of calves to haul wood and corn.

"In 1851, Ezra T. Benson came with the message that the Saints at Council Bluffs should start for Salt Lake City, and he assisted them in making arrangements. The Saints were advised to go to the woods and chop down wood for wagons. This they did and after the wood was seasoned, THOMAS proceeded to make his own wagon, which he accomplished with the exception of some iron work, which was done by the blacksmith.

"The family was anxious to get started; but corn was only 10 cents a bushel, and there was no sale for their land as all the people were selling. They gave their land to a Brother McPherson, and borrowed $100 from Brother Almon W. Babbit who was there from Utah. With this they purchased a yoke of oxen for $50. They also bought factory for the wagon cover and cooking utensils. After living in Council Bluffs for 2 years and 3 months, they left in the summer of 1852 . . . Daughter HELEN was left to come on in the Russell Company. THOMAS and others joined the Capt. Howell Co. of 100 wagons—divided into groups of 50s and 10s. They met Indians, killed buffalo, and crossed Sweet Water River (Platte) fourteen times. They traveled down Echo Canyon to the Weber River and then down through Emigration Canyon to the Salt Lake Valley. They were with the thirteen wagons that arrived in the valley on the 2 Sep 1852. On one occasion in Wyoming, the Sioux Indians painted up and came into camp. Brother John Toone had a fiddle (cello) and the Saints sang '*Oh stop and tell me Red Man, who you are, why you roam, and how you get your living . . . etc.*' charming the Indians, who departed in peace."

[Note: In Salt Lake, they found their daughter JANET and husband JOSEPH SHARP settled in the Tenth Ward. THOMAS and HELEN SHARP CONDIE established a home on the corner of 1st West and 7th South. President THOMAS S. MONSON, a descendant of brother GIBSON and CECELIA SHARP CONDIE, told us at a dinner with the stake presidency when he was the visiting apostle at the Enterprise Utah Stake Conference that his grandfather, another THOMAS CONDIE, had farmland in Granger, and it was quite commonly known that ducks were not permitted to fly over his farm.]

The next years were eventful. On 6 April 1853, the cornerstone of the Salt Lake Temple was laid and the wall around Temple Block was being built. In June, 1854, twins were born—CECELIA ANN and JOSEPH. On 12 May 1855, daughter HELEN married GEORGE THACKERAY. On 25 October 1855, HELEN and THOMAS went to the recently completed Endowment House for their own endowments and sealing.

The Death of Chief Walker

On 26 January 1855, Chief Walker who had caused so much sorrow and bloodshed in Utah, died at Meadow Creek, Millard County, Utah, and was buried in the mountains up Walker Canyon. Meadow, today, is a small town about four miles below Fillmore, Utah, where many of my husband GROVER SWALLOW's ancestors are buried; in fact, he was born there. The following was written by his aunt LAURA DUNCAN (Edwards):

"Chief Walker seemed to be a very cruel man, and most of the whites were afraid of him. At that time our town [Meadow] was a vast meadow of tall grass and the pioneers ran their cattle here in the summer time, and they would also cut the grass and use it for winter feed. The men would always return to the fort at Fillmore to spend the night as they were afraid the Indians would make trouble for them.

"One day the cattle stampeded and all came running to Fillmore and they were shot full of Indian arrows. The leader at Fillmore asked someone to volunteer to go to Meadow and try and find out what the trouble was. At that time Chief Walker and his band were camped on the northeast corner lot of our town today. The old creek ran from the mountains right down through the green meadow and the Indians were camped on the creek. My grandfather JAMES DUNCAN volunteered to find out, if possible, what the trouble was.

"He started out on foot along the foothills in the thick cedars. A little while after he started he met a man named King . . . looking around for his cattle . . . He came on to Meadow with Grandfather. As soon as they were near enough so they could see the Indians they hid behind Cedar trees and watched. The Indians were all dancing around in circles and moaning and carrying on like they did when one of their tribe had died. One Indian left the dance and ran out a few steps and shot a pony, then in a few minutes another one would run out and do the same thing until they had killed several ponies. These were killed so Chief Walker would have them to ride in his happy hunting ground. They ceased dancing and some of the braves tied Chief Walker (who had died) on one of the horses. They all formed in a line and went up the canyon.

"The story goes that they buried alive one of the papooses with him. The papoose worked its head up though some of the pickets they placed over the grave. He was seen and heard crying, but the Indians gave the white people strict orders not to go into that canyon and not to even try to make a road up there as that canyon was their chief's happy hunting ground."

GROVER's father, THOMAS C. SWALLOW told us one day, that they had buried two of his wives up to their necks and some young boys to herd his cattle, and when great-grandfather JAMES DUNCAN heard that the child was alive and crying, he jumped on his horse and galloped up Walker canyon to try to save him; but he had already died. In January, there was probably heavy snow and ice.

⟶ 22 ⟵

THE "HOT AND BLOODY" ELK MOUNTAIN MISSION BY THE COLORADO RIVER

"An Indian Mission known in the history of the Church as the Elk Mountain Mission was established for the purpose of educating a tribe of Indians who occupied the region of country in south-eastern Utah in the vicinity of the Elk Mountains (now the La Salle Mountains). Their main rendezvous was in a little Valley on the Grand River [Colorado River] where the city of Moab is now situated. Those who went on this mission were called at a general Conference of the Church held in Great Salt Lake City in April, 1855. Forty-one men were called, namely . . . JAMES [A.] IVIE, JOHN LEHI [IVIE] . . . Wm. W. Sterrit, ANDREW JACKSON ALLRED . . . Martin Behunin, Wm. Behunin . . . Alfred N. Billings was appointed president of the mission by President Brigham Young. [From Gottfredson's *Indian Depredations*]

"The company, after being partly organized for traveling, left Manti, Sanpete County, Monday, May 21, 1855. It consisted of 41 men, 15 wagons, 65 oxen, 16 cows, 13 horses, 2 bulls, 1 calf, 2 pigs, 4 dogs, and 12 chickens, besides implements, seed grain, etc., and provisions. After a hard journey they arrived on Grand [Colorado] River on the evening of June 11th. On the 12th they crossed the river, came to some land that was cultivated by Indians who were friendly and wanted the white people to settle among them. By July they had built a stockade corral of logs, set three feet in the ground and six feet above, and put in their grain, etc. and started work on a stone fort. The fort was finished July 19th.

"One of the settlers writes: 'Sunday September 22nd we changed herd-ground, feeling apprehensive of mischief intended by some Indians as they were very saucy and impudent. On inquiring why we had changed herd-ground, the boys began loading their guns, which caused the Indians to cool down, the Indians went off a short distance to consult together.

Soon three of them started for the field in the direction of the cattle, and in a few minutes James W. Hunt started with a lariat to get his horse. Charles, a son of Suit-Sub-Soc-Its or St. John, followed him [James W. Hunt] on horse-back; he kept telling him to go ahead of him, asking what he was afraid of, Hunt kept turning his head occasionally towards him, as though being apprehensive of danger; they got nearly a mile from the fort when [Indian] Charles told him to look at the stock. He did so, raising himself on tip-toe. That instant Charles shot him, then shouted to another Indian, not far off, to run and take the horses.

"The ball entered Hunt's back . . . This happened about half past twelve o'clock. Ephraim Wight and Sheldon B. Cutler were herding the stock. The Indians left and went across the river, Cutler came to the fort on horse-back and told what had happened. President Billings jumped on behind him. Peter Stubbs followed, and while John Clark and another followed with water . . . The boys carried Hunt in a blanket; but before they got within one fourth of a mile of the fort, the Indians re-crossed the river and came charging towards the boys and stock, raising a war whoop.

"Wm. M. Sterrett, Sheldon B. Cutler and Clark A. Huntington acted as rear guard to the boys who were carrying Hunt and fired upon the Indians who had fired some eight or ten guns before our boys commenced shooting. President Billings was wounded by a ball passing through the fore finger of his right hand. The bullets whistled briskly all around. The men arrived safely with the wounded man and the horses and cattle were taken inside the corral, except those the Indians had driven off. Every man was engaged.

"Soon one of the Indians set fire to our hay stacks which were adjoining the north end of the corral; they were entirely consumed, as also the corn, and it took five or six men steady to carry water to save the corral logs, so as to keep what stock we had on the inside. The firing was kept up by the Indians till after dark. We succeeded in saving the corral, although some of the logs were nearly consumed. Seven Indians were seen to leave, Charles at their head, going to the mountains.

"The day previous (Saturday) two of the boys, Edward Edwards and William Behunin went hunting, expecting to return Sunday afternoon. Captain Capsium, a Tampa Ute, came down to the corner of the fort and corral and talked to Clark A. Huntington for some time when a few more Indians came. They said we had killed two or three of them and wounded as many, and they would not be satisfied till they had killed two more 'Mormons.' They at first denied having killed the two boys who were out hunting and [the Indians] wanted bread. We gave them all we had. The Indians had turned the water off from us. They finally acknowledged killing the two boys out hunting. Hunt expired the following day.

"Early in the morning of Monday, September 24th the Indians came to the fort and said they were glad the three Mormons had been killed; they had killed the two boys as they were coming down the mountain. Thus three of our boys were killed. Three Indians had also been killed and three others wounded, who would die. It was now thought best to move out right away, or we should all die, as the Indians had sent runners out into the mountains for help. We packed up and without breakfast left about eleven o'clock in the morning, leaving fifteen head of horses, twenty-four head of cattle and a calf, besides six head which we gave the Indians. When we got to the north side of Grand river, a brother of St. John an uncle to Charles, the leader, came to us. Clark A. Huntington told him all that had taken place, and what we had left behind. He said it was too bad, but he was only one against many. He said we should have our cattle, and he would see that the bodies of the boys who had been killed were taken care of and buried. Together with his sons he went to the fort and talked to the Indians. He had some difficulty with them, when they began shooting the cattle. The friendly Indians who succeeded in driving away fifteen head of cattle, delivered to us eight cows and kept seven that were wounded. They butchered three head and brought us a little of the meat.

"We arrived in Manti, Sunday, September 30th, between 4 and 5 o'clock p.m. John McEwan who was left behind the last morning driving his pony which was tired, some three miles from where we started, got bewildered and lost his way. The trail being dim and not very easy to follow, left all he had except his gun, and traveled eating nothing from Saturday night the 27th till Wednesday forenoon the 3rd of October about eleven o'clock a.m. when he was met by three men, viz: Nathaniel Beach, John Lowry, Jr., both of Manti and Lyman A. Woods of Provo . . . They arrived at Manti Thursday morning 7:30 o'clock."

In considering my great-grandmother, MARY CATHERINE BARTON IVIE, during her husband's mission in 1855, I have wondered where and what she was doing. She was only 18 years old, and had already buried two children. JOSEPH ALMA IVIE had died the day he was born in Provo. Her second child, PHEBE ELLEN, was buried in Ephraim, 25 July 1854, while the big fort was being built during the previous summer. Alone again, would she have remained in Ephraim with the many Danish immigrants? Would she have returned to Bountiful, where her parents, family, and former friends were still living, or would she have gone to Provo?

MARY CATHERINE's third child, MARY SUSANNAH, would be born in Provo, 7 June 1956. Wherever she was that summer, it was probably difficult and lonely for her. Her husband's family was from the southern United States and her family was from Pennsylvania, a northern state. Utah was becoming multinational very rapidly, and the beginning of the United States Civil War was on the horizon.

JOHN came back home the end of September, 1855—driven from his mission by the Indians. Some had died. With more Indian problems brewing, the little family returned to Provo. MARY CATHERINE was pregnant again.

Early in 1854, Provo had a militia with seven battalions of infantry. In 1855, they were organized into a brigade with Colonel Peter W. Conover unanimously elected as brigadier-general. Colonel Conover needed the militia to go after more cattle an Indian Chief called Tintic had taken. JOHN's brother JIM had been called to go to Fort Supply again. This time he would take his family with him.

— 23 —

THE TINTIC INDIAN WAR—
TROUBLE ON THE SWEETWATER RIVER

Across Utah Lake, on the northwest side, lived a sub-tribe of the Ute Indians that claimed the Cedar Valley and westward—what later became known as the Tintic Valley. They had been stealing cattle and horses there and in the western Utah Lake area. In February, 1856, Chief White Elk walked into the settlement at Cedar Valley and handed them a bunch of arrows with a dead rattlesnake attached. This was the Indian's way of declaring war. That night there were dozens of fires burning along the foothills to the southeast of Cedar Fort.

Deputy Marshal Thomas S. Johnson came to Provo and enlisted a posse of about ten men who, armed with writs of arrest, issued by Judge Drummond, started from Provo and went by way of Lehi where they camped the first night. Colonel Conover accompanied the posse as far as Lehi, at which point he left for Salt Lake City to seek advice from Governor Brigham Young, who was also superintendent of Indian Affairs. The posse stayed at Cedar Fort during the night and on the following morning sent interpreter John Clark to the Indian camp, about a mile southwest of the fort, to talk to Chief Tintic and his followers. Tintic treated the matter with contempt, and spoke vilely of President Young. The Indians were talking of keeping Clark there until dark, and when he left, they planned to kill him. Clark understood their language, he had on an overcoat and carried two revolvers under it on his belt. He had walked to the camp, and, as he was a fast runner, he intended to dodge round.

A squaw on the outside called out, "*Mormons coming.*" The Indians, while talking, had stripped and painted on their war-paints, prepared for fight. They had their spears set up against the tent, easy to get at. When the company came up, Deputy

Sheriff Parish got off his horse and came into the tent, walked up to Tintic, caught him by the hair with one hand, and with revolver in the other said, "Tintic, you are my prisoner."

Tintic grabbed the pistol with one hand and jumped, the pistol went off and shot him through the hand, breaking loose, he slipped through the back of the tent. Then the firing commenced. Tintic's brother, Battest, aimed his rifle at George Parish and fired, but the gun-barrel was knocked aside and missed its mark. One of Parish's friends then drew his revolver and shot Battest through the head, killing him instantly.

George Carson, one of the posse who was outside on his horse, saw an old squaw aim her spear at him, and he raised his leg to ward off the blow, but her spear struck him in the leg. Shots rang out and Carson fell to the ground mortally wounded. One squaw and three or four Indians were also killed and several wounded.

> "John Clark, the interpreter, ran back into the tent and got two guns and four or five bows and quivers of arrows, ran out, untied Tintic's and his brother's horse, jumped onto Tintic's horse and led the other. He laid down on the horse as he rode away, with bullets whistling by him, but escaped without injury." [Gottfredson, *Indian Depredations*]

The posse left; the wounded George Carson was taken in a wagon to Fairfield and laid on a blanket on the exact spot where the monument now stands. He died soon after. The Indians ran for the dense cave banks near Utah Lake. That night they killed two young herders, Henry Moran, and George Carson's brother, Washington Carson, 21 February 1856. As the posse returned in greater numbers, Chief White Elk led his band over the frozen Utah Lake. About one third across, the ice began to break, and from the shore, the posse watched as Chief White Elk defiantly waved his tomahawk at them as he and his band sank into the icy waters.

Meantime, Governor Young had given orders to Colonel Peter W. Conover to raise a company of the Utah County Militia to pursue the Indians and recover the Hunsaker herd of stock which had been driven off. So Colonel Conover, with eighty men crossed Utah Lake on safer ice, and followed the trail of the Indians across the mountains.

Bishop Nephi Packard said:

"While at the fort, the citizens brought in the bodies of Moran and Carson, frozen stiff. Their bodies had been mutilated, and when they were thawed out with warm water for the purpose of dressing them, it created a stench which together with the sight of their mutilated bodies, made him sick. They were buried there."

From *Tullidge's History, Vol. 3* by John Banks:

"Peteetneet, the chief of the Indians on the Spanish Fork, being friendly disposed was consulted. Peteetneet was grieved at the hostilities of Tintic and his band, and remarked that Tintic had ears that were no good and of no use to him. He had good council given him, but he would not hear it, and (Peteetneet) wanted Peanitch, the Indian guide, and three others, when they would find Tintic, 'to cut off his ears, as they were of no good.'" This talk took place just before the marshall, with about seventy-five men, left Palmyra for the western mountains.

John Banks writes:

"We camped the first night on the north end of . . . west mountain, where we experienced an extremely cold night, without any bedding except our saddle blankets, and were not allowed to have any fire after sundown. When day dawned we learned that several of our men had frozen feet, and consequently had to return home." [Across Utah Lake they came to the dugout where Hunsaker's two herders had been killed in the cedars.] "The sight of [the blood] caused quite a sensation."

Peter Conover told his story:

"It was February and very cold. I took eighty men and went over the Tintic mountains. It took us all day. We found a good many cattle dead on the trail, for when one mired down in the snow, they killed it.

"My horse slipped off the trail in one place, and down he went, but I stuck to him and he brought me out all right. At daylight, we passed through where Eureka now stands and camped about one and a half miles down in the valley, but not to sleep. To sleep would have been death, it was so cold. I walked from one fire to another all night. Some of the men got so cold that they burnt out the fronts of their boots while their heels were freezing. The next morning we had no trouble getting breakfast, as we had nothing to cook . . . we followed down where Jericho, now stands, twelve miles below Eureka [to the west]. There the Indians took to the right, into the cedars in the hills.

About noon we came upon their camp where they had about a dozen kettles of meat boiling, almost done. The boys soon put themselves outside of the most of it. We then followed the Indians, who had left upon seeing us, over the hills into the valley. Tintic had now divided the cattle, part to the right and part to the left. We took the left hand trail with the whole Company. In about an hour we espied them. I ordered a charge. We followed on with a rush until we overtook the cattle south of Cherry Creek, at a big sand ridge."

John Banks stated:

"We saw cattle standing up, braced in the snow, frozen quite stiff . . . we picked out the best beef from seventy-five head, having had nothing to eat that morning. Our Indian guide informing us that it was about six miles to the Sevier River, orders were given to march thither to water our stock. There was no trail to follow—the Indians having scattered in every direction. Our horses had been without water since we left the Utah Lake. We camped on the Sevier river that night. Early next morning we found thirty head of horses, but no Indians."

Conover continues:

"[We] espied twenty head of horses. We stopped, held a council and decided to go after them. I ordered Br. Pace to take his company and go to the left side of the ridge, while I went to the right with my men. Al. Huntingdon, and an Indian belonging to John Berry, of Spanish Fork, laid down on the side of their horses and ran right around the horses, and drove them down to us. We got all of them we wanted and started to camp. The boys had killed another beef . . . The next morning we started up the river and got to the mouth of Chicken Creek [near Mills on Interstate 15]. There we turned north to Dog Valley and camped there and killed another beef. Next day we came to Nephi, had supper and breakfast and fed the cattle and horses hay in the tithing yard. We then came on to Provo as fast as we could. I issued an order for the people that owned the horses and cattle to come and prove them and take them away. This the Tintic War was my last Indian raid. We then put in our crops."

John Banks adds to this account:

"[We] came out at Nephi. The inhabitants had rallied to a point on the north side of their herd to save the cattle." When they saw the troops, they "supposed the Indians were making for the settlement, and would take the town before any of the citizens could get back." Both parties rejoiced, when they found they were their friends; and the militia rejoiced when they were treated to "plenty of good food to eat, having had nothing to eat for seven days previous except fresh beef, without salt—weary and tired, we appreciated the comfortable beds and happy rest afforded us that night."

From the *Deseret News* of March 5th, 1856:

"Tintic, head chief of the disaffected band, and who was wounded in the skirmish near the south fort in Cedar Valley, is reported dead."

Fort Supply — Artist's conception of Mormon fort near Ft. Bridger before it was burned

Grandfather JAMES OSCAR IVIE tells us that his father, JOHN LEHI IVIE, participated in this war, and was with Colonel Conover's troops.

In April 1855, some 19 missionaries were called to the Fort Supply Mission, including ISAAC BULLOCK, HENRY W. SANDERS, MOSES M. SANDERS, and Elijah Barney Ward.

On 24 February 1856, the *Journal History* lists more colonists called to Fort Supply. Among the twelve families from Provo we find the names of JAMES A. IVIE and Peter W. Conover. Many others were sent from Great Salt Lake City and a few from Springville, Palmyra, Tooele, Payson, Nephi and Lake City. They brought their families with them and had fine gardens and community life. It was in October of 1856 that these stalwart colonizers came hastily to the aid of two large companies of handcart emigrants, the Martin and Willie Handcart Companies, and also the wagon company that had followed behind to aid them.

Fort Supply residents helped rescue marooned Willie and Martin handcart pioneers

To accomplish this, all of the men at Fort Supply with Judge ISAAC BULLOCK as the leader, had taken all the oxen down to two years old. They had hoped to meet the desperate parties by November 21st and bring them to Fort Supply and Fort Bridger where they could stay until spring if necessary; but relief came from the Salt Lake Valley, also, and all but a few journeyed on and were in the Salt Lake Valley by December 16th, 1856. It is certain that the aid given the Martin and Willie Handcart Companies by the people of Fort Supply was instrumental in saving the lives of several hundred of the unfortunate emigrants. The name of JAMES A. IVIE (JIM) is listed with those who came to their aid. Coming with his wagon from Bountiful was second-great-grandfather JOHN BARTON.

REDDICK N. ALLRED, former sergeant in the Mormon Battalion, and later the captain of a seventy-two wagon train that had arrived in Salt Lake City 16 November 1849, at first lived with his family in Salt Lake County. In 1852 he was called on a three years mission to the Sandwich Islands [Hawaii], and on his return, he found his family had moved north to Davis County. He brought his wagon to General Conference in Salt Lake City in 1856, and was there when the news of the handcart companies arrived. When the call came to rescue the snowbound companies, he, as a captain of ten, took his wagon loaded with supplies. At the Sweetwater River near South Pass, Captain George Grant asked R. N. ALLRED to remain there in the freezing blizzard with his men and their wagons and be ready to help when the rescuers returned with the handcart pioneers.

They first found the Willie Handcart Company—freezing, dying and starving. Captain Grant left part of his men to help them and took others into the unmerciful storm in search for the Martin/Tyler Company. Helping the Willie pioneers up the Rocky Ridge, the rescuers were greatly relieved when ALLRED and the other supply wagons brought them food, clothing, and got them into wagons for the journey to Salt Lake City.

But Captain George Grant had not returned with the Martin pioneers. As the weeks passed and the blizzard continued in its fury, blowing the snow into high frozen drifts, two of his companion wagoners decided they had waited long enough and started back, against the wishes and determination of the stalwart REDDICK ALLRED. He would wait as ordered. Those who returned took wagons, supplies, and turned seventy-seven wagons around that were coming to help, until President Young sent messengers to them to continue the search.

REDDICK ALLRED had waited three weeks in the turbulent icy winds before Captain Grant arrived with the even more destitute Martin Company. Grant's supplies were running low. ALLRED's persistence in realizing "they also serve, who stand and wait," gave comfort and new life to the hundreds. ELIZA CUSWORTH BURTON and her two young children, JOSEPH, seven years old, and MARTHA, four years-old, were among those who were rescued from death. She is a step-great-grandmother of my sister ADELIA's husband JOSEPH RILE.

A year later, in 1857 in Pleasant Grove, she married his second-great-grandfather, the widower NATHAN STAKER. They moved to Mount Pleasant in 1859. Her story was written by Mrs. A. V. Miner, Longsdorf's book of *Mount Pleasant*, it reads:

"January 19, 1924 marked the 100th anniversary of the birth of ELIZA C. B. STAKER. In England she was a flower girl and carried flowers and sang "God Save the Queen" at the coronation of Queen Victoria. She married Joseph Burton in 1846. While making preparations to emigrate to Utah her husband died, leaving her with two small children, a boy and a girl.

"She and the children left England in the early spring of 1856 on the good ship *Horizon* . . . and were seven weeks on the ocean. They went by train and boat from New York to Council Bluffs, waited . . . for handcarts to be made . . . Joseph walked the entire distance and often helped push the cart. They came in Martin's and Tyler's company and did not reach

Salt Lake until November 30, 1856 . . . The company comprised 500 men, women, and children, one fourth of which died while on the trip . . . The first and larger streams they ferried, but later in the season, they waded the streams. Mrs. STAKER waded the Sweet Water three times in one evening, first taking the boy across, then the girl, and then her handcart. At one time there were nine persons, one man, two women, and the rest children, died in one night. They died of Cholera. They thought the Cholera was caused by drinking alkali water. They buried them in their clothes, and had no tools, they put them in the washes and kicked dirt over them. In Wyoming they ran entirely out of food. They were given some pelts of deer and mountain sheep that were old and dry. They scraped the hair off from them and cooked them thickened with a little bit of flour. This mixture was almost like glue. The company was cheerful and sang songs every night and tried to cheer each other up.

"When the snow came, they cleared it away as much as possible and made their beds on the ground. One night Joseph was very wet and cold and in the night his feet were frozen. His big toe and one other came partly off. After a time teams came from Salt Lake and helped them into the valley. They would not let them have all they wanted to eat as it would have made them ill. Mrs. STAKER had gold in her pocket and could buy nothing to eat."

This was a time of phenomenal stories of faith, spirituality, and struggle, and a Church Visitor's Center called *Martin's Cove* has been constructed in this area of Wyoming, where several 100,000 travelers stop every summer and hear their stories.

During this winter, on 23 January 1857, JOHN LEHI IVIE married his second wife, MARY ETT CARTER. She was fifteen years-old. MARY CATHERINE BARTON IVIE was nineteen, and JOHN was twenty-three. To take a plural wife required the permission of the first wife, who remained in charge of the household. Living in Provo at this time, they had only tiny six month-old, MARY SUSANNAH. MARY ETT's father had two wives, who were sisters and lived in two separate houses in Provo. JOHN LEHI IVIE's three older brothers each had two or three wives. Plural marriage was encouraged by Brigham Young at that time. Single women had few ways to support themselves, and safety was a large problem. If they were unmarried, they remained the maiden aunt in their parent's household—something few women wanted to be. Their children were their jewels. MARY CATHERINE probably welcomed the younger MARY ETT, from a Northern family, with similar experiences, much like her own—at least for awhile.

~ 24 ~

Johnston's Army and the Invasion of Utah Territory and Government

When Wilford Woodruff was president of the St. George Temple in the 1880s and George Washington and other early patriots appeared to him and requested that their temple work be performed for them, Woodruff quickly had their temple ordinances done. (MOSES M. SANDERS was the proxy for Benjamin Franklin.) They did the temple work for all the presidents of the United States who had died prior to that time except—Van Buren and Buchanan. When Van Buren had been asked for his help against the Missouri atrocities, he had refused, saying, "Your cause is just; but I can do nothing for you."

Buchanan, a conciliatory Pennsylvania U. S. President (1857-1861), who preceded President ABRAHAM LINCOLN, tried to avoid civil war by compromise. Jefferson Davis, who would become the President of the Southern Confederacy, had been the Secretary of War for President Franklin Pierce. When Buchanan took office, the strong Democrat Senator Jefferson Davis worked hard to extend slavery into Kansas and further west to California. Democrat Senator Stephen L. Douglas of Illinois was his strong opponent, and a break occurred in the Democratic Party, opening the way for the Lincoln/Douglas debates and the Republican Party.

As this division of the nation widened, Missouri and Kansas became a focal point with the abolitionist Jayhawkers of Kansas, against the secessionist Bushwhackers of Missouri. Violence and demands increased. Missouri's hatred of the Mormons had not subsided and still continued with horrendous lies, even with the distance between them. The culmination was Drummond's falsified letter of resignation as Associate Justice of Utah Territory (Drummond had hoped to be appointed Governor of the Utah Territory). Buchanan chose to believe all his lies without confirmation, and sent an army of 2500 to Utah to destroy the Mormons.

A second, more subtle, reason for this army was the hope of the Southerners to bankrupt the nation and greatly weaken its financial and military capacity— thus giving the South as much advantage as possible in the civil war that was approaching rapidly. A war with the Mormons would cost the country considerably, and it would be excellent training for the southern troops. Drummond's letter was published widely and gave the president the public support he wanted. On 20 May 1857, President Buchanan issued his extermination order and chose *Squaw-killing Harney* (the general who had escalated the prairie war) to lead the U. S. Army against the *rebel Mormons* of the Utah Territory.

It was not until the tenth anniversary celebration of Pioneer Day, 24 July 1857 that the Utah people became aware of this new order of extermination. Porter Rockwell arrived at the Big Cottonwood Canyon party with his first *Pony Express mail delivery* and the news that the troops were on their way to destroy Mormondom. When Brigham Young received the news, he called the large group of saints together and repeated his words of a decade ago, "Give us ten years of peace, and we will ask no odds of Uncle Sam or the Devil." He then pronounced, "God is with us and the devil has taken me at my word." He then told them of the forthcoming invasion of their territory and the extreme folly of sending an army to subdue a people guilty of no crime. To vent the strong feelings of the group, they continued with their singing and dancing.

Playing the fiddle at this dance was JOHN NIELD, a brother of GROVER's great-grandmother ALICE NIELD who married WILLIAM HENRY STOTT of Fillmore, Utah. JOHN in his short autobiography tells us his remembrance of the occasion:

"July 24, 1857, we celebrated pioneer day. We had a good time—Firing the cannon, music procession, a fine program at the bowery. I played the fiddle at a dance for the first time. This 24th, Brother A. O. Smoot arrived from the east and reported that they refused to deliver our mail to him at Independence, Mo. A fuss is sure to come. 2500 troops are started out here. They will come and raise what they call a 'standard of liberty' and expect that enough will rally to them from amongst us to wipe out the rest. Our military forces are called out to drill and ordered to be on hand for service at any time with wagon and four horses to each ten men, with arms, ammunition and provisions . . . A good deal of excitement was raised with some; but the people generally were cool and collected and were ready to defend our liberties to the death if necessary."

The NIELDs had come from Oldham, Lancashire, England. They had heard the gospel and joined the LDS Church—father, LUKE NIELD, had been baptized 8 February 1843. By working ten hours a day in a cotton mill and carefully saving, but still participating in Church activities, they were able to sail for America from Liverpool on the ship *Marchfield*, 8 April 1854. Of the LDS Church in England, JOHN NIELD wrote:

> "After my ordination to the priesthood I attended an average of 5 meetings a week and two for music and Mutual Improvement . . . These religious meetings furnished sweet morsels to my soul, which I never can forget. Testimonies, singing and speaking in tongues and prophesy will remain among the saints . . . My whole soul was in the Lord's work. But of course, making allowances for nonsense and blunders sometimes common to poor mortals."

They arrived in Salt Lake City 24 October 1854. Unfortunately, their mother, MARTHA WILD NIELD, contracted cholera and died. She was buried eleven miles from the temple site in Jackson County, Missouri. They first settled at Lehi. Daughter ALICE married WILLIAM HENRY STOTT of Fillmore, Utah, 27 December 1855.

The U. S. Army that was moving westward included the Fifth Infantry and eight companies of the Tenth Infantry and was supported by twelve artillery pieces. Strangely, the United States War Department sent ahead the assistant quartermaster of the U. S. Army, Captain Stewart Van Vliet, to learn what fuel and forage could be obtained from the Mormons and to locate a suitable campsite near Great Salt Lake City.

Upon being questioned, Governor Young informed him politely that theirs was an invading army and would not get any fuel, and moreover, they would not be allowed into the valley. He then asked him to take them a letter written by Mormon Adjutant General James Ferguson, in which he requested of them their manuals on infantry tactics, cavalry tactics, fortification, and any others that they felt might be useful.

Van Fleet returned east and reported:

> "I told them that they might prevent the small military force now approaching Utah from getting through the narrow defiles and rugged passes of the mountains this year; but next season [there would be] sufficient

troops to overcome all opposition . . . I attended their service on Sunday, and [in a sermon] . . . Elder Taylor . . . referred to the approach of troops and declared they should not enter the Territory.

"He then referred to the probability of an overpowering force being sent against them, and desired all present, who would apply the torch to their own buildings, cut down their trees, and lay waste their fields, to hold up their hands. Every hand, in an audience numbering over four thousand persons, was raised at the same moment."

Van Vliet boldly protested against the coming "Mormon War," but was unable to convince his commanding officers. He also learned that a new commander had been chosen to replace Harney, Colonel Albert Sidney Johnston. Johnston was a Southerner who intensely disliked Brigham Young and all those "abolitionist Mormons" from the North and foreign countries. He felt that while slavery was a blessing to the African, the white people of the South, and therefore the state, Mormonism was a curse that must be stopped.

In a few years, the Southern General Albert Sidney Johnston would join with the Confederacy, taking with him most of the troops he now commanded. In Johnston's class of 1824 at West Point were his friends—Jefferson Davis, Robert E. Lee, and Joseph E. Johnston. The real rebels to the United States of America at that time were not the Latter-day Saints, but President Buchanan, Jefferson Davis, Colonel Johnston and their many friends, and loyal followers.

As the soldiers advanced westward and negotiations continued to fail, on 15 September 1857, Governor Young declared martial law. By the 27th of September orders came from the Church to Fort Supply and Fort Bridger, which was now owned by the Church, to evacuate everyone. Both forts were to be burned to the ground. Fort Supply would never be rebuilt. By the 29th of September, around 1,250 Mormon militia men were ordered into Echo Canyon, as that appeared to be the U.S. Army's proposed entrance route into the Salt Lake Valley. Our relations who had been called to Fort Supply with their families, who may still have been there at the time it was to be burned, were JAMES A. [Jim] IVIE, MOSES M. SANDERS, HENRY W. SANDERS and ISAAC BULLOCK [GROVER's relative-in-law].

Traveling the same route across the plains that summer of 1857, on the north side of the Platt River across from Johnston's Army on the south side, were additional LDS pioneers. Grandfather GIBSON A CONDIE tells us of these memories of his mother, HANNAH SWANN, who was nine years old as she walked most of the way. He wrote:

"My great-grandfather, EPHRIAM SWANN was born in Ninevah, Worcestershire, England, January 2, 1792, and died Nov. 11, 1862. His wife, ELEANOR BROOME, was born July 15, 1798 and died April 8, 1894. They had 4 children, JAMES, ELLEN, EPHRIAM, and HANNAH. My grandfather, EPHRIAM SWANN, was born in Ninevah, near Tenbury, Worcestershire, England, May 25, 1824. He married FANNY JONES, who was born May 26, 1828 in Lathly House, Berford, Worcestershire, England.

"They were baptized into the LDS Church, about Sept. 1856. They sailed from Liverpool, England on the ship *George Washington*, Mar. 28, 1857, landing in Boston in three weeks [claimed by the captain to be a record crossing]. They had three children, two of them died as the journey continued to Zion. Mother shared the family sorrow when a brother and a sister died the same day [of an infectious disease], yet were buried 100 miles apart, as the company of Saints were en route to Florence, Nebraska. The railroad afforded very poor accommodations, some of the people being crowded into cattle cars. At the R. R. Terminus, oxen and wagons were obtained and a caravan of Prairie Schooners was soon equipped for the company to start on the tedious journey of crossing the plains.

"Grandfather's outfit consisted of 2 yoke of oxen and a wagon, pretty well loaded. A hand-cart company was on the way, also the flower of the U. S. Army moving across the plains intent on destroying the reported rebellious Mormons. Mother related incidents along the journey wherein these companies passed and repassed each other. The army mule drivers were notorious for their profanity. This was the year Lot Smith was sent by Brigham Young to harass and delay Johnston's Army, stampede cattle, wreck supply trains, etc. Mother relates that they were humiliated when Lot Smith with 30 men halted a long train of wagons loaded with army supplies, told the teamsters to load some flour and bacon on a few wagons and go while he and his men burned the rest of the wagons and the supplies.

"When camp was made in the evening the wagons were left in a circle forming a corral to hold the cattle while yoking them to the wagons. The cattle were turned out to graze during the night. Sometimes they would take fright and stampede. This happened one morning after the cattle had been corralled and were being hitched to the wagons. All of a sudden the animals turned wild and jumped wagons or whatever was in the way and made for the open plains. Three persons were killed. The men pursued the fleeing cattle, seeking to recover them. It was a serious and exciting time. Some of the animals were lost. One of Grandfather's oxen was missing, another man was in the same trouble. He proposed that SWANN leave part of his load (a cook stove and other heavy articles) and make room for some of his effects and take his lone ox to make a team, thus SWANN had two yoke on his wagon and the other man one yoke and a lighter load. They arrived in Salt Lake City, Sept. 12, 1857."

They had moved onward before Fort Bridger and Fort Supply were burned. During the move occasioned by the advent of the Army to Utah, the SWANNs moved south to Beaver, Utah. Returning to Salt Lake City they soon after settled in Ogden. In the spring of 1860, they moved to Weber valley, living on Dalton Creek, near Milton, Morgan County, Utah.

JOHN LEHI IVIE was chosen as major of the Provo militia Fourth Battalion only shortly before the news of Johnston's army arrived. In the Church Historical Records there is mention of the "two IVY brothers, JIM and JOHN" delivering a message from the army to General Daniel H. Wells later. My cousin, WILLIAM (Bill) IVIE, insists that great-grandfather JOHN L. IVIE and his brother JIM (still in their mid 20s) were with Lot Smith, and everywhere Lot Smith was, they were there.

Peter Conover was not in Echo Canyon until mid-October. His journal states:

"Brigham got a telegram to the effect that Colonel Harney was coming out to handle all the Mormons. Brigham sent me an order to take a Company of men to meet the Army. After I had gotten my Company organized, he concluded that we did not have ammunition enough, so he ordered me to take ten men and go west, get the Carson Valley Missionaries to come in, and he would send my orders and a guide to Ruch Valley to meet me. Other men were with him, and I had ten men with me. We did not travel on the northern route as the Indians were so bad there (the Snakes). I met the guide, he was O. B. Huntingdon . . . We left Provo on 17 August 1857."

They had a difficult journey south of the Great Salt Lake, across the salt flats. They did not see any Indians; but food and water were very scarce. Traveling thirty-five to sixty miles a day, he mentions Redding Springs, Deep Creek, Antelope Springs, the head of Steptoe Valley, a spring at the south of Ruby Valley, through a canyon known as Railroad Canyon, passing between the Ruby and Humbolt Mountains to a fork of the Humbolt River. They traveled west up the stream until they came to the Hastings road which shortly became so steep they had to dismount and lead their horses until they got to the top of the mountain. The other side was so steep that Hastings and his group had taken their wagons apart and let them down with ropes, one at a time. Hastings had cut poles and slid their boxes down on them. Conover and his party led their horses down, being very careful of their footing. It was called Break-down Pass. The view from the top was wonderful. At the bottom, they discovered the poles that Hastings used.

> "We kept on our trail, the one the guide had taken years before . . .when there was plenty of water. We traveled on, man and horses almost perishing with hunger and thirst. I was worrying along with my pack animal. She had given out, but I . . . would not . . . leave her to die. GEORGE BEAN stayed with me to help . . . BEAN's tongue as well as mine, were swollen so badly we could scarcely keep them in our mouths . . . about 4 o'clock . . . the guide had given up. He could not see, hear or make a loud sound. Steve Moore and Joe Dudly said they believed he was lost, and they were going to find water . . . They did find some and thereby saved the lives of the company."

They had a lively time with plenty of water, killed Conover's pack mule for food, jerking all they didn't eat. Then filling every available container with water—plus the entrails of his slaughtered mule, they traveled on for two days to the sink of Walker's River, and then, after most of the company had passed by a poison spring, one man and his horse tried it out, and suffered severely for their few swallows. Traveling on until about 11 o'clock that night, they reached the south side of the sink of the Carson River.

> "I had taken some men and rode on ahead and found a band of Indians. Wheeler had been there for years before and was acquainted with some of them, and could talk their language. We rode right into the camp of about fifty lodges. They were drying fish. [With Wheeler's assistance, the Chief agreed to pilot them to Rag Town] where they could get provisions." Arriving around 2 o'clock, they gratefully accepted dinner, obtained their supplies, and travelled back to their delighted company.

Traveling up the Carson River, they came to a saloon kept by a man called Dutch John, ate supper about dark, then started over the mountain until around midnight. Awaking early they reached the top of the mountain and viewed with thankfulness the Washoe valley below, where the President and the missionaries and their families lived. They found the President at breakfast.

> "I gave him my message [from President Brigham Young] . . . it asked for all the ammunition we could find and for me to take the money and go to California. [The President furnished $5,000] that he had received for

tithing and which he was planning to take to Salt Lake with him."

He would be leaving soon to attend the October General Conference in Salt Lake City. Meetings were called throughout the Washoe Valley, Genoa, and the Carson Valley—another $7,000 was raised.

Arrangements were made for Bob Walker to go to San Francisco with $1260 in gold to buy the ammunition with orders to deliver it to Stockton by steamboat.

"Bob Walker was a clerk to a merchant in Genoa and was going to San Francisco to pay for some goods he had got and get some more . . . he was well known there. At the council I decided to go with O. S. Huntingdon after the ammunition if they would furnish the horses, saddles, blankets, etc., and they agreed to that . . . The next morning we got the horses and started on over the mountains [Sierra Nevada]. It was the sixth of September. Two young men volunteered to go with us as there were reports of robbers on the road."

They rode all day, rose early and about two o'clock they came to the Big Trees, where they got their dinner and fed their horses, then rode eighteen miles to a place called Angel's Camp. Conover had a letter of introduction from Nickerson with him. He was treated kindly. In the morning he sent a telegraph to Walker asking, "if he had got what he went after." And the answer came back positive. It was all ready to be shipped on the steamboat.

"On the fourth day I got up very early in the morning and went over to the tavern. The news boy came and threw the daily paper in on the stand. I picked it up and read it. The first thing I saw was that Harney had started with, I am not sure whether the number is 15,000 or 1,500, to handle all the Mormons. And that on the 22 of July, the Mormons and Harney had had a fight, and that the Mormons had killed six-hundred of his men; and that he had gone back for reinforcements. That the Mormons had sent for two thousand dollars worth of ammunition and as many pistols and guns, and that the Mormons with the ammunition must be stopped at some point; and the Governor had issued orders to stop them at Angel's Point . . . . I read this in the Sacramento Bee. I laughed, for the ammunition had not even got there yet . . . Travers, the Tavern keeper said, what's up now. I told him I was laughing at this d----d lie in the paper. Said he, how do you know that it is a lie? I said, because I started out on the 17th, and the Mormons were all at home, minding their own business . . . Said I, John two heads are better than one. He called me into a back room and asked me what was up. We sat down on a sofa and I told him the whole truth and what we had come for, and all about it. Well, said he, you have paid for it and you shall have it, and it is a shame that you should have such a time after buying anything from the Government, to have it taken away by the Government. He said that I should have what I bought if he had influence enough to get it for me. I had my teams already hired and in the yards, ready to load the ammunition as soon as it should arrive. Walker had bought 12,000 pounds of other goods with the ammunition.

"Next morning Travers handed me the key to his warehouse, to where the goods were consigned to. Our horses were stabled close by where the warehouse was. We had a tent and slept in it to guard them. When we went in to breakfast, the same paper came up again, with the statement doubled. The miners that boarded at the Tavern were determined to take the ammunition away from me as soon as it arrived. It arrived on the 15th, in the night, in a big rain storm. We were laying at the warehouse watching for it. I opened the gate myself for the wagons to come in. As soon as the wagons stopped I slid under and loosened the trail wagon, and we ran it into the warehouse, and locked it up. Then came out and took the hind end gate out of the big wagon where the twelve thousand pounds of goods were. Just as I got that done about fifty men came pouring in, with a big Missourian at their head. I said to them gentlemen, I am very glad you have come, for I want help to unload so that I can get away from here as soon as possible. The Captain said what they had come for was the ammunition and that they were going to have it. The first thing that presented itself in the hay wagon was a big barrel of whiskey. The captain took hold and helped me set it on the scales to weigh. When it was weighed we set it on a platform and took a big auger down from overhead and bored a hole and drawed a bucket full. We called on all hands to come and have a drink. They came to a man. Then the Captain and I got into the wagon and began handing out the goods. Walker weighed and loading into the other wagon, with others helping him.

"The Captain did not know anything about carrying powder in boxes, so we handed out the cases of canister, the same as the other goods, and kept on until we had it all unloaded and loaded into the other wagons. It was now about 11 o'clock at night. The Captain was very much disappointed at not finding a keg of powder in the wagon and got very mad over it and swore that if he had the man that printed that newspaper he would hang him in a minute, for there was not a pound of ammunition, nor a gun, nor a pistol.

"Then they began to go by twos and threes, until there was not one of them left with us. After they had all left us, we sat down and rested; as we were very tired and warm, as it was very warm weather. After all was still, we rolled out the trail wagon. I had reserved two small wagons to haul the ammunition in. We weighed it and loaded into these two wagons. Then as the moon had just risen, the boys hitched up their teams and started right out. G. B. Huntington, Walker and myself staid until the morning of the 10th, to settle up with the Tavern keeper and get our breakfast."

They caught up with their teams around noon. The journey back to Salt Lake with the ammunition and the twenty families of returning missionaries was still very difficult; but they were at least prepared with much more water and food for the journey.

Conover was elected as captain of the guard by the group. After the long journey across Nevada and the salt flats, they crossed the mountains into Grantsville and stopped at JAMES COOLEY's place on the second of October. "They were very glad to see us, as they had heard we were killed and had not heard to the contrary." Conover found his family all well at Provo and glad to see him. He had been at home four days when orders arrived for him to go to Echo Canyon and help with the preparations that were in rapid progress there. He had been gone for two months.

Brigham Young had mandated the Utah militia was to "defeat the U.S. Army, but do not shed blood." How this was to be accomplished was not given to them. "The advancing troops were supplied with food and ammunition, and eager to try their strength with their Mormon foes," wrote militiaman Junius Wells.

The Utah militia still called themselves the *Nauvoo Legion*, to show respect for their former leader, General Joseph Smith. Preparations were made in Echo Canyon as their spies had confirmed this was to be the way the U.S. Army planned to enter Great Salt Lake City. This was the same trail the Saints had come through to enter the valley, and the LDS were well acquainted with it. They dug trenches above the canyon and built breastworks, rolling huge boulders to the precipice of the mountain tops. They had hidden trails, known only to the Nauvoo Legion. To force the army to stay on the canyon road, the river was dammed. There was quicksand that could be made active by soaking.

Jesse W. Crosby wrote:

"Here the enemy could be raked from all our positions, and immense rocks were pried up and fixed in readiness to roll down some hundreds of feet at a given signal; here the body of our men took up their quarter; but the horse companies formed themselves into scouting parties and proceeded near the enemies' camp."

Porter Rockwell had been placed in command, and he next decided to focus on the Army supply trains. One train consisting of twenty-six wagons filled with supplies had preceded Johnston's Army by several months. The supply trains were camped on the Big Sandy, the Green River, and at Ham's Fork, ahead of the infantry. Alexander's infantry marched quickly ahead and caught up to all three supply trains. He gathered up two of them and continued his march to the Rocky Mountains. One of his teamsters reported:

"Soon after we passed through it [collecting the supply trains] a force of Mormon cavalry under Bill Hickman descended upon it, set fire to the wagons and consumed them and their contents . . . The same night or early next morning Hickman's and other Mormon cavalry [referring to Lot Smith's activities] burned up the two large supply trains [collected from] Green river and Big Sandy—thus depriving the army of about 500,000 pounds of provisions intended for its maintenance during the long and severe winter settling in."

It is said that among the civilian supply teamsters with the U. S. Army were eleven year-old William F. Cody, "Buffalo Bill" and James B. Hickok, "Wild Bill."

Porter's next step was to burn the two forts. Fort Bridger had been purchased by the Church from Jim Bridger, although he spread rumors that it was still his as he guided Alexander's infantry to the burned-out ashes. There are receipts still in existence with his signature showing it was paid for. Fort Bridger was the first to be fired—the sky of the entire valley was lit like a meteoric shower. They next galloped to Fort Supply. One of the militia officers reported:

"We took out our wagons, horses, etc., and at 12 o'clock set fire to the buildings at once, consisting of 100 or more good hewed log houses, one saw-mill, one grist mill, one thrashing machine, and after going out of the Fort, we set fire to the Stockade and grain sacks, etc. After looking a few minutes at the bonfire we had made, thence on by the light thereof."

It was the end of Fort Supply—lost mostly in old memories that are rarely recalled. Only a small marker remains on the vast prairie. Fort Bridger was rebuilt by the U.S. Army and many of their homes and belongings can still be viewed by the interested travelers on Interstate 80.

General Wells next wanted Rockwell to enlist forty men to take the cattle; but the army had placed them behind the infantry, so they started to burn the surrounding grass that fed them. The men were shot at by the army cannon; but the cattle feed was gone.

Lot Smith, whose name was not mentioned in Rockwell's report, tells his story:

"October 3rd... We rode nearly all night, and early the next morning came in sight of an ox train headed westward ... On calling for the captain, a large fine-looking man stepped forward and gave his name as Rankin. I informed him that we wanted him to turn his train and go the other way, until he reached the States. He wanted to know by what authority I presumed to issue such orders. I replied, pointing to my men, that there was part of it, and the remainder was a little further on concealed in the brush. He swore pretty strongly... however, he faced about and started to go east ... After traveling fourteen miles, we came up to the train, but discovered that the teamsters were drunk, and knowing that drunken men were easily excited and always ready to fight, and remembering my positive orders not to hurt anyone except in self-defense, we remained in ambush until after midnight."

At midnight Lot Smith and his men advanced into the army camp. They discovered, to their surprise, that they were outnumbered. It was too late to turn back. Then, as they approached the Army's campfire, Smith looked back and realized "that we had the advantage, for looking back into the darkness, I could not see where my line of troops ended, and could imagine my twenty followers stringing out to a hundred or more as well as not. I inquired for the captain of the train. Mr. Dawson stepped out and said he was the man. I told him that I had a little business with him. He inquired the nature of it, and I replied by requesting him to get all of his men and their private property as quickly as possible out of the wagons for I meant to put a little fire into them. He exclaimed: 'For G-- sake, don't burn the trains.' I said it was for His sake that I was going to burn them, and pointed out a place for his men to stack their arms... Captain Dawson and I shortly after went up to the second train. Dawson, shaking the wagon in which the wagon-master slept, called loudly for Bill. 'Bill' seemed considerably dazed and grumbled at being called up so early. Dawson exclaimed with peculiar emphasis, 'D--- it man, get up, or you'll be burned to a cinder in five minutes!' Bill suddenly displayed remarkable activity.

"One old man, shaking with St. Anthony's dance or something ... tremblingly said he thought we would have come sooner and not waited until they were in bed and some of them liable to be burned up. My big Irishman told him we were so busy that we nearly left him without calling him up at all.

"When all was ready, I made a torch . . . At this stage of our proceedings an Indian came from the Mountaineer Fork and seeing how the thing was going asked for some presents. He wanted two wagon covers for a lodge, some flour and soap. I filled his order and he went away much elated. While riding from wagon to wagon, with torch in hand and the wind blowing, the covers seemed to me to catch very slowly. I so stated it to James. He replied, swinging his long torch over his head, 'By St. Patrick, ain't it beautiful! I never saw anything go better in all my life.' About this time I had Dawson send in his men to the wagons, not yet fired, to get us some provisions, enough to thoroughly furnish us, telling him to get plenty of sugar and coffee for though I never used the latter myself, some of my men below, intimating that I had a force down there [though it was non-existent], were fond of it. On completing this task I told him that we were going just a little way off and that if he or his men molested the trains or undertook to put the fire out, they would be instantly killed. We rode away leaving the wagons all ablaze.

"On the morning following we met another train . . . we disarmed the teamsters, and I rode out and met him [the captain] about half a mile away. I told him that I came on business. He inquired the nature of it when I demanded his pistols. He replied: 'No man ever took them yet, and if you think you can, without killing me, try it,'—his eyes flashing fire; I couldn't see mine—I told him that I admired a brave man, but that I didn't like blood—you insist on my killing you, which will only take a minute, but I don't want to do it. We had by this time reached the train," where he and the others were disarmed. Smith then told them "to hurry up and get their things out, and take their two wagons for we wanted to go on . . . We then supplied ourselves with provisions, set the wagons afire and rode on." Lot Smith raided three government supply trains and captured and burned 75 wagons, all near Green River.

Porter Rockwell was told he was near the government cattle camp at Ham's Fork, and the Army camp was at the moment unguarded. Pressing on, he discovered that his old rival, Lot Smith, was already there. Gathering one hundred of their militia, Smith described their next adventure:

"Rockwell and I were good friends, on the following basis: I did as I pleased and he, regularly, d----d me for it. When we arrived in sight of the camp, I discovered a herd of cattle numbering about fourteen hundred head on the bottom lands below. We were on the bluff. I told Porter we would take those cattle. He said that was just like me. The stock was left there as a trap laid on purpose to catch me. The troops had found out what a [fool] I was, and that I didn't know any better than to put my foot into that kind of a trap. The willows were full of artillery, and the minute I exposed myself among the stock they would blow me and my command higher than Gilderoy's kite.

"I told him to sit down and I would go and take the cattle myself. He replied very roughly that he would see me in 'limbo' first, and said that he had waited forty years for such a chance, and now I wanted to spoil it. While he stopped to survey the situation with his glass, I started down the bluff, only about one-third of them being able to keep up as we rushed down the steep descent. Porter came on in a terrible rage, swearing at me for going so fast, and at the men for being so slow. He wanted me to wait for them all to catch up. There was, however, no time to wait. We had to run about two miles to reach the cattle, and by the time we got to them the guards had yoked up teams . . . We intercepted them, unyoked the cattle and turned their heads the other way . . . The boys then gave a shout . . . The guards were frightened as badly as the cattle and looked as pale as death. They came to me and asked me if we were going to take the stock. I replied that it looked a little as if we would. Captain Roupe, the head wagon master [who had sworn the teamsters should have no pay because they would not fight when the trains were burned] was with this company of guards and appeared to be as badly scared as any of them. When he recovered a little from his fright, he asked me to let him have enough cattle with which to take his wagons to camp . . . I gave him about twenty head, and when we returned to where his men were, they made what appeared to me at the time a most singular request. They wanted to know if I would give them their arms back. As we hadn't seen their arms, this request led to an inquiry, when we found that on seeing us coming down the bluff, so much like a lot of wild men, they threw their guns away, some one saying if we found them unarmed we would spare their lives. I told the men they could go and get their guns as we had all we wanted . . . We rode on and soon overtook our men with the stock. We divided the cattle into suitable herds and drove all night. Porter and I piloting the way. As we rode along in the darkness together, he thoroughly enjoyed reflecting upon the events of the day . . . Rockwell went in with the cattle, very much to my regret. I never found many men like him. I think our officers were afraid that he and I could not get along together. But we could."

There were 624 steers and four mules that arrived in the Great Salt Lake City. Additionally, Rockwell left hundreds of the steers for the Mormon patrols to eat in the mountains. Lot Smith ended his narrative of his final weeks in the war by telling us:

> "General Wells had told us that our numbers would be magnified in the eyes of the enemy, and it proved to be so. We passed [in their eyes] . . . for from five hundred to a thousand men, while in fact the whole number never exceeded at any time one hundred, and generally was not half that many . . . President Young said it was providential for all parties [of Smith and Rockwell not finding other Army supply trains], for if we had burned another train we would have been compelled before the end of winter to feed the enemy to keep them from starving."

Left in charge of Rockwell's as well as his own men, Lot Smith continued: "We took our stand, receiving deserters from the enemy daily, and sending them to the Valley. When General Johnston turned towards Salt Lake, after going up Ham's Fork, one would have thought that he would go right through in a few days, but the General began to see how far off Salt Lake really was. Our duty was to watch the troops as they slowly came up to the ruins of Bridger and went into winter quarters. I suppose that it was this position, which the 'London Punch' so graphically pictured in a cartoon in which the flower of the American army is being herded by ten Mormons.

"It soon became evident that the army would settle for the winter. The snow fell and covered the ground a great depth, but it was not so deep as our chaplain prayed for. He asked for twenty feet . . . The word came to us to leave *ten men* on the Yellow Creek Mountains to guard the army. The detail of this illustrious little band was made, and the rest of us turned towards home. When crossing the two mountain ranges, I felt satisfied that Uncle Sam would not attempt to follow."

General Wells wrote:

"Every night those troops encamped I had men among them. Their conduct showed significantly what they meant to do to us. They had doggerel songs, copies of which were captured, announcing their intention to make a barrack of Brigham Young's house, and enjoy his family. These songs inflamed our people, and united us as one man in the defence of our settlements."

On 5 November, Colonel Johnston, before he arrived at Fort Bridger, reported to headquarters in the east that in his opinion "the time for further argument was past and that the time for prompt and vigorous action had arrived, as the Mormons had, with premeditation, placed themselves in rebellion against the Union, and entertain the insane design of establishing a form of government thoroughly despotic and utterly repugnant to our institution." He then commenced his thirty-five mile advance toward Fort Bridger. The snow was heavy, the cold so intense, and the loss of draught mules, oxen and battery horses so tremendous, that it took them fifteen days to arrive at the burned-out fort. "On the night of the 10th the mercury went 25 degrees below zero, and on the morning of the 11th . . . three wagons were abandoned . . . two of them empty and the other hidden in the brush and filled with 74 extra saddles and bridles and some sabers." On November 15th, Johnston reached the Green River and crossed on the ice, and on the 16th, nine wagons and forty-two mules were left there. Lieutenant Colonel Cooke reported that:

> ". . . on reaching Johnston's headquarters . . . I have 144 horses and have lost 134. Most of the loss has occurred, much this side of south Pass, in comparatively moderate weather. It has been of starvation. The earth has a no more lifeless, treeless, grassless desert: it contains scarcely a wolf to glut itself on the hundreds of dead and frozen animals, which for thirty miles nearly block the road, with abandoned and shattered property. They mark, perhaps beyond example in history, the steps of an advancing army, with the horrors of a disastrous retreat."

In the Salt Lake Valley there was little if any snow—they received gentle rain. The anti-Mormon writer John I. Ginn wrote, "No Mormon seemed to question that this simple occurrence was anything short of a direct, visible and tangible interference in their favor on the part of Heaven, so simple and credulous were these ignorant zealots." The Saints, I'm sure, were not totally ignorant of the usual difference in the weather of Wyoming and the Salt Lake Valley, at least those who spent the winters at Fort Supply and the rescuers of the Willie and Martin Handcart Companies. To these we could add the many of us who today have traveled Interstate 80 during inclement weather.

At the officer's mess, many bold statements were made. Captain Albert Tracy passed through the canyon and reported the Saints could not have actually held off the Army—that their artillery could have knocked the Mormons' boulders "about their ears," where guerillas were located atop the canyons. Van Vliet, the scout, disagreed:

> "There is but one road running into the valley on the side which our troops are approaching, and for over fifty miles it passes through narrow canyons and over rugged mountains which a small force could hold against great odds."

On 30 November 1857, Johnston reported:

"Since my last report the troops and all the supply trains have arrived at this place, and will remain here, or in this district, during the winter."

On 30 December 1857, the general had given up on Fort Bridger and moved to Black's Fork. Here he conducted a rather strange court in which his grand jury indicted over one thousand Mormons for "wickedly and maliciously" conducting war on the United States. Johnston sent men south through the blizzards into New Mexico to purchase additional supplies, and livestock, for their attack on the Mormons in the spring, when the weather cleared. Then as the weather began to clear, Johnston received a visitor—Colonel Thomas L. Kane, who had befriended the Saints in Nauvoo and at Winter Quarters. His friendship still intact, he finally, after three weeks, convinced the new Governor of the Territory, Cumming, to go with him to Great Salt Lake City and actually meet and talk to Brigham Young about a peaceful solution. So, on 5 April 1858, Cumming set out on his journey with Kane and no armed escort.

From a letter of John Kay:

"They travelled about fifteen miles, upset one of the carriages in the snow, and there stuck for the night. It so happened that W. H. Kimball, E. Hanks, O.P. Rockwell, Howard Egan, and myself, with a few other good boys, were out scouting in that vicinity, and on the morning of the 6th April, we took the Governor and his small party under our protection."

As they progressed further into Echo Canyon, they were constantly halted by the militia. Campfires burned all night along canyon walls, and when Cumming reached the mouth of the canyon, he estimated he had seen between two and three thousand militiamen. But it was a staged affair. The campfires were unmanned. The numerous bands of militiamen had simply been the same single band circling back over and over again to reproduce the same scene—stopping the Governor's buggy, interrogating him, and letting him pass. Great-grandfather JOHN L. IVIE was undoubtedly there. One of our family histories claims that he and five other men went around and around the mountains of Echo Canyon in an attempt to convince Johnston Army that their small group was a very large army. Cumming was convinced that Johnston's army couldn't succeed . . . even with reinforcements. The negotiation of peace at any price seemed very plausible. Convincing Johnston was more difficult, his pride was at stake.

As he entered Great Salt Lake City, Cumming was surprised to find it quite empty of inhabitants—they had gone south to Provo, or beyond. But with his escort, they soon located President Brigham Young. Cumming had another surprise. President Young proposed that he would turn his entire gubernatorial powers over to Cumming. Peace became even more beautiful. On 3 May 1858, Porter Rockwell escorted the Governor back to Johnston's headquarters.

Back in Washington D.C., President Buchanan, this same week, had started a peace commission towards Utah to release the Mormons from all indictments of treason. He was becoming embarrassed. The press was having a field day at his and Johnston's expense.

From the *New York Times*:

[If we have] "been the means of driving away 50,000 of our fellow-citizens from fields which their labor had reclaimed and cultivated, and around which their affections were clustered, we have something serious to answer for . . . Was it right to send troops composed of the wildest and most rebellious men of the community, commanded by men like Harney and Johnston, to deal out fire and sword upon people whose faults were the result of honest religious convictions? Was it right to allow Johnston to address letters to Brigham Young, and through him to his people, couched in the tone of an implacable conqueror toward ruthless savages? . . . Posterity must not have to acknowledge with shame that our indiscretion, or ignorance, or intolerance drove the population of a whole State from house and home, to seek religious liberty and immunity from the presence of mercenary troops."

From an editorial of the *London Times*:

"Does it not seem incredible that, at the very moment when the marine of Great Britain and United States are jointly engaged in the grandest scientific experiments that the world has yet seen, 30,000 or 40,000 natives of these countries, many of them of industrious and temperate habits, should be the victims of such arrant imposition? [It further stated:] Does it not seem impossible that men and women, brought up under British and American civilization, can abandon it for the wilderness and Mormonism? They step into the waves of the great basin with as much reliance on their leaders as the descendants of Jacob felt when they stepped between the walls of water in the Red Sea."

Reynolds' Newspaper, which represented the British Republicans, said:

"There can be no doubt that, in one thing at least, Mormonism has been eminently successful. It has, in the great majority of instances, really improved the earthly condition of those who have embraced it . . . the Mormons, not as fanatics or sectaries, but as heavily-oppressed, long-suffering, and earnestly struggling men, are entitled to the sympathy of the enslaved classes throughout the world. But they have a claim to something more than sympathy. Their heroic endurance and marvelous achievements entitle them to the respect and admiration of their fellow-creatures . . . and how many thousands of the down-trodden and penury-stricken victims of European tyranny were leaving the land of their birth, in order to find in the Mormon territory, that hope and encouragement denied to them in their native countries; how all this has been accomplished by the reviled followers of Joseph Smith, all Europe and America have heard, and, though hating, admired."

Again from the *New York Times*:

"Whatever our opinions may be of Mormon morals and Mormon manners, there can be no question that this voluntary abandonment by 40,000 people of homes created by wonderful industry, in the midst of trackless wastes, after years of hardship and persecution, is something from which no one who has a particle of sympathy . . . pluck, fortitude, and constancy can withhold his admiration . . . we think it would be most unwise to treat Mormonism as a nuisance to be abated by a 'posse commitatus.' It is no longer a social excrescence to be cut off by the sword . . . When people abandon their homes to plunge with women and children into a wilderness, to seek new settlements, they know not where, they give a higher proof of courage than if they fought for them."

However, when the peace commission arrived, three weeks after Cumming had returned back to Johnston's army, they decided that Cumming was too soft on them. The Mormon's must submit. They wrote to the U.S. Secretary of State: "this deluded people [shall] submit quietly and peacefully to the civil authorities." The commission consisted of thirteen men, plus Senator Lazarus W. Powell of Kentucky, and Major Ben McCullough of Texas.

On 11 June 1858, after being escorted through Echo Canyon, the commissioners arrived and met with Brigham Young and other leaders. They presented their case, after which Brigham Young gave his response. He was interrupted by Porter Rockwell, who whispered to him that Johnston's Army was on the move toward the city. Brigham arose and severely stated:

"Are you aware, sir, that those troops are on the move towards the city?"

"It cannot be! We were promised by the General that they should not move till after this meeting."

"I have received a dispatch that they are on the march for this city. My messenger would not deceive me." The Peace Commission could give no explanation.

Brigham Young's response was to sing the following song in his bold, strong voice, which conveyed his message:

O ye mountains high,

Where the clear blue sky

Arches over the vales of the free;

Where the pure breezes blow,

And the clear streamlets flow,

How I've longed to your bosom to flee.

O Zion! Dear Zion! Land of the free.

My own mountain home,

Now to thee I have come,

All my fond hopes are centered in thee.

Here our voices we'll raise,

And we'll sing to thy praise,

Sacred home of the prophets of God;

Thy deliverance is nigh,

Thy oppressors shall die,

And the gentiles shall bow 'neath thy rod.

O Zion! Dear Zion! Home of the free.

In thy temples we'll bend,

All thy rights we'll defend,

And our home shall be ever with thee.

[This song was written in England by the SWALLOWs' beloved friend, Charles Penrose, who wrote it barefooted while a young missionary, as he walked the dusty roads of Essex, England, before he came to America—changing only a few words after his arrival. The SWALLOWs joined the LDS Church in Essex, England, on 9 November 1854.]

Tullidge wrote:

"The action of Brigham had been very simple in the case, but there was a world of meaning in it . . . There have been times when the singing of that hymn by the thousands of saints has been almost as potent as that revolutionary hymn of France—the Marseillaise."

~ 25 ~

MOUNT PLEASANT SETTLED—
SANPETE COUNTY PROBATE COURT RECORDS

It was March, 1858, that the *Big Move* of forty thousand people from Salt Lake City began in earnest, an exodus that left the city uninhabited. After peace was established, Cummings became governor. The army marched the forty miles to establish Camp Floyd—then the populous started to return. The CONDIEs had moved into a church at Springville. After returning to their home in the city, great-grandfather THOMAS made bricks for Camp Floyd and was paid five dollars a day. He was glad for the employment.

The SWANNs returned from Beaver and moved north into Morgan County. Many who had moved into Fort Ephraim had wanted to stay, especially the Scandinavians, who had just arrived. The larger Fort Ephraim became crowded and the pioneers looked longingly at the open lands to the north. But there were the ghostly remnants of old Hambleton and Springtown to remind them that the Indians were a force of unknown quantity.

In August 1858, JAMES RUSSELL IVIE, Benjamin Clapp, Joseph R. Clement, ISAAC ALLRED Sr., RUEBEN W. ALLRED and RICHARD IVIE were chosen at Fort Ephraim as an exploring committee to select a suitable location for a settlement. Their choice was Pleasant Creek. We know that JOHN L. IVIE was in Ephraim before this time, because their fourth child, ROSELLA ANN, was born in Ephraim 2 February 1858. She would also die in Ephraim, 24 April 1859.

A meeting was called and a petition drafted and signed by sixty men who wanted to accompany them there. After some discussion, in mid August of 1858, it was decided that second-great-grandfather JAMES RUSSELL IVIE with his uncle JAMES ALLRED should take the petition and present it personally to

Brigham Young to obtain his advice. Leaving Fort Ephraim on 2 September 1858, they arrived in Great Salt Lake City on 6 September 1858. They met Elder Orson Hyde on the street and he escorted them to the President's office. Upon studying the petition, Brigham Young expressed himself as favorable. JAMES R. IVIE then told him the petitioners were desirous that he appoint someone to take the lead. President Young declined but drafted the following letter:

Great Salt Lake City, Sept. 6, 1858

Brother John Reese and the rest of the brethren whose names are on the list:

I am perfectly willing that you should go there (Pleasant Creek) and make a settlement, but you must consider whether it will be safe or not. You wish to know my mind on the subject. It is this, that you must build you a good substantial fort and live in it, use every precaution that is necessary against the Indians. Your fort must be twelve feet high and four feet thick, built either of stone or adobe and laid in lime mortar. I also want you to select one of your number for president and one for bishop. You will have to be very careful of your stock or you will lose them. In choosing your farming land get it as nearly together as possible. It would be better to have only one piece fenced. Then you are compact in case of an attack on you by Indians or white men. God bless you is my prayer and that of all other good men.

(Signed) BRIGHAM YOUNG [*Mount Pleasant* by Longsdorf]

The two returned to Fort Ephraim and on September 14th a meeting was held by the group and JAMES R. IVIE, Joseph Clement, and ISAAC ALLRED (probably the brother of JAMES ALLRED) were appointed to 'wait upon' the surveyor, Albert Petty, of Manti, to help them in the survey of the city lots; choice of the site where the Fort would be built, and the survey of the farm land into twenty acre lots. Upon returning to Fort Ephraim around the middle of October, the settlers gathered and drew by number for the various lot locations to begin their land preparations for planting crops the following spring. On 10 January 1859, another meeting was called in the school house to organize and make preparations for the move.

"After discussion of some length, JAMES R. IVIE Sr. was chosen their president and REDDICK ALLRED was chosen bishop. Later, however, REDDICK ALLRED, not being sure he would move north with the party in the spring, declined to accept the position."

About the middle of February, twenty men pitched their camps in a ravine in the cedar hills and began cutting fence posts. The snow was about two feet deep at the town site. ALMA ALLRED was with this group. Later they were joined by ALMA ZABRISKIE, JAMES ALLRED, and SIDNEY ALLRED, who had already brought their cattle and horses north to winter. On 20 March, through snow and mud they moved their wagons and tents to where the fort wall was to be built. On 10 April, others came with a supply of wheat, grain, and farming tools. They were accompanied by President JAMES R. IVIE, ISAAC ALLRED and his sons. More settlers arrived from Utah County, President IVIE added 1200 acres to the original 1300 acres. The land was "a vast area of native grasses in abundance and huge patches of sage brush." Plowing began 16 April with the people living in their tents and in covered wagon boxes. In a month's time, with many unaccustomed to such work, slow oxen, and mostly homemade tools, one thousand acres of ground were cleared and cultivated. Some irrigation ditches had been dug. There were many nationalities; but the Danish people predominated.

President IVIE sent a letter dated 20 April 1859, to President Brigham Young explaining the progress, and Young sent the following answer:

Great Salt Lake City, May 6, 1859
JAMES R. IVIE, Pleasant Creek, Sanpete County.
Dear Brother:

In reply to your letter of the 20th inst. I have to inform you that I have heard no complaint concerning your new settlement and trust there will be no grounds for any reasonable complaints by anyone disposed to do right. In your location it would seem to be an easy matter to manage your affairs justly for the benefit of all concerned, and to make early and efficient steps for building a secure fort that you may be safe in an Indian country and conduct your affairs upon wise principles, living industrious and humble that you may make your settlement beneficial to yourself, the country and the territory at large. In all of which you have the best wishes of your brother in the Gospel.

(Signed) BRIGHAM YOUNG

On 28 April and on 2 May 1859, large numbers of families arrived from Battle Creek [Pleasant Grove]. Included in this number were William Stuart Seeley, JOHN CARTER, MORONI SEELEY, Jesse W. Seeley, Justus Wellington Seeley, and ORANGE SEELEY. They were given a hearty welcome; however the peace of this new settlement was about to change.

The Manti court records began in March 1852. My sister, IVIE BABBEL, and I searched through to 1866. These were the original records, which were old but mostly readable. Manti was part of the First District Court, County of Sanpete, and Territory of Utah. Brigham Young was governor of the Utah Territory, until the office was conferred upon Governor Cummings in 1858.

The records were few and quite briefly recorded. JAMES T. S. ALLRED was one of the Selectmen of Manti and probably, in several cases, the JAMES ALLRED referred to in these early records as giving the prayer and being present.

I have included this case shown on page 16 as it was written as it reflects on the procedures in 1856 regarding a bodily injury case in their Probate Court in that year.

Territory of Utah	)	Probate Court
San Pete County	)	for said County
The People of US	)	March term 1856
in the Territory of	)	Hon. Geo. Peacock
Utah. vs	)	probate Judge
	)	for an assault
ANDREW J. ALLRED	)	on Indictment with intent
		to commit a bodily injury

March 6, 1856

Court in Session

Daniel Henrie, Sheriff returned a warrant having arrested ANDREW J. ALLRED; the Prisoner brought into Court; Indictment read.

George Snow prosecuting Attorney made a motion to stay all proceedings agreeable to the 29th Section of 'an Act regulating the mode of procedure in Criminal cases.' The court dismissed the case and discharged the prisoner.

Court adjourned.

George Peacock

The following court record of March 7, 1859 is as recorded to show the changes made in the judge and jury selection. Evidently the Utah Territorial Legislature had met and allowed the Probate Court to handle the criminal cases.

Manti Sanpete Co. U.T.

Mar 7th 1859

Court in Session

Present—Gardener Snow probate Judge, C. G. Edwards & J. T. S. ALLRED, Selectmen.

The Clerk then arose and gave a brief Statement of the business to be acted at this session. There being a vacancy of Selectmen occasioned by Gardener Snow being Elected Probate Judge: on motion of C. G. Edwards, H. J. Christisen was appointed to fill said vacancy until the ensuing Aug. Election, and was duly qualified and took his seat.

The following named persons were selected to serve as Jurors according to an Act of Legislative Assembly approved Jan 21st 1859.—

Court adjourned till one P. M.

Fifty men were named with their occupations listed, eleven of which would be called as jurors in the trial of THOMAS C. IVIE the following June. It is interesting that C. G. Edwards, a selectman named above, was the twelfth member of this jury. The occupation of the eleven selected jurymen was *farmer* except Martin Lindsay who was shown as a *painter*.

Territory of Utah / Manti Sanpete Co.

June 6th 1859.

June Term of the County Court

present Hon Gard\r Snow Probate Judge

C. G. Edwards, J. T. S. ALLRED & H. J. Christison selectmen, & Geo Peacock Co. Clerk—all present.

Court called to order by the Judge. prayer by his Honor: . . .

A petition was presented by Geo W. Bradley for the right to work a Road into Twin Creek Kanyon (sic) and to control the same. A Remonstrance from Pleasant Creek Settlement was present by Mess\rs Morrison & Clements signed by 111 persons. The matter was duly considered, and Geo W. Bradley and JAMES B [R.] IVIE were appointed Overseers over said Kanyons and working and controlling of Roads and timber thereof, to wit—Pleasant Creek & Twin Creek Kanyons agreeable to an Order of Court passed June 28th 1852 . . .

~ 26 ~

"A House Divided against Itself" Murder in the First Degree

Two days later, in the newly developing city of Mount Pleasant, this sad event occurred. Entitled *The First Murder* in *Longsdorf's* book, it reads:

"On the 11th day of May, 1859, on the south side of the street of what is now known as Main, between State and First West, a certain THOMAS IVIE, assaulted with a fire brand, ISAAC ALLRED, a church veteran and a member of Zion's Camp, breaking ALLRED's skull, and inflicting other injuries upon him, causing his death the following day. The dispute had resulted from a quarrel over the difference of a small herd bill. On the 12th day of May, THOMAS IVIE was arrested and taken to Manti, where he was bound over by Justice Elisher Averett.

"On the 13th of June, a grand jury was impaneled which on the 14th presented a true bill for murder against IVIE. A trial jury was then chosen and the case proceeded; the trial lasted until the 16th when it was admitted to the jury, who returned a verdict of guilty, on Friday, June 17th, Judge Garner [sic] Snow pronounced a sentence of death upon the prisoner."

The above history was written eighty years later in 1939. It glosses over many questions and includes many errors that become apparent upon further study. As a child, I was not told this bit of history. Perhaps it is best left partially buried; however, with the age of computers, this is impossible. Friends of uncle TOM have been slow to tell. My bereaved ALLRED cousins have been more vocal. For myself, not a direct descendant of either, but related to both, I feel the story should be included. I have attempted to locate the original documents. This has taken many journeys and hours of time. The event occurred on 11 May 1859 and came within the jurisdiction of the First District Court of Utah. The great division of our nation was eminent at that time and a new personality,

ABRAHAM LINCOLN, would be elected President in the fall of 1860. South Carolina passed an ordinance of secession on 20 December 1860. Although duels were illegal, a man's pride was still very important and an insult to him or his family was not taken lightly. Fighting was not an uncommon way to settle a dispute.

In Lincoln County, Nevada, I searched some of the old records of their court cases, as Pioche, Nevada, founded in 1865, was considered by many to be the most violent town in the west. They claimed 75 deaths occurred before there was one from natural causes. These cases are from the early 1870s, as the 1860s, although wilder, were not as carefully recorded.

A few cases condensed from the Pioche, Nevada, Court Records:

June 29, 1870—A man killed at Pioche—Hard feelings between the parties the cause.

September 4, 1870—A man was killed at a mill (near Pioche)—He was an important witness in a lawsuit over the title to a ranch. The killer escaped over the line into Utah.

October 30, 1870,—R. H. Carson, alias "Kit" was killed at Pioche by parties unknown.

February 15, 1871, John Clappy, with several aliases, was killed by Jas. D. Kennedy, in Pioche. Kennedy was convicted of murder in the second degree, and obtained a new trial. The case was finally 'nolle prossed.'

March 12, 1871. Thomas Gorson was killed by Mike Casey, at Pioche—A business settlement was the cause.

May 30, 1871, Mike Casey was killed by James Levy, at Pioche—Acquitted.

July 7, 1871, Samuel Cooklin was killed by a Sheriff's posse, at Pioche—He resisted the officer, firing at them; they had to shoot him.

August 5, 1871, George M. Harris was shot and killed by D. A. Myendorff at Pioche. Harris slapped Myendorff across the face, thereupon the latter killed him. Myendorff acquitted.

November 26, 1871, James Butler was killed by Special Officer Shea, at Pioche. Insulting and threatening language was the cause--Acquitted.

November 26, 1871, John G. Wood was killed by Pres Standifer, at Pioche. The citizens held that the killing was justifiable.

October 2, 1872, Charles Hickey was killed by Mike Holland, at Pioche—A newspaper article reflecting on Hickey and contributed by Holland was the cause. The grand jury ignored the bill against Holland.

November 5, 1872, John F. Strain was fatally shot in an altercation between George Manning and a man named Dow, at Pioche. Cause—an election row. Manning, charged with the shooting, was examined and discharged.

November 20, 1872, William McCarthy was killed by James Woods, at Pioche—Quarrel over a game of cards. Woods was acquitted, as McCarthy struck first.

May 1, 1873, Thomas Welch was killed by Frank Soule, at Pioche—old business transactions. Soule acquitted.

May 8, 1873, S. D. Potter was killed by Jeff Howard, at Pioche—Quarreled over a game of cards. Howard got 10 years in the State Prison.

July 6, 1873, John H. Lynch was shot and killed by James Harrington at Pioche—Dispute over a dog. He wounded three other men at the same time. Harrington was sentenced to 15 years in the State Prison.

August 1, 1873, Morgan Courtney was shot and killed by George McKinney, at Pioche, who lay in wait for him and shot him in the back. McKinney was acquitted.

August 1, 1873, B. H. Kistle was shot and killed by D. W. Cherry at Pioche. He was stealing Cherry's barley. Cherry was acquitted.

September 2, 1873, John Manning was shot and killed by Deputy Sheriff McKEE at Pioche in self-defense. Acquitted.

October 5, 1873, Antonio Cardinos was killed by Charles Peasley at Pioche in a bar room fight. Acquitted on self-defense.

November 2, 1873, Joseph W. Thomas was killed by William Rosamurgay at Pioche. Dispute concerning wages. Sentenced to 15 years in the State Prison.

November 3, 1873, Mathew Cahill was killed by Robert McCollough at Pioche in a Hurdy House. McCollough got out on bail and went to work in a mine and had both eyes blown out by a blast. He left Pioche for medical treatment and thus got free."

In all the above cases, and those not mentioned, there was no death sentence given.

It seems appropriate to give a brief summary of the lives of these two relatives, whom the court records claimed had been good friends prior to this event.

ISAAC ALLRED, the son of JAMES ALLRED, has been quoted quite often from his autobiography throughout the early chapters of this book. He was born 28 June 1813, in Bedford County, Tennessee. At seventeen the family moved to Missouri, where he joined The Church of Jesus Christ of Latter-Day-Saints in 1832. On 11 October 1832, he married JULIANN TAYLOR. He was a member of Zions Camp. In the year 1835, he moved to Clay County and the next year to Caldwell County. He went on several missions for the Church, traveling into Tennessee, Illinois, Kentucky, and Missouri. He and his family were driven from Missouri in the fall of 1838 and arrived early in Nauvoo, participating in the Nauvoo Legion as a colonel of the 5th Regiment when the Prophet and his brother Hyrum were killed. He worked on the temple until it was finished, and he "took an active part with the Brethern in quelling the mob." He "went into the temple and laboured during the endowments." In February 1846, he was driven from Nauvoo, perfectly destitute. He stayed at Garden Grove two years, and in the spring of 1848, moved to Council Bluffs. He was elected constable at the August election and was called on by President Joseph Young to travel and preach to the branches of the Church. He built a flat boat and got a petition for a ferry across the Missouri River. He "tended the ferry the spring 1850 and was put in as Justice of the Peace by the voice of the people." He served a two-year mission to the Sandwich Islands (Hawaii) and then returned to his family in Bountiful for awhile, until they came to Fort Ephraim. He was greatly loved and respected by his very large family, who idolized him, and by his close relations, as well as their many friends throughout Sanpete County. His death was a great shock and deep feelings for him and his family appear quite universally. He was 46 years old when he was killed [the same age my father was when he died of cancer in 1939; I know the heartache that comes to a ten year-old child with the death of their father.]. ISAAC ALLRED was buried at Ephraim. He had three wives and 20 children.

Third-great-uncle THOMAS CELTON (KELTON) IVIE was the son of ANDERSON and SARAH ALLRED IVIE, an older sister of ISAAC's father, JAMES ALLRED. TOM was born 25 August 1820 near the Duck River in Bedford County, Tennessee—seven years younger than his cousin ISAAC. His family moved to Missouri in 1829, when he was 9 years old. He is mentioned in *Parley P. Pratt's Autobiography* as the young man who took Pratt to the JAMES RUSSELL IVIE home to hide, after Parley P. Pratt had escaped from prison. He stayed with the Church through the persecution and moved to Nauvoo, and was married there to AMANDA JANE MOORE by his mother's brother (also named) ISAAC ALLRED. Their lot in Nauvoo is recorded in the early Church records of Nauvoo. The couple received their endowments in the Nauvoo Temple. THOMAS C. IVIE left a small family behind in Council Bluffs, when he enlisted in the Mormon Battalion in 1846 as a member of Company C, and he was one of the three guards chosen from his Company, as "the strongest, best horse riders and survivors," and therefore he returned with General Kearny, who left earlier than the others to report to the President of the United States after peace was established with Mexico. TOM was discharged at the Bear River (Soda Springs, Idaho). He was still in Council Bluffs when his son was born in December, 1848. He probably went on a mission to the early settlement of Genoa about 1851, as his next child was born in Nevada. He was building a larger home in Provo in 1854. He went with his brother to build Fort Ephraim, and then to Mount Pleasant. He was 38 years old when this incident occurred. He and his wife had seven children.

When TOM was jailed on first degree murder charges, his brother, second-great-grandparents JAMES RUSSELL and ELIZA IVIE, stepped in to help TOM's wife AMANDA and their fatherless children. JAMES RUSSELL IVIE and my great-grandfather JOHN LEHI IVIE were called as witnesses for the defense, although neither of them were apparently present at either location where the altercations occurred. In the court record, THOMAS IVIE does not express any belligerence towards his deceased cousin or members of the court or jury, and although admitting that he killed his cousin ISAAC, he claimed it was not premeditated or intentional, and further claimed he was not guilty of the first degree murder charge.

The Manti records are detailed as to the dates and members of the court; but they have recorded very little of the actual testimonies of the various witnesses, or the questions of the prosecuting, or defense attorneys. The first pages were quite readable; but very limited in actual value as to understanding what actually happened. I have recorded them as given. The final two pages were much more difficult to read, but more informative. I have copied these two and recorded such words as I considered correct—other parts are left for your own speculation.

~ 27 ~

COURT RECORDS OF THE TRIAL—
SHOT UNTIL DEAD! DEAD! DEAD! —AND AFTER

As recorded on microfilm in the State of Utah Archives:

Territory of Utah   )   Probate Court for said Court

Sanpete County   )   June term June 13th 1859

)   Presiding: Hon. Gardner Snow

Court called to order by the Judge and cried open by the Sheriff —
Officers of Court present as follows,—

Hon. Gardner Snow,	Judge
Geo. Peacock Esq	Clerk
F. C. Robinson	Reporter
George P. Billing	Sheriff
Daniel B. Fink	acting Bailiff

A Venue having been issued by Clerk on the Fourth day of June 1859 for a
Grand Jury was returned and duly certified by the Sheriff with the names
of following persons thereon indorsed:

Malcome Chapman,		
Numan Brown	Sam'l A. Gifford	Riley G. Clark
David P. Bennett	Danish Howrie	Titus Billings
Augustus E. Dodge	John Patten	John Lowry Sen.
Oliver Demill	James A. Lemon	Asuriah Little
Sanford Fortworth	Rob't H. Brown	--------------

As the Jurors names were called by the Clerk, they took their seats, being
asked by the Judge if they were American Citizens. They answered in the
affirmative. The judge then appointed Malcome Chapman [as] Foreman,
the usual Oath was administered to him, after which the Jury were Sworn.
Collectively, the Judge then delivered his charge to them . . . The Jury retired to their Room under the Charge of Bailiff.

    Court adjourned till 1 o'clock P. M.

---

1 o'clock P. M.

Court Cried open by Sheriff

Office of County prosecutor, A. (?), witnesses having been duly called with the following names duly ordered as written . . . on the behalf of the "people," the witnesses: JOHN A. ALLRED, Benj'm Jones, MOSES M. SANDERS, David H. Jones and Isaiah Cox, who on their appearance in Count were duly sworn by this clerk, then admitted to the Grand Jury Room.

Court adjourned till tomorrow

9 A. M. Tuesday June 14th, 1869

Gardner Snow, Judge

Tuesday, June 14th 1859, 9 o'clock A. M.

Court cried open by the Sheriff

Present Officers of County

Judge Snow Hearing—

Court called Records of yesterday heard and approved by the Judge. The Grand Jury came into Court and answered to their names. The Judge then asked if you have any presentiments you will make them to this Court _____. The Foreman then presented "A True Bill" against THOMAS IVIE for the Murder of one "ISAAC ALLRED." The Judge instructed the Grand Jury upon this further, stating in comparison with other offenses that the dignity of the Law must be preserved. The Jury then retired to their Room.

The Attorney of Defence, Esq. James A Sly was presented to the Judge and Officers of the Court of this County and was duly Sworn.

The Clerk then called for the following Case on Docket.

| The people of the United States in the Territory of Utah vs THOMAS IVIE |) June ___ The Probate Court, 1869
) Indictment
) _____
)
) Attorneys for the defence
) Jonathan (?) Hatch and
James A. Sly |

The Prisoner was then brought into Court. Indictment was read by the Clerk (the original on file in office.) The Judge then inquired of Prisoner are you guilty or not guilty as charged? The prisoner pled "not guilty." The Prosecution and Defence both announced that they were ready to proceed with the case and requested that a jury should be impanelled. A venue was returned by Sheriff with the following names of persons duly summoned as a Trail (?) Jury, to wit,—

George W. Bradley —	Martin Lindsay	
F. W. Cox Sen'r	Jerzareal Shoemaker	Elisha Edwards
W. L. Seeley	Alford N. Billings	Abner Lowery
Nelson Higgins	Isaac Herrings	Caleb G. Edwards
Oriville L. Cox		

As their names were called they appeared and took their seats in the Jury Box. The Prosecution and Defence both said they had no objection to the Jury. The Clerk called their names again. The Judge asking each Juryman if He had given his opinion in the present case. Each one answered in the negative. Their names were called and tallied by the Sheriff again. The Jury were then complete and Geo. W. Bradley appointed Foreman (and the usual oath was then administered to the Jury).

Court adjourned till 1 o'clock P. M.

1 o'clock P. M.

— Court called, Prisoner in Court.

The following persons having been duly subpoena'd appeared and were sworn witnesses on the part of the Prosecution to wit—Benjamin Jones, Rosanah Jones, MOSES M. SANDERS, MARY J. SANDERS, JOHN A. ALLRED, Isaiah Cox, James W. Lemon, David H. Jones and MARY J. ALLRED.

The names of jurymen were called and tallied, all being present.

Attorney G. Snow on the part of the Prosecution, then proceeded _____ to lay before the Court the _____ facts or particulars touching the Murder of ISAAC ALLRED, and during his remarks stated that though he had no private malice against Prisoner, yet he intended to prosecute this case with utmost vigor that the dignity of the Law might be vindicated, and be retained a court, and we are ready to proceed with the examination of witnesses.

MOSES SANDERS and Benjamin Jones were then examined after which the Court took recess—for 5 minutes.

Court resumed its listing and proceeded to the examination of Isaiah Cox.

The Court then ordered the Jury to retire to their room under the Charge of the Bailiff, with the instruction that no person be allowed any communication with them except through the proper Officers.

Court adjourned till tomorrow 9 A. M.

Gardner Snow Judge.

W'nesday June 15th 1859
9 o'clock A. M.

Court called.

The Minutes read and agreed by the Judge.

The Jury being called into court and answered to their names.

The Prisoner brought into Court.

Isaiah Cox recalled resumed his testimony. Rosanna Jones, MARY J. SANDERS, and J. W. Lemon each gave in evidence in the case.

During the examination of J. W. Lemon, a question arose with the attorneys on the propriety of introducing family affairs of Deceased into evidence. Prosecution making the objection. Court ruled that private family affairs being disconnected and just touching this case was out of order.

When Jury retired to their Room,

Court adjourned till 1:30 P. M.

1:30 P.M.

Court called.

Jury brought into Court answering to their names and all present. Prisoner in his Seat.

Court proceeded with the case and with the testimony of JOHN A. ALLRED.

At the close of which the Prosecuting Attorney stated that he had no more testimony to offer, but asked the privilege of recalling any of his witnesses should he desire or feel it would be expedient, which the Court granted.

Witnesses for the Defence on Subpoena,

The following persons then came forward, witnesses on the part of the defence who were duly sworn, to wit, — JAMES R. IVIE, JEROME ZABRISKEY, WILLIAM A. ALLRED, JOHN L. IVIE, William Bouch, and JAMES (?) A. ALLRED, all of whom were duly examined (this report (?)).

Which closed the evidence on both sides and on the Jury retiring, the Judge enjoined the silence of officers, and witnesses of both, the Sheriff and Jury regarding the necessity of the Jury being kept from illegal communications, etc.

The Prosecuting Attorneys gave notice that they would be prepared with their pleas by tomorrow 10 A. M.

Court adjourned till June 16th, 1859 – Tomorrow 10 A. M.

Gardner Snow Judge

Thursday, June 16th, 10 o'clock A. M.

Court called

The Jury brought into the Court answered to their names. All present. Prisoner in his seat. M. Snow on the party of the Prosecution took up the case in Comprehensive manner, reading the "Indictment" and commenting upon the testimony given before the Court. Allowed by his Colleague R. W. Glenn Esq. who commented upon the Indictment and the Legality of the handling and further commented upon the various testimony touching the case and concluded by expressing his conviction that the Jury had no other alternative but to convict the Prisoner of Murder in the First Degree.

W'm Hatch for the Defence made a very impressive and affecting plea to the effect that though it was acknowledged that the prisoner at the box (?) did kill the Deceased, ISAAC ALLRED, that he maintained that said act was not premeditated or wilful as far as killing applied, but was committed under the influence of excitement and intensity (?) and dwelt largely upon the principle of Mercy.

Mr. Sly then followed also for the defence, who commented upon the testimony and the Law, dwelling some what on the prisoner's Friendship that existed between the Prisoner and the Deceased and expressing perfect confidence in the integrity of the Jury and submitted the case to them on the part of the Defence, asking the Jury to be Merciful.

(Closing Plea) Attorney G. Snow rose and made his closing Plea by expressing his confidence in the Jury and being assured that they would render their verdict according to Law and evidence. He willingly and confidently submitted the Case.

Jury retired to their Room

Court Adjourned till 1 P. M.

1 o'clock P. M.

Court called

The Grand Jury was called into Court, names called, all present. The Foreman reported no further business in progress. The Grand Jury joining the (present) Session of Court. Attorney G. Snow not knowing of any further business in progress for this session of Court. The Court discharged the Grand Jury.

The Trial Jury was then brought into Court and answered to their names, Prisoner in his seat.

Mr. Glenn then delivered the final plea on the part of the Prosecution.

Then the Pleas closed on the part of both Prosecution and Defence.

Judge Snow then charged the Jury on all the points of Law and evidence touching the Case, (see charge on file) then ordered the Sheriff to take charge of Jury, to confine them, and see that they held no communication or interruption (?) of an unlawful nature, and have no food or drink, save water, till they had agreed upon their verdict or were discharged of the Court.

The Jury retired at 2:30 P. M.

Court took recess for 15 min.

2.45 P.M.

Court resumed its Sitting

At 5 P. M. the Jury notified the Court that they had agreed upon their Verdict, upon which the Judge ordered the Jury to be brought into Court, who appeared, took their seats and answered to their names.

The Court inquired if they had agreed upon their Verdict. The Foreman replied in the affirmative and presented to the Court the following sealed Verdict. —

Territory of Utah	)	Jury Room, Manti City
	)	June 16th, 1859
Sanpete County	)	------------

We the undersigned Jurors being duly sworn before the Probate Court of said County on Tuesday the (14th) fourteenth day of June, one thousand eight hundred and fifty nine to hear and determine the Case of the people of the United States in the Territory of Utah and THOMAS IVIE Defendant arraigned upon an Indictment, finds the Prisoner guilty of Murder in the First Degree as witness our signatures—

Foreman: Geo K. Bradley Martin Lindsay
(The original on file in Office)

P. K. Cox Sen'r	Jerzareal Shoemaker	Orville A. Cox
W`m L. Seeley	Alford N. Billings	Elisha Edwards
Nelson Higgins	Isaac Herring	Abner Lowry
C. G. Edwards		

The Court ordered the prisoner to stand and hear the Verdict which was then read aloud by the Clerk. The Jury were then called by name and Jurors in turn being interrogated by the Judge answered 'That is my verdict.'

The Jury were then discharged.

The Judge ordered the Sheriff to take Charge of the Prisoner until tomorrow, Friday, June 17th, 10 A. M., and deliver him into Court for his sentence of the "Law" with the pronouncement on him.

Court then adjourned until

Tomorrow 10 A. M.

Gardner Snow Judge

Friday June 17th 1859
10 o'clock A. M.

Court called

[very difficult to read—see the copy on page 289] . . .

[The defendant THOMAS K. IVIE is speaking—]

I do not deny the wrong of the death of ISAAC ALLRED, but it was not done intentionally or with premeditation; but I desire to be reconciled to all men always be on the (?) side of Justice. I know its within _____ my honor _____. I desire that this Court will prolong the day of my demise—all for settling some difficulties and that I may have sufficient time to arrange for the matters of business and I furthermore request (desiring of himself) the alternative of being shot instead of being hung such being the allowance of the Law.

The Judge addressed the Prisoner and the Audience setting forth his feelings on the present occasion and touched upon the importance of his present responsibility as that of pronouncing the sentence of death upon a fellow being, then added,

"Prisoner stand up and receive your sentence. You, THOMAS IVIE, have been indicted by a Grand Jury of your countrymen, have then been arraigned before this Court upon that Indictment, and have had a fair and impartial trial before a Jury of your own choice. That Jury have rendered a verdict against you of "Murder in the First Degree"; it now becomes my duty to pronounce the Sentence of Death upon you, which is—that you be remanded back into the hands of the Sheriff from whence you came, there to remain until the eighth day of July eighteen hundred and fifty nine between the hour of 9 A. M. and 1 P. M.. Then to be taken to some place that shall be appointed and prepared by the Sheriff within the Limits of Sanpete County, Utah Territory, then and there on the day and between the hours aforesaid to be executed by being SHOT, and your blood to flow until you are dead, dead! dead! and the Lord help you and have mercy on your Soul."

The Judge then commanded the Sheriff to take charge of the Prisoner to carry out the order of the Court and execute the Sentence Just put upon THOMAS IVIE, the Prisoner.

The Court then discharged the Jurymen and witnesses who were still in attendance before the Court and ordered—Court adjourned Sine die which adjournment was announced by the Bailiff

---

Gardner·Snow Judge

While this trial proceeded in Manti, the building of the fort at Mount Pleasant, under the leadership of second-great-grandfather JAMES RUSSELL IVIE was progressing rapidly and crops were being planted.

Somewhat discouraged that these court records were not more explicit regarding the circumstances and testimonies of those involved, I was excited when I found additional references to this trial in the *History of Brigham Young,* stating that the news of the killing arrived in Great Salt Lake City on Wednesday, 18 May 1859. These were days of suspicion and false accusations against *Mormons* from the new officials that were appointed in Washington D.C. to govern this people. The accusations and suspicions extended beyond the LDS pioneers, however. The occupation army now stationed at Camp Floyd had a commander who was extremely pro-South regarding the Civil War that was erupting throughout the nation, and there was strong friction between him and any U. S. government appointed person from the *Yankee* states, which, in his mind, included these Northern and foreign *Mormon* people.

Young's history states:

"Intelligence arrived in this city that ISAAC ALRED of Fort Ephraim was killed by THOS. IVEY. The difficulty originated about herding some sheep. Bro. ALRED took two teachers and visited IVEY to try to settle matters. ISAAC (sic) took a stick of wood off the fire and struck him with it and thereby caused his death."

On Thursday, 23 June 1859, after the trial, the case is again mentioned.

"Evening—Geo. A. Smith at the President's office—present Prest. Young,

[YOU SHALL] BE EXECUTED BY BEING SHOT, and your blood to flow until YOU ARE DEAD! DEAD! DEAD! —and the Lord help you and have mercy on your soul.

I do not deny the wrong of the death of Isaac Allred, but it was not done intentionally or with premeditation.

Daniel H. Wells, Albert Carrington and George Peacock. [The clerk of the Court in Manti.] The minutes of the Probate Court held in Manti City, Sanpete Co., June 6th were read. The minutes show that the proceedings were got up in good form and with legal skill. A Grand Jury empaneled and . . . an indictment was found against THOMAS IVEY for the murder of ISAAC ALRED of Ephraim. He was put upon his trial, found guilty of murder in the first degree, and sentenced to be (according to his own request) shot on the 8th day of July next. From the evidence it appears that the difficulty originated about the herding of some sheep. The quarrel commenced in the morning and in the evening Bro. ALLRED took two teachers, visited IVEY and tried to settle the matter. IVEY took a stick of wood from the fire, which was part of a pole burnt in two, and gathered it slyley (sic) up the side of his leg until he got it onto his knee. He then struck ALLRED with it twice, which caused his death, saying, 'There you will keep out of my way now!' He also threatened to kill ALRED's son."

It seems at this point that the trial took on a new dimension. Apparently this criminal trial was heard by a Probate Court, and although the previous Territorial Legislature had granted them this power, the Federal judges who were appointed by the U. S. President were questioning the authority of a probate court to hear a criminal case. Fearfully, Geo. Peacock brought his records to Brigham Young, and told the additional information in his own words.

Evidently, they were more concerned at that time with the trial procedure being correct and accurate than the final decision of the court. No one seemed concerned that the Prosecuting Attorney was the son of the Judge, or that one of the Manti Selectmen was a brother of the victim, or that the other Selectman served on the Jury, or that all references above seemed to refer to BRO. ALLRED and the defense was stopped from any personal references about the victim by the Judge. It was not noted that after the morning quarrel, ISAAC brought two witnesses, one of which was his son, [called teachers] to the *home* of THOMAS IVIE, who had no witnesses present, was also a brother in the gospel, served in the Mormon Battalion, and also lived in Fort Ephraim with a wife and seven young children—which facts are not indicative of premeditation on IVIE's part. Evidently, ALLRED's attempt to *settle the matter* by bringing the two additional men with him, a three to one settlement, was not totally peaceful or impartial. ISAAC was not dead when they left, so it would seem unlikely that THOMAS would use the term *kill,* if he threatened ISAAC's son and his companion with some of the same treatment.

On 30 August 1859, Judge Eckels, in Salt Lake City, gave the following instructions to his Grand Jury, regarding a different trial and person, which helps us understand his position in criminal cases:

> "In reference to the crime of dueling you will see that at every step that can be taken every person concerned, whether as principal or in any other capacity, all are guilty of an offence, and I really think that those who aid and abet are often more guilty than the principals. For, as in cases of murder, the principal actor may be the victim of momentary and excited passion: while those who aid, abet and encourage it, are acting coolly and deliberately. When a person kills another under the influence of momentarily excited passion, he CANNOT be regarded as GUILTY OF MURDER of the FIRST DEGREE, but of a LESS OFFENCE, PUNISHABLE by IMPRISONMENT for a TERM OF YEARS only." [Caps added.]

From the *Encyclopedia Americana [1945 Ed.],* "Murder and Manslaughter are distinguished from each other by the intent which causes or accompanies the act. If a homicide be not justifiable or excusable, and yet be not committed with malice aforethought, it is manslaughter and not murder." It then describes the four degrees of manslaughter according to the laws of New York. According to the Court record, THOMAS IVIE stated, "It was not done intentionally or with premeditation." The fact that the three men came to *his* home, would indicate that he had not been planning the incident.

Quoting again from the *History of Brigham Young:*

> "25 June 1859 . . . Evening—Geo. A. Smith at the president's office—present, Prest. Young, Daniel H. Wells, Albert Carrington and others. Geo. Peacock came in and stated that he had present[ed] Gov. Cumming with a copy of the proceedings of the Probate Court at Manti, in the case of the people versus THOMAS IVEY, for murder. The Governor sent for Judges Eckels and Cradlebaugh, the proceedings of The Court were read. The Judges said they were got up in excellent style, everything was right, but they thought the court could not exercise criminal jurisdiction, though the Legislature had given it to them in good faith. Mr. Peacock also said that he had heard after leaving the Governor's office that the Judges had *concluded to let them execute the law on IVEY and then arraign the judge, juries and sheriff for murder.* [italics added] Gov. Cumming went to see Genl. Wilson on

the subject, but he was sick and could not be seen.

"Mr. Curtis E. Bolton states that after Mr. Peacock went out of the Governor's office, Judge Cradlebaugh said this man (Peacock) was one he had issued a bench warrant for and he supposed that he had been in the mountains ever since. Gov. Cumming told him that he (Cradlebaugh) had formed an erroneous opinion of Peacock as (the Governor) had been acquainted with him ever since he had been in the Territory and that he was an honest and upright man and he had no doubt but that he had been at home attending to his business. The governor seems to have forgot that the Judge tried to arrest good men only and that others he happened to get into his custody he discharged. There was a short discussion in the President's office in relation to the authority invested in the Sheriff to execute the sentence of death upon IVEY . . . 28 June 1859,

"Thursday . . . Evening . . . Gov. Cumming informed Geo. Peacock that the papers were ready to be sent to Sanpete Co. to stay the execution of THOMAS IVEY until the 13th of August . . . 30 June 1859 . . . Judge Eckels manifests a disposition to rely considerably upon the influence of the military power. You will recollect that THOMAS IVEY a short time ago, killed ISAAC ALRED, both of Sanpete County. In accordance with the laws of the Territory, IVEY was tried, convicted and condemned to death by the Probate court of that county, he choosing, also according to law, the mode of his death, viz:—Shooting.

"Judge Eckles without application from the criminal or his attorney issued a writ of Habeas Corpus upon Geo. Billings, Sheriff of Sanpete County, returnable at Camp Floyd. There are three objectionable features in this transaction, first—issuing a writ of Habeas Corpus without application by the criminal or his attorney, second—making a writ returnable in the midst of an army at Camp Floyd, this being justly repugnant to the feelings of the citizens and decidedly opposed to the tenor of the instructions of Gen. Black and as he emphatically observes—the spirit of our judicial system. Third—since the October term of 1858, no U. S. Court has been held in that district, except the illegal one by Judge Cradlebaugh at Provo, and he refused to punish any crime or even to suffer any criminal cases to be tried, but immediately a case is tried by a lawful tribunal in an unexceptionable manner and there is a prospect of the law being magnified, Judge Eckels straightway thrust in his cloven foot and does his best to hinder the due administration of Justice. IVEY's crime was a cold blooded murder and he has long sustained the reputation of being a perfect desperado."

In all my findings so far, I have found no reason in the life of THOMAS IVEY to make such a statement. But this is undoubtedly the report Clerk Geo. Peacock gave Brigham Young.

A letter from John Jacques to Geo. Q. Cannon reads:

G.S.L. City, July 7, 1859.

Bro. Geo. Q. Cannon: THOMAS IVEY, the man condemned to death for murder by the Probate Court of Sanpete County, was at Camp Floyd at last advices in answer to the writ of Habeas Corpus issued by Judge Eckels. The Judge proposes to sit in Chambers at Camp Floyd to hear the question of the jurisdiction of the probate courts argued. There is a probability that this whim will not be gratified . . . Judge Eckels said a day or two ago that he was informed that Gen. Johnston would order them to be set at liberty, for he would keep them no longer. 12 July 1859 at one o'clock . . . Judge Snow showed me the injunctions issued by Judge Eckels against the case of THOMAS IVEY. Bro. John Eager wrote these notes both morning and evening.

[*HBY* 1859, p. 579, 580]

In a letter from Wilford Woodruff to Geo. A. Smith, 12 July 1859:

Bro. Geo. A. Smith:— As brother Jacques has given you most of the news, I will only write a few lines. The army flour inspectors are condemning nearly all the flour taken there under the Holliday Contract. We cannot ascertain what amount of forged drafts upon U. S. were found in the possession of Brewer and McKenzie. Report says from $5,000 to $500,000. Who is connected with them in it we have not learned.

When Col. Crossman found that McKenzie had a hand in it, he jumped up and down like a crazy man, saying, 'By ___, we will make this stick on Brigham Young this time. Our lawyers will not go to Camp Floyd to argue any case.' Wilson says he thinks Cradlebaugh and Sinclair will join issue against Buchanan and Judge Black. If they do the Executive of the nation must be in danger.

Here are some excerpts taken from the First Judicial District Court records:

"Monday, Aug. 22, 1859. Court met pursuant to appointment in the court house. Nephi city, Juab county. Hon. D. R. Eckels presiding . . . 2 p.m. . . . The court then ordered the bailiff to call G. P. Billings sheriff of San Pete county, who had the charge of the prisoner, THOS. IVIE. At this juncture the judge received thro' a deputy, Sheriff Billings' memoranda, etc., which announced the escape of said prisoner.

"The judge said, 'I enter a rule against Geo. P. Billings, sheriff of San Pete county, to be returnable on the 29th day of August 1859, to show reasons why he has not brought before this court the said prisoner, THOS. IVIE, according to writ issued by me . . .'

"Tuesday, Aug. 23, 8 a.m . . . 2 p.m. . . . The Judge said in the case of the people v.s. . . . McDonald Earl and others, there was a rule against the Sheriff of Utah county, to produce the prisoners, who had been committed on mittimus, and who had escaped. Also in the case of the people v.s. THOS. IVIE there was a rule against the Sheriff of San Pete county, for same cause. On Friday, Sept 3, 8 a.m., two cases were dismissed. The reason given was that the probate court had no jurisdiction to hear, try or determine this action. He summarizes by saying:

"The territorial legislature has no power to give or take away the jurisdiction conferred by the Organic Act . . . The Probate courts having neither common law nor chancery power, had no jurisdiction of case; and this court not having by the appeal, more power than the tribunal from whence it came, it follows that this motion to dismiss must prevail. The suit is therefore dismissed at the cost of the plaintiff . . . 11 a.m. Court resumed its sitting . . . People of the United States v.s. THOMAS IVIE. Rule against G. P. Billings, Sheriff of San Pete, continued and alias for IVIE ordered for next term."

From these records, it appears Judge Eckels, greatly concerned about a probate court trying a criminal case, stepped in and stayed the execution of IVIE without his request. THOMAS IVIE was brought to Camp Floyd and into a judicial battle. Southern General Johnston, hating both the North and the *Mormons,* turned the prisoner loose. Judge Eckels, wanting to keep the case alive, attempted to blame Sheriff Billings for IVIE's supposed escape. If IVIE had come to trial in his court, the Judge would probably have dismissed the case, as he felt the probate court had no jurisdiction to try a criminal case. If he had actually held a second trial, it is likely that his sentence would have been less severe than First Degree Murder.

THOMAS IVIE went to Missouri, where his mother, SARAH ALLRED IVIE, lived—leaving his wife and seven children in the care of his brother, JAMES RUSSELL IVIE. He was no longer welcome in Mount Pleasant. His father, ANDERSON IVIE, had died in 1852.

Mount Pleasant—The Fort and its People

[Note: Two days after the fight between IVIE and ALLRED, on May 13, 1859, JAMES RUSSELL IVIE called a meeting to discuss the building of the fort wall. Assigned the First Ten, North Line were JOHN A. ALLRED, Captain; JEROME ZABRISKE; SIDNEY ALLRED; REUBEN ALLRED; ISAAC M. ALLRED; Wm. C. BILLINGSLEY; ALMA ZABRISKIE; Warren P. Brady; Benjamin Jones; David H. Jones; John Cox; and Issiah Cox. Assigned to the First Ten, South Line, were Ora Sutton, Captain; JAMES R. IVIE; RICHARD A. IVIE; JAMES A. IVIE; JOHN L. IVIE; WILLIAM A. IVIE; Daniel Page; Joseph S. Allen; Joseph Page; Jacob Julander; Porter Dowdell; Peter C. Christensen. There were nine more similar groups. M. M. SANDERS was Captain of the First Ten, West Line with Wellington Seeley and JOHN F. SANDERS; Ole Olsen; DAVID W. SANDERS and others in this group. HENRY W. SANDERSON and EDWARD DALLEY were in the Second Ten, West Line. HENRY McARTHUR was in the First Ten, East Line. Four men were called to supervise the construction: Jahu Cox was allotted the north side; Thomas Woolsey Sr., the west side; W. S. Seeley, the south side and John Tidwell Sr. (who had arrived recently with several other Tidwell and Seeley families from Pleasant Grove) was assigned the east side. From Andrew Madsen's Journal: "During the month of June, we were kept busy in attending to our crops and the building of the large fort wall."]

On 10 July 1859, Apostle George A. Smith and Amasa Lyman visited the settlement and "organized the Saints on Pleasant Creek into an ecclesiastical ward. William Stuart Seeley was chosen and ordained Bishop. The office of President no longer existed and JAMES R. IVIE was released of his duties." Brother JAMES R. IVIE felt very much pleased when released from the responsibility that had been placed upon him in the establishment of the colony for which he had worked so hard. As it was a very pleasant place in which to live, the name Mount Pleasant Branch was chosen." On 18 July, the fort was completed—the finest in the County.

The fort at Mount Pleasant enclosed the block later known as the Tithing Yard. It was 26 rods by 26 rods or about 5½ acres of land between Main Street and First North and State Street and First East. It was made according to Brigham Young's instructions and was built of native rock taken from the surface or dug out of the ground and laid with mud mortar. The wall was twelve feet high, four feet on the bottom and tapering to two feet on the top. This wall, in order that the maneuvers of the Indians could be watched from inside was built with port holes every sixteen feet, which were seven feet from the ground. The holes were about two feet wide on the inside, about four inches on the outside and about eighteen inches high.

The inside of the wall was utilized for one wall in the erection of houses, sixteen feet square, with one port hole in the middle of the one wall of each house. There was a flat-roofed house in the northwest corner of the fort upon which guards could stand and view the country. It had two large gates, one in the center of the south wall, with a small gate adjoining it, giving a thoroughfare in passing. These openings had heavy wooden gates. Small entrances were in the east and west walls, which made it convenient exiting in various directions.

The water supply was obtained from Pleasant Creek, which passed almost parallel east and west through the center of the fort. A large bridge was erected over the stream. All corrals for the livestock were built just outside the north wall of the fort leaving a roadway between. It remained a tribute to second-great-grandfather JAMES RUSSELL IVIE and his leadership for many years. There is a statue on State Street today that honors him and the other hardy pioneers that first settled at Pleasant Creek. His name is mentioned with honor in the early histories.

The following is from a letter sent by George Peacock and published in the *Deseret News*:

> "At a convention held at Manti, on the 16th, EDWIN WHITING [an ancestor of cousin JAMES (Jimmy) C. BAIRD's wife, EVELYN WHITING BAIRD] was nominated for councilor and JOHN L. IVIE for member of the House of Representatives of the next Legislative Assembly." Great-grandfather JOHN L. IVIE was 26 years old.

Indian problems were at a minimum about this time, so the old burned-out and deserted Allred Settlement was resettled. REDICK N. ALLRED was one of the leaders who returned to what was also known as Springtown. In 1870, it was incorporated into a city, under the name of Spring City. The Danish people predominated, and at times it was called *"Little Denmark."* These skilled and enterprising people would build a beautiful tabernacle, patterned after the wonderfully beamed churches of their old country, Denmark. In the nearby city cemetery, there is a large tombstone of GROVER SWALLOW's ancestor, LUKE NIELD, who came from England.

In 1930, Tina Ericksen Nelson described her memories of her early home life in the Fort at Mount Pleasant:

> "The first homes built within the fort were nearly all one-roomed huts in which the fort wall formed the back of the house. They were made of

adobes with a roof which slanted from the fort wall toward the center of the fort. In each were two small windows and one door. There were only dirt floors. They were crudely plastered within. A huge fireplace served, in nearly all of them, for both heating and cooking, as stoves were very scarce articles at that time. Across these fireplaces hung a great iron rod on which their kettles hung—among them the water kettle, from which they could always obtain hot water. Anything which required boiling was cooked in a kettle which hung from the rod above the fire. When it was necessary to bake, coals were raked out a bit, on which the bake skillets were placed and more coals placed upon the lid. Those who were fortunate enough to have flatirons, heated them by standing them on end near the coals of the fireplace. The pioneer homes were noted for their hospitality. There were then, as now, certain groups who especially enjoyed associating together. Because of the variety of nationalities represented, even in so small a community, they were better able to understand and enjoy the association of those who came from their mother countries."

There were Danish groups that met at their different homes and enjoyed dancing to the music of the fiddlers. There were Norwegians. Then there was the English group who met in the evening parties, enjoying an early supper after which they sang, chatted and had speeches. They were Bishop Seely and wife, Mr. and Mrs. William Morrison, DAVID CANDLAND, JOHN IVY, and JOHN BARTON.

"In the midst of the joys and sorrows, the work and play which went on within these humble homes, there was a spirit of love and contentment and gratitude for blessings which perhaps would be difficult to duplicate today. All were united in their struggles to exist and to succeed, and in the united effort, home ties were established which could never be destroyed. There were but few homes, if any, where the mothers and children were not called together daily by the fathers for family prayer. They loved their God and they loved each other. Their home life was complete." [Ibid]

In 1860, JOHN LEHI IVIE made a trip to Bountiful. ELISHA KEMBER BARTON, youngest brother of MARY CATHERINE IVIE, wrote:

"In Bountiful, they farmed the upper piece of ground which did not thrive for lack of water. Barton Creek now stands where they settled . . . JOHN IVIE . . . urged the family to come to Mt. Pleasant where he claimed the water was more plentiful and farming was good. After a journey to Mt. Pleasant and investigation of the land, JOHN BARTON returned to Bountiful to take his family to Mt. Pleasant. They came in the year 1860. Most of the people were living in the fort then."

Mount Pleasant had been settled only a year, when DAVID CANDLAND, who was the convert from England and temple clerk in Nauvoo and who married JOHN BARTON's youngest sister MARY ANN BARTON, came to Mount Pleasant in 1861 from Salt Lake City.

"Realizing the need of recreation and entertainment, in 1860, a dramatic company, which always played to packed houses, was organized by a number of people, among them was W. W. Brandon Sr., [great-grandparents] JOHN IVIE and his wife, KATHERINE IVIE, Rudolph Bennett, George Porter and Joseph Smith Day. As time went on, the personnel of the company would change, but W. W. Brandon and KATHERINE IVIE played with them for years. During the winter months, their plays were put on in the log meeting house in the center of the fort, using wagon covers and other such material as they could provide for scenery. Among other plays, they presented the *Merchant of Venice* and *Good for Nothing Nan*." [MP—Longsdorf]

The 24 July 1860 celebration at Mt. Pleasant was reported in the *Deseret News*. On this program we find that JOHN LEHI IVIE was Marshal, and an address was given by Elder JAMES RUSSELL IVIE. The day was ushered in by several volleys of musketry from companies of infantry who continued firing at intervals throughout the day. A spacious bowery had been erected for the occasion, with fresh green limbs brought from the mountains, under which the citizens, old and young, assembled en-masse at 9 a.m., where the proceedings were conducted throughout the day. There was a morning program with songs by the choir, orations, poems, solos, and music by the quadrille band. The BARTON boys were very musically talented and played in many of their bands and dances.

At noon a large dinner was served, after which the bowery was cleared for dancing. In the evening, toasts were given to their community, the church, and the nation. According to grandfather JAMES OSCAR IVIE, who was not born until 1863, this was an annual event that was looked forward to by everyone. He tells us that there was a competition between the men to see who could win in a standing broad jump—with weights. His father, JOHN L. IVIE would usually win, jumping twelve feet forward from standing position or eleven feet backwards. This has always seemed incredible to me.

It was shortly after this 24 July 1860 celebration that second-great-grand-father JAMES RUSSELL IVIE and his wife, with most of their posterity left the fort at Mount Pleasant and moved back to Ephraim. Evidently many of the community still regarded their brother, uncle, or father, THOMAS IVIE, as an escaped *murderer* and tried to administer their own form of persecution against those he loved, especially his children. It became worse than the family cared to deal with. Their stay in Ephraim was only a stopping place until they could find another suitable location.

The extended family group had grown considerably in numbers, and the larger valleys with good farm land and water were limited. They investigated Rose Valley, near Pioche, Nevada; but felt it already had sufficient settlers. Round Valley (now Scipio) was their final decision, and in 1862, they said "Goodbye" to Sanpete County and moved to Milliard County. An exception to this departure was my great-grandfather JOHN LEHI IVIE and his family, including the BAR-TONs, who stayed in the Fort at Mount Pleasant. They loved and were loved as community leaders. They, also, remained close to the members of his family who had left Sanpete County. Their love for his father, mother, brothers, sisters and their families is very evident in all the records I am aware of—both spoken and written. Great-grandmother MARY CATHERINE BARTON IVIE would have twelve children; the last eight were born in Mt. Pleasant, none of which died as babies. My grandfather, JAMES OSCAR IVIE, was her sixth child. He was born 9 May 1863.

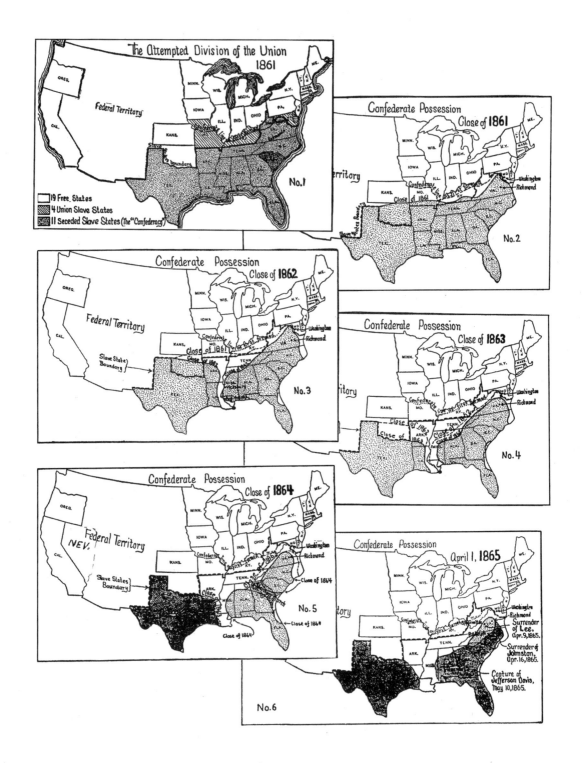

~ 28 ~

MISSOURI, OH MY!
INTO THE MIDDLE OF THE
BUSHWHACKERS AND JAYHAWKERS

At a special spot in Yellowstone National Park, three small streamlets begin their crystal clear descent. One goes west and joins the Snake River whose force turns the huge generators that light up and water the deserts of Southern Idaho and Eastern Oregon and joins with the Columbia River in Washington State, finally arriving at the Pacific Ocean. The second tiny stream goes South into the Green River, traversing western Wyoming and eastern Utah until it reaches the great Colorado that bores its way through the vast and treacherous Grand Canyon which empties its contents eventually into the Gulf of California, having powered Hoover Dam and lit up the spectacular casinos of Las Vegas. The third tiny channel of water makes its way east—a beginning on the Great Divide of the Rocky Mountains that adds and increases until it becomes the mighty Missouri River that crosses the Great Plains and enters the State of Missouri a little above the western center between Jackson and Clay Counties—named earlier after the two opposing candidates for president in 1831, Andrew Jackson and Henry Clay. Appropriately, Jackson County is south of the Missouri and Clay County is on the north. The Missouri River cuts through the state and at St. Louis joins the wondrous Mississippi, which empties into the Gulf of Mexico.

And so, in the 1830s, in Jackson and Clay Counties, Missouri, where the Kansas River joins the Missouri River, making it more navigable, the designated western boundary of the United States and a one-way gateway into Indian Territory was located. The nation had a concern—the British were trying to claim the Oregon Territory. A federal outpost was established in Jackson and Clay counties, followed by the Oregon Trail and cheap land incentives in an effort to once more beat the British and expand the country. This trail went through the little explored wilderness with miles of flat plains, roaming herds of buffalo, then through the high—almost impassible—Rocky Mountains to descend again to the Pacific Ocean. Get there, and get land, before the British do. There may be Indians—Oh, well!

Living in this distant outpost of the United States and Missouri, was Alexander Doniphan, born in 1808 in Kentucky, a lawyer, and three times elected to the Missouri legislature. He was a Brigadier General in the Missouri militia. He served in the Mexican War, capturing Chihuahua after an unexpected encounter with an army of four thousand men. He was one of the peace commissioners at the convention which met at Washington city previous to the Civil War. He later died in Richmond, Missouri, in 1887. But in the 1830s, he was living in Liberty, Clay County, Missouri, practicing law—one of the few lawyers, and considered the best, in the territory. Doniphan had watched as the *Mormons* had purchased land and peacefully settled in Jackson County. He had seen them driven from their lands in Jackson County into his county, Clay; then driven out of Clay to the counties further north. At times, he had spoken and acted strongly in their defense. Probably the most remembered was his refusal to carry out the order of 1 November 1838:

> "Brigadier-General Doniphan: Sir:—You will take Joseph Smith and the other prisoners into the public square of Far West, and shoot them at 9 o'clock to-morrow morning.
>
> Samuel D. Lucas,
> Major-General Commanding."

His insubordinate reply, for which, he was never called to task, was:

> "It is cold-blooded murder. I will not obey your order. My brigade shall march for Liberty tomorrow morning, at 8 o'clock; and if you execute these men, I will hold you responsible before an earthly tribunal, so help me God.
>
> A. W. Doniphan,
> Brigadier-General." [*HC Vol. III, p. 272, note*]

It is understandable why Joseph Smith, as a prisoner in Liberty jail, hired him as his lawyer. On one occasion General Doniphan had Joseph Smith brought from the prison to his law office in regard to his defense. While he was there, a resident of Jackson County came in and requested to pay his account with some land in Jackson County. Since his partner was out of the office, Doniphan postponed a decision for his approval. After the Jackson County man had left, Doniphan later reported that Joseph Smith, who had overheard the conversation, said:

> "Doniphan, I advise you not to take that Jackson County land in payment of the debt. God's wrath hangs over Jackson County. God's people have been ruthlessly driven from it, and you will live to see the day when it will be visited by fire and sword. The Lord of Hosts will sweep it with the besom of destruction. The fields and farms and houses will be destroyed, and only the chimneys will be left to mark the desolation."

General Doniphan lived to see and testify that this prophecy was fulfilled after General Ewing's "Order No. 11" was dutifully executed by the Union Army in 1863. [L. M. Lawson, after interview with Doniphan in 1863. See *The Fate of the Persecutors of the Prophet Joseph Smith*, and *Black Flag* by Thomas Goodrich.]

In 1854, with the legislative compromises that continued to go on in the nation's capitol, the Kansas-Nebraska Act opened that territory to settlement by the whites. The Missourians felt that Kansas, which bordered them on the west, should have slavery. When elections rolled around, New England abolitionists paid for the passage of those who would immigrate to Kansas and vote the free-soil ticket. The Missourians, however, crossed the lines and voted the pro-slavery ticket, winning the election quite handily. Quite unhappy with the ballot box stuffing, the angry free-state settlers ignored the election and set up their own government.

It was the beginning of their personal civil war. Gangs of Missouri mobs, backed by a pro-Southern federal government harassed the free-staters. They were chased from their homes, occasionally jailed, and at times, brutally beaten or killed. But northern emigration continued. In desperation, the pro-slavery men from Kansas and Missouri surrounded the abolitionist capital of Lawrence, Kansas, plundering it on 21 May 1856. Several days later, the abolitionists retaliated, killing five pro-slavery settlers. They were slashed with sabers—their heads and bodies mutilated. The pro-slavery settlers accused John Brown. They collected

300 men and attacked John Brown's abolitionist stronghold of Osawatomie.

Then, as the vengeance for one act breeds revenge by the other side, the atrocities increased, until during the next two years, the territory became *Bleeding Kansas*. In January 1858, Kansas voters overwhelmingly rejected the pro-slavery constitution and with this decisive vote, the U.S. Congress prepared to admit Kansas into the Union as a free-state.

The trouble shifted south when free-state marauders—Jayhawkers—attempted to drive pro-slavery settlers out of the territory. In 1859-60, a severe drought ruined crops and impoverished the Kansas farmers and merchants. [This was the period of time that THOMAS C. IVIE returned to eastern Missouri and the home of his mother, SARAH ALLRED IVIE.] By 1861, the eve of acceptance of Kansas as a free-state, Kansas was starving, while western Missouri, a more established area, still had plenty. Envy and hatred burned inside the Kansas settlers as they observed their Missouri neighbors. It was a tinderbox just waiting for the spark.

The spark came when the Yankees lost at Fort Sumter. Missourians were ecstatic. They were now Southerners, through and through, and thousands of their best defenders joined military organizations. It was not long, however, before Missouri was invaded by the North, and the rebel army, led by former governor Sterling Price (the Colonel Sterling Price mentioned in the Mormon Battalion history and earlier mobbings) was pushed into the southwest corner of Missouri. Only old men and young boys were left behind and the Kansas Jayhawkers, under Charles Jennison, found it easy to rob and destroy those who had been left at home.

The Missourians formed guerrilla bands to attempt to help the Southern cause, and retaliate whenever possible on the Kansas Jayhawkers. Rising from the ranks to the leadership of these Missouri guerrillas, known as Bushwhackers, was Bill Quantrill—a tall, harmless-looking young man with sandy hair, originally from Ohio. He had received his schooling from Abraham Ellis, a Kansas man. It seems that in March 1862, Ellis, with four other Kansas men went to Leavenworth to petition the Union Army for the protection of Kansas along the Kansas-Missouri border. He had liked Bill Quantrill, until his pro-slavery violence could no longer be ignored. The Union Army denied their request, believing that the border was already sufficiently patrolled. Ellis and the other Kansans worried about Quantrill's band as they journeyed home.

While sleeping at Aubrey, they were awakened by the cry, "The cutthroats are coming." Before they could dress, the raiders surrounded the house and "were yelling and screaming and swearing like devils."

Five men were upstairs and about thirty outside—those in the lower rooms attempted to escape by running—three were shot and robbed, two being riddled with bullets. Ellis looked out the upstairs window; Quantrill saw him, tipped his hat and shot him in the forehead. He fell and was thought to be dead—the others went downstairs and surrendered. Two of Quantrill's men were upstairs in a moment, each with a cocked revolver pointed at Ellis' head.

One yelled out, "If you have any money G-- d--- you, give it to me in a minute or I'll blow you to H---." Ellis handed them $250, and they ordered him downstairs. After Ellis had been helped into a chair, Quantrill recognized him and got a cloth and some water and washed his face and told him he had done it himself and was d--- sorry for what he had done as he was one of the Kansas men he did not want to hurt, and that not one more thing of his would be touched. [see *Black Flag* by Thomas Goodrich]

Soon after, Ellis fainted away and lay on the frozen ground, unconscious, for about four hours—presumed dead by those who saw him. He did recover, but the tide was turning against the Jayhawkers as the Bushwhackers brought destruction back into Kansas, leading to Quantrill and his men nearly destroying the city of Lawrence, Kansas, in August 1863.

The *New York Times*, 24 August 1863:

"Quantrill's massacre at Lawrence is almost enough to curdle the blood with horror. In the history of the war thus far, full as it has been of dreadful scenes, there has been no such diabolical work as this indiscriminate slaughter of peaceful villagers . . . There have been many displays of rebel barbarity, but none that have approached this. It would seem that even the rebel authorities in Richmond, steeped in wickedness as they are, cannot yet be so dead to all human feelings as to sanction such monstrous outrages . . . It is a calamity of the most heartrending kind—an atrocity of unspeakable character."

As the horror of the details arrived throughout the North, there was a demand that Quantrill be condemned and punished for his atrocities. But the Confederates withheld comment until all the facts were known. The headlines on the Charleston, South Carolina, *MERCURY*, read, "The whole town swept— A perfect success."

The Richmond, Virginia, *EXAMINER* stated:

> "The expedition to Lawrence, Kansas, was a gallant and perfectly fair blow at the enemy . . . as the population of Kansas is malignant and scoundrelly beyond description."

But the *eye for an eye* retaliation came soon, as thousands of angry Union pursuers crossed the border into Missouri, burning and killing as they went, and four days later, border commander Thomas Ewing signed into law "General Orders, No. 11," ordering all persons occupying the four Missouri border counties in his district, about twenty thousand people, to be off their land in fifteen days. Everywhere, the homes of Missourians in the doomed region went up in flames. Just one squad of men claimed to have burned 110 houses, some of them worth as much as $20,000. The road from Independence, Missouri, to Lexington was crowded with women and children, babies in arms, and packs on their backs—hungry.

A Kansas soldier wrote:

> "The border counties of Missouri have almost as desolate an appearance as before the soil was trod by the white man. Not a man, woman or child is to be seen in the country to which Order No. 11 applies . . . Chimneys mark the spot where once stood costly farm houses, cattle and hogs are fast destroying large fields of corn, prairie fires are burning up miles of good fencing every day or two, and turn which way you will, everything denotes a state of utter desolation and ruin."

After "General Orders No. 11" had devastated the four border counties below the Missouri River in the summer of 1863, the inhabitants along the Kansas border, even into Topeka, lived in horror of the Bushwhackers' revenge. They slept with their revolvers and sometimes with their clothes on, and all available guns nearby and fully loaded. Every house was an arsenal. But the real terror was postponed, for Quantrill had tired of the killings. However, when spring arrived, his former lieutenants Bill Anderson, George Todd, and Dick Yager arrived from Texas with additional hundreds of Bushwhackers. In the ravaged southern counties there were dense and tangled forests with steep drop-offs that offered guerrilla protection. North of the Missouri River, they were welcomed by the secessionist settlers. If caught, they fought to the death, as they knew no mercy awaited them.

The fury of 1863 intensified in that bloody summer of 1864. Both sides had become callous to human suffering. Men were usually shot in the head, and their bodies mutilated. Scalps, dried ears, eyes, or tongues might adorn the saddles and necks of the raiders. An enemy's decapitated head might be nailed to a tree or post as a warning. Since the Bushwhackers often wore Union army jackets for warmth, signals of various kinds were used by the North, only to be discovered by their spies. As the *seceshs* helped the guerrilla bands, the Federal army's response came—"Let the people *feel* the war," and the remaining settlements became targets as the junior officers seemed to delight in their destruction. They looted, raped, and torched, leaving desolation and death behind them as the confrontations moved east and south. Family history records place THOMAS C. IVIE's death by the Bushwackers at about 1863 in Missouri.

Twenty-five year-old Bushwhacker Bill Anderson and his gang seemed to lead the central Missouri turmoil, and the gang included such men as George Todd, Frank James, and his seventeen-year-old brother, Jesse. Bill Anderson wrote a letter explaining his reasoning to a Lexington newspaper, 7 July 1864:

> "I lived in Kansas when this war commenced. Because I would not fight the people of Missouri, my native State, the Yankees sought my life, but failed to get me. They revenged themselves by murdering my father, destroying all my property, and have since that time murdered one of my sisters and kept the other two in jail twelve months. But I have fully glutted my vengeance. I have killed many. I am a guerrilla."

There was a small railroad town about twenty miles south and west of *Florida*, Missouri, called Centralia. In September 1864, it was held by Union troops. Bill Anderson's camp of around three hundred was close by. The Yankees had made him the North's *Public Enemy #1* and in an ambush had killed and scalped seven of his men. So to even the score, he and about eighty of his men raided Centralia—taking goods, boots, and liquor, and holding up a stagecoach. A train approached; there were twenty-four Federal troops aboard. All the passengers were robbed, some shot without mercy. All the troops, except one, who he hoped to exchange, were lied to, disarmed, and then ruthlessly shot. The train was burned—also, another one that steamed its way in while they were pursuing their bloody business.

One witness reported:

"The guerrillas seemed transformed into fiends, half drunken with the whiskey they had stolen . . . Those who have never seen men unrestrained, can have no idea of how those guerrillas conducted themselves."

The following is quoted from the *History of Monroe and Shelby Counties, Missouri (1884)*:

"It was from Paris [Missouri] that Maj. A. V. E. Johnson started (September 26, 1864,) with detachments of Cos. A, G and H, Thirty-ninth Missouri, in pursuit of Bill Anderson, George Todd, John Thrailkill, et al. The next day, September 27th, the fight occurred near Centralia, where Johnson and 122 of his men were killed."

General U.S. Grant had his headquarters in Florida, Missouri, for awhile during the Civil War. From the above mentioned book on Monroe County we read:

"When the first gun was fired upon Fort Sumpter (April 12, 1861), little did the citizens of the remote county of Monroe dream that the war which was then inaugurated would eventually, like the simultaneous disemboguement of a hundred volcanoes, shake this great nation from its center to its circumference . . . Little did they imagine that war, with all its horrors, would invade their quiet homes, and with ruthless hand tear away from their fireside altars their dearest and most cherished idols . . . Monroe county, as did the State of Missouri generally, suffered much. Her territory was nearly all the time occupied by either one or the other antagonistic elements, and her citizens were called upon to contribute to the support of first one side and then the other.

"We have tried in vain to obtain the number and names of the men who entered the Confederate army from Monroe county. No record of them has ever been preserved, either by the officers who commanded the men or by the Confederate government. It is supposed about 600 men went into the Southern army. Hon. Theodore Brace raised the first company at Paris for State guards, numbering about 70 men. These men went into camp on Elk fork of Salt river, six miles south of Paris. After being in the service six months they were discharged, when some of them entered the Southern army at the battle of Lexington."

The following events within Monroe County are described in this history:

The Battle at Monroe City—8 July through 14 July 1861. Most of the inhabitants fought for the South; but in the end the Northern troops were reinforced by Grant, then in Illinois, and the Southerners dispersed. *Skirmish near Elliott's Mills*—spring of 1862. *Florida fight*—22 July 1862. The Federals retreated to Paris and the Confederates go south. *The capture of Paris*—30 July 1862. Southern Col. Joseph Porter sent Joseph Thompson with a force of men. Porter came north that night with his men and after a few hours went further north. Porter arrived at Kirksville on 6 August 1862 with about three thousand troops. Porter lost this vicious battle at Kirksville and retreated to the south. He was reported near Florida, Monroe County, on 25 August, threatening Paris with one thousand men. Palmyra was captured and desperate fighting continued between the armies—winning and then retreating. Col. Porter was wounded in January 1863, but stayed with his army into Arkansas, where he died from his wounds near Batesville 18 February 1863. *The fight at Paris*—15 October 1864. The history states that:

"Up to December 31, 1863, Monroe county had furnished 41 men for the regular United States service; in the Missouri State Militia, 38. For the Union Army: 'Under calls previous to December 19, 1864, Monroe county furnished 474, being 7 more than her quota. Under call of December 19, 1864, the county furnished 134. There was no deficiency under the draft.'"

[Note: Third-great-grandfather ANDERSON IVIE had died in May 1852 before the war started, and his wife, SARAH ALLRED IVIE had died before 8 May 1861, when some inheritance settlement papers listed her as being dead. Nine slaves are listed in these court papers. Remaining in Monroe County in the 1860s were their children, ISAAC and SARAH. They had married MELISSA and WILLIAM H. LONG—close neighbors. Sons, JOHN ANDERSON IVIE and WILLIAM SHELTON IVIE (deceased before his mother's death), and daughters POLLY ANN BILLINGTON and ELIZABETH ALLRED had moved further north to Kirksville, Adair County, Missouri. Third-great-grandmother SARAH ALLRED IVIE's brother JOHN ALLRED and his wife NANCY were also in Adair County at this time. Both of these Kirksville brothers, JOHN A. and WILLIAM S. IVIE, had a son named JAMES RUSSELL IVIE.

Of WILLIAM's son, JAMES RUSSELL IVIE, we read, "He fought on the confederate side of the Civil War. He was taken prisoner and later joined the Federal army. After the war he married. He died, probably from war wounds, 24 Dec 1866, leaving no children."

The county court records in Paris, Monroe County, Missouri, show that on 12 May 1864, SARAH M. (IVIE) LONG is listed as the administrator of the Estate of [her husband] WILLIAM LONG (deceased). Other heirs listed were their children SARAH J., JOHN A., WILLIAM N., ANITA A., KITTY A., and ROBERT L. LONG. There are also later records where the court was searching for second-great-grandfather JAMES R. IVIE and his brother THOMAS C. IVIE who had not claimed their inheritances—both had died prior to these court records. Second-great-grandfather JAMES R. IVIE had been killed in Scipio, Utah, by the Indians on 10 June 1866.]

A record by a granddaughter of THOMAS C. IVIE stated that he was killed by Bushwhackers. It is possible that his brother-in-law, WILLIAM H. LONG, was one of those Southern Bushwhackers, as some records indicate that he might have killed him. It would also seem likely from the date of his death, May 1864, that WILLIAM H. LONG was also a Civil War casualty. According to ALLRED records in Utah, Brigham Young had told them after THOMAS C. IVIE's *escape* from prison on murder charges, that they were not to worry about his punishment as he would be killed in a cornfield in Missouri and the buzzards would pick his bones. It would seem from the Missouri court records, that his sister SARAH IVIE LONG, WILLIAM LONG's wife, was unaware (or unsure) of her brother TOM's death or an inheritance would not have been left to him.

General Johnston, who had released THOMAS C. IVIE from prison in Utah, left Camp Floyd a few months later. He feared that the Civil War would begin before he arrived in the South with his troops to support his close friend Jefferson Davis. Many of his troops joined with him in the Southern Confederate Army. He was an excellent general for the South; but was killed in the Battle at Shiloh, Tennessee, fighting against the forces of Ulysses S. Grant.

The battle got its name from a log church named Shiloh, which interpreted by their Bible scholars meant "a place of peace." It was located on the west side of the Tennessee River as it flows northward, through Tennessee and Kentucky to the Ohio River. Southward were the three converging borders of Alabama, Mississippi, and southern Tennessee. Grant's army had camped in this peaceful area, having driven the Confederate Army out of Missouri. They were waiting for General Beull's army to join them—coming southwest from the Nashville area. It was early April, 1862.

Southern General Beauregard had been transferred from the east with the purpose of reassembling the scattered Confederate troops into a larger army. He had managed to assemble an army of forty thousand by the end of March at Corinth, Mississippi, near the northern border—fifteen thousand from General Albert Sidney Johnston's group, ten thousand from General Polk's command and another fifteen thousand troops as far away as the Gulf of Mexico and Texas. Major General Braxton Bragg was appointed Chief of Staff of this Army of the West.

Knowing that Buell's army had left Nashville to join with Grant, Johnston's plan was to catch Grant's forces by surprise and destroy them before they could evacuate across the river. With Grant's army eliminated, he would then move against Buell's army. This would open the way for a large Southern advance across Tennessee and Kentucky. As they started their move on 5 April 1862, they encountered several skirmishes and Beauregard wanted to turn back; but Johnston determinedly refused. He had been correct. The northern army was taken completely by surprise. Grant was away from the camp in a strategy planning conference. Only Brigadier General Benjamin A. Prentiss, whose division was all raw recruits, was sufficiently concerned that pickets had been posted on a perimeter one and a half miles from camp shortly before dawn. Theirs was the only alarm that was sounded in the Union camp when the 40,000 Confederate troops bore down on them from the forest that Sunday morning of 6 April 1862.

Sherman's troops stubbornly held their ground around the Shiloh Church; but Prentiss' recruits held only briefly, giving way under a combined flank and frontal attack. By 9:00 a.m. Sherman's camp had also been taken, and the Union troops had fallen back to secondary lines along the Purdy and Hamburg River Roads. The continuous firing had early alerted Grant and other divisions, who rushed to the scene. On arriving, Grant was still not convinced that it was indeed a major battle. He could not believe that Johnston would risk a full-scale attack on his encampment; but within the hour he had called for all his reserves and was more than convinced as the Confederate forces continued to surge forward in almost continuous waves. The Union position appeared more and more hopeless. The morale of their troops was declining, while the Confederate soldiers sensed victory. Quoting from Shelby Toole, *The Civil War, A Narrative:*

> "It was a frantic mass of keyed up men crowded into an approximate battle formation to fight a hundred furious skirmishes strung out in a crooked line. Confusing as all this was to those who fought . . . it was perhaps even more confusing to those who were trying to direct them. And indeed how should they have understood this thing they had been plunged into as if into a cauldron of pure hell? For this was the first great modern battle. It was Wilson's Creek and Manassas rolled together, quadrupled, and compressed into an area smaller than either. From the inside it resembled Armageddon."

Johnston decided the battle could be quickly won by directing his forces more fully against the Union left flank; but encountered staunch resistance at a point which the Confederates nicknamed *The Hornet's Nest,* where the rebel attack was opposed by the divisions of Hurlbut, Wallace and Prentiss. It was the scene of one of the epic battles of the war. The battle raged, twelve separate times the armies collided with neither side accomplishing much more than increasing the piles of dead bodies that were walked over without ever touching the ground.

Shelby Toole continues:

"At the end of the battle line, on the far flank of the Hornets Nest, there was a ten acre peach orchard in full bloom. Hurlbut had a heavy line of infantry posted among the trees, supported by guns whose . . . bullets clipped the blossoms overhead . . . Johnston saw that the officers were having trouble getting the troops in line to go forward again. 'Men they are stubborn; we must use the bayonet,' he told them . . . they still seemed reluctant . . . Riding front and center, he stood in the stirrups, removed his hat, and called back over his shoulder: 'I will lead you!' As he touched his spurs to the flanks of his horse, they surged forward, charging with him into the sheet of flame which blazed to meet them there among the blossoms." It seems unlikely that those present thought much about the blossoms.

So intent on his battle, Johnston failed to realize that he had been hit in the femoral artery near one of his knees. It was bleeding quite profusely into his long boot and it went unnoticed until, weak from the loss of blood; he fell unconscious from his horse. His life still might have been spared, if those who surrounded him had applied a tourniquet above the wound instead of searching unsuccessfully for a more experienced doctor. He literally bled to death. Some records speculate that had Johnston lived a few more hours in command of his troops, the victory would have been his, not Grant's.

The battle continued with Beauregard in command of Johnston's division. He had kept Johnston's death a secret from the troops; and had rallied them until a discouraged group of 2,200 Union soldiers surrendered; but the whole attack and battle had been orchestrated by Johnston, sometimes against the wishes of General Beauregard. He did not exhibit the same stamina and determination and twice retreated, when a forward thrust might have brought victory. At one point, part of the confused Union army were trapped in a ravine and shot down without mercy. It was later named *Hell's Hollow.* Grant remained firm, believing in the eminent arrival of Buell's army. After twelve hours of continual battle both armies slept. Grant's sleep was more relaxed. He felt sure that Buell and his army would arrive with their fresh troops before morning. It became Grant's victory when Beauregard gave up because his ammunition was nearly gone and retreated into the South, opening the doors for Grant's future victory in Vicksburg.

[Note: ISAAC IVIE died in Kirksville, Adair County, Missouri, 4 April 1883. POLLY ANN IVIE BILLINGTON's husband EZEKIEL died in Kirksville 16 November 1857. POLLY ANN and her son NATHANIEL BILLINGTON came to Spring City, Sanpete County, Utah. Her other children evidently remained in Kirksville. POLLY died in Spring City on 15 December 1887. Her son, NATHANIEL BILLINGTON died in Spring City, 29 December 1922. ELIZABETH IVIE ALLRED died in Grayson, Texas, 22 March 1870. Her husband WILLIAM H. ALLRED [the oldest son of JAMES ALLRED] survived her and came to Spring City, where he died 1 August 1890. Uncle JOHN ANDERSON IVIE took his family to Alabama.

THOMAS C. IVIE's wife, AMANDA and her family accompanied the IVIEs when they moved to Round Valley [Scipio]. She later married again and took her family with her to Payson. This family had two additional children—for a total of nine children. According to the record of aunt PEARL IVIE (Stanford), one of her daughters, SARAH JANE IVIE married SYDNEY ALLRED, and they had six children. Their daughter ELIZA IVIE married ANDREW J. ALLRED, 1 January 1875, and they had two children. All of their nine children grew to adulthood and were married. Although the grandchildren's names are not listed, Aunt PEARL's record claimed a total of fifty-one grandchildren. No attempt was made to number their great-grandchildren.]

Samuel Clemens and his brother Orion boarded a stagecoach going west on 25 July 1861. Orion, with proper connections after LINCOLN's inauguration, was appointed to the post of Secretary of the new territory of Nevada, and Samuel signed on as Secretary's secretary. Tickets by overland stage to "the straggle of wooden houses on the desert" called Carson City, Nevada, were one hundred and fifty dollars—it would take twenty days. Samuel Clemens had given up being a Confederate soldier. His comment:

> "I could have become a soldier myself if I had waited. I had got part of it learned. I knew more about retreating than the man that invented retreating."

He left behind his experiences in New York City, his advancement from pilot of the slow freight Mississippi steamboats to that of piloting the fancy riverboats of the wealthy patrons. It had been great fun; but this occupation had ended with the shots at Fort Sumter. When he returned to the east five years later, age thirty-one, he would no longer be the obscure brother of Orion, Sam Clemens of Hannibal, Missouri; but he returned as the famous Mark Twain— "The Wild Humorist of the Pacific Slope."

Back in central Utah, the mostly unknown Indian, Black Hawk, had also grown older. His bold leadership would create new troubles in what the Saints had hoped would be quiet, spiritual communities. JOHN LEHI IVIE's days in the saddle had not yet ended, nor were his family ties as tranquil as hoped for.

The Black Hawk War story will be told in BROAD are the BRANCHES—an American Saga, Part II: STANDING FIRM, along with stories of another U. S. Army—this time from California—advancing into Salt Lake City and northern Utah. There are stories of freighting into violent Pioche; missionaries into the troubled Northern and Southern missions of the United States. Part II includes briefly the problems created by the early church practice of polygamy, and the commandment, in 1890, that stopped the practice within the Church—even to the excommunication of those who continued this practice, against the laws of church and state.

There are bare politics in Idaho, Utah, and Nevada, and some incredible spiritual experiences. Searching further into genealogical records, I discovered early 1600s relationships into all the pristine thirteen original colonies, including French Huguenots and Canadian Catholics.

Part III: REBELLION and Part IV: UNITED STATES? are the stories of founding a nation from these fragmented people and uniting them through multiple wars, political factions, and foreign diplomacy into ABRAHAM LINCOLN's "This nation, under God" with its new birth of freedom. It ends with the question of the UNITED support of a God-inspired Constitution still remaining.

~ ABOUT THE AUTHOR ~

Born just before the beginning of the Great Depression of wonderful parents, Brookie Condie spent her early childhood on a large sheep and cattle ranch near Carey, Idaho, by the Craters of the Moon National Monument. Just before Hitler started his invasion of Europe, her beloved father died of cancer, leaving her mother with the ranch and seven young children. Brookie was the third oldest child at ten years old. Shortly after Pearl Harbor, the family moved to Twin Falls, where she graduated from Twin Falls High School with high honors.

Excelling in math and science, she chose pharmacy as a career and attended Idaho State College in Pocatello, Idaho, where she met and married her handsome husband, Grover Swallow, also a pharmacy major, in the LDS Manti Temple in 1948. World War II had ended and there were over two hundred new pharmacists in her 1950 graduation class. They were mostly GI Bill veterans. She was one of only three women pharmacists and graduated summa cum laude. The couple worked many low pay jobs to finance their educations. At college, Brookie played the violin in the Idaho State Symphony orchestra.

To become a registered pharmacist, Brookie worked in Logan and Smithfield, Utah, and Preston, Idaho, where her husband was also working. In 1954, he became a partner in a drug store in Montpelier, Idaho. Always active in church and community activities and playing violin solos, Brookie wrote short plays for local entertainment, and directed one of her ten minute road shows that placed first in the area. Four children were born during these years. As always, Grover was chosen as a leader in church and community organizations. They also became interested in the genealogy of their families. Brookie loved to teach adults and taught in the Gospel Doctrine class—the New Testament, Acts through Revelations. The class more than doubled in size.

Wanting their own drugstore, they purchased the Pioche Pharmacy in Nevada. Brookie sold her first publication to *Sunset Magazine* in 1957 to promote tourism into the area, while writing a fiction novel she chose not to try to publish. She then enrolled in Art Instruction, Inc., later graduating and specializing in illustrations. In the fall of 1958, they purchased a second drugstore in Caliente, which Grover managed, while she was pharmacist in Pioche and did the accounting for both stores.

Living in a three bedroom home, cut into the mountain behind the drugstore in the mining town of Pioche, became more difficult as the children grew and became more numerous. So with the birth of number seven in 1962, they purchased and remodeled a larger home in Panaca with extra acreage, driving north and south to their two businesses. The high school for the three towns was located in Panaca. Ever interested in the education of her children, Brookie was elected as the only woman on their five member Lincoln County school board.

The mandatory U.S. Reapportionment legislation by the Supreme Court in 1964 left the county without a legislator, and the destruction of their local economy began rapidly descending towards zero. They closed the Pioche Pharmacy in 1968. Grover, ever the leader, was unable to find anyone else willing, so he filed for the Nevada Assembly. The odds of his election were one in twenty, but someone at least needed to try. Brookie became his campaign manager. He won, giving the Republicans their first majority in forty years. Keeping all his campaign promises, he won again in 1970. Brookie became the Caliente pharmacist, a strong lobbyist for morals and school boards, and mother of ten during the legislative sessions. In addition, Grover became a member of the LDS Stake Presidency, and drove home every weekend for this assignment—450 miles.

With another reapportionment after the 1970 census, Grover filed for the state senate race in 1972. This area included the south half of Nevada, except Clark County (Las Vegas). He lost this race by a very few votes, in spite of Watergate and the descent of the Republican Party, and was not quite successful in his bid for the one seat in the assembly in 1974, but Lincoln County was no longer ignored in Carson City.

Four children had attended Brigham Young University, a missionary had returned from Guatemala, three children were married, and with a pharmacist/

manager in Caliente, they decided in 1976 to move closer to BYU and pur-chased a drugstore in the University Mall in Orem from Walgreen's, who with high interest rates and a shrinking economy had decided to sell all their stores in Utah. It was 15,000 square feet and included a restaurant. Brookie worked from 10 a.m. to 3 p.m., with her children in school, mostly doing accounting with some management and pharmacist duties. They later expanded into the Layton Hills Mall in Layton, Utah; but with the national economy still going sour and interest rates zooming near twenty percent, they closed it in 1982.

At home in Provo, Brookie became a typical LDS mother with a mission-ary in Colombia, Arizona, and Dominican Republic at the same time. She had a gymnast/cheerleader, a girl's basketball star at Provo High, two exciting el-ementary students, a BYU bishop husband with his office at home, interviewing his single members, while she was Relief Society chorister, Primary teacher and chief cook, laundress, chauffeur, and genealogist. Time brought more marriag-es, family history consulting, auditing freshman French at BYU, and more in-tensive research at the best genealogical library in the world, the Family History Library in Salt Lake City. When the lease ended in 1995 for Swallows Drugs in the University Mall, they sold it, and she began to compile and edit her vast col-lection of genealogical records, which became more and more exciting as new discoveries were made in these and other historical records.

They sold their Caliente store and built a retirement home on their vacant lot, and celebrated their sixtieth wedding anniversary in 2008. In 2009, Gro-ver died. Today Brookie is still in Panaca, Nevada. She has 47 grandchildren, including a Green Beret in the Middle East, and 32 great-grandchildren. After her physical examination, her doctor told her she was eighty years old, going on sixty, so she traded her old Lincoln clunker for a red 2010 Ford Fusion.

— BIBLIOGRAPHY FOR PART I —
DRIVEN

Alexander, Thomas G., *Things in Heaven and Earth. The Life and Times of Wilford Woodruff, a Mormon Prophet,* Signature Books, Salt Lake City, 1991.

Allred Family Oranization, Quarterly Magazines

Allred, Isaac, *ISAAC ALLRED – MY GREAT GRANDFATHER,* His Autobiography on microfilm in the Family History Library, Salt Lake City, Utah 1849

American Genealogical Research Institute, *Barton Family History,* Heritage Press, Inc. Washington, D.C., 1977

Ancestor Files AF, computerized records of ancestors, The Church of Jesus Christ of Latter-day Saints.

Anderson, Richard Lloyd, *Investigating the Book of Mormon Witnesses,* Deseret Book, Salt Lake City, 1981.

Arrington, Leonard J., *Great Basin Kingdom, Economic History of the Latter-day Saints, 1830-1900* University of Nebraska Press, Lincoln, 1958.

Barton, Elisha Kemmer, brother of Mary Catherine Barton, *Life Story*

Barton, Margaret, granddaughter of Elisha Kemmer Barton, *Historical and Family History Records.*

Berret, William Edward, *The Restored Church,* The Deseret News Press, Salt Lake City, 1936.

Bigler, David L. and Bagley, Will, *Army of Israel, Mormon Battalion Narrative,* Utah State University Press, Logan, 2000.

Billington, Ray Allen; Ridge, Martin, *Westward Expansion, A History of the American Frontier* Macmillan Publishing Co. Inc., New York, 1982

Brown, Matthew B., *Plates of Gold, The Book of Mormon Comes Forth,* Covenant Communications, Inc., American Fork, 2003.

Brown, S. Kent, Cannon, Donald Q., Jackson, Richard H., *Historical Atlas of Mormonism,* Simon & Schuster, New York, 1994.

Buchannan, Ida Belle Gledhill Christensen, and her aunt, Dix, Ida Ivie Stanford, *History of their mothers, Lillie Belle Ivie Gledhill and Mary Catherine Barton Ivie Peters.*

Burt, Olive, *Brigham Young,* Julian Messner, Inc., New York, 1956.

Carter, Kate B., *The Mormon Battalion,* 1946 & 7, *Our Pioneer Heritage,* Daughters of the Utah Pioneers, Utah Printing Company, 1956.

Carter Pioneers of Provo, Utah, Part 1, Historical Sequence, self published

Chicago, 1911, FHL US/CAN 974.531 D2go, Salt Lake City, Utah

Clay, Lillie Ida Condie, *They Chose to Serve,* Self Published, Provo, 1998

Clint, Florence, *Northumberland County, Pennsylvania, AREA KEY,* FHL 974.831 D25a. 1977, SLC, Utah

Condie, Lillie A. Ivie, vast collection of Ivie, Condie, Barton, and personal records

Conover, Don W. (Grandson), from *Utah Pioneer Biographies, Volume 7, Journal of Peter Wilson Cownover,* begin page 8 – 1849-1946

Day, Sherman, *1843, History, Northumberland County,* Pennsylvania

DeLafosse, Peter H., *Trailing the Pioneers,* Utah State University Press, Logan, 1994

Deseret News, 24 July 1860 and others

Dewey, Richard Lloyd, *Porter Rockwell, A Biography,* Paramount Books, New York, 1986

Dixon, Madoline C., *These Were the Utes,* D. Appleton and Company, 1913

Daughters of Utah Pioneers, *100 Years of History of Millard County,* Art City Publishing Co.

Dyer, Gustavus W. & Moore, John Trotwood, *The Tennessee Civil War Veterans Questionnaires,* US/Can 976.8 M2dg V.3

Emigration of 1848, LDS Historical Library, Church Office Building, 1848

Ephraim's First 100 Years, a committee, Milton G. Armstrong, Chairman

Family Search, IGI, ordinance records of The Church of Jesus Christ of Latter-day Saints. computer, microfiche, internet, archives, and card catalogue of Family History Library, Salt Lake City, Utah

First Judicial District Court Criminal Records Index and microfilms

French, Ellen Cochran, *Barton & Hummell Family Histories, Early Pioneers,* Pennsylvania, Ohio, Iowa, Tribune Printing Company, Fairfield, Iowa, 1967, FHL US/CAN 929.273 B285f

Ghost Town Gazette Fall, 1996, Vol. I, No. l, *Pioche, Nevada—Nation's Liveliest Ghost Town*

Gottfredson, Peter, *Indian Depredations in Utah,* Skelton Publishing Co., Salt Lake City, 1919

Goodrich, Thomas, *Black Flag,* Indiana University Press, Bloomington and Indianapolis, Indiana, 1995

Gowans and Campbell, *Fort Bridger, Island in the wilderness, Fort Supply, Brigham Young's Green River experiment,* Brigham Young's University Press, Provo, Utah, 1975, 1976

Grant, Carter E., *The Kingdom of God Restored,* Deseret Book Company, 1955

Gunn, Stanley R., *Oliver Cowdery, Second Elder and Scribe,* BookCraft, Inc., Salt Lake City, 1962

Haslam, Matthew J., *John Taylor, Messenger of Salvation,* Covenant Communications, American Fork, 2002.

HC *History of the Church, seven volumes,* copyrighted by Joseph F. Smith for The Church of Jesus Christ of Latter-day Saints, 1904.

History of Monroe and Shelby Counties, Missouri, from the Most Authentic Official Sources, St. Louis National Historical Company, 1884.

History of Sanpete and Emery Counties, Utah, FHL US/CAN 979.85 h2b, W. H. Sever, Ogden, 1940

Ivie, Evan, *Land Deeds and Court records collected in Monroe County, Missouri* 1833–1867

Ivie, Grant, *The Story of James A. Ivie,* as researched by his father, Lloyd O. Ivie, and other stories.

Ivie, Horace Leon, genealogical records

Ivie, James Oscar, his personal writings of his life and that of his father, Colonel John Lehi Ivie and mother Mary Catherine Barton Ivie Peters.

Ivie, Lloyd O., *James Alexander Ivie,* family history, genealogical, Japanese and early church records

Ivie, William Elbert, *My Memories*

Jenson, Andrew, *Encyclopedic History of The Church of Jesus Christ of Latter-day Saints,* Deseret News Publishing Company, Salt Lake City, Utah, 1941; *History of Provo*

JD *Journal of Discourses, Volumes 1 through 26, by Brigham Young, his two councilors, Twelve Apostles, and others* F.D. and S. W. Richards, London, 1851, Reprint Salt Lake City, 1964.

Kearl, J. R., Pope, Clayne l., & Wimmer, Larry T., *Indexes to the 1850, 1860 & 1870 Censuses of Utah,* Genealogical Publishing Co., Baltimore, 1981 Knaut, Andrew L., *The Pueblo Revolt of 1680,* The University of Oklahoma Press, Norman, 1995.

Korns and Morgan, *West from Fort Bridger,* Utah State University Press, Logan, 1994

LDS Collectors Library, 1995 Infobases Inc.

Larson, Gustive O., *Outline History of Territorial Utah,* Brigham Young University, Provo, Utah, 1958

BIBLIOGRAPHY

Leonard, Glen M., *Nauvoo, A Place of Peace, A People of Promise,* R. R. Donnelley and Sons, Crawordsville, Indiana, 1995.

Longsdorf, Hilda Madsen, *Mount Pleasant, 1859 – 1939,* Stevens & Wallis, Inc., Salt Lake City, Utah, 1939

Lund, Gerald N., *The Fire and the Covenant,* BookCraft Publishers, Salt Lake City, 1999

Lundwell, N. B., *The Fate of the Persecutors of the Prophet Joseph Smith,* BookCraft Publishers, 1952

Madson, Truman D., *Defender of the Faith, The B. H. Robert's Story,* BookCraft Publishers, 1952

McNeer, May, *The California Gold Rush,* Random House, New York, 1979

Meltzer, Milton, *Mark Twain, Himself,* Random House, New York, 1950

Millard County Court House Records, Fillmore, Utah, 18

Moffitt, John Clifton, *The Story of Provo, Utah,* Provo, Utah, 1975

Mortensen, Don M., *Stories, Legends, and Lore of the James Allred Family,* Allred Family Reunion, 2002

Mortensen, A.R., *The Valley of the Great Salt Lake,* Reprinted from Utah Historical Quarterly' Utah State Historical Society, Salt lake City, 1959

Nelson, Lee, *The Black Hawk Journey,* CFI, Cedar Fort Incorporated, Springville, Utah, 1999

Nevada State Historic Preservation Office, *Nevada's Historical Markers,* Carson City, Nevada, 2000

NEVADA, THE SILVER STATE, Volumes 1 & 2, Western States Historical Publishers, Inc. , Carson City, Nevada 1970

Northumberland County, Pennsylvania, Genealogical and Biographical Annals, J.L. Floyd & Co.

Parkman, Francis, *The Oregon Trail,* The John C. Winston Company, Philadelphia, 1921

Peterson, John Alton, *Utah's Black Hawk War,* The University of Utah Press, Salt lake City, Utah, 1998

Porter, Larry C., *BYU Studies, Vol. 9, No. 330-336*

Pratt, Parley P., *Autobiography of Parley P. Pratt,* The Deseret Book Company, Salt Lake City, 1938

Provo City Records, Provo Public Library

Probert, William, *A Letter to Peter Gottfredson,* July 1, 1915, from Provo to Springville.

Pyper, George D., *Stories of Latter-day Saints Hymns,* Deseret Book Press, Salt Lake City, 1939

Reay, Lee, *Lambs in the Meadow,* Meadow Lane Publications, Provo Utah, 1979 Roberts, B. H., *A Comprehensive History of the Church of Jesus Christ of Latter-day Saints, Century 1, in Six Volumes,* Published by the Church, Brigham Young University Press, Provo, 1926.

Robins, Nettie N., *The History of James Russell Ivie & Wife Eliza McKee Fauscett,* (great-granddaughter)

Rollins, James, *James Rollins Autobiography,* BYU p. 9-10

Russell, David H., McCullough, Constance M., and Gates, Doris, *Trails to Treasure,* Ginn and Company, New York, 1949

Shipps, Jan, and John W. Welch, *The Journals of William E. McLellin 1831-1836,* The Church of Jesus Christ of Latter-day Saints, BYU studies, Provo, 1994.

Sanpete County Court Records, located in Manti, Utah.

Slaughter, William W., Landon, Michael, *Trail of Hope,* Shadow Mountain, Salt Lake City, 1997.

Smith, Joseph Fielding, *Essentials in Church History,* Deseret News Press, Salt Lake City, 1950.

Stone, Conway B., *Ships, Saints, and Mariners, 1830-1890,* FHC, BX 8673.4 So59hs Orem Park Stake, Orem, Utah, 1987

Strouse, Jean, *Morgan, American Financier,* Perennial, Harper Collins Publisher, 1999.

The Allred Family in America, FHL US/CAN 929.273 Al57a, Wm. R. Bischoff, Salt Lake City, Utah

Times and Seasons, Vol. 4. p. 36-38

Toole, Shelby, *The Civil War, A Narrative, Volumes I and II,* Time-Life Books, Alexandria, Virginia, 1999

Tyler, Sgt. Daniel, *The Concise History of the Mormon Battalion in the Mexican War, 1846-1848*, Tyler collected the journals of many members, including Sergeants William Hyde and Reddick N. Allred, The Rio Grande Press, Inc., Clorieta, New Mexico, 1881.

United States of American, Census and Taxpayer Records, 1790-1860

Utah Pioneer Biographies, Utah State Historical Society, Volume 7, G.S. 1947, includes the journal of Peter Wilson Cownover., starting where he comes to Provo. pages 181 to 218. Genealogical Society 22157, 1946

Utah State Archives, Early Criminal Records, Salt Lake City, Utah

Watson, Kaye C., *Life under the Horseshoe, a History of Spring City*, Publishers Press, Salt Lake City, Utah, 1987

Welsh, Douglas, *The Complete Military History of the Civil War*, Brompton Books Corp., Greenwich, CT, 1990

Winik, Jay, *A Civil War Saga, APRIL 1865, The Month That Saved America*, Perennial, Harper Collins Publishers, 2002

~ INDEX FOR PART I ~
DRIVEN

[NOTE: MAIDEN NAMES ARE USED FOR SOME WOMEN.]

Part II

STANDING FIRM

Brookie Condie Swallow

Contents

~ CAST OF CHARACTERS ~

All passed on to a happier world, but not forgotten!

JOHN LEHI IVIE, known as the colonel in the Utah militia, born in Florida, Missouri, 11 June 1833. He was my great-grandfather and the husband of

MARY CATHERINE BARTON, who was born in Pennsylvania, 30 June 1837, my great-grandmother and daughter of

JOHN BARTON and **SUSANNAH WILKINSON** of Pennsylvania. His parents were NOAH BARTON and MARY COOLEY of Hunterdon County, New Jersey. She was the daughter of AARON WILKINSON, who married MARY SUSANNAH POYER, both of Pennsylvania.

JAMES RUSSELL IVIE, born in Georgia in 1803, father of JOHN LEHI IVIE, and married to **ELIZA McKEE FAUSETT** in Tennessee. She was the daughter of RICHARD FAUSETT and MARY McKEE. His father and mother were ANDERSON IVIE, born in Virginia in 1774, and SARAH ALLRED of North Carolina.

JAMES ALEXANDER (JIM) IVIE, older brother of JOHN LEHI IVIE. Accused of starting the (Utah) Walker Indian War.

JAMES OSCAR IVIE, my grandfather, born in Mount Pleasant, Utah, in 1863, son of JOHN LEHI IVIE. Married **ANNIE C. MORTENSEN,** whose parents were JENS F. MORTENSEN and METTE M. HANSEN from Denmark. Their daughter and granddaughter was

LILLIE A. IVIE, my mother, who married **MARION A. CONDIE,** my father, son of GIBSON A CONDIE and EMILY E. TUCKER, daughter of JAMES TUCKER and BETSY LERWILL of England.

GROVER SWALLOW, my husband, son of THOMAS C. SWALLOW and VANDA DUNCAN, grand-daughter of JAMES and JANET SNEDDEN DUNCAN of Scotland and WILLIAM H. and ALICE NIELD STOTT from England. [see Part I: DRIVEN] GROVER's grandfather was

CHARLES SWALLOW, who was born in England and married **ISABELLE DEARDEN,** daughter of THOMAS DEARDEN and CHARLOTTE DAVIES, from England and Wales.

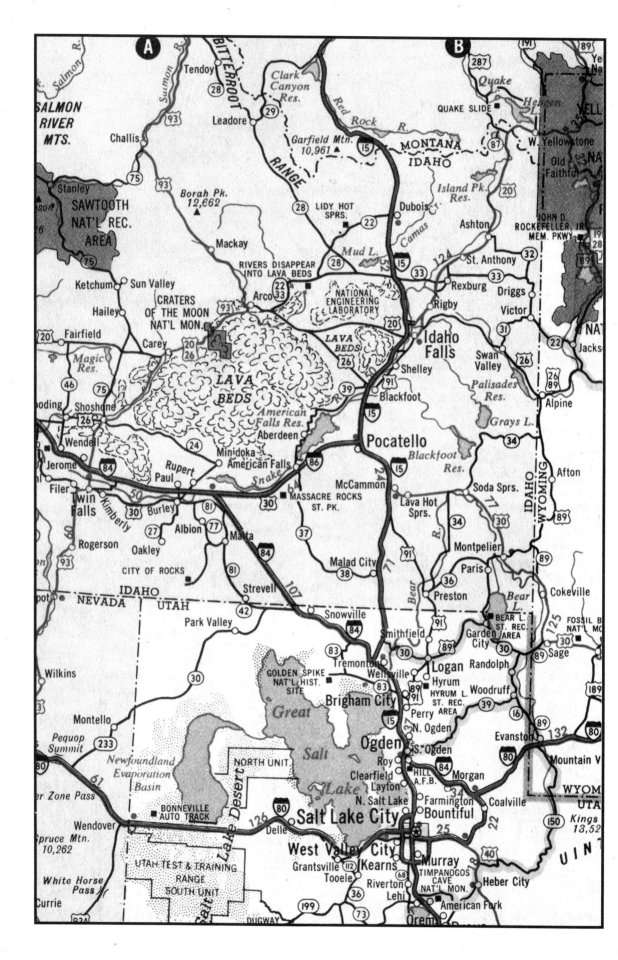

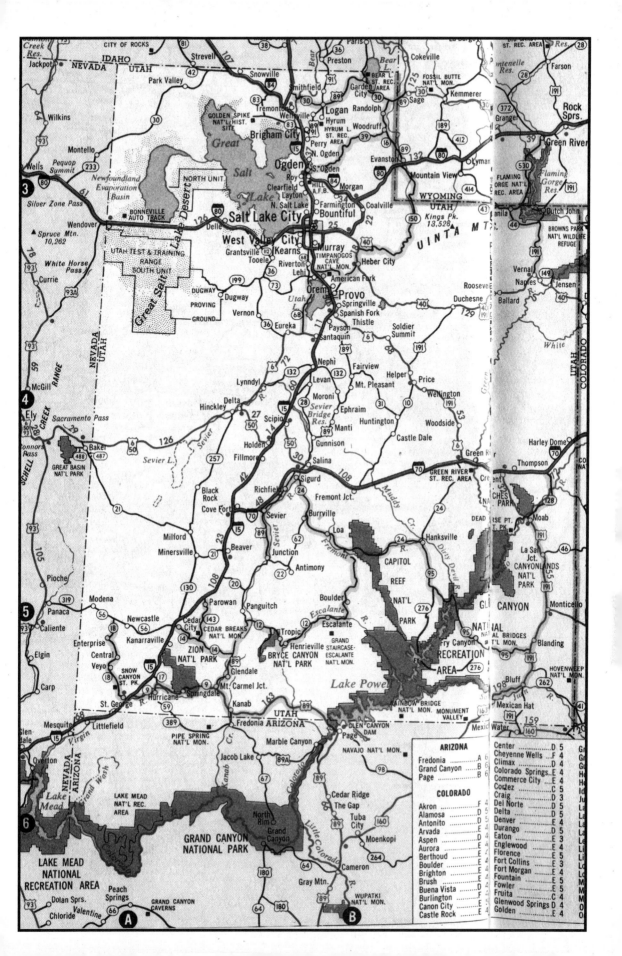

~ 29 ~

A Shoemaker from
Devonshire, England

"Does it not seem impossible that men and women, brought up under British and American civilization, can abandon it for the wilderness and Mormonism? They step into the waves of the great basin with as much reliance on their leaders as the descendants of Jacob felt when they stepped between the walls of water in the Red Sea."

[*London Times 1857*]

"Their heroic endurance and marvelous achievements entitle them to the respect and admiration of their fellow creatures . . . and how many thousands of the down-trodden and penury-stricken victims of European tyranny were leaving the land of their birth, in order to find in the Mormon territory that hope and encouragement denied to them in their native countries?"

[*Reynolds' Newspaper* of the British Republicans, 1857]

"Posterity must not have to acknowledge with shame that our indiscretion, or ignorance, or intolerance drove the population of a whole State from house and home, to seek religious liberty and immunity from the presence of mercenary troops. . . . When people abandon their homes to plunge with women and children into a wilderness, to seek new settlements, they know not where, they give a higher proof of courage than if they fought for them."

[*New York Times, 1857*]

These three quotes are from major English and American newspapers during 1857, when the United States sent Johnston's army of 2500 troops on a march of over 1,000 miles to destroy Mormondom, as they called it. The above articles seem to cry out against this action and ask the question, why?

Why would tens of thousands of people be willing to leave all their worldly possessions behind and plunge into the unknown with only their families and their faith in God?

Still in England at this time was great-grandfather JAMES TUCKER, born 22 Jul 1836 in Eastdown, Devonshire, England. He left us a few short paragraphs of this early period of his life.

> "My schooling was very limited—only about 4 months. Most of my early life was passed in my father's tailor shop where under his instruction I learned the tailoring art. When 14 years of age, I was bound out by contract for five years to my uncle, JOHN BLACKMORE, to learn the cordwainer trade. After two years my uncle died, and I served under Robert Canebear two years. Then for one shilling per day I served one year under John Prediux. When about 19 years old, I went to Exeter, the capitol of Devonshire, for further instructions, for one year. Returning to the residence of my father, at Kentisbury, at the age of 20, I started business for myself as a cordwainer or shoemaker. [This was shortly before the above three articles were written.] This continued for three years. About the age of 23, I became acquainted with Mormon Elders who visited that locality, teaching the everlasting Gospel. Study of the scriptures and earnest prayer brought me a testimony that what they taught was true. I was baptized in October, 1859, and thus became a member of the L.D.S. Church. The unpopularity of the Mormon Doctrine caused some of my friends and patrons to forsake me. The spirit of gathering to Zion rested upon me and in March 1860, I made preparation to emigrate."

When GROVER and I attended the First International Genealogical Conference at the Salt Palace in Salt Lake City, Utah, in August 1968, we purchased a book, *TUCKERS HALL, EXETER* by Joyce Youings, Reader in Tudor History, University of Exeter. I thought it would contain information about the TUCKER family in Devonshire; but instead, I discovered that the word *tucker* is a trade dating back in history to the early gild system in England. Exeter was a center for manufacturing cloth as early as 1200 A. D. Another name for a tucker is a fuller. There were weavers, tuckers, and shearmen in Exeter. With time the shearmen became fewer, and the tuckers took over the total work of finishing the cloth. I think we can safely say that our earliest TUCKER ancestor belonged to the tucker gild. But what does a tucker do?

"When the woollen cloth had come from the loom the raw web . . . had still to undergo a series of processes before is was ready for use. Apart from dyeing, which in Devon was carried out after weaving . . . the cloth had to be . . . subjected to treading or hammering so that, with the aid of water and a chemical alkali such as soap or fuller's earth or, as was the practice in Exeter and elsewhere, of stale urine, it was cleansed of grease and the fabric shrunk and felted, the latter resulting from the entangling of the wool fibres to give the cloth a more or less close texture. The fulling mills were, for their time, elaborate installations. Each mill comprised a number of 'stocks' which in turn consisted of two or more gigantic wooden hammers, their heads weighing several hundred-weight, which were lifted in turn by tappets on a revolving shaft. They fell with great force on the cloth which lay in the stock pit or trough, the shaft itself being connected to a large undershot water-wheel. Cloths were pounded thus for several hours or even days, until the fuller [tucker] was satisfied. . . . After milling the cloth was carried out to the rows of racks or tenters, parallel wooden bars on which it was fastened by tenterhooks and thus stretched into shape and partly dried. Next the cloth was taken into the workshop and burled, that is the whole length was searched for knots and other imperfections which were removed with small metal pincers or burling irons. After this it was rowed or dubbed, the still damp cloth being hung on vertical frames and its nap raised with the aid of teasel heads set in wooden handles. After rowing the cloth was sheared to give it as smooth a surface as possible, the instrument used being the large, broad-bladed, and very heavy cloth shears, sharpened to a fine cutting edge. . . . The finished cloth was then pressed, often after being further immersed in hot water, and finally folded and packed."

After the Roman Empire was no longer able to maintain itself, because of its own sheer weight and corruption, it fell to the barbarians in 476 A.D. The remains of this European civilization, which included much of the British Isles, was soon converted into highly fortified manors (castles) with the strongest *lords* controlling their countrysides, giving some protection to their *serfs* who in turn worked tiny strips of land to survive and pay their taxes to their *masters* and fight under their command. Then as the desire for finer clothing, furniture, music, and other desires increased, artisans of various talents were chosen to fulfill these duties. Villages grew into towns for merchandise exchange, and mayors and magistrates increased in power. The various artisans joined into gilds to protect their interests, demanding more and more specialization and perfection in their occupations. Shoemakers only made shoes; cobblers only repaired them. The gilds enforced Sunday closure.

The following Old English poem, written about 1362-99, from *The Vision of William concerning Piers the Plowman*, describes the duties of the tuckers.

"Cloth that cometh fro the wevying is nought comly to were,
Tyl it is fulled under fote or in fullying-stokkes,
Wasshen wel with water and with taseles cracched,
Ytouked, and ytented and under taillores hande.
And so itt fareth by a barne, that borne is of wombe,
Til it be crystened in Crystes name,
and confermed of the bisshop,
It is hethene as heveneward and helplees to the soule."

Unlike our schools and universities of today, an apprentice had little to say about his own occupation. He did what his father contracted him to do. JAMES TUCKER spent five years as an apprentice and another year of specialized training to become a *freeman* and work for himself. When able to afford it, he could become the master of a new apprentice, if the gild agreed. It limited the applicants to protect the group. Moving in any direction beyond the occupation you were cast into was extremely difficult, and as stated in the early writing, they extended their control to include his immortal soul. When JAMES TUCKER joined the *Mormon* church, his lack of friendship and patronage would in itself drive him from the shores of England into a new world, where he could support himself as well as maintain his own faith in God. His story continues:

"Previous to this I had formed a very friendly acquaintance with BETSY LERWILL, who also had joined the Church. She and I in company with our esteemed friend RICHARD FRY, and wife ANN RAWLE, [a cousin] and about 500 others sailed on the ship 'Underwriter' March 29 [1860] and landed after about five weeks in New York. From there we journeyed by boat and railroad to the outfitting post at Florence, Nebraska. Here about 5 weeks were consumed in making preparations to continue the journey across the Great Plains to the valleys beyond the Rocky Mountains.

"In the month of June, 1860, I and BETSY LERWILL were married by Elder D. J. Ross. RICHARD FRY and I purchased 2 yoke of oxen, 2 cows, and a wagon. Thirty wagons made up the train which started in June from Florence, Nebraska, and arrived in Salt Lake City Sept. 11, 1860.

Early picture of
JAMES TUCKER AND BETSY LERWILL

"Brother FRY and I now divided our interests, he going to Weber Valley [Morgan], while I secured a house and lot in the Tenth Ward S. L. City, and resumed my former occupation as a shoemaker working for other parties. In the spring of 1862 we also moved to Morgan and purchased a farm and like good pioneers started to make a living in a new place with very few tools to work with. Followed general farming and stock raising. When the Morgan Z.C.M.I. was established, again took up my trade of shoemaking having charge for years of that part of the business. In 1888 the firm of TUCKER and TONKS opened up a real shoe store, which was quite successful not withstanding robbers several times depleted the stock."

Arriving into the farm lands of the Weber Canyon about the same time was the young son of THOMAS and HELEN SHARP CONDIE, also named THOMAS. His family arrived in the Salt Lake Valley in Sep 1852 after they joined the Mormon Church in Clackmannan, Scotland in 1849—told by my grandfather GIBSON A CONDIE in Part I. His uncle GIBSON, 13 years old when he crossed the Atlantic, adds these interesting personal details:

"In 1847 Elder William Gibson introduced the gospel of Jesus Christ in this place. There were many converted in the church and were baptized in the Church of Jesus Christ of Latter-day Saints. a few of the many were JOHN SHARP, the Russells and Hunters and Patersons. It caused an excitement in the place for a new religion coming in. They were prejudiced in their feelings against Mormonism. They slandered them of their character and called them False Prophets to come in the last days to deceive the elect, etc. My mother was the first in the family to embrace so called Mormonism. JOHN SHARP baptized her. The branch began to increase . . . . My mother was persecuted by her friends and my father was very bitter against mother joining that wicked sect. Father was a great reader of the Bible and he had a good memory to quote passages in the Bible to prove in his own way that Mormonism was not from God but from the devil. JOHN SHARP and other Elders would come to Father's house and discuss for hours with him. Father was bitter for months against Mormonism. Mother had no peace. Father would abuse her. She went to bed. She did not lay long. The evil spirits drug her out of bed to the floor. She prayed continuously before the Lord to endure all the trials and be able to overcome them. Elder William Gibson had a discussion with a . . . minister named Scott. It caused many to come to hear for themselves. Also at another time JOHN SHARP had a discussion with the two or three diviners or ministers—it lasted two or three days. There were hundreds went to hear for themselves. They were surprised that a Coalminer, JOHN SHARP was to debate with three learned men from the college. When these ministers came into the meeting with the same feeling that the Great Giant, that we read about in the Bible and Little David, —they thought they could kill him. The result was that little David slew him and took the sword from the Giant and cut his head off. So it was with JOHN SHARP the Lord was with him and gave him his Holy Spirit to advocate the principles of the Gospel to expound the scriptures which were laid down by our own Savior and his apostles. He spoke boldly and testified that he embraced the same gospel that was taught anciently and also knew that Joseph Smith was a Prophet of God. He confounded them . . . Mr. Alexander Dow . . . an old acquaintance [told] Father the vision he had and related to him what he saw. The tears came flowing from his eyes while he was relating those experiences. He stated that those who had embraced the gospel and that knowledge and turned aside and denied their Lord and Master he knew their doom to be turned over to the buffetings of Satan until he paid the penalty. . . . Father's heart began to soften . . . my sisters JANET, HELEN, MARGARET and myself were baptized . . . Elder John Russell presided over the Clackmannan Branch. JOHN SHARP presided before and left with other saints and went to America. Father shortly got baptized in Dumfermline by Alexander Dow . . . Father then wanted to immigrate to America with the body of the Church."

The group left Liverpool on the British ship Zetland whose records state that they landed in New Orleans 3 Apr 1849. GIBSON was 13 years old. THOMAS (my great-grandfather) was only 7. They had three sisters: JANET–17; HELEN–11; and baby MARY–12 months. Also listed were JOHN

CONDIE–25; GIBSON CONDIE–32; CECELIA–33; and their children CECELIA–15; JANE SHARP–13; GIBSON–3; PETER–Inf.; JOHN and GIBSON were THOMAS' brothers.

[Note: Young 13-year-old GIBSON CONDIE listed the following relatives: PETER SHARP married to MARY STRANG; WILLIAM SHARP married to CECELIA SHARP; MARAGRET SHARP married to THOMAS STRANG; his uncle ROBERT CONDIE with his wife JANET HUTTON with their children; JOHN's wife, JEAN RUSSELL; uncle THOMAS STRANG and wife, MARGARET SHARP and family; uncle WILLIAM SHARP and family; also his aunt MARY STRANG; uncle PETER; uncle FRANCIS PATERSON and his wife JEAN CONDIE and family.]

Continuing his narrative, he wrote:

"We boarded the train bound for Glasgow and arrived all safe there . . . . We then went aboard a steamer to take us to Liverpool . . . . The people thought if you went a hundred miles away from home it was a great distance. They would be astounded at the long distance we were going. There are folks in Scotland who live where they were born and die in the same town. They do not care for traveling—satisfied where they be. I was surprised in Liverpool—the bands of music, brass instruments would play in the street on Sunday. It was different in Scotland where I was raised any kind of instruments playing on Sunday was forbidden. They were very strict in observing the Sabbath Day more than England. They would not allow anyone to go fishing, playing ball, playing marbles. If you were to shave yourself or blacken your shoes or if any kind of play whatever it was strictly forbidden. They would be prosecuted and punished."

The Church of Scotland was Presbyterian; in England, it was the Church of England—called Episcopalian in America. Third-great-uncle GIBSON CONDIE's eye-witness journal told about how he found the Elders that blessed his baby sister to recover after she drank the sulfuric acid. The large group of Mormons leaving at that time were placed under the direction of Orson Spencer, with his counselors James Ure and Brother Mitchell—Orson Pratt was in charge of the mission and blessed them that all would be well and they would arrive safe if they followed their leaders. He admonished them to be clean, respectful of each other, and not forget their prayers, as they journeyed across the Atlantic. They were pulled from the docks by a steamer into the Irish channel. 20 Jan 1849.

"The people then began to be sick, dizziness, began to vomit and could not sit up for anything and could not eat. They call it sea sickness. . . . They feel as though they could not live. I was about a week myself before I was able to be around again . . . the first mate got drunk and neglected his duty. . . but [the captain] saw for himself the danger . . . took charge and changed the course of the vessel. He then took the first mate into custody. . . . He was a prisoner all the way to New Orleans. The Lord was with us and preserved us from the jaws of death. Another circumstance—our galley fireplace caught on fire . . . no way to escape only to jump into the sea and be drowned. We succeeded in then checking the flames. We all felt thankful to our Heavenly Father in preserving us from the two narrow escapes we had. . . . It was a great sight to see Jamica Island when it came in sight. The natives in their canoes would come along and bring different kinds of fruit to sell. . . . We would then see another island . . . We were about nine weeks on the ship while we were in the gulf. . . . I think we stayed a day waiting for a steamer to tug us up the river to New Orleans . . . about 100 miles. . . . . There was another vessel waiting also in the gulf. That ship came from Africa with a load of slaves (Negroes) to sell. . . . We would go over to the other ship and see the Negroes—how they were fed on corn bread (this was the first that I ever tasted corn dogger) . . . I like it very well. Liverpool to New Orleans . . . is over 5,000 miles. . . . The surroundings all around New Orleans down the river is like a paradise. The slaves were sold at this place commanding high prices at auction—the same as they do selling horses. . . . New Orleans to St. Louis is 1800 miles. We arrived at night [on the steamer.]"

On the Mississippi, his father (my second-great-grandfather) was robbed of his watch while he was sleeping —they cut the chain. His son wrote:

"It appears there are a class of men on the steamers who steal and plunder for a living. Next morning Father thought he would go ashore and took one of our boxes on his shoulders. He walked along one of the planks. It appears the plank sprang up. He then lost his balance. He and the box fell in the river. He sank and rose again. He swam and grasped one of the ropes and climbed on deck. We were surprised to see him on deck—all his clothes wet. No one saw him fall in the river. He undressed and put on dry clothes. We were all thankful to our Heavenly Father in preserving Father from being drowned. That day we all went on shore with our boxes. I think it was the first part of April that we arrived in St. Louis. Here we found some of our old acquaintances from Clackmannan. They came here in 1848—the SHARPs, Fifes, Wilsons, and others.

"They advised us to come to Grovi Diggins—seven miles from St. Louis. . . . It is a coal mining place. . . . Coal miners were making good wages.

Laboring men lived well. . . . We worked for a few months . . . . My sister, JANET, was married to JOSEPH SHARP, brother of JOHN SHARP, from Clackmannan, August 28, 1849. . . . My mother was confined—a son— [He] died shortly in confinement. Since then we named him ROBERT. Cholera set in Grovi Diggins raging fearful. Also in St. Louis, along the river there were many thousands attacked by the destroyer. Hundreds died of that plague. They would live not many hours. The saints were attacked as well as the Gentiles. I have seen the Fathers of Mothers and children be the only one left to tell the tale. . . . They were very humble and sorrowful all alone in the world with no one to attend to their wants and stay the plague. We did have a good time—the spirit of God rested on the speakers, the gifts of tongues and interpretations of the spirit, prayers and singing. It was a comfort to the saints. About that time in St. Louis a fire broke out destroying many blocks, hundreds of houses, mostly stores in the main part of the city. You could see the blaze of fires at night for miles around. It was a fearful sight to look at. I went to St. Louis next day and saw the remains. There were millions of dollars destroyed. That large fire quenched the plague. My little sister, MARY, took sick and died in 1850. She was going on three years old. In that part of the country fever and plague pre-vailed. Father was attacked with that disease. It lasted four weeks . . . . He suffered fearful and had no hope of recovery. The Lord had mercy on him. He gradually recovered again.

"One day father went to St. Louis. There was an auction sale—con-demned Government guns. They were in large boxes. I suppose 50 in a box. They were barrels—the stocks were not there. Father bought I think a couple of boxes. . . . He went to a gunsmith to see if they would stock them. Arrangements were made, prices were fixed. . . . Father then went around selling them. Father was anxious to leave. . . . We left about the first of March, 1850. . . . We left behind my sister JANET and husband also my Uncle GIBSON and family. They were going to start that spring for Salt Lake City."

THOMAS CONDIE and family took a steamboat up the Missouri River to St. Joseph, Missouri. Second-great-grandmother HELEN SHARP CONDIE had a miscarriage while on board. THOMAS and four men carried her ashore. They stayed in St. Joseph until she was better. Her son, GIBSON continues:

"We were thankful to see Mother getting better. She had a narrow escape of death. Some thought she could not live, her being so low, but the Lord preserved her for a wise purpose. . . ."

"That spring 1850 there was a great excitement of Gold Fever; all going to California for gold. There were thousands of gentiles with their teams camping all around Council Bluffs, waiting for grass to grow. What little produce that was in the country became very scarce. The corn began to raise in prices every day. When we came here we could buy the corn for 10 cents a bushel. The drought continued. The poor saints had not money to pay for corn. They had to trade or exchange their good clothes for corn. . . . Orson Hyde presided over Iowa. He expected Brother Orson Pratt from Liverpool and Brother Wilford Woodruff from Philadelphia. The latter was going to the mountains . . . I think it was the 10th of May. The meeting was held in a large grove about a half mile from Kanesville. There was a large attendance. A good many gentiles were there for curiosity to hear the Mormons preach. . . . Brother Pratt opened with prayer. He asked the Lord to bless the saints that they may have rains for the grass to grow—that the saints may cross the plains and to bless the farmers that rains may come in the seasons that they may be blessed with good crops, etc. The prayer was offered fervently and all said Amen. All were united. President Hyde then arose . . . he referred to our conditions—the poor saints suffering for bread. He said the Lord was displeased for our not seeing to the poor. He also spoke of our having no rains for months; crops were all dried, grass, etc. He wished before we go into business the first thing is to see the poor saints provided, give them employment so they can have bread to subsist and other things. He wished the Clerk of the Conference to write the names of all those who had businesses or jobs that they could give to the poor and needy and attend to their wants. He then prophesied in the name of Israel's God that we would have rains and also blessed us with good crops and abundant harvest. Those of the saints who were well off promised they would comply with the request of Elder Hyde. It was a clear, beautiful morning. No clouds whatever could be seen. Just as the brethren were handed their names to the clerk, you could see in the sky a black spot the size of your hand. It began to increase until it became very black. It then began to sprinkle. A good many were scared of the rain and going out Brother Hyde wished them to remain until the meeting was dismissed. The rain began to come down heavily before the meeting (forenoon) was dismissed. From that time we had regular rains. The Lord showed the manifestation and power of God to his saints. We did all rejoice and gave praises to our Heavenly Father for his mercies and goodness towards the gentiles who were at the meeting. They were surprised at the Elders prediction. Reality came to pass within an hour. They called Brother Orson Hyde the rain prophet. The grass then began to grow rapidly. The saints and gentiles then began to move out with their teams on the plains. The place we lived in—it was called Carterville. The Branch was presided [over] by James C. Snow, [who had ordained his father a teacher August 15, 1850]. My mother gave birth to a son, ORSON HYDE CONDIE. . . . Brother Ezra T. Benson . . . went all around the different branches . . . He wanted all those who had no wagons to go to the woods and chop down timber and make their own wagons. He promised there would be a way opened. . . . My father and I . . . chopped down different kinds of timber. We then hauled it home and seasoned it . . . . My father then did all the wood work except getting the jobs. They had to be in a turning lay. He then completed the wagon gears. Now he wanted some blacksmithing done—bolts made—tire iron for the wheels, etc. . . . Next was how we were to get the oxen. "

No one was buying land or houses. Everyone was going west. They had a letter from their son-in-law JOSEPH SHARP, who was then in Salt Lake City, promising Brother Babbit if he would loan them $100.00, he would repay him plus interest when they arrived in Salt Lake City. With this money they were able to purchase all they needed for the journey. They were in Captain Howell's Company of 100 wagons. Brother McCulloch was the captain of their ten, which included Brother Limeon Curtis, Joseph Hunter, and Brother Banks.

"We then bought a yoke of oxen (Buck and Bill) . . . We put in the middle a yoke of cows, Dick and Lion. They were the leaders . . . . We crossed the Missouri River. There was a flat boat to carry the wagons and the folks across. The cattle had to swim to the other side about a mile wide. We left my sister, HELEN, to come in another company. . . . He bought machinery to make sugar from beets. He made a present to the church, brought it to Salt Lake City."

They arrived in the Great Salt Lake valley on 2 Sep 1852, the day before the first company of the perpetual emigrating company led by Captain A. Smoot came in. His sister JANET CONDIE SHARP had "a very fine boy," JOHN C. SHARP. They lived in the 10th ward. The masons were working building the wall around temple square—"part in rock and other adobies." They purchased a "lot in the lower part of the city," south in the 4th ward. Father THOMAS built a shanty with the wagon box next to it. Little 16-month-old ORSON HYDE CONDIE, took sick and died 13 Nov 1852. At first, GIBSON drove an ox team for the SHARP brothers, hauling rock from Red Butte Canyon for the Church. He was paid $1.50 a day by the tithing office. The 14 Feb 1853, he attended the ground breaking for the Salt Lake Temple. On 6 Apr 1853 the corner stones were laid.

"It was a beautiful day. It seemed to me that the angels in heaven did rejoice that a house was to be built to perform work for the dead. . . . I will never forget the speeches and the prayers that were made by the brethren and the beautiful singing. . . . My father and I did some ditching for President Heber C. Kimball and President Willard Richards. They had a large pasture west of the city adjoining the Jordan River. We worked by the rod; we made good wages. Sometimes when we were spading we would come against bones, skulls, human beings, also pieces of crockery. It was supposed the Nephites occupied this region of country. Flour was scarce. Brother Kimball offered us the money for our work. Father told him he had a large family to feed. He wanted flour. Brother Kimball had a grist mill and we had what we wanted as long as we worked at the ditch. . . . In 1854 President Willard Richards died March 11th. I attended his funeral. . . . He was editor of the Deseret News. In April 7th Jedidiah M. Grant was chosen to fill his place as second counselor to President Brigham Young."

On 22 Jun 1854 my second-great-grandmother HELEN SHARP CONDIE gave birth to a pair of twins. CECELIA came first, then JOSEPH. In July the grasshoppers came and destroyed most of their crops:

"the loss and suffering was aggravated by drought. . . . For months we had to suffer but after all I never heard of any who died of starvation. The grasshoppers left. The farmers commenced again to till the ground. They were blessed with a bounteous harvest. . . . Ever since passing through the trial of scarcity of bread stuff I do not like to see bread get wasted."

In September the first Handcart Company arrived with much celebration, but at the October conference word came that those still coming needed help.

"President Young went out but he took sick. There were a good many brethren with their teams. They went back as far as 100 miles. . . . They were in a deplorable condition, the cattle died. . . . Death stared before them. . . . The brethren wept when they heard of their suffering. They would bury as many as eleven in one day. My Bishop called on me to drive an ox team, three yoke, and haul a load of hay to meet the companies for their horses and animals. The feed was all covered with snow. I then got everything ready to start. I traveled as far as the foot of the Big Mountain, could not go any further on account of the snow being so deep. A young man named Bill Jide traveled with me from the City. Assisted me and also company for me. I went with the few brethren with our shovels to clear the roads. There were drifts of snow piled up when we reached the top of Big Mountain. The snow was deep as sixteen feet of snow on the road. We all went to work and cleared the snow for the teams to pass as there was a large company on the other side of Big Mountain. We were just in time. . . . We all then descended down from the Big Mountain to camp. It was dreadful cold and stormy. We had to have a large fire burning at night to keep from freezing to death. My feet were frozen. I could hardly walk. We travelled and then crossed the little mountain and on to the city . . . . I suffered considerable with my feet. I could not go home for days. In November the last companies arrived in Salt Lake City. On Sunday the streets were well crowded to see the emigrants had places to go and were well cared for. It was a sad time for the poor saints to suffer as they did. Edward Martin Handcart Company suffered the most, it being the last company. Some had their legs frozen.

"December 1st President Jedidiah M. Grant died. . . . He was a great noble man for the truth. . . . I attended the funeral. . . . President Heber C. Kimball related . . . . I laid my hands upon him and blessed him and in minutes he raised himself up, and talked about an hour as busily as he could telling me what he had seen and what he understood . . . he said to me: 'Brother Kimball, I have been into the spirit world, two nights in succession and of all the dread that ever came across me, the worst was to have to again return to my body, though I had to do it, but O says he, the order and government that were there when I was in the spirit world.'"

He told him of the perfect order and harmony he saw—it was just as Brother Brigham says; there were no wicked among them. He spoke to his wife Caroline who had in her arms their daughter Margaret, who had been eaten by the wolves, but she was all right.

"To my astonishment he said when I looked at families, there was a deficiency in some. There was a lack, for I saw families that would not be permitted to come and dwell together, because they had not honored their callings here. He asked his wife where Joseph and Hyrum and Father Smith and others were; she replied, they had gone ahead, to perform and transact business for us. . . . He said that after he came back he could look upon his family and see the spirit that was in them and the darkness that was in them; and that he conversed with them about the gospel and what they should do and they replied, 'Well, Brother Grant, Perhaps it is so and perhaps it is not'; and he said that is the state of the people to a great extent, for many are full of darkness and will not believe. This imperfect account of the wonderful vision of those two nights was listened to with rapt attention by the large audience and was repeated for years after by many who heard it. A profound sensation was produced by its narration for it unfolded to many minds details of the glory of the spirit world. . . . He was forty years of age when he died but had spent those years to such advantage in labouring for the welfare of his fellowmen that he was mourned by thousands and left in their memories a name that will be forever.

"Throughout the Territory the Presidency of the Church called out missionaries to preach repentance to the saints, to arouse them from their lethargy and turn unto God with a sincere heart. . . . It was a general reformation throughout the church. If anyone stole they had to return and make restitution, the winter was excessively severe, snow falling to a depth of eight feet in places in the valleys in 1857."

Third-great-uncle GIBSON CONDIE proposed marriage to ELIZABETH ROBINSON, who had come in the Captain E. Martin Handcart Company. They were married 24 Feb 1857. Living first with his parents, he stated:

"I do not think any person on the earth was so poor as we were to be married as we were, but the Lord knew our hearts and the Lord blessed us."

The ROBINSON's had joined the *Mormon Church* in Bradford, Yorkshire, England in the spring of 1856. GEORGE ROBINSON made furniture and was a mechanic. They had left soon after their baptisms to join the saints in Salt Lake City. It was late in the season; but they obtained handcarts in Iowa. Shortly after, the youngest child, GEORGE ran away—a man "made great promises if he would live with him. He would give him a horse, money and he could be rich." His father, GEORGE, after finding him, tried to convince him to continue on with the family, but he was determined to stay. His father would not leave him. An equally determined daughter, ELIZABETH, would not stay, although good wages with a respectable family were promised. So her mother, MARGARET ANGUS ROBINSON, and sister, DOROTHY, joined her in the Martin Handcart Company, leaving their father and younger brother behind.

"They passed through severe trials and hardships, hundreds died of starvation and cold. . . . I do think the ones who passed through this trial will have a great reward. God will bless them. . . . Shortly after we were married her sister DOROTHY got married to SOLOMON ROSSITER."

[Note: His wife's mother, MARGARET ANGUS ROBINSON, who had crossed the plains in the Martin Handcart Company, suffered a number of years from this hardship she had gone through. She stayed with GIBSON and ELIZABETH CONDIE until she died in 1862. He does not mention whether her husband and son that were left in Iowa ever arrived in the valley. He described her as a good woman who fed the Elders in England and gave them shillings—also the poor beggars. "What good she has done on the earth cannot all be counted."]

"July 24 (1857) the saints celebrated the day in the head of Big Cottonwood—ten years since the pioneers entered the valley. I happened to be working in that canyon making roads to get granite for the temple. I took my wife with me in ox teams with others to the head of Cottonwood. We then had a rejoicing time. Hundreds of saints with the Presidency and Twelve. There were bowers built for the saints to enjoy different exercises, also dancing, brass band, all enjoyed themselves. There were fine lakes with fine trout. Some enjoyed bathing, others fishing. They had swings for the young folks. There were speeches made by the Presidency and Twelve. While we were enjoying ourselves some of the brethren arrived from the state bringing news that they were deprived of bringing the mail and that General Kearney (sic) with two thousand infantry and a proportionate number of artillery and cavalry ordered for Utah and were on the road to fight the Mormons. President Young told the saints not to be alarmed about the troops. The saints had been persecuted and driven to these mountains and we do not calculate to leave here. We are here in the chambers of the mountains and if we keep the commandments of God our enemies would never drive us more.

"September 15 the territory declared under martial law by Governor Brigham Young. . . . In the fall our regiment was called out. We went to Echo. We were under Col. Harmon. All the regiments stationed at Echo and other points to intercept the soldiers and prevent their access to the valley. I stayed out a few months when we were called to go home. The counsel of the servants of the Lord was not to fire first, promised us if we would obey orders from our leaders we would not be hurt.

"Sometime in November the United States Army General Johnston reached Fort Bridger and took possession of the supply fort of Mormons on Green River. . . . In the spring we were all called out. Reports came out that United States troops were on the road to Salt Lake. Our camp was a great many miles up Echo Canyon. Ours was infantry. We were not many miles from our enemies. Reports would come in continually. Our enemies were on the road expecting at any moment to conflict with our enemies at camp. Night and morning we would have orders. Our prayers were offered to our Father in Heaven to preserve us from our enemies. February 24th Col. Thomas L. Kane arrived in Salt Lake City by way of California, had interview with President Young and Governor Cummings. March 21st the citizens of Great Salt Lake City and the settlements north of it agree to abandon their homes and go south. Some were supposed to be going to Sonora in Mexico. April 10 Governor Cummings and Col. T. L. Kane with a servant, each having left the army to proceed to Salt Lake City arrive with an escort of mormons whom they accidentally met on the way.

"When Gov. Cummings arrived in Salt Lake City the Mormons were very kind and was treated everywhere with respectful attention. The Gov. and Col. Kane visit the Utah Library. J. W. CUMMINGS showed them the records and seal of the United States District Court said to have been burnt up, which was one of why the army was ordered to Utah. In May citizens of Utah residing north of Utah County leave their houses and travel south, a few remain in each settlement. They were instructed to burn homes and everything else in the event that the approaching troop should prove hostile. . . . We were called home, had to shoulder our gun and pack our bedding, very tired traveling across the mountains. My wife and my father's folks had all gone south. There was not a mormon or child left in the city; a forsaken place. Traveled all the way to Spanish Fork.

"My wife and other families occupied one of the school houses. After resting a few days I made a dug-out for us to live in. June 26 Col. Johnston and army passed through Salt Lake and camped outside of Jordan River. Later the army proceeded to Cedar Valley and located at Camp Floyd."

My grandfather GIBSON A CONDIE wrote:

"When the Johnston Army came to Utah and established Camp Floyd, west of the city, though a boy in his teens, my father, THOMAS CONDIE, [son of THOMAS] earned big wages helping make adobes to erect barracks for the soldiers. He made $5.00 a day. In 1862, when settlements were being made along the Weber river, he located on Lost Creek (Croydon) in Morgan County, Utah. He was searching for lost cattle when he discovered the area. He built the first log house there and used to walk to Henefer to attend meetings and dances. Several times he walked to Salt Lake City. One incident I will relate. Having finished the log house to shelter him and his effects, he went to Salt Lake City for a visit. Returning in company with others to Henefer, he was surprised as he came to his house. It had been broken into and the provisions he had stored for the winter were gone. He had a part of a loaf of bread. Very early the next morning he started out on foot back to the city following the old emigrant trail over the mountains. It began snowing and by the time he reached the Big Mount Ridge the snow was knee deep. Tracks of bear and other wild beasts were numerous. A few occasional bites of the crust of bread was all the food he had on this arduous journey.

"In early spring, 1863, he returned and established his bachelor home. It seems he brought with him a choice yoke of oxen, Dick and Lion. He often spoke of them as a fine team. In that year, fifteen or twenty families were settling on Lost Creek and among them was the family of EPHRAIM SWANN. The shy young man watched [daughter] HANNAH SWANN milk the cows and ventured near enough to ask her if she was engaged. They went by ox team to Salt Lake City and were married in the Endowment House, July 15, 1864. My mother [HANNAH] was born 19th of December, 1847, at Knighton Tem, Worchestershire, England. She came to Utah in 1857 with her parents [the same time that Johnston's Army journeyed across the plains, *Part I: DRIVEN*] and first lived in Salt Lake City, then to Beaver, Milton and Croydon. Here she met and married [young] THOMAS CONDIE.

"In the early years of pioneering the area, they had little meat, but were healthy on coarse grains, pig weeds, nettles, sego lily bulbs and many other greens. That they were blessed is evident by the record that of the 20 families . . . there were no deaths for the first 8 years."

THOMAS' father and mother lived with them the winter of 1864/1865. The snow came early and deep. Feed was short and many of their cattle starved.

"In the spring of 1865, Grandpa was determined to return to his home in Salt Lake City. Father, Uncle GIBSON and Uncle GEORGE joined in the task of moving their parents. The wagons were loaded and the journey commenced down Echo, Coalville, Silver Creek and Parley's Park. The melting snow had raised the water of the streams to overflowing their banks. No bridges then. When our folks arrived at the crossing of the Weber River, it looked rather hazardous. . . . Uncle GIBSON had a yoke of young oxen and they thought they would be fine leaders. This proved disappointing . . . As soon as the lead teams got into water above their knees, they refused to face the current and turned to the right going down stream. . . . Before the leader could gain footing on the bank the swift current carried the wagons and rear team so fast that it swung the outfit around. . . . This caused the wagon rack to break. The oxen took the front wheels back to the starting point, the hind wheels were left in deep water. The wagon box, and the cook stove and boxes of articles . . . tipped off and floated down the river. It was near a miracle that Grandpa was not thrown out also. As the wagon's box was floating near some overhanging brush, he grabbed some limbs and got safely away from the dangerous stream.

"Father could swim . . . so he stuck with the wagon box until a place where the river took a westward turn and he could wade and draw the box to the edge of the water on the bank. He walked a mile or so upstream to the ford and joined the others. . . . The top of one hind wheel of the wagon could be seen way out in deep water. Father stripped off most of his clothes, took his team, Dick and Lion, got on the back of one of them with a chain in one hand. Some places the oxen swam, some places their feet touched bottom. As they passed near the wheel he hooked the chain to the rim and soon had the wheels on the bank. The wagon was put together. The team was driven down the river to recover the wagon box. Most of the day was thus occupied. When ready for another start, Dick and Lion were put on lead and Father rode on Dick's back and led the outfit across. No wonder he thought so much of these oxen."

On March 13, 1854 young sister MARGARET CONDIE married JOSEPH SHARP—as a second polygamous wife. Her sister, first wife, JANET CONDIE SHARP died 19 Jan 1859 after childbirth; inflammation set in—the baby girl survived (named JANET.) (Brother) GIBSON CONDIE wrote:

"It was a sad affair to lose my eldest sister JANET. She was beloved by all. She was kind and affectionate and a good mother and a true Latter-day Saint. We miss her greatly.

"March 27 [1859] Governor Cummings issued a proclamation against the troops in Provo. [There were] reports of a conspiracy on the part of the United States officials to secure the arrest of Brigham Young. July 7, 1861 my wife gave birth to a male child. The child was very sick and we did not think he would live—sent for some Elders to come to the house to give a blessing. Brother WILLIAM FASSETT was mouthpiece. Gave the name THOMAS. He began to mend from that time."

[Note: The child's full name was THOMAS ROBINSON CONDIE. The family would later move to Croyden, Morgan, Utah. This THOMAS married first CATHERINE JONES. They had one child, ALMA, who would later live in Preston, Idaho. CATHERINE died after the birth of her son, and her husband married her sister NELLIE JONES. They had five children. Two of them, IVAN and LUCRETIA, grew up in Preston, but would come to Pioche, Nevada, where IVAN married ROSE MARIE AUSTIN—the parents of BRUCE CONDIE, ROSE MARIE CONDIE (Delmue), and five more children. His sister,

LUCRETIA is the mother of WILLIAM and FRANK LLOYD, who married two of our early capable and beautiful teenage clerks, who worked for us in the Pioche Pharmacy—MARY PECTOL and ANN HARTLEY. Today, WILLIAM (BILL) LLOYD, one of my third cousins, recently retired as one of our county commissioners.}

"October 3 John W. Dawson was appointed Governor . . . October 18 first telegram crosses the overland wire from Utah sent to President ABRAHAM LINCOLN by Brigham Young. October 24 the first telegram was sent to San Francisco.

"In autumn a large number of saints were sent to southern Utah. My brother-in-law GEORGE THACKERAY went to Lost Creek. . . . In July 16, 1864 my brother THOMAS married . . . HANNAH SWANN. JOSEPH SHARP, my brother-in law died on the plains bringing a train of goods for Utah. Brought his body to Salt Lake City and interred [in] cemetery.

"My sister, MARGARET CONDIE SHARP, raised all the children . . . . She passed through great trials and afflictions. While she was sick one day Sister Eliza Snow and Sister Smoot took a walk together. When they came to my sister's house in the 20th ward she felt impressed to call in. My mother was in the house at the time attending to MARGARET . . . . Sister Snow had never been in the house before and did not know that MARGARET was sick. She laid her hands upon MARGARET's head and blessed her that she would live and the angels of God would preserve her. The enemies would not have any power over her and she would conquer her enemies. She began to mend from that time and prospered."

— 30 —

THE BEAR RIVER MASSACRE, NORTHERN UTAH, SOUTHEASTERN IDAHO

While severe Indian problems were being experienced by those sent south by Brigham Young into the center of the Ute and Piute Indian tribes' favorite hunting and fishing areas of the Utah Territory [Utah, Sanpete, Juab, and Millard Counties] The Salt Lake Valley and north to Ogden had fewer Indian problems. Further north, along the Oregon Trail were the Shoshone, Blackfoot, and Bannock tribes. Chief Walker of central Utah was at war with these tribes, and became angry when the church members would not support him in his leadership against them.

In 1855 a group of Mormons were sent north to settle *Fort Limhi* by the Salmon River in Idaho. The Bannocks consented at first—on the condition that they did not sell their produce to the emigrants or outside of their area. Some of the ALLREDs were with this group. Things went quite well for a year or so, until one of the settlers took a cart filled with salmon to sell in Great Salt Lake City. The angry Bannocks retaliated, and the settlers quickly returned to Utah.

On 14 Apr 1860, a group of L.D.S. colonists founded Franklin, Idaho, near the Utah/Idaho border–believing they were still in Utah. This was Idaho's first town. They built a common corral and arranged their wagon boxes for protection while a fort was constructed. The pioneers dug their ditches and on 26 May planted their first gardens and fields. A sawmill, gristmill, and store soon followed, marking the birth of agriculture in southeastern Idaho.

On 15 Sep 1863, General Charles C. Rich with thirty to fifty colonizers crossed the smaller mountains east from Franklin and chose a site eight miles north of Bear Lake to establish their new town of Paris, Idaho. Having personally lived several years in both of these valleys in our early married life, GROVER and I know about the deep snow and severe cold of their winters. The Bear Lake Valley was much worse with winter temperatures reaching forty degrees below zero while we were there. Mosquitos were rampant during the summer evenings.

The early pioneers reported that the grasshoppers routinely destroyed their crops in the Bear Lake Valley, where other small towns had sprung up— Montpelier, Ovid, Bennington, Bloomington, St. Charles, and Fish Haven. During those difficult years, flour was hauled from Logan or Brigham City, which were settled earlier. During the winter months, mail had to be carried twenty-five miles over the mountains from Franklin on snowshoes. It is said that Charles C. Rich sometimes performed the task. Many early converts from the Scandinavian countries came. When Brigham Young visited their towns in 1864, he encouraged them to build substantial houses and the small log cabins quickly disappeared.

Non-Mormons were rare in these settlements until the 1880s, when the railroad came through Montpelier bringing industry and people more diverse in their religions and moral standards, but the L.D.S. were still greatly predomi-nant when we were there in the 1950s. We really enjoyed and loved the people of Montpelier. The main highway to the south was then through the magnificent Logan Canyon, where the heavy snowplows blew the snow into high ridges that would tumble down the steep dugways onto the tall spruce and pines below— wherever sufficient land remained for their roots to cling onto in those massive rugged rocks. The view from the summit above the pristine blue Bear Lake is breathtaking.

At first, in the 1850s, Idaho was part of the Oregon Territory. Acceptable to the politicians in Washington D.C. in 1859, Oregon became a state and the re-maining territory was called the Washington Territory. The state of Washington came thirty years later in 1889, with Idaho following closely behind in 1890. The much more populous Utah still remained a territory.

There are many emigrant/Indian tales of depredations and horror in Idaho during the 1850s. It was said that the Bear River Massacre really began dur-ing the summer of 1851. A train of emigrants going to California under Dr. Patterson, were trying to locate a suitable campsite, and chose one that was oc-cupied by Indians. They refused to leave when the doctor arrogantly ordered them off. Patterson discharged his shotgun into the air and then, with some of his men, chased the Indians off on horseback. The next day the Indians retaliated and shot three of the company—one died from his wounds.

The following incidents were recorded that year: the Shoshones and Bannocks stole eight horses and four head of cattle from travelers near Bear River; the Shoshones stole 74 oxen from three wagon trains at old Fort Hall; eight oxen were lost to the Indians near American Falls, and four horses were stolen near Shoshone Falls (located in the deep water-carved channel of the Snake River, by present day Twin Falls city;) a wagon train was attacked at Black Rock Creek—four people were killed, a woman wounded and abused, and 22 horses taken; the Shoshones stole 26 horses from travelers north of Fort Hall; the Bannocks took 3 valuable horses from a doctor, and four men were killed and 13 horses taken. "They feared for their lives."

A picture of Shoshone Falls on the Snake River near Twin Falls, Idaho. Taken in June 2011 when the water supply was sufficient to allow a full flow over the falls.

The United States government felt responsible for the U.S. mail delivery and the large number of emigrants that were moving into the coastal states and along the Oregon Trail. Agent Elias Wampole reported that he ascribed most of the Indian unrest to white traders who plied the natives with whiskey and sold the Indians guns and ammunition. This was verified by Agent J. H. Holeman of the Utah Territory, who claimed that the road from Salt Lake City to California was lined with traders who usually had nothing to barter but whiskey—their unkindness to the Indians was slowly making the natives hostile to all whites. Some of these renegade whites even offered to buy any cattle or horses that the Indians could steal from the emigrants. Holeman complained that when he warned these men that the laws would be enforced against them,

> "They laughed at me . . . they told me . . . 'they could and would do as they pleased, law or no law.'"

In August of 1854, a party of Digger Indians attacked an emigrant party under Mr. Ward--only two of the 21 escaped the slaughter. It was said that many were women and children, whom they had tortured to death in a most brutal manner. The Indians also took 41 head of cattle and about $3,000 in cash. It was believed that these Indians were a band of thirty "Winnestah" Snakes (Shoshones) residing east of Fort Boise. Three other whites were shortly killed in Camas Prairie, and the Shoshones informed the Indian Agent that they were determined to rob and kill all who trespassed through their country. A military force was sent to catch the renegade Indians, but was not very successful. Confronted, they blamed it all on the Blackfoots, Crows, or Diggers.

Early statistics number the Shoshones at 3,000 and divide them into three groups: the Green River Snakes, 1,500; Fort Hall Snakes, 1,200 (200 were Bannock); and the Sheepeaters, 300. The "Wineptas" of the Boise River area numbered about 400 and were looked down upon by the Shoshones and Bannocks as inferior. [From *Bannocks of Idaho* by Brigham D. Madsen]

It was August, 1859. A Bannock-Shoshone band attacked a wagon train in a canyon of the Goose Creek Mountains, about 15 miles from Raft River. Seven white men were killed and a number wounded. The Indians tried to sell their plunder to the early L.D.S. settlers. A company of U.S. dragoons from Camp Floyd, set up a headquarters at the Bear River Crossing, [near Tremonton, Utah] and patrols were sent out to try to catch the guilty Indians--Major Isaac Lynde was in charge. Lieutenant E. Gay was sent to investigate and, arriving in Box Elder Valley, he was told by the settlers that a band of from 150 to 200 Bannocks and Shoshones was camped in Devil's Gate Canyon [Wyoming]. A surprise attack was made there by 42 soldiers. Six soldiers were wounded and 20 Indians killed. Twenty horses were taken by the Indians, which were not recovered, as they quickly climbed the steep mountainside—the troops were unprepared.

At this same time 200 Bannocks arrived in Cache Valley (Logan) to join a group of 300 Shoshones. Another detachment of dragoons was sent up from Camp Floyd, as 300 wagon trains passed the Bear River Crossing area every day. One day Chief Pocatello visited the camp and was captured by Lieutenant Gay, who finally let him go, claiming he hadn't any proof of his guilt.

There were more attacks and four white men were killed near Fort Hall. Eight of a train of 19 men, women, and children were attacked and killed 25 miles west of the fort on the Snake River. A place we called "Massacre Rock." The survivors traveled three days to get help.

In mid-June, 1861, a large band of more than 1,000 Indians from Oregon entered Cache Valley threatening to kill all the white settlers. They camped on the future Brigham Young College lands in Logan, in an excellent position to guard against surprise attacks. For over two weeks the Cache Valley militia stood guard. The Indians left, claiming many of the Cache Valley horses. The Indians later stated that this location was a very spiritual and sacred place. The L.D.S. people appear to have agreed for they built their Logan Temple in that area.

With the news of the fall of Fort Sumter in 1861, the United States War Department became concerned about their Overland Mail Route and the new telegraph line. Camp Floyd was vacated and Johnston with most of his troops joined with the Southern army. On 24 Jul 1861, the Secretary of War asked Governor Downey of California for one regiment of infantry and five companies of cavalry, to serve for three years, to guard the route from the Carson Valley to Salt Lake and Laramie. Pat E. Connor of Stockton, California, disliked by his military groups for his Union beliefs, enlisted in the Union army in August 1861. Major Fred B. Rogers wrote,

"Captain Connor was a mark of especial detestation by some of those men

[Southerners]. His life was a hundred times threatened, and he walked those streets day and night for two or three years when he was not certain that he could live a minute. But he was always resolute for the government and the Union, and courted rather than avoided danger."

Mustered in at Camp McDougall as colonel of the Third California Infantry, he was presented with a fine horse, saddle, and bridle, value—$600.

In March 1862 the Shoshones allegedly raided stations of the Overland Mail between Fort Bridger and Platts Bridge, drove off the stock, and rifled the mails. The 11ᵗʰ Ohio Volunteer Cavalry began to guard that part of the trail. In Utah, Brigham Young wanted the Utah Militia, under Daniel H. Wells, to protect the mail line from Great Salt Lake City to Independence Rock, which was eventually approved. Colonel Connor, designated for duty on the Overland Mail Route, greatly loved his country. His first hatred was for the rebels of the South, close behind were the detested Indians, with the Mormons ranking a close third. His men in general were not happy with their assignment. They felt the war in Virginia could use some strong Union westerners.

The "Utah Column," which became known as the "California Volunteers" with Colonel Connor, of Stockton, at their head, received their orders on 5 Jul 1862 to start their march for Salt Lake City. A soldier from Company G, Third Infantry, made daily entries of their long hot trip across the Sierra Nevada Mountains, crossing the desolate Great Basin and the Salt Flats of Utah to the Great Salt Lake. The *Deseret News* of Salt Lake City described an Indian attack which ended near Box Elder:

> "They were five days without food, and fortunately met a large company of emigrants some six miles beyond Bear River, bound for Humboldt, from whom they obtained relief. . . . The Indians, in addition to their horses, blankets, etc., got a considerable quantity of ammunition and most of the arms with which the company was well supplied. How many of the Indians were killed and wounded was not known, but many were seen to fall. This is reported to have been the fifth or sixth company of emigrants, some of them large and having a great amount of stock, which has been attacked and used up in that vicinity within the last six or eight weeks by the same band, as supposed."

It was during their camp at Ruby Valley (Nevada) that Connor received a report that 23 emigrants had been killed by Indians in various attacks near

Gravelly Ford on the Humboldt River. Connor issued the order to Major Edward McGarry on 29 September to proceed after the guilty Indians. Their instructions included in part:

> "On the route thence you will examine every valley or place where you have reason to believe guerrillas or hostile Indians are congregated, whom you will capture; but if they resist you will destroy them. In no instance will you molest women or children. If on the route to Humboldt friendly Indians deliver to you Indians who were concerned in the late murder of emigrants, you will (being satisfied of their guilt) immediately hang them, and leave their bodies thus exposed as an example of what evil-doers may expect while I command this district . . . You will destroy every male Indian whom you may encounter in the vicinity of the late massacres. This course may seem harsh and severe, but I desire that the order may be rigidly enforced, as I am satisfied that in the end it will prove the most merciful."

Major McGarry's troops killed a total of 24 Indians under these orders and were gone throughout most of October. They had a problem, however—hanging the Indians in the non-existent trees of the desolate territory. The *Monitor*, a Catholic newspaper, stated:

> "The two corroborating circumstances of their capture near the scene of the murder and many similar murders amounted to reasonable probability, that this party were the guilty ones. So the twenty four were shot."

The newspaper further spun the story suggesting they were probably Mormons, disguised as Indians, and stated,

> "We fear very much that the country will have reason to mourn over the unchristian butchery of Major McGarry."

The correspondent for the *San Francisco Bulletin*, traveling with the troops, reported that Colonel Connor, before crossing the Jordan River into Great Salt Lake City, issued

> "forty rounds of ammunition . . . to each man, and that the four 6-pounders are abundantly furnished with destructive missiles, and the two 12-pound mountain howitzers [were] amply supplied with shells. . . . Colonel Conner sent word to the chief of the Danites (meaning Brigham Young) that he would 'cross the River Jordan if hell yawned below him;' and the battle fields of Mexico testify that the Colonel has a habit of keeping his word."

After breakfast and a speedy march of 15 miles, the California Volunteers crossed the Jordan at two P.M. on Sunday, 20 Oct 1862. Disappointed that no one was on the eastern shore to fight them, the correspondent observed,

> "It was a magnificent place for a fight, too, with a good-sized bluff upon the western side from which splendid execution could have been done."
> San Francisco readers were told,
>
> "You may imagine our surprise—-strive to imagine the astonishment of the people . . . as the column marched slowly and steadily into the street which receives the overland stage, up it between the fine trees, the side-walks filled with many women and countless children, the comfortable residences, to Emigration Square, the Theatre and other notable landmarks were passed, when, about the center of the city, I should think, it filed right through a principal thoroughfare to Governor Harding's mansion—-on which . . . . waved the same blessed stars and stripes that were woven in the loom of '76. Every crossing was occupied by spectators, and windows, doors and roofs had their gazers. Not a cheer, not a jeer greeted us. . . . Standing in his buggy, Governor Harding made a long welcoming speech. . . . Toward the end of his speech, the governor issued this precautionary warning: 'I believe the people you have now come amongst will not disturb you if you do not disturb them in their public rights and in the honor and peace of their homes; and to disturb them you must violate the strict discipline of the United States army, which you must observe and which you have no right to violate.'"

At the conclusion of his speech Connor called for three cheers for country, flag and the governor. The march through the city resumed with the bands playing. They continued east for two and one-half miles to the slope between Emigration and Red Butte Canyons, where they built their camp. Connor called it Fort Douglas, remembering his good friend Stephen L. Douglas of Illinois.

In the past 1860 presidential election, Douglas was the only candidate of the three-way split Democratic Party that got votes from the Northern states. He campaigned vigorously—something Lincoln and the two Southern candidates refused to do. It was generally believed that it was not dignified to campaign for president. LINCOLN won with 1,866,452 votes; Douglas received 1,376,157; Beckinridge got 849,741, and Bell received 588,879 votes.

Third-great-uncle GIBSON CONDIE was among the many who watched Colonel Connor arrive in Salt Lake City. He wrote:

"October 24 Colonel P. E. Conner with a body of soldiers (Volunteers) from California passed through Salt Lake City and located near the mouth of Red Butte Canyon . . . named Camp Douglas. The saints were surprised—they were not aware they would camp near Salt Lake City and did not approve their choice. Seem to bring us trouble all the time because we are Mormons. December 10 Governor Harding delivers his annual message, extra copies of which the legislature will note, viewing it as insulting."

In 1862 Virginia, the Army of the Potomac's performance, under General McClellan, was proving his ineptness, or unwillingness to aggressively lead them against the Southern army at Fredricksburg and the vicinity. In Tennessee, Ulysses S. Grant had managed a victory at Shiloh, after Southern General Albert Sydney Johnston, formerly of Utah's Camp Floyd, had died from his wound. Grant was moving south, planning and preparing for his attack on the Southern fortress of Vicksburg. The North needed control of the Mississippi. Connor wished he could go east.

The following is taken from the first Idaho Day, Franklin County *Official Program of 14-15 Jun 1910.*

"During the fall and early winter of 1862 large bands of Indians under Chiefs Hunter, Sagwitch and Pocatello had collected at the site that would be known as *Battle Creek,* twelve miles northwest of Franklin on the west bank of the Bear River. The settlers had adhered to the policy requested by Brigham Young, 'It is cheaper to feed the Indians than to fight them.' This 'tax' hit heavier on the Saints in the outlaying settlements, and it didn't guarantee that the Indians would not strike with treachery. 'No Mediterranean pirate ever levied tribute with more impunity and persistency than did these Indians. Their begging, exacting and stealing had gone on until a large supply of provisions had been collected which [formed] a base of supplies for an organized system of raids to be made upon the settlers later on in the spring.'"

Soon after Christmas, 1862, David Savage and William Bevins, with a small party of men, came from Leesburg, a mining camp on the Salmon river, to Cache Valley—staying on the west side of Bear River. After a heavy snow storm, they found themselves west of Richmond, Utah. They made a boat of boxes, and crossed the river. While the last boatload were still in the river some of the Indians from the Battle Creek camp, who had followed them, began shooting at them. One man of the party was killed and several others were wounded. The survivors hid in the brush and during the night arrived at Richmond, six miles south of Franklin. In the morning Bishop Marriner W. Merrill (later Apostle Merrill), sent men to recover the dead man and horses. Attacked by a large band of Indians, they still returned with the body and some horses.

Bishop Merrill sent the message with Savage and Bevins to Salt Lake City which brought Colonel Connor with 200 soldiers from Fort Douglas. The previous day, Bear Hunter and a party of his warriors had come to Franklin, received twelve (two bushel) sacks of flour and demanded more. The people hesitated, because flour was scarce. The Indians surrounded Bishop Preston Thomas' house, held a war dance, flourished their tomahawks and threatened the people. The next morning Bear Hunter came again to Franklin for wheat. As they collected three large sacks, the soldiers came in sight over a small ridge about one mile south of town. The old warrior did not seem worried. Someone said to him: "Here come the soldiers, you may get killed."

He coolly and carelessly remarked, "May-be-so soldiers get killed too," and he started for camp with his burden of wheat.

It became evident later, that the old fellow was worried—as one sack of wheat was picked up a mile out of town, and the rest near the future site of Preston.

Colonel Connor chose a 220 man detachment from Companies A, H, K, and M. They left Fort Douglas on 24 January and marched north in frozen snow for 68 miles, spending the first night in Brigham City. He records:

> "The second night's march . . . I overtook the infantry and artillery at the town of Mendon and ordered them to march again that night. I resumed my march with the cavalry and overtook the infantry at Franklin, Utah Ter., about twelve miles from the Indian encampment. I ordered Captain Hoyt, with the infantry, howitzers, and train, to move at 1 o'clock the next morning, intending to start with the cavalry about two hours thereafter, in order to reach the Indian encampment at the same time and surround it before daylight, but [because of] the difficulty in procuring a guide . . . Captain Hoyt did not move until after 3 a.m.
>
> "I moved the cavalry in about one hour afterward, passing the infantry, artillery, and wagons about four miles from the Indian encampment. As daylight was approaching I was apprehensive that the Indians would

discover the strength of my force and make their escape. I therefore made a rapid march with the cavalry and reached the bank of the river shortly after daylight in full view of the Indian encampment, and about one mile distant.

"I immediately ordered Major McGarry to advance with the cavalry and surround before attacking them, while I remained . . . to give orders to the infantry and artillery. On my arrival on the field I found that Major McGarry had dismounted the cavalry and was engaged with the Indians who had sallied out of their hiding places on foot and horseback, and with fiendish malignity waved the scalps of white women and challenged the troops to battle, at the same time attacking them. Finding it impossible to surround them . . . he accepted their challenge.

"The position of the Indians was one of strong natural defenses, and almost inaccessible to the troops, being in a deep, dry ravine from six to twelve feet deep and from thirty to forty feet across level table-land, along which they had constructed steps from which they could deliver their fire without being themselves exposed. Under the embankments they had constructed artificial covers of willows thickly woven together, from behind which they could fire without being observed. After being engaged about twenty minutes I found it was impossible to dislodge them without great sacrifice of life. I accordingly ordered Major McGarry with twenty men to turn their left flank, which was in the ravine where it entered the mountains. Shortly afterward Captain Hoyt reached the ford three-quarters of a mile distant, but found it impossible to cross footmen. Some of them tried it, however, rushing into the river, but, finding it deep and rapid, retired. I . . . ordered a detachment of cavalry with lead horses to cross the infantry, which was done accordingly, and upon their arrival upon the field I ordered them to the support of Major McGarry's flanking party, who shortly afterward succeeds in turning the enemy's flank. Up to this time, in consequence of being exposed . . . while the Indians were under cover, they had every advantage of us, fighting with the ferocity of demons. My men fell fast and thick around me, but after flanking them we had the advantage and made good use of it.

"I ordered the flanking party to advance down the ravine on either side, which gave us the advantage of an enfilading fire and caused some of the Indians to give way and run toward the north of the ravine. At this point I had a company stationed, who shot them as they ran out. But few tried to escape, however, but continued fighting with unyielding obstinacy, frequently engaging hand to hand with the troops until killed in their hiding places.

"The most of those who did escape from the ravine were afterward shot in attempting to swim the river, or killed while desperately fighting under cover of the dense willow thicket which lined the river banks. . . . The fight commenced about 6 o'clock in the morning and continued until 10. At the commencement of the battle the hands of some of the men were so benumbed with cold that it was with difficulty they could load their pieces. Their suffering during the march was awful beyond description, but they steadily continued on without regard to hunger, cold, or thirst, not a murmur escaping them to indicate their sensibilities to pain or fatigue. Their uncomplaining endurance during their four nights' march from Camp Douglas to the battle-field is worthy of the highest praise. The weather was intensely cold, and not less than seventy-five had their feet frozen, and some of them I fear will be crippled for life. I should mention here that in my march from this post no assistance was rendered by the Mormons."

Many L.D.S. people objected. Perhaps, he meant in the actual fighting and killing of the Indians. In the *Franklin County Citizen*, 1 Feb 1917, William Nelson states:

"When the army came to Franklin on their way to the battle field many of the soldiers accepted the invitations of the people to go into their homes and cook their suppers. The people furnished wood for those who remained outside to build large camp fires. We also furnished hay for their animals and I did not hear of anyone charging the soldiers for such accommodations. Mr. Connor appeared to be a perfect gentleman and I can hardly believe that he was responsible for that statement."

From Colonel J. H. Martineau's Military History of Cache Valley:

"In January, 1863, Col. P.E. Connor . . . fought the battle of Bear River . . . . The river was full of running ice, but was gallantly forded, many . . . men getting wet, and afterwards having their feet and legs frozen . . . met a deadly fire from the Indian rifles; but without wavering pressed steadily on; and, after a bloody contest of some hours, in which the Indians fought with desperation, the survivors, about one hundred in number, fled. Pocatello, and Saguich, two noted chiefs, escaped, but Bear Hunter was killed while making bullets at a camp fire. When struck he fell forward into the fire and perished miserably. For years he had been as a thorn to the settlers, and his death caused regret in none.

"A simultaneous attack in front and on both flanks, finally routed the Indians, whose dead, as counted by an eye-witness from Franklin, amounted to three hundred and sixty eight, besides many wounded, who afterward died. About ninety of the slain were women and children. The troops found their camp well supplied for winter. They burnt the camp and captured a large number of horses . . . On their return the troops remained all night in Logan, the citizens furnishing them supper and breakfast, some parties, the writer among the number, entertaining ten or fifteen each . . . In crossing the mountains between Wellsville and Brigham City the troops experienced great hardships. They toiled and floundered all day through the deep snow, the keen, whirling blasts filling the trail fast as made, until, worn out, the troops returned to Wellsville. Next day Bishop W. H. Maughan gathered all the men and teams in the place and assisted the troops through the pass to Salt Lake Valley.

"This victory was of immense value to the settlers of Cache Valley and all the surrounding country. It broke the spirit and power of the Indians and enabled the settlers to occupy new and choice localities hitherto unsafe. Peter Maughan, the presiding bishop of the county, pronounced it an interposition of Providence in behalf of the settlers; the soldiers having done what otherwise the colonists would have had to accomplish with great pecuniary loss and sacrifice of lives, illy spared in the weak state of the settlements."

Unfortunately for the settlers in central Utah, Connor refused to help them; they were not part of the U. S. mail route.

The present-day Wellsville Canyon road between Logan and Brigham City was built in the mid-1930s, when I was a child. Prior to its construction, the narrow oiled highway crossed the mountains on a steep winding dugway through Sardine Canyon. It had many sharp high curves, and we honked the horn on the automobile when approaching these blind turns as a warning to any approaching vehicle. The highway was barely wide enough for two cars to pass. The scene was beautiful with the added excitement of the view of the cliffs below. This road became only a dangerous trail after the much wider and shorter Wellsville road was completed.

The Bear River begins its journey on the north side of the highest peaks in Utah—the Uinta Mountain Range. It flows north past the Bear Lake to Soda Springs, then changes to the southwest, past Preston and into the eastern fresh water bay of Great Salt Lake. When I was very young, on a trip to Logan from Carey, Idaho, my father, with business in Twin Falls, took the Snowville highway to Tremonton. To avoid Sardine Canyon, he chose to cross the Bear River.

South of our ranch home near Carey, Idaho. BROOKIE, IVIE, and MARION ASHER (front) with our father MARION A. CONDIE, about 1930.

The very old dilapidated bridge over the Bear River had a large *DANGER* sign, forbidding anything over 5000 pounds. Debating, he finally drove across. I scanned the horizon for the bears that should inhabit the green shores of the Bear River—relieved, yet disappointed, there weren't any.

Our usual trip to Logan from Carey was over the dusty, narrow dirt road between the lava beds of the Craters of the Moon and the Pioneer Mountains to Arco, where a better road turned southward. In 1962, I wrote the following about my early fears. I called it *Faith*.

> When I was young, the road wound round past Dead Man's Hill
> And past the dark long miles of lava beds that
> Lay in endless waste to the horizon.
> A marsh of quiet bulrushes stood sentinel to
> Seepy bogs of quicksand on the way.
> And yet a little further—Danger Curve that
> Made its "U" upon the crest,
> In trees beneath, the skeletons of fearless model T's.
> At night, each silent sagebrush on the road,
> Licked its wolfish jaws and waited
> The ubiquitous flat tire,
> When rattlesnakes and coyotes could descend upon
> Their helpless prey.
> How much do we proceed from fear to fear?
> Or burying our fear, refuse to go?
> Faith knows the way as straight and light, and
> Contemplating danger--prepares before,
> Then sees the beauty in the rock and marsh,
> And loves the lonely creatures of the road.

This old narrow dusty road around the foothills was changed in the middle of the nineteen thirties and replaced with an oiled road straight across the lava beds into Arco when U.S. Highway 93 became a reality. There was much rejoicing in Carey, Idaho.

Reading from third-great-uncle GIBSON CONDIE's journal, I found that in Jul 1862 the U. S. Congress passed an Anti-Polygamist bill, and the Church challenged this law in the courts. He wrote:

"March 22[1863] overland mail with four passengers attacked by Indians near 8 mile station. Tooele County driver killed and one passenger wounded. Judge Mott, who was in the coach, took the reins, drove for life and escaped.... The Governor, Judges and soldiers at Camp Douglas, tried to force President Young and take him to Camp Douglas, [with] no trial. Their feelings were to imprison him for life. Also be tried for treason. If they had it in their power he would be killed. The saints knew their feelings and hatred. I was working ditching at the church pasture at the time the soldiers from Camp Douglas marched toward the city. A signal flag was raised from the top of President Young's house. I would have to walk five miles to get to the President's residence. There were hundreds of us guarding night and day expecting every minute they would come to battle. We were prepared for them and determined to defend our President and leaders. It was an exciting time. The soldiers knew we were prepared."

$\sim$ 31 $\sim$

A WEAVER FROM HJORRING,
ISLE OF JUTLAND, DENMARK

METTE MARIA HANSEN was born in the little town of Emb, Hjorring, Denmark, on 27 Jun 1830. She was the daughter of HANS CHRISTIAN THOMSEN and JOHANNA MARIA POULSEN. Emb is located in the most northerly part of the Isle of Jutland. In the times when the Holy Roman Empire made their conquests in Germany, they were never able to conquer this little place. The people were brave and fearless of the threatening tyrants and took up their arms. Catholicism was consequently never introduced there, and the saying was that the north side of Limfjoren was the north isle of righteousness. The greater portion of the people on the Isle of Jutland gained their livelihood from the soil. The land was tilled by large numbers of people, who owned title to their plot of land. They loved and honored their precious mother earth, some of which was handed down from father to son for many generations. As this was a small land, every inch of it was made to produce all it could.

According to the memory of my grandmother ANNIE CATHERINE MORTENSEN (Ivie,) her mother "METTE MARIA HANSEN ... worked as an apprentice in a weaving factory before she became an expert weaver for fine linens, damask and sheets for two years. Then she took her trade to Sinby, a city on the opposite side of Albaek ... and hired a woman to help her. She took in weaving. During this time she was thinking of joining the Baptist Church. One night she dreamed of seeing the tabernacle in Salt Lake City, and later, when she went to Salt Lake City for her endowments, she recognized the building of her girlhood dreams.

"It was about this time that METTE MARIA became engaged to be married. The marriage was even advertised when her mother quarreled with the groom's father about property, and her parents forbad the marriage. There social customs were a bit different from ours today, and a baby son was born to METTE MARIA by this union. In spite of this, METTE MARIA gave back all of her presents and lived with her parents as a dutiful daughter. Her fiancé tried to assist in every way, and they were waiting for reconciliation between their parents when METTE MARIA heard about the Church. She did not agree with the Lutheran Church on baptism, and was ready to listen when the Elders brought the Gospel to her. After praying, she felt assurance that Mormonism was true and accepted it. Having a desire to join the Saints in Salt Lake, she left her home on April 5, 1862. [Other records say that her parents made her leave their home when she joined the church and her fiancé wanted nothing more to do with her.] Taking her son, CHRISTIAN JORGENSEN, and her savings, she left from Hamburg, Germany.

"JENS FREDERICK MORTENSEN was born the 9th of May, 1833, in Albaek, Fredrickshawn, Denmark [other records show Tveden, Albaek, Hjorring, Denmark]. When grown, he was about 5 ft. 9 inches tall, weighing 165 lbs, with a chest size of 41 inches. He had brown hair and blue eyes. He was a hard working man who never complained of being sick . . . He was chased away from his aunt's home in Denmark because he was a Mormon. He filled a 3 year mission for the Church in Denmark before coming to Utah. The last part of his mission had to be finished in England, because the prejudice in Denmark was so great that he could not finish his mission there. When told that smoking was against the teachings of the Church, he threw his silver pipe into the river. His uncle thought this a lack of judgment as he figured the silver should have been saved for commercial sale. He married METTE MARIA HANSEN in 1863 at sea on the ship *Franklin*. JENS adopted her son CHRISTIAN JORGENSEN."

According to Church records: JENS FREDRICK MORTENSEN was baptized and confirmed by L. Nielsen on 7 Feb 1858. METTE MARIA HANSEN was baptized by Jens Christian Anderson Weibye on 11 Aug 1861. She was confirmed a member of the church by C. A. Madsen on 12 Aug 1861.

On 15 Apr 1862, the *Franklin* sailed from Hamburg, Germany, carrying 413 Mormons from Denmark. Commanding the ship was Robert Murray. Their church leader Jens Christian Anderson Weibye [who had baptized METTE MARIA HANSEN, and was a counselor of the L.D.S. mission president, Christian A. Madsen, the other counselor was Lauritz Larsen] divided the emigrants into eight districts, each with a president. The youth Anthon H.

The ship *Franklin* was 708 tons and one of four German flag square-riggers, measuring 163' x 31' x 15'. It was built at Rockland, Maine, in 1854. She was a three-master with two decks, no galleries, a round stern, and a figurehead. In 1866, she was reported sold to Norwegian owners.

Lund who later became an apostle and a member of the First Presidency of the Church, was among the emigrants. He was very accomplished as a linguist and acted as an interpreter. Later, in Mount Pleasant, he boarded at the home of second-great-grandparents JOHN and SUSANNAH WILKINSON BARTON.

The vessel *Franklin* had 160 bunks below deck, which were wide enough for three persons to lay side by side. It had eleven lanterns–six belonging to the ship and five to the emigrants. To feed everyone, it carried beef, pork, peas, beans, potatoes, pearl barley, rice, prunes, syrup, vinegar, pepper, coffee, tea, sugar, butter, rye bread, sea biscuits, water, flour, salted herring, and salt. The menu on Sunday included *sweet soup*; Monday, pea soup; Tuesday and Wednesday, rice; Friday, barley mush; and Saturday, herring and potatoes. It arrived in New York City on 29 May 1862, after a forty-four day journey.

Elder Jens C. A. Weibye described the voyage: "Some of the emigrants carried the measles with them from home and the disease soon spread to all parts of the ship, so that no less than forty persons, mostly children, were attacked at once. Many of the emigrants were also suffering with diarrhea, which caused much weakness of body. We lost the appetite for sea biscuits, but learned to soak them in water or tea for eight or ten hours, which softened them so that they became more palatable. The sick were served twice a day with porridge made from barley, rice or sago, and almost every day pancakes could be had by the hundreds for the sick, who could not eat the 'hardtack' (sea biscuits). Wheat bread was also baked for some of the old people. We held a council meeting every night and the sanitary condition of the ship's apartments were attended to with great care. Three times a week the decks were washed and twice a week the ship was thoroughly fumigated by burning tar. A spirit of peace prevailed . . . The captain and crew were good-natured and obliging and so were the cooks who even served the sick when they were not on duty.

"We held at times meetings of worship on the upper or lower deck, and every morning at 5 o'clock the signal for rising was given by the clarionet or accordian. At 7 a.m. and 9 p.m. a similar signal was sounded calling the Saints to assemble in their several districts for prayer. Most every day we amused ourselves a short time by dancing on deck to music played by some of our brethren or members of the crew. We could thus have had an enjoyable time, had it not been for the sorrow occasioned by the many sick and dying amongst us on account of the measles. Up to this day (May 27th) three adults and 43 children have died, nearly all from measles. During the last few days, the chicken-pox has broken out amongst us and four cases have already developed. We had had head winds most of the time; otherwise we could have been in New York before now for the 'Franklin' is a first-class ship. We have been very little troubled with sea-sickness."

Our family history states that great-grandmother METTE MARIA HANSEN boarded the *Franklin* with a large trunk filled with linens she had woven. Most of these linens were used to wrap the dead, as they were lowered into the ocean. After their marriage and the adoption of her young son CHRISTAIN by JENS, his surname became MORTENSEN. Danish genealogy is patronymic, which means that the surname changes in each generation. For this reason, it is difficult to follow a genealogy line. Instead of <u>son</u>, like the Swedes, the Danish used <u>sen</u>. If JENS had continued this Danish method, his son CHRISTAIN would have had a surname of JENSEN, not MORTENSEN. METTE's father's given name was HANS.

Forty-eight of the original passengers had died by the time the ship arrived in New York. At Castle Garden the Saints were quarantined. Eighteen were hospitalized, and the remaining emigrants were returned to the *Franklin*, where they remained shipboard two more days and a night. On 31st of May they were greeted by elder Charles C. Rich and other Church representatives at Castle Garden. However, before the company reached Utah there were fourteen more deaths, bringing the total to 62 dead of the original 413 emigrants.

Brigham Young assigned the young MORTENSEN family to go south to Salina, Utah, because METTE was skilled as a weaver. They were delayed on their southward journey, in 1863, at Pleasant Grove, Utah, (known then as Battle Creek), where METTE became ill with Rocky Mountain spotted fever. She was very sick, and her recovery was slow. Going further south, the cold, snowy fall weather stopped their further advance to Salina. They chose to make a small lean-to against a cliff by Mount Pleasant and remained there during the harsh winter. Grandmother, ANNIE CATHERINE MORTENSEN was born in this lean-to on 26 Nov 1863.

When the spring of 1864 broke, they continued on to Salina with their beautiful baby girl. JENS built a strong solid home with the first shingled roof in the town. It had walls nearly three feet wide and was two stories high. The large flat north window sill in the kitchen was used as a refrigerator through many years. The house stood solidly in its place for over 100 years, when my mother sold the four-acre lot to a developer that tore it down and built a gas station with a mini-market. The lot is located one block from the center of Salina on the west side of the highway that joins I-70 within a few rather long blocks. As a child, I remember the home as being quite cool, without air-conditioning, throughout the hot summer months. A large grizzly bear rug with head and claws was in the center of the living room floor.

GENERAL ERASTUS SNOW

COL. JOHN R. WINDER

COL. JOHN LEHI IVIE
of Mount Pleasant, San Pete County,
Utah. He fought in seven battles
with Indians and led three of them.

ELDER ORSON HYDE, Apostle
Spring City, Sanpete County

BISHOP WM. S. SEELY
Favorite with the Indians

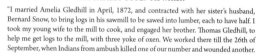

PETER GOTTFREDSON, the author of *Indian Depridation*,
and FAMILY 1882. He writes:

"I married Amelia Gledhill in April, 1872, and contracted with her sister's husband, Bernard Snow, to bring logs in his sawmill to be sawed into lumber, each to have half. I took my young wife to the mill to cook, and engaged her brother, Thomas Gledhill, to help me get logs to the mill, with three yoke of oxen. We worked there till the 26th of September, when Indians from ambush killed one of our number and wounded another.

In 1882, at the age of 26, when this picture was taken, I was requested by the editor of our local paper, the Richfield Advocate, to write up the circumstances for publication, which I did, with the assistance of my wife, her brother Thomas, and my brother-in-law, Colonel JOHN L. IVIE, which was the beginning of the compilation of this history."

COL. HEBER P. KIMBALL

COL. GEORGE A. SMITH

JOHN LOWRY
Lieutenant in Wm. Bench's Infantry company. Indian
interpreter of experience, explorer, pioneer, colonizer.

PRESIDENT ANTHON H. LUND
First Telegraph Operator at Mt. Pleasant, Utah.
Lieutenant, Capt. Frederick Neilsen's Infantry Company.

BRIG. GENERAL WM. BYRAN PACE
Commander Utah Militia led the battle at
Gravelly Ford, June 11th, 1866.

~ 32 ~

THE ANGRY CHIEF BLACK HAWK
DECLARES WAR AND DESTRUCTION

[Note: Here is a listing from *Indian Depredations in Utah* supp. pp. 11-13 of white people killed by Indians in the early Utah history. I have placed a * by the counties of Millard, Juab, Piute, and Utah, and ** by Sanpete/Sevier.

1850	Mar. 10	One killed at Provo*	Joseph Higbee
1853	July 18	One killed at Payson* (Walker War)	Alexander Keel
	Aug. 17	Three killed at Parley's Park	John Quaile, John Dixon, John Dickson
	Sept. 13	One killed at Fillmore*	William Hatton
	Oct. 1	Four killed at Uinta Springs** (Fountain Green)	J. Nelson, W. Luke, T. Clark & W. Reed
	Oct. 4	Two killed at Manti**	William Mills, John Warner
	Oct. 14	One killed at Santaquin*	Farnee L. Tindrell
	Oct. 26	Twelve killed at the Sevier River*	Captain Gunnison & eleven others
1854	Aug. 8	Two killed at Cedar Valley*	William & Warren Weeks
1855	Sept. 23	Three killed at Elk Mountain (Mission)	J. Hunt, Wm. Behunin & E. Edwards
1856	Feb.	Five killed at Cedar Valley (Tintic)*	H. Moran, W & G Carson, Hunsaker & Cousins
		Two killed at Kimball Creek	John Winn, John Catlin
1858	June 4	Four killed at Salt Creek Canyon*	Terkelsen, Kjerluf, Jens Jorgensen & wife
	Oct. 7	Two killed at Chicken Creek*	Josiah Call, Samuel Brown
1860	July 26	Two killed at Smithfield	John Reed, Ira Merrill
1865	April 10	One killed at Twelve Mile Creek**	Peter Ludvigsen
		Two killed at Salina Canyon**	Barney Ward, James P. Andersen
	April 12	Two killed at Salina Canyon**	Jens Sorensen, William Kearns
	May 25	One killed near Fairview**	Jens Larsen
	May 26	Six killed in Thistle Valley**	John Given, his wife and four children
	May 29	One killed near Fairview**	David H. Jones
	July 13	One killed near Salina**	Robert Gilispie

	July 14	One killed at Gravelly Ford **	Anthony Robinson
	Oct. 17	Seven killed near Ephraim**	Khure & wife, Petersen, Thorp, Hite, Jespersen, Black
	Nov. 2	Four killed near Circleville*	Froid, Hansen, Barney, Heilersen
1866	Jan. 8	Two killed at Pipe Springs	J.M. Whitmore, Robert McIntyre
	April 2	Three killed near St. George	Joseph & Robert Berry & wife
	April 13	Two killed near Salina**	Johnson, Chris Nielsen
	April 22	Two killed in Marysvale*	Albert Lewis, Chris. Christiansen
	June 10	Two killed in Round Valley (Scipio)	*JAMES RUSSELL IVIE, Henry Wright
	June 24	One killed in Thistle Valley**	Charles Brown
	June 26	Two killed in Spanish Fork Canyon*	Albert Dimie, John Edmiston
1867	Mar. 21	Three killed near Glenwood**	Jens P. Petersen & wife, Mary Smith
	June 1	One killed near Fountain Green**	Louis Lund
	June 2	Two killed at Twelve Mile Creek**	J. W. Vance, Heber Houtz
	Aug. 13	Two killed near Spring City**	James Meeks, Andrew Johansen
	Sept. 4	One killed near Fayette**	John Hay
1868	April 5	One killed at Cedar Ridge**	Alexander Justesen
		One killed at Rocky Ford**	Henry Wilson
1872	June 16	One killed at Twelve Mile Creek**	NIELS HEISELT
	Aug. 10	One killed near Fairview**	Nathan Stewart
	Sept. 26	One killed near Spring City**	Daniel Miller

This list does not include any that were killed in Wyoming, Nevada, or Idaho. It is not totally complete in Utah, as other histories have mentioned some that are not included here; but this is an excellent guide to the events given in this book as to time and place. There are ninety-nine listed above. Many were Scandinavians.]

The Ute Indians' beloved *Provo (fishing) River* in Utah County, where the IVIEs were sent with the first group to build Fort Utah, was very difficult for the Indians to relinquish. The IVIEs were with the militia for the battles of Fort Utah and the Walker War that included Sanpete County (with the ALLREDs), and Millard County (the home of Chief Walker). The STOTTs and DUNCANs (GROVER SWALLOW's ancestors) were living at Fort Fillmore. As Utah County became more populated, the Indians centered their thefts and violence further south with Sanpete, Juab and Millard Counties being easier prey for food, cattle, and horses, which they took whenever the opportunity and inclination arose at the same time. The Indians who did this justified themselves by saying that all the land really belonged to them, ignoring all peace treaties, promises, and gifts. Often the ones they killed were the herders, or the single

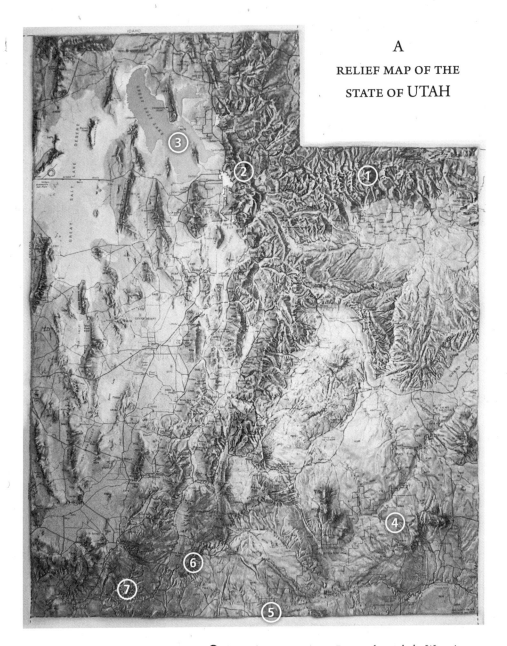

A

RELIEF MAP OF THE
STATE OF UTAH

Most of the state of Utah is uninhabitable. ❶ The High Uinta Mountain Range is beneath the Wyoming border. ❷ The Wasatch Mountain Range descends down the center of the state. ❸ The Great Salt Lake of the north and west is the last remains of the massive old sea water Lake Bonneville, whose salt water remains destroy most of the vegetation in its western lands. ❹ The central east to southeast corner is a geologist's dream area, which displays the rocky remains of the eons of creative time, dating back before and including the dinosaurs. It forms the hot, horseshoe-shaped canyons—❺ the beginning of the deep Grand Canyon of northern Arizona. The multicolored southwest shows great volcanic and earthquake activity, which created the marvelous wonders of ❻ Bryce Canyon and ❼ Zion National Parks. Most of the state's useable water comes from the snow along the Wasatch western front that creates the winter-wonderland for a skier's paradise.

family traveling, or living apart from the forts in the less protected areas. War would start when a malevolent chieftain could persuade sufficient braves to join him. Young JOHN L. IVIE (great-grandfather) was first a private in the Utah County Militia, where he participated in the Utah (1850), Walker (1853-4) and Tintic (1856) Wars. He was chosen as a major just prior to the arrival of Johnston's Army and served under the command of Lot Smith (1857-58). He had been called with his brother JIM to the Fort Supply Indian Mission (winter of 1853-4) and then to the Elk Mountain Indian Mission (1855), where the Indians killed three of the missionaries and the others were forced to return to their homes in Ephraim and Manti. [Part I: DRIVEN]

A peace conference had been held between Brigham Young with his retinue and Chief Walker on Chicken Creek (by Mills, Utah) in Walker's tent in May 1854. Chief Walker is quoted as saying:

> "Walkara has heard all the talk of the good Mormonee chief. Walkara no like to go to war with him ... Mericats [Americans] kill Indian; Indian kill Mericats! Walkara no want to fight more. Walkara talk with Great Spirit, Great Spirit say, 'make peace!' Walkara love Mormonee chief—he is good man. When Mormonee come to live on Walkara's land, Walkara give him welcome ... Walkara talk last night to Paiute, to Utah, San Pitch, Pauvan— all Indian say 'no fight Mormonee or Mercats more.' If Indian kill white man again, Walkara make Indian howl."

Chief Walkara (Walker) remained friendly until his death, which occurred on Meadow Creek, Millard County, in January of 1855, where my husband would be born in 1927.

Efforts were made by the Territorial Government to further establish peace with the Indians by setting aside farm lands for their use. In Sanpete County, it was attempted at Twelve Mile Creek (Mayfield), and in Millard County it was at Corn Creek (Kanosh). The land near the mouth of Spanish Fork Canyon in Utah Valley was designated for their use. Special agents were appointed to help them farm the land. The United States government was supposed to send money to help with these land reservations; but none was forthcoming—instead they sent Johnston's Army against the Mormons, which brought this effort rapidly to a standstill.

[**Note: Back in Mount Pleasant in 1860:** JOHN LEHI IVIE had married, as a second wife, young MARY ETT CARTER of Provo, on 23 Jan 1857. She had a separate house close to great-grandmother MARY CATHERINE BARTON IVIE's home. MARY ETT's oldest son was JOHN CARTER IVIE. He was born 16 Feb 1860. They had three more children: ELIZABETH (1863); ARLETTA (1865); and THOMASON HARRISON IVIE (23 Feb 1867). For whatever reasons, MARY ETT divorced JOHN LEHI IVIE during the troublesome Black Hawk War days. Taking her children with her, she returned to Provo and her parents, saying she wanted a husband of her own. She later married William Abner Haws.

JOHN and his vivacious first wife, MARY CATHERINE BARTON (Ivie), had helped to persuade her parents, JOHN and SUSANNAH WILKINSON BARTON, to leave Bountiful and move with their children to Mount Pleasant in 1860. By 1863, mother SUSANNAH was taking in boarders, including the young Danish interpreter, Anthon H. Lund, who had sailed to America on the ship *Franklin* with our Danish great-grandparents. DAVID CANDLAND, who married JOHN BARTON's youngest sister MARY ANN, with his family, arrived in Mount Pleasant the spring of 1861. DAVID CANDLAND was very active teaching school, postmaster, clerk, and farming. MARY ANN had died in Salt Lake City 23 Feb 1859. Her death had left him with six young motherless children, five daughters and a son; but he had another wife, ANN WOODHOUSE (Candland). They would have ten children between 1856 and 1879. Then there was another wife, HANNAH ANN WRIGHT, who had twelve children between 1858 and 1883. With his wife, KATHERINE ANN JOST, he had seven more children (1859-1875). In the Ancestral File, he is listed as having seven wives, but no additional children. This adds up to at least 35 children and at least 3 additional wives in Mount Pleasant.]

As the Indian hostilities increased in Sanpete County during 1863-4, JOHN L. IVIE was appointed first as captain of this vast county of Sanpete, which included Thistle on the north and extended south through Piute County. He was under the command of stalwart Colonel REDICK N. ALLRED of Spring City, son of his great-uncle ISAAC ALLRED, [a brother of third-great-grandmother SARAH ALLRED (Ivie)]. REDICK was the efficient quartermaster and later a captain in the Mormon Battalion.

The settlers in Mount Pleasant built a second fort specifically for their cattle and horses which bordered the original fort. It was the duty of the militia to guard this fort at night. During the day, it was often necessary to guard the farmers as they planted, cared for, or harvested their crops. With the firing of the shots, these minutemen would leave immediately to help wherever Indian problems took them—sometimes for many days.

[Note: Grandfather JAMES OSCAR IVIE was born 9 May 1863 in Mount Pleasant, when his mother MARY CATHERINE was 25 years old. His older brother, JOHN LAFAYETTE IVIE, was born 10 Nov 1860. Second-great grandfather JAMES RUSSELL IVIE, with most of his children and their families left Sanpete County in the spring of 1863. They moved across the mountains to the sparsely settled Round Valley of Millard County, which is now Scipio.]

Although the date for the beginning of the Black Hawk War is usually set at 9 Apr 1865, the Mormons never declared war on the Indians. Their wars were self-defense and preserving their homes, herds, food, and other supplies. This date is also of great national interest, for on this date General Robert E. Lee conceded to Grant's terms for surrender at Appomattox Courthouse. Five days later, on 14 Apr 1865, ABRAHAM LINCOLN was assassinated by John Wilkes Booth. His vision of uniting the country with the least difficulty and pain was ended, and the reconstruction would be harsh and restrictive. The hatred that resulted had long tentacles, but these events had little evidence in central Utah. Mostly, the Civil War passed them by.

During the winter of 1864–65, a small band of Indians was camping near Gunnison and contracted smallpox, which resulted in the deaths of several Indians. They blamed the white people and threatened to kill them and steal their cattle. The threats festered into action, and they took some of John Lowry's herd. In trying to get compensation and avoid war and further problems, a special meeting with the Indians was called in Manti on 9 Apr 1865. They met outside, at Jerome Kempton's place. One young Ute Chief Jake Arapeen, whose father had died during the winter, was a thorn in the peace talks. He would not be pacified. John Lowry was one of the Indian interpreters and perhaps equally arrogant. The discussion heated up. Arapeen, on horseback, reached for his arrows. John Lowry stepped up, caught hold of the Indian and pulled him off his horse. Arapeen struck Lowry. Lowry threatened retaliation; but was restrained by the others present. The Indian swiftly rode off to the Indian camp at Shumway Springs near Moroni with his report; riders were sent to the distant Indian camps, which were quickly moved to the mountains, and the young Ute Indian Chief Black Hawk gathered his warriors for a conflict.

Not as quick to discern the danger, but hearing reports that the Indians were planning to take the stock at Twelve Mile Creek (Mayfield), a small party of men from Manti was sent out to collect their animals. Black Hawk and his braves were already there. They killed Peter Ludvigsen whose companions took flight back to Manti. The Indians drove the animals south and were joined by the Richfield Indians who had added most of the Salina stock, then drove the herd east up Salina canyon. Barney Ward, a prominent mountaineer and interpreter, and James Anderson were in Salina Canyon—quite unaware that Black Hawk was on the warpath. Their mutilated bodies were found the next day— shot with both bullets and arrows. It appeared that they had first been severely tortured, and then scalped and most of their clothing taken.

A call was made throughout the settlements for well-armed cavalrymen by Colonel REDICK N. ALLRED. Responding from Mount Pleasant according to the journal of Andrew Madsen were,

> "A party of about twenty men, JOHN IVIE, Dolph Bennett, ORANGE SEELEY, George Frandsen, Christian Jensen, ALMA ZABRISKIE, Peter Fredricksen, N. Peter Madsen, Mortin Rasmussen, myself and others, with three baggage wagons . . . started out at daybreak. At our arrival at Manti, we were told what had transpired at Salina Canyon and of the killing of Ward and Anderson. We were ordered to hurry on at once.

> "We arrived in Salina early in the evening where we were joined by a number of men from other settlements. Preparations were made during the night and early the following morning. Colonel REDDICK ALLRED with eighty-four armed men started up Salina Canyon (I-70–going east) in pursuit of the Indians. About ten miles east of Salina, where the canyon was very narrow, we were compelled to travel in single file. Here the Indians were in ambush waiting, and suddenly, without any warning, from behind trees, bushes, and rocks, volley after volley were poured upon us by the Red Skins. We were panic stricken and compelled to retreat into a clear opening, pursued by the Indians who had all the advantages. During the encounter, Jens Sorensen, of Ephraim, and William Kearns, of Gunnison, were killed. The bodies lay in the mountains for two days; then it was reported an Indian, the Chief Sanpitch, came in the night and said it would be safe to get the bodies. The bodies were then taken to Salina. Sorensen's body had been terribly mutilated."

Efforts had been made by the Indians to preserve the body of Kearns, because he was a close friend to some of the Indians who had killed him.

Having successfully taken all the cattle and horses from Salina and nearby lands, Black Hawk moved north toward Thistle. On 25 May 1865, while gathering his sheep four miles north of Fairview, JENS LARSEN was shot and killed. His daughter PAULINE later became the wife of JACOB DASTRUP of Sigurd. Great-grandmother METTE MARIE MORTENSEN's oldest son CHRIS, who was born in Denmark, would later marry into this family.

> From *Indian Depredations:* "Between daylight and sunrise on the morning of May 26, 1865, the same murderous band attacked John Given and family who had moved up Spanish Fork Canyon into Thistle Valley and

intended locating there for the summer. [The family] were sleeping in a hut constructed of willows, [two men] Leah and Brown being in a wagon box at one end. The former was awakened by hearing the cattle running wildly down the canyon, and shortly afterwards the firing of the Indians through the brush of the hut apprised him of the cause of the alarm. To their concealed position in the wagon box the two men owe their escape. The other occupants of the hut were speedily killed, the blood thirsty Indians completing with arrows and tomahawks the work which their first volley had begun. Quickly gathering up the flour, axes and guns of their victims, they surrounded a herd of stock, and after killing the calves, drove off between one and two hundred head of horses and cattle into the mountains."

MARY CATHERINE IVIE's seventeen-year-old brother OSCAR BARTON was one of the rescuers from Mount Pleasant. He reported:

"On the morning of the killing, between daylight and sunrise, Andrew Larson of Mount Pleasant who had camped during the night with the Wing family passed the Given place on the road . . . he heard calves bawling in the corral. Thinking that the people had not yet arisen, he passed on, but . . . about where Indianola railroad station is now located, he saw horsemen about half way up the valley, driving stock eastward toward the mountains. His first impression was to . . . ride up to them, but . . . concluded to travel on. One of the men who escaped ran to North Bend (Fairview), and reported what had happened. An express was immediately sent from Fairview to Mt. Pleasant. Twenty armed men were soon in their saddles and on their way to Thistle Valley. A few more men joined this Mt. Pleasant company at North Bend, and they all arrived . . . before noon. Here they found Mrs. Given outside of the cabin stripped and lying on her back with her head towards the shanty, and John Given Jr. lying on the floor on his back with his feet toward the door, where he had fallen, being shot in the breast.

"The three girls lay in the wagon box, each with a deep tomahawk gash in the left side of the head. They were all stripped, with the exception of a small waist which the savages had left on each. The bedding had all been taken away, together with much of the house furnishings, guns, etc. The murdered people were taken to Fairview for burial and Charles Brown and Charles W. Leah, after attending the funeral, went back to Spanish Fork by way of Salt Creek Canyon and remained there. Ten or twelve of the young calves which had been left in the corral on the Given premises were found . . . tomahawked across the loins and were dragging their hind parts. The supposition was that the Indians, fearing that the calves would be a hindrance in driving off the stock into the mountains, had thus crippled the poor animals to prevent them from following their mothers. The massacre of the Given family in Thistle Valley represents one of the most horrible deeds committed by the Indians during the Black Hawk war."

Indian Depredations: "On Friday, May 29, 1865, three days after the massacre of the Given family . . . David H. Jones, a member of the Mormon Battalion and a resident of Fairview, was killed by Indians about three miles northwest of Fairview. This killing was supposed to be done by the same band of Indians that had murdered the Given family. Comrade JAMES M. ALLRED says that ten persons killed by Indians are buried in the Fairview cemetery."

On 8 Jun 1865, Colonel Irish, superintendent of Indian Affairs, accompanied by Brigham Young and other white leaders met with Chiefs Kanosh, Sowiette, Sanpitch, Tabby, and other smaller chiefs in an attempt to negotiate a peace treaty. All but Sanpitch signed. Sanpitch claimed to be suddenly indisposed. Perhaps the negotiations should have been with Black Hawk for in July, two more men, Robert Gilispie and Anthony Robinson, were killed near Salina. The news of the double murder infuriated the settlers. Militia General Warren S. Snow, with about 100 men, endeavored to prevent further depredations, and they were on the march on 15 July.

From *Mount Pleasant* by Longsdorf, we read, "There were twenty-eight men from Mount Pleasant, among them Captain IVIE, ORANGE SEELEY, JOSEPH GLEDHILL, Jefferson Tidwell, William Stevensen, and Neils Madsen. In a valley east of Salina, this military expedition surrounded a number of Indians who commenced shooting."

Joshua W. Sylvester, of Gunnison, described the battle: "At daylight, on the morning of the 18th, we had a good view of the whole valley. Descending the mountain, we reached a creek, and un-saddled, resting just opposite a large cedar grove near the present site of Burrville. The picket guard was sent out and returned in a very short time. We were aroused and told that the cedars were full of Indians. The horses were soon saddled and we surrounded the grove. The first shot was fired by an Indian who lay behind a fallen log, the bullet entering the breast of Marine York of Richfield. Captain Beach ordered his men to dismount and enter the cedars which was done and the Indians were soon routed. It was part of the band that had killed Robinson, as we found some of his things with them; the main gang had gone on ahead.

"E. C. Petersen (Chris Feuting) says that there were six Indian tents below the hill and that Colonel IVIE's company were on the outskirts of the grove and did not see many Indians; that after the fight some of his boys wanted to go back and look for dead Indians and guns, but the Colonel said: 'No, let the squaws go and hunt up their papooses.' Then IVIE's company drew off, while some of the others searched the grounds.

"It was reported soon after the fight that only one Indian got away and a dozen or more had been killed, including some squaws and papooses; the militia had fired into a large bushy cedar where a lot of them were concealed. It was also said that Louis Thompson of Ephraim and a man from Casper's Company came onto a bunch of squaws and papooses, and that they were left there to guard them. One of the squaws tried to get away, and when prevented by Thompson, she picked up a stick of wood and struck him with it; he then shot her. This excited the others and they were soon dispatched. This event has been dubbed 'the squaw fight.' We returned through the head of Grass Valley, down Salina Canyon to Salina, where we stayed a couple of days jerking beef and getting provisions ready for a trip into the mountains."

The militia found the tracks of the Indians who had driven off the stolen stock. The officers now divided their men into three companies, some remained in Salina as guards, some went north with Colonel ALLRED to secure more men and to start over the mountain in pursuit. The main bodies of soldiers, with General Snow, tracked the Indians southeasterly.

Copied from Andrew Madsen's Journal: "ORANGE SEELEY, N. P. Madsen, ALMA ZABRISKIE, myself, and others from Mount Pleasant were in Snow's Company. As soon as possible, we started on the trip, trying to secure the cattle from the Indians. We camped the first night at the head of Salina Canyon. Then went down the canyon into a large valley (now Emery County). We did most of our traveling at night in order to avoid the attention of the Indians. We crossed a large creek and journeyed over Buck Horn Flat where we were joined by ALLRED and his company who had taken the trail to the north."

Mr. Sylvester continues:

"On the evening of the 20th we started out again, and when about half a mile from town a sad accident happened; as we stopped by a large boulder to gird our saddles, Jack Harper set his gun (a Joslin) down against a rock and in some way discharged it, the ball passing through the cheek of the horse which James Mortensen was riding and lodged under Mortensen's collar bone; he still (1917) carries that ball and another with which he was shot later. The company stopped there while some of the boys took him back to Salina."

This was not great-grandfather JENS MORTENSEN of Salina, [died 9 Jan 1886.] From Colonel ALLRED's journal:

"I crossed the mountains with eighty men. We found three or four lodges of Tabby's Indians returning from a hunt, and the boys wanted to kill them, but I restrained them because they had their families with them. We formed a junction with General Snow's men on Price River and went to Green River without seeing the marauders."

Again from Andrew Madsen's journal:

"We camped on the Price River that night and the following morning we moved on south and east to Green River by day light. We did not see any Indians but could see where they had driven the cattle through the river. Here the company stopped for breakfast. On the other side of the river we could see fresh wickiups made of green trees. The river was too high to ford. Dolph Bennett, of Mount Pleasant, JOHN SANDERS, of Fairview, and Jens Larsen of Ephraim, were chosen as advance guards to swim across to investigate. JOHN SANDERS very nearly drowned, but was rescued by Bennett. The advance men, upon reaching the other shore found a great many fresh tracks of the Indians, and called back to tell of their find. After scouting about a short time, they returned across the river to the balance of the company. Most of the company wanted to follow the tracks, but upon taking inventory of their supplies, which now consisted of cracker crumbs only, the officers decided, on account of the jaded condition of the horses and the lack of supplies, to give up the chase and return home. Years later, Chief Jake Arropine [sic] told that the Indians were in hiding among the bushes and trees and could easily have shot and killed the advance men and others had they wanted to; when asked why they had not done so, he said that they had intended to fire when all the men were across or crossing and had gotten into the river, 'then the water would have been red.' We started our homeward journey across the mountains, over rough trails, through canyons and deep washes, by way of the place called 'Hole in the Rocks.' We were two days and a half without food, with the exception of a spoonful of cracker crumbs dished out to each man for a meal. While we saw no Indians, we were interrupted now and again by wild beasts of the mountains. In Rock Canyon, on the other side of the mountain, we were met by a party from home who brought provisions to us, they, in attempting to reach us, had been delayed by losing their way in the mountains. There was much rejoicing the following morning when we pitched our camp in Ephraim, having been gone about two weeks."

On 26 Jul 1865, there were *very few houses in Glenwood*—at the foot of the mountains east of Richfield. It had only started to be settled the previous year. Blacksmith Merritt Staley went out after coal to start a fire in his forge. After collecting his basket of coal, he was fired upon by Indians who lay concealed under the creek bank—one bullet went through his right breast, one seared his lip under his nose, and still another grazed his forehead. He placed his hat over his breast and shouted, "Help murder!" as he fell down the steps into the dugout where the family was living. Staley's wife jumped out of bed and ran to the house of Peter Allen, across the block, screaming,

"My husband is shot! My two little girls are in bed and will surely be killed!"

Isaac Allen, a mere boy, grabbed a gun and ran up through the lot into the dugout. He seized the two little girls, one in each arm, and ran with them, the bullets flying all around him. Neighbor, Solomon Case, had heard the shot, cried "Indians!" and grabbed his gun. As he opened the door his fourteen-year-old step-son, Thomas Goff, slipped outside in time to see Staley fall into the dugout and his wife run to the Allens. An Indian called out,

"Sol Case! Shoot him!"

A volley from the Indians on the hill was fired at the young boy Goff, bullets hitting all around him. Running back into his house, he opened the back door which had no hinges, laid it on the floor, and ran down to Main Street. Solomon's wife was in bed with a baby girl—two days old. The nurse grabbed the baby girl and ran into a nearby patch of corn. Mrs. Case demanded,

"If you don't take me down town, I will get up and run!"

Case wrapped a quilt around her and carried her on his back to Main Street. There was constant fire from Indians behind the rocks on the hill. Bishop Wareham, with a Sharp's rifle, remarked:

"There sits a beggar on a rock,"

He handed his gun to George Pectol, who crawled out to a wagon box, and fired. The Indian fell backwards off the rock, now without a jaw.

Runners were sent to Salina and Richfield for help. The Richfield group got through and brought a company of men, which included young Peter Gottfredson who related:

> "There were ten of us and we were ordered to get through [to Salina], if we had to fight our way," [The Indians were seen at Cedar Ridge on the east side of the river moving north.] "The road at this place [Willow Bend] passed along the river bank on the west side. No doubt, if we had followed the road, we would have been shot at but we circled up toward the west mountains, out of gun reach and came back into the road about a half mile north of the bend."

Crossing the Sevier River at a cattle ford they arrived at Salina, only to be told that:

> "Most of the men had gone to Manti to mill, but was expected home the next day. We all stood guard that night. Soon after, five of us started home."

Peter was wearing a big red flannel shirt.

> "About three miles out of Richfield we scattered out hunting rabbits. Some one outside of town saw us and reported that the Indians were coming; he knew that it was Indians, for one had a red blanket. The drum beat and all the people gathered at the meeting house . . . when we got to the public square we saw the people at the meeting house, and when things were explained it was learned that we were the Indians that had been seen. Many of the men with the best guns were out in pursuit of real Indians who had driven away a lot of stock." [*Indian Depredations*]

About 28 July, (1865) Captain Niels L. Christensen with a company of men from Richfield and Captain ISAAC M. ALLRED with a company from Spring City were stationed at Fort Gunnison to guard the trails between Salina and Twelve Mile Creek. The guard duty was for sixty days, but ended after fifty days.

> Andrew Madsen wrote: "At a special meeting held at Manti, August 6th, attended by Bishops of the various settlements and several of the military authorities, it was decided to have a standing Army in Sanpete County and that the men doing Military duty should be paid. The system of paying the men was by assessment upon the settlers. My portion was $75.00 a year. Some of the men could not fit themselves out and we were ordered to

let them have such articles as they could use, and receive credit for them. Besides the above assessment, I furnished them a horse, bridle and saddle, kept it on hand for them, along with one Ballard rifle and one cap and ball revolver. Others did likewise. JOHN IVIE was appointed commander of the northern settlements in Sanpete Valley and 22 men were called from Mt. Pleasant."

On 7 August, the community gave a party to honor the boys who had returned from the difficult and dangerous expedition to Green River in pursuit of the Indians. On 8 August, the standing Army left Mount Pleasant, armed and equipped for an Indian encounter; however, they temporarily stationed them in a hay field to cut their hay. With that completed, they marched to the north end of the county to discourage Indian attacks from that direction. During the three years of their enlistment, they were called out for encampments and inspections, which were held at Chester, Ephraim and Manti. The home guards remained at home and were called out by the call of the bugle to answer to roll call; some were detailed for guards each day. *Indian Depredations* recorded:

"Nearly two months had passed since there had been any serious outbreak. But Indians were prowling around Circleville, and it was reported that they had a rendezvous somewhere near Fish Lake, east of Sevier Valley. General Warren S. Snow with 103 men went up the River as far as Circleville; he had with him Colonel JOHN IVIE's company of cavalry from Mount Pleasant, and Captain N. W. Beache's company from Manti, with some recruits from other companies; they went to investigate the conditions of affairs and arrived in Circleville September 18, 1865. On the 19th they marched up the east fork of the Sevier to Clover Flat, where they encamped for the night. There they got onto the Indian's trail, which they followed over the plateau between Grass and Rabbit Valleys. Night overtook them before reaching the latter valley; it was raining and very dark; they made camp in the head of a very rough canyon. Early next morning (September 21st) Ezra Shoemaker and another man went out to reconnoiter; they found the track of a pony which had come within half a mile of camp and turned back; they reported what they had seen. The company then worked their way down the canyon. When they reached the flat country, at a small lake or pond called Red Lake, near Thousand Lake Mountain, they made a halt.

"General Snow and Col. IVIE went up a black, rock ridge to get a view of the country and its surroundings. When near the top, Col. IVIE saw a ramrod wiggling behind a brush only a few paces away, and exclaimed, 'There they are,' when a volley was fired from ambush, one bullet hitting and seriously wounding General Snow in the shoulder. The men retreated to the company, when a general battle ensued; the Indians firing from ambush on top of the hill.

"The Indians over-shot, the bullets singing over the heads of the soldiers, striking in the water, fairly making it boil. Orson Taylor of Richfield received a serious gun-shot wound in the side. George Frandsen of Mount Pleasant, while concealed in a gully, trying to get a shot at an Indian he had seen, received a bullet high in the forehead, the missile plowing through his hair and filling his eyes and face with blood, but it caused no further injury. A short retreat was ordered for the purpose of getting flanking movements on the savages, when it was noticed that one of the pack animals had been left behind. Ezra Shoemaker of Manti and another man went back, and in the midst of a shower of bullets from the enemy recovered the animal with the pack. The fighting continued till night and several Indians were killed. The militia crossed back over the mountain in the night to Grass Valley and made camp. Next day they marched down King's Meadow Canyon to Glenwood, where they separated and returned to their respective homes."

Grandfather JAMES OSCAR IVIE adds this:

"At the Rabbit Valley Battle, near Thurber, which was built afterwards, Warren Snow was shot off his horse. The Indians fired near twenty shots at father [Colonel JOHN L. IVIE] not over three or four rods; one bullet going through his hat and one going through his coat tail."

That fall (1865) Brigham Young proposed extending the telegraph throughout the territory for faster communication. Several thousand dollars were subscribed by the people of Sanpete. Armed guards were placed along the line in the canyon in order to protect the laborers from the Indians, while the line was being constructed. Grandfather JAMES OSCAR IVIE recorded this memory from his very early childhood,

"I remember companies of men gathering together and going to the mountains to get poles to put up the telegraph line to Manti and seeing men putting up the poles and wire. The men had to go in companies because the Black Hawk war was on."

On 3 Oct 1865, a letter was received from President Brigham Young in which he told the people to make peace with the Indians, as it is cheaper to feed them than to fight them. All militia were disbanded as a consequence. It would seem that Black Hawk was unaware of any peace negotiations, unless it was the part that they were to be fed without conflict; for with his warriors, he made a raid on Ephraim, 17 October, attacking, capturing, torturing, and killing in various places seven white people.

The two-year-old son of Pedersen Kuhre and his wife Elizabeth was found later--still alive by his mother's dead body. Black Hawk and his braves had gathered their winter supply of beef. Taking 200 head of cattle, they returned to their mountains without losing an Indian.

On 18 October, when the news of the raid at Ephraim was received in Mount Pleasant, a meeting was called in the evening and a strong guard was appointed. The following arrangements were made:

> "Each company of fifty men should stand guard twenty-four hours and use the Social Hall as a guard house."

During the night between the 19th and 20th, two brethren on guard supposed they saw two Indians jump over a nearby fence. They gave the alarm and in a few minutes every man who had a gun was prepared to meet the enemy.

At a meeting held 1 November, agreeable to Elder Orson Hyde's counsel, the guard at Mount Pleasant was reduced to ten men every twenty-four hours. They also called missionaries to settle on the Muddy. JOHN L. IVIE was first on the list; he may have gone for awhile, but his family remained in Mount Pleasant.

[Note: The mountains south of the Meadow Valley River that flows down Rainbow Canyon into the Colorado River, (now Lake Meade) are called the Muddy Mountains. Early pioneer maps of this area refer to these valleys as the Muddy. There is also a Muddy Creek in Sanpete County.]

On 26 Nov 1865, Black Hawk and his band attacked Circleville, driving away all their cattle and four white people were killed. Mrs. Mads Nielsen, a sister of ELIZABETH DAINTY, who later married on 19 Sep 1870, SAMUEL ALLRED, the son of ISAAC ALLRED and MARY HENDERSON, told her story of this Indian raid on Circleville.

> "My husband and I were . . . returning from a visit to Salt Lake City. When within ten miles of home we passed another team which was driven by my Brother-in-law, James Monsen. Being so near home we thought there would be no danger of Indians . . . about three miles from town . . . we saw a herd of cattle being driven toward the mouth of the canyon. I became

very much frightened . . . and I begged my husband to turn back. But as he thought the Indians had already seen us, he suggested that by driving fast we might reach a company of men who were in pursuit of the Indians. In a few minutes the Indians left the stock and with a yell started towards us. Our horses were very tired, but we urged them on . . . The Indians rode up to us, and one of them was in the act of shooting my husband, who, however, frightened him away some distance by pointing an old revolver at him. I suppose I am now safe in telling that the revolver was an old broken one, but of course, we did not tell the Indian so. Mr. Redskin now turned and shot our best horse, which of course stopped the team . . . I with my two year old brother in my arms, jumped from the wagon, while the Indian was reloading his gun. Willows were growing along the road, but as they were low they did not afford much protection. The Indian again mounted his horse and rode around trying to get a chance to shoot my husband.

"At this juncture I jumped into a slough that was near, in which the water reached up to my neck, but I preferred drowning to being captured by the Indians. My husband again pointed the revolver at the Indian who again turned back. My husband then took my little brother whom I was holding up out of the water and I climbed out of the slough. We walked a short distance and tried to cross the swamp at another point, but were headed off by ten Indians. Hence we got into the water again. The little boy began to cry because the water was so cold, and we left the slough once more. The Indians did not follow us into the willows, but turned their attention to the wagon and its belongings. They cut the harness from the wounded horse, leaving the collar, and took the wagon cover off. They emptied the flour on the ground, cut the feather bed tick and scattered all the feathers, threw all the dishes out of the wagon, breaking all but one plate, which I still have. They also took all of our clothing. While they were destroying the contents of the wagon, an old man named Froid, who had traveled in our company, arrived at the top of the hill and saw the Indians. He might have escaped all right if he had gone back himself at once, but he ran around his steers to drive them back. The Indians saw him, and followed him into the hills about a mile and killed him."

The Nielsens remained hidden when others found the wagon, believing they were Indians . . . after dark they started for home.

"It was late in the evening; we were both bareheaded and my clothes were frozen stiff on my body. My little brother had gone to sleep. When we entered the house it was full of people who had gathered because it had been reported that we had been killed."

One of the first settlers at Circleville was JAMES T. S. ALLRED, who was called on an Indian Mission to Circle Valley, Piute County, in 1864. He built a home, but was driven out in 1866 by the Indians and returned to Ephraim.

The winter of 1865 was a very cold, hard winter. Not even the Indians cared to come forth. They preferred enjoying their bountiful supply of beef that they had harvested from Sanpete, Sevier, and Piute Counties. Some depredations occurred in the warmer St. George area. The L. D. S. were against the practice of the Arizona Navajos, who liked to capture children of any color and sell them into slavery in Mexico, and so some strong animosities existed. Joining with the Utes, they killed Dr. J. M. Whitmore and his hired man, Robert McIntyre.

As the weather warmed, peaceful Chief Kanosh sent word to General Snow and Colonel ALLRED that a lot of Indians who had stolen cattle were camped in the Nephi Hills. Chief Kanosh had a son, Jake, who had been raised among the white people, and Kanosh volunteered to send him to pick out the renegades. Twelve armed men from Sanpete were called to aid their militia and bring the prisoners to Manti. Chief Sanpitch was among the prisoners.

R. N. Bennett reported:

> "The outcome was they secured a bunch of those who had killed, and started with them to Manti to be tried and put in jail. However, on the way we had some trouble. At daybreak we heard the dogs barking. We camped in a flat. Jake called to the other Indians in a tone that made the mountains echo and told them to keep still or be killed. The Indians were unruly and in the skirmish one was killed. They held court at Manti. Jake gave evidence against the Indians; four were condemned to be killed, and the rest put in jail."

Indian troubles continued in Kane County in the south. Joseph Berry, Robert Berry and wife, Mary Smith were killed by the Indians, as they journeyed from Spanish Fork to their new home in Long Valley. Apostle Erastus Snow called for armed men from St. George to move all of the settlers out of Long Valley.

BLACK HAWK TIMES
Composed by F. Christensen, Fairview, Utah
Tune: TA-ra-ra-boom-deay
(sung often to his grandchildren by JAMES OSCAR IVIE)

Black-Hawk and his red-skin band,
Was a terror in the land,
Proud he was the Indian chief,
Who could live on Mormon beef.

CHORUS
Singing heyeh, heyeh, yah,
Singing heyeh, heyeh, yah,
Heyeh, heyeh, heyeh, yah,
Heyeh, heyeh, heyeh, yah,

Ev'ry "Hawk" has piercing eyes--
From the hills his prey he spies--
Waits till Mormons pray and sleep,
When he takes their cows to keep.

I have always heard folks say
Men should watch as well as pray,
True, they did quite early rise,
Scratch their heads and rub their eyes.

Then they find their cattle gone--
Beat the drum and sound the horn;
Get your guns and don't bewail,
But get on the Indian trail.

Up the canyon big and wide,
Watching ev'ry mountain side,
While ahead some twenty miles,
Black-Hawk with his red-skins smiles.

After hours continuous tramp,
Strike they Black-Hawk's breakfast camp;
Scraps of hide and roasted bone,
But the hawks had long since flown.

Hungry and with weary feet,
Turn about and make retreat;
Having learned this truth that day,
Better watch as well as pray.

sketch by
B. SWALLOW

405

~ 33 ~

INDIANS KILL FATHER JAMES RUSSELL IVIE
TO TAKE THE LARGE HERD

On 15 Apr 1866, a call was made by the church for men to go east for immigrants. Thirteen men from Mount Pleasant responded. Among them was OSCAR BARTON, a younger brother of great-grandmother MARY CATHERINE IVIE. Accompanying this group as night guard was LYMAN PETERS, the future partner of JOHN L. IVIE. They were fitted out with eleven wagons and 44 oxen and left for Salt Lake City, where they joined the others. The entire company leaving Salt Lake City would consist of 456 teamsters, 49 mounted guard, 89 horses, 134 mules, 304 oxen and 397 wagons.

[Note: They returned 20 Oct 1866 with a company of immigrants who were chiefly Scandinavian. George Farnsworth rendered a great service in helping the cholera patients, fifty-six of whom died on the plains, and he was left in charge of fifty-three orphans, whom he distributed among the Saints in Utah who applied for them.]

Prior to the departure, Black Hawk with thirty mounted braves intercepted three teams from Glenwood, Sevier County, who were on their way north to join the others in Salt Lake City. The three teamsters escaped and fled to Salina; but the nine yoke of oxen and everything in their wagons were either carried away or demolished by the attacking Indians. The young herder Emil Nielsen of Salina told his story:

"I was helping to herd the Salina cow-herd while the men were employed building a fort. We were on the west side of the Sevier River northwest of town, distant about two miles, near the old wagon ford. My brother, older than I, was with me. We had been talking about Indians and he said that if the Indians came after him he would run and jump into the river. We saw the Indians on the east side of the river, but did not know they were Indians; they had attacked the three teams from Glenwood just before we saw them. They came over the river after the cow-herd.

"When we saw the Indians coming, Chris, my brother, ran to the river and was evidently killed there in the river as he was never found, but one foot with shoe on was found down the river during the summer. An Indian came after me and shot an arrow into my head and pulled it out three times. I thought if I could make the Indians think I was dead, he might leave me, and as I did not flinch when he shot me in the head, he evidently left me for dead.

"I lay there from about ten o'clock in the morning till near sundown. I dared not get up, fearing that the Indians might be near and see me and come and finish me. When I got up, I went to look for my brother, but could not find him. I then waded the river, the water being above my waist, and I started for home . . . When I reached the edge of town, I met my father, who picked me up and carried me home. I carried the arrow spike in my side for two weeks before it could be taken out. The old doctor lady, Maria Snow, of Manti, put poultices on the wounds and it drew out the spike. I was eleven years old."

Six-years-old great-uncle CHRISTIAN J. MORTENSEN remembered:

"On April 13, 1866, the Indians made an attack on Salina and drove away all their cows—they being in a herd. They also drove away all the stock on the range. We lost 3 cows . . . and a yoke of cattle that day. The Indians also killed the sheep herder and one of the cow herders. One of the cow herders, a boy ten years of age was shot with five arrows and left for dead. He however revived and waded the river and walked home. On the night of April 15, teams came from Gunnison and took the women and children away. We arrived in Gunnison bout sunrise on April 16. Salina was soon abandoned and was settled no more—[for] years."

The Indians took 200 head of cattle and killed a sheepherder from Fairview named Johnson. He was in the foothills northeast of Salina. The people of Salina had lost nearly all of their stock.

On 14 Apr 1866, the Indian prisoners, who had been brought from Nephi in March, escaped from prison in Manti. Two were killed in Manti during the escape, but five, including Sanpitch, made it to the West Mountains between Fountain Green and Nephi, south of Salt Creek Canyon. On 19 April, Dolph Bennett and Amasa and George Tucker found their tracks and were joined by others from Moroni. They found the escaped Indians, who were desperate and attacked these men. All five Indians were killed in the skirmish that followed.

When word came to Mount Pleasant of the Salina raids, they organized twenty-five minute men at once, and divided the remainder of men in the town into four parts—each division to attend roll call at least once each day. The horses were kept for service at once in case of a raid. The twenty-five men were immediately mustered in and placed under the command of JOHN L. IVIE. This cavalry company was to act as picket guards for the settlement and went out every day, scouting in the hills and cedars and around the settlement. When the beating of the drum was heard, fear spread, the people congregated, and the minutemen quickly assembled.

On 28 Apr 1866, this letter was received by Bishop [and Major] William S. Seeley.

"Spring City, April 27th Midnight

"Major Seeley:

"We have just received an express from the central station that the Indians attacked Alma Sunday night. No particulars of the attack. The men from Richfield and Glenwood pursued the Indians and at the corner of Marysvale field, were fired upon by the Indians, killing Alfred Lewis and wounding three other men. They then pursued the Indians up the canyon leading to Grass Valley. The Indians attacked the settlers of Circleville, taking twenty-five head of cattle, two mules and two horses. The men were at once in pursuit of them and followed them up into the canyon, but could do nothing as the Indians had secured positions and it would not be safe to attack them.

"We learned also, that the Indians had fired upon two of our men at Bear Creek above Circleville, wounding one slightly. The other man shot and killed one Indian and wounded another. [Major] ALLRED, of Circleville, took two bucks, six squaws, and six papooses, tying them hand and foot, and on the 22nd they broke the cords that bound them and sprung upon the guards. The guards fired upon them, killing all but four papooses. I think we will have to take the field and order men to be on hand . . . Prepare at once, without delay, in case of a forward move.

"Captain IVIE will take charge of the men. I have suggested to the General the impropriety of drawing our men from here while we are menaced by the Indians from Spanish Fork Canyon. We shall make no draft upon Fairview. We shall want them to be prepared in case of an attack. Please copy and forward to Major Larsen of Fairview.

"Yours truly,

"Col. R. N. ALLRED." [Longsdorf *Mount Pleasant* p 108-9]

On 29 Apr 1866, near Fairview, the Indians killed picket guard Thomas Jones and wounded William Avery. The third guard managed to get Avery away on a horse to a place he considered safe, then hurried on for help. Elias Cox, WILLIAM ZABRISKIE and others joined in pursuit of the Indians. They saw the murderers, but did not overtake them. Colonel ALLRED's journal reads:

> "The people in Sanpete had a Co-op herd of stock in Thistle Valley in charge of Noah T. Guyman who camped there in the valley together with his family. The Indians made a raid on Fairview killing one man and wounding another. Fearing for the safety of the herd and family with it, I went into the valley with a company in the night, it being so dark that we could not see the man next to us in line. Thomas Coates of Mount Pleasant piloted us safely through; we found the family and stock safe and moved all into the settlement next day and delivered them to President J. A. ALLRED.
>
> "The following day (May 1st) President Brigham Young issued instructions to the people in Sanpete, Sevier and Piute Counties to move together, in bodies of not less than one hundred and fifty men, arm themselves well, and protect themselves and their stock. The people in the small settlements in Piute County moved to Circleville; those at Monroe and Glenwood in Sevier County to Richfield; those at Fayette, Sanpete County to Gunnison; those at Fairview, Sanpete to Mount Pleasant, and those at Fountain Green and Wales to Moroni in Sanpete County."

Colonel ALLRED learned from the Indians at Circleville, whom they had imprisoned there, that the Utes, Piedes, Pauvans, and Navajo Indians had all joined together, supplying themselves with ammunition to assist Black Hawk in his bloody depredations and massacres.

Quoting R. N. Bennett:

> "DAVID CANDLAND was sent with the epistle for the people of Fairview to move to Mount Pleasant, the people of Fountain Green to Moroni, and the people of Spring City to move to Ephraim. JOHN L. IVIE and myself were sent as CANDLAND's body guards. After these families had moved, the minute men of Mount Pleasant and other settlements had to go as guards for the men while they did their work."

The people of Mount Pleasant sent teams to Fairview to help the people move, which was accomplished in one day. The men then went to Fairview to build a fort for their protection. They completed this in August and all returned to their homes.

The fort to protect the cattle in Mount Pleasant enclosed the block which was later known as the North Sanpete High School Block. It bordered the old fort. Herders were appointed and paid by the head. The tingling of the cowbells was heard every morning at seven o'clock as the cattle were taken to pasture. In the evening one man was assigned as gatekeeper, and after the cattle were accounted for and claimed by the owners, the gate was locked. The guards would patrol both ends of the fort and would call out to each other at specified times throughout the dark nights, "All is well!"

Grandfather JAMES OSCAR IVIE loved to tell us the following incidents:

"During the Indian troubles in the 60's—the Indians had stolen some cattle, and driven them up North Creek Canyon, between Fairview and Mount Pleasant. Father JOHN L. IVIE and his company of minute men were in pursuit, and going up the mountain they gathered up several head of cattle which had been left along the trail, on account of not keeping up with the herd. And up among the timber was discovered a lone Indian covered up with leaves; he was sick, and not able to travel with the rest. Some of the boys wanted to kill him, but father said 'no, we will not shed blood, unless it is necessary,' so they left him and went in pursuit of the Indians and stock till nearly night, when it was decided to give up the chase and return home, taking back what stock they had. On their return they came across the sick Indian sitting up against a tree smoking a pipe. The men still wanted to kill him, but father wouldn't let them."

Some time after that, his father, JOHN L. IVIE was home with his family, but felt disturbed in his mind about the safety of the guards. Unable to relax, he left his home and went to check on his men who were guarding the livestock fort.

"[They] had got together at the north side of the fort, when they heard and saw the cattle getting up from their bed ground and moving away from what they thought might be Indians crawling among them. The cattle kept getting up nearer and nearer to where the three men stood, when father spoke to the others and said, 'that they must be close by.' After that they saw the cattle moving as if something among them was going away from them. When morning came nothing had been molested.

"In the beginning of the 70's—after peace had been restored, an Indian and his family came to our house and spent a day or two. He told father of the occurrence at the fort, explaining that he and four other Indians were there on that occasion and had their guns lying across a cow ready to shoot the three men, when they heard father speak and say, 'They must be close by.' He said he knew father's voice and would not let the others shoot as father had saved his life on the mountain when he was sick. In appreciation he had now saved father's life."

Franklin H. Heath of Wisconsin had succeeded Colonel Irish as Indian Superintendent in March 1866. The militia throughout all the counties of Utah was reorganized. By 1 May 1866, several companies from Davis, Salt Lake, and Utah Counties were on the march, and upon arriving in Sanpete County they reported to Brigadier General Warren S. Snow.

A company of cavalry from Salt Lake City under Colonel Heber P. Kimball and Major John Clark, reached Manti on 5 May, and was ordered to march up the Sevier River and assist the settlers in moving into Sanpete County. About 10 May, a company of cavalry arrived from Utah County (A. G. Conover, captain). They occupied a picket post near the abandoned town of Salina on the Sevier River. They were under the command of Brigadier General William B. Pace. Other counties responded, including Brigadier General Lot Smith of Davis County who mustered a company of cavalry for ninety days of service. All of this extra help allowed the Sanpete County settlers to plant and harvest their crops.

With the increasing militia in Sanpete and Sevier Counties, Black Hawk looked for opportunities in the southern, western and northern counties,

"as far south as Washington County where, under instructions of Brigadier-General Erastus Snow, a company under Captain James Andrus had taken the field and had lost in one expedition private Elijah Everett Jr., slain by the savages." [*Indian Depredations*]

The Everett brothers, George, Elijah and Elisha were converted to the church in Hamilton, Illinois, 1835, during WILLIAM SHELTON IVIE's mission.

"As far north as Cache County there was the same alert and unceasing watchfulness against hostile inroads or outbreaks, and at one time during the year as many as twenty-five-hundred men were under arms. The number killed during the season's campaign was—of whites about twenty and of Indians between forty and fifty. The settlers stock herds were reduced nearly two thousand, and rarely were any of the animals recovered."

In the months of April through September, Wasatch County [Heber City] experienced five raids. The Black Hawk war was expanding rapidly.

JAMES RUSSELL IVIE and most of his children with their families were living in Round Valley (Scipio) after the spring of 1863. His great-granddaughter NETTIE M. ROBINS tells us:

"[When they arrived] the settlers were still in Graball or Robinsville where there was a branch of the church. The IVIES . . . went west a little further south up in the valley about two miles from Graball. . . . A stream of water came from the little lake about seven or eight miles further south in the valley. It separated into two streams. The west stream went by the settlers at Graball. The east stream was just running to waste. It was on the east fork that JAMES RUSSELL IVIE and family stopped. It was known as Ivie Creek for years. Not long after this President Young visited the people here and advised them to all locate closer together on the townsite in the valley . . . The IVIEs were the first to build homes on the new townsite. The first home built was a room put up of logs. It was the old stable on the Joe Miller lot. It was built by WILLIAM FRANKLIN IVIE, son of JAMES RUSSELL IVIE. His family lived there until he could get logs out to build a place for them to live. This stable was used to keep a fine stallion in. He had brought it there with other live stock of horses and cattle. Grandfather JAMES RUSSELL IVIE built his home and owned the old Joseph Stone lot. It is on the northwest corner from the public square. . . . JAMES RUSSELL IVIE was interested both in his church and civil affairs. Both he and his son, WILLIAM FRANKLIN IVIE were block teachers and JAMES RUSSELL IVIE was president of the Field Committee and Water Master. He was also very interested in education. He helped with the loan of his teams to move the log school house from Graball to the new townsite.

"Great-grandfather and grandmother had shared their home with an Indian boy whose father was a half-breed French and Indian and whose mother was an Indian woman. They were from New Mexico. Their names were Perble. The Indian boy's name was Shindy Perble. After his mother's death the father was on his way to Colorado. However, his son was sick, so the father left him with the IVIEs. The father stayed through the winter and went to Colorado in the spring. Great-grandmother, ELIZA McKEE FAUCETT IVIE, cared for Shindy Perble, the little Indian boy. She always thought of him as a son. My mother, a little girl then, called him Uncle SHIND. I have heard her say she thought as much of him as she did of any of her uncles.

"Great-grandmother ELIZA was one of our good pioneer mothers who nursed and cared for many babies and helped them see the light of day . . . So far as wealth or worldly goods, we find theirs was a limited supply. I think I would be safe in saying that in Spiritual goods theirs will be a rich supply. They left their all for the Gospel's sake. Great-grandfather gave his life helping to build a community and surrounding his family with the necessities of life.

"Both grandparents had received their patriarchal blessings. I can remember . . . seeing dear little grandma going to the old black box or chest, as she called it, reach in and bring out her blessing, hand it to my mother and ask her to read it. It seemed such a source of strength and comfort to her in her last days. The one thing I remember in it was that their posterity should be as Jacob's of old and as numerous as the sands of the sea. From their thirteen children, twelve of them grew to maturity, marrying and are parents of large families. A host of grandchildren, some over one-hundred and twenty-five. I am happy to be counted among their great-grandchildren."

Near the end of May 1866 according to great-grandson, LLOYD O. IVIE:

"JAMES RUSSELL IVIE . . . happened down by the town store to encounter some men who were idling, whittling and in general panning some of the authorities as such were sometimes wont to do. He listened for a few moments, and then, looking them squarely in the eye said, 'I know the Gospel is true and I only hope I can prove faithful to the end,' not knowing, of course, that he was leaving his final testimony for generations to come."

Two weeks later, on 10 Jun 1866, JAMES RUSSELL IVIE, age 63, was awakened early that Sunday morning by a neighbor and told that one of his cows had freshened down by the lake. He walked down to the herd to bring her and her calf in, accompanied by his twenty-year-old son MARTIN. After they had gone a short distance, Father IVIE turned to his son and said:

"Maybe, you had better go back and help with the chores to be in time for church. I can make out all right."

The pasture lands were located a little northwest of the settlement of Scipio in what was called the pond field. A lake was there at that time, but with the reservoirs today it is rarely seen. The area is located west of Interstate-15—driving by one spring, with the melting of heavy snow, I saw it.

"As he neared the cattle, the Indians came out of the cedars southwest of the lake. There were two or three hundred of them. Father IVIE ran out into the water in an attempt to escape. But the bullets of the savages reached him, and his body was hard to find because only one elbow showed above the surface." [Records of my uncle LLOYD O. IVIE]

Some records say he had three Indian arrows in his body.

An Indian war-hoop rang throughout Round Valley. This alerted the people of the town and they rushed to look for the kindly, 63-year-old Father IVIE. When they found his body, he had been stripped of his clothing except his boots, which the Indians were unable to get off. The young herder, Henry Wright, was also killed. The Indians drove off 500 head of stock, according to *Indian Depredations*. Included with this stock was the beautiful stallion, which belonged to the IVIEs. Black Hawk quickly claimed this prize and rode him during the battle—only hours later on the eastern side of this mountain range.

The Indians drove the complete herd eastward–past Scipio and into the canyon towards Salina. This unexpected first Indian raid in Round Valley on a Sunday, when even the horses were pasturing and resting, left the church-going Scipio militia without the means to pursue the Indians. A messenger was dispatched to Fort Gunnison on one of the few remaining horses, knowing that General William B. Pace with a company of thirty men was stationed there—but he and a few of his men were on their way to Manti. They caught him at Twelve Mile Creek (Mayfield), and the company hurried to Gunnison through a heavy thunder storm. Here he organized his men and started east. Vacated Salina was reached by daylight, where they planned to rest, but one of the pickets discharged his gun—the signal that the enemy was within sight.

From *Indian Depredations* page 201:

"Looking to the southwest, and just opposite the Gravelly Ford could be seen a band of Indians driving a bunch of cattle. [This is near the town of Vermillion, where both Colonel IVIE and grandfather JAMES OSCAR IVIE would later have farms and where my mother was born. Grandfather IVIE had a large collection of Indian arrowheads that he later found in his fields.] The Indians were evidently trying to make the ford, which if reached in time would give them the passes to the mountains on the east [Interstate 70], and insure them a clean getaway with the stock. General Pace ordered an advance, and the distance of eight miles to the Gravelly Ford was covered under whip. The advance guard was about two hundred yards in the lead when the point of the mountain was reached [and this first group passed it without harm], but when the [rest of the] company reached that place they were fired upon by the Indians from ambush at the close range of sixty paces.

"The whites were commanded to cross-fire, and the Indians were routed, but about this time the Indians were reinforced from the band driving the cattle on the west. A guard of Indians was left over the cattle on the west side of the river, while Indians to the number of seventy-five or eighty engaged in fighting on the east side. The whites retreated to higher ground and made the crest of a hill serve as breast-works for them. While making this retreat, William Tunbridge was wounded in the leg just as he was mounting his mule, but when assisted in his saddle, he continued to fight.

"After reaching the higher ground, the Indians surrounded the whites and began to close in on them until by command the militia began to fire by platoons; this manner of fighting proved very effective, for at every fire an Indian or his horse would drop. Then the Indians began to circle around, and when a point of advantage was gained, they fired on the whites. There was one particular point from which most of the shooting was done. A wash led in the direction of the point, and James E. Snow determined to put a stop to the practice of firing from it. He followed the wash nearly to the mouth, and then dropped behind a large sage-brush, which he used for a rest to shoot from. He soon got range on an Indian who was trying to put one of his wounded on a horse. The horse being between Snow and the Indian, he could not see the body of the Indian, but judging from the position of his feet and legs, he decided that by shooting the horse through the body in the region of the heart the same shot would get the red man. The aim proved true, for at the report of the rifle the horse fell and the Indian was wounded. He was picked up by two of his braves and spirited away.

"The wounded Indian was none other than the famous Black Hawk, though at the time it was not known. [And the horse that was killed was the beautiful stallion belonging to the IVIEs.] Mr. Snow had a narrow escape in this affair, for he was fully 600 yards from the rest of the whites and was closely pursued by three of the enemy. While getting away from them, Snow caught his saber between his legs and fell. Four men were dispatched to rescue him and thus he was saved from the torture of the red men."

[Note: More will be said about this incident later. Remember, Snow was 600 yards away. His vision of the Indian was blocked by the stallion. Another wounded Indian was being placed on a horse. The action was very rapid. It was later decided that it was Black Hawk.]

"When the tide of the battle seemed turned in favor of the whites, though their ammunition was by this time exhausted, a cloud of dust from the direction of Round Valley [Scipio] suggested to the militia that more Indians were coming; a retreat was therefore ordered. Black Hawk's good fortune again befriended him. The approaching horsemen were a company of Fillmore cavalry, seventy strong under Captain Owens. Before they effected a junction with General Pace the slippery foe were safe in their mountain fastnesses."

Millard Milestones records:

"Many men in Millard County were called upon to join a posse to follow Black Hawk and his warriors, who had killed JAMES [RUSSELL] IVIE and Henry Wright, young son of Jonathan C. Wright, who was herding cows at Round Valley (Scipio). The Indians had swooped down on this section and taken three-hundred head of cattle, driving them up the canyon towards Sevier County. Runners were sent to the north, but by the time sufficient help arrived, orders came to Captain Owens not to pursue the Indians any farther.

"Jacob Croft and John Powell were working at a sawmill at the mouth of the canyon just before the Black Hawk raid. Jacob Croft dreamed the Indians came and killed the two men; he was so impressed by this dream, that he and Mr. Powell immediately left for Fillmore, or no doubt they, too, would have been killed."

Accompaning the group of Captain Owens were several men from Scipio. The Filmore group brought them extra horses and several of JAMES RUSSELL IVIE's descendants were amongst them.

My husband GROVER SWALLOW's ancestors, JAMES DUNCAN and WILLIAM HENRY STOTT were with Captain Owens, as they were Black Hawk War veterans with his militia. Great-grandfather JENS F. MORTENSEN was probably with the militia from Gunnison at Gravelly Ford. A very young (Grandmother) ANNIE C. MORTENSEN (Ivie) later recalled,

"I remember that while we lived in Gunnison, Father would get up at night every time a whistle would blow and get dressed and go after the Indians. It seemed like they beat a drum some of the times."

From a *Sketch of WILLIAM FRANKLIN IVIE* of Scipio by his granddaughter ELIZA ANN IVIE JOHNSTON—there are inaccuracies, but it gives her memories:

"The raids on the stock had cleaned all horses and cattle from their fields—240 horses, 6 mules and 800 head of cattle including the work oxen and milk cows. Some few head of stock and horses escaped the Indians and came back home. A few milk cows and work animals had been procured from neighboring towns.

"Just about this time an incident occurred that had and still has a direct effect on the IVIE clan. The town of Gunnison across the mountains east on the Gunnison River was attacked by Indians and completely wiped out, not a person left alive. This was a terrible blow to the colonizing plans of the church and the plans of Brigham Young. A so called friendly Indian visited Scipio on one of his begging trading trips. [He] stayed around several days eating and visiting with the people. No one was afraid of him as he was thought to be a good man. He was visiting in a crowd of men in the open space of the Fort one day. Of course the subject to the late disaster of the neighbor town of Gunnison came up. This Indian said he was one of the Braves who accomplished the great victory--laughing and bragging. He was talking to men who were all members of the [HENRY] McARTHUR'S Minute Men Co. These men were not armed at the time except the two IVIE boys, who were the Official Scouts of the Company and who always wore their guns and knives—WILLIAM ALFORD IVIE, son of WILLIAM FRANKLIN IVIE, and a distant cousin JOSEPH JOHNSTON IVIE . . . JIM IVIE, son of the murdered JAMES RUSSELL IVIE was standing near scout JOE—hearing the Indian talk—suddenly he seized the gun of Scout JOE and shot and killed the bragging Indian spy. Later JIM IVIE was arrested by the county officers on a charge of murder. At his trial at Fillmore, Utah, he was found guilty and was sentenced to be turned over to the still warring Indians for torture and death. The McARTHUR Minute Men Company was at once assembled by the Scipio people and they did some driving up and down the streets of Fillmore, talking loud. At an afternoon session of the same court the same day, a new hearing was had. JIM IVIE was found to be justified in the shooting and was paroled to McARTHUR's Company . . . But even to this day, we often hear the old cry 'JIM IVIE killed an Indian and that brought on the Black Hawk war.'"

The Fillmore court records of 15 Jul 1866 state that Capt. HENRY McARTHUR of Round Valley had ordered the shooting of the Indian Pannikay--according to his own statement under oath before the Probate Court. Evidently, JIM IVIE had taken the gun from the young militia scout, JOE IVIE, after the two scouts were reluctant to follow the order. Some testimony stated that JIM IVIE followed the Indian who had left the fort, and shot him a distance away.

As we are all aware, the Black Hawk War had been in progress on the other side of these mountains for over a year before this incident occurred. Since this was the first incident in their valley, the settlers may have considered it the beginning for them. Militia had already come from Salt Lake, Davis, and Utah Counties to aid the Saints in Sanpete and Sevier Counties, to allow them to plant their crops. Perhaps it was the massacre of Captain Gunnison and his exploring party that the granddaughter referred to in this account, which happened in October 1853 on the Sevier River near the town of Deseret in Millard County, where twelve innocent United States army soldiers were killed in revenge by the Indians in retaliation for depredations committed upon them by a group passing through to California. A detailed account of this incident can be found in *Indian Depredations* by Gottfredson. I have not found any references to a massacre such as she described in the town of Gunnison, which was named after the US military Captain Gunnison. My Salina ancestors moved to Gunnison for safety. Panacara was probably bragging about aiding in the killing of these soldiers. Although ELIZA's account is undoubtedly hearsay, she grew up in Scipio and as a child knew the two scouts who were there. Her account reflects the feelings and rumors circulated throughout that community.

On 12 Feb 1914, William Probert of Manti, Utah, wrote a letter, claiming to tell the true story of the events. This letter is also hearsay, as he was not there; but it seems to be the version recorded and accepted by most historians. In Probert's story he seems to whitewash the dead Indian Panacara, and condemn JIM IVIE as a vindictive man. This much is true; JIM IVIE was indicted by the Grand Jury in Fillmore for murder, not at the fort, but after following the Indian a short distance. The prisoner was released to the military by the Probate Court when Captain HENRY McARTHUR testified under oath that he had ordered "Pannikay" to be killed. With the Captain's testimony, the court released JIM IVIE and censured HENRY McARTHUR. (Copies of these court records are included later.) Probert's letter was written about 40 years later.

Thirteen years before, during the Walker War, 17 Jul 1853, JIM IVIE, in self-defense of his family and himself, killed an Indian and was blamed by some to have started the Walker War. [See Part I: DRIVEN] It was a totally different incident, but confusing later perhaps to some.

The following is copied from the *Deseret News Weekly*:

"The Colonel [JOHN LEHI IVIE] requests us to publish the following card with regard to some statements made by a city contemporary: 'SALT LAKE CITY, July 2d, 1872 Editor Deseret News: I wish to correct a statement which appeared in the Herald this morning regarding my deceased father, who was murdered by Indians at Scipio in 1866. The statement that my father was killed by Indians out of revenge for having himself killed an Indian is totally untrue. My father came to Utah in 1848 and from that time till he was massacred he was a friend to the Indians, and was well known for his mild and peaceable character.

"I will also state that the circumstances which led to the killing of an Indian by my brother JAMES were as follows: The Indian whom he killed came to Scipio the evening before the raid was made, in which my father was killed, and carried intelligence to the marauding party of Indians concerning the condition of the settlement. After the raid was made this treacherous Indian returned, pretending friendliness, while my father's blood was scarcely dried on the ground. Under these circumstances my brother killed him. These are facts which I can prove at any time. I had the Indian interpreter in Sanpete County inquire about the matter of the chief who led the marauding party who killed my father, and he states that the Indian who was killed was in communication with the party for ten days before the raid was made.

"I may say, in addition to the above, that besides killing my father they took $10,000 worth of property which belonged to him, and about $7,000 worth which belonged to my brother.

Respectfully,   J. L. IVIE."

In Sanpete and Sevier Counties, after the Battle of Gravelly Ford, the militia continued to follow the wounded Black Hawk and his braves to regain their animals. The march went on for several days until

"the condition of the troops was seen to be perilous. A retreat was again ordered, and it was none too soon; the command was scarcely able to get out of the desert, owing to the weakness of both horses and men; of the latter there were several whose mouths and tongues were so sore that they could scarcely speak." [*Indian Depredations* page 206.]

A few days later on 21 Jun 1866, Captain Albert Peter Dewey of Colonel

Kimball's command was ordered to establish a post in Thistle Valley in the north end of Sanpete County. His command consisted of twenty-two cavalry and thirty-five infantry, the latter under Captain Jesse West, who started from Moroni on the 21st of June. Since this battle was written and told to us as children by my grandfather, JAMES OSCAR IVIE, it is included as he wrote it:

"On the 21st of June, 1866, a company of men or soldiers were sent to assist the Sanpete people with their Indian troubles and landing in Thistle Valley on the 23rd, they camped on the east side of the valley by a deep wash on the south and near the mouth of Indian Hollow. They were told not to camp there, because of danger; but the reply was, 'We'll show the Sanpete *wooden feet* how to fight Indians!"

The term wooden feet came from the wooden shoes that many of the Danish people of Sanpete County liked to wear.

"The result—as the Captain Peter Dewey told me himself, about 1906, when Father and I were in Salt Lake City. Mr. Dewey knew Father and hailed him and after shaking hands, Father introduced me to him. Mr. Dewey put his arm around me and said 'Young man, do you know that I look upon your father as a savior?' I asked, 'How is that?'

"He said, 'I was Captain of the company that went to help the Sanpete Wooden Feet fight the Indians. When I pitched camp in Thistle Valley, they told me to go to the center of the valley; then it would be safer in case of an Indian attack; but I knew more than they did and was not afraid of Indians. We put our wagons in the shape of a circle and camped in the most dangerous place in the valley--a large wash 35 yards on the north; cedars 75 yards on the east and the Indian Hollow southeast of us. We turned our horses out to graze, except two that we kept in the circle in case of need. Twenty-six were turned out, which the Indians took first thing in the morning.

"'We got up early and saw the smoke of a fire about two miles north of us on the point of a hill. A few minutes later, west of the valley, we saw two more smokes, then one south--an Indian custom to call them together. A short time after the smoke appeared, we saw Indians coming in all directions. When they got closer, I could see there would be too many for us, so I told two men to take the horses in the circle and go to the valley for help as we could count 150 to 200 Indians coming upon us.

"'The two men started, but were chased by the Indians and one was killed. The Indians surrounded us and took to the cedars where they had protection. We only had our wagons. We fired on them and a battle ensued which lasted most of the day and our ammunition was gone, except myself, and I only had 25 loads left. I got on the front wagon wheel where I could watch and every Indian that stuck his head above the bank, I tried to hit him and let all the other parts go. The Indians were closing in on us and the men were walking in the circle of the wagons and wringing their hands, saying, 'What will we do? We will all be massacred in a short time!'

"'At this stage of the action, one of the men saw horses—white men or Indians?—coming on the road southwest and reported that help was coming. By looking through the glasses, we saw they were white men.

"'All day, the Indian Chief was on the hill giving commands. He was busy at that time commanding his men and about seventy-five Indians lined up between the help and our wagons, which looked impossible for aid with the help that was coming.'

"The rest, I will tell as father told it to me. Father said, 'When word reached Mount Pleasant that the company were overpowered with Indians, I was three miles east of town looking for fresh signs. Hagard Wilcox came and soon found me by firing a gun, a signal that I was wanted.' Father joined Wilcox and learning the particulars, they hurried to town, changed horses, and were on their way to the scene of trouble. They started with only ten men and rode very fast, making eighteen miles in about one and one-half hours. Eight more joined them when they got to the divide. There were Indians on the road in the cedars, firing on them and trying to delay them or their speed in getting to the company. By crossing a hollow, they kept out of range of their guns. Then about thirty-five Indians fell in behind them and when father neared the Salt Lake Company, there were seventy-five Indians lined up between him and the wagons and those coming behind.

"Father called a halt and looked over the situation. Seeing the Chief on the side hill, about three hundred yards, giving orders or commands, he jumped off his horse and said, 'Boys, watch the Chief!' Father had a new Henry rifle, one of the first that came to Utah. Taking aim, the chief rolled off his horse at the crack of father's gun. Another Indian by him picked up the chief, put him on his horse, jumped on behind him and went up through the cedars, through the canyon.

"After shooting the Chief, Father jumped on his horse and said, 'Boys, fight your way through to the wagons.' The men all started on the run; but not a gun was fired. The Indians seeing their chief shot, run in every direction toward the canyon. The men went through to the wagons and found the men all alive, but one wounded.

"Father followed the company of Indians to the canyon and found that the Indians had washed the Chief's wound and gone up Rock Canyon, which was very rough. Father, knowing that it would be dangerous to go into the canyon, returned to the wagons. He put harnesses on their saddle horses, drove the wagons into the center of the valley and camped for the night. The next day, he went to Mount Pleasant with all the company."

So—there were eighteen men with great-grandfather Colonel JOHN L. IVIE. There were about thirty-five Indians pursuing them and seventy-five Indians blocking their approach to Captain Peter Dewey's trapped fifty-six soldiers, who were nearly out of ammunition. The Chief was directing from a nearby hill. With one shot from IVIE's rifle the Chief fell from his horse wounded. Concerned for their Chief, the Indians rushed to his side. The rescuers arrived at Dewey's camp without another shot being fired. There were no raids for another six weeks.

Four of my male IVIE cousins surrounded me after viewing Sibley's video of the "Blackhawk War," in which I had a small part, and emphatically informed me that the IVIE family says that the chief was Black Hawk, and they strongly disagreed with the historian's assessment that Black Hawk was wounded severely at Gravelly Ford, for the following reasons:

1. This Chief was of such importance that the whole encounter was immediately ended.

2. The settlers knew the Indian chiefs. Black Hawk was the only one known to be wounded.

3. The raids continued after Gravelly Ford, but ended after this encounter for six weeks.

4. A bullet, from the usual rifles of that day, going through a horse and then wounding an Indian as is claimed at Gravelly Ford would not have had sufficient strength to have resulted in the severe wound that Black Hawk was known to have received.

5. Colonel IVIE was a peaceful man. He loved the Indians. Some were like brothers to him. His parents had raised a half-breed Indian/French as their

own son. Colonel IVIE had no desire to be notorious in this way. He did not want to wound any Indian. The shot was only fired in defense of his men, himself, and to save the lives of Captain Dewey and his men.

6. In most raids, Black Hawk usually led the raid. His usual pattern did not include sitting on a hill to direct his braves, but an already slightly wounded Black Hawk might do this.

"This [the incident with Captain A. P. Dewey] was the last military event of importance in Sanpete County that season, and a few weeks afterwards the larger part of the troops from the northern counties returned [to their homes] and were mustered out . . . But with the withdrawal of the outside militia, the efforts of the local militia organizations were not relaxed. The men rendered uncomplaining service on picket guard and in occasional reconnaissance into the mountains, and the officers were vigilant and full of energy. Their scanty crops had to be harvested, and winter's supply of fuel gathered, protection furnished their remaining flocks and herds, and winter's forage provided. All this work had to be performed by men under arms or attended by an armed escort. And it is remembered that the sleepless foe ranged over and ravaged a district three hundred miles in extent, burning saw-mills, ranges and isolated ranches, and causing the abandonment of a number of flourishing villages. The heroism of the settlers in resisting by night and day the terrifying attacks of the marauders is worthy of the warmest praise. In nearly every part of the Territory regular guard duty was ordered." [Indian Depredations]

ELIZA McKEE FAUSETT IVIE,
widow of JAMES RUSSELL IVIE

THEIR GRAVES ARE LOCATED IN THE OLD WEED-COVERED PIONEER CEMETERY NEAR SCIPIO, UTAH.

~ 34 ~

THE NOTORIOUS JAMES ALEXANDER (JIM) IVIE

JIM IVIE is often characterized as the villain in many of the Utah histories. This prejudice and bigotry precipitated his excommunication from the Church. His posterity asked my uncle LLOYD O. IVIE to help them clear his name. This chapter gives this brief history.

JAMES ALEXANDER IVIE was born in eastern Missouri on the 17 Mar 1830—just a few weeks before the L.D.S. Church was organized on 6 Apr 1830. His family and close relations soon joined the Church. In the early church records these members were referred to as the Salt River settlement, organized in 1832, with his uncle JOHN ANDERSON IVIE presiding elder. This eastern Missouri settlement became the meeting place of the three groups of Zion's Camp coming from various directions to aid the devastated saints driven from western Jackson County. JIM's father and many of his close relatives joined Zion's Camp as they continued west across the state. His family moved to Far West in Caldwell County. They were driven back to eastern Missouri, and helped, in 1839, Parley P. Pratt after he escaped from prison and needed to cross the Mississippi River. Nine-year-old JIM and younger JOHN L. IVIE recognized "Brother Pratt" and helped him hide until their father returned. JIM IVIE gave him his new straw hat to help with his disguise.

Seven years later, sixteen-year-old JIM and thirteen-year-old JOHN L. IVIE watched as their older brother RICHARD married, and joined the Mormon Battalion at Council Bluffs--along with many of their cousins and close associates. The young boys befriended the local Indians and were given the only horse that could outrun the buffalo. They greatly helped by providing buffalo meat. The family was with Brigham Young's first company crossing the plains in 1848.

In March of 1849, his family was called to go south and build a fort on the Provo River. This was called Fort Utah. The valley was a favorite home for the Indians with the best fishing rivers in the area. Indian problems came. All able-bodied men and boys were members of the militia and fought in the Battle for Fort Utah.

In 1853, the settlers were tired of living in the fort and many had moved onto city lots and others to the more isolated areas. Twenty-three-year-old JIM had a small home near the river by Springville with his wife and two tiny children. The Indians had been capturing children from other tribes and selling them as slaves into Mexico in exchange for guns and ammunition. The territorial authorities tried to stop this practice. Tension between the whites and the Indians was increasing. Historians like to keep things neat, so they name the various wars with the Indians, although the Mormons never declared war on the Indians at any time. When the Indians sent war parties to kill the whites and steal their herds, the pioneers were told to move into the forts, form militia, and protect themselves and their animals.

The following, written by my uncle LLOYD O. IVIE, is in the records of the Church Historian Archives:

"On that fateful July 17, 1853, JIM IVIE was at work on a well on his own property. When the squaw came on his premises to trade fish for flour, he knew he would have to humor her. There was nothing to be gained for him in the bargaining. Anyone who knew the streams in those days, during spawning season, could testify that it was possible to go along the banks even without hook and line and in a few moments time pull out with bare hands all the fish he could carry. Flour, on the other hand, was scarce, and hard to get at any price. In July the old crop of wheat is exhausted and the new is still not harvested. Uncle JIM simply did not have the flour to trade. A pint of flour for a fish was at that time all he could spare to pacify the Indians.

"After the trade was made, Uncle JIM returned to his work in the well, and with the squaw still in his house, two armed Indians came up. One of them went over to the well and watched Uncle JIM. They could not possibly have known the outcome of the barter. ...

"Imagine yourself down a well six or seven feet deep, with nothing but a small pole for a ladder, and with an armed Indian looking down on you. Suddenly your wife, who is alone in the house with two small babes, comes to the door and screams, 'Come quick, JIM. He's beating her shamefully.' . . . Critics have damned Uncle JIM because he went running; they would have damned him worse, if he hadn' t. . . . When Uncle JIM reached the house the Indian was beating, jumping on, and kicking his squaw, whom in an insane outburst he had thrown on the floor. JIM seized the Indian and shoved him out the door. The Indian, who had set his gun down at the door, seized the weapon and aimed it straight at Uncle JIM. He would have shot Uncle JIM on the spot--and behind Uncle JIM were his wife and family.

"The ensuing struggle took place in the yard. Uncle JIM gained possession of the barrel of the gun. It broke. The Indian struck Uncle JIM with the stock on the left cheek, laying the flesh open to the bone. It left a scar which he carried to the grave. In return, Uncle JIM dealt him a blow with the barrel, which later proved fatal. The other Indian had his bow in readiness and shot the arrow, which sunk deeper than an inch into Uncle JIM's shoulder--not merely passing through his shirt. A blow from the gun barrel was Uncle JIM's answer to the arrow and the second Indian fell to the ground. At this point the squaw rushed out with the stick of firewood and struck Uncle JIM a smashing blow across the mouth, and he was forced to meet her onslaught as he had the others. The cheek wound and the arrow had already roused him to the terror of a life and death struggle, or it is doubtful that he ever would have struck the squaw. In each case, the Indian had been the aggressor. It is significant, too, that as soon as his assailants were overcome, Uncle JIM turned to assist them.

"At this point, William Kelly, who was passing, came upon the scene. A fourth Indian appeared, who, when asked to go to the stream for some water, broke for the Indian camp instead--as fast as he could go. On Kelly's advice, Uncle JIM quickly hitched up a team and with his family drove into town.

"It is hard to believe that anyone could think of Uncle JIM's 'relishing' such a fight. It is an unfortunate happening. Uncle JIM regretted it more than anything else in the world. In spite of the mistakes which he made later and which he acknowledged in tears to my father in his declining years, history should grant him the full measure of truth to which he is entitled in the Springville incident."

The two brothers fought with the militia in Utah and Sanpete Counties until peace was somewhat established. A few months later JOHN L. IVIE was called on an Indian mission to build Fort Supply and to teach and preach to the

Indians in the Wyoming area--and shortly after, JIM IVIE was called to join him. During the cold winter months, lessons were given to the men to help them speak and understand the Indian language. The two young men were next called on the Elk Mountain Indian Mission near present day Moab. The Indians killed a few and drove the rest out of this area. The IVIE families helped build the larger Fort Ephraim. JIM IVIE was called again to the Fort Supply mission the following year, with his wife and children. They would be of great service to the Willie and Martin Handcart companies. He is listed on the memorial plaque as one of the rescuers.

JIM and JOHN IVIE packed their wagons and joined with Lot Smith in Echo Canyon. We find their names delivering an express from General Daniel H. Wells to Church headquarters—

"The above express was forwarded by JOHN L. IVY and JAMES IVY. They started at the rising of the moon. Gen. Wells was on Bear River and the army had moved up Ham's Creek."

Fort Supply was burned and never rebuilt with the approach of Johnston's Army, 1857.

JIM went with the rest of the IVIEs when they settled in Round Valley (Scipio) in the spring of 1863. Here his father was killed by the Indians in June 1866. Here JIM IVIE killed the Indian "Pannikary," and was first charged with murder and then acquitted. Uncle LLOYD O. IVIE continues:

"In those days the apostles lived out among the people. Orson Hyde was in Spring City; Moses Thatcher was in Cache Valley, and Erastus Snow was in Dixie. One of the apostles from the south came through Scipio on his way to Salt Lake City. He heard, so the story in the family goes, the testimony of the opposition and forthwith cut Uncle JIM off the church and proceeded on to Salt Lake where he reported the matter to President Brigham Young, whose response was as follows: He reared up out of his seat, brought his fist down on the table and said, 'You go right back down there and reinstate that man!' These words represent Uncle JIM's own testimony to my father (JAMES OSCAR IVIE). The subsequent happening also attests their veracity. Elder Snow did return to Scipio (or the apostle who did excommunicate Uncle JIM; father was not sure of the name.) He went to Uncle JIM's home, and because the latter was out in the field, waited in the front room until evening. Uncle JIM came in from the yard through the kitchen door, where he was apprised of the Apostles' presence. He washed his hands and face, 'tidied up a bit' and went into the front room and shook hands.

"'JIM,' the apostle arose and said, 'I have come back to fix things up, if I have put any straws in your path, I want to remove them.'

"Reference to the excommunication as a 'straw' cut Uncle JIM to the quick. 'If its straws,' he replied, 'I can remove them myself.' He turned and walked out of the room. The interview was ended.

"At this time Uncle JIM was thirty-six years old. His whole life had been for the church. He knew of mobs, traitors, and treachery before he came west––and he had come for the Gospel's sake, he had faced gunfire and arrows on the Provo, in Sanpete and at Moab. He had endured trouble and turmoil all his days because of the Prophet and the cause he loved. A Straw?—It might as well have been a dagger in his heart.

"Of course, he erred seriously in this attitude. Without doubt he should have been more humble. The excommunication stood. The rest of his life was spent at his ranch at Maple Grove in Scipio and then at his rock home in Salina––on the west after crossing the creek southward. I was born a mere block north of it in mother's parent's place and my father's homestead was eight miles south of the river at the point of Rocky Ford hill. We always passed his home when we went to town. Father stopped often to pass the time of day, eat dinner with Uncle JIM and Aunt LIBBY, or say 'Hello' to their children: JIM WILL, CHARLEY, or WILLIS, whose homes were in a row adjoining their father's.

"And here is a very pertinent fact in the later years of Uncle JIM's life––he never at any time to the day of his death denied his testimony of the gospel. When my father was called on a mission in the early 1890s, Uncle JIM was as proud of the call as was his brother JOHN––my grandfather. He rejoiced in the work and often talked about his life in the church. He admitted that those were the happiest days of his life.

"Hear this testimony from Hilmer Peterson who came from Sweden as a ten-year-old boy in a convert family. Hilmer related this to me in 1935, while I was doing audit work for the government: 'One thing I remember about Salina is Old Man IVIE. I hadn't been there long and couldn't speak English very well. One day he put his hand on my shoulder, there on the sunny side of the street, and talked to me about the church for a long time. He asked me many questions about why we came to Utah,—why we joined the church and how we liked America. And I always remember the last thing he said, 'Young man, I would be willing to crawl on my belly from the

Atlantic to the Pacific if I could say that I knew Mormonism was not true.'

"One evening near the end of his life—(He died March 15, 1926, age 96)—on his way home from town, he met father on the creek bridge where they stood leaning on the railing and talking for a long time. 'OSCAR,' he said, 'I know the gospel is true just as well as you do.' He allowed that the reason he didn't live it any better was 'because of the old nick' in him.

"In those declining days father was closer to him than his own children. Not because of estrangement, however. Most of them had moved away. In fact, it was father and I who sat at his bedside during the last hours of his life. I have in recent years asked neighbors--then children who played with his grandchildren--what they remembered of Uncle JIM. Was he kind–honest–a good neighbor, etc.? Could they remember anything evil . . . or disagreeable, or objectionable about him? Nothing.

"On the contrary, I received this witness of his oldest son, JIM WILL, who was the nearest like his father. It came from a stranger who came one day to my office in the Federal building. Hearing the name 'IVIE' he remarked, 'I used to live next door to an IVIE. He was the finest gentleman, and one of the best neighbors I ever had in my life'.

"In my humble belief . . . Uncle JIM will be exonerated. He may have to face charges of pride and stubbornness of heart in not being patient--in not schooling his feelings sufficiently to reconcile with Apostle Snow. But the charge of murder will not stick forever, because he was not that kind of man. He was not a murderer.

"October 12, 1964

LLOYD O. IVIE: Salt Lake City, Utah."

[After prayer and consideration, his priesthood was restored to him, as affirmed by the following letter addressed to my uncle LLOYD.]

An older
JAMES ALEXANDER IVIE

"Idaho Falls, Idaho –
November 21, 1965

Dear Cousin LLOYD,

Elder [Ezra Taft] Benson . . . met us at the temple as scheduled and by the laying on of hands conferred (restored all the blessings of the priesthood I.E.—all the previous blessings) upon him. It was a wonderful spiritual occasion. . . . The spirit was there. . . .

Most gratefully your cousin, FLORENCE T. REES."

JAMES ALEXANDER IVIE—Trial Records

Case of Murder   Fillmore City, Millard County

The People of the
United States in
The Territory of Utah   In Probate Court of Said Co.

V.S.

James A. Ivie   Hon. T. R. King Presiding

We the Grand Jurors of the aforesaid County, having been duly empanelled, sworn and charged to inquire into all crimes that have been committed in the aforesaid County do xxx and present. That one James A. Ivie, of Scipio, did on or about the 15th of June A.D. 1866 in the County aforesaid commit the crime of Murder by shooting a certain Parawan Indian named Pannikary in or near the town of Scipio which act is contrary to the Laws and statutes in such cases made and provided.

Hirum Mace   Foreman

Official Documents concerning James A. Ivie

Territory of Utah	)	In the Probate Court
Millard County	)	of said County
	)	July 12th 1866
Indictments	)	Shooting an Indian
Against James A. Ivie	)	named Pannikay
for the crime of Murder:	)	Hon. Thomas A. King Presiding.

Counsel for Defense in behalf of his Client Pleaded not guilty and wished the Court to issue an order for the appearance of Lieutenant General Wells and Gen. Snow. Court ruled that it had no power to call military officers from the field while in active service and therefore it declined issuing a compulsory order for the appearance of aforesaid gentlemen. Defense refused to proceed to trial without those gentlemen unless the prosecution would admit what they wished to prove by them Viz. That James A. Ivie was acting under the military orders of General Wells and Snow.

Court called for the proof and ruled that it could not accept of Defendants plea of not guilty and at the same time to plea that he was justified in killing the Indian on account of Military Orders, whereupon Defendant withdrew his plea of "not guilty" and pleaded guilty to the killing and justification of the act on account of military orders from the aforesaid generals.

Capt. H. McArthur Commander of Round Valley Post was called and sworn. He stated that James A. Ivie had killed the Indian Pannikay under his orders. Question by the Pros. Attorney— Did you have any orders from Col. Callister the Commander of this District to kill said Indian?

Answer: No I had no order to kill him nor any to the contrary.

Have you received any exterminating order through your Col.

Ans. Col. Callister ordered me to defend the place to the best of my ability.

Court ruled that the indictment and other necessary papers together with the prisoner be delivered over to Col Callister, the Commander of the Military District for his action thereupon as the present court had no jurisdiction in the case.

(Signed) Thos. R. King
Probate Judge

Fillmore City, July 15th 1866
Hiram B. Clawson Esq.
Adjutant General of the Nauvoo Legion.

Dear Brother Clawson,

Enclosed I send you the Indictment found and presented by the grand Jury of Millard County against James A. Ivie, also a transcript of the proceedings of the probate court in the case. You will see by the ruling of the court that it considers it has no jurisdiction in the case as the act of killing was done under military orders. I therefore submit the case for the action of the Lieutenant General.

I present also the name of Capt. Henry M. McArthur of Round Valley as being guilty of a Capital offense in ordering the shooting of the Indian Pannicary, according to his own statement under oath before the Probate Court as you will see by the synopsis of the proceedings—

Capt. Henry A. McArthur commands the fourth division of this military district and I present him agreeably to the sixty fifth section of an act to provide for the further organization of the Malitia of the territory of Utah approved February 15, 1852.

For the particulars of the killing of the Indian Pannicary and his peaceful disposition I refer you to a letter written by me to George A. Smith. The above matter is respectfully submitted for consideration.

I Remain Yours Very Respectfully,
J. Callister
Colonel Commanding
Parawan Military District

P.S. Please let President Young have the perusal of these papers on their arrival. I did not think I had anything to do in the case of James A. Ivie as he had committed no act against the Militia laws of the Territory. I consider it a civil case and the civil authority in full force but I consider that Capt. McArthur has altogether exceeded his bounds acting without any orders for his exterminating proceedings.

$\sim$ 35 $\sim$

INDIAN FIGHT AT THE J. C. LEE RANCH—
DEARDENS AND SWALLOWS

R. N. Bennett states: "About September 1866, the Black Hawk Indians drove off a herd of cattle. JOHN L. IVIE, ORANGE SEELY, myself and others, were with the company that followed them over the mountains east of Ephraim, via Joe's Valley, from there down Cotton Wood Canyon, on to Huntington River, where the town of Lawrence now stands, a distance of about seventy-five miles. Then we came back to the Cotton Wood River, and there camped and patrolled the valley two days, searching for Indians. We were gone from home about ten days."

J. P. Lee's Ranch in Beaver, 22 Oct 1866, by Lucinda Lee (abridged)

"It was sunset before the load was completed, and all the busy workers noticed that the wolves were very noisy, and seemed to answer each other from many directions. They took no hint, however, even when a neighbor from town, Mr. Elliott Willden, remarked that Indians often used wolf howls to signal each other and to drive cattle together. After the guest went on his way, Mr. Lee said to his helper, Joseph Lillywhite: 'Joe, it does seem foolhardy to live on a lonely place like this and pay so little attention to our firearms. Say we clean them all up tonight and get our ammunition all ready . . . . The firearms consisted of one large double-barreled shotgun, one new excellent repeating rifle, and one good six-shot revolver. The stock of ammunition was found to be pitiably small and Mr. Lee resolved to buy some on the morrow while in town. The magazine of the rifle contained the whole of its stock of cartridges . . . . All night the wolf howls continued and the two dogs barked and fretted.

"Before light next morning, the family was astir and as the back door was opened, the dogs barked so furiously toward a low ridge on the north, that the two men took their guns to reconnoiter. 'Mr. Lee,' said Lillywhite,

'I see something moving. Shall I fire?'

"'Hail first, Joe,'" answered Mr. Lee, 'for if it should be Indians, and we fire first, it will be said that we brought trouble on ourselves.'

"Accordingly the young man hailed; and for reply received a volley of bullets, one of which went through his right shoulder. He reeled and the gun fell from his helpless hand; but he staggered into the house before he fell. Mr. Lee . . . fired one barrel of his shotgun at the place where he saw the flashes, and sprang into the house, forgetting to recover the rifle.

"The doors and windows were hastily closed . . . . The front door had only a wooden button on a screw for a fastening, and the west one had a broken gimlet stuck nail-fashion into a small hole. These doors were reinforced with furniture. The windows, fortunately, had strong wooden shutters, secured with iron hooks on the inside. For the first few minutes the whoops and yells of the Indians, punctuated as they were with heavy blows on the doors and with shots through both doors and windows, were something terrific . . . a tallow candle had to be lighted to enable Mr. Lee to reload the empty barrel of his shotgun. There were six children, five belonging to Mr. and Mrs. Lee and a young English girl, who was temporarily with the Lees.

"After raising such a hideous storm around the house for what seemed an age, the Indians grew quiet and one advanced to parley. The Indian spokesman who hailed Mr. Lee by name, said that he was Too-witch-ee-Tick-a-boo, a very good friend, who was hungry. Would his friend John open the door and give him bread-milk-matches, etc.? Mr. Lee, after some talk, said to his wife, 'We have always been such good friends with the Indians, can it be . . . a mistake?'

"'Not possible!' she replied, 'that all this shooting is any mistake.'

"The Indian continued to plead and protest until Mr. Lee said again to his wife, 'I have so little ammunition . . . when it is all gone . . . they would be still more angry . . . What do you think?'

"'I think just this: They are not angry at all . . . They have simply made up their minds to kill us. We will fight as long as there is one shot left, and trust in God. Let me answer once.'

"'No!' she called to the Indian, 'you are not Tick-a-boo! We will not open the door! If you come in here, we will shoot you!'

"The Indian laughed, 'Oh! Squaw shoot! Now me scared! Yes, now me scared!' Mr. Lee hastened to speak again lest the enemy suppose . . . he was disabled.

"Now the defenders learned the real reason for the stay of proceedings and the parley. Little puffs and lines of smoke began to come in between the roof and the walls of the unceiled rooms. The Indians had brought sagebrush and pushed bundles of it with poles under the eaves, and fired them. Providentially, there had been snow sometime lately, and the roof of boards and slabs was so damp it would not blaze . . . [but] poured into the rooms clouds of bitter smoke—baby Rose gasped and struggled so that she seemed about to die. Under the best bed was better air, and Mary, age fifteen, was appointed to take the child there and tend her. There was a little water in the house, which was hoarded carefully. The wounded man continuously moaned for water, the baby drank eagerly, the others must have a few sips, and there was very little to spare for the fire, but that little was cautiously applied so as not to waste one precious drop.

"Charles, age ten, and Janey, the young English girl, went together to the mother to ask what they could do to help.

"'You poor children,' she answered, 'there is nothing more you can do with your hands; but you might pray with all your might for God in heaven to help us—He only can;' and those two children knelt down amidst all that blood and smoke and uproar, and prayed with all the unstudied earnestness of trusting childhood; and who shall say they were not heard?

"About this time some Indians inserted the tines of a pitchfork into the closing of the east door, and burst off the frail wooden button, but the cupboard barricade did not allow the door to open more than an inch or two. Here the darkness within gave Mr. Lee his first real advantage over his assailants. He saw, without pressing near enough to be seen, an Indian raising his gun to fire through the crevice; and he turned loose the old shotgun at point blank range.

"A wild yell, followed by dreadful shrieks, groans and howls, was the result of this. The second shot from the gun fairly tore away the right shoulder of the Indian. Almost immediately, Mr. Lee saw another Indian at a few rods distance ramming a load into his gun. He sent the load from the other barrel after this besieger, and handed the gun to his wife to be reloaded; while with his revolver in hand . . . continuing his watch through that dangerous . . . opening. . . . The Indians cautiously removed the pitchfork, and the besieged hastened to drive in a stout nail.

"Emma, age twelve, found an ax in the kitchen and stationed herself by the west door, saying grimly that she would do her best to chop off a leg from the first Indian who came in there. Her mother smiled drearily at such training for a dainty girl, but her keenest anxiety in this terrible situation was for her daughter Mary. She found and gave to Mary a small dagger in a sheath attached to a narrow leather belt; and while directing her to buckle it around her waist, said solemnly: 'My daughter, our case is desperate; and if the worst comes, if the Indians do break in on us, your father, I and most likely all the rest of us except yourself will be killed at once; but I fear they would take you alive and put you to tortures worse than death, as is their way with women prisoners . . . wear this dagger and do not let them take you alive.'

"The uproar outside gradually subsided. The baby, pale and gasping, grew so weak and faint, that the mother in desperation took her to a west window which she opened enough to give the child a few breaths of outside air. The father took up his guard there as long as they both dared. Then he said, 'I will rush out and get water to drink and to throw on the fire.'

"'If you are killed,' she urged, 'the others very soon would be.' He yielded to their entreaties, and Mrs. Lee . . . and Mary, who had already concluded that an Indian bullet would be far better than a dagger in her own hand, took buckets, and when the barricade had been removed from the back door . . . ran to the stream, only a rod or two from the south end of the house and secured water, and with it they finally extinguished the fire.

"There had been no demonstration whatever from the enemy for nearly an hour when Charles [asked] that they allow him to run to town and ask for help . . . . ' I know I can go and not be shot.' . . . 'God is with the child,' said the father, and laying his hands on the head of his grave little son, he solemnly blessed him. The mother kissed him just as solemnly, with all the dust and blood upon him. Then they opened the west window looking toward town and the boy sprang through and ran like a deer until lost to sight among . . . cedars and sagebrush on the hillside.

"The sequel proved that at this very time the Indians were really gone to join their companions who were passing with droves of cattle; and happy would the Lees have been could they have known it. The men of Beaver followed, but never recovered the herd. Joseph Lillywhite recovered from his wound but did not live to reach middle age."

"In after years the Indians said Mr. Lee was a Big Chief—a Brave— and that he had killed three bad Indians who had tried to kill him. These were the Piutes, whose home was in Beaver County, and who knew every member of Mr. Lee's family well, and often visited them at the farm."

[Note: Young seven-year-old Ellen Lee would later become Mrs. ELLEN L. SANDERS of Nacozari, Sonora, Mexico, and would be considered one of Utah's foremost literary women.]

On 28 Dec 1866 the Deseret Telegraph Line opened to Manti. The project of covering Utah with a network of electrical wires began as early as 1861, the year the Overland Telegraph Line was completed. In November 1865, a letter was sent to all bishops from Rich County, Idaho, in the north to St. George in the south with instructions for getting out poles and collecting money for the service. By January 1867, 500 miles had been laid across Utah at a cost of $150 per mile. This first circuit of local line extended from Cache Valley to Dixie with a branch line running through Sanpete County. President Brigham Young called a number of young men to learn telegraphy. Anthon H. Lund, of Mount Pleasant, was among those called. He gave a large clock to Andrew Beckstrom in part payment for his site and built a telegraph office and also conducted a daguerreotype photograph gallery. It became a popular gathering place for the young people.

Colonel IVIE needed help, especially during his absence on military duty, and LYMAN PETERS became his partner. PETERS was born in Vermont in 1837, but his family had moved to Michigan, when as a young man, he left his parents and sought his fortune in the west—perhaps heading for the gold or silver fields of California and eastern Nevada. While traveling through Salt Lake City, he met a beautiful girl, CAROLYN LYTLE, a daughter of Lieutenant Andrew Lytle of the Mormon Battalion. LYMAN joined the L.D.S. Church and they were married and sealed in the Endowment House. The Lytles were sent to the Carson Valley in 1854, and the young couple went with them. They had two children, a girl born in Nevada, and a boy after they returned to Salt Lake City. According to one history, LYMAN was called on a dangerous assignment, (perhaps as the guard for the emigrants coming west). When he returned to Salt Lake City, his wife and two children had moved to Saint George, Utah, where her parents were called to settle. Before she left Salt Lake City, she had persuaded Brigham Young to give her a divorce. In St. George, she became a plural wife to a man who would have seven wives. She changed her two children's surnames to her new last name, Whipple. With great-grandfather JOHN LEHI IVIE needing help, the lonely, heartbroken LYMAN PETERS took the job, after observing JOHN's lovely outgoing wife, who was his own age.

From Longsdorf's *Mount Pleasant:* "In the year 1867, the Indian difficulties became very serious in different localities. The Black Hawk warriors started out with more vigor, and the destruction then became more serious than ever before. It seemed the Indians, with a determination to massacre all the white people, came in great numbers from the south and the east. The Militia was sent from the north to assist southern settlements in their struggle in combating them. No longer was it the bow and arrow; ammunition was smuggled to the Indians, who also traded freely the stolen cattle and horses to the immigrants who were en route to California, thereby obtaining fire arms.

"During the first warm days of March, when the settlers of Richfield were contemplating their farm work, the Indians dashed through the town towards Glenwood, where they attacked a family traveling with ox team, murdering Jens Peter Petersen, his wife, and Mary Smith, all of Richfield. The citizens of Glenwood made a vigorous fight, but the Indians were victorious and [got] possession of about one hundred head of stock which they drove into the mountains.

"April 1st, President Young counseled the settlers to abandon their homes and move north into older and stronger towns for safety . . . . The move was made about May 1st, and nearly all the settlements on the Sevier and those in Kane County were deserted.

"April 30th, Daniel H. Wells visited Mount Pleasant and spoke to the people about the necessity of building a wall around the town . . . . It was originally intended to build a wall twelve feet high, but as the trouble . . . grew less serious, the wall was never completed.

"As wealth was then counted, Mortin Rasmussen, who owned a home and land, two pair of mules, a team of horses, kept one horse in readiness for the Minute men, and had two good wagons, was considered one of the wealthy men of the community.

"General Snow, confined to his bed with illness, was released from his command, and General W. B. Pace was placed in charge of the entire Military District of Sanpete, then comprising all of southeastern Utah . . . all the stock of several settlements was placed under strong guard day and night. This . . . checked their ravages for a time."

Cowherd–Louis Lund killed [*Indian Depredations*] "At Fountain Green, Sanpete County, it was customary for a guard of ten men to be with the cowherd, but in the morning of June 1st 1867 only five were with it, and Mathew Caldwell, the man in charge of the guard, was detained in the settlement and getting his horse shod. Feed being plentiful the herd only went a short distance from town to graze. Two of the herders were stationed . . . east of the herd on a knoll where their horses were feeding just below. The other three herders were on the north. Wm. Adams, Jr. . . . saw ten persons riding fast from the east hills towards the herd.

"Before the Indians reached the herd, they separated, six going east and the other four west of the herd. Jasper Robertson, Swen Anderson and Louis Lund . . . north of the herd, had killed some rabbits and were cleaning them . . . [in] the water hollow ditch, and did not know anything about the presence of Indians until the savages rode to the brink . . . and shot Lund through the region of the heart. He immediately fell forward into the water, and the other two jumped up and ran. Jasper Robertson was shot through the thigh, while Anderson escaped unhurt . . . . The Indians tried to head them off, but the boys had the start . . . . W. H. Adams and Thomas Caldwell, hearing the shooting . . . mounted their horses and went to the scene . . . as speedily as they could . . . they were informed that Louis Lund had been killed . . . Adams knew where the shooting had been done, they soon . . . found him [Lund] lying with his head in the ditch with water running through his hair. He had also been shot in the center of the forehead at short range, his face being powder-burned . . . . Most horses are frightened at the smell of blood, and as Adams had a gentle horse and PARLEY ALLRED had a saddle on his horse, they took the saddle off and put it on Adams' gentle horse, placed the corpse in it in an upright position, and with Swen Anderson walking on one side and Adams on the other, they held it in the saddle until they reached the edge of town, where they met Thomas Crowder with a wagon. They then placed the body in the wagon and took it to the fort, only about two hundred yards distant. Bro. Lund's body was taken to his mother's room; he was her only child."

[Note: "Springtown, June 12th, 1867
"Editor Deseret News:—

"In regard to the Indian raid at Fountain green, some people may wonder why forty-five men, coming up with twenty-one Indians could not kill or capture them and recover the stock,– we were led to believe, from the report of the express riders and telegram from Moroni, that twelve Indians had gone with the stock, and that a war party was left behind fighting for two hours. On learning this, and that Major Bradley had sent assistance, I raised fourteen men from Springtown and followed Col. IVIE as fast as I could to Thistle Valley, to intercept the Indians. He (Col. IVIE) arrived in Thistle valley with twenty-three men from Mount Pleasant and Fairview, and saw the Indians about three miles distant, and near the canyon. Finding themselves hard pressed they killed and wounded some of the cattle, mounted fresh animals, driving only horses before them and reached the canyon before Col. IVIE came up. He took the precaution to flank the canyon, not knowing but that a heavy reserve was lying in wait. In a few moments he became satisfied that twelve Indians were about the whole number in the canyon, but supposed that the war party was still behind, and kept a rear guard to watch for them. That guard twice reported Indians in the rear, but they proved to be our re-inforcements. Col. IVIE pursued the Indians about three miles, into the mountains, but finding that their jaded horses were unable to compete with the fresh horses that the Indians had just mounted, they gave up the chase. I formed a junction with Maj. Guyman and twenty-three men from Fountain Green and Moroni, in the south end of Thistle Valley, and met Col. IVIE at the mouth of the canyon.

After hearing his report I decided to return. The distance our men had to travel was from fifteen to thirty miles, which was done on the run. I believe that the officers and men generally did their best in trying to capture the raiders, but the want of vigilance on the part of the guards gave them the advantage; and the want of a telegraph office in each settlement was all that prevented us from cutting them off. The distance rode from the point of attack till I met Col. IVIE was at least fifty miles.

"Yours,   (Signed) R. N. ALLRED."]

Grasshopper Invasion–1867 From Andrew Madsen's Journal: "The year 1867 promised to be a prosperous year and conditions were favorable for large crops in Mount Pleasant; but in the midst of our trouble with the savages, another enemy appeared on the scene. During the month of June, grasshoppers, in great numbers, came flying into our fields, moving on through the field, working their way of destruction and destroying most all crops as they advanced, leaving the land and garden spots as barren as the road bed. They were so numerous, that when flying they would darken the rays of the sun. Chickens, turkeys and all poultry were moved to the fields and assisted very much in reducing the number of grasshoppers. Trenches were dug ahead of the marching army, where they fell in great numbers and were buried by the millions. Another system was adopted--that of spreading straw ahead of them where they would seek refuge at night. The straw was then burned. Many were destroyed that way. But they were so great in number, their power of destruction continued on until nearly all our crops were destroyed and little saved. It was due only to the economy and conservation of the settlers during the years previous, having foresight to lay aside a portion of their crops for such emergencies, that they were prepared and did not suffer from hunger."

From Levi Edgar Young's *The Founding of Utah:* "Every bushel of wheat and corn had to be carefully harbored from the Indian raids, and when a beef was killed, the people shared the meat. It was a time when all shared alike, and there was consequently developed a spirit of kindliness toward all people. If one family had food, they gladly shared with their neighbors."

Raid on Spring City, 13 Aug 1867, Marinus Lund of Spring City, Utah, wrote:

"About twenty men with teams left Spring City for the hayfield which was about six miles south-west of the town. Contrary to the usual custom, the scouting ahead of the cowherd was not done that morning. A company of Indians, who evidently had spent the previous night in the stone-quarry hills, about a half mile south of the hay road, saw the cow-herd coming over the hills north of the road. In their effort to reach the herd the Indians encountered the hay teams; the minute men were guarding the cow herd and were attracted by the reports of the guns fired by the Indians in their attack on the hay teams. William Scott, SANFORD ALLRED and myself rode to the place where the firing was heard. On our way we saw Andrew Johnson [Johansen], a driver of one of the hay teams, going north with an arrow in his back. He had been shot by an Indian while on his wagon. SANFORD ALLRED, who was armed with a cap and ball pistol, went to Spring City to report . . . .

"When I reached Scott, I asked him where he was going? He said that he was afraid his father-in-law, James Meeks, had been killed. I then left Scott and rode north to the cow herd . . . I met William Blain who had been shot through the ear by the Indians . . . . I showed him the nearest way to town and told him to go there as fast as he could. The Indians were then all south of us."

HYRUM SMITH IVIE, ten-year-old son of THOMAS K. and AMANDA IVIE wrote:

"About nine o'clock . . . I was riding down to the hayfield with SIDNEY H. and JAMES R. ALLRED, when about half way between the stone-quarry and the meadows we heard some shooting. Christian J. Larsen, who had a pair of gray horses (pretty good runners) was not far behind us. About eight Indians on horses came from . . . Pigeon Hollow [direction] towards him. Larsen who had a small boy with him, whirled his team around and went back as fast as he could go, while the Indians rode along beside the wagon, shooting at him and the boy. They shot several holes through his clothes, and also shot his gunstock in two, but he was not hurt. The main lot of Indians had been hidden in the cedars above the stone-quarry, south of the road. When we saw what was up, we turned and drove back till our horses got out of wind. The ALLREDs unhitched the horses and went to where the fighting was going on. Two men from Ephraim came along and one of them took me on his horse over the hill and let me down, when Con Rowe, who was coming out, took me into town on his horse. When we got to the foot of the stone-quarry hill, we saw James Meeks lying by the road dead; he had been shot through the right breast and under one eye; his pants and hat had been taken; his pipe lay by his side and his ox team was out in the brush a short distance from the road."

Marinus Lund continues:

"The Indians had stolen twenty-eight head of horses and started to the mountains . . . We followed the Indians up the trail south of BILL

ALLRED's canyon and the militia had a small engagement with them on the mountain-side. The Indians were followed to the top of Horseshoe Mountain, and on the way up my horse gave out. Thomas Coates, and a tame Indian from Moroni, and I followed to the top . . . we returned to Springtown where we arrived about nine o'clock at night . . . we learned that William Scott's father-in-law, James Meeks, had been killed, and also that Andrew Johansen . . . died that night."

Colonel REDICK N. ALLRED's journal says:

"I went to Ephraim to meet General Pace and General Robert T. Burton . . . . I knew not that a band of Indians were lying in wait in the cedars to take the herd as soon as it was driven out . . . When we arrived at Ephraim we received a telegram from Mount Pleasant giving the news of the raid, and we joined Captain Louis Larsen's Minute men who later joined men from Springtown and Mount Pleasant under Colonel IVIE. But the Indians had made good their escape into the mountains, taking only the horses from the herd. We pursued them to the top of the Horseshoe Mountain."

Black Hawk suggests a possible peace. The *Deseret News* 28 Aug 1867 stated that Superintendent Head, of Indian Affairs met with the notorious chief Black Hawk at the Uintah reservation. Black Hawk said he had twenty-eight lodges under his sole control, and that he was assisted by three Elk Mountain chiefs who each had ten or twelve lodges with them. These Indians were scattered all along the valleys from the north of Sanpete County to the southern settlements watching opportunities to make raids. Nevertheless, he expressed a personal desire for peace and said that inasmuch as the others looked to him as head chief, he thought he could influence them to bury the hatchet and perhaps consent to a peace conference. He had not cut his hair since the raids and fighting had begun. Now, with peace in mind, he asked Superintendent Head to shear his locks for him.

The Semi-Annual October L. D. S. Conference in Salt Lake City was the first one held in the new great Tabernacle, which was still not completely built. During the conference, 163 families were called to strengthen the settlements in southern Utah, and the Saints were requested to assist liberally towards the immigration of all who were still coming west.

On 1 Nov 1867, the first issue of the *Deseret Evening News* was issued. The 12 Mar 1868 issue included DAVID CANDLAND's description of Mount

Pleasant:

> "a shingle and saw mill; the brass band of fifteen instruments; $4,000 raised for the emigration; young elders sent out two by two to preach in the city; more lands cultivated; an eight-foot vein of coal at Fairview; five schools; their flour mill and blacksmith shops, and a request for a railroad and high school."

In March 1868, a meeting consisting of President Hyde, the bishops of all the towns in Sanpete County, Bishop Bryan of Nephi, Indian Chief Joe, and three other noted Indian warriors was held in Mount Pleasant; an interpreter from Nephi was also present. Chief Joe made a speech favoring peace, saying that Tabby and Black Hawk also desired peace. Many heated words were exchanged; but the desire for peace seemed to prevail, and the Indians promised that their tribes would not molest the settlers in the future, if the settlers gave them 1000 pounds of flour---delivered to Santaquin. This promise was soon broken after the goods were delivered.

On 4 Apr 1868, settlers moving south to Richfield were attacked, and Axel Justensen and Charles Wilson were killed and others wounded. Scipio was raided and the Indians succeeded in driving away the stock. Shortly after, Ephraim's cattle were driven away; but the settlers gave chase and the Indians retreated into the mountains leaving their cattle. The Indian campfires could be seen on the mountain side, where they were engaged in song and dance, and numerous powwows were held by various tribes; at times the hideous sounds could be heard in the valleys below. Their attacks on the livestock were usually unsuccessful.

At a powwow held in Strawberry Valley, Sanpete County, 15 August, Colonel Head succeeded in forming a treaty with chieftains of the Indian bands. Black Hawk claimed he had kept his pledge and used his personal influence in forming the treaty. Young warriors were slow to consent and boasted of their cunningness in deeds of bloodshed. The treaty was signed and generally observed until the final treaty was signed 17 Sep 1872, in Mount Pleasant, at which General Morrow, Apostle Orson Hyde, three bishops, Colonel REDICK ALLRED, and many Indian chiefs were present.

Black Hawk was not with them. Feeling that death was awaiting him, in 1869–70, Black Hawk obtained permission from military authorities of the territory to visit all the places where he and his tribe had caused trouble. With seven or eight warriors, Black Hawk visited every town and village from Cedar City on the South to Payson on the north and made peace with the people. He feared going to Scipio, as he felt JIM IVIE had sworn vengeance. Black Hawk's original telegram to Brigham Young expressing this concern is in the museum in St. George, Utah. But, of course, JIM IVIE was not a problem. Black Hawk died in his wickiup at Spring Lake Villa, a small settlement between Payson and Santaquin, Utah County, in 1870.

By 1868, pioneering into the Salt Lake Valley and the surrounding areas was changing rapidly. My husband GROVER SWALLOW's second-great-grand parents, HENRY and SARAH BOLTON DAVIES, with his great-grandparents, THOMAS and CHARLOTTE DAVIES DEARDEN, and their children arrived at Laramie, Wyoming, by railroad and were met there by a mule train of wagons that brought them into Salt Lake City. This journey from New York City had

THIS PHOTO WAS TAKEN IN LIVERPOOL JUST BEFORE THEY SAILED ON
11 AUG 1868. THOMAS AND CHARLOTTE's BABY DAUGHTER SARAH DEARDEN DIED
EIGHT DAYS BEFORE ARRIVING IN THE SALT LAKE VALLEY. HENRY AND SARAH's TINY SON
HENRY DAVIES DIED TWO DAYS LATER. BOTH WERE BURIED ON THE PLAINS OF
WYOMING, PROBABLY NEAR DEVIL'S GATE.

taken only three weeks, but it was one of hardship, sickness, and death.

The older family members had been baptized in November of 1848. After struggling twenty years to save money for their ship passage on the *John Bright,* filled with a large company going to Zion, they left Liverpool, England, 4 Jun 1868. As the ship sailed out of the harbor, young THOMAS DEARDEN, with his brother, waved farewell to his wife and tiny daughter from the dock. He and his brother had good jobs in the steel mill. He would come later. Suddenly changing his mind, he hired a small more rapidly moving boat and joined his family on board for the voyage. His brother later stated that he wished he had gone, too. The *John Bright* arrived in New York harbor on 13 Jul 1868.

Living in the Cottonwood area where Murray is now located, HENRY and THOMAS worked for the railroad when the Golden Spike was driven in at Promitory Point, north of the Great Salt Lake and west of Ogden, in 1869, joining the east and west coasts with the first transcontinental railway. HENRY DAVIES was a sawyer by trade, and after two years, the two families moved to Springville and built their own successful sawmill. After two more years elapsed, Brigham Young and Bishop Partridge of Fillmore called them to build the first steam-powered sawmill in Utah. The DAVIES-DEARDEN sawmill was built on the right-hand fork of Chalk Creek with a lumberyard nearby in Fillmore behind the cooperative store. It was quite successful for a few years, until an early spring thaw created heavy flood conditions and the mill was washed away.

Back in England, in Essex County, next to London, the SWALLOW family was still saving to obtain sufficient money to finance their journey and join the saints in Salt Lake City. THOMAS and CAROLINE CROW SWALLOW had joined the L.D.S. Church in 1854. He was a gardener and laborer on the estate of the *Lord* of Stebbing Green. When they were baptized, they were part of the Braintree Branch, east of Stebbing. As the converts became more numerous the branch was divided and they became part of the Dunmow Branch to the west, where THOMAS became branch president for eighteen years. Their home became a center for most of the traveling missionaries throughout the area. His wife, CAROLINE CROW (Swallow) was a persistent student of the Bible and had memorized chapters throughout it. Her father, WILLIAM CROW, was a dissenter from the Church of England, and the family names are listed earlier with the non-conformists that met in Dunmow, although they were residents of Braintree at that time. The distance between the two towns was approximately twenty miles, with Stebbing between. CAROLINE was a wonderful teacher and missionary. Some of her associates claimed she had the gift of prophesy.

Visiting at their home near the end of 1865 was Charles W. Penrose, then president of the English mission at London. He would later become a member of the First Presidency of the L.D.S. Church. But the SWALLOWs knew him originally as the young missionary that traveled barefoot through the dusty roads of Essex composing the hymn, "O Ye Mountains High," when he day-dreamed of uniting with the Saints in the Rocky Mountains in those mid-1850s. However, in 1865, GROVER's grandfather, their youngest child, had just been born a few weeks before on 3 November. Elder Penrose admired their young son, and they asked him to give him a blessing. He consented to do so, on one condition—being allowed to choose the name. They agreed, and he named him after himself, CHARLES.

Years later, GROVER and I became well acquainted with one of Charles Penrose's granddaughters—Lucetta Hollinger, wife of Lorraine Hollinger of Pioche and Panaca, whom GROVER happily worked with many years in the Church and communities.

Third-great-uncle GIBSON CONDIE, then in Salt Lake City, wrote:

"October 7, 1869 there was a mass meeting held in Salt Lake City, with a view of again appealing to congress for the admission of Utah as a state. October 8th one hundred and ninety Mormon missionaries were called at the General Conference in Salt Lake City to go to different States of the Union and preach. . . . One night I had [a] very simple dream. My spirit wandered into the spirit world. I saw some outside of the wall. It appeared to me that THEY HAD BEEN SHUT OUT BY THEMSELVES. The men looked very sad and dejected. I conversed with them. I said: 'do you have any more communication from the heavens than what we have on the earth? They said "no." While they lived on this earth they were wicked and did not live good lives. You see the results, they were not happy; they were cast out by themselves outside of a high wall. There countenance betrayed them. I felt very sorry for them. They gave me good advice not to do as they had done. They were very free in the conversation, advised me not to be in the same predicament as they were. That dream I will never forget. I am in hopes it will be a lesson and a guide for me to pursue on this earth.

"August 28 [1970] MARTIN HARRIS, one of the witnesses of the *Book of Mormon* arrived in Salt Lake City. He was 88 years old. I was at the tabernacle on Sunday to hear him speak. He bore a powerful testimony concerning the *Book of Mormon*; also he saw an angel and heard the voice of God. I felt glad to see and hear for myself one of the three witnesses to the *Book of Mormon*. "

From his family group sheet, great-uncle GIBSON CONDIE had then moved to Croyden, Utah, as his 5th through 12th children's births indicate. Three of them died as very young children: CICILIA, about 18 months old in 1874; then the next two daughters MARTHA and ETTIE died of diphtheria in March and April 1878—ages 3 and ½ years old, and about 21 months. Their father wrote:

"After I lost my two last girls . . . my mind got to be darkened as to whether there was a future or not. Everything seemed to me to be in darkness, no light whatever. I would say to myself. I would give all I possess if I could have that light as I used to have . . . what have I done for the Lord to withdraw his spirit that I should have doubts? "

In 1880, he wrote:

"I was called by the presidency of this stake, Morgan Co., with Brother John London as a home missionary. It was a great trial for me to preach to the saints, to exhort them to faithfulness. . . . I did not know what to do, whether to fulfill it or reject it. . . . At last I decided I would do my best . . . . Brother London and I went to Morgan to be set apart. The next Sunday we went to South Morgan for the first time to address the saints. The house was about full. . . . I told them for the last two years my mind had been darkened, etc. and now being called to preach and exhort the saints I should be the one to be preached to and be comforted. . . . That darkness that had been on me disappeared. That bright light came back again. The doubts left me. The spirit of the Lord rested upon me. . . . It gave me a great testimony, double fold, money could not exchange for the testimony I had on the future."

[Note: His companion John London was the father of ALICE REBECCA LONDON who married THOMAS A CONDIE, my grandfather GIBSON A CONDIE's older brother. They were married 9 Dec 1897. They had 5 children before he died 7 Feb 1919.]

He then tells us about the death of his mother, second-great-grandmother HELEN SHARP CONDIE in Salt Lake City, 21 Feb 1883—at noon.

"She suffered pneumonia for a few days. . . . A few minutes before she died we were all around her bed . . . . Her eyes looked up toward heaven with a beautiful smile. It seemed she saw heavenly messengers to escort her to her abode. She died with a beautiful smile on her countenance and made her young. She looked about thirty years of age . . . . She was a good, kind mother to her children and also kind to her husband and her neighbors. Well respected, she was a true Latter-day Saint . . . . I have never known her to talk light of the principles of the gospel or of the leaders of the Church but she would defend them."

After she died my great-grandfather had his youngest daughter CECELIA (twin) live with him. Second-great-grandfather THOMAS CONDIE died 9 Nov 1887. His daughter CECELIA married ARTHUR H. KIRK in 1890. I, BROOKIE SWALLOW, remember him. He had a wholesale general merchandise store in Salt Lake City and invited my mother to come there on one occasion after my father died and buy anything she needed at wholesale.

It was on 14 Jul 1868 that GEORGE SWALLOW, the second child of THOMAS and CAROLINE, stood alone on the deck at Liverpool, England, and listened to the preparatory ceremonies before the departure of 600 Saints to America on the steamship *S.S. Colorado*. He had just turned seventeen.

From the *Mormon Immigration Index*: President Franklin D. Richards addressed the Saints saying:

"upon the great blessing conferred upon them by the Almighty, in delivering them from bondage and opening the way for their escape to Zion . . . they were now beginning to experience the realities of the journey, and had an opportunity to exercise their patience and all those good qualities which should be possessed by Saints of God. . . . Said this was the last company of Saints for the season, and expressed his great gratitude to God for the great deliverance which had been wrought out for so many of his people, the company swelling the number to about 3,170 souls [that season]."

Elder William B. Preston, a returning missionary, was appointed president of the company and then addressed them. Charles W. Penrose dedicated the ship and its company to the service of God on this voyage, by prayer. They sang a few hymns.

"About 4 P.M. the noble vessel steamed out to sea, the sun shining brightly, the sky without a cloud, and no sadness appearing on a single countenance, except of those who returned to shore after bidding their friends farewell . . . the sea was as calm as a mirror, and no one had experienced any symptoms of seasickness."

They arrived in New York on 28 Jul 1868, crossing the Atlantic in two weeks. What a difference this steamship voyage was from that of the DAVIES and DEARDENs, which had sailed from the same port that year 4 June and arrived in New York 13 July. GEORGE SWALLOW would follow them across the plains by railroad to Laramie, Wyoming, departing there on 14 August in Captain Daniel D. McArthur's Company that arrived in Salt Lake City 2 Sep 1868. GEORGE would proceed on to Fillmore, where he is found in the 1870 U.S. Census:

"GEORGE SWALLOW, age 18, single, occupation –- laborer, living with Chandler Holbrook in Fillmore, Utah."

GEORGE sent money back to England to help other members of his family immigrate to *Zion*. His older brother, FREDERICK joined him in August 1871.

JOSEPH and JAMES came in June 1872. Their mother, CAROLINE CROW SWALLOW had walked with her two sons the five miles from Stebbing to Braintree to see them off on the train to London. Traveling alone, two men asked them who their parents were and where they were going, then gave each a piece of money. Arriving in London, no one met them and they were frightened. A policeman took them to Joseph V. Robison, conference president in London at that time, who had arranged their passage to America and should have met their train. Lizzie Robison was placed in charge of them during their voyage on the steamship *Manhattan,* which also had two masts, and left Liverpool on 12 Jun 1872 and arrived in New York City in fourteen days. The boys were sick the first four days on the ocean.

JOSEPH SWALLOW, wrote a short history on a paper bag of their journey:

"Captain Britton on ship. Started to cross. Storm came up. Water came in ship. Washed dishes off wall. Decided to pray. Captain then said, 'We have started for Zion and that's where we are going.' I was 14 years old. Birthday on water. Storm subsided. Joseph V. Robison paid Joseph's immigration from England to America. Mother and Father bid good-bye and told children to keep up their faith. Lizzie Robinson came with Joseph, 12 years, and James, 14 years. Holbrook took JAMES to raise. Parents came out two years later. 2 ½ years schooling."

JAMES later described the storm as follows:

"I have seen the (ocean) when it resembles an immense boiling cauldron covered with white foam; while the roar of the winds and waves was like the bellowing of a thousand wild bulls."

JOSEPH SWALLOW's son, WILLIAM later wrote:

"A big storm came up, and they couldn't dip the water out of the ship fast enough and it filled up almost to the first bunk. Father said he was sitting on Mrs. Robison's lap. She was talking to them, trying to console them, cause they were crying. They were scared, cause they were afraid the ship was going to sink. People were dishing water out of there and throwing it over the deck as fast as they could, but it just kept filling up. It was making an awful noise and scared the kids almost to death; but Mrs. Robison kept telling the boys to keep quiet and don't cry, cause we are going to Zion— we're going to get there alright. There were people praying. You know, when you get caught in a thing like that, you might get pretty humble. . . ."

Brother Britton knelt on the table to pray to keep out of the water. It was said the storm almost stopped while he was praying.

"Grandfather JOSEPH went to live in Joseph V. Robison's home and his brother JAMES went to Mr. Holbrook's home.

"JOSEPH was sick for eleven weeks after he first came to Utah with the Rocky Mountain Fever. The Robisons were very good to him and treated him like he was their own son. JOSEPH worked seven years for Mr. Robison to pay for his board and room, his clothes and his immigration to America . . . . [He] became an American Citizen 24 April 1888."

Their father and mother, THOMAS and CAROLINE CROW SWALLOW, with the two youngest children, ELIZA and CHARLES arrived in September 1874. Son WILLIAM came about 1885. It had taken 32 years from the parent's baptisms for this family to all join together in Fillmore, Millard County, Utah.

THOMAS AND CAROLINE CROW SWALLOW

~ 36 ~

INDIANS STOP COLONEL IVIE IN SALT CREEK CANYON—A RACE FOR THEIR LIVES

From the *Deseret News Weekly*, 10 Jul 1872:

"INDIANS—We met Brother Henry N. Larter of Moroni, Sanpete County, today. He arrived in town yesterday, in company with Col. JOHN L. IVIE and the latter's family. He reports that when they were about four miles below the divide in Salt Creek Canyon [east from Nephi], six Utes, among whom was Tabiona, rode up to them and demanded to know of Col. IVIE whether he was 'JIM IVIE,' the colonel's brother. On being answered in the negative they passed on. In a short time, however, they returned, rode in front of the wagon, stopped it, and reiterated the question. One of the Indians then said that it was not 'JIM IVIE,' but his brother. At this time, Tabiona had his hand on his arrows, and another Indian had his rifle ready for use.

"The Indians, however, again passed along and after going a short distance they stopped and held a consultation. The team was then made to travel at a lively pace. When the Indians saw this two of them started after it, coming towards the wagon about 300 yards, but seeing their companions did not follow, they stopped and went back.

"One Indian was so drunk he could scarcely sit on his horse, and the others had also been drinking, but they knew what they were doing.

"Since writing the above Col. J. L. IVIE called at our office and, being well acquainted with Indian character, says that he has no doubt that had himself and those who were with him not got away, the Indians intended to murder them."

According to grandfather, JAMES OSCAR IVIE, one of the children in the wagon, his mother covered the smaller children with the bedding in the wagon, and his father, Colonel IVIE later said,

"If the Indians had overtaken them the second time, he intended to jump out of the wagon and let it go on and take his chances with them. He was well armed."

LILLIE BELLE, two years younger than grandfather, was under the bedding and told her daughter, IDA BELLE, she, "remembered the story very well and said the bedding was a feather bed as her mother thought that feathers would deflect the arrows. Mother told us how frightened they were, and that they were told not to cry or make a noise in the hopes that the Indians would not know that they were there."

COL. JOHN LEVI IVIE OF MOUNT PLEASANT,
SAN PETE COUNTY, UTAH.
HE FOUGHT IN SEVEN BATTLES WITH
INDIANS AND LED THREE OF THEM.

CHIEF TABIONA (TABBY)

Grandfather JAMES OSCAR IVIE told this story quite often when he visited us at our ranch in Carey, Idaho. I remember the excitement and fear he engendered in me as he told it. But my older brother, MARION (ASHER) CONDIE, remembers an interesting addition to this story. Grandfather was known as OSCAR IVIE by his relatives and friends, not by his first name JAMES. According to my brother, after the Indians had questioned his father about his identity as "JIM IVIE" and he had told them he wasn't, the Indians passed on. Then he, young JAMES OSCAR IVIE stood up in the wagon bed and shouted after them, "I'm not JIM IVIE, I'm OSCAR IVIE!" The Indians then consulted together and decided at that time that JOHN L. was his brother, and some started the chase. LYMAN PETERS (or maybe the man mentioned in the news article) whipped the team immediately to full speed. His mother,

MARY CATHERINE BARTON IVIE, pushed her young son back into the wagon bed and his father, JOHN L. IVIE, aimed his rifle to discourage further pursuit. His reputation with a rifle may have played a part in discouraging the Indians from further attack. It is highly doubtful that the colonel would have repeated this part to the press. The Indian Tabiona, mentioned above, was a brother of the former Chief Walker, which means that he was also a brother of Jake Arapene and Sanpitch. His name is often shortened to Tabby in the historical accounts. He would later lead his tribe to the Indian Reservation near the Uintah Mountains.

OLD DANISH STYLED SPRING CITY CHURCH

Early in 1872, Special Indian Agent G. W. Dodge tried to pacify the Indians and distributed large quantities of flour, beef, and other supplies among them. The more warlike refused to be pacified and saw no reason to submit to treaties. On 12 June, they made a raid on Sanpete County, again— at Twelve Mile Creek, and NIELS C. HEISELT, Jr. was killed. It was difficult for the settlers to determine who was friendly and who was not. Superintendent Dodge asked the friendly Indians to return to the reservation. Councils were held in Nephi and at Fountain Green in July. The Indians agreed, but never fulfilled their promises. Affairs appeared to be progressing toward greater difficulties. The Indians were stealing the finest horses right from the stables. Militia activities had been curtailed under orders. A party of Indians went to a stable in Ephraim. When they were unable to get the horses out, they crawled in by a small opening and cut the animals in a horrible manner. On 12 Aug 1872, General D. H. Wells received the following message from Colonel R. N. ALLRED of Spring City:

"Tabby sends word to all the Bishops, that he can control his men no longer. He was in Spanish Fork Canyon yesterday. I with a detachment brought the herd from Thistle Valley yesterday, having started as soon as I got word of the raid at Fairview. The wounded boy Stewart is dead."

The following day a telegram from Fountain Green asked Indian Agent Dodge for troops to defend the people against some of the bands of savages who had become angry at Dodge's order not to feed them, as he would furnish them plenty on the reservations.

Great-grandfather Colonel JOHN L. IVIE of Mount Pleasant sent another telegram:

"Mount Pleasant, August 17, 1872

Gov. Geo. L. Woods, care of Daniel H. Wells–

Indian depredations here last night. Shall I call out the militia to defend the place for services generally in this county? The Indians attacked the telegraph operator about 11 o'clock last night in front of the office and, we fear, fatally wounded him.

JOHN L. IVIE, Colonel of Militia"

Another message went out that day:

"Mount Pleasant, Aug. 17th.–Gen. D. H. Wells–2

As the telegraph operator, Jeremiah D. Page, was leaving the office last night about 11 o'clock, and when near the gate of the office, an Indian pounced upon his back and struck him three blows, with a tomahawk, upon the head, inflicting severe wounds, one penetrating through the skull. He was in a critical condition all night, but seems a little better this morning. There were five Indians seen in town about the same time that the attack was made upon Mr. Page. Col. J. L. IVIE detailed a scouting party from the home guard this morning, and they were scouting the base of the east mountain. One scout reports no sign of Indians in that direction.

J. S. Wing."

But the culprit was not the Indians. Bishop William Seely, of Mount Pleasant sent the following to the *Deseret News:*

"On Saturday evening suspicion rested on Richard Smyth as being the person who assailed our operator on the 16th. He was arrested . . . he pleaded guilty . . . and was committed to a higher court. The operator said that he was telegraphing a message to the operators of the county, and while so doing observed Smyth go into an adjoining room and return and place himself behind him. He stood for about a half an hour, and as quick as the operator had finished the message and closed the key, he was struck down and knew no more until he found himself lying on a lounge . . . with his head all mangled and his clothing all soaked in blood, and Richard Smyth pacing to and fro with a hatchet in his hand, making remarks about the deed he had done. After making a pause for some duration, he said, 'Jeremiah, hold up your hands, I cannot spare your life any longer, your head is all chopped into pieces and your brains are running out. I have murdered you. The operator says he resolved in his mind, weak as he was, if a chance offered itself, to spring upon Smyth, take the hatchet and kill him, but there was no chance, so he thought again the best way was to direct his mind upon the best means of liberating himself and cover up the deed; so from that Smyth made him swear not to reveal what had happened for six months, and still kept him there for about five hours; without any assistance, soaked in his blood and perishing with cold. He was so weak and frightened that he dared not reveal anything after he got among friends until Smyth had confessed he did the deed . . . .

Signed—W. S. Seely."

Peter Gottfredson explained:

"The office in which Jeremiah Page was assailed by Richard Smyth was under the supervision of Anthon H. Lund. Besides the telegraph office Brother Lund also kept a daguerreotype picture gallery in an adjoining room. It was quite customary for young people to meet and visit there. Brother Page was well thought of and a favorite with the young people, but not so much with Smyth, and it was general supposition that Smyth was jealous of Page and that this had much to do with the act."

The last man killed in the Indian Wars of Utah was Daniel Miller of Nephi, Juab County. According to Peter Gottfredson:

"The tragedy took place on the morning of the 26th of September, 1872, at Snow and Douglas' saw mill, in Oak Creek Canyon, Sanpete County, three miles east of Spring City. The mill had shut down about a month before, it being considered unsafe to work there because of Indians, but William Higbee stayed there as watchman.

"I had a contract to get out a bill of lumber to finish a new school house which was being built in the Second District at Mount Pleasant, and

THOMAS GLEDHILL, my brother-in-law, sixteen years old, was helping me. [THOMAS GLEDHILL would later marry Col. JOHN L. IVIE's
daughter, LILLIE BELLE IVIE.] I was working three yoke of oxen, getting logs to the mill to be sawed on shares. Miller was building a house at
Nephi, and he and his son, (Dan M. Miller), thirteen years of age, were
working a pair of mules getting out logs for lumber to finish his house. All
told, there were five of us at the mill.

"The 26th of September, 1872, was Saturday. We were all going home
except Higbee. The house in which we camped was about two hundred
yards below the mill, between the road and creek, with the door toward
the road east. About thirty yards east of the house at the side of the road
lay a pile of poles, one on each end of the pile, and a large pole on top of
them, making an opening to put their guns through. There were marks in
the dust where five Indians had lain, ready to fire, if we had all gone out
together.

"I called GLEDHILL to go after the oxen which were in the hills about
a mile south. He left the house shortly after I did. Soon afterwards, Miller
came up to the mill and loaded his wagon, and in a short time Miller's boy
came up to the mill. GLEDHILL brought the oxen, yoked them, left them
in the mill yard, and returned to the house. Soon after this I went down
to breakfast and Miller and his boy started away. They passed the house
with their load of lumber, drove about one hundred yards below the house
around a patch of oak brush, which hid them from view, and then stopped
to tighten the binder.

"The Indians had run down behind a low ridge where their horses
were tied to the oak brush, and from ambush fired five shots, most if not
all, taking effect. Miller was shot through one arm and in the side under
the arm, and one bullet passed through his bowels, breaking his back. The
boy was shot through one thigh and through one wrist, the ball passing
between the two bones.

"We heard the shooting, but thought the Millers were shooting at a
rabbit or wolf and took no more notice of it. We finished our breakfast and
all three started up to the mill after my team. When about half way up, we
heard the rattle of a wagon, and in looking back we saw a man standing up
on the wagon driving as fast as he could make the horses go.

"TOM GLEDHILL said, 'That fellow is driving pretty fast up hill.'

"I remarked, 'He must have had one drink too many this morning.'

"Just then the man shouted, 'There is a man shot all to pieces below
the house.'

CHIEF ANTERO, A UTE WARRIOR

COL. REDICK N. ALLRED
SPRING CITY

"We then knew what the shooting was we had heard and started back to the house as fast as we could run. We saw some horsemen south west of the house coming at full speed through the brush, and thought they were Indians trying to head us off from the house, where we left our guns. When we reached the house, we saw that the men were from Spring City.

"The Miller boy, when shot, tried to run to the house, but the Indians headed him off. They had not yet re-loaded. The boy turned and ran down the road toward Spring City and met these men going out to look for stock. They received word that Indian signs had been seen the previous evening in the foot hills. Some of the men took the boy who was very weak from the loss of blood to Spring City and sent a telegram to Mt. Pleasant. Col. JOHN L. IVIE gathered up a small posse with which he pursued the Indians, but never overtook them. Later Colonel ALLRED took young Miller home and kept him until he recovered. Brother ALLRED's wife attended him like a mother without compensation . . .

"The Spring City men carried Miller, one at each corner of the litter, and GLEDHILL took Miller's wagon with one yoke of oxen. I drove my wagon with the other two yoke. Having traveled about half the distance to Spring City, Miller said he was tired and wanted them to lay him down in the road to rest. . . . I asked him if he would like us to take any word to his family, if he should not live to see them. He said he had nothing on his mind, but would like to see his twins before he died. We learned later that a pair of twin baby boys had recently been born to him. We asked him if he wanted us to take vengeance on the Indians. He said, 'No, they don't know any better.'

"'He said he knew some of the Indians, one was Taby, and there were five of them. . . . In a short time the poor fellow expired. Colonel ALLRED came up with a wagon, and his body was carried down to Spring City. That night his family, who had been telegraphed at Nephi, came to Spring City and took charge of the remains.

"It was generally believed that the Indians mistook Mr. Miller for Bernard Snow, as they had the same kind of team, a gray and a bay mule, and Snow often had a boy with him. The Indians did not like Bernard Snow. In one of the raids on Ephraim, Bernard Snow, the veteran actor who was building a mill at the mouth of the canyon near the settlement sustained during several hours a lonely but heroic siege; the savages surrounded the mill, but the gallant defender kept up a fire so vigorous that they were forced to retire."

[Note: Bernard Snow's wife was VIOLET GLEDHILL, a sister of THOMAS GLEDHILL.]

IDA BELLE GLEDHILL wrote this experience her mother LILLIE BELLE IVIE (Gledhill) had while a young girl:

"After the war was over . . . [JOHN LEHI IVIE] worked with Indians and they were always camping at our place. One time mother was baby sitting the smaller children and heard a noise downstairs. She lit a lamp and came down . . . to investigate. In the light as she came down she saw a room full of Indians who wanted her father. She was so frightened the lamp shook and she had to put it down. They left, but one Indian buck would keep coming back, putting his arms on the door and grinning at her. She was very glad to have her parents return. Mother never overcame her fear and dislike of Indians. We hid from them whenever we could. She frightened us by telling us Indians would get us if we didn't wear our bonnets."

Grandfather JAMES OSCAR IVIE wrote:

"Father was a good hunter and provider—always keeping the family in meat and provisions. As there was no law against killing wild game, he always kept plenty of meat and especially deer meat, both fresh and dried. He had plenty to help his neighbors, and was always big hearted and willing to share and to do good to mankind in case of need. . . . One evening when father was going to camp, the snow was deep and hard walking and he got to the top of the hill above the creek. He saw two bear cubs by the creek about fifty yards from him. The snow was waist high. He looked for the old bear in the willows; but he couldn't see her, so he shot one of the cubs, which fell. The old grizzly came out of the bush and slapped and bit the cub trying to get it up and get away—but it was dead. While it was working with the cub, father got behind the tree. He just got out of sight when the bear looked up, smelt around and couldn't see anyone. It took the other cub and started away. . . . Then it would come back for the other cub. It would smell around and then go away; then it would return and repeat its performance. It kept father there for two or three hours. Father said that if he had shot and only wounded her, she might have got him, as he would have had no show to get away or climb a tree. His gun was a muzzle loading gun. He had to go to camp after dark."

~ 37 ~

FREIGHTING TO PIOCHE, NEVADA
DRAMATICS IN MOUNT PLEASANT

Grandfather JAMES OSCAR IVIE wrote:

"I was born in Mount Pleasant, Sanpete County, on the ninth day of May 1863. I was two years old before I remember anything. One incident I remember—we lived west from the North Fort and father was trying his gun at a mark. I wanted to shoot the gun so father took aim and told me to pull the trigger, which I did. We hit the mark—which made me a 'big boy.' Mother lived on the northeast corner of the lot and MARYETTE (Father's second wife) lived in the middle of the lot. We moved to the south side of town where Father had traded for an unfinished house and lot. I remember carrying shingles to father to finish the roof."

[Note: In 1867, or soon after, MARY ETT divorced JOHN and went to Provo.]

"I would keep a fire in the fireplace to keep warm. I seen the house finished and mother and family moved into a comfortable two room house where we lived until 1884, when father sold it and his Chester Farm and went to Vermillion, Sevier County, Utah."

[Note: Aunt IDA described the home as a two-story home with a porch across the front.]

"When I was . . . about six years old, I went to Auntie Hyde's school, in a one room log house with slabs for seats, having four holes bored in them and wooden sticks for legs. We took turns going to the corner to do our writing on a desk and a fireplace to get warm by. When let out for recess the teacher would come out and holler, 'To Books! To Books! many times. If any didn't come right in, they got a pair of leather straps over their backs. I went to school for three or four winters and I would herd cows in the summertime and during the years 1871, 2, 3—Charles Didham, Joseph Branstead and myself. I used to go to Sunday School where we would receive a little card about the size of a postage stamp for each Sunday's attendance with some scripture line or verse, which we were asked to learn and tell where it was found. I took great delight in learning them. When we got ten of the small cards, we would give them to the teacher and receive a larger one with a verse on it to learn. Ten of them would be changed for a larger one (about 8x10) with the Lord's Prayer. The one getting the most and learning them all was praised and given a token of reward, which always made him feel good for being at the head.

"As we grew older, we would take turns reading a few verses from the Bible and would commit them to memory—long chapters. I was at the head or near it—most of the time. While in my early teens, I worked on the farm at Chester, Utah, and was always ready to do my part. Machinery was scarce. People had to mow hay with a scythe and cut grain by hand with a cradle. I have raked hay by hand and followed a man that cradled the hay, three acres a day. I bound the grain in bundles when only thirteen or fourteen years of age. I could bind my share with any of the men. Wages were two bushels of wheat per day. One time a man only gave me one bushel per day, because I was only a boy and I always looked upon him as an unfair man.

"While young, I went freighting with my father (JOHN LEHI IVIE) and my brother, JOHN LAFAYETTE—to Frisco [by Beaver, Utah], Oscila [Osceola, by Mount Wheeler, Nevada], Pioche, Bristol [north of Pioche], and many other camps during all the seventies. I learned many foolish ways of the world as all camps had saloons and rough people in them. The saloons were the only place to spend the evenings, where gambling, drinking, dancing with lewd women and sometimes a lot of words and shooting took place; but while seeing things of this nature going on, I can truthfully say that I kept myself clean from the above and I believe I kept many Mormon boys from going to places that would lead them down."

The western Nevada silver mines in Pioche were discovered a little before 1864. Later that year, Nevada was made a state to help President Lincoln with the financing of the Civil War and to pass the 13th and 14th Ammendments of the Constitution. Pioche grew rapidly to around 10,000 people. It was the second largest city in Nevada—Virginia City was larger. It is said that there were 240 claims on Treasure Hill at one time. Many gunfights resulted. Hired killers were brought in to settle some of the disputes. Seventy-five were killed and buried in "boot hill" before there was one natural death. The old "Million Dollar Court

House" has been restored (1970s) along with the lower story of the scary old rock jail that was dug into Treasure Hill. Originally, the jail was entered through a door in the back from the upper road. The Court House looks over the steep descent into the broad valley below and the distant mountains to the east that border Utah.

NORTHERN PIOCHE IN 1870, SHOWING THE YET UNFINISHED
MILLION DOLLAR COURTHOUSE AND JAIL BEHIND
THE HIGH COST WAS MOSTLY FROM GRAFT AND HIGH INTEREST RATES WHEN THE MINES
WERE LESS PROFITABLE AND PAYMENTS BECAME MUCH MORE DIFFICULT.

I [Brookie Condie Swallow] had never heard of Pioche before we purchased our first drugstore there, nor was I aware of Enterprise [Utah], Panaca, Caliente, or Alamo, Nevada. We were told that it was at the end of the earth, and joked that if you went any further, you dropped off into nothing. We arrived there in February 1957 with four very young children to live in a three-bedroom home built in the dug out mountain behind the drugstore with many cement steps going up the side to the next highest level. Only memories of the violent days of the past remained, but it was still a great adventure.

Grandfather JAMES OSCAR IVIE continued:

"While in Pioche, I was spending the evening in a saloon with three Mormon boys. One said, 'Let's go up to the chippies'—(lewd women). The two said, 'All right.' and then said, 'Come on, OSCAR.'

"I said, 'Boys, there isn't money enough in Pioche to get me to go there and if you think anything of your character and the teachings of your father and mother, you wouldn't go to such places!' The result was they didn't go there and they told me afterwards that they were glad they didn't go. They wished I was with them always. One pointed to a man and said, 'He is the man that led me there.'——a lewd Mormon raised boy.

"At another time, I was in the company with two of the men above mentioned and taking a load of bullion ore to Milford—the train depot to ship the bullion. There were goods there to be taken back to Pioche. So we loaded our wagons—four loads and being winter and 30 degrees below zero. One of the wagons had three barrels of whiskey and every noon and night, the three barrels were tapped and much liquor was drunk to ward off the cold by the three men—while I rode the wagon. So one of the three men said to me, 'OSCAR, why is it that you don't drink with us? You ride all the time and we walk and drink and then can't keep warm.'

"I told them, 'I could freeze them to death.' Our loads were delivered and we loaded bullion back to Milford. Then we left to go home—myself being the lead wagon. The snow was about a foot deep. The men tied their teams behind my wagon and then they all got into my wagon to have some fun with me. They had liquor and told me I had to drink with them. They wouldn't take 'No!' for an answer. I saw they were too many for me and were going to force me to drink with them. I took the bottle and made out like I was drinking. After a few drinks, I played I was happy. They would laugh and wink at each other, thinking I was getting full--so I played that much harder and just before night, we turned east toward Cove Fort.

"The snow was getting deeper (about eighteen inches.) All three men were dead to the world and lying in my wagon, so I got to the cedars and I camped for the night and had to shovel the snow away for a fire, then take a horse and snake some wood. The fire was made, coffee pot put on and I put a handful of salt in the coffee. Then I got the men around the fire, gave them some coffee, then went to taking care of the horses, while the men stayed around the fire—sick, as a result of drinking the coffee. It was 30 degrees below zero.

"I finally got the ten heads of horses fed and then made the beds. I got the men to bed at two o'clock A. M.. The next morning, they got up rubbing their eyes and hair wondering where they were and how they got there. They thanked me over and over again for not getting down with them, because some one or all of us would have perished that cold night.

"I had the laugh on them afterwards. One of the party, Dell Nebeker, told the workers at the Manti Temple, in my presence, that I taught him the best lesson that he ever had and it caused him to repent and live a better life. He related the circumstances to all the workers and said that one or all would have frozen to death."

The first fire in Pioche by Peter Gottfredson, compiler of *Indian Depredations:*

"Hans and I, with five other Mount Pleasant boys, went to Pioche, Nevada, spring 1870 . . . . In August, 1871, Pioche burned. It was caused by a lantern falling on a porch of a boarding house kept by two women. The wind was blowing and it got too much of a start before it was noticed. Nearly the whole town burned and there was no hay left in town.

"Felsenthal's powder magazine exploded and threw a stone door weighing more than a thousand pounds over the town and up to the Burke Mine. Some men were killed in a saloon where some liquor barrels exploded. It was said that thirty men lost their lives by the fire. A small church on Meadow Valley Street was used as a morgue. We went to see the dead. Some were burned to a crisp. Others with arms, legs, or heads gone. It was a gruesome sight . . . .

"The night Pioche burned Hans and I camped about two miles east of Pioche. We were loaded with twenty eight thousand pounds of hay on the two teams. As we drove into the lower part of town, we were met by men who wanted hay. We were offered five cents a pound by the bale. When up main street about halfway C. H. Light who we had sold hay to before met us. He said he would give us seventy five dollars a ton and take the job lot. I asked Hans if we had better let him have it, which we decided to do provided he would give us a contract to deliver a hundred tons more at thirty six dollars a ton. We got the contract, and got a thousand and fifty dollars for our two loads. Fourteen tons. We delivered the hundred tons and some over, and got our pay according to agreement.

"Then in the spring of 1872, Hans and William Higbee brought their teams to Mount Pleasant. They worked various places throughout the summer; then in the fall, [Hans] loaded with rails at York railroad station for Pioche. [Peter] loaded at Mount Pleasant with chopped barley and they met at Round Valley [Scipio] and went together to Pioche where they hauled cord-wood to the quartz mill at Bullionville [across the swamp from our 1962 SWALLOW home in Panaca, Nevada] till spring." Hans stayed at Pioche until fall, then he loaded "with quartz-mill machinery and went to Eldorado Canyon, Nevada. He worked for the mill company for a time." Before Christmas, Peter returned to Mount Pleasant and Hans remained in Pioche—the ancestor of the Gottfredsons of Caliente, Nevada. Eldorado Canyon is now covered by Lake Meade, north of Hoover Dam.

Hans "ran boats on the Colorado river freighting cord wood and salt from up the river for the company. He had a crew of thirteen Piute Indians and learned their language and some of their traditions."

FREIGHTERS AT YORK RAILROAD STATION. GRANDFATHER JAMES OSCAR IVIE IS ON THE LEFT.

Ute and Piute Traditions by H. J. Gottfredson:

"They believe when the earth was created that it was level and beautiful, that fruit and vegetation grew spontaneously, that game was plentiful everywhere and that all was peace, that God (Towats) lived in the south, and that the Lord had two sons. The elder son, who was independent and could always take care of himself, was the father of the Indians who inherit his nature; the younger was a cry baby always wanting everything he saw, and he is the father of the white people. The Lord granted him his desires, and the whites inherit his disposition, that is the reason why the white people are smarter in getting and in inventing and making things. But as orators they are not the equals of the Indians. At one time the father became vexed at his children for some cause or other and tearing through the country from south to north he tore up the land as he went along, leaving it in the present condition, with mountains, hills and deserts and not fertile as it was. But that he will sometime come back and level the land and make it as it was before. The Indians are superstitious and believe there is some kind of charm about writing and making pictures. They also believe in Satan (Shin-nob) who is always bent on doing harm that he delights in seeing people do wrong. They do not serve God, because he is good and will not harm any-thing; but they serve Satan through fear; they want to keep peace with him . . . . When trouble comes to them, they think, that if they do something to please him, it will stop the trouble."

Hans later lived and died in Salina. My grandmother IVIE's best friend in her old age was her elderly neighbor lady of Scandinavian descent who lived across the street from her. She called her *Gottfredson*.

A comment on early Nevada freighting is recorded by Boyd E. Quate, *Pioneers of Snake Valley*, 8 Nov 1894:

> "Tonight we visited with freighters . . . from Sanpete County, Utah one of the best agricultural counties of the state, but markets were poor and money was a scarce article with them. These men had loaded their crops of honey, flour, dried fruit, butter and eggs and were hauling them some 200 miles to the Nevada towns where they could change them for money. It was a long hard trip which took them nearly 3 weeks to make and then sometimes they did not get much for their loads. . . . The money made on these trips was about all they had for a year.
>
> "Since the rich strikes in eastern Nevada in 1869, White Pine and Lincoln counties had been the purse for southern Utah. For years the prices of foods had been high and these farmers had made big money by hauling their products to Nevada. But now times were hard; and many of the good camps had closed down and what people were left were just hanging on and waiting for better times to come. So these tireless men still hauled their loads over the mountains and deserts [and told] when times were good and money was plentiful, when their loads used to net them from $300 to $500. Now they had to haul to a failing market; and if their loads netted them from $100 to $150, they were happy to get that and made it go as far as it would."

By 1871, young GEORGE SWALLOW of Fillmore, Utah, the first child of THOMAS and CAROLINE CROW SWALLOW to arrive from England, was also hauling freight between Milford, Utah, and Pioche, Nevada. He was then age 19. In 1872, he worked on a cattle drive that took him into the Elko area. Returning back, he stayed the night at the Benjamin Kimball ranch at Shoshone, Nevada, which borders the western side of the foothills at the base of Mount Wheeler, the highest mountain in Nevada. Mr. Kimball was impressed with the young man and asked him to care for the ranch while he made a quick trip to Salt Lake City. Kimball was even more impressed when he returned, and he offered him a partnership in 1873. GEORGE accepted the offer and sold one-half of his lot in Fillmore to the HENRY DAVIES and THOMAS DEARDEN families, who had arrived to build their steam-powered sawmill on Chalk Creek. They had met and travelled south with his two brothers JOSEPH and JAMES, when they first arrived from England. In time, GEORGE SWALLOW would become the single owner of this large ranch in White Pine County.

The DAVIES and DEARDEN families loved Fillmore. At first the mill and lumberyard were very successful. Then a very harsh winter arrived and the snow piled higher and higher. The spring thaw came rapidly, flooding the valley and washing away the whole sawmill. HENRY and THOMAS then began hauling freight from Salt Lake City to Fillmore and to the mines and ranchers in Nevada. SARAH BOLTON (Davies) died in 1884. Her husband, HENRY DAVIES, lived until 1896. Their daughter CHARLOTTE had twelve children. She died from a lingering illness on 5 Jan 1889. She was only forty years old.

Husband THOMAS DEARDEN added to his small income by building a general merchandise store in Baker, Nevada, that year, but his younger children remained mostly in Fillmore, where they could attend school and church until he could build a home for them. He purchased a second store in Garrison, Utah, about 1904, and called them the *Ranchers' Store*.

My husband GROVER SWALLOW's grandmother, ISABELLA DEARDEN, was the oldest child living at their home in Fillmore. Much of the responsibility of the younger children fell upon her, until she married CHARLES SWALLOW in 1891. She wrote:

"About a year after my mother's death, the family became ill with diphtheria . . . . There were six of us . . . . They sent for father to come home. No one was allowed to come into the house except two quarantine physicians, who would . . . blow some medicine down our throats. One night Lizzie, a younger sister and I were sleeping in the same bed, and we were both ill. Father had returned and [was] sitting by the bed watching us. [Her sister] CHARLOTTE [who had married JAMES SWALLOW] had come to help. [She] was tired and worn out, and father was also tired from traveling and loss of sleep. Both had fallen asleep for just a moment. Suddenly a dog by the window howled three times. Father jumped up and hurried to the bed and found little Lizzie was dead. From this time on, it has always made me feel awful to hear a dog howl."

ISABELLA DEARDEN ON HER WEDDING DAY

AN OLDER THOMAS DEARDEN

THE OLD SWALLOW GENERAL STORE IN MEADOW, UTAH

Early Dramatics in Mount Pleasant, Utah by Dora Day Johnson as told by Valentine L. Anderson, 1924 (Longsdorf):

"I came to Mt. Pleasant March 1860. I was at that time eight years old. That winter the log meeting house, in the center of the fort, was the play house. Some of the players who took part at that time were Wood Brandon, JOHN IVIE and his wife, [MARY] KATHERINE IVIE, Dolph Bennett, George Porter, Joseph S. Day and others whom I do not now remember. They played 'Good for Nothing Nan,' and the 'Merchant of Venice.' The scenery was wagon covers and other materials mixed together, but didn't we children enjoy it! And so did everyone else. The next play house was the Social Hall, with real scenery. Wood Brandon and KATHERINE IVIE were the only two members who stayed with the company. In 1869 a new dramatic company was formed. Those belonging to the company from time to time were . . . KATE CANDLAND . . . KATHERINE IVIE . . . and myself. The men were . . . Peter and Hans Gottfredson, Wood Brandon, and a number of others would join the company.

"During the winters of 1869 and 1870 the company would play three successive nights a week in Mt. Pleasant, and would also play in the neighboring towns, traveling, of course, in bob sleighs or wagons. They played such dramas as 'The Rose of Elrick Hill,' 'Night and Morning,' 'The Skeleton Witness,' and the 'Carpenter of Roan.' These were always followed with a farce, such as 'Matrimony,' 'Swiss Swane,' 'The Forest Rose,' etc. Each player received three complimentary tickets, and a settlement was made each spring. I remember once each player got two and a half bushels of wheat for their winter's work. Tickets were about twenty-five cents each. The company after a while owned their own scenery. They played in the Social Hall and in Jessons' Hall. There was no entrance to the stage in the Social Hall, and the crowds were so large they could not pass through the aisles, so the cast had to crawl through the windows to get to the stage. . . . The company played Little Fontleroy, with ANNIE WOODHOUSE CANDLAND dressed in a black velvet suit and with white collars and cuffs, as Lord Fontleroy, she looked swell. It was unusual to see a girl dressed in boy's clothing in that day. The Bishop and family, the Bishop's counselors and families always had free tickets. . . . The players used no makeup, excepting flour on the hair to make it gray. Thunder and lightning was made by using gun powder and sheet iron . . . Later, the upstairs of the Co-op Store was used for plays. The audience always bought peanuts and enjoyed them between acts. It was very common for almost all the men in the audience to go outside between the acts, and rush in when the bell rang."

PLAY, by Malvina Crane, written in 1926:

"After the scenic equipment had been put in, our troop held forth at regular intervals, crowds of eager people always packing the house to its utmost capacity. You should have been there to witness some of those classical plays! We had no very great artists, of course, but those who took part did the job to the satisfaction of all who came to witness the shows . . . . I am unable to recall a complete list of the men and women who took part in our theatricals . . . . The real leader and organizing genius was the Englishman, John Wallis, who had considerable ability and did much towards securing the formation of an efficient troop. Assisting him were the following gentlemen, according to my recollection . . . R. N. Bennett, W. W. Brandon, JOHN CARTER . . . ALBERT CANDLAND, THOMAS GLEDHILL . . . Among the ladies were . . . ANNIE and KATE CANDLAND . . . MARY KATHERINE IVIE.

"The popular dances were: Plain quadrille, Tucker quadrille, French Four, Upper Reel, and some Danish dances. Then there was the Flying Dutchman, the Mazurka, the Tyrola Polka or Danish Glide, and many kinds of fancy waltzes too numerous to mention, but which were a great improvement upon the present jazzy movements in the sober judgment of the old people."

Organization of a **BRASS BAND**–By Louise Hastler, written in 1923:

"In the autumn on 1869, the Governor of Utah sent notice to the citizens of Sanpete County, that a military drill would be held the first week in November. The gathering place would be between Ephraim and Manti. All captains and officers of the Indian War Organization should be represented, also the Military Bands . . . . John Hastler, who had arrived in Mt. Pleasant in October, had brought with him a full set of instruments from Switzerland, [was] engaged to organize a brass band . . . . He distributed instruments, and they started practicing every evening; he was greatly handicapped in not knowing the English language, but Brother Winkler and Jacob Hafen acted as interpreters.

"Many amusing stories are told about how hard he strove to express himself. If any of the members would miss a note, he stopped all proceedings and would call out 'Stop! Stop! It is Falsch.' While they were playing at the drill, some of the members played out of time and he stepped up . . . and took hold of the instrument, and tried to tell him not to play any more. He often tried other means to be understood, he was quick to memorize words he thought would emphasize a meaning, which would often be a swear word. [John Hastler had been director of the cavalry band in his company in Switzerland.]

"The gathering was largely attended and a great success, for which the brass band received much encouragement. It was, however, the last drill we were allowed to celebrate. In 1870, the Mormons were prohibited from bearing arms. [But] the brass band had come to stay. For more than twenty-five years it existed under the same leadership. . . . At the present time, March 24, 1923, of the group, only OSCAR BARTON and Olaf Rosenlof are with us. . . . Later he [John Hastler] took the leadership of the ward choir."

~ 38 ~

MARY CATHERINE BARTON IVIE
LYMAN PETERS

My mother's first cousin IDA BELLE GLEDHILL (Christensen Buchannan) wrote the following about MARY CATHERINE BARTON (Ivie Peters) after visiting with aunt IDA IVIE (Stanford Dix) in 1960:

"My father, THOMAS GLEDHILL, used to say Grandmother MARY CATHERINE was the most beautiful woman he'd ever seen. She was refined, kind spoken, thrifty and made a fine home. She had black curly hair, and laughing eyes. Aunt IDA told me she had met an old friend of her mother's in Bountiful, who said, 'She was the prettiest, and most popular girl in their crowd. She was loved by everyone who knew her. When she married we all hated to have her leave Bountiful.'

"Grampa JOHN LEHI [IVIE] was made a Colonel in the . . . Black Hawk Indian War. He was away much of the time, so she raised her family alone much of the time. Also, he had another wife, MARETTA CARTER, and after the breakup between he and MARETTA, he married VIOLET GLEDHILL, sister to my father. He was in Sevier Co. much of his time and Grandmother saw some really hard times there alone with her family at Mt. Pleasant. Food was scarce and her family had to come to her rescue many times to keep them from starving.

"She didn't ever whip her children, but her talks to them was punishment enough. One time, Aunt IDA took a dollar and ran off to school. Of course, she had many friends who could suggest ways to spend it. So they bought candy and sloughed school and went home late. Grandmother just talked to her and it was agreed that as punishment Aunt Ida was to sit in the High chair all day. She was to tell everyone who came in what she had done, as she received any money, she paid 10 cents of it until the dollar was paid back. But all of that didn't hurt like hurting her mother and knowing how bad her mother felt."

MARY CATHERINE lost three children as infants,

"then two later sons at Mt. Pleasant. SEYMOUR CLIFF was 6 years old when he died of dropsy [accumulation of body fluids, usually from congestive heart failure or kidney failure.] JOHN LAFAYETTE died at 20 years of age . . . they had a good crop of grain and he was carrying large sacks of grain up a steep stairs to put out in the loft. He became overbalanced and fell and injured his back on the steps. He suffered terribly. Grandmother took him to a doctor in Salt Lake, but he died and was buried in Mt. Pleasant. She was just heartbroken."

MARY CATHERINE
BARTON IVIE

"MARY CATHERINE was a nurse and midwife in her spare time, she treated the sick and set bones. She had many old pioneer remedies, salves and liniments. One salve was made of bees wax, sticky pine gum and mutton tallow. One time she was making a liniment on wash day, the boiler boiled over and somehow her liniment caught fire. She burned her hands badly, but instructed the children to grate up potatoes, put them in 2 salt sacks, then she put her hands in the sacks. It cured her. She had no blisters or trouble with them.

"She carded wool, made lye, soap and did much sewing. After she and Grandfather separated, she did much sewing for a very wealthy woman, a Mrs. Lewis. She did much of her cooking in black iron pots which hung in the fireplace that had to be white-washed every morning. That was Aunt IDA's job, while she was still in the IVIE home. She knitted all the socks, caps, and sweaters for the family. She could walk and go right on knitting. The socks for the girls were flowered patterns, white for summer and black for winter. Of course, they all wore long-legged underwear, too.

"Then trouble came to this couple. You see, Grandfather had a business partner, LIME PETERS, who lived much at their home, even when Grandfather was away. People talked. Grandfather believed the gossip and so Grandmother went away with LIME PETERS, taking the four youngest children with her. Aunt IDA says she remembers Grandmother telling her own mother, Grandma BARTON, it was unfounded gossip. She and LIME were married in Provo and went on into Idaho to live. I guess divorce was a formality and not required in those days."

Actually, the Decree of Divorce of JOHN L. IVIE, Plaintiff vs. MARY C.

IVIE, Defendant, dated 14 Feb 1881, is recorded in the Sanpete County Probate Minute Book A, page 212. It ratified and confirmed the original agreement of 5 Feb 1881, signed by said parties as to alimony, care and custody of children. It was signed by JAMES A. ALLRED. JOHN L. IVIE did not marry VIOLET GLEDHILL until later in September of that same year. VIOLET, according to my mother's records, had been married previously to BERNARD SNOW, who died. She was teaching school. From great aunt IDA's story, it appears that great-grandmother MARY CATHERINE did not acknowledge her divorce to her young daughter and perhaps others of the community until months later, as IDA seemed to believe VIOLET was a plural wife.

Grandfather JAMES OSCAR IVIE was seventeen when his parents were divorced. He was the oldest child at home, although he was their sixth child. His older brother JOHN LAFAYETTE IVIE had died the previous year, and his remaining older sister MARY SUSANNAH IVIE had married JOHN TAYLOR HENINGER five years earlier on the 13 Nov 1874. They were living at Chester, which is about 10 miles west of Mount Pleasant. LILLIE BELLE was teaching school at Chester—staying with her older sister and husband. This arrangement became unsuitable when her sister's husband decided that she would make a desirable second wife. LILLIE BELLE quickly returned to Mount Pleasant.

MARY CATHERINE, had a problem--how to support the four younger children and herself without male help. She sewed for wealthy Mrs. Larsen; she was a nurse and midwife; but this did not provide enough for the necessities of daily family survival. Her parents helped from time to time, but she was in-dependent. JAMES OSCAR and LILLIE BELLE had chosen to remain with their father, JOHN LEHI IVIE, who was courting VIOLET and had moved to Vermillion (southwest of Salina). In desperation, great-grandmother con-vinced her son JAMES OSCAR, who had just turned eighteen, to marry ELSIE ELIZABETH DALLEY and manage the farm in Chester to help her. The young couple married August 1881. It didn't take my grandfather long to realize his mistake. ELSIE was a termagant (tumultuous, scolding woman) in his opinion. A child was on its way, or the marriage would have been shorter. For the sake of his new daughter, VIOLA SUSANNA IVIE, born 11 May 1882, he tried, but could not endure. His father married VIOLET in September of 1881 and they lived in Vermillion.

WEDDING PICTURE OF JOHN LEHI IVIE WITH HIS WIFE VIOLET GLEDHILL (SNOW, IVIE)

MARY CATHERINE, finding her income still at starvation level, gave up her struggle to reunite her family and married LYMAN PETERS in Provo— (date unknown, but between the fall of 1881 and March of 1882). In 1884, the Chester farm was sold and JAMES OSCAR IVIE went to Vermillion, now divorced—leaving his former wife and young daughter with her parents.

JAMES OSCAR IVIE's young daughter VIOLA was taught by her mother to dislike her father. When she grew older she became acquainted with him and his family and loved them very much. My mother became a very special friend of VIOLA all her remaining life. She married FRANK SHEPHERD. Their son LAVAR would deliver a large truck load of coal to us every winter at our ranch in Carey, Idaho. We were always excited and looked forward to his overnight visits with us.

IDA BELLE continues:

"Determined to escape (Mr. HENINGER), LILLIE BELLE came back to Mt. Pleasant, and there she and Father fell in love. Father (THOMAS GLEDHILL) and Mother were married on Oct. 8, 1881 in Uncle PETE and Aunt MILLIE [GLEDHILL] GOTTFREDSON's home in Vermillion with Grandfather and Aunt VIOLET as the witnesses. [LILLIE BELLE and THOMAS lived in Mt. Pleasant until after their first son, RAY, was born 13 Feb 1883, and then moved to Vermillion] . . . . Mother was a good seamstress and made all the clothes for the family; coats, hats, pants, dresses and anything else.

"LIME, according to my father, was not a refined man. I doubt [he was] even a member of the church and [he] was a drinker. So with her refinement and ideals, she must have had a bad life, as he beat her and the children. He was often mean to them; but Grandmother felt that marriage was sacred and she was bound to him.

"At some time in her life she lived at what is now known as Sun Valley, [Idaho]. It was a big cattle ranch. They didn't own it though. LIME PETERS managed it. Many men were working there at that time and Grandmother took care of supplies and a Chinese cook, who died cooking. While PETERS had all vices, he wanted her and the children and held home in very strict circumstances. She was very clean, and one time a hired girl brought them body lice. Grandmother worked very hard to get rid of them and felt so ashamed about having them around.

"She had pierced ears and pierced the ears of all her girls. She heated a needle and put linen thread in it and while the needle was hot put it through the ear lobe. Every day the thread would be pulled a little till the ears healed and left a hole for earrings.

"She was interested in mines and staked out many claims herself. One of her claims got jumped and it became the biggest mine in Idaho. [Probably the Triumph Mine at East Fork.] Aunt IDA hurt her leg and it got to be a very bad sore. Her mother healed it by using wagon grease on it, and while it was healing, her mother pulled her in a wagon until the sore was gone.

"When Aunt MAY was just past 14, a man named Solinder, almost PETERS' age and his friend, asked if she could go to visit the Catholic church with him. Grandmother said, 'Yes, if ALDEN went along.' But at the door, they left ALDEN and Solinder took Aunt MAY right up to the front and was married to her. Uncle ALDEN ran home for grandmother, but by the time she got there, they were on horses and gone. She (her sister MAY) only lived with him a short time. She had ARTHUR who lived, and twin boys who died by this man. Her husband drank, beat and choked her. Grandmother had to send money to feed them, and finally sent money for her to come home. Then Grandmother built an extra room on the house for she and the child to live in."

According to family records, MAY married JOHN SOLENDER in Boise, Idaho, 18 Apr 1882. Around 1935, her son, ARTHUR SOLENDER and his wife lived in Carey and had a daughter, KATHERINE, who was in my (BROOKIE CONDIE's) first and second grade classes. I liked her. During the noon hour, if we girls walked to the store for candy, she would stop by the pool-hall door, and her father would leave his card game and give her money. They never came to church. Around 1937, they moved to Mackay, Idaho. I didn't know that we were related.

"Grandma had one other mining claim which she expected much of. One August day [1888—fifty-one-years-old] she set out with a buyer for her mine. Uncle RAY [10 years old] was in the buckboard with her, with a horse tied behind to go to inspect it and probably sell, if the right price was offered. They went as far as they could in buckboard, then got on horses. This was at Minamore Mt., Red Fish Lake. Something frightened the horse and though Grandmother was a good horse woman, she was thrown; but her foot caught in the stirrup. She was dragged a long way--being kicked in the head and chest, and bounced on rocks. She got loose, but was badly hurt. They got her to the buckboard and brought her home. She was in great pain in the head and lungs. Her leg was twisted at the knee. She had no crutch, so she would put her leg on a chair and dragged the chair about a little. In October, she went back to bed and never got up again. Death came December 24, 1888. A fine article was written about her life in the Deseret News. It told of her devotion to family and nurse for the community. Her friends were the influential people of the town, the banker, the hotel owner, etc. Her body was sent to Mt. Pleasant for burial. She was dressed in black, which hurt my mother very much.

"After the funeral, Uncle RAY and Aunt IDA sat on the doorstep wondering and crying—who would take care of them? [RAY was 10 years old and IDA was 13.] Now, Aunt MAY had married a man named PIERCE and was living in Salt Lake. Uncle ALDEN wanted to stay there and work in the mine. He did and forgot some of his mother's teachings, and took up the bad habit of smoking. However, before his death he warned his family against it, and getting lungs like his. Uncle RAY and Aunt IDA came back to their father's home where in a few years, Aunt IDA got courted by Eddie Gottfredson. . . . Later, she went to Salt Lake with Aunt MAY, and still later to Idaho and to her brothers, where she met Uncle TOM STANFORD, whom she married. Aunt MAY [and her second husband, PIERCE, a drunkard,] lived in Salt Lake. . . . He had three children. She couldn't stand the life and left him and went to live with her brothers ALDEN and RAY at East Fork. Later, they came to Carey, Idaho, and lived in the EVERETT DIX home."

[Note: After great uncle TOM STANFORD died, aunt IDA married EVERET DIX.]

"Aunt MAY married ERNEST GILES. She lived happily with him and raised her son [and other children]. ARTHUR. GILES was a Captain in World War I, but was never heard of after the war was over. She died of cancer of the liver, brought on they thought by a bruise made by the horn of the saddle when her horse reared."

Aunt IDA IVIE (Stanford) and Aunt MAY IVIE (Giles)

MAY died on 8 Mar 1935 at Carey, Idaho. I, BROOKIE CONDIE, remember being lifted up to see her in her coffin. I have vague memories of her visiting us earlier at the ranch with grandpa and grandma IVIE.

When the four children came to Carey to live, the boys had one pair of nice shoes between them, so they took two sisters to the dances and would divide the time dancing with the shoes. This Photo of them with their families was taken around 1923, probably in East Fork, south of Ketchum, Idaho. ALDEN and MARY ANN AINSWORTH IVIE are on the left. They had only daughters. RAY and MAUDE ELLEN AINSWORTH IVIE are on the right. Their only daughter NEVA is holding their son DREXEL and their son ALDEN is standing by his mother.

My grandfather JAMES OSCAR IVIE wrote:

"Trouble had got into the family and a separation came between father and mother. She went to Ketchum, Idaho, and he to Vermillion, where he married VIOLET GLEDHILL SNOW, and mother married LYMAN PETERS, the man that caused the trouble. And mother told me, when on a visit to see me, in 1888, that she thought more of father's little finger or a hair on his head than she ever did of LYMAN PETERS and while telling it she cried like a child and wished she had her life to live over again. She would hang on to father. When I told father, he said he always thought a lot of mother and was willing to accept her back. We went to the temple after mother's death, 24 Dec 1888, and former blessings were pronounced . . . and they were sealed for time and eternity, my wife ANNIE C. IVIE being proxy. I am writing this to let my brothers, sisters and relatives know the true feelings of father and mother . . . and I hope they take cognizance of it and think more of the Gospel and Father's Kingdom. I could tell more of the viper that made the trouble; but, I will say no more at the present and he will get his dues in the next life."

Young Peter Gottfredson, herding sheep for his father in Thistle Valley in 1864, before the Black Hawk War, wrote about PETERS:

"My brother and I were a short distance west of the herdhouse when an Indian who had seven or eight dogs with him, came after us and made for our sheep. We had a large brindle dog which had been brought in with Gen'l Johnston's Army. We sicked him after the Indian dogs and he threw them right and left; this stopped their rush for the sheep. The Indian then came towards me. He had, besides a gun and bow and arrows, a large painted wagon spoke, with a string through the small end, hung on his wrist . . . acting as if he wanted to hit me with it, I kept backing away from him . . . I asked him what he wanted . . . but he would not talk . . . I squatted down, cocked my gun and with my finger on the trigger pointed it at his face. He jerked his horse back . . . and rode to the herdhouse where all the Indians had gathered . . . They broke open the door and . . . carried away all our bedding, provisions and cooking utensils, and other things, and started towards Fairview . . . they met LYMAN PETERS, coming to Thistle Valley, and when they saw his head over the ridge, they pulled their guns out of their cases. PETERS saw it, got off his horse, turned it between him and the Indians, laid his gun across the saddle, pointing it towards them, and asked what they wanted. They answered 'navish' nothing, placed their guns back in the cases and came on. As they passed PETERS, one of them made a grab for PETERS' gun, but as PETERS struck at the Indian with his gun, the Indian dodged and [he] hit his own horse on the shoulder, laming him.

"PETERS then came down to where we were . . . . Just then one lone Indian . . . came down through the brush on foot. When he was about three hundred yards, PETERS rested his gun on a knob on the corner of the house, cocking it and said, 'Now see me make that Indian jump ten feet in the air.' I told him not to shoot as that would cause trouble. He answered, 'No one will ever know it.' Believing that he intended to shoot, I pushed the gun off the knob.

"Before the Indian came up, PETERS had set his gun against the house; it was a large new rifle. The Indian took hold of the gun to look at it, but PETERS took the gun from the Indian saying, 'You let that be.' The Indian answered, 'You mad.' PETERS said, 'Yes, I am mad.' The Indian said, 'Hombo (what) make you mad?' and shoved his finger around on his body, saying 'You bullets no pass.' LYMAN PETERS took a handful of large bullets from his pocket and, showing them to the Indian, said, 'Don't you think they will pass?' The Indian started off, looking back over his shoulder till he got a long way off."

PETERS is buried in the cemetery at Hailey, Idaho, next to the grave of great-uncle ALDEN IVIE. My mother told us LYMAN PETERS had bragged around Mount Pleasant that he would get the Colonel's wife. He hung around the house at every opportunity and was available for any errand, especially when the Colonel was away. He deliberately started ugly rumors.

Today, 2009, one of PETERS' great-grandchildren, LAIRD WHIPPLE with his wife DEE ANN, lives in the Panaca valley, where they have beautiful farmland and a gorgeous home. They are our very good friends and solid members of the L.D.S. Church. Presently, he is a member of the Panaca Nevada Stake high council. According to our IVIE relations in Hailey, PETERS was very good to the children after MARY CATHERINE died.

Both aunt IDA and uncle RAY lived in Carey, Idaho, when I was growing up. Uncle RAY's son ALDEN helped my mother on our ranch for a while after my father died in 1939. We enjoyed knowing him better. Although IDA and RAY were not very active in the church when I was young, they were very active later and both were sealed to their spouses in the temple prior to my mother's death in 1989.

Uncle RAY's son DREXEL was a little older than my brother MARION. He was an excellent skier, not very tall, and doubled for Claudette Colbert during her skiing scenes in a movie made at the Sun Valley Ski Resort.

I was about four years old, when DREXEL IVIE was a Boy Scout and had received his life-saving merit badge. A large, deep canal ran through Carey and directly in front of the home of uncle JIM and aunt ADA CONDIE BAIRD's home. When the water was turned onto the farm land to the north, the canal would be empty with wonderful sand in the bottom. Sometimes we were allowed to play in the sand for a short while and build small sand castles. My cousin JIMMY BAIRD, two years older, was playing in the sand, unknown to his mother. The water was turned into the canal, and he was quickly washed away. Several blocks south, DREXEL IVIE saw him in the stream and jumped in, pulled him to the bank, and gave him artificial respiration. Aunt ADA arrived and wanted her young son moved to a warmer place; but DREXEL would not budge. It took forty-five minutes before he began to breathe on his own. Our family arrived at the BAIRD's home that evening, and my father and grandfather CONDIE gave JIMMY a blessing.

MARY CATHERINE's nephew, [ELISHA KEMBER BARTON's son,] AMOS BARTON, lived in Carey, Idaho. His daughter, MARGARET was one of my favorite people. She taught us tap dancing, played the piano in church, was very talented on the accordion, and, in addition, she was a beautiful young lady. If our class was ever short a teacher in Sunday school, she was always our first choice. I didn't know we were related. When I was baptized at age eight, our new bishop, R. E. Adamson, placed a large picture on the wall of our chapel where our class was seated in Sunday school. It had spaces for 16 2x4 photos. With only two photos already in the upper left-hand corner, the bishop stated that the empty 14 spaces would be filled before the two recently sent missionaries returned from their missions—about two years. Our ward was small. Carey had a sign that said its population was 269 people (probably the surrounding farmlands were not included.) I was old enough to think that twenty-four would be quite an accomplishment, and watched the pictures increase. Near the end of the two years, the final two photos of two young women were added to the 14 young men. MARGARET BARTON was one of them. One of the highlights of my youth was the homecoming speeches of these young L.D.S. missionaries who seemed so spiritual and energetic. The *Church News* wrote an article giving a special recognition to the Carey Ward for this effort.

TREENY MORTENSEN (seated)
with sisters MARTHA, and HANNAH

My grandmother ANNIE CATHERINE MORTENSEN was called ""TREENY" in her early teens. She was taught by her mother the art of weaving. and was sent to Salt Lake City to learn dressmaking. She made all the dresses in this picture of the three sisters. Their embroidery work was exceptional. In her older years, she claimed to be one of two women still living in Utah who could shear a sheep, card the wool, spin it, dye it, and weave it into cloth on her loom. A beautiful embroidered crewel floral picture by her sister MARTHA is folded in a glass cabinet in the Manti Temple. My sister, LILLIE CLAY, has the mate—signed in embroidery "Treeny."

Their older brother
CHRISTIAN MORTENSEN

JENS FREDRICK and METTE MARIE HANSEN MORTENSEN

(BEFORE HE DIED 9 JAN 1886)

⇥ 39 ⇤

JENS F. MORTENSEN's
NORTHERN STATES MISSION—MINNESOTA

When "TREENY" was sixteen years old, [1880] her father wanted to go on a church mission back to Denmark. The following is taken from his handwritten journal which he wrote in English:

"I, JENS FREDRICK MORTENSEN was moved upon by the spirit of God to Preach the Gospel and to prepare for it. I went to St. George to go through the Temple to have the 2 oldest of my children sealed to me and to administer in [the] temple for some of my Dear Friends and relatives. We had a hard trip in the winter but had good luck and had it satisfactory attended to and when I came home there was a letter to me from John Taylor, President for the twelve apostles of the Church of Jesus Christ of Latter Day Saints that I was called to go to the United States to Preach the gospel which required me to give an immediate answer. [Brigham Young died in 1779]

"I wrote [the] following answer. I am willing to go but I would sooner go to Denmark to Relatives and Friends and get Genealogy. I then received the following: . . . I am required to tell you that you are requested to fit out for a mission to Minnesota but after laboring for a year or so you can have the privilege to finish your mission in Denmark to get your genealogies and so on. I then made preparations and sold the best span of horses and some stock to raise money to travel for and the young ladies made up a dance for Hyrum Jensen and me who at the same time was called to go on a mission and $3.50 cent for each. On April 1st [1880] I was ready to start but had to go through Sanpete to deliver my horses. I bade farewell to my wife and children and left them in care of [Him] that is the protector for the widow and the father of the fatherless and depending on God my heavenly [Father] to help them in need.

"I left town with the horses . . . . I looked back on the town where for several years back had gone through a good deal of hardship and spent many happy days with my family and good many thoughts crossed my mind as I had never before being called to leave family for any length of time . . . stopped in Mayfield and went to Manti on the 2nd and settled up with Brother Christensen about the wagon and arranged with Hans Jensen the morning on the 3rd. I got my money and started for Moroni after that I bid goodby to my sister and relations my nephew N. C. NIELSON gave me $5.00 to help me out. The 4th I left my friends in Moroni. Andrew Jensen later took me with Br. Wesley and family to Fountain Green where, I visited the meeting in the afternoon and was called upon to preach. Had long conversations with my Aunt K. HEISEIT in the evening and stopped with my cousin H. HEISEIT and him and Jens Jensen both took me and Wesley to the depot at Nephi on the 5th. I met with Brother Lund and Erickson from Mt. Pleasant coming from Minnesota and [they] gave some information and Brother Nielsen and Hansen address in Linden [Minnesota]. I then took the [railroad] cars for Salt Lake City and stopped at Thomas Jens and attended conference the next day April 6th and was highly edified and instructed by hearing the Twelve Apostles speak and it was the year of Jubilee. [50 years after the founding of the Church on 6 Apr 1830. JENS was born 9 May 1833 in Denmark.]

"They had spoken about helping the poor and indebted . . . the rich brethren was counseled to give their notes back to their poor brethren and 1000 cows and 5000 sheep was given to the poor and the General RS Society voted to send their wheat to sow for the poor. There was good many missionaries called to go on missions. On the 9th we was set apart for our missions by the twelve apostles . . . . Brother Joseph Young pronounced the blessing on my head. The next day I got books at the [Juvenile] Instruction Office [and] had my appointment confirmed by F. D. Richards and started the same day for Farmington with H. Jensen with me. Stopped with his uncle and was well entertained. Sunday on the 11th we went to meeting and I was called upon to preach to a large assembly. I stayed to the 13, took the cars to Ogden and with 39 more missionaries started for Omaha. We enjoyed ourselves well on the train. Myself and Brother W. Palmer, C. Bolin, C. Jensen, Stayed in Council Bluffs for the night and in the morning of the 16th started for Sioux city. Stayed at Br. Giles and had visit in evening. Started for Madelin arrived there at 6 am on the 17th and started for Linden on foot. Stayed and had breakfast with a Norwegian named Martin and a conversation about the gospel. Arrived at Linden . . . found Brother Larsen from Moroni."

Great-grandfather JENS F. MORTENSEN's mission was mostly in the south central third of Minnesota, which from his journal included many people from Denmark, Norway, and Sweden. There were Lutherans, German Catholics, 7th Day Adventist, Cambellites, Methodists, and he seemed to be able to converse in the various languages. He administered to the sick; preached at meetings and in their homes. He distributed the "Voice of Warning" to many, and some were baptized. There was some persecution. The following was recorded in his journal:

"Sunday [May] 23 stayed at John Gofe in forenoon. Meeting in Grapeland schoolhouse in the afternoon . . . written on the blackboard. 'Apostles from Salt Lake around Grapeland to make proselytes at $40 per head. They are partakers in the Mountain Meadow Massacre they call themselves Elders when they ought to be called outlaws.' . . . I was called upon to open their Sunday school with prayer. In discourse I make some remarks about the prejudice against us. . . .

"Monday 24 Started for Albert Lea. Stayed for the night at Mr. Nels. 3 miles before we came to Albert Lea on the 25 in the afternoon, we found a Danish boardinghouse where I found good many there acquainted with my relatives from Denmark and had a pleasant time. Went to bed about 9 o'clock but 2 hours later the house was surrounded by a mob--the news 2 Mormon Elders had come to town. Had roused the whole Scandinavian population notwithstanding there was 8 different churches in town. When we awoke there was 10 or 12 persons in [the] room and demanded us to come down forthwith as they wanted to see me. I told them that I was tired and sleepy but would be happy to wait on them in the morning. They said that they was working men and had no time through the day. I told them that to oblige them we would wait until evening. They said that there were 500 Scandinavians and they were all united that they would not hear us. I told them that they need not hear us unless they wanted and tried to explain to them the impropriety of coming this time of night to disturb strangers in a boarding house, we could hear yells from underneath, 'down with them—down, down with them, as they are the servants of God, let them try whether he can protect them or not.'

"I felt all the time that God would protect us. After a little the Proprietor Christian Peterson came and told them to go down. . . . I had nearly fallen to sleep again when the lady came up and told us that they was not satisfied and wanted us to come down and talk to them. She said there was not police enough in town to keep order. We then dressed ourselves and went down to talk with them. We heard yells and was in a fearful fright. And one Paul Jensen there had been in Utah . . . . He commenced by finding fault with the Latter day Saints and their children. I told him that the Latter day Saints in Utah was the best people on the face of the whole earth. After some conversation, I told of an event 2 years ago [when] there was about 16 persons from here who slept in my house all night and never was disturbed. He said he was one of them and he did not like this. I found after I came back again that a clerk at the livery store by name Hans was the cause of it. We were very thankful to God for delivering us out of their hands.

"26. left Albert Lea early in the morning and found an emigrant woman with 4 children whose mother & Aunt & Grandmother I had baptized into the church in Denmark was very poor but was glad to see us."

It was a very cold winter. He described it at different times as "fearful cold . . . The winter turned very hard . . . . I did see on the road how they worked the snow plow on the railroad . . . . Very stormy in the afternoon . . . . It was a very heavy snow storm. I helped to keep the snow off the loft." He tells some of his conversations in defense of the church, and of several members that were administered to and healed. His last entry was on 18 Mar 1881, in which he records that Hugh R. Williams "and wife said they want to be baptized the next day."

Minnesota is north of Iowa and close enough to Missouri and Illinois to be quite aware that the *Mormons* were driven from those states. The Mountain Meadows Massacre and polygamy seemed to be their battle cry against these missionaries. His answer to the first was that Brigham Young had sent word on 10 Sep 1857, that

"You must not meddle with them. The Indians we expect will do as they please but you should try and preserve good feelings with them."

Unfortunately, according to court records, the massacre took place before President Young's letter arrived. Later, a trial took place and John D. Lee was executed for the offense.

These emigrants from Arkansas that were killed in the massacre had passed through Salt Lake City earlier, and had made ugly threats claiming they would raise an army from California and return to join with Colonel Johnston and the 2500 U.S. army troops that were approaching from the east to destroy the *Mormons*. They had sneered remarks for the Indians, and had killed livestock, tore down fences, poisoned wells and watering places as they journeyed south, creating an intense hatred among the Indians that spread fear and a spirit of retaliation within the tribes, who in turn put tremendous pressure on the white people of the Cedar City area to cooperate with them. It was a sad and regrettable story; but Church headquarters had not sanctioned it.

Polygamy was defended in great-grandfather MORTENSEN's journal— usually by referring to the Old Testament and the wives of Abraham, Isaac and Jacob, and God's acceptance of it at that time. The *Book of Mormon*, between 544 and 521 B.C., on the American continent, condemned plural marriage:

> "Jacob 2:27–31—*Wherefore, my brethren, hear me, and hearken to the word of the Lord: For there shall not any man among you have save it be one wife; and concubines he shall have none; for I the Lord God, delight in the chastity of women. And whoredoms are an abomination before me; thus saith the Lord of Hosts. Wherefore, this people shall keep my commandments, saith the Lord of Hosts, or cursed be the land for their sakes. For if I will, saith the Lord of Hosts, raise up seed unto me, I will command my people; otherwise they shall hearken unto these things. For behold, I, the Lord, have seen the sorrow, and heard the mourning of the daughters of my people in the land of Jerusalem, yea, and in all the lands of my people, because of the wickedness and abominations of their husbands."*

The twelfth Article of Faith of the L.D.S. Church reads:

> *"We believe in being subject to kings, presidents, rulers, and magistrates, in obeying, honoring, and sustaining the law."*

A decade after great-grandfather MORTENSEN left on his mission to Minnesota, on 6 Oct 1890, Church President Wilford Woodruff issued a Declaration that became known as the "Manifesto" in which he stated, after the Church was accused of breaking the recently adopted Territorial law that prohibited it:

> *"We are not teaching polygamy or plural marriage, nor permitting any person to enter into its practice . . . Inasmuch as laws have been enacted by Congress forbidding plural marriages, which laws have been pronounced constitutional by the court of last resort, I hereby declare my intention to submit to those laws, and to use my influence with the members of the Church over which I preside to have them do likewise . . . And I now publicly declare that my advice to the Latter-day Saints is to refrain from contracting any marriage forbidden by the law of the land."*

The penalty was very soon the same as it is today—excommunication from the Church.

At least five years prior to this "Manifesto," JENS FREDRICK MORTENSEN did take a second wife. He had a dear friend whose last name was Nielson. On his deathbed he insisted that JENS marry his wife, after he died. JENS consented. I haven't discovered the date this occurred; but I believe it was after his mission. Her name was JENSENNA HANSEN (Nielson.) There were no children from this union, and my mother seemed to believe that it was basically a favor to his friend, in order to take care of his widow. We can see from the experience of MARY CATHERINE BARTON (Ivie Peters) that women were at an extreme disadvantage in supporting themselves during the time period that polygamy was practiced. She had only her sewing for the wealthier woman to bring in money to support her family in Mount Pleasant. It was a man's world—physically and economically. Utah was the second State in the Union to give women the full rights of equality including the right to vote. Their original constitution was ratified on 5 Nov 1895.

[Note: Wyoming was the first state to allow women the right to vote, because they became a state in 1890. The Utah Territorial Government had already granted the women equal rights in the 1870s.]

Utah's constitution's fourth article reads:

> "both male and female citizens shall enjoy equally all civil, political and religious rights and privileges."

The nation was not quick to follow. The Constitution of Utah also stated,

> "Perfect toleration of religious sentiment is guaranteed and polygamous or plural marriages are forever prohibited."

After the Civil War had ended and after peace was established with the Indians in the early seventies, the Utah Territorial Government increasingly persecuted the men who had polygamous marriages, and many were imprisoned while these laws were being challenged in the various courts. To avoid being jailed, many of the men escaped by moving their families to Mexico, where polygamy was permitted, sometimes taking only one of their wives.

Grandmother ANNIE CATHERINE "TREENY" MORTENSEN (Ivie) told us the following:

> "The last time I saw Father alive was in 1885. I was decorating the Christmas tree in the meeting house, being one of the committee, when my brother,

FREDDIE, came and told me my mother wanted me. When I got home, she told me Father was called to go to Mexico, and I was to fix his food for him. So I baked some pies and bread and fixed it as good as I could and then went back to the Christmas decorating. When I came back, he was ready to go. He left Salina at 7:00 p.m. that night. Then we did not hear anything from him until Brother Thriber came and said Father wanted me. He thought Mother was not well enough to take the trip, but mother went instead of me. But they did not get there before he died. They say the last thing he had asked them was to raise him up and then he said, 'I am going to preach the gospel!' And those were his last words.

"When I returned that Christmas Eve, I was very sad. Some of my friends came in and wanted to know what was wrong. I did not tell them. When we got the news about his death, we received a telegram. The operator told me to go to Father's other wife's parents and tell them to send word to Kanosh as that was where his wife had gone on a visit to her sisters. I was not to tell anyone else. I went and told them, and I got Sister Gates to do up his temple clothes.

"No one can describe the sadness that came over us when he left, or of when they brought him back a corpse."

He died 9 Jan 1886 at Koosharem, Utah, from pneumonia, caused from exposure to the *fearful cold,* much like he had described in his Minnesota mission journal.

JEN's wife METTE had been driven from her parent's home in Denmark when she joined the *Mormon Church*; yet these parents came to her in a dream, after they died, and asked her to do their temple work. They left METTE over $3,000 as an inheritance. She spent most of it on the genealogical research of her family in Denmark. When their beautiful Manti Temple was completed and dedicated on 24 May 1888, the IVIE and MORTENSEN families remained very busy throughout their lives working in the temple for these relations.

Early in the year, before METTE MARIE MORTENSEN died, 17 Jul 1905, age 75 years, she became quite ill and needed her daughter "TREENY's" care. She promised to give the JAMES OSCAR IVIE family her home and the four acre lot when she died, if they would move to town and take care of her. There was one condition, her youngest son FRED would be able to live with them as long as he chose to. The family accepted the offer and moved to Salina. My mother was in the third grade. FRED lived in the home until he married later in his life. They never had any children.

~ 40 ~

VIOLENCE IN THE SOUTHERN MISSION OF
GRANDFATHER GIBSON A. CONDIE

Grandfather GIBSON A CONDIE of Croyden, Morgan County, Utah, wrote:

"It was a dismal day on the 15th of October, 1866, when I first opened my eyes in this world, Mother has said it was about four o'clock and it was snowing fast. The house in which I was born was built of logs. The cracks were daubed with mud, a white clay hauled from a nearby hill, which stuck pretty well to the logs. The floor was lower than the level of the ground . . . a step down about six inches. This prevented drafts from the floor and prevented cold feet. The roof was covered with soil and sometimes leaked. It contained one room in which was a door, a window, and fireplace. Adjoining this was a lean-to which father used as a blacksmith shop.

"The next important house was the school house. It was a log building with a dirt roof and perhaps 18 by 30 feet in size. This was our meeting house and recreation hall as well as a school room. Near it was three walls of a fort. The walls were built of sand stone laid up with mud. In the school house I attended day school a few months each year.

"I was quite sick soon after birth and from what I can learn was not expected to live. James Walker, then president of the Croydon Branch was called in to bless and give me a name. The name given was GIBSON, after Father's oldest brother which was after his Grandfather CONDIE who was named GIBSON in honor of a particular friend of his father.

"As I grew older I had a good memory and could learn little pieces with ease, and many a time have I said pieces for candy. I was taught to preach a little sermon as soon as I was in pants, and like the ministers recited it at every opportunity. At this time I remember being quite a favorite. I was about three years old at the time."

[NOTE: My brother JAMES could sing first verse and chorus of *Praise to the Man* when he was 17 months old. Mother asked him to do it quite often. My oldest son, TOM, has a memory perhaps much like his great-grandfather. When he was in the second grade in Pioche, Nevada, he wanted to participate in an elementary school talent show, so I found him a reading to give—maybe eight or ten pages in the small book of readings. He took it upstairs to study. He was back in about five or ten minutes claiming he was ready to give it. I couldn't believe him, but took the book to test him. He gave it perfectly. Needless to say, he won the talent show. He was very near-sighted, one eye 300 the other 400. We never knew it until he was in the fourth grade, because he passed all the school eye tests. When we asked him how he did it, he simply stated, "I memorized the chart before I took the test while I was waiting my turn;" however his early baseball games were disasters.]

Grandfather CONDIE continues,

"When I was about 6 years old the smallpox broke out in the family. Our neighbors were quite alarmed when my brother CHARLES became sick and small spots began to show on his body. They called a meeting and thought our family should move some distance up the creek to a small log house. Well, Father refused to move. Then he consented if a house could be moved to the bottom of his field near the bank of Lost Creek. . . . Now Grandfather SWANN had a one room lumber house, unfinished. This was put on skids and on a Sunday morning, men gathered with several yoke of oxen and drug the building to the spot designated. A little fixing and cleaning and our family moved in. There were five of us children, the youngest a babe of two month. . . . During the exposure of this move, the baby caught cold and as a result, left this world of misery and suffering for a better. The rest of us had smallpox in a light form. Father, Grandfather SWANN, and Uncle GIBSON buried little HELEN ELIZA at night, a very sorrowful time . . . May, 1873. . . . Although I was not seven years old, I was so impressed with the sorrow this caused my parents and the hardship we all endured the following months that time can never erase from my memory the incidents of those days.

"The weather was very stormy. For weeks we had lots of rain. The creek overflowed the banks and it was unsafe to cross. I saw many cows and steers carried by the stream down a considerable distance before they could get footing and wade out.

"The following summer I remember as one of great poverty, even flour was a scarce article . . . the necessities of life were luxuries. We children were barefoot and destitute of decent clothing. My brother, THOMAS, had but one shirt. When he [was] baptized this was taken off so he would have it dry to put on when leaving the creek to go home. He had on only a pair of old pants when he was immersed in the cold water. Before the wheat was ripe flour was scarce. I carried a few pounds that half mile from the home of Grandfather SWANN more than once and hungrily waited

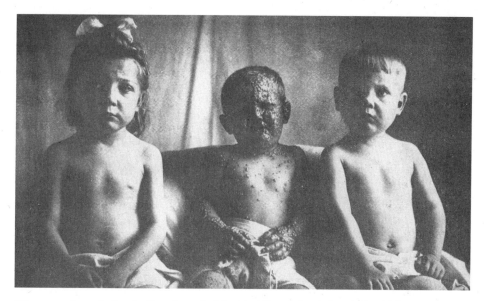

"Three members of a Family, Brought to the Municipal Hospital with the Mother, 'Who was Suffering from Small-pox.' The child in the centre was unvaccinated; the other two had been vaccinated a year before because of the school vaccination requirements. These two children remained in the small-pox wards several weeks, and left the hospital perfectly well." (Welch and Schamberg.)

Photo is from *Library of Health* 1923 Edition, Historical Publishing Co., Philadelphia, PA.—not any relations. This very fat medical book belonged to TOM and VANDA SWALLOW. My family had one, too. We called it our *Doctor Book*—larger in size, but thinner.

till mother could bake it for us to eat.

"Mother had a hard time. She had no broom to sweep the rough floor. I've often got some willow branches to sweep the floor. Father was busy getting out logs for lumber to build an additional room . . . . The farms in Croydon were small, five to twenty-five acres each. Father had divided his with his brother so his farm consisted of fifteen acres only, eleven acres of which was tillable. The settlers had no tame hay such as alfalfa. They depended on meadow grass that grew wild along the creek or public land . . . . When I was 8 or 9 years old I hunted the cows on foot and generally milked them until I was 15 years old, when the chore fell to the lot of CHARLEY.

"The spring of 1878, the diphtheria broke out and took away a number of children. We were all sick, but CHARLEY was the worst and suffered much. Father was going past the stables for help with the illness. He heard a heavy groan and sent TOM and me to look at the animals. That night CHARLEY began to get better and one of the mules began to fail. One morning she couldn't be found. After some time we learned of her whereabouts and found she had died with a swollen throat . . . . I remember one Sunday in August in the year 1878. We were returning home from Sunday school. The sun seemed to be obscured by a cloud. Suddenly grasshoppers began to fall like hail or snow and soon covered the ground . . . . The most of the crop . . . was matured and harvested. The grasshoppers deposited their eggs and disappeared. The following spring, crops were planted as usual and the fields were green and prospects looked good for a favorable crop. Alas! A few hot sunny days and myriads came out of the ground and began to leap and eat. They left our fields as barren as the traveled street. A few patches of potatoes survived.

"In September of 1885, I received a call from President John Taylor to go on a mission to the Southern States, leaving on about October 12. Notwithstanding many obstacles that stood in the way, I determined to accept the call which I knew was from God, and accordingly began preparations to go. I attended conference in Logan in October, and then I went through the Temple to receive my endowments and returned home. I came up on a freight train and had to jump off it below the quarry as it would not stop. I got home about 1 or 2 o'clock that night.

"October 10ᵗʰ: I was at home with many of my friends and relatives gathered around to bid me goodbye and God bless you. . . . I just began to realize I was actually going to be away from my family connections for a length of time . . . . That night as I lay on my bed, sleep had departed from me. I thought how different my situation would be in a few days. I then began to count the cost this way. Am I willing to leave this comfortable home and sleep in the cold? Can I stand it to be away for 2 or 3 years in the midst of strangers? Can I endure the persecutions that the servants of the Lord meet from mobs while preaching the Gospel of peace? Do I think enough of my religion to lay down my life if required? Yes, any thing the Lord requires, I am willing to pass through . . . . I left home October 11 and went to Salt Lake City and was set apart on the 12ᵗʰ by Apostle Erastus Snow. I left Salt Lake on October 15ᵗʰ on the Denver Rio Grande Railroad."

With only two missions in the United States, the Southern States mission included all of the Civil War South plus Kansas and other southwestern states. Grandfather CONDIE's mission began at Chattanooga, Tennessee, where he continued eastward into Rutherford County, North Carolina. After leaving the railroad depot, they traveled on foot without purse or script, relying on the goodness of God to help the two companions find food and lodging and people willing to listen to their message in an area that was basically anti-Mormon.

GIBSON A CONDIE
THIS PICTURE WAS TAKEN IN SALT LAKE CITY
BEFORE HE LEFT ON HIS MISSION.
IT WAS HIS BIRTHDAY. HE WAS NINETEEN YEARS OLD.

One example of the animosity of some of these citizens of the southern states had taken place on 13 May 1857. Our friend Parley P. Pratt journeyed into Arkansas, near Fort Gibson, [now Fort Smith] to help an innocent member in a court case before the Civil War had began. "His assassins followed him some twelve miles from the place of trial, and then, taking advantage of his lonely position, shot him."

My sister, LILLIE IDA CLAY now of Bristol, Tennessee/Virginia, tells us:

"In 1884 in Lewis County in middle Tennessee, two Mormon missionaries had been killed when holding a church meeting in the home of Brother James Condor on Cane Creek on Sunday, August 10th. Mrs. Condor was crippled and two of her sons were killed by the mobbers. Elder John H. Gibbs was shot with a Bible in his hand looking up a text. Elder William S. Berry pushed a gun aside so that Elder Thompson could escape out the back door, but then he fell riddled by bullets. There is a monument on the site which my husband and a Priesthood group from Nashville went to see. A grandson of Elder Gibbs happened to live in our branch at the time. There are no roads now and the whole community is gone.... The anti-Mormon feeling is still evident in this area even today but nothing like what the Elders in the 1880's had to endure."

GROVER SWALLOW's great-grandfather THOMAS DEARDEN served a mission to the Southern States, beginning in 1882. He left behind his family; the baby, ELIZABETH, number nine, was one year old—daughter ISABELLA, GROVER's grandmother was nine years old.

A LATER PICTURE OF DAVID DUNCAN,
THE FIRST WHITE CHILD BORN IN MEADOW, UTAH.

GROVER's grandfather DAVID DUNCAN, born 4 Feb 1859 in Meadow, married MARY JANE STOTT on 8 Dec 1880. He left us a small book, printed by *Deseret News Co., 1886, The Martyrdom of Joseph Standing or the Murder of a "Mormon" Missionary, A true story—written in prison by John Nicholson, A convict for conscience sake.* His prison mate, under the Edmund's Act [antipoligamy] of 1884, was Rudger Clawson, the missionary companion of the murdered Joseph Standing, whose life was equally in danger. The JAMES FAUSETT mentioned as the captain of the mob might have been a distant cousin to second-great-grandmother ELIZA McKEE FAUSETT (Ivie). Abridged from part of this book:

"In 1879, Rudger was called . . . on a preaching mission to the Southern States. . . . He labored in the State of Georgia, associated with Elder Joseph Standing, [who] had accomplished a good work in Whitfield County; particularly in the neighborhood of Varnell's Station, where he had succeeded in raising up a branch of the church. . . .

"Brother Standing had a dream . . . . 'I thought I went to Varnell's Station, when suddenly clouds of intense blackness gathered overhead and all around me.' He visited a family connected with the church. 'The moment I entered their house the most extreme consternation seized them, and they made it clear beyond any possibility of doubt that my presence was objectionable.' He suddenly awoke, without knowing the end.

A missionary conference was called in Rome, Georgia. As they journeyed southward, Standing's dream was literally fulfilled.

"They reached that place on the evening of Saturday, July 9th . . . . They said that threats had been made and the feeling toward them in the neighborhood was bitter and murderous. They declined to allow them to stay over night, because if anything happened they would have to share the trouble. This reception chilled the feelings of the Elders, and Rudger said to himself involuntarily: 'This is the fulfillment of Joseph's dream.'

"'What shall we do?' said the missionaries. 'It is now nine o'clock, and getting quite dark. Can you tell us of a place there we can find shelter?'

"'Yes,' said J—, 'you can go to Holston's, a mile and a half further on. He will doubtless entertain you.' Henry Holston . . . was not a member of the Church, but had shown a very friendly disposition toward the Elders. They trudged through the thickly wooded country . . . in pitchy darkness." Holston hesitated but invited them inside explaining,

"Threats of mobbing, whipping and even killing the Elders had been freely made, and he expected to get into trouble . . . however, that he would take his chances . . . and would defend them so long as they were under his roof.

"When the guests entered the room assigned them Standing appeared pale, anxious and determined . . . impressed with a premonition of approaching danger. He had always felt an intense horror of being whipped and more than once had declared that he would rather die than be subjected to such an indignity. He carefully examined the windows and securely fastened them, then got hold of an iron bar and placed it in such a position as to be within easy reach stating, 'I expect the mob to-night, and I want to be ready to receive them.' 'I don't think we will be disturbed,' said Rudger, who slept soundly until Sunday morning.

"The weather was clear and beautiful. The two Elders set out to go to the house of the fearful J— where they had left their satchels . . . returning quickly on the densely wooded road toward the Holston home . . . turning a bend, the two young missionaries suddenly came in full view of a posse of twelve men. Some were mounted . . . and all were armed. As soon as they caught sight of the Elders they set up, unitedly, the most demoniacal yells of exultation, and came rushing toward them like a pack of hungry wolves who had discovered the prey they were about to tear to pieces and devour . . . . The sensations that passed through Rudger's mind and frame were entirely new to him, as he was now facing a danger that had no parallel in any former incident of his life, which he thought he was about to be compelled to surrender.

"The names of those who composed this bloodthirsty band of murderous ruffians, whose cruel and dastardly deed will cause them to be branded with eternal infamy, are: David D. Nations, Jasper N. Nations, A. S. Smith, Benjamin Clark, William Nations, Andrew Bradley, JAMES

FAUCETT, Hugh Blair, Jos. Nations, Jefferson Hunter and Mack McLure. The expressions upon the faces of those fiends incarnate were in unison with the vengeful sounds which had just escaped from their throats. They were laboring under the excitement of passion to such an extent that their frames shook and some of them foamed at the mouth.

"As soon as they came up Joseph Standing, in a clear voice, loud enough to be heard by all of them said: 'Gentlemen: By what authority are we thus molested upon the public highway? If you have a warrant of arrest or any other legal process to serve upon us, we would like to examine it, that we may be satisfied as to your authority to interfere with our movements.'

"'We'll show you by what authority we act.' some of them shouted.

"One of the mounted mobbers then jumped from his horse and approached Rudger with a cocked revolver. He flourished this weapon, whirling it menacingly in the face of the young man, who looked down the muzzle of an implement of that character for the first time . . . . The murderous fellow . . . accompanied his threatening antics with the most foul and blasphemous abuse, while his companions were moving around and indulging in vile and profane coursings. The excitement of Bradley--a large and powerful man—was singularly noticeable. He was on horseback and was holding a double barreled shotgun in front of him, across his animal, with both hands. He shook so that the weapon bobbed about as if he were about to drop it. 'Come with us,' was the command from the mob. The singular procession then started back in the same direction from which the Elders had come. Standing appeared to be laboring under a terrible strain. His face continued overspread with a deathly pallor . . . he kept pace with the front line of the mobbers, with whom he constantly reasoned and expostulated. 'It is not our intention,' said he 'to remain in this part of the State. If we had been unmolested we would have been away in a very short time. We use no inducements to persuade people to join our Church. We preach what we understand to be the truth and leave people to embrace it or not, as they may choose.' They said: 'The government of the United States is against you, and there is no law in Georgia for Mormons.'

"Rudger manifested no hurry in accompanying the gang . . . . He expected he was going to his death, and he had no desire to meet the grim monster any sooner than might be compulsory . . . One of the ruffians, becoming exasperated at his tendency to lag, came up behind and struck him a terrible blow on the back of the head . . . . Rudger reeled and fell forward, saving his body from the full shock of the fall by extending his hands. Recovering speedily, he was on his feet in an instant, his heart fired with consuming rage."

He turned and found the cowardly assailant to be a young man, whom he looked at with great contempt. This seemed to enrage the wretch.

"He raised a heavy club and was about to bring it down upon Rudger's head with all the force he was capable of using, when another member of the band seized his arm and told him to desist."

The group journeyed onward meeting an old man who spoke briefly and then passed on, then a young girl, who had hoped to warn the missionaries of the mob. One of the men said to her:

"You see we have got your brethren. As soon as we dispose of their case we purpose attending to you."

"The Lord is with them and my prayers are forever for them," replied Mary, the tones of her voice evincing deep emotion. She then went on her way.

"At this juncture three of the members of the party who were on horse-back left the main body . . . . The remainder, in charge of the two intended victims of their satanic hate, proceeded a short distance further, when they reached a lovely spot—a spring of clear water, overshadowed by a huge, outspreading tree. Here a halt was made and the party seated themselves around the mirror-like pool."

Standing was offered a chance to drink. Fearful, he refused.

"You needn't be afraid; you can drink, as we will not hurt you while you do so."

Standing took a copious draught. He was still very pale, his features rigid, and overspread with an expression of deep anxiety.

After he had returned to his place JAMES FAUSETT, aged about sixty years, and who was seated upon a horse addressing the Elders, delivered himself as follows:

"I want you men to understand that I am the captain of this party, and that if we ever again find you in this part of the country we will hang you by the neck like dogs."

"A general desultory conversation ensued, in the course of which the vilest accusations were laid against the 'Mormons,' the beastly talk of the mobbers merely serving to show the depravity and corruption of their own hearts. . . . The space of about one hour was consumed in this way, when the three horsemen who had left the party came in sight. As they rode up, one of them exclaimed: 'Follow us.' . . . Joseph Standing was sitting with his back toward the horsemen . . . he leaped to his feet with a bound, instantly wheeled so as to face them, brought his two hands together with a sudden slap, and shouted in a loud, clear, resolute voice—'Surrender.'

"A man seated close to him pointed his pistol at him and fired. Young Standing whirled or spun three times round upon his feet, fell heavily forward upon the ground, turned once over, bringing him face upward, and spread his arms widely out his form being in such a position as to be in the shape of a cross . . . all . . . rose to their feet. Suddenly a member of the party, pointing to Rudger, said to his companions, in an authoritative tone—'Shoot that man.'

"In an instant every weapon was turned upon the defenseless young missionary, who felt that his last moment on earth had come and that in a few seconds he would be launched into eternity . . . . The murderous wretches paused a moment with their weapons leveled upon their proposed victim, who folded his arms—showing an outward calmness at the most extreme variance with his inward feelings—and said with apparent deliberation: 'Shoot.'

"The suspense of a lifetime seemed to be thrown into the next few seconds. A whirling sensation passed over his brain and then all was dark. This condition was but momentary, and when he recovered the position was unaltered—the murderous ruffians still stood with their guns and pistol pointed at him. The man who had directed that the young Elder be murdered suddenly changed his mind and countermanded the first order by shouting 'Don't shoot.'

"The men at once lowered their arms. They then appeared to sense the horrible character of the deed that had been committed . . . . As soon as it flashed fully upon them, they were seized with sudden consternation and instinctively rushed together in a compact group, as if seeking mutual protection from each other, from the probable consequences of the bloody act.

"Rudger walked over to where young Standing was lying, stooped and looked into his face. The spectacle that met his gaze sent a shock through his system that can never be erased from his memory. There lay his companion, recently in full vigor of life and health—bright, capable and intelligent—in the throes of death. There was a large ghastly wound in the forehead, directly above the nose, the right eye had been torn out, the brain was oozing from the place where the bullet entered, and the death rattle was sounding in his throat. Rudger gently raised the dying man's head and placed his hat under it to keep it out of the dust . . . . As Rudger stood gazing at his friend and companion, he was approached by one of the Nations brothers, who said with a strong emphasis upon the last word of each exclamation: 'This is terrible! This is terrible! That he should have killed himself in such a manner.'

"The missionary perceived the intention to resort to the suicide theory, and deeming it both imprudent and unsafe to openly repudiate it, replied: 'Yes, it is terrible.'

"Then realizing the danger of giving the gang any time to sense the fact that to permit him to escape alive would be a menace to their safety, he saw there was no time to be lost.

"He exclaimed: 'Gentleman, it is a burning shame to leave a man to die in the woods in this fashion. For heaven's sake either you go and procure assistance that the body may be removed and cared for, or allow me to go.'

"He urged this point so earnestly and vehemently that the gang consulted a moment and then, turning to him, said: 'You go.'"

Rudger went at once, not as rapidly while in their view as he did when that view was blocked by the dense trees. His first stop was at Mr. Holston's home--about two miles away. He asked him to go and look after the body while he obtained the services of the coroner. Holston agreed and left at once, giving Rudger a horse to speed him on his journey to Catoosa Springs, where the coroner resided. Traveling as rapidly as possible, he turned at a curve only to see a group of armed men approaching—part of the mob. He rode on and confronted them.

"'What have you done with Standing?' one of them exclaimed.

"'I have not disturbed him, and I presume he lies just where he fell.'

"'Where are you going?'

"Rudger extended his arm westward and, pointing with his index finger, said: 'I am going in that direction.' Some of them smiled, and all rode on, their departure lifting a load from Rudger's mind that seemed like the removal of a mountain."

They evidently believed he was fleeing the country. Pushing on to Catoosa Springs he first sent two dispatches, one to the Governor of Georgia, another to mission president John Morgan in Utah asking him to inform Standing's family and promising to bring his body home. With help from the sheriff, his deputy, his friend Holston and the Lord, after much persuasion, Rudger was able to fulfill that promise.

The body, mutilated additionally by the mob with perhaps a bullet from each of the members, was placed in a casket. It started to smell. At the railroad station this casket was placed in a larger casket and surrounded tightly with heavy straps to lessen the odor. The total weight was over 900 pounds. Rudger returned with the casket to ensure its safe arrival. He with his deceased companion was greeted in Ogden by a brass band, members of the Young Men's Improvement Associations, and a multitude of people on 1 Aug 1879.

> "The obsequies were conducted in the Tabernacle on Sunday, August 3d, in the presence of about 10,000 people. The speakers on the occasion were President John Taylor and President George Q. Cannon. The body was interred, in the Salt Lake City cemetery, the same day."

After Rudger had been at home about eight months, he received a subpoena issued by the Circuit court of Whitfield County, Georgia, requiring him to appear at Dalton the following October (1880), and testify in the cases of Jasper N. Nations, Andrew Bradley and Hugh Blair, charged with the killing of Joseph Standing. He went without any regard for his personal safety. He arrived in Dalton in September, 1880, where he was joined by Elder John Morgan, the President of the Southern States Mission. He found the feeling amongst the populace to be exceedingly bitter, with an imminent danger of an outbreak of open hostility. He had a duty to perform, however, and he was determined to accomplish it. The people of Georgia could not say that the murderers went free because the witness had failed to do his part. At Dalton, Rudger met with his friend Henry Holston, whom he had promised that he would return and attend the trial. Numbers of men declared he would never come back. Holston had confidence that he would.

In the meantime, Mr. Holston had passed through a trying ordeal, "where he stood strong against a nocturnal attempt to take his life."

He told of repeated threats on his life. The deputy sheriff also told Rudger how he had placed pressure on the sheriff to pursue and capture the three men, who were then on trial. The book further describes the trial and the difficulty of finding unbiased jurymen willing to judge their neighbors. There were five lawyers for the defense. The judge throughout the trial showed his bias in favor of the defense. The courtroom was crowded in excess throughout every session. Rudger, Holston, the old man, and the young girl were the witnesses for the prosecution. The defense was allowed to let the three prisoners testify for each other regarding their supposed innocence, claiming they were armed to go turkey hunting, or another was taking his gun to the blacksmith to have it repaired.

While the jury was deliberating this three-day trial,

> "The sheriff came into court dragging with him a negro, whose eyes were rolling wildly in his head, his grotesque contortions giving every indication of his being in a state of mortal terror. He was charged with stealing a gallon of whisky. A jury was empanelled on the spot and he was forthwith tried and found guilty. He pleads . . . for mercy, on the ground that he had a large family and was extremely poor. The judge paid no attention to his pleadings, but arose, gravely and severely . . . elaborated upon the heinous character of the . . . offense, and sentenced him to one year in the chain gang."

Finally the jury in the Standing case returned into court with a verdict of not guilty. The announcement of this result was greeted with a demonstration among the spectators, favorable to the accused, and increased the popular feeling against Rudger.

Rudger Clawson later was called to be a member of the Twelve Apostles and was their president when I was a young child in the 1930s. The picture and his following testimony is from the 6 Apr 1930 Centennial Celebration booklet of the L.D.S. Church.

> "The Christian world of today is witness of the fact that the very things which the great image pictured in Nebuchadnezzar's dream stood for have occurred as far as time has gone. [see Old Testament, Daniel: Chapter 2] History certifies to the fact that King Nebuchadnezzar was the head of gold. The Medes and Persians, an inferior kingdom to Babylon, were the arms and breast of silver. The Macedonian kingdom, under Alexander the Great, was the belly and thighs of brass: and the Roman kingdom under the Caesars was the legs of iron. For, mark you, later on the kingdom, or empire of Rome, was divided. The head of the

RUDGER CLAWSON

government in one division was at Rome, and the head of the government in the other division was at Constantinople. So these two great divisions represented the legs of iron. Finally, the Roman empire was broken up into smaller kingdoms, represented by the feet and toes of iron and clay, and, as there were ten toes on the image, we might well conclude that the following ten kingdoms stand to represent the toes: Italy established in 496 A.D.; France, in 733; England, 853; Germany, 896; Holland, 922; Portugal, 1138; Persia 1139; Austria-Hungry 1159; Spain, 1171; Greece, 1829 A.D. The stone cut out of the mountain without hands, representing the kingdom of God, was established April 6th, 1830, with six members, and is known as the Church of Jesus Christ of Latter-day Saints. Thus the work of the Lord in our own time, designated by revelation as a marvelous work and a wonder, had a very humble beginning, but it has grown apace. Today the Church of Jesus Christ of Latter-day Saints has a membership of about 700,000. It cost the best blood of the nineteenth century to establish this work on the earth. Its founder, the Prophet Joseph Smith, and his brother Hyrum Smith, the Patriarch, were martyred for the cause of truth, in Carthage, Illinois, in 1844. The Latter-day Saints have passed through the fire of persecution and have stood the test of one hundred years. Never was the prospect brighter for our people than it is today. We sincerely believe, and, I may say, have every assurance that this Church will stand forever. It is, indeed, the Church of the Son of God, the Redeemer of mankind."

We might add that in 2011 the Church has increased in population to over 14,000,000—with more than half of them located outside the United States and Canada.

But back to grandfather GIBSON A CONDIE from his journals. On Friday, 1 Apr 1887, grandfather sat in the Turkey-Tail Railroad Station waiting three hours for a very late train to go to Chattanooga. He was being transferred to Missouri to complete his mission. He sat alone, as his two past companions felt unsafe and had hurried on. They had "met a crowd of fellows who hailed us with profanity, called us carpetbaggers and other epithets." While waiting, he summed up his mission in North Carolina.

"I had walked more than 3000 miles since I got off the train, about two miles east of this place, nearly 18 months ago. During that time I had, with my various companions met insults and threats of violence from enemies of the truth. I have not been injured nor have I had to sleep out and seldom got right hungry. Without money for months at a time, the Lord provided friends who shared their humble fare with us. We visited the sick and blessed many who recovered. We sat up with some who were bedfast. We have preached at many firesides, at meetings held in private homes and in a few churches. 'What will the harvest be?'"

On Saturday 2 Apr 1887 at eleven o'clock A.M. grandfather arrived in Chattanooga. He checked his luggage and walked directly to the Post Office.

"In a minute Elder William Spry walked in to get the Mission mail. A joyful meeting. He invited me to go with him to the depot to meet some elders from Utah. In about 30 minutes they stepped off the train. Elders Thomas, Price, and Powell were strangers to me, but I knew David Benion, A. J. Stookey & J. M. Browning, slightly. The elders were led to a hotel. I accompanied Brother Spry to his office and shared his room and meals with Brother & Sister Tillman.

"After dinner we elders visited the National Cemetery, where 12,965 union soldiers, who were killed in the Civil War, are buried. We also visited the big nail factory. Some of us took a trip to the top of "Lookout Mountain."

Earlier in his mission, in the Carolinas, he spoke of viewing Kings Mountain in the distance from another lookout point—a battlefield site of great importance during the Revolutionary War. On Wednesday, 6 Apr 1887 at 8:30 A.M., grandfather arrived in Kansas City and had to wait twelve hours for another train to take him to Holden, Johnson County, Missouri—southeast of Jackson County.

"I walked around the city for hours. I also rode some distance on the street cars which were pulled by an endless cable. All the street cars I had previously seen were drawn by mules. It was 10:40 p.m. when I arrived at Holden. . . . I secured a bed for 25 cents."

He finds that a letter had been sent to Church Headquarters by Elias Thomas who resided in Holden. Thomas had been baptized in Wales 20 years before.

"He had drifted around in several states and mingled with many of the apostate groups formed after the death of the Prophet Joseph Smith. The Strangites, Hendrickites, Whitmerites and the Josephites. He had failed in business and his desire seemed to be to get in fellowship with the Church in Utah. He studied the Book of Mormon and the Doctrine & Covenants and had many arguments with such Apostates as William E. McClellan. It had been proposed at that time to call the Elders home on account of the Anti-Mormon crusade at that time, but President John Taylor said, 'No.'"

After many inquiries, he was able to find Mr. Elias Thomas, his companion.

"There was a Mr. Henry James living in the home of his brother who was at someplace in California preaching. He was a minister in the Baptist Church . . . . He (Henry) is well acquainted with the Bible and unlike many professed Christians, he believes it. He had been baptized by an elder of the Josephites, or the Re-organized Church, but was not satisfied that they had the authority to act for the Lord as did the Apostles of the Lord anciently. They taught the first four principles of the Gospel as well as any Bible student could do it. But there was no spirit manifested.

"Mr. James asked me many questions. His wife and mother listened with interest until Brother Elias Thomas and I were about to depart." Grandfather was able to baptize Henry James into the Church.

"Friday, April 29, 1887: Sister Thomas made a hop poultice to put on my face and I went to bed until noon. After dinner Brother James came for me to come and baptize his wife. Immediately I made ready and went with him. Arriving at the house we found the devil in the person of a Josephite Elder Warneky from Independence trying to persuade Sister James to refuse to be baptized. We repaired to the big room and held a lively discussion for nearly three hours. He was a clever speaker and led me along until I said I accepted only what was contained in the word of the Lord as given in our standard works. This seemed to please him. 'Let us take a text,' said he, turning to St. John 3:34, 'For he whom God hath sent speaketh the words of God.' I accepted that as a true scripture. His face beamed as if he had won a victory quite easy. He then began repeating garbled sayings of Brigham Young. Many remarks I never before had heard, which if true, were only words of Brigham, a mortal man, and out of context.

"The Lord sustained me as I replied to his sophistry. 'The text, obviously referred to Christ, but included perhaps all men sent with a message from God. If we apply your reasoning, we must reject many of the prophets and apostles who did not always speak the word of God,' said I. 'What of Peter who cursed and swore and denied his Lord, and erred on other occasions? What of Paul who confessed he was giving the saints ideas of his own, and how about Aaron whom God called to be the High Priest to Israel yet he led the people to sin. Moses had his weaknesses, and many other servants of God.'

"Brother James rose to his feet and said, 'I never told a falsehood to any person in this town, then why should my word be doubted? I was baptized by Mr. White of the Josephite church and I did not receive any more spirit than that chair and when Elder CONDIE baptized me I did receive the spirit witness to the truth. Is that not sufficient proof?' At this point, Brother Thomas came in and the conversation took a different turn. After supper we went to hold a meeting on the lot. We started singing to attract attention. Someone threw eggs and a few fell at our feet. About 100 listened while I spoke an hour.

"Friday, June 10, 1887. It had rained most of the night. Brother Henry James saw me in the late afternoon. His brother had arrived from California and some argument had taken place. For hours the Rev. Brother had tried to induce Henry to give up and turn against such unpopular people as the Mormons. Henry asked him many questions but received no answers. He asked his brother's consent to meet a young Mormon Elder who would answer any questions about the Gospel he might wish to ask. He said, 'I'll have him here in 15 minutes.' The minister said, 'No.' All the sophistry brought to bear did not shake the testimony Henry had received. Sister James was asked if she received any spiritual gift when the Mormon Elder baptized her. She replied, 'Yes, I received the gift of faith.' I told Henry the Lord would sustain him and I would pray for him. I felt truly thankful for the integrity of Henry James and his kind hearted wife.

"Sunday, June 12, 1887: This afternoon Brother James came to us. He felt much troubled; they could hardly endure to remain here under the conditions. He desired to go to Utah. I did not know what advice to give him. Times are dull. Men glad to get jobs at a dollar a day. Our church is in debt. The United States Marshall has taken over all the church property he can get and the outlook is none too bright for our people. I said be patient, the Lord will direct you.

"Thursday, June 16: [now in Kansas City] I accompanied Brother Morgan to the various R. R. Offices where tickets were obtained for the Holden group to Salt Lake City. I purchased a ticket to Hutchinson, Kansas. Traveled with the company. We had a very fine time. It was nine o'clock then I said good-bye to those on board. I found the way to the Windsor Hotel. It was crowded. One guest had just left. I fell heir to the bed he had just vacated.

"After returning from my mission the latter part of July, I again worked up on the Cedar Canyon farm. Father and CHARLES went to Price, Utah, to take care of a homestead on Miller creek. This left the harvesting of the crops to me and my brother, THOMAS . . . During the month of March,

I closed a sale of most of our claims and improvements to John Hopkins for seven hundred and fifty dollars. This was done with Father's consent. The few acres retained were sold after I left Croydon. The money received for this place was used during the summer to build five more rooms to the house and the remainder to help pay schooling expense for the fourth oldest of us at the Brigham Young College. . . . I was 23 when I attended the Brigham Young college of Logan one year. This comprised the period of school life which I feel grateful it was no worse.

"I have taught schools as follows, Croydon, 3 months, beginning January, 1888, Enterprise 3 months, beginning December, 1888, South Morgan 7 months, beginning November, 1890 and 1891. Croydon, 8 months, beginning September, 1892. Enterprise, 6 months, beginning November 1893, and again at Croydon 5 months, beginning October, 1994."

As children we were told by our mother that grandfather CONDIE was the valedictorian of his class at Logan, with classmates that included these future apostles of the Church: James E. Talmadge, John A. Widsoe, and Richard R. Lyman. George Q. Cannon was the president of the college, who upon meeting grandfather several years later asked him why he never continued his education, whereupon grandfather referred to his beautiful wife and newly born son of 1892, my father, MARION ASHER CONDIE, and answered, "I would not trade them for all the education in the world." Years later, aunt ADA CONDIE (Baird) told my sister that grandfather would have liked to have had more education, but his lack of money and the cold, miserable; attic living conditions had made him quite ill and unable to continue.

[Note: GIBSON A CONDIE, b 15 Oct 1866, in Croydon, Utah, married EMILY ELIZABETH TUCKER 3 Sep 1891, in the Logan temple. She was the daughter of JAMES and BETSY LERWILL TUCKER of Devonshire, England, and was born in Morgan, Utah, 25 Nov 1869.

Grandmother CONDIE, whom I was named after, was always called EMILY in our Carey community. I remember being bounced on my father's foot as a small child when he asked me, "Would you like to be called Emily or Brookie?" In my very young mind, I thought about it. I thought of my beloved grandmother, and it seemed that it was her name, not mine—everyone called me Brookie; so I said, "BROOKIE." Years later after grandmother had died, Grandfather CONDIE watched me silently and then quietly asked, "Whatever happened to your name EMILY?" He really loved and missed her. His actions towards her were very protective.]

Their courtship probably began at the dances in Morgan, Utah, when grandfather was teaching school. She had grown up in Morgan, but was then working as a housekeeper for the Wright family who owned a department store in

Ogden, Utah. She loved to dance and grandfather didn't; but he loved to call the square dances. Grandmother always stood tall and sat straight, and tried very hard to get me to do likewise. She always said, "You won't get as tired if you sit up straight." She was immaculate in her dress as well as her posture, and her housekeeping and cooking were perfection. She insisted on mopping her own floors. No one could do it well enough to please her, so after they left, she would do it again. She made very large loaves of white bread, a slice of which, with butter, was a better treat than any candy.

~ 41 ~

THE MARRIAGE AND SOUTHERN MISSION OF JAMES OSCAR IVIE

Grandfather JAMES OSCAR IVIE and Grandmother ANNIE CATHERINE MORTENSEN met in Salina at the home of his friends and freighting companions, Peter and Jake Gottfredson, who lived across the street from her home. They fell in love and were married when he had just turned twenty-four and she was still twenty-three. Prior to this time, Mother told me that grandmother had been raised to accept polygamy as all right, and when a married man asked her on a date to go dancing, she accepted. He gave her a bag of candy and they stopped by his house to introduce her to the family. While she was there, his wife stole her candy. That was the first and last date this husband or any other had with my grandmother.

On their Golden Wedding, uncle LLOYD O. IVIE wrote the following:

"Couple Notes Golden Wedding—Mr. and Mrs. JAMES OSCAR IVIE "RICHFIELD, July 12 [1937]—About five years ago, I had occasioned to drive father and mother over the old route from Salina to St. George. Every half hour, or thereabouts, father pointed to the roadside and said, 'That's where we camped the first night,' or 'there's where we camped the second night,' etc . . . Six days journey by team and wagon, accompanied by a load of salt and flour to defray expenses, is the romantic story of JAMES OSCAR IVIE and ANNIE CATHERINE MORTENSEN, when they went to get married in 1887. There were simpler and easier means of meeting the legal requirements of marriage, but in the light of their teachings, there was no other way. It had to be a trip to the temple. On July 6, they celebrated their golden wedding. . . .

"JAMES OSCAR IVIE is a son of Col. JOHN L. IVIE, who was well known in Central and Southern Utah during the days of Indian troubles, a

521

man who claimed the distinction of having been fired at more and at closer range without having been hit, than anyone who lived through those days.

"ANNIE CATHERINE MORTENSEN was the first child of her parents born in Utah, her father and mother having emigrated from Denmark the year before she was born, in 1862, her mother having walked all the way from the Missouri River to Salt Lake City beside an ox team.

"They were married on July 6, 1887."

THIS FAMILY PICTURE WAS TAKEN BEFORE JAMES OSCAR IVIE WAS CALLED TO THE SOUTHERN STATES MISSION—CHILDREN: LLOYD AND MATTIE (STANDING)

JAMES OSCAR IVIE wrote:

"On the 28th of May 1892, I got a letter from Box B, Salt Lake City telling me to be prepared to go on a mission to the Southern States and to leave Salt Lake City, Sept. 21st 1892. It didn't say 'will you go' or 'can you go,' but 'to be ready.' Now I want to say it was a surprise to me and to get ready in the short time was a question, because I was prospering financially. I had 12 hundred head of sheep, about 30 head of cattle, the farm at Vermillion—all paid for. So a battle was on hand in my mind—to go, I would have to sacrifice much of my substance and not to go—my family was on my mind. Lucifer had me going out and studying what to do and as the word went out that I was called on a mission, my relatives in Salina said to me, 'You are not a big enough fool to go on a mission and leave family and all you have accumulated to please those leaders in Salt Lake City.' And they said, also, if I was fool enough to go, they hoped the people would give me a whipping and tar and feather me for being such a fool. These were 'Job's comforters' and they weighed heavily on my mind, with the other things to look at.

"I was herding sheep on the east mountain two weeks out of every month (as Albert Brown and I had mixed our sheep and taken turns herding.) While herding all kinds of thoughts were upon my mind, so I would go to God in prayer night and morning and sometimes during the day and told God I wanted to know what to do and wanted him to reveal it to me. So, about the middle of June, while praying alone, a still voice said to me, 'Go on your mission, for your family is of more value than all your earthly considerations, and your example is wanted before your family in obedience.' From that time on, I made up my mind to go and when I got home, I told the folks I was going—also, I wrote Box B office I would be there at the appointed time to go on my mission, and from that time on I worked and prepared for it, selling some of the livestock and sheep, and to rent everything I had—to get ready to go. Some sheep were sold at $2.50 per head, calves $2.50 to 4 dollars per head and cows about 15 dollars per head . . . . I rented the farm to Haden Poff and sold some of the cattle and sheep to Isaac Colby. The farm brought my wife the next year 28 bushels of wheat and about five tons of hay to live on and pay taxes. The second year, 50 and 60 bushels of wheat and about 15 ton of hay.

"The wife and two children (MATTIE and LLOYD) I left at home and one boy was born after I left. She named him PARLEY PRATT, as he was born on Parley Pratt's birthday. The trial and hardships were greater on the wife and family than they were upon me; but thank the Lord, she never complained or wrote me discouraging letters, but always encouraged me on the mission. Had I of known her true situation, I might have asked to be released, but thank the Lord for the experience we both had and we stood faithful to the gospel cause and we gained a testimony of God's work and had our prayers answered in many ways.

"Ma told after I returned home of being out of flour and didn't know where the next meal was coming from. She laid the matter before the Lord in earnest prayer and before night [Bishop] Jacob Dastrup and wife came in a wagon, brought her a sack of flour and provisions that lasted them for some time. Her prayers were answered. [Bishop Dastrup had been spiritually prompted 'The IVIE's need food!'.]

At times he would show them a picture of himself with a long beard, and tell the people with a twinkle in his eyes, "This is my wife's first husband." Grandfather IVIE, with his kind humor, was loved by all who knew him—at least, from my observation.

"There were 6 missionaries called from Vermillion Ward to go to different parts that fall. THOMAS GLEDHILL (my brother-in-law) was to go to England; August Malmquist to go to Sweden; Frank Nebeker to go to New Zealand; myself to the Southern States. The others didn't go on their missions and one told me after I got back, if he had went when called, he would have been ahead, as he lost his store, cattle and farm and was left single handed in the two years I was gone. The other man that didn't go didn't fare any better."

Grandfather IVIE's mission took him into Virginia and Georgia, where he met some distant cousins and was able to copy and bring back many genealogical records of his early Norfolk, Virginia, ancestors and their descendants.

One of his missionary jokes, when he was quizzed about polygamy was,

"I have a wife and three children at home, and I haven't seen one of them."

Young CHARLES SWALLOW, born 4 Nov 1865 in England, attended school in Fillmore, Utah, after arriving in 1874. They had three grades in one classroom. One of his chief sports was marbles, of which he was the champion. His oldest son, THOMAS CHARLES SWALLOW (GROVER's father), also excelled in this sport. GROVER has told me that his dad could shoot a marble with such speed that it would crack his opponent's marble into two pieces. TOM also excelled in basketball and was on the B.Y.U. Academy team. He also was the bass in many quartettes at the academy and throughout his life—but back to his father CHARLES SWALLOW. In 1891 he married ISABELLA DEARDEN, and on 11 May 1898, he was called on a mission to England. He left behind his wife and three small children, serving for two years and four months.

His son TOM told us:

"I could tell of many close calls in my life, but I will tell one ... that happened while Dad was on his mission. The big sweet apples were still green and hard, but they had the sweet taste to them. They were very hard to digest and would often give people what they called colery marbus. Aunt Fan and I took the salt duster and proceeded to do away with some of the apples. After awhile mother called me to get her some wood. I chopped an armful and was on my way to the house when a pain struck me, and I fell to the ground. I finally got up, gathered up the wood; when I reached the house, I fell on the porch unconscious. This lasted for over two hours. They gave me up for dead. Mother had Bro. J. D. Smith, President Hinckley, and Bro. Thomas Colister come and administer to me, but there was no change. Mother had a lot of faith and pleaded with them to administer again.

CHARLES SWALLOW ON HIS MISSION TO ENGLAND

President Hinckley said, 'There is no use; it is too late; but we will do as you say.' As they took their hands off me they could see life.

"While this was going on, Father was in England over three thousand miles away. He was just going out tracking when a voice said to him, 'There is trouble at home.' He went back to his room, kneeled down and prayed. He told the Lord he was in his service and would he please correct the trouble at home. He sat down and wrote to mother asking what was wrong, and I guess she had a letter of explanation on its way before she received his. I have seen the wonderful faith of Mother a good many times when the power of the Priesthood was all they had to depend on. There were no doctors."

~ 42 ~

DIPHTHERIA, CHILDBIRTH, AND RED MEASLES

Throughout the history of the world, plagues, infections, and famines have been a constant in shaping the history of nations and in determining populations and their decrease, and throughout the centuries the world population remained much the same—until man began to conquer the tiny disease enemies that could be much more devastating than armored men. The heros that devoted their lives to conquering these virulent villains deserve much praise. Unfortunately, there remains much to be done, but our twenty-first century world has changed immensely from the world of the nineteenth and early twentieth century.

After grandfather JAMES OSCAR IVIE returned from his Virginia mission to his family in Vermillion (near Salina, Utah,) and two months after their fourth child, my mother, LILLIE, was born on 5 Dec 1895, an outbreak of diphtheria struck the small village. Inoculations today have practically eliminated this disease; but even in my early childhood in the 1930s, it was greatly feared. I still recall crossing the street with my friends to totally avoid a home that was quarantined. The large posted sign was placed in view of the front door entrance by the public health department with its warning against entering or exiting--diphtheria was inside. We had been told that five members of the family were infected with it. At least one of them died, creating a darkness and fear that I still remember.

In the home of my grandparents, their oldest child, MATTIE CATHERINE IVIE, age 7, was the first to go, 7 Feb 1896. Mother told us that just before MATTIE died, she sat up, stretched out her arms toward the unseen world and cried out to her mother,

"The angels are coming. I can see them. They are coming for me!"

Her brother PARLEY PRATT IVIE, age 3, followed his sister two days later, 9 Feb 1896. Devastated, grandmother, in an effort to save her two-month-old baby girl, LILLIE, grabbed the (consecrated-for-the-sick) olive oil and fed a teaspoonful to her–only to discover through her tearful eyes that the medicine was not olive oil, but the carbolic acid she had been using to disinfect her home. Grandfather IVIE quickly administered a blessing on my infant mother, which, it was fervently believed by the family, saved her life. Two small graves were dug to the south in the nearby Sigurd cemetery.

THEIR TWO REMAINING CHILDREN LLOYD AND LILLIE WERE FIVE YEARS APART.

Two years later, on 20 Jan 1898, my mother was pleased at the arrival of a baby sister, IDA PEARL. The two girls would be close companions during their lives. Afterwards, in about two-year intervals, three more boys were born: JOHN ELMER, 20 Dec 1899; HORACE LEON, 7 Mar 1902; and ALDEN LEROY, 5 Feb 1904.

LEFT TO RIGHT: LILLIE IVIE,
INFANT MARTHA RONNOW, PEARL IVIE
IN FRONT, JOHN ELMER IVIE,
WHO LATER DIED OF THE MEASLES.

STEP-MOTHER MRS. C.P. RONNOW WITH
MARTHA WHEN SHE WAS A YOUNG GIRL
IN PANACA, NEVADA

[Note: MARTHA RONNOW was the daughter of my grandmother IVIE's sister, MARTHA MORTENSEN (Ronnow,) who died when her first child was born. Her husband was C. P. RONNOW of Panaca, Nevada. They gave the new baby girl her mother's name. My mother, LILLIE IVIE (Condie), wrote on the back or the photograph on the left: "My mother raised MARTHA as a baby at our farm, I tended her and cried when she went to live at Panaca with her stepmother."]

While world events tell of the early births of the automobiles and airplanes, and former "Rough Rider," President TEDDY ROOSEVELT was contemplating his second-term fall campaign for president, (then completing President McKinley's term, after he was assassinated on 14 Sep 1901), the tiny settlement of Vermillion, Utah, had an epidemic of red measles in February of 1905. Grandmother ANNIE C. IVIE needed to get groceries and other items from the stores several miles away. She left her recuperating-from-the-measles children in the care of a good neighbor, who volunteered to help her. When she returned from her errands, she found all the windows in her home wide-open. The good-neighbor woman believed that fresh cold air was needed in this home of the ill. Unfortunately, the children took a turn for the worse.

My mother recalled:

"In the spring of my third grade in school, an epidemic of measles swept through the community and closed the school. Mr. Despain [her teacher] came to visit my mother while I was sick with the measles. I saw him through the window and tried to get to him. He called Mother's attention to me and she was able to save me from falling on my face onto a red hot stove. It was a few days later, February 22nd, that my baby brother, LEROY, died. On March 12, 1905, my brother JOHN, age 5, died. They were buried in the Sigurd Cemetery."

Mother, LILLIE IVIE (Condie), wrote the following story about her younger brothers, JOHN and LEON:

"When I was six years old, my parents sold the farm and moved to a small log home in the town of Vermillion. While residing there, I attended the one room rural school taught by Mr. Orson L. Despain. I never thought of us as in need. . . . We always had shelter and plenty to eat and wear. I loved my cousins even though their father, Uncle TOM, made it clearly understood that his children were socially superior to our family. We still loved them and visited regularly. At this time, we lived in a small two room house, and he took the new larger house that my father had made arrangements to buy. Our home was a two room house with a lean-to on the back. On the west side of the south lean-to were elevated beds built on the wall. This is where I slept. It was in this home that my brother LEROY was born. The house was one block east of the mail stop. My mother took over the care of the mail and would put it all in a bag and place the bag on a special post by the track. The men on the train could reach over and grab it as the train went by. Then the train would not need to stop or even slow down as [it] passed through this small community unless they had passengers who wanted to get on or off at Vermillion.

"West of the mail sack was a family whose surname was Stringham. Their four year old daughter, Alta, and my brothers, JOHN and LEON were always seen playing together. LEON was 2 years old at this time. They usually played in the vacant lot next to our house. One day a neighbor saw the three of them sitting near the ties of the track as the train passed by. They were heard to say, 'This train surely does shake the track while we are sitting here.'

"One day while I was at school, a knock was heard at the door of our one room school. Mr. Despain answered the door. These three children walked into the room. JOHN removed his hat. 'We are visiting the school, today.' They took the seats Mr. Despain gave them. How relieved I was when they all stood up and said, 'we need to go now.'"

Years later, about 1943, my mother was severely burned when a pressure cooker exploded. She went to see Dr. Rees of Twin Falls. In giving him her medical history, she mentioned the early deaths of her siblings from these contagious diseases. His comment was:

"Today their deaths from diphtheria would not have happened; but people underestimate the virulence of the red measles. It's a very serious disease with many possible dangerous side-effects."

Since that time, inoculations for the measles have become equally common.

～ 43 ～

THE SOUTHERN DIVISION AND DEATH
OF COLONEL JOHN LEHI IVIE

Cousin IDA BELLE GLEDHILL (Christensen, Buchannan) tells us:

"Grandma IVIE (MARY CATHERINE), now PETERS, lived near a mine in Idaho and the miners there would wear their clothes until they were dirty and then just throw them away, so Grandma would pick them up, wash them, and then send them to Mother to make into clothes for her children. She could tat, crochet, and embroider and her home was made beautiful.

"Mother [LILLIE BELLE IVIE (Gledhill)] had many fears of being left alone, especially at night, when Father was gone. If someone approached, lamps were not lighted and no noise was made by the children until she was sure who was calling on us. While Father was on his mission [to England,] a Brother Adshead used to bring little gifts to us and drove a long way to do it. But one night mother kept him out of the house all night, because she couldn't tell who he was.

"A dugway ran along south of our farm and many times people tipped over there into the bushes or the river and would have to be rescued, often at night, by my parents. This river was the summer swimming hole and the whole family would go in together, and Uncle OSCAR's family would often join us."

"When FRED was 11 days old, Father left her [mother] and went on a mission to England after only three days of preparation. He rented the farm to Billy Carter, but he wasn't much of a farmer and so Mother was hard pressed for money all of the time that Father was gone. She always had faith that money would be provided. Many people were kind to her and gave her food and clothes and money to send to Father. I think that $208.25 was sent to him by friends in the two years he was gone. She really had a hard time and told of many times being down to the last mixing of flour and going to the door to find a sack of flour or other eatables left there by known or unknown friends. She felt that they'd always keep well and have enough while Father was gone, and they did. After Father returned from his mission, I was born to them and then my sister Amelia May.

LILLIE BELLE AND THOMAS GLEDHILL WITH THEIR TWO YOUNGEST CHILDREN, IDA BELLE AND YOUNGER SISTER AMELIA MARY GLEDHILL

(NOT PICTURED) THEIR OLDER SONS WERE: THOMAS RAY, HUGH LAFAYETTE, JOHN IVO, ALDEN OSCAR, HERBERT FRANCE, AND FRED OVI.

After my sister was born, Mother was dangerously ill. We all stayed over at Uncle OSCAR's farm while she was recovering. We'd get lonely for her and Father, and would walk up the railroad tracks to get to see them. I remember Dr. West getting out of his buggy and threatening us with a whipping with his buggy whip if we didn't return and not bother her.

"Mother never whipped us. She hit our heads with a thimble or would tell us to go and get a stick. When this happened Sis would bring in the smallest stick she could find . . . and of course, Mother would laugh and everything would be alright. She liked parties and having people over to eat. Our pantry in the rock house was large and at party time, every shelf would be filled with pies, tarts, cakes, and so on. Mother was known by many for her pies. At the foot of the cellar she kept a large barrel of dill pickles, and in the winter she kept a crock of mincemeat in her bedroom window. Mother liked costume parties and was as young as anyone. She liked to play charades, other guessing games, and checkers. In spite of her lack of education, she was well read. She liked to go swimming in the canal or wading in a stream. She liked anything that was good clean fun. The people around sent for her in sickness or to lay out their dead for burial. She helped deliver all of the babies in the family as well as many others. I think that all of her grandchildren but 4 or 5 were washed first by Mother.

"Mother loved flowers and worked early and late to keep the yard beautiful. She was always bringing home a new flower start to plant . . . . Mother, as well as Uncle OSCAR, could pick up handfuls of bees and not get stung, at least not very often. She was always getting another swarm. One time she was getting a swarm from the top of our cherry tree and she had stacked tables, chairs, and boxes to get her and hive up to the swarm, but got off balance and fell. This time she really got stung, but still saved the bees . . . . Every one loved her; me too, though it took a long time for me to think that she loved me.

"When Mother was so dreadfully sick after the birth of my sister, she was delirious part of the time. But as she recovered, she prayed she would be spared to raise her children. Then she slept and dreamed that a man in white came to her and told her that her time wasn't now. He told her that she would live many years. Then a train of cars came by with just old ladies in it with white hair and a man with the train. The man told Mother that sometime she would be given charge of this train of ladies and that she should prepare herself to that end. So when she was given charge of the Sevier Stake Relief Society . . . she felt that this was the train in the dream. There were many old ladies then in Relief Society. So when she was released from this position, she knew that she wouldn't live much longer. An autopsy was never done, but Dr. Gottfredson thought that she had died from cancer.

"From 1895 to 1913, Mother held many positions in the Church. On June 23, 1913, they all went to stake conference in Richfield and after the morning session went to Ray's home for dinner. LILLIE BELLE was late and went into the bedroom. As they tried to get her to come out and eat, she'd be on her knees praying and crying. Finally she told them that she had been called to be the Stake Relief Society President and would be sustained in the afternoon meeting.

"Each Tuesday was designated as Relief Society day, and the General Board began sending lessons to the Wards including genealogical ones. Their job was to promote temple excursions, scripture reading, and home evenings. While she was president, a burial department was set up in the Stake Tithing Office. During World War I, they checked food and sold bonds. During the 1918 flu epidemic, all meetings were canceled for two months. A children's clinic was established and operated. Up until 1921 there had been all of Sevier County and Marysvale in the Stake, comprised of 21 Wards. In 1921, the Stake was divided into three Stakes: Sevier, North Sevier, and South Sevier. Mother stayed on as Stake Relief Society President in the Sevier Stake. In March of 1929 [very near my birthday—BCS] a very successful pageant was put on in the High School for the 50th anniversary of the Relief society. [The Relief Society was organized 17 Mar 1842 by Joseph Smith in Nauvoo, Illinois. It is the largest women's organization in the world. The 50-year celebration referred to the reorganization after the church came to Utah.]

"She wasn't very well the last 10 years of her life. She had dysentery that was hard to check. She tried anything that someone thought might work and had many doctors, but they couldn't help her much. . . . When Stake Conference time came around again, the visiting Apostle and the Stake Presidency came by the house to tell her that she had been released. When they left she turned her face to the wall and cried and told us that she wouldn't live much longer. She died in the late evening of May 1, 1929 . . . just before she did, Father asked, 'Do you still love me?' and she answered, 'You bet I do.' and those were her last words.

"Grandpa IVIE (Colonel JOHN L. IVIE) and LUTA (his daughter by VIOLET) made their home with us after Aunt VIOLET died [of typhoid fever]. One day he was sitting by our stove in the rocking chair when he died and he then slumped in the chair and burned his knees on the stove.

Mother carried on so, and promised so much, that he was brought back to life and lived for three months in terrible agony. Mother had no real rest night or day with death's rattle in his throat for so long. It was a terrible thing for her to have to go through. She said that never again would she try to change the will of God. Losing IVO, BERT, LAFE, JANE, and MAGGIE all in about this same period of time made an old woman of my mother . . . Having a great deal of work to do was the only thing that kept her going."

THE ADULT CHILDREN OF COLONEL JOHN LEHI IVIE (AFTER HIS DEATH, 1909)
JAMES OSCAR, ALDEN, RAY, RUSSELL (SON OF VIOLET AND JOHN L. IVIE)
LILLIE BELL, MAY, IDA

My mother LILLIE IVIE (CONDIE), wrote about her grandfather:

"I remember my grandfather [JOHN LEHI IVIE] as a quiet, non-talkative man. He did not play games with us. I did not know [then] he had the title, of 'Colonel' and had even led in some of the battles that stood out in Utah history. . . . He lived with Aunt BELLE and Uncle TOM. Uncle TOM was a stanch Republican and worked to get TEDDY ROOSEVELT and Howard Taft elected President. My Grandfather was a Democrat and was very disappointed at the defeat of William Jennings Bryan. He and Father had many heated discussions with Uncle TOM about it.

"When I was ten, my family moved to Salina. On [grandfather's] visits he would crack nuts and sometimes shared them with me. He would make shadow pictures on the wall by putting his hands together and moving his fingers to form the shapes of animals. He also played checkers with PEARL, my younger sister. With his help, they always beat me at that game.

"I can remember the long string of buggies that followed his casket from Vermillion to Richfield where he was buried. I really missed him."

JOHN LEHI IVIE'S GRAVESITE
IN RICHFIELD, UTAH

THE TALL TOMBSTONE WAS PAID FOR BY THE
MEN HE HAD COMMANDED AND READS:

COL. JOHN L. IVIE
OUR COMMANDER

IT THEN GIVES HIS BIRTH, DEATH DATES,
WITH A VERY SPECIAL TRIBUTE NEAR
THE BOTTOM OF THE SPIRE.

COUSIN GRANT IVIE, SON OF UNCLE LLOYD,
HOLDING THE COLONEL'S SWORD AND METAL.

(ABOUT 1996)

After I [Brookie Condie Swallow] was married and was looking for family histories in the Logan Genealogical Library, I discovered the book *Prominent Men and Pioneers of Utah*. Each of the thousands of histories in this large book had only a short paragraph or two with a small picture usually accompanying it. His picture and history were among the others. When I told Mother about it, she was surprised. She said that when the book was being compiled, they went around the state and charged those who were included $60.00. Her grandfather felt this was wrong and told them quite bluntly that after all he had done for the state of Utah, and after spending over eight years in the saddle for their benefit, if he had to pay money to have his picture and history included in a history book, he didn't care if it was included or not.

My mother, LILLIE IVIE (Condie) wrote:

"The name, Salina, was derived from the salt hills in the east and from the taste of the water. . . The story was told to me that when Salina became a town, fifty men met at the Presbyterian Church to . . . find a way to get rid of Mormonism in Salina . . . They took an oath that they would sacrifice their life if necessary to see that every Mormon left that town even if they had to wade in blood from the church to the river. Their church was located about a mile west of Salina.

THE ORIGINAL MORTENSEN HOME IN SALINA, UTAH, ABOUT 1914. J. OSCAR AND ANNIE IVIE ARE IN THE WAGON. MY MOTHER AND HER SISTER ARE STANDING BY THE TREE.

They had to sign their names in blood, and they proceeded to harass the Mormon families in the area . . . bad and unpleasant things had happened to all the members of this group . . . In any event, it didn't stop the church from growing in Salina."

Salina had two wards of the church and she was in the third grade when they arrived there. There was an opera house and a saloon. Mother continues:

"there were two men alive who had been members of that group--Ott Cuttaback and a Mr. Rex. Mr. Rex was the manager of the post office and he lived a block west of our home. . . . He was a quiet type of neighbor and he walked past our house . . . to and from the post office. Ott Cuttaback was the father of three grown daughters. One . . . was my teacher in school. Mr. Cuttaback [who had been the sheriff who hunted and caught any man who had more than one wife,] spent most of his time standing somewhere on

Main Street or where the public could see him . . . Usually he was in front of the General Store or in the Post Office or the Saloon. He had all his teeth capped with gold. I would pass him when I was sent to town on errands. . . .

"Miss Cuttaback was my first teacher in Salina and perhaps because I was new to the school or shy, or both, or maybe because I was a Mormon, she decided that I needed to take the third grade over, and I was retained and she had the pleasure of teaching me for two years, my second third grade and the fourth grade."

Mother's sister, PEARL, wrote that her brother:

"JIM (JAMES OVI IVIE) was born 12 March 1906, when Mother was 42 years old. The tenderness born of the sorrow for the loss of four of Mother's children centered upon JIM. Nor was it wasted, for he thrived from affection. JIM was a healthy happy baby but delayed in walking and talking by his wants being [quickly] supplied.

"There was a great tragedy in Salina the year after JIM was born. Salina had an epidemic of typhoid fever. There were 75 cases and 7 deaths. Two of our neighbors died with it. In late summer I took vegetables to a relative and a neighbor who was a Christian Scientist. I helped myself to a glass of water from the water pail at her house. It was not long after that I had typhoid fever. Father had just dug a new well out next to the road so that others could use it also.

"The well was condemned as a source of infection and was abandoned (it was 60 feet deep). VIOLET [wife of great-grandfather JOHN LEHI IVIE] died and Brother Nordfelt across the corner died. I had the fever for about three months. By Christmas my arms were the size of a broomstick. With good care I recovered. In March my brother LLOYD took the disease, and in the summer my sister and my Mother each occupied a front room in their fight to survive."

My mother, LILLIE IVIE CONDIE, told us as children that she was whirling around and around with her arms outstretched on their front lawn. She became dizzy and fainted. She hadn't any memory of the fever until she was recovering. The typhoid was so virulent that she lost all her hair. It was just starting to grow back when school started. Embarrassed about her missing hair she wore a parka type cap over her head. A bossy classmate insisted that she take it off. She refused, and the girl asked the teacher to make her do it. Miss Cuttaback complied. Totally submissive, she obeyed, shocking the whole classroom with her bald head—the cap was put back on.

Aunt PEARL continues:

"At this time I and my baby brother JIM were left to be cared for by two of my aunts. First at my Aunt EMELINE's and second at Aunt BELLE's. In both cases I was expected to manage tending my brother while he was awake and wash his diapers while he was asleep. Once at my Aunt BELLE's home we were in the garden and JIM ate some raw green beans. These were not chewed, and he was very sick following this experience. We made a bed for him in the dining room by tying two chairs together, and I sat beside him wiping his face with a wet cloth and giving him frequent drinks of water. JIM got well, but he was very heavy for me to lift and to manage. In this same room a couple of years later, I was giving drinks of water to my Father's father [Colonel JOHN LEHI IVIE] and rubbing his head to ease the pain; here he died when he was 75 years old (on 10 Mar 1909).

[Note: EMELINA DASTRUP married uncle CHRISTIAN J. MORTENSEN, 26 Jan 1887; they had six children by 1909]

"As a result of the typhoid epidemic, Salina managed to get a water system. A cement cistern to hold spring water was built on the hills south of Salina. Electric lights and telephones came soon after. It was in this early period of JIM's life that he became absorbed with invention. When he was asked to turn the washing machine, he worked to contrive a way to turn the wheel by a treadle similar to the one on the sewing machine. Invention became his life's work. 'Have JIM do it!' became the request by which JIM learned many skills. Eventually he majored in physics and earned a Master's degree."

JAMES OVI IVIE was born 12 Mar 1906. When her brother JIM was born my mother, LILLIE, expressed her feelings:

"I looked at him wonderingly. My four year old brother, LEON, went to the cupboard and brought the baby a slice of bread and held it to his mouth. 'This baby in not quite old enough to eat bread,' said my father. Someone suggested that LEON was unselfish in wanting to give the new baby some food. A feeling of love and thankfulness came to me. I had not reconciled myself to the deaths of JOHN and LEROY, although it was a year since they had died. At church a feeling of peace had come to me when I looked at the Anderson boy who resembled by brother JOHN. . . . 'What shall we name him?' asked my mother, 'Shall we name him JAMES after you?'

"'We already have one of our children named OSCAR, so . . . I would like to name him JAMES IVO, but that would not be the same initials as I have. Why don't we turn those letters around and call him JAMES OVI

UNCLE JIM, AUNT BENOLA AND THEIR ADOPTED SON BEN
THE COUPLE HAD THE RH FACTOR AND HAD EIGHT
CHILDREN THAT WERE BORN, BUT LIVED ONLY A BRIEF
TIME. THIS WAS BEFORE THE MEDICAL PROFESSION STARTED
THEIR TRANSFUSION OPERATIONS ON THESE CHILDREN.

IVIE?' This is the name they finally decided upon. I idealized my cousin IVO, so I was glad."

Uncle JAMES OVI IVIE, from my memories, worked hard on air purification from the tall factory smoke stacks in the Salt Lake City area. He continued with his inventions in eliminating air pollutants, teaching and inventing at a southern California university, and then in Vienna, Virginia, near Washington D.C. He was listed in *Whose Who in America* for his contributions in air sanitation. My brother, JAMES M. CONDIE, was also listed that year for his expertise in statistics during the early computer days, while working for the Federal Reserve.

Uncle LLOYD OSCAR IVIE, received his call to go on a mission to Japan 28 Dec 1910 (age 20.) During this mission he helped translate the L.D.S. hymnbook into the Japanese language. He was in Japan until World War I required his return home. After this war, he married aunt NORA BLAMIRES and returned to Japan as the Mission President. This mission was closed later when the troubles between China and Japan began to erupt into open warfare. The mission remained closed until after World War II ended and peace was established. Uncle Lloyd was in Tokyo, Japan, when the devastating September 1923 earthquake struck, followed by the fires that demolished 65 percent of that city and leveled Yokohoma with its 750,000 people.

Uncle LLOYD O. IVIE always loved the Japanese people and later directed the genealogical program that allowed their temple work to be performed for their dead. After his retirement, he was called as a bishop over the Japanese ward in Salt Lake City, Utah. He was greatly loved by them, and many tears were shed for him upon his death by these loving members.

Uncle Lloyd O. Ivie in Tokyo, Japan, after the September 1923 earthquake, which demolished and created fires throughout much of the city. Uncle Lloyd was the L.D.S. Mission president in Japan at that time. The mission would be closed a few years later, when the signs of the coming war between Japan and China were eminent.

"On 1 September 1923, an earthquake, followed by a tidal wave and fire, almost completely destroyed Tokyo, Yokohama, and all towns within a radius of 40 miles with an appalling loss of life and property." [*Americana, 1945 edition*]

These postcards were sent to my mother and father by Uncle Lloyd. This one is a picture of a hospital in Yokohama that was destroyed by the devastating fire.

Commuting into Tokyo after the electric power was destroyed by the earthquake

~ 44 ~

THE CONDIEs, SWANNs, AND TUCKERs
OF MORGAN COUNTY, UTAH

There are two male given names in the CONDIE line that are so common it becomes somewhat confusing—GIBSON and THOMAS. The first GIBSON CONDIE was my third-great-grandfather, who was named after a dear friend in Scotland. He never came to America.

1. GIBSON CONDIE – married – JEAN RUSSELL

2. (his sons) – THOMAS married HELEN SHARP and GIBSON married CECELIA SHARP [They stayed in SLC] [both were converted by missionaries William Gibson and JOHN SHARP]

3. THOMAS (son of THOMAS, who later married HANNAH SWANN) had a brother GIBSON (his journal included earlier) [numbers 2 and 3 came to America on the ship *Zetland* in January 1849]

4. GIBSON A (my grandfather and son of #3 THOMAS, married EMILY E. TUCKER) had a brother THOMAS

5. My grandparents named their second son <u>THOMAS</u> LEE and his youngest son <u>GIBSON</u> ADELI CONDIE. I knew them in my youth as Uncle LEE and Uncle <u>GIBSON</u>.

<u>THOMAS</u> S. MONSON, now the President of the L.D.S. Church (2008), has a grandfather named <u>THOMAS</u> SHARP CONDIE, whose father was the #2 <u>GIBSON</u> CONDIE, who married CECELIA SHARP. President MONSON's mother was GLADYS CONDIE, the youngest of this THOMAS' children.

[Note: Although THOMAS S. MONSON was born the same year as my husband, GROVER SWALLOW, [1927, the year Charles Limburg flew non-stop across the Atlantic Ocean,] he is a third cousin to my

father, which makes him my third-cousin-once-removed. This age difference is created because his ancestors were the youngest children, and I am descended from the older children.]

My great-grandparents THOMAS and HANNAH SWANN CONDIE had nine sons and five daughters.
One son and two daughters died in infancy, smallpox claiming one and spinal meningitis another. The
children shown above are: GIBSON A, HANNAH ELIZABETH, JOSEPH W., GIDEON, NEPHI, and
PARLEY CONDIE.

HANNAH SWANN's parents were EPHRIAM SWANN from Ninevah,
[near Tenbury,] Worcestershire, England, and his wife, FANNY JONES
(Swann), who was born 26 May 1824 nearby in Lathly House. The family arrived in Salt Lake City, 12 Sep 1857, having crossed the plains at the same time
Johnston's army crossed the western plains. They were sent south with the many
families that had evacuated the city to Beaver, Utah. When the emergency
ended, they moved to Ogden. In the spring of 1860, they moved to the Weber
Valley—living on Dalton Creek, near Milton, Morgan County, Utah. It was
during the spring of 1863 that the family moved again—this time to Croydon
for the next 21 years. There were then 5 children: HANNAH; ELEANOR;
FANNY ELIZA; EDWARD WILLIAM and JAMES EPHRIAM. In 1884, my
second-great-grandparents EPHRIAM and FANNY moved to Preston, Idaho.

Grandfather GIBSON A CONDIE described his grandfather EPHRIAM SWANN as:

"5 feet 10 inches tall, weight 160 to 180 pounds, eyes dark, hair dark, top of head bald ever since I remember him. He was a farmer and stock grower, a veterinarian without a school diploma, a very useful man in any community, generous and hospitable to everybody. His house in Croydon near the school and meeting house and the side of the main road afforded shelter to neighbors and strangers alike. He served as presiding Elder until the organization of the Morgan Stake, and a Bishop, John Hopkin, was given charge. I would say EPHRIAM SWANN was a good, honorable man, a true saint. I grew up near him, worked beside him in the field, slept with him on the ground, and on the floor away from home. Never was he heard to complain of his lot or condition during adversity, poverty or prosperity. He died 13 Sept 1896 and was buried in the cemetery near the farm he homesteaded [in Preston, Idaho.]"

Grandfather CONDIE describes his grandmother SWANN:

"FANNY JONES SWANN, a great woman, a true wife, a real helpmate, a wonderful mother. She mothered many besides her own children. An excellent midwife and nurse, she assisted at over 2,000 births, nursing the mother and child for no compensation in many cases. [Her usual fee was $5.00 for the birth and subsequent care.] One of these was Mathew Cowley, later a member of the Twelve Apostles. She was also present at the birth of all of my mother's children. Often leaving her sick bed to go and help the afflicted, it was never too stormy. She fed the hungry, patched the clothes of the orphaned. An angel of mercy, her life was occupied with useful service. The Bible refers to one person as a 'Great Woman.' It was not Pharaoh's daughter, nor the Queen of Sheba, but a farmer's wife. You can read about it in the 4th chapter of 2nd Kings. The one and only woman to whom the Bible gives that title. Well, I pass the title to Grandma SWANN, 'A Great Woman,'—what more can be said?

"She died January 28, 1909. Her remains were placed in a brick vault beside EPHRIAM SWANN, in the cemetery near the Homestead in Preston [three miles from the city.] The grave was dedicated by her oldest grandson present, GIBSON A CONDIE. Her four surviving children were present, vis. HANNAH, FANNY ELIZA (LILA), EDWARD W and MARY ELLEN, beside many grandchildren and about 600 friends attended the funeral services. It was a very muddy road, almost impassable, yet 18 vehicles followed to the graveyard."

In England, Fanny had worked with a medical doctor as a nurse. When she left for America, he gave her a large medical book to take with her. Her services were called upon frequently as she crossed the plains. At one time she set a broken leg, which she was able to do successfully. In Croydon, she was the only person with any medical experience between Park City, Utah, and Green River, Wyoming. In Preston, Idaho, her medical training took her to Lewiston, Utah, to as far north as Soda Springs, Idaho—and further distances at times to help her family and friends. We were told in Preston that she delivered some of the relatives of L.D.S. Church President Ezra Taft Benson, whose early family home was in Whitney, Idaho. Ezra Taft Benson was delivered by a Doctor Cutler.

[Note: We knew a Dr. Cutler when we arrived in Preson in 1951. GROVER played tennis with him at times. He was older, but an excellent tennis player.]

Grandfather GIBSON A CONDIE states that his father's sister, HELEN CONDIE THACKERAY, in 1887, took up the study of medicine and obstetrics and became the doctor and midwife of Croydon and surrounding areas. There was no store in Croydon for many years, and supplies had to be brought from Henefer or over the mountain from Salt Lake City. Grandfather CONDIE continues:

> "Our parents had real pioneer experiences. The Indians, the grasshoppers, killing frosts in mid summer all combined to test their endurance. Instruments and tools were scarce. All kinds of make shifts were prevalent. Men and women made such articles they needed to get along. I saw my father make ox yokes and ox bows, ax handles, wooden rakes and wooden forks to handle unbound bundles of grain, also spokes for wheels and fitted tires on the wheels. I remember he had a set of blacksmith tools and he made ox shoes and horse shoes and nailed them on. He made a wooden plow with a steel point.
>
> "He was always active in Ward Teaching. The General Authorities often stayed in his home when they came to Croydon. Father always taught us that we should take the Lord as a partner in our enterprises and pray as we go about our work. His monument is the family he left, their honestly and integrity and high moral character and a testimony of the gospel, a beacon to others. His greatness is the name which will endure through generations and receive honor in eternity."

Great-grandfather THOMAS CONDIE died in Croydon, Morgan County, Utah, on 11 May 1921. He had been sick for about six weeks with some trouble of the liver and his feet swelled considerably. He endured his suffering very patiently and was very little trouble to anyone. He was buried in the Croydon Cemetery, where my sisters IVIE and CeCELIA, aunt HELEN CONDIE SMITH and I were proud to place the "Faith in Every Footstep" marker on his grave stone as well as that of our great-grandmother HANNAH SWANN CONDIE—to honor them on the 1997 Sesquicentennial of the Utah Pioneers. We also located his parent's graves in the Salt Lake City Cemetery; EPHRAIM and FANNY JONES SWANN's gravestones in Preston, Idaho; JAMES and BETSY LERWILL TUCKER's grave stones in Morgan, Utah, as well as our ancestors in central Utah.

AUNT HELEN, IVIE, AND BROOKIE AT MORGAN CEMETERY
OUR SISTER CECELIA TOOK THIS PHOTOGRAPH OF JAMES AND BETSY TUCKER's
GRAVES IN THE CEMETERY ABOVE MORGAN, UTAH

When GROVER and I lived in Preston, we met many of the descendants of EPHRAIM and FANNY SWANN. Three of grandfather CONDIE's brothers with many of their families lived in Preston. JAMES BROOM McQUEEN, a SWANN grandson and a member of our ward, shared the following:

"During the summer of 1952 the writer [visited] one of the oldest living cousins, HANNAH SWANN COPLEY at her home in Coalville, Utah.

Great Grandmother, ELEANOR BROOM was a bond servant in the home of a wealthy Englishman . . . Among the conditions of her bondage was a stipulation that she remain unmarried for the duration of her bond. However, her master agreed to permit her to enter a common-law relationship and have her home in a servant's cottage on his place. There were two other provisions in this permit. The spouse must be approved and must agree to all the conditions of her bondage, and, second, that any children born to the couple must bear the surname of the mother during the life of her bondage. Under these conditions and arrangements, a farm laborer, employed by the master, by the name of EPHRAIM SWANN, became her common-law spouse. By this means the master was practically assured of the continuous availability of his two servants.

"Several children were born to this couple and they grew up under the name of BROOM. Later on, perhaps at the termination of her bondage period and the lifting of the restrictions incident thereto, a church marriage solemnized and legalized the family relationship. The children adopted the surname of their father. Thus we became SWANNs instead of BROOMs.

"This story was interesting to me because it explained why Grandfather SWANN had me given the name of JAMES BROOM, to honor the name of his beloved mother—the bond servant of an English lord. . . . I honor their son EPHRAIM who recognized the Message of Salvation brought by the missionaries of the Church of Jesus Christ of Latter Day Saints and transplanted the SWANN Family name to a country that promises freedom from bondage of any kind. May God bless their memories and prosper all their descendants.

JAMES BROOM McQUEEN"

[Note: His mother was FANNY ELIZA SWANN, who married JOHN NESBIT McQUEEN the 6 Sep 1880. ELEANOR married L. I. TOONE on 25 Dec 1879, and MARY ELLEN married RICHARD C. TOONE in 1892. One of their descendants leased our ranch at Carey for a short time during World War II.]

[Note: In 1952, 100 years after his grandparents THOMAS & HELEN SHARP CONDIE settled in Salt Lake City, grandfather GIBSON A CONDIE attempted to count their living descendents at that time and give a brief history of each family. He claimed the numbers were still incomplete but his total was 617 living at that time. In 1952, my parents had only seven children and one grandchild. Their small contribution of less than one and one-half percent has increased to about 400 living in 2008, a multiple of fifty times as many, maybe indicating that currently their descendents may be in the tens of thousands. GIBSON and CECELIA SHARP CONDIE's descendants are not included in these numbers. According to grandfather's summary in 1952, their were 22 school teachers, 8 nurses, 4 doctors, 4 attorneys, 2 judges, 1 state water commissioner, 1 state superintendent of schools, 1 sheriff, 1 chief of city police, 6 real pioneers, 8 bishops, 29 stake presidents, 1 mission president, 48 missionaries, 1 patriarch, 5 members of school boards, and 9 in the armed forces. He added, "I know of but one millionaire and I have no knowledge of any of our kinfolks on relief or drawing support from the state or the church."]

FOUR GENERATIONS OF THE SWANN FAMILY
HANNAH SWANN (Condie), her daughter and granddaughter, and FANNY JONES (Swann)

Grandfather CONDIE gave much honor to the women and their accomplishments as mothers. In a SWANN family reunion I attended about 1952, he countered a previous speaker that had said that Mothers Day was celebrated much more than Fathers Day, and that we need to remember our fathers, by pointing out that the opposite was true, and that women are seldom given the honor they deserve. The Bible and history is filled with the contributions of men and only a few women are even mentioned.

Grandfather GIBSON A CONDIE taught school in Star Valley, Wyoming, which includes the towns of Afton, Grover, and Freedom. It is quite close to Yellowstone National Park, which is often sited as the coldest place in the nation. They then moved to Carey, Blaine, Idaho—also cold. About 50 miles west of Carey is the Sun Valley Ski Resort, which was chosen for its powder snow and mountain slopes by the Union Pacific Railroad in 1934. Going east, Carey borders the volcanic Craters of the Moon National Monument.

THE GIBSON A. CONDIE FAMILY

This picture of the family, taken while they were in Grover, Wyoming in 1898, has rarely been seen by our family. My father, MARION ASHER CONDIE, is standing in the rear with his ringlets and a Lord Fauntleroy tatted collar. ADA and LEE are in the front. It was obtained from aunt HELEN CONDIE SMITH's photo album. Grandmother EMILY ELIZABETH TUCKER CONDIE is obviously very proud of her husband and children. She tatted all the lace collars and the inserts, as well as sewing all of their clothing. Years later, when I was married in 1948, I inherited her old Singer treadle sewing machine, and used it until we could afford an electric one. According to family stories, my father cried when they cut off his naturally curly ringlets; but he told my mother, he was very glad when they were gone. His tears were for his mother, who was crying profusely.

SUN VALLEY, IDAHO, NESTLES IN THE HEART OF THE SAWTOOTH MOUNTAINS

UNIQUE CHAIR SKI LIFTS AT SUN VALLEY, IDAHO

1934 PICTURES OF EARLY SUN VALLEY, IDAHO, SKI RESORT. THERE WAS NO ROAD INTO IT AT THIS TIME—THEY HAD TO ARRIVE ON THE UNION PACIFIC RAILROAD.

From the journal of JAMES TUCKER of Morgan, Utah, the English shoe-maker from Devonshire, England:

"In 1892, the later part of August, I was afflicted with typhoid fever, also 3 other members of the family were attacked, (LUCY, ROSE, and NETTIE). In April 1894, I rented my business and responded to a call to perform a mission to England. I received a very honorable release and returning home, I found my business in much worse shape than I left it. After working years paying off my debts, and suffering losses from thieves, I finally sold all my store, also my interests in the Morgan Z.C.M.I. I served in various positions such as water master many years for thanks, school trustee for 12 years, member of city council, city treasurer, County treasurer for two terms, and County commission for two terms.

"But in positions in the Church I have also done a little. For many years I was secretary of the 35th quorum of Seventy, one of its first presidents as long as I was connected with it. After being ordained a High Priest, I served in the presidency of that quorum. Was Genealogical Representative for Morgan Stake for many years. I have labored in the temple four years and have had 82,289 baptisms and 8,000 ordinances performed for the dead. Both for my kindred and my wife's people also.

"Much more could be said but something should here be said concerning my wife who as a faithful helpmate assisted me in many of our accomplishments and endured the privations incident to pioneers. In the year 1863 after our second child was born, she was very sick and for 13 weeks lay confined to her bed. At one time her spirit left her body for 38 hours, and during that time I heard her sing twice. The burial clothes were being prepared, but she was restored thru faith, and lived after and bore ten more children. She was a faithful Latter Day Saint, a devoted wife, and a wonderful mother. Largely thru her faith we succeeded in raising all twelve of our children to maturity. She taught all ten of her daughters real domestic science, and the art of home making. Their success as wives and mothers has been the result of her instructions. I hope they will cherish her memory and emulate her many virtues.

"I would describe her as above the average size of women these days; Height five feet seven inches, Bust forty inches, Weight 150 lbs, Grey eyes and beautiful black hair.

12 ADULT CHILDREN OF JAMES AND BETSY LERWILL TUCKER
MY GRANDMOTHER EMILY E. TUCKER (CONDIE) IS SITTING FIRST ON THE LEFT
GREAT-GRANDFATHER JAMES TUCKER IS SITTING CENTER, HIS WIFE HAD DIED 20 JUN 1909
JAMES TUCKER WOULD DIE 19 JUN 1925

[Note: "The names of our twelve children are:

Mrs. Charles Kingston of Ogden, Utah, [MARY PRISCILLA LERWILL TUCKER, born 3 Jan 1862];

Mrs. Fred J. Muir of Grey Lake, Idaho, [LYDIA ANN TUCKER, born 28 Aug 1863];

Mrs. John J. Simmons of Oakley, Idaho, [SUSAN TUCKER, born 20 Oct 1864];

Mr. James Henry Tucker of Morgan, Utah, [born 3 Apr 1867, md. Rebecca Tonks];

Mrs. Gibson A Condie of Carey, Idaho, [EMILY ELIZABETH TUCKER, born 25 Nov 1869];

Mrs. Edward Jones of Penrose, Wyoming, [LUCY GRACE TUCKER, born 30 Oct 1871];

Mrs. George Spackman of Farmington, Utah, [BERTHA AUGUSTA TUCKER, born 24 Sep 1874];

Mrs. James Clark of Carlin, Nevada, [ANNIE TUCKER, born 13 Sep 1876];

Mrs. Charles Van Orden of Idaho Falls, Idaho, [LILLIE LERWILL TUCKER (twin) born 28 Jun 1878];

Mrs. Willis A. Smith of Rexburg, Idaho, [ROSE LERWILL TUCKER, (twin) born 28 Jun 1878];

Mrs. Norman Gorder of Milton, Utah, [JENETTE LERWILL TUCKER, born 24 Aug 1880];

Mr. Lerwill Tucker of Morgan, Utah, [born 29 Nov 1885, md. Nona Vincent.]

I have 84 grandchildren—seventy-four now living, and 41 great grand children."]

JAMES TUCKER did not date his autobiography. He spent many of his last years with my grandparents GIBSON A. and EMILY TUCKER CONDIE who lived on Main Street in Logan, Utah, just below the L.D.S. temple, where he did much temple work for our dead English ancestors. The CONDIE home was sold and replaced with the *Dinner Horn Restaurant* in the 1930s. He was buried by his wife in the Morgan, Utah, cemetery in 1925.

~ 45 ~

TWO SISTERS FROM SALINA, UTAH, AND TWO RETURNING VETERANS OF IDAHO

SISTERS PEARL IVIE AND LILLIE IVIE ABOUT 1917

PEARL IVIE (Stanford's) early life record states:

"So soon the years slip by. The summer of 1913, I went to my Aunt HANNAH's home to help her for six weeks while her 13th child (GEORGE) was born. Father had been called to assist with the harvesting of the wheat in Alberta, Canada. With the coming of World War One, the

Canadian boys were called into the fighting forces, and it was difficult to get farm help in Canada. My brother LLOYD was in Japan on a mission. The creamery work at Salina had been stopped by the Jensen Creamery Company paying higher prices for cream and creating losses for the cooperative where my father had made butter for several years. Father went to Canada and later sent for Mother, LEON and JIM. LILLIE and I stayed in Utah to go to school. In 1915 the harvest from my cousin's farms in Canada would total to a train 23 miles long with each car filled with wheat.

[Note: MARY SUSANNAH (the oldest living child of JOHN LEHI IVIE) married JOHN T. HENINGER. The family had left Chester, Sanpete County, Utah, and bought a ranch near Raymond, Canada.]

"At Christmas in 1912, I had the measles at the beginning of my first year at high school. It was a busy year, especially in music. I played in the band [flute] along with my sister [LILLIE on the clarinet.] We played in the orchestra and played for dances and picture shows. We sang in the ward choir as well as in the school choir. We took part in the operetta and light opera. We planned to stay in Salina to go to school. A strange thing happened after consolidation of Salina and the county schools. There was conflict, and the music program folded up, so we went to Snow Academy at Ephraim. [1913-1914—At that time it was owned by the LDS church.]"

LILLIE's records of this period state that their mother thought that it would be only a week or two before arrangements would be made for the two young girls to join them in Canada; but as the days passed, and arrangements were not made, she spent all her spare time in prayer for their protection. The girls were young and could see no danger. They attended L.D.S. Mutual, a Mutual dancing class and tried to keep the house clean. They sewed and LILLIE prepared for a third year of high school. She wrote:

"We also had two boyfriends that came from Redmond, a town three miles from us to take dancing lessons also. I felt able to meet any responsibility that was necessary and was shocked that one of our neighbors made some remarks that parents should be home caring for their girls instead of sending a son on a mission."

After Snow Academy, the girls attended Brigham Young Academy at Provo, Utah. Mother found this to be too close to Salina, because a young man came every weekend from the Salina area, and she was not that fond of him. The following year, the two girls went further north to the college at Logan, Utah, where they got their normal teaching degrees in 1915.

In 1915-16, LILLIE taught all the grades in a one-room school house at Hillsdale, Utah.

[Note: son-in-law HYRUM HAYNES' mother MONA WILSON (Haynes) was born in Hillsdale, Garfield County, in 1917, and both her parents were school teachers.]

In 1916-17, she taught the fourth grade at Salina, Utah. The following summer mother spent in Raymond, Alberta, Canada, where her father was still working. In 1917-18, she taught the 1st, 2nd, and 3rd grades at Grouse Creek, Utah; and in 1918-19 she taught the 3rd and 4th grades at Carey, Idaho. One of LILLIE IVIE's future pupils was asked what her teacher's name was. The young girl replied that she wasn't sure; but she thought it was Miss Bouquet.

Before the sisters went to Carey, where their father was managing part of the farm of his sister IDA's husband TOM STANFORD, LILLIE and PEARL made a trip into Salt Lake City. They splurged and bought themselves the latest fashions from hats to shoes. Later in her life, Mother was told by Stake President Lennox Adamson:

"LILLIE, I can still remember when you and your sister arrived in Carey. All of us thought you were the most beautiful girls. You were like a fresh breeze in our small community and so intelligent and capable."

The United States was at war; but on 11 Nov 1918, the World War I armistice was signed. The servicemen would soon return from France to their homes on the farms, or whatever. A popular song of that time period was *How you gonna keep 'em down on the farm, after they've seen Paree?*

When I was the LDS Panaca Nevada Stake Record Extraction Director for seven years, among the many records we extracted were the Death Records for Shelby County, Tennessee, which included the city of Memphis. In early October of 1918 the pandemic Spanish Influenza struck the nation. Page after page in these records listed as cause of death—Spanish Influenza. No one was exempt from this death toll. There were doctors, nurses, pharmacists, lawyers, farmers, housewives, infants, children, whites, colored, travelers, and so forth. They far outnumbered the soldiers of that city that were killed throughout the war, which included their local student airplane base with their many airplane crashes, and this was just one county—even tiny Carey, Idaho, was not exempt.

Aunt PEARL's history tells about arriving at Carey and her romance:

"When I was 12, my father's sister IDA, visiting in Salina with her husband TOM STANFORD . . . . a brother to SEDLEY's father CYRUS, said to me, 'I have a nephew in Carey that I am saving for you.' In 1918, I was age 20 and SEDLEY was 27. . . . Most of the boys were already in the service, and . . . there were about four girls to every boy, it was decided that, as a going away party we would have a picnic up in the East Fork area (near the future site of Sun Valley). Together eleven girls locked arms, with some competition about who should walk beside the boys:

AUNT ADA CONDIE (RIGHT) GRADUATES
FROM NURSING SCHOOL

Beauford Kirkland and Stanley Sparks. We walked around the twist in the road . . . past Aunt IDA's house, Wilford Patterson's house, the farm house that had been the home of SEDLEY's father—now managed by Rowe and Thomas . . . the next house, clean and white was set back from the road in a setting of large Cottonwood trees and a large lawn in front. It was twilight, and the last colors of sunset hovered over Queen's Crown, the crested mountain that stood above the foothills to the west.

"In the neighborhood where the gang had grown up together, there was the call to come out, SEDLEY came down the four steps of the angled porch, across the long path, opened the gate, and there we were, a group of young folks determined not to let the clouds of war dampen our quest for fun. Henry and Wren McGlochlin and Milford Sparks were drawn into the group, [for] our celebration on July 23rd and 24th on the jamboree at Warm Creek above Ketchum.

"Greetings and introductions were made, and as LILLIE, my sister, and I were new in the group, SEDLEY took his flash-light pen from his pocket and turned the light on our faces to see what we looked like . . . . LILLIE rode in the car with him on our trip, but she was already wearing a diamond, so he turned some of his attention to me. Songs and chatter made the time pass quickly as we traveled to the tall evergreen country. . . . Wren was considerate of my comfort and gave me a box of chocolate covered Brazil nuts, which I shared. . . . Food was abundant as we circled around a huge bonfire and filled our plates with the good supply that each had added to make it a feast. We sang; we cooked and played tag as we circulated around the fire. In time my stomach rebelled, and as some of the group grew drowsy during the story-telling, my cousin ESTHER and I sought retreat in the car parked close to the fire. We tried to go to sleep, but sleep wasn't on the agenda for that night. First one person came to talk to us, then another. Wren came several times, but SEDLEY persisted and . . . we began to feel quite well acquainted. . . .

"When the first call for breakfast came, we each took some fruit or what we could eat while hiking and set out to climb the hills.

[Note: East Fork, below Ketchum, is in the Sawtooth Mountain Range. North of Ketchum is the high rugged mountain pass into northern Idaho called Galena Summit. East Fork is where the Triumph Mine was discovered. Great-grandmother MARY CATHERINE BARTON (Ivie Peters) and her second husband, LYMAN PETERS, came there after they were married.]

"I don't remember which hills we climbed, but . . . SEDLEY . . . was walking on one side while Wren walked on the other. Nature provided much for us to observe; but I soon found out that SEDLEY was much better informed about nature than anyone I had ever met before, and I liked to hear his explanations. When we got back to camp, I was holding on to a white moth and several kinds of flowers and was fascinated with the instructions to step over logs, not on them, and was initiated into the pattern of burrows that were heaped with dirt on the top of the ground as the holes were made for underground passage.

"We had lunch, then tried our skills at rhymes to include in a letter to be sent to Milford . . . in the service . . . [then] to the warm springs bath house in Ketchum . . . splashing water as we were all in the swimming pool together, and there was a certain amount of showing off to get attention. In time we tired of it and got out of the water and sought some entertainment.

"We found a dance hall where we could drop in a coin and the music would play for dancing. It was a day when songs like 'Cuddle up a Little Closer' were sung in daring expression of supervised recreation; but we prided ourselves in not being that kind of people. Of course, as school

PARTY AT EAST FORK

teachers, my sister and I were expected to set the examples of good behavior; . . . however, we enjoyed the nonsense of a day to be remembered; ate chocolate bars, popcorn and soda pop, and talked about serious things whenever there was a slowdown in activity. Soon we were on our way back to Carey. At Lola Sparks' place we washed our faces, combed our hair and put on fresh clothes for the dance that was to be held at the Phippen Hall.

"At the hall I met SEDLEY's three sisters. Each one of them was pushing a baby carriage—Loma Adamson, Dayle Cooper, and Denton Richards would in the following year be my niece and nephews . . . . I danced with SEDLEY four times . . . . The next day, most of the girls went to the station to bid the boys goodbye. LILLIE and I did not go. We were on the lower ranch . . . of . . . Uncle TOM. It was a log house with two rooms with a slant roof kitchen where we stuffed sagebrush into an iron stove to get heat for cooking. And the summer days were hot, but the nights were cool. [There was] a swing and a hammock. . . . Philbert Lind came from Lind, Utah, and begged . . . LILLIE to return her ring to Bill Frost. He . . . was not worthy of her. Then one day LILLIE got word to meet Bill [and] get married at Seattle or Portland. LILLIE decided to go.

"Mother was worried. Father took LILLIE to Picabo, where she was to catch the train that came from Hailey to Shoshone. Father had his work to do, and so he left LILLIE there by the crossing. It was hot in the sunshine and there was no shade nor shelter there. At the ranch that day, I knew that Mother was praying frequently. There was a cloud over our hearts as we sensed the terrible slaughter of our boys on foreign soils and that many marriages were made hastily because of the war. . . . She had lived at the Frost home while [she] taught school at Grouse Creek. . . . He gave her a beautiful diamond, and they sat there in the parlor . . . and made their plans.

"All day we listened for the train, but we did not hear the usual whistle that was the signal for the crossing. Perhaps we had missed hearing it. We watched the sunset and had supper. My younger brothers, JIM and LEON, were at supper (LEON was 16 and JIM was 12). They were my father's main help on the farm. Twilight was closing into night. We could hear the crickets chirping. Then we heard the sound of a motor, a step, and then the motor drove away. Mother went to the door to look, and there was LILLIE. We were all glad to have her back again. She was tired from the long wait at the track. At evening Forrest McGlochlin stopped by and offered to bring her home. He said he had never known the train to be so late before. We all went to bed early. . . . Somewhere about midnight, we heard the sharp whistle of the train as it went on its way. The next day we heard that something had gone wrong with the engine.

"After the war we learned that Bill's big weakness had been drinking. We felt grateful that the Lord had answered Mother's prayers."

The long wait and her own prayers convinced my mother LILLIE to send the diamond back to Bill. PEARL and SEDLEY were soon engaged.

My mother, LILLIE, wrote:

"A dance was an event that we country people never missed. As my sister was going and I had no date, I decided to stay home—but she and Sedley insisted. I went and was watching the first part of the dance from the balcony when some returning soldiers came in and I was very impressed with one of them. He greeted his friends and was shaking hands with most of the people. A feeling came over me. Why couldn't I attract that kind of a man. I knew that if I ever had an opportunity and nothing came to change my mind, he—or one as good as he—would be the kind of man with whom I would like to spend my life.

"Well, I met him. Later in the evening, my sister's fiancée brought him over and introduced him to me. Several days later, while with SEDLEY and PEARL in the drug store, he came over and invited us for a ride in his car. His young brother, GIBSON, was with him. To my surprise and delight he asked me to go with him to a dance the following Friday night."

At the dance, MARION asked her if she would like to accompany him in his automobile to Salt Lake City for a General M.I.A. Conference. She was glad to accept. They would stop in Logan at his parents' home. Mother already knew his father, GIBSON A CONDIE. They had spoken at the post office several times, and she had enjoyed his conversations. The family owned the Condie Hot Springs Ranch, northeast of Carey. Offering rides to others in this limited automobile society of 1919 was not unusual, and she appreciated his offer. She wanted to attend the conference, and we already know she liked the driver.

They arrived at Logan as planned. After a wonderful meal, the family gathered around the piano and sang songs. Joining in these activities was the beautiful brown-eyed "girl next-door" whose name was Enid. It was obvious Enid had every intention of claiming MARION for herself, and MARION was kind and gracious to her. As the family started to retire, MARION took Enid out on their front porch. The talk seemed endless, until

PRIVATE FIRST CLASS MARION A. CONDIE WAS STATIONED NEAR NEW YORK CITY WAITING FOR THE SHIP TO TAKE HIM TO FRANCE WHEN THE ARMISTICE WAS SIGNED 11 NOV 1918.

Grandpa TUCKER, who was staying with the CONDIEs doing temple work, brought an alarm clock and set it off in the front window, which ended Enid's stay. My great-grandfather JAMES TUCKER told his daughter EMILY,

"I've seen in a vision MARION's wife, and she has blue eyes, not brown!"

After, my mother explained, MARION and she sat on the couch and they "reached an understanding." While talking, she happened to look up and saw Enid looking through the glass on the front door. As their eyes met, Enid ducked and disappeared. PEARL and SEDLEY had set their wedding date for 25 Jun 1919 in the Salt Lake Temple. Since her parents were planning to attend the wedding, they felt that it would be helpful if it was a double wedding. It was a very long day at the temple. With so many veterans returning and anxious to begin their own family life, over 100 couples were in their temple session.

MARION had purchased a beautiful solitary diamond ring with a plain wedding band when he was stationed in New York City. After he had returned home, his sisters were pressing his pants and discovered the two rings. Not knowing that he could hear them, his sister HELEN stated that as disagreeable as the idea was to the family, Enid would probably get the rings. However, the rings were not purchased with Enid in mind. He had felt that at the age of 26 years he should find the right wife, and New York City was the best place to buy a diamond.

His friend SEDLEY STANFORD had suggested in Logan, before he came to Carey, that there were two IVIE sisters, who were the very best—but he, SEDLEY, got his first pick. Uncle SEDLEY would often tell us this in later years. Daddy would just smile and indulge him; but privately mother was told that he got his pick, too.

Young GIBSON A. CONDIE with his mother EMILY TUCKER CONDIE on his eighth birthday in Logan, Utah.

Their honeymoon was in the Salt Lake City area. Mother mentioned that Daddy took her to Saltaire, on the shore of the Great Salt Lake, and to the old Salt Lake Theater to see a stage production of *Maytime*. When Jeannette McDonald and Nelson Eddie later performed it in the early 30's "talkies," it became her favorite movie. But she always added that it never began to compare to the stage production.

The couple made their home on the Hot Spring Ranch in Carey, Idaho. Mother became a full-time homemaker with plenty of work; but she had a husband she loved deeply and was very proud of. Through the years, she has claimed his qualities to be only perfection.

Mother did not become pregnant and in 1921, MARION was called to the California Mission under President James McMurrin. Serving in the Arizona District, he was called as the District President over the whole state. Grandfather CONDIE managed the ranch. Mother taught school at Glenwood, Utah, to finance his mission. During the summers, she stayed with the CONDIEs in

MARION AND LILLIE CONDIE MARRIED 25 JUN 1919
IN SALT LAKE CITY TEMPLE

Logan, attending summer-school at the Agricultural College. Enid was in her Home Economics class and suggested that when MARION returned, they should give him a dinner together; of course, it never materialized.

After her husband MARION returned from his mission, mother was able to correct her uterine problem, and their first child was born 18 Dec 1925. Their eldest son, MARION ASHER CONDIE was followed quite regularly by six more siblings. Uncle SEDLEY and aunt PEARL went east to Cornell University in Ithica, New York. He got his Doctorate Degree and taught Zoology at the Agricultural College in Logan. They bought a home just across the street from College Hill. Their first son STEPHEN was born in New York State. They would have nine children.

DIANE, MARIE, ELAINE, KATHERINE, PEARL, SEDLEY, STEPHEN, MELVIN, and GLEN STANFORD —Missing, their son and one of our favorite cousins, TED, an air force navigator whose plane went down over the Pacific Ocean during World War II. Their daughter VESTA died as a child.

LEON and RUTH ASHBY IVIE
with children, EVAN, JOY, RAY
and CAROL

— 46 —

POLITICS AND EARLY EVENTS IN
NEVADA, IDAHO, AND UTAH

Nevada was the first of these three states to gain statehood. ABRAHAM LINCOLN declared it a state during the Civil War in 1864 because he needed another free state to pass the 13th and 14th Amendments to the Constitution and also to help finance the Union and preserve the nation. Virginia City and Pioche were the rich mineral producers at the time, which helped Congress to designate the eastern and western boundaries of Nevada. The state was very sparsely populated; but the mineral wealth was enormous and greatly needed by the North. Lincoln County on the eastern side included some small towns that were settled by the Mormon pioneers, including the small communities of Panaca, Logandale, Hiko, and Las Vegas. These pioneers believed their areas were part of the Utah Territory. Lincoln County, Nevada, extended north from the southern tip of Nevada—now Clark County—to about 50 miles north of Pioche, where it bordered White Pine County and the mining area that surrounded the present city of Ely. The Colorado River defines Nevada's southern tip, whose importance was not realized until the Hoover Dam was constructed as one of President Hoover's land reclamation projects in the early thirties.

President Herbert Clark Hoover's value as a president is usually minimized by the majority of the people of our nation. He was born on the 10 Aug 1874 in West Branch, Iowa. When he was six years old, his father died. At the age of 9, his mother died. Alone, he prepared himself for Leland Stanford University, and at age 21, he graduated from the University as an engineer. At age 23, he managed large mining projects in Australia. Two years later, he was the chief engineer of the Department of Mines for the government of China and was married that same year, fighting in the Boxer uprising in China. Between the ages of 27 to 39 years, he worked as a mining expert in geological expeditions in Australia, Russia, Italy, Central America, and other lands, and became a millionaire by the time he was 30. He was 40 years old, when the First World War broke out, and personally assumed the task of helping 150,000 stranded Americans get home, heading the Commission for Relief for all victims of war-stricken Europe—successfully carrying on the most gigantic philanthropic enterprise ever attempted. President Wilson appointed him Food Administrator for the United States when he was 43 years old. At the close of the World War, he became head of the Supreme Economic Council for the relief of war victims. At age 46, he was the Secretary of Commerce, and at age 55, this quiet, skilled technician became the thirty-first president of the United States, taking office shortly before I [BROOKIE CONDIE (Swallow)] was born in March 1929—at the peak of the roaring 20s, with its run away world inflation that had destroyed the German mark and set the stage for Adolph Hitler's dictatorship. It was an unfortunate time. "Black Thursday" came on the 24th of October that same year, when the bottom dropped out of the stock market. That afternoon a group of New York bankers succeeded in temporarily halting the plunge, but five days later Wall Street was in a panic again and continued to skid downward for three-and-one-half years. Although only a small part of the population of the United States was directly affected by the market, it seeped into the very fiber of the country's economy and, with the added drought that attacked the farmers and created the Dust Bowls of the Midwest, banks floundered, and the nation found itself in what became known as the "Great Depression" by 1932.

A recent article in *Money and Markets* put it this way:

"in 1929, the dumb money lost their shirts; in 1930, the smart money lost their shirts, and in 1931, the very smart money lost their shirts."

In 1932, election year, the bear market had ended and a bull market was beginning. In *The Challenge to Liberty,* author Herbert Hoover (1933) states:

"Five years ago there came the earthquake of world-wide depression from world-wide causes. Business men and farmers suffered bitter distress. Three to four million families lost the earnings of their breadwinners, poverty stalked in the land as we had not known it since the like aftermath of the Civil War.

"In view of the character of the storm, the nation may thank God that twenty-one millions of families still had their living. It is one of the greatest testimonies to the staunchness of the structure of American Liberty that immediately upon this disaster the country was organized and giving unfailing food and shelter to those in distress, supplied through the idealism of the nation which accepted its responsibilities and through the sacrifice of those who were kept at work. Manfully the nation was adjusting to the strains of the depression and was accomplishing it without strikes and without social clash.

"And it might be observed through it all that the structure which was builded over these years was not so much in 'ruins' that it did not produce more goods than bureaucracy could tolerate, that some 30,000,000 children continued to attend school in the 'ruins'; that millions of people continued to find spiritual inspiration in churches still standing in the 'ruins'; that other millions daily attended games, theatres, and recreations in the 'ruins'; and that 23,000,000 automobiles were running about in our 'ruins' at ever increasing speeds."

Herbert Hoover, before his death in 1933, at his home in Palo Alto, California, was concerned about the creeping destruction of American Liberty:

"For many years in the practice of my profession in public service I journeyed to other countries. My occupation was not as a tourist but as one engaged intimately with those peoples, associated in their daily lives and problems, in contact with their social systems, their governments, their thoughts, their hopes and their progress. In England, in Germany, in France, in Italy, in Russia, in China, in India, in Latin America, and in Australia alike, the great mass of people viewed the progress and the liberty of America as an ideal. And to me every homecoming was an inspiration. I found again a greater kindliness, a greater neighborliness, a greater sense of individual responsibility, a lesser poverty, a greater comfort and security of our people, a wider spread of education, a wider diffusion of the finer arts and appreciation of them, a greater freedom of spirit, a wider opportunity for our children, and higher hopes of the future, than in any other country in the world. . . . In proportion to our numbers we have developed ten times as many laboratories of scientific research and invention. Our application of scientific discovery has grown at a pace far beyond that of any other nation. . . . We have come into a fuller life for all of the people, have given increasing scope to creative power and expansion of every man's mind.

"More than any other leading country, we have advanced the realities of human justice—not alone in education but in a vast series of protection to children, to public health, to conditions of labor, and regulations of business activities—making firm an open door of opportunity."

Hoover warned the nation in his book of the rising revolutionary spirit and regimentation that was coming about in the world in the form of Communism, Fascism, and Nazism. He feared for our own National Regimentation, explaining changes that had occurred since he had left office only months before:

"The first step of economic Regimentation is a vast centralization of power in the Executive . . . omitting relief and regulatory acts, the powers which have been assumed include, directly or indirectly, the following: To debase the coin and set its value; to inflate the currency; to buy and sell gold and silver; to buy Government bonds, other securities, and foreign exchange; to seize private stocks of gold at a price fixed by the Government; in effect giving to the Executive the power to 'manage' the currency; to levy sales taxes on food, clothing and upon goods competitive to them (the processing tax) at such times and in such amounts as the Executive may determine; to expend enormous sums from the appropriations for public works, relief, and agriculture upon projects not announced to the Congress at the time appropriations were made; to create corporations for a wide variety of business activities, heretofore the exclusive field of private enterprise; to install services and to manufacture commodities in competition with citizens; to buy and sell commodities at minimum prices for industries or dealers; to fix handling charges and therefore profits; to eliminate 'unfair' trade practices; to allot the amount of production to individual farms and factories and the character of goods they shall produce; to destroy commodities; to fix stocks of commodities to be on hand; to stop expansion or development of industries or of specific plants and equipment; to establish minimum wages; to fix maximum hours and conditions of labor; to impose collective bargaining; to organize administrative agencies outside the Civil Service requirements; to abrogate the effect of the anti-trust act; to raise and lower the tariffs and to discriminate between nations in their application; to abrogate certain governmental contracts without compensation or review by the courts; to enforce most of the powers where they affect the individual by fine and imprisonment through prosecution in the courts, with a further reserved authority in many trades through license to deprive men of their business and livelihood without any appeal to the courts."

He further explained that most of these powers could be delegated by the Executive to any appointee and the appointees are mostly without the usual confirmation by the Senate. Hoover's book was published prior to the midterm elections of 1934, during Franklin Delano Roosevelt's first term, which was after the death of its author, former President Herbert Hoover, in 1933. Roosevelt's attacks against individual liberty and enterprise in favor of bureaucracy, powerful labor bosses, and his own greatly extended executive powers, of which this was only the beginning, increasingly stopped individual initiative in favor of executive power—delaying the economic recovery of our nation. The second bear market began later in 1933 and lasted until 1938, 62 months, losing 60 percent of its value. The bulls emerged then until 28 May 1942 after we entered World War II. This third bear market lasted until 13 Jun 1945, 37 months with a loss of 29.6 percent of its value—after VE Day (victory in Europe), and Roosevelt's death.

Hoover's main theme in his 205-page book, *The Challenge to Liberty,* centered on this theme:

> "Thus our American Republic was the first of the modern nations to place into the structure of government the whole social philosophy of Liberty, with its care for the worth and integrity of the individual, with its security of unalienable human rights. Thereby came the emancipation of the lives and minds of American men and women into the mastery of their own destinies, for they were the masters of the state, not the state the master of men. Thereby they gave the light of freedom to the whole New World and a workable system of government for its protection. Our fathers died willingly that we might come into this, the most stupendous inheritance men could bequeath to a race."

In 1890 Idaho became a state, but did not allow their Mormon population in southeastern Idaho to vote, for the Mormon vote was strongly Democrat, and they feared their rapidly increasing population. Anti-Mormon sentiment and literature was rampant in the northern and western parts of the state. This subsided somewhat after Church President Wilford Woodruff issued the "Manifesto," which eliminated the practice of polygamy (also in 1890).

My mother had strong Democratic roots, and Grandfather GIBSON A CONDIE was always registered as a Democrat. My parents changed their registrations to Republican in 1932. Mother would tell us how delighted she was at first when FDR announced his candidacy. Then she began to study the issues and listen to the campaign speeches and changed her party, voting for Herbert Hoover that year. Utah remained Democrat. Dwight Eisenhower was the first winning president she ever voted for. I asked Grandfather CONDIE why he was a Democrat. He smiled and replied,

"I am a Jeffersonian Democrat; but I always vote for the man and not the party."

My uncle GIBSON CONDIE was freshly out of Salt Lake City's law school in the early 30s. In 1932, age 22, he was elected Probate Judge for Blaine County, Idaho, against a long established opponent. He became the leader of the Young Republicans in Idaho. When Idaho Representative Dworshak went to Congress in Washington D.C., he accompanied him as his secretary, being groomed to replace him when Dworshak ran for the Senate in a few years. Senator William Edgar Borah had been the stanch Republican Senator from Idaho since 1907 and in 1936 he filed as a candidate for the Republican nomination for president, then withdrew his name in favor of Governor Alfred M. Landon of Kansas. Senator Borah had studied and practiced law in Kansas before coming to Boise around 1892. He was noted for his *strong opposition* to imperialism, American adherence to the League of Nations, the World Court, and other related issues. He was getting older and died 19 Jan 1940. Idaho mourned the loss of this respected and beloved Senator.

My personal interest in politics began one Saturday afternoon in the fall of 1936, when I was in the second grade. Uncle GIBSON had come to visit my father—his oldest brother—at our ranch near Carey, Idaho. He had with him a lot of posters, campaign buttons, and other campaign materials with Landon's picture and name on them. As they talked in our living room, I slipped quietly in and listened. My handsome 6' 4" uncle GIBSON had married the popular 5' 1" [aunt] MARGARET CAMERON. She had stayed in Carey that day, visiting her aunt and uncle. The two brothers talked for hours, and I remained—listening. It was a new world to me and very fascinating.

When Election Day arrived in November, the voting took place in our school gymnasium. Our school house had two floors. The gymnasium was attached on the north with a rather large stage, and extended north on the second floor, where it was reached by the public on many outside steps. Operettas, plays, dances, community programs and rallies—as well as sports events—were held in the gym.

During our lunch hour, after emptying our lunch boxes, the unsupervised children separated into various groups of their own choice, engaging in activities and games that were only limited by their imaginations. The high school boys usually could be found in the center of the one-mile circular track playing baseball. [Most of the central part of the track was filled with sagebrush.] Softball was popular with the girls; but in the second grade we liked jump ropes, swings, tetter-totters, giant strides, and various group games.

On that Election Day, while I was engaged in a rather limited game of tag, I ran past the gym. Gazing upward, through one of the many barred windows, I could see my father voting in one of the temporary booths. He was studying his ballot and didn't see me. However, this inspired me into believing that I needed to do a little campaigning for the Republicans. With my cousin HELEN and our friend Luene we proceeded to try to make Republicans of all the second and first grade girls. They looked at us strangely and refused to join our campaign—continuing with their own various activities. The real blow to my supposedly intelligent undertaking came the next day, when my friend Luene told HELEN and me that she had spoken with her father that night, and he had told her emphatically that she was a Democrat. HELEN and I were horrified by this revelation—it didn't help, either, that Landon had lost his election for president by a landslide.

The three-letter abbreviations for the ever-extending powerful bureaucracy would continue for another four years. A few of them, I can still remember. There was the PWA; the NRA; the WPA; the AAA with Henry A. Wallace; the CCC; the IRS; the SSA; the CIO; the AFL of earlier origin, with John L. Lewis—all very powerful in collecting votes, stifling individualism, creating strikes, and enlarging the federal government with the "New Deal." When the courts objected to some of his policies, Roosevelt unsuccessfully attempted to increase the size of the Supreme Court, so he could control it.

And while private enterprise was being suppressed by bureaucracy in

America, our family placed a large world map on the wall next to where I sat at the dinner table. It contained pictures of all the major world leaders, including that of "Adolph Hitler, Dictator of Germany." I thought he was the best looking of all the leaders—including another three letter abbreviation, FDR; but Hitler had an ominous look about him that created a silent fear within me. This fear increased when his speeches were broadcast on the radio—and interpreted into English. It was an angry, controlling voice. The Russian Stalin and Communism also worried me. Japan and China were engaged in a devastating war; Spain had their civil war with General Franco leading the array. We saw the *March of Times* documentaries of the devastations before every movie (called talkies).

Great Britain was in pink on our map with the slogan "The Sun never sets on the British Empire." It included India, Palestine, Gibraltar, Canada, Australia, New Zealand, and Kenya, to mention only a few of their larger colonies. Although Great Britain and Northern Ireland contained a combined land area of only 94,490 square miles with a population of 46,011,000, they controlled a land area world wide of 12,943,358 square miles with a total of 501,201,000 people. In addition, the Empire ranked first in sea power. Pink was definitely the predominant color on that map. If we compared the home Islands of Great Britain to the State of Nevada, Nevada had an area of 110,540 square miles, just slightly more land area, with a population of only 110,247 people in 1940—almost one person for every square mile.

When Hitler and his German Army marched into Czechoslovakia in September of 1939, it was another of those European wars in the minds of most of the American people. The powerful Brits did nothing. It was stated later that if Lord Chamberlain, their prime minister, had challenged Hitler at that time, the Germans had orders to turn back; but he smiled and tried to negotiate his own peace, while the black tentacles of the swastika spread throughout Europe.

[Note: The early traditional meaning of his clockwise swastika was bad luck (Hitler used it to mean evil); the reverse swastika anti-clockwise meant good fortune.]

With World War I only twenty years behind us, the majority of Americans remembered that terrible slaughter, when Woodrow Wilson had joined our nation in that foreign war. About ten veterans of our own Civil War were still living in the 1930s. Helping the English Empire maintain their superiority was not the priority of our struggling nation. *"While the Storm Clouds gather far across the sea,"* we were *"grateful for our land that's free,"* as Irving Berlin wrote in his song, *God Bless America.* We watched films of the goose-stepping German Army and their militant dictator.

Seeking his hotly debated third term as president of the United States in 1940, Roosevelt promised the Americans he would keep them out of war. It was a promise he really never intended to keep. When the Germans marched across Europe, and the English became involved, he soon directed Irving Berlin to write a new song, *"Arms for the Love of America, and for the love of every mother's son, who's depending on the work that must be done—by the man, behind the man, behind the gun."*

Roosevelt shut down the automobile and other industries and started building weapons, tanks, airplanes, etc. We were supposed to be neutral; but our ammunition and weapons were being shipped to England, China, and Russia. The new words to remember then were "Lend Lease," but we knew it was only his prelude that would pull our people into the actual fighting, again. And, of course, the Germans, Italians, and Japanese Axis knew it, too.

But back to the earlier days of the Great Depression, which began before my recollections, historian David M. Kennedy in his book *FREEDOM FROM FEAR* (1999), covering 1929-1945, claims it began slowly after World War I with the heavy movement of European immigrants and war refugees into the United States, who mostly congregated in the cities, overpopulating the factory work forces and keeping wages low. The war had created a needed excess food production, and with tractors increasingly replacing horses after the war, large farm surpluses were still being produced. Congress closed our borders from further immigration, and increased the tariffs to keep prices higher for our own people. Foreign governments retaliated by not purchasing our excess food supply, which our government bought, but couldn't sell. Without dollars for distribution, much of the surplus was destroyed.

The German mark inflated beyond control to meet the demands of the heavy debt that was placed upon that nation by the peace treaty. England went off the gold standard in order to save the English pound—the British and French owed America for our help in the war. The U.S. tried to stabilize our dollars and kept the gold standard intact. Brokers were allowed to sell stocks on high margin with broker calls, which led to the false valuations of our American corporations.

There were low wages, unemployed immigrants, and the struggling farmers, who were heavily in debt buying tractors, automobiles, refrigerators, radios, phonographs, and so forth. There was mass marketing, advertising, and extensive consumer financing. The numbers of unemployed steadily increased. The U.S. federal government was small. They increased their taxes to balance their budget and subsidize farm market expenditures. Bank regulations were minimal, and small underfunded banks flooded the nation—creating a spendthrift nation in debt, with the larger world economy on the skids. The world dictators built war machines and smothered individual liberty, but got cheers from the masses, who felt overwhelmed by events.

TOM AND VANDA DUNCAN SWALLOW WITH OPAL. ABOUT 1919.

Hoover tried to keep the economy in balance and our liberty intact. In 1932 he started many new relief programs; the market turned bullish, but did not change the fall election. His strength was in written words and figures; Roosevelt, less knowledgeable, was the politician who had been preparing from his youth to charm the people, avoid hard facts, and gloss over commitments by listening and agreeing with everyone—sort of. No one really knew where he was going. The people sang "Happy Days are here again" and waited for a chicken in every pot.

An example of the banking problem happened to my

husband GROVER SWALLOW's parents. They had a beautiful farm in central Utah with plenty of flowing water and beautiful soil. Their mortgage was nearly paid when the crisis arrived; they needed only $2,000 to pay it off. All loans were called in when their bank was forced into liquidation. Unable to raise this total in immediate cash, the bank foreclosed—taking their valuable farm to clear the debts of the bank, but left his neighbor unscathed, who owed much on his mortgage. There was no advantage in taking that farm, as the debt was higher than it would sell for.

YOUNG GROVER SWALLOW ABOUT 1934

In Salt Lake City, my father's parents had nearly paid for a boarding house they had purchased after selling their Logan home. Their bank called in their $3000 loan. Borrowing from another bank to pay off the mortgage was impossible. Losing their income and property, they returned to Carey and lived near us on the ranch.

On 14 May 1940, I received a small reward for prefect attendance during the 1939-40 school year, *Know Your Presidents* by Grayhul Features, Wichita, Kansas, 1934. It had a one-page picture and history of all the presidents of the United States. Franklin Delano Roosevelt's page gave his birth in 1882, wealth, his infantile paralysis, but the bold printing read:

"The Son of a Great Banker, and Only President to Close All Banks of the United States."

Centered in the city of Twin Falls, Idaho, a group established an organization called "Production Credit." The story goes that the young banker Carl Haynie had lost his job. Without work, he approached one of their more successful ranchers in the Twin Falls area asking for work. At first, he was told there wasn't any job available. The young man persisted, saying, "I don't want a banker's job. I want work. I'll do anything you need done, including digging ditches. But I need a job and will work hard." On that basis he was hired. When Production Credit was organized, young Carl Haynie became their secretary, a full-time job. His employer became the president—not a full-time job. My father, MARION CONDIE, also a successful rancher, became their field man. He was trusted with the responsibility of determining which farmers were worthy of credit and for what amount. He was also to advise these ranchers and farmers in ways to increase their production of needed commodities, to help insure the safety of the loans. Daddy was loved by these farmers and ranchers throughout the area and he loved them. It was an organization that brought real help to many people during a very troubled time.

According to David M. Kennedy,

"Fully 70% of American industry was powered by electricity in 1929, much of it from generating plants fueled by oil from newly developed fields in Texas, Oklahoma, and California. By 1925, a completed Model T Ford rolled off the continuously moving assembly line at Henry Ford's Highland Park plant every ten seconds. Just a dozen years earlier it had taken fourteen hours to put together a single car. . . . Yet even this fabulously successful strategy had limits. Mass production made mass consumption a necessity. . . . But . . . the increasing wealth of the 1920s flowed disproportionately to the owners of capital."

The industrial workers' wages fared better than the agricultural income. By 1928 average per capita income among nonagricultural employees had reached four times the average level of farmers' incomes. There was a great migration from the rural areas into the cities.

"By 1920, for the first time in American history, a majority of Americans were city dwellers. . . . Forty-four percent of the population were still counted as rural in 1930 . . . More than forty-five million of them had no indoor plumbing in 1930, and almost none had electricity."

Included in this number of 45 million without electricity or indoor plumbing was our ranch home near Carey.

We had a hot spring on our ranch with water flowing close to the boiling point. Our sterile drinking water was carried into the house in buckets from the spring and left to cool until it reached a drinkable temperature. The center crater of the vast lava beds that bordered our ranch on the south was about 30 miles northeast, and I suppose this water was an escape from the volcanic proximity beneath. Large steam bubbles would rise through the orange red striated moss that covered the bottom and continued upward with rising spirals to the surface where it spread into crusty masses, which broke into smaller islands that flowed rapidly into the continuous stream. The steaming water spread, and then narrowed–cooling slightly as it tumbled over the crusty mineral formations behind our two swimming pools on the west—then continued its flow to the bordering Carey Lake on the west. Many old plumbing pipes reminded us of previous attempts to plumb the home; but the moss had collected too rapidly and had always clogged the pipes.

There were no trees near the home. Less than two feet beneath the land surface lay a "hard pan," which, if penetrated three to four feet, water would appear. The remains of the old carbide tank and a few of the gas lights it supplied were still around; but these had also been

THE HOT SPRING

abandoned. Electricity would not reach our (two-and-one-half miles from Carey) ranch until 1940. Indoor plumbing never arrived. Today the home is unoccupied. The new owners built a home further south from the spring, where cold water, without moss, could be acquired, and trees would grow. They built a large building over the spring and bottled and sold the never ending mineral water.

Shortly before Pearl Harbor, Roosevelt had chemical toilets publically constructed on most of the farms throughout America, in an effort to control flies and help the rural areas. They were white with green trim. They had a cement base and a lid covered the hole, while chemicals destroyed the refuse. The lid was raised with a rope when the door opened. We called them "Roosevelt Monuments." Ours was constructed with little cost to us around 1940. Many self-sufficient farmers were not particularly impressed. Black widow spiders found their way inside, and the farmlands, with their animals, still breed innumerable

MARION A. CONDIE ON HIS HORSE. HE ALWAYS SAT TALL IN HIS SADDLE. HE GOT HIS DEERSKIN GLOVES FROM THE INDIAN RESERVATION AT FORT HALL NEAR BLACKFOOT, IDAHO. HE WOULD ALWAYS BUY SEVERAL PAIR WHEN HE WAS THERE.

flies; but the toilets dotted the landscape.

One morning in the fall of 1936, I dressed, came downstairs and saw my father's grey-patterned shirt hanging on the back of one of our kitchen chairs that surrounded our dinner table. It was spattered quite heavily with blood on the collar and upper shoulder area. He had a large bandage on a part of his forehead that extended backward over part of his hair. He was dressed and appeared fine in other ways. My mother was still in bed, and a strange doctor was dressing a wound she had near one of her eyes. We were quickly told that she would be all right.

We were told there had been an auto accident during the previous evening as they were returning from a Twin Falls shopping trip. Grandmother CONDIE had gone with them and was in the back seat. She escaped physically uninjured, because a five gallon can of honey they had purchased had stopped the front seat from crushing her in any way; however, emotionally she became disoriented. After climbing out of the wrecked blue 1935 Ford sedan, which lay on its side, they had her wait inside the sheriff's car. She immediately locked all the doors and then refused to unlock them until my father was able to persuade her to do so. Mother, who was very early pregnant with my youngest sister ADELIA, had a problem, also. She didn't want to step on the steering wheel of the demolished automobile to get out of it—feeling she might scratch or break it.

My grandparents were living in their home in Carey by this time. Grandfather

CONDIE hadn't gone with them to Twin Falls. He became carsick easily. That fateful day, he was working in his garden when a feeling of dire desolation came over him with a strength that he could not ignore; it was around 4:00 o'clock in the afternoon. The patriarch retired to his bedroom and prayed desperately for several hours, evidently pleading with the Lord.

At 6:00 o'clock P.M. the stores in Twin Falls closed their doors and the shoppers started for home. At Shoshone, after crossing the railroad tracks, they stopped for gas. At this intersection there are two ways to go to Carey. The shortest and usual way was a 40-mile washboard dusty gravel road. The alternate longer route was oiled and continued on to Bellevue, Hailey, Ketchum/Sun Valley, and then north over the Galena Summit of the Sawtooth Mountain Range. At Bellevue, an equally graveled dusty washboard road turned east 23 miles to Carey.

Light-heartedly my parents discussed their options and decided to indulge and take the longer route, totally unaware of the consequences that would follow that decision. In Hailey, a drunken Chevrolet salesman left one of the bars, staggered into his demo and turned south, weaving back and forth across the narrow highway at a great speed. The sheriff tried to stop him; but the salesman's speed exceeded his speed capability—we were told it was over 80 mph on an oiled, narrow road with a 50 mph speed limit. As the chase continued through Bellevue a newspaper man quickly jumped into his car and followed them—he knew there would be a story of some sort.

These two witnesses told their story. The two cars met head-on with the salesman completely on the wrong-side of the road. Strangely, or miraculously, the two cars shot up into the air, instead of smashing bluntly into each other, and rolled rather harmlessly into the gutters on each side of the road. The drunken salesman walked away uninjured, although his car was also mutilated. Daddy later told mother that, as their car was flying through the air, he felt a spiritual battle going on within him for his life. We were told that grandfather CONDIE's prayer had prolonged his mortal time on earth—at least, for a few short years.

Against their wishes, believing the distance was closer, the sheriff drove them to Shoshone instead of Hailey and their personal doctor, Dr. Fox. Grandmother CONDIE arrived home just before daybreak and told grandfather he was lucky to have a wife. His response was quick and definite, "Come to bed and get your sleep, I already know all about it."

The Chevrolet dealer in Hailey gave my parents a new tan 1936 Chevrolet—feeling responsible for his drunken salesman, who was driving one of his cars, which was insured. Mother liked the mirror he added to the visor on her side. I liked the new car, but felt a little compromised when the usual debate among my schoolmates would begin, regarding the best automobile. I had always defended the superior performance of the Ford, now we were driving a Chevy.

The November 1938 mid-presidential term election in local Blaine County was memorable. My uncle GIBSON had discarded his dream for Washington D.C. The young politician had been diagnosed as having a serious case of diabetes, and the Washington D.C. location, (perhaps its elevation, climate, or stress,) was causing a fast deterioration in his health. He had returned to Hailey ashen pale to become their Blaine County Probate Judge—a year or so before this election. Shortly after becoming the Probate Judge, Blaine County needed him as District Attorney, and grandfather CONDIE was appointed to finish the

UNCLE GIBSON ADELI CONDIE

term of Probate Judge. In the fall of 1938, both were up for reelection. Another relation was added to the election when uncle JIM BAIRD threw in his hat for County Commissioner. Cousin HELEN had told me about it privately as our friend Luene's father was his opponent on the Democrat ticket.

Uncle GIBSON won by a landslide. Uncle JIM became County Commissioner, but grandfather CONDIE lost his position as Probate Judge. It was said that the "pool hall crowd" wanted a more liberal, easygoing judge that could better appreciate their point of view. That was not grandfather! "Liquor by the Drink" seemed to always be on the ballot in Idaho. Sometimes it passed; sometimes it failed, but it was always there. Grandfather, then retired, returned to Carey. Of course, FDR won his third term election with all the ballyhoo, fireside chats, and strong-arm union support.

Earlier in October of that year, Daddy and Mother took my sister IVIE and me to Salt Lake City to attend LDS General Conference. Our father was a first counselor in the Blaine stake presidency and always attended these meetings, usually taking his patriarch father with him, who would sit in the front seat of the car and bring a bag of dried bread to control his car sickness. Mother ordinarily stayed home with the seven children, where we listened to the three days of two-hour morning and afternoon sessions on KSL radio, even at times with bad static. That fall the four of us stayed at the Hotel Utah. It was an exciting time: the wide six-lane oiled streets; the elevators and lobby in the hotel; the oval-dome-topped grey tabernacle with its great organ, choir, prophet, and all the church authorities; the restaurants; the movie theaters; the trip to the Salt Lake City airport to watch the passenger planes take off and land; Brigham Young's statue; the church museum with real Indian mummies and John Taylor's watch that had saved his life at Carthage jail; Eagle Gate, the State of Utah Capitol building—a long awaited dream.

When conference ended, my father went to the Veteran's Hospital that was located in the city. He was a private first class in World War I and had remained active in the veterans' organization. He believed he had a goiter that had been slowly enlarging for several years. They agreed to remove it in early December. The family (mother and seven children) went with him to say good bye when he caught the train to Salt Lake City in Shoshone. My memory of that trip was the restaurant dinner. Daddy ordered large fried oysters—perhaps three inches in length. This was new to me, so I ordered them, too. I liked them. It was February 1939 before we saw our father again.

Shortly after he left, mother joined him in Salt Lake City. All was not right. The enlargement of the thyroid gland was not a goiter. Brand new names like Hodgkin's disease and cancer were added to my vocabulary. Adults whispered and looked at us with sorrowful eyes. A few days before Christmas, Mother returned alone with many packages. It was good to see her again; but she looked stressed and weepy. Christmas presents to the children kept arriving from our aunts and uncles, and they were placed under the tree. Christmas morning came.

Santa had never been quite so generous; but the carefree happy feeling and joyous multifamily get-together was not there. My memories of that Christmas are accompanied by feelings of darkness.

Daddy was soon sent to the huge Veteran's Hospital—Sawtelle in Los Angeles. We wrote letters. He was pleased and answered all of them. They gave him X-ray treatments. When he returned home in early February, he was very weak. He sat in the chair with the footstool Mother had bought for him and attempted to rise and view the ranch he loved so much. I was very sad when he chose to lie down in his bedroom. I don't recall him ever leaving it, though he probably did at times. Many visitors came and went—usually wiping their eyes.

Shortly after, I woke up one morning with a rash. My brother JAMES had one, too—the red measles. We were sent back upstairs to bed with plenty of blankets, an application of Vick's Vaporub, and a soft strip of flannel around our necks. When our high fevers broke a few days later, five other siblings were sent upstairs with the measles. JAMES and I were allowed to go downstairs and attempt to help Mother, who had a cancer-patient husband downstairs and five new cases of red measles upstairs. The hired manager of the lambing crews on the ranch often came in seeking directions from Daddy in his bedroom.

Aunt ADA and uncle JIM BAIRD were quick to arrive and helped to ease the heavy load. When the measles disappeared, it was decided that JAMES and I would stay with aunt ADA in Carey, until school ended in May. The three youngest children, LILLIE, CeCELIA, and ADELIA, were cared for by our grandparents in Carey with the help of aunt HELEN SMITH, who had arrived from Kaysville., Utah. The two older children, MARION and IVIE, would stay on the ranch and help before and after school. Living with my cousin HELEN, who was one week younger, in Carey was much easier than being on the ranch. We slept in the same bed, did the dishes, gathered eggs, walked to school and everyone treated me wonderfully. LILLIE IDA was in the first grade, JAMES in the third grade, and I was in the fourth.

In mid-May, school ended and JAMES and I returned to the ranch. By then, there were large gunnysacks filled with carrots. Carrot juice, it was hoped, would cure the cancer that had spread throughout our father's body. Endless hours I helped others scraping the carrots, which were grated and put into the lard press to extract the juice. Our father drank about two quarts of carrot juice every day. We all believed it was helping him. IVIE would make him custard and junket to add to his diet. We had a gas refrigerator then; but no electricity. We still had coal oil and gas lamps and no indoor plumbing. The visitors were still coming, and shortly before he died Dr. Fox brought a hospital bed for Daddy and he was lifted onto it. I felt sure he was getting better.

He died on Friday, 13 Jun 1939. At his funeral I sat next to my aunt HELEN with my cousin HELEN next to me on the other side. Cousin HELEN was more emotional than I was, and in a way I resented this. I remember thinking, "He's my father, not yours;" but, of course, I said nothing. At the cemetery cousin HELEN informed me that there would be two dinners given for our many out-of-town guests by the Relief Society women of our church. All the CONDIEs were to go to her home in Carey, and the IVIE relatives would go to my home on the ranch. It was an obvious division, and I'm sure HELEN intended no harm

The CONDIEs left us at the cemetery and went to their dinner. We remained with the IVIEs at the cemetery until the last shovelful of dirt was placed on the rounded heap, piled higher and higher above the casket. Then the beautiful flowers were placed over the raw dirt. Uncle SEDLEY STANFORD had his camera and took our picture, while the wind blew a small gale. To the east of the cemetery is the Carey Lake, our ranch, and then those never-ending lava beds. It has been said by some that it was the saddest picture they had ever seen. Uncle LEON IVIE is holding ADELIA's tiny hand. She wouldn't stand still for the picture. Aunt PEARL STANFORD is next to them. It was a lonely group that returned to that dinner on the ranch, which had lost its excitement, fun, and security. The family grew up a great deal that day.

in telling me; but a feeling of isolation came over me. Did the death of my father mean that the CONDIEs no longer cared about us? Were we now only going to be important to our IVIE relations, none of which lived very close? It was a second sadness; but still no tears.

CONDIE CHILDREN, AUGUST, 1939, AFTER THE DEATH OF THEIR FATHER
STANDING, LEFT TO RIGHT – MARION ASHER, IVIE, BROOKIE, JAMES,
SEATED — LILLIE IDA, ADELIA, CECELIA

ON THE EAST SIDE ADDITION OF OUR TWO-STORY LOG RANCH HOME
THE IVIE FAMILY LINE UP FOR A PHOTOGRAPH.
THEY DID NOT BRING ANY OF OUR YOUNG COUSINS.
MY MOTHER LILLIE, HER UNCLE FRED MORTENSEN,
PARENTS ANNIE & OSCAR, PEARL, LLOYD, JIM, LEON
SPOUSES AUNTS NORA, BENOLA, RUTH, AND UNCLE SEDLEY WERE THERE ALSO.

Golden Wedding Anniversary at the Sun Valley Ski Resort Lodge, 3 Sep 1941
The children are seated. The spouses are standing behind. Left to Right.
HELEN CONDIE, b 30 Mar 1903, Freedom, Wyoming, md FARRELL SMITH
THOMAS LEE CONDIE, b 3 Jul 1898, Grover, Wyoming, md BLANCHE PHIPPEN
Standing behind: LILLIE A. IVIE, wife of deceased MARION ASHER CONDIE,
(not shown) b 9 Aug 1892, Morgan, Morgan, Utah,
EMILY ELIZABETH TUCKER and GIBSON A CONDIE
ADA B CONDIE, b 6 Apr 1894, Morgan, Morgan, Utah, md JAMES A. BAIRD
JAMES IRA CONDIE, b 21 Jan 1901, Grover, Wyoming, md MARY LLOYD
ABIGAIL T CONDIE, b 29 Aug 1905, Carey, Blaine, Idaho, md CYRIL CALL
GIBSON ADLAI CONDIE, b 19 May 1910, Carey, Idaho, md MARGARET CAMERON
Their daughter CECELIA CONDIE, b 15 Jul 1896, died as an infant, Grover, Wyoming.

My father is missing at the celebration., MARION A. CONDIE, who had died in 1939.

— 47 —

SEVEN FATHERLESS CHILDREN
FACE THE WORLD

Daddy had told Mother prior to his death, "Don't worry about the children. If they have to struggle, it will be good for them."

I was never particularly happy about the idea of struggling being good for me. When I was a sophomore at Idaho State College in Pocatello, I applied for the sophomore woman's $100 scholarship given yearly by the women's faculty and administrators. I knew my grades were the highest, because the Graveley Hall grade averages over 3 points were posted in our dormitory to allow us extra hours outside the dormitory in the evenings. As for need—who could need it more than a girl who was putting herself through college, with three other siblings attending various colleges, and a widowed mother with a very small income? I had a job in the dining hall, which paid my room and board, barely. I worked summers, so I could afford the textbooks. There was no tuition for Idaho residents. I needed five dollars to join the Women's Pharmacy Organization. I didn't have it, so I never joined. Mother paid for my violin lessons. I made or bought my own clothes. Recommendations from teachers, church, and community were superb.

Shortly before Women's Day, the secretary to the Dean of Pharmacy called me into her office. She informed me kindly that, although I deserved the scholarship, they were giving it to another girl, a B+ student, who would not be able to attend college without it. Their group all felt that regardless, BROOKIE CONDIE would make it through college. I smiled—no tears; but I mostly felt cheated. I could have used that money. Inwardly, I blamed my father a little and his remark that struggling was good for his children.

Back in 1939, again, shortly after my father died, our L.D.S. bishop, R. E. Adamson, called Mother as the Carey Ward Relief Society President. Some seemed to think it would be an extra heavy burden on her, but my view was different. She was very capable, and this gave her an excellent opportunity to become closer and develop strong friendships with the women of Carey, rather than being isolated into what might otherwise have been a man's world of farm management. Her first counselor, Margaret Eldridge, became her lifelong friend and confident.

In 1940, my grandfather JAMES OSCAR IVIE died. Then my uncle GIBSON died about a year after that. Death and funerals became very real. Uncle GIBSON's death was not expected. His diabetes was under control. He caught cold and went to see Dr. Fox. A new drug for infections had just been discovered. Dr. Fox thought it might help him, and gave him some. Within a few days, he was dead. It was not until I was in pharmacy school that I realized that the new drug was probably sulfanilamide, which was soon replaced by safer sulfa medications, because it crystallized in the kidneys. A diabetic would be very vulnerable.

When the Japanese bombed Pearl Harbor 7 Dec 1941, we were still living on the ranch, now with electric lights. U.S. Highway 93 with its oiled highway had been completed several years before. We enjoyed our new heated 1937 red school bus, which replaced our old unheated Fish Creek bus—a grey wooden box, with benches and gunnysacks on the windows and door. It had been strapped on the back of Mr. Judy's large cattle truck every fall. One time, before I attended school, the box became loose and fell off the truck into the gutter just before it arrived to pick up MARION at the end of our lane. No one was seriously hurt. We had to stamp our feet to keep warm in those cold winter months. There was great excitement when the first electric lights were turned on at the ranch, and we welcomed the electric irons and appliances, and the old wind up Victrola was replaced with a fancy radio, record-player combination.

In April 1942, Mr. Judy's large cattle truck was loaded to overflowing with furniture and other belongings and widow CONDIE and her family moved to Twin Falls, Idaho, into a new FHA-home development area on the President's Streets. The ranch had been leased. She had paid cash for this modest home. It

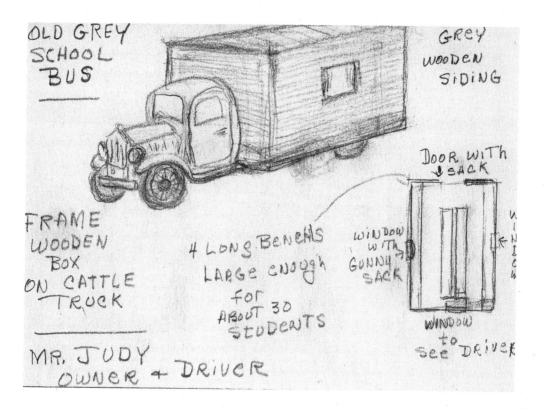

was a decision she had made with some very strong advice from grandfather CONDIE. The seven children and their future education were very important to both of them. All of us had been promoted early to the next grade in school before we left Carey, but Mother insisted that we march into the large Twin Falls High School/Junior High building and register for band and orchestra for the remainder of their school year.

I felt quite overwhelmed as our steps resounded in the vacant hall as we journeyed past the endless lockers on each side to go to the junior high side of the three-story building with the band and orchestra rooms in the dome. School was in session and some classroom doors were open, revealing part of the hundreds of students—totally unknown. I was placed in the Intermediate Band with my alto saxophone and the Intermediate Orchestra with my violin. JAMES was also there with his coronet and violin. IVIE and MARION got the Senior Band with their clarinets. Mother insisted on private lessons on these instruments, as well as piano lessons for most of the children. IVIE also played the accordion. LILLIE IDA would play the clarinet, CeCELIA the cello, and

ADELIA took voice lessons, and sang in the choir. At home (a two-bedroom house with a full basement, where we had added another bathroom, bedroom and recreation room) practice times were scheduled, and to the consternation of our next-door neighbors, some of them started at 6:00 A.M. That summer the Carnegie Public Library and its contents became one of our constant companions. My choices were usually the fiction area and included the unabridged translated works of Alexander Dumas, Sir Walter Scott, the Bronte sisters and similar classical authors. IVIE found work at Newberrys—a "five & dime" store. MARION worked in the fields with a tractor. Later in the summer, our L.D.S. bishop Fredrickson gave me a job as the popcorn girl in his ice cream store. I was 13-years-old. Pay was 25 cents per hour—better than the 10 cents paid for babysitting.

Twin Falls had two L.D.S. wards when we moved there. The Twin Falls stake included the surrounding smaller towns that had small wards and branches. Before I left for college, the two wards were each divided making four wards in the city. Twin Falls was distinguished in some national survey as having more different churches in proportion to its population than any city in America. Shoshone Street ran on the diagonal in front of the high school, and had an intersection nearby with four very large different denominational churches on each corner. We were told that the *Mormons* were only 10 percent of the population; but they still had more members than any other religion in the city. While we were there, the distant Idaho Falls Temple became the 8th temple in our Church—the first L.D.S. temple in Idaho. We attended its dedication, as part of this large temple district. In 2008, Twin Falls had fourteen stakes when the Twin Falls Temple was constructed, making 127 L.D.S. temples worldwide.

The Rim-to-Rim Bridge, that crossed the deep chasm where the Snake River found its way west through the deep black rocks, was located four miles from our home on Tyler Street. This bridge was notorious in those days for its suicides, perhaps it still is. My nephew and his friends would later, around 2000 A..D., enjoy sky-diving from it with their parachutes. Four miles further up the Snake River to the east was the dramatic Shoshone Falls. It was partially dammed to supply the power and irrigation water necessary to turn this formerly sagebrush desert into a city surrounded by lush farmland—adding to the production of the famous *Idaho potatoes* and other crops.

In October, with World War II taking all our young men 18 years or older, our high school and junior high closed their doors for two weeks, and many of the students would go to the fields to pick potatoes. We needed extra money, so the four older CONDIE children joined the pickers to help the war effort. It was a back-breaking job. JAMES and I would work together. MARION and IVIE always surpassed us in the quantity of sacks picked. We were paid 10-cents a sack, which was split between the two pickers.

THE SNAKE RIVER AT THE BOTTOM OF THE DEEP CHASM BELOW THE SHOSHONE FALLS, FLOWING WEST. THIS PICTURE WAS TAKEN IN JUNE 2011 WHEN THE WATER SUPPLY THROUGH THE WINTER WAS SUFFICIENT TO ALLOW A FULL STREAM OF WATER TO FLOW ON TO THE COLUMBIA RIVER.

Several miles above the Shoshone Falls on the Snake River were the Twin Falls, from which the city got its name. The water was seldom allowed to flow over both of them. The greater attraction was Shoshone Falls, which had picnic grounds and a more exciting view. My memory of the Twin Falls ends in sadness. JAMES with two of his friends from our ward decided to explore the surrounding steep rocks. On a very narrow trail, one of the boys slipped and fell to his death below. JAMES edged down to the bottom to try and help his friend;

the third boy returned back to get help. It was a grim experience for JAMES, and the loss of this handsome young boy affected all of us.

Adapting to Twin Falls High School and Junior High was not difficult scholastically for any of us. MARION turned 18 years old in December 1943, during his senior year. He had petitioned the draft board earlier and had taken difficult tests that allowed him to finish his high school and qualify for officers training—only two were accepted that year in Twin Falls high school. One of his friends, whose birthday was near his, was on Normandy Beach on D-Day. He survived the ordeal, and told us about it in a ward fireside. Not all our young men were as fortunate. It was a time for mourning, fear, and patriotism.

MARION filled his last semester's class schedule with all the science and math courses he could. He was questioned when he wanted to take trigonometry, along with his physics and three-hour afternoon radio lab that had been offered to help young men with scientific ability. His problem with trig was his lack of geometry, advanced algebra, and solid geometry, which were all required prerequisites for admittance. MARION persisted and the teacher finally gave her approval, although she strongly questioned his ability to understand it. To her amazement he received an A in the math class. He also received the Bausch and Lomb science award—two were given that year with permission; the other male student was the valedictorian of the class, who was accepted into the Navy V12 officer's training. MARION, at first, was accepted into the Naval V5 pilot training; but these slots were filled when he had completed his fourth semester at Carroll College, a Catholic school in Helena, Montana, so they then gave him V12. He finished his Bachelor's Degree in Science at the University of Colorado at Boulder, and

ENSIGN MARION ASHER CONDIE

became an Ensign in the Naval Reserves. From there, he was able to go to Cal Tech for his Master's Degree. Later, he would get his Engineering Degree from Stanford. He was first employed by Ryan Aeronautical Company in California as an electrical engineer. This was the (much larger) aircraft company that had built the *Spirit of St. Louis* for Charles Lindbergh—the first to fly nonstop over the Atlantic in 1927. When the Korean War exploded, MARION was frozen on his job with a top-secret security clearance, while most of the other reserve officers were called to duty.

MARION started, and was president of Condie College, a business and computer school in San Jose, California. He later sold it, and is now retired. He loves skiing, has taught it, and still loves to ski, go snowmobiling, and play tennis in his 80s.

IVIE was also a hard act to follow. I happened to get her English literature teacher, who embarrassed me when she asked me to stand up, after she read my name on her roll call. She then told the large class that BROOKIE would be an excellent student; she had taught her older sister. IVIE excelled in typing and shorthand classes and after graduation, she attended Woodbury Business College in Los Angeles, which was considered the ultimate by our uncle JAMES IRA CONDIE, who insisted that she live with them in Alhambra, where he was the Chief of Police. IVIE graduated as a Business Accountant.

I knew my weaknesses. I was not an expert typist anymore than I could ski or ice skate. I was loose-jointed, and my knees dislocated at times with little provocation. To fill in my electives, I took Latin, Chemistry, Math, World History, and, of course, there was Senior Orchestra—by then I had dropped band and piano lessons: my schedule was too full. JAMES had dropped orchestra and piano in favor of the coronet. He played first chair before he graduated, and played his trumpet with the local dance band at the Radio Rendezvous. This was a large dance hall that would at times host the Big-Name Bands, and pictures of their leaders with their signatures surrounded the extensive walls. JAMES favored Harry James. His *Flight of the Bumble Bee* was his favorite record. The record album I spent my 25-cent per hour wages on was Jascha Heifetz's rendition of *Brahms Concerto in D for the Violin*. It was expensive; but I loved that music. I played the album while I ironed the clothes with tears streaming down my cheeks—it was heavenly music that tore at the very heart strings; but the record we danced to the most in our basement recreation room was Glenn Miller's "In the Mood." The jitterbug had arrived with the screaming bobby-soxers and boyish tantalizer, Frank Sinatra. I loved to dance.

BROOKIE CONDIE
Twin Falls high school

It was early in the spring of 1946 during my junior year of high school. Inwardly I was trying to decide on a suitable career. My mother and aunt ADA pushed toward business school. Another acceptable career for a girl was nursing. I didn't want that either. My talent was in math and science; but what could I do with it in a small city or town? In a few years I wanted to be married and have children. Most scientific careers didn't want women. My biology teacher called me Dr. CONDIE; but that took eight years of school plus the intern years. It took a lot of money and prestige to even be admitted, and women were not wanted. I passed over that idea.

One week, our school newspaper printed a short announcement. The University of Chicago was giving nationwide scholarships to high school juniors who were talented in science. It was a four-year scholarship that included all tuition, books, room, board, with a little extra for personal expenses, and the winners would begin in the fall and miss their senior year of high school. Anyone interested in taking their test should apply through the principal's office. The University of Chicago had a cyclotron and was one of the foremost colleges in the new field of nuclear science. I really wasn't confident about winning; but why not try. It would help with the family's financial problems, if I were able to get it. I filled out the papers.

Shortly after, my mother told me that she had a call from our principal, Mr.

Flatt. He was concerned. He told her that he would send in my application, if she wanted him to. If he did, he felt sure I would get the scholarship, especially with the recommendation that he planned to give me; however, did she want me to go alone to Chicago at that time of my life? He was not L.D.S.; but he knew we were. Together, they decided to offer me an alternative. I could graduate with the present class in May and choose a college or university nearer to my home, where I would meet men of my own religion more readily. Mother seemed relieved when I consented. She would pay for my college education, somehow.

My chemistry teacher was the one that solved my career problem when she suggested pharmacy and recommended the pharmacy school in Pocatello as the best one west of the Mississippi. I had never had a prescription drug and seldom went into a drug store. Earlier in our junior high P.E. we were supposed to get our family doctor to sign our health slips. Our family had not needed a doctor, so I had gone with my friend, [unknown fourth-cousin] CAROL BEAN, to her physician to be checked. I wrote Pocatello for their catalog, which was promptly sent. There was no tuition for Idaho residents and the pharmacy course included exciting and challenging courses in chemistry, pharmacology, bacteriology, math, pharmacy Latin, drug assaying, and so forth. Even small towns have drugstores. Why not try it?

At that time, it was the 2-year Southern Branch of the University of Idaho at Moscow. The one exception to their 2-year status was their Pharmacy School, which required four years. It was a time of change, and before I had completed my freshman year, we had a new name, Idaho State College—offering

CAROL BEAN AND I IN FRONT OF MY HOME IN TWIN FALLS, IDAHO, THE SUMMER BEFORE I WENT TO IDAHO STATE COLLEGE.

4-year-degrees in the Liberal Arts and Sciences.

The colleges and universities in the fall of 1946, throughout the nation, were bulging with students. The World War II veterans had returned home with their new G.I. Bill that allowed them great benefits. There was no longer a shortage of men at the dances. Our college had five men for every woman; of course, many of them were married or much older. The old barracks, where the former V-12 officer trainees had lived during their educational pursuits, were made into practice rooms for music students. One of those former officer trainees was the pianist Louie Wertz, who would later change his name to Roger Williams. He came back to his old college every year and played a concert for the faculty and students. During my sophomore year, he dated and then married Joy Dunsmore, who roomed down the hall on my dormitory third floor. She was a beautiful, popular girl from Jerome and had previously dated GROVER SWALLOW's roommate.

I loved college—socially and educationally. The first dance I attended was at the L.D.S. Institute. It was of necessity a short dance, since the Graveley Hall freshmen girls had to be back in the dorm by 8:15 P.M. on school nights, and all out-of-town girls were required to stay in the dormitory. Sophomore girls could stay out until 9:15. Honor students were allowed 10:00 P.M. My roommate was a cute short blond girl from Gooding, Idaho, Shirley Stevens. There was a large shortage of girls at the dance, so brooms were given to the extra men who cut in constantly by tapping the male partner and handing him the broom. Getting your partner's name and major was about all you could find out before you had a new partner. I remembered GROVER SWALLOW was a sophomore in pharmacy, and he was quite handsome. He didn't even remember that short exchange. His first memory of me was as one of the students in our dining hall, where he was a waiter. I had a band-aid across my nose, which he remembered. Our first football game had been the night before. I had fallen on my face in the long snake-line when the girl ahead of me tripped and fell, creating the domino effect. My nose was a little scraped and swollen, and I considered the band-aid more becoming.

He was the Sunday School Superintendent at the Institute and the president of the Beta Chapter of Lamba Delta Sigma, the L.D.S. fraternity. Everyone seemed to like him, and our Institute Director Eugene E. Campbell chose him to introduce church president George Albert Smith when he came one evening to address the students. I stood at the door and greeted the prophet with a handshake as my part. GROVER always seemed to be involved in leadership positions. At times we danced together, but were mostly just acquaintances.

Institute M.I.A. was on Tuesday evenings—followed by a short record dance; their was a college "Coffee Dance" at the Student Union building dance hall, from 6-9 on Wednesday evenings; Thursday evening the Idaho State Symphony practiced; sports events were on Friday evenings. Saturday nights at 9:00 P.M. there was always a dance on the large upper floor of the Student Union Building, which became a major formal dance every three to six weeks throughout the year. Downtown Pocatello had three movie theaters. Dancing was my favorite activity, not GROVER's. He played tennis and had run cross-country on their track team during his freshman year.

Idaho State had two very musically-talented brothers, Jay and Dell Slaughter. They were L.D.S., and lived in Pocatello. Jay was the oldest and spent his time in the Navy during World War II as a musician entertaining the troops. He played the trumpet and his college dance band (and pep band) rivaled the "Big Name Bands" in my opinion. He played trumpet in our symphony orchestra, Dell the clarinet. Their older married sister was our ballroom dance instructor.

I dated a young veteran who would only do the jitterbug. It was not the throw-them-around kind, but more sedate and graceful, depending on the speed of the music, of course. He was easy to follow with a keen sense of rhythm. Dancing together, we stood out, and our reputation as dancers became known—at least to GROVER. It seemed to me that we were being paired off, and I didn't want that. I wasn't serious; I believed him to be. The Valentine Sweetheart Formal Dance was coming in February. It was girl's choice, so after the Christmas vacation, I joined several L.D.S. friends in a dorm room, and we brain-stormed the situation. Collectively we agreed I should ask GROVER SWALLOW—you had to kiss them during the grand march going through the heart. Other girls would ask him; so I asked him early—actually three weeks before. He was surprised, but said "Yes!"

He then asked me to several movies. I truly believed he liked me, as we continued to date after the Valentine's dance. Then the night for the Engineer's Ball approached. He hadn't asked me. No one else did; they thought I would be going with GROVER. It was Saturday night and the dance began at 9:00 P.M. My girl friend, Barbara, from across the hall didn't have a date, either. The two of us watched from my dorm window, which was on the third floor, and where we could see the men in their fancy suits bringing their corsages to be pinned on their beautifully dressed partners. Barbara and I were not happy as we watched; in fact I believe we bordered on being very angry.

Then my room was buzzed. I had a telephone call. There was one telephone booth in the center of each floor. I expected it to be GROVER; but it wasn't. It was Ken, a tall, handsome, talented piano player I knew from the L.D.S. Institute. Barbara had expected him to ask her out. He wanted me to go to the movie with him. I said, "Yes!" I had barely arrived back in my room to tell Barbara when her room was buzzed. This time it was GROVER. He wanted to take her to the movie. She said, "Yes!" Evidently, they had concocted this great joke (?) between themselves with the idea that they would trade dates before we walked the many blocks downtown. Ken and I became increasingly angry as we followed behind them while they blatantly giggled and laughed together, turning to look at us occasionally with a facial expression that resembled a smirk—all the way, through the subway under the railroad tracks, to the theater. If Ken had asked me if I would like to leave them and return to the dorm or anywhere else, I would have said, "Yes!" It was the most miserable movie I had ever attended, and the walk home did not improve—although their smirks and laughing became more subdued and anxious. We sat in the dormitory lounge; each probably hoping one of us would make the effort to straighten out the situation. No one did. When the formal dancers began bringing their dates back to the dorm, our group

BARBARA MCGREGOR

grudgingly said, "Good night,"—but it was not "Good night, Sweetheart," which was always played as the final dance at the balls.

Sunday after, Barbara and I remained friends. We went to Church and the dining hall dinner together then returned to the dorm to commiserate together. We were sure that if they didn't straighten it out that day, we would forget both of them. Both of our roommates were gone with their dates and the dorm in general was quite empty. No one called. We studied a little and prepared for school the next day. Barbara was a sophomore and majoring in English.

The following Tuesday was my eighteenth birthday. School kept me very busy during the days. Classes were in the mornings and three-hour labs were in the afternoon. After that I needed to practice the violin at least an hour in the scheduled practice room. With top grades, I was taking 21 credit hours so I could also take the L.D.S. Institute classes and violin. Returning to my dormitory room, I found a vase of twelve long-stemmed deep-red roses waiting for me. They were beautiful. The small green gift card from Atkin's Flower and Gift Shop said, "With Love," and was signed "Grover." Joy Dunsmore stopped by to admire them, telling me what a fine person he was—and prob-

MY ROOMMATE SHIRLEY STEVENS WITH HER FUTURE HUSBAND VAN SCHIESS IN FRONT OF GRAVELEY HALL

ably made her report on my reaction. She was dating GROVER's roommate, Byron Lemon. GROVER called later that evening and asked me quite properly for another date, which I accepted. A dozen deep-red roses have been a tradition in our personal lives ever since on special occasions—the births of our children and Mother's Day, especially.

GROVER and I continued to date through the semester, and when summer arrived, wrote regularly to each other.

About a month later, in the spring, I got a phone call from Marty, a Jewish

AN AFTERNOON IN ROSS PARK

boy attending Idaho State College from Manhattan Island. (I had dated him, among others, the previous fall, and we had a date for the Pharmacy Ball—the first ball of the school year. I broke it and went with another man when I had found our ideologies were uncomfortably different.) In his phone call, he wanted me to join with him and some other students in a welcoming rally for the new Progressive Party candidates that were coming to Pocatello—Henry A. Wallace, former vice-president to Franklin D. Roosevelt was the candidate for president, and Senator (Idaho) Glen Taylor, the singing cowboy, for vice-president—not even close to my favorite people. I told him they were a front for communists and I wanted no part of it. He was very enthusiastic, which I thought strange; anti-Semitism had kept him out of the eastern universities he would have preferred to attend. Later, Marty would become a reporter for the New York Times, assigned to the political arena of Washington D.C.

[Note: According to *Europe, A History page 1328* by NORMAN DAVIES: "The Holocaust: the genocides of Jews by the Nazis, 1939-45: in Poland, 2,350,000 minimum to 3,000.000 maximum were killed; in the Soviet Union, it was 1,500,000 to 2,000,000; throughout the rest of Europe, it totaled 1,021,000 minimum to 1,271,500 maximum." Stalin, with his communism, was not a friend of the Jews.

The Progressive Party was not successful and got very few votes. They became insidious, and plotted against capitalism. Nitika Khrushchev had stated that Russia would destroy our country from within. Progressivism moved into the universities, especially in the departments of education, sociology, and political science.]

That fall our steady dating continued. In the spring, since we were both paying our way through college, working as waiters in the girl's dining hall (added in the basement of Graveley Hall), we became engaged. We were married in the Manti Temple 7 Sep 1948—GROVER was twenty and I was nineteen. It was not quite the same financially as we had expected. GROVER then had four jobs—I had three.

Grover & Brookie in wedding clothes

I was one of the four women taking pharmacy in a class of over 200 pharmacy majors. It was not unusual to be the only girl in some of our smaller classes. We were always treated with respect by our male classmates and the faculty. After graduating, I found the employers less willing to accept a woman pharmacist than anything I had experienced at college, although most customers were accepting. I smiled when one male customer in Pioche would drive the 25 miles to Caliente, where my husband worked, to get his insulin, because he wouldn't trust a woman pharmacist to take it out of the refrigerator. I had graduated summa cum laude. GROVER has often jokingly stated,

"BROOKIE graduated with high honors and I was honored to graduate."

Probably the strangest exclusion came from those of my own sex. When we moved to Preston, Idaho, some of the women college graduates wanted to join the U.S. National Association of University Women, and they recruited me to be one of their charter members. My friends were sad to tell me a few weeks later that I couldn't join with them. This association would not allow any women into their membership that had a degree in a field that they considered to be a male profession. I could be an associate member and work for more acceptance of women into the profession; but my degree would not be honored by membership. I turned that down. The only university bias I had discovered against women was theirs.

My brother JAMES has excelled scholastically at whatever he tried to do.

JAMES M. CONDIE

HIGH SCHOOL GRADUATION ·

His plan had always been to return to the ranch after graduating from the Agricultural College in Logan, Utah. His freshman year he came to Idaho State. When he was 19 years old, he served an L.D.S. Mission—one of the early missionaries into the war-torn Frankfurt Germany Mission (ca. 1949-52).

During World War II, the foreign missions and most of the domestic missions of our church had been closed. Europe, who was devastated with hungry refugees, needed help. The Church had built, and filled with wheat, a very large grain elevator and was prepared to send the entire contents into Europe along with clothing, bedding, and other needs right after the armistice was signed. One of our young men from Twin Falls, FRED BABBEL, was chosen to accompany Apostle Ezra Taft Benson as his secretary on this first expedition into Poland, Germany, and the other bombed out nations to help relieve the great suffering of the people with food, clothing, and other necessities. FRED spoke excellent German. On their return, FRED wrote a book about their almost unbelievable experiences, *On Wings of Faith*.

My sister IVIE soon after married FRED's youngest brother, BYRON—a returned naval veteran. The wonderful parents of this large BABBEL family had joined the church in Germany and had immigrated into Idaho many years before the war. BYRON and IVIE were married in the Salt Lake Temple by Apostle Benson in 1949. BYRON got his degree in mechanical engineering at the University of Utah. They then moved to Seattle and Boeing Aircraft. They had eleven children. After his retirement they moved to Manti, Utah.

When JAMES' mission to Germany of over 2 years was completed, JAMES returned home and soon married pianist MARILYN LINCOLN of Twin Falls in the Idaho Falls Temple. His college years were interrupted again by the draft board and the Korean War. Returning, he completed his degree in agriculture and took over the ranch at Carey, Idaho.

My sister IVIE and BYRON BABBEL stand for a photo with the CONDIE temple wedding party in Salt Lake City before escaping on their honeymoon 7 Sep 1949 (left to right)

Our mother LILLIE CONDIE (living in Logan), GROVER, BROOKIE,

cousin MARY LOUISE CONDIE BUNKER, LILLIE IDA CONDIE, JAMES CONDIE,

the bride IVIE, cousin AFTON CONDIE, the groom BYRON BABBEL,

grandfather GIBSON A CONDIE, and BOB BUNKER.

[Note: IVIE worked as an executive secretary for Arthur Franks downtown Salt Lake City store while Byron was completing his education at the U of U. BOB and MARY LOUISE were married and had brought grandfather and her sister AFTON to the wedding from Alhambra, California. Husband BOB was a scientist at Jet Propulsion Laboratories, having graduated from Cal Tech. Today, 2011, both are still living. He is still a consultant at JPL for the high definition satellite box he designed with replaceable parts. MARY LOUISE is a graduate dietitian and has been a member of the Alhambra City Council for many years, taking her turn as mayor when it came around. Her sister AFTON became an osteopathic physician specializing in anesthesia, and married FRANK TAYLOR—a classmate who specialized in eye, ear, and throat. My sister LILLIE IDA was attending nursing school, and my brother JAMES was making final preparations for his L.D.S. mission into the war torn Frankfurt Germany mission. BOB and MARY LOUISE's oldest son BOB, like his father, graduated from Cal Tech and works for JPL. He would stay at our home when he came to B.Y.U. and U of U to interest their top science majors in JPL. At that time he was working on the Mars project. GROVER and I were celebrating our first wedding anniversary. in this picture. He had a new job in Smithfield, Utah, and I was then completing my final semester in Pharmacy at Idaho State. We had no car, so we had come with Mother and the family. I commuted weekly to Pocatello on the Greyhound bus.}

JAMES HAD THIS AERIAL PHOTO TAKEN OF THE RANCH HOME AND SURROUNDING BUILDINGS WHILE HE WAS ON THE RANCH. HE HAD MADE A FEW CHANGES, BUT IT IS VERY SIMILAR TO THE RANCH OF MY YOUTH.

After ranching in Carey several years, he then worked for the United States Department of Agriculture (crop reporting service) stationed in Boise, Idaho. We were living in Pioche when the news arrived that there had been a car accident as they journeyed to Boise and the new job. It was reported in the *Twin Falls Times News* on 17 Oct 1960. From the front page:

> "Gooding Traffic Accident Claims Baby Girl's Life—A 14-month-old girl became Gooding county's third traffic victim within four days when she died Sunday morning at St. Luke's hospital, Boise, of injuries received in a truck-car accident about 4:30 p.m. Saturday four miles west of here on highway 20-26. The baby, MARGARET CONDIE, was taken to Boise after the accident in which her parents, Mr. and Mrs. JAMES CONDIE, two brothers and a sister also were injured. Mrs. CONDIE, 28, was listed in 'critical' condition at the Gooding Memorial hospital, but an attendant reported Monday morning she was 'slightly improved.' She received internal injuries and a broken pelvis. . . . The CONDIE baby was a passenger in a 1958 Plymouth station-wagon driven by her father which collided with a 1946 Chevrolet pickup truck driven by Ben Raymond, 60, King Hill. Raymond received cuts but was not admitted to the hospital. [He apparently went to sleep while driving.]

Others in the CONDIE family injured were the father, 30, cuts and bruises; JOHN CONDIE, 2, cuts and bruises; EMILY CONDIE, 3, right leg broken above and below the knee, and ELDON CONDIE, 5, treated and released from the hospital Saturday. . . . Both vehicles were demolished and CONDIE's station-wagon caught fire and burned while being towed into Gooding by a wrecker. MARGARET CONDIE was born August 11, 1959, in Hailey. . . . Funeral services will be held at 2 p.m. Wednesday in the Carey LDS ward chapel with Bishop Lynn Adamson officiating."

MARILYN WITH BABY

My sister, ADELIA RILE, who lived in California, and I drove to Gooding together, and then to the funeral of the young child at Carey. MARILYN was not doing well. The boys and EMILY with her broken bones seemed in fair spirits putting picture puzzles together in their various hospital beds. JAMES survived with minor physical injuries. MARILYN died a few days later. GROVER and I attended her funeral at Twin Falls. She was buried by her baby in the cemetery lot where my father was buried. Mother was helping me in Pioche with our many children and in the drugstore, while GROVER was driving to Caliente and our second store. A greater need was at hand, and Mother moved to Boise to help JAMES with his young children.

As time passed and his sadness dimmed a little, JAMES was given a short agricultural assignment for a few days in our area of Lincoln County, Nevada. We were still living in the home behind the drugstore in Pioche, but were remodeling an older home in Panaca, located in a valley between the two stores. Number seven was on her way. We could drive two directions.

That Friday evening we took JAMES with us to a Rotary Club party in Caliente. We arrived before the store closed and GROVER introduced him to one of our clerks, whom we greatly admired. She had two children and was fairly recently divorced from her wayward husband. After the party ended, we stopped by the darkened drugstore for milkshakes. JAMES was interested.

James, John, Emily, and Elden at the Yosemite Park reunion.

He called JERRY, asking to take her and her two daughters, COLLEEN and KARYN, to the public swimming pool at Veyo (near St. George, Utah) the next day (Saturday). She accepted with persuasion and GROVER's volunteering to cover her shift.

That Saturday, 30 Jun 1962, remains in my memory. It was the day our daughter EMILY was born around ten in the evening in the Caliente hospital. JAMES and JERRY still hadn't returned. GROVER had returned from the hospital to Pioche, when around 1:00 A.M., JAMES came in, all smiles, sat down, stretched out his legs on the footstool and said, "Well, I guess I won't have to look any further." They had swum at Veyo, drove on to Zion National Park, Bryce Canyon—then to Cedar Breaks, above Cedar City. Back in Caliente, with his trumpet somehow nearby, JERRY, accompanied him on her piano, until they finally realized it was late at night and the neighbors might not appreciate the after midnight concert. Three weeks later JERRY was wearing the ring (claiming it was much too fast). They were married in the St. George Temple.

Not too long after, JAMES transferred to the central office of the Department of Agriculture in Washington D.C. during which time he was able to do post graduate studies in Ames, Iowa. Later, he worked with the Federal Reserve Board, where he became highly involved in statistics and the early computer development of that department of government, which extended into helping other countries in the International Monetary Fund (IMF) at times with their computers and statistical projections. When Paul Volcker met to decide on their new plan of action, after the financial mess of the Carter administration, JAMES and his large group furnished the board with their long-term projected statistics to help them plan their course.

JAMES and JERRY added four more highly talented children to their family of his, hers, and ours—a total of 9 living children. After JAMES retired from the Federal Reserve, he continued to act as a consultant to the IMF. JAMES was a bishop, high councilman, and patriarch in the L.D.S. Church. JERRY was president of many church women's organizations, including stake Young Women's counselor and stake Relief Society president. She and all of their daughters were very proficient on the piano. JAMES and JERRY filled a full-time couple L.D.S. mission in India, and now work in the Washington D.C. Temple. He plays trumpet in a neighborhood dance band. JERRY and one of their talented daughters add their expertise to this group on the keyboard.

I was three years old in the fall of 1932 when my sister LILLIE IDA was born on our ranch by Carey, Idaho. Grandfather CONDIE's job was to tend the four older children at his home next to ours at that time. He didn't let us go into his house, because grandmother CONDIE was at our home and he needed to keep their house in order; but he gave us all the watermelon we could eat. It was an unusual round

LILLIE IDA CONDIE
HIGH SCHOOL GRADUATION

melon, and he laid out some newspapers for us to spit the seeds on, as he wanted to save them to plant in the spring. Three-years-old, I accepted that explanation, although the summer season in Carey was never long enough to grow watermelons or tomatoes. The black automobile in our parking lot belonged to Dr. Fox, but we were told not to go to our house until he left.

While Dr. Fox's black automobile sped down our lane to the highway, leaving a trail of heavy dust behind it, our smiling father joined his children and informed us that we had a new baby sister. Would we like to see her? When it was my turn, I was lifted up to view a 9-pound baby in her bassinet. She had a tuft of black hair at least an inch long. She was wrapped tightly in a small white blanket. Her eyes were tightly closed. Strangely, Mother was in bed, and grandmother CONDIE appeared to be taking care of her. It would be several years before I learned about the birth of babies. The comic strips would tell about the stork bringing them; but I knew that was just a joke. Living on the ranch, we had been in the lambing sheds where hundreds of lambs were born every spring. We knew that cows had calves; cats had kittens; dogs had puppies and mares had colts; but the comparison escaped me for some time.

It was in August of 1934 that Daddy took Mother to Logan, Utah, before she gave birth to my sister CeCELIA, who was born in the Budge Memorial Hospital where I had been born. He wanted Mother protected from the heavy work on the ranch with large crews of hay-men and thrashers to cook for over a hot coal stove. My brother MARION returned back with him to the ranch.

Aunt PEARL STANFORD lived in Logan, across the street from the Utah State Agricultural College. Until she went to the hospital, Mother with JAMES and LILLIE IDA stayed with her. IVIE and I stayed at the home of uncle SEDLEY's sister who lived across the street from the entrance to the Logan L.D.S. Temple with its grey-stoned towers and beautifully groomed landscape that smelled of sweet alyssum and petunias. There were goldfish with lilies in their pond. Our older cousin KATHERINE STANFORD took us on a quiet tour of the grounds a few times; but we were warned that it was a sacred place and we couldn't go inside until we were older.

Those were the days when a woman was kept in the hospital for two weeks after childbirth. On the tenth day she could sit up and dangle her feet over the side of her bed. This seems odd today; but they didn't have ergotrate to help stop the bleeding. Penicillin, sulfa, and the antibiotics were still in the future. Deaths in childbirth from bleeding and infections were not unusual.

Pioneer Day, July 24, was always celebrated in Carey, and a small traveling carnival would arrive and setup their booths and rides. In 1937, Mother was in the hospital at Hailey, Idaho, with my infant baby sister, ADELIA, when the holiday arrived. Daddy gave each of his children a silver dollar to add to our savings from our small weekly ten cent allowance, and we went to the celebration. He was amazed when we all returned home that evening with our silver dollars—more valuable to us than the rides. We did spend most of our allowance money, however. They had hired a woman to take care of us on the ranch. IVIE was only 10 years old; but the woman was better at bossing IVIE than doing—I was to help, too. IVIE and I did the washing in our gas-operated Maytag washer in the washhouse by the hot spring the day Daddy brought Mother and ADELIA home. IVIE had put too much bluing in the rinse water, and the blue sheets were still hanging on the line when they arrived home. I felt quite proud of our (mostly IVIE's) accomplishment, but our parents never let the woman come back again.

One of our household's major duties each summer was bottling fruit. The vegetables were purchased already canned by the case. Some corn was dried in small sacks on the clotheslines. There were lugs of various varieties of cherries, raspberries, gooseberries, and apricots, and later the bushels of peaches, and pears to bottle. When the wild currents ripened in the lava beds, Mother sent the children with small buckets to pick them to make jelly. Another favorite jelly was the wild chokecherries that grew on our range land. The children helped in preparing the fruit, while Mother would do the bottling on the hot cook stove, during those hot summer days. To add some fun to the process, Mother would appoint one of the older children to read to the young workers. *Treasure Island, Ivanhoe,* and *Pride and Prejudice* were among my favorites.

When IVIE went to Los Angles to Woodbury's business school, I inherited a new sleeping companion in our basement bedroom in Twin Falls—LILLIE IDA. Before going to sleep, I would read to her, for perhaps a half-hour, the large thrilling volume of *Ivanhoe*. She continued this practice, after I left for college, with CeCELIA, who in turn read to ADELIA. We all loved the book.

LILLIE IDA chose nursing as her career and attended the University of Utah. It was here she met WILLIAM CLAY, a lineman on the University of Utah's football team. He was tall, strong, good looking and a strong member of the L.D.S. Church. They were married in the Idaho Falls Temple, before they finished their college—like the rest of us. BILL got his degree in Business Administration. He managed many companies through those early years living in California, Oregon, Texas, Tennessee and then into southwestern Virginia, where he started his own insurance business. They have been very active in the L.D.S. Church. BILL served as a stake president, while LILLIE IDA taught early morning seminary for years, along with her multitude of other church callings. When their eleven children left home, they served a couple welfare mission in the Philippines for two years. It was a time when heavy guards were required at their church office building in Manilla, and they were personally driven to their offices by escorts of the church. Taxi cabs could not be trusted.

BILL and JAMES are both patriarchs. BILL died in 2007 near Abingdon, Virginia.

CeCELIA CONDIE
HIGH SCHOOL GRADUATION

ADELIA CONDIE
HIGH SCHOOL GRADUATION

CeCELIA first attended Utah State University at Logan, Utah. Her major was business and accounting. After ADELIA graduated from Twin Falls High

School, the two sisters attended B.Y.U. at Provo, Utah. ADELIA had been dating Naval Korean War veteran JOE RILE (medic), and, not wanting to lose her, he promptly enrolled in B.Y.U. also—although he had a baseball scholarship to another university. WAYNE P. WILSON from Ogden was also attending B.Y.U. Both WAYNE and JOE were majoring in school administration. CeCELIA and WAYNE were married 1 Jun 1956. ADELIA and JOE followed closely behind on the 11 Sep 1956. Both were temple marriages for time and eternity. The two sisters with their newly born daughters were pictured in the local newspaper when they had their second babies, NANETTE WILSON and STEPHANIE RILE, on the same day in the same hospital—Utah Valley Hospital in Provo, Utah.

After WAYNE and CeCELIA graduated with their degrees, WAYNE found a teaching position in Stockton, California. JOE obtained his degree at the same time, and ADELIA and he moved to Fontana, California, where his teaching position was located. Both WAYNE and JOE began their teaching careers at the salary of about $5,000/year. We were paying our clerks $1/hour. This may seem low; but I was glad to get 60 cents an hour when I worked in the Blue Room and stockroom at college. When GROVER graduated as a pharmacist, his first salary was $250/month with a work-week average of 52 hours. He received $325/month when he worked in Preston. During his partnership in Montpelier, Idaho, in 1954, he received $400 per month. Utah teachers were not paid as much as the teachers in California or Nevada.

JOE RILE advanced into school administration. JOE and ADELIA moved to Indio, California, where he was a high school principal. They had a swimming pool in their backyard, which was not unusual in this hot, dry area just south of Palm Springs. Swim teams within this area of Southern California were very competitive athletically, and the four RILE children excelled in this sport. Then the family moved to Riverside, California, where JOE was employed as the principal of Poly High School. Nine years later, he would become the assistant to the superintendent of the district. ADELIA completed her college education, obtaining a degree in nutrition and obtained certificates in elementary and secondary education, teaching many years. They became the parents of four children. Their daughter, MELANIE, received a four-year swimming scholarship to

B.Y.U. in Provo, Utah. While attending, she broke five of their records. Two of them are still standing. While at the University she married Brazilian Olympic swim team member RONALD MENEZES. Their two daughters would later receive swimming scholarships at B.Y.U. MELANIE was added to the B.Y.U. Hall of Fame. ADELIA and JOE remained very active in the church. ADELIA, with her organ, piano, and voice, was constantly used in music, but also served as Relief Society president in both ward and stake. JOE died in 2009, recuperating from a new knee implantation. At that time they were working in a church program that helps church members overcome their addictions.

WAYNE and CeCELIA added a walnut farm to their activities in Stockton. After MARION built Condie College in San Jose, WAYNE and CeCELIA sold their farm and joined him. WAYNE became the vice president, and CeCELIA taught business law and handled the accounting. MARION had married CONNIE JOHNSON of San Diego in the temple. [Some of her grandparents lived in Morgan, Utah.] They had six children. Their oldest son, CRAIG, helped to teach the newly developing courses in computers along with his father. Daughter JOAN became MARION's private secretary. CeCELIA became very skilled at government programs that could help the students as well as the school. CeCELIA and WAYNE had six children.

JOE AND ADELIA CONDIE RILE AT YOSEMITE REUNION
WITH THEIR CHILDREN RICHARD AND STEPHANIE—
MELANIE AND BECKY HAD NOT BEEN BORN.

Condie College kept growing and prospering. MARION had his own airplane and a second smaller ski home with a sail boat at Lake Tahoe. Unfortunately, MARION's wife CONNIE developed giant cell melanoma. Only their two youngest teenage daughters, JANICE and KAREN, were still living at their lovely home in Saratoga, California, when their mother died. To add to the great distress of that sad day, one daughter left the curling iron plugged in when she rushed to the hospital. Their home caught on fire. The neighbors called the fire department, when the smoke became visible. It was not yet the suffering of the Biblical Job, but a start.

MARION AND CONNIE CONDIE'S FAMILY (EARLIER)—THEIR FOUR OLDER CHILDREN: TODD, JUNE, JOAN AND CRAIG—JANICE AND KAREN WERE BORN LATER.

After MARION married his next wife, SUE SCHILLING (Couper), they sold Condie College to another company, and also sold their home in Saratoga, for a very decent price, and moved to Reno, Nevada. Their new home was in a building development among the ponderosa pines on the road to the skiing facilities of Mount Rose. SUE became pregnant, and they welcomed their new young son, JAMES, into their lives. MARION turned sixty years old that year. Their dream of going on a church couple full-time mission was changed to a stake mission and ordinance work in the Reno Temple. But the joy and challenges of raising this new son more than compensated. Young violinist JIMMY was concert master in their youth symphony orchestra while attending high school and his first year at the University of Nevada.

The new owners of Condie College, who had many business schools throughout the nation, needed a president for their newly acquired San Jose business school. Marion recommended and WAYNE applied for the position, and was accepted. The school was quite profitable, and WAYNE was sent into Oregon to another newly acquired school; then in a few years the family was again uprooted and sent to Riverside, California, and another college. The RILE and WILSON families were once more in the same location. Their home in Oregon had sold quickly for an excellent price, and the WILSONs were able to purchase a beautiful large colonial-style dream home in Riverside. Then WAYNE had a quadruple-bypass on his heart. He recovered and was soon nearly up to pace.

But the national economy is constantly changing and double-digit interest rates, rising as high as 22%, were destroying businesses. It was the later 80s, and home sales were on a downward skid. WAYNE was transferred to Salt Lake City, Utah. Their beautiful home in Riverside was slow to sell and they took a bad loss, but in a few years they were able to build a lovely new home in South Jordan, near the temple.

CeCELIA CONDIE WILSON developed breast cancer. She continued in her work and went through chemical therapy, losing her hair, wearing cute hats, and barely surviving day-by-day.

Their son CHARLES, alias CHUCK, changed universities and came to stay with them in South Jordan. He had become very skilled in diving during his swim team years in California.

CHUCK, like MELANIE RILE, had qualified for the Nationals. I suppose it was only natural that his love for diving would extend into sky diving. While I was working in our drugstore in Orem, I glanced at a front-page article in the Salt Lake Tribune that told of some daring young men that had jumped off the twenty-six story L.D.S. Church Office Building with their parachutes. The name CHARLES WILSON was included in the three names. According to his mother, CHUCK had slipped out of the house before they were awake. The smiling police were waiting for the adventurers when the three safely landed on a rather busy street. The three young men promised not to do it again, and efforts were made by the church to stop further attempts.

CeCELIA became a breast-cancer survivor. She and WAYNE had been very

In loving memory of
our son, brother and uncle

Chuck Wilson

October 3, 1969 - January 14, 2001

active in many leadership and teaching positions of the L.D.S. Church. WAYNE had been a bishop for many years in California, and was especially helpful with the youth of the church. They were living close to the L.D.S. Jordan Temple, and the two of them attended regularly. Then CeCELIA was called to be the Stake Relief Society president of her South Jordan Stake. In a few years, the cancer returned, this time with a vengeance. Of the 45 tests on her lymph nodes, 37 tested positive. CeCELIA knew her time on earth was limited. It wasn't helpful when WAYNE was diagnosed with hepatitis that had come from the transfusions he had received earlier during his heart surgery. The day-by-day survival had become hour-by-hour survival; but still they persisted in doing their regular work activities.

Then one winter morning CeCELIA received a phone call. CHUCK had been sky diving in Mesquite, Nevada. The group of nine had returned that evening to find that the Salt Lake City airport was completely clouded over and no planes could land. They were directed to a smaller airport across the Great Salt Lake. Their plane never made it. The nine dead bodies were recovered from the salt water. It was a time of great sorrow; but daily activities demand attention, and life goes on. Many spiritual experiences helped them through those days with the sweet comfort that comes from the knowledge that a loving God is there, and that there is a purpose in our mortal existence.

CeCELIA, with her great skill in student loans and government grants, was very helpful in the business, and when Provo College was experiencing financial difficulties, the owner asked WAYNE for a recommendation for a new president. He suggested CeCELIA. She got the appointment. Provo College specialized in business, computer graphics, dental assistants, and other business-related programs. With CeCELIA at the helm, it prospered, and the owner, with her consent to also be its president, opened a new school in the Salt Lake valley called Eagle Gate. Both schools are highly successful.

CeCELIA CONDIE WILSON, born 23 Aug 1934 in Logan, Utah, died Sunday, 11 May 2003, in South Jordan, Utah. She was survived by her husband, WAYNE PAXTON WILSON and five children: BUD; NAN; MICH; CONNIE KAY, and MATT, and of course by her many grandchildren and six siblings. A few days previous to her death, she delivered her two commencement addresses as president of the two colleges, leaving her wheelchair to stand with only the slim speaker's stand to support her This is a copy of the large portrait which the owner had made and hung as a welcome when the students entered the main doors of the two colleges.

(From her funeral program} "She Lived with Faith." Her life is an inspiration to all who struggle against difficult circumstances.

GROVER SWALLOW

Windows shattered, *condemned and disconsolate building known (for good reason) as the Million Dollar Courthouse is a landmark in the mining town of Pioche, Nevada*

THREE CHILDREN BY THE OLD JAIL

ONE OF THE CELLS

If you drive U.S. 93 in Nevada . . .

Don't by-pass old Pioche

Travelers find little reason to pause along most of U.S. Highway 93 between Nevada's Lake Mead area and the Ely crossroads 250 miles to the north. About midway, however, the highway passes near three state parks, not far from Pioche. This historic mining town is a good base from which to visit the parks, and it's well worth exploring itself.

The parks are Cathedral Gorge, where nature has carved majestic formations in stone; and Kershaw-Ryan and Beaver Dam, scenic preserves in a wooded, mountainous region that attracts many hikers and campers. Cathedral Gorge is only 5 miles from Pioche; Kershaw-Ryan is about 30, and Beaver Dam about 45.

Despite the fact that Pioche's former population of 8,000 has shrunk to 800, its residents bridle at any reference to it as a "ghost town." Two of its mines are in full operation, and others are maintained by skeleton crews against the day when mineral prices may again make them profitable. Meanwhile civic improvements and new construction prove the town is very much alive.

Pioche got its start in 1864 when William Hamblin staked a mining claim where Indians had shown him high-grade silver ore. The town was named for F. L. A. Pioche, San Francisco importer who invested heavily in the area's mines. Within two years the new camp was rivaling Virginia City in its silver yield. In 1872 one mine produced in three days a record

36 bars of silver worth $60,000.

During this period six stage lines carried away the silver and brought back more prospectors, many of them veterans of the California gold rush and the Comstock silver strikes. With mushroom growth came all the violence and color of the typical early Western boom town. Seventy-five men were buried in the cemetery before one died of natural causes.

The main street today is just where it was 90 years ago, and though some buildings have been rebuilt or renovated, many are unrestored relics of the early days. Among these are the "Million Dollar Courthouse," Mountain View Hotel, Masonic Temple, and opera house. The cemetery and the tramway from the mines are much in evidence. So are the colorfully-walled "glory holes" created by huge cave-ins at the old Prince Mine.

The Million Dollar Courthouse got its nickname from the fact that graft during its construction and repair, plus a spiraling accumulation of interest on bonds unpaid for decades after the price of silver dropped, actually brought the total cost to more than a million dollars—for a modest stone structure on which the original bid was $26,400, and which was crumbling and condemned by the time its debt was finally paid in 1937. A year earlier Lincoln County built the modern courthouse now in use.

Pioche has two motels, two hotels, two restaurants, and three trailer courts.

SUNSET

A TOUR IN THE COMBINED METALS HARD ROCK MINE 1200 FEET BELOW PIOCHE, AND BELOW THE WATER LEVEL . . . WITH MINE SUPERINTENDENT BLACKMAN AND RULON PECTOL—AFTER THE LEAD/ZINC MINE WAS CLOSED FROM ALL PRODUCTION.

Photos by GROVER SWALLOW

~ 48 ~

SWALLOWS IN NEVADA—THE BOMB, NEVADA LEGISLATURE—ABORTION BILL

The accompanying article "Don't by-pass old Pioche" was the first writing I ever sold. It was written after the mines closed in 1957 in an effort to try to increase tourism into the historic mining town. Sunset Magazine distilled my much longer story to the two columns with no byline and purchased the picture of the Million Dollar Court House from the photos GROVER had taken, which included our children in the old stone jail that was cut into the mountain behind. It was an eerie place with shackles still on the floor, black widow spiders in the corners, and rodents roaming around with little fear.

In the early 1970s the courthouse and jail were restored and made safer for tourists. It is still fun to see with all its additional photos, furniture, dummies, and histories; but it has lost its old ghost-town charm. Our oldest son, TOM, judged

SEATED WITH THE OLD JURY ARE GRANDSON ALEX AND HIS UNCLE BENJAMIN ORME.

his childhood trials in those early days. He is now a lawyer in Los Angeles.

Shortly after this article was published, author Louis L'Amour came to Pioche to do some research. Because I had researched this article, they sent him to me. I wasn't able to help him; but we talked for about a half-hour.

Dressed in his typical rugged western outfit, he appeared to be in his mid-forties. He tried to encourage me to write about the area; which he considered a writer's dream location. After telling how he got his start by writing short stories for the Saturday Evening Post, that made him write under a fictitious name because they thought his name was not appropriate for western stories, he volunteered three suggestions, which I will pass on:

1. Never start at the beginning. Always start your story with an interesting incident and then go back to the beginning. He said they had wanted him to write a few episodes for the "Wells Fargo" television series (in black and white.) It needed a boost and was struggling at that time. He had agreed to do one or two. We had just got our first black and white television set with the tall antenna a few months before. I thought the series was stiff and lacked action, and had told GROVER so several days before.

2. Never go to college to learn how to write. He stated flatly that if the teachers knew how to write, they wouldn't be teaching college. He claimed his editors helped a little sometimes.

3. Always go to the area you are describing, such as a water hole, and view it first hand. Five minutes might be enough; but make it authentic.

With drugstores and children, writing was not my priority. Within six months of our purchase, President Eisenhower, the first president we were old enough to vote for (at twenty-one years), lowered the tariffs on metals, and all the larger mining operations in the area ceased. At that time they were mining lead, zinc, copper, and manganese, with traces of silver. We had been told before we bought the store that the mines were down, and could only go up. I wrote Eisenhower a letter of complaint, and included one of the small pieces of lead-zinc ore they had chipped off for me when they showed me the mine. I did receive an answer from the Secretary of the Interior, expressing his regrets—but nothing would be changed.

[Note: They wouldn't take me down in the mine when it was open. The superintendent explained that half his crew would have quit immediately if he had allowed a woman to come down—an old superstition. The power went off for about ten minutes while we were riding the ore train. Our only lights were our battery hats. The pumps to keep the water out and bring in fresh air also stopped, and the skip would not have been able to take us to the surface without power. Showing us the fault line, they explained, the faults were important because they allowed the heavy metals from the center of the earth to move into the vacant spaces. We were shown old iron mining cars that were crushed flat by the heavy weight of the earth in the walls when an older mine had been vacated.]

Fortunately, we were able to purchase another drugstore in Caliente in November 1958, which was 25 miles south of Pioche. Since GROVER and I were both pharmacists, the children and I remained in Pioche and with my mother's help; I became the pharmacist/manager in Pioche, and chief accountant, while GROVER commuted to our more lucrative store in Caliente, which still had a doctor, a hospital, and the Union Pacific Railroad.

THIS PICTURE OF PIOCHE MAIN STREET WAS PROBABLY TAKEN IN THE EARLY MORNING DURING WORLD WAR II. OUR DRUG STORE WAS THE CLOSEST ONE WITH THE VACANT LOT NEXT TO IT. WE DIDN'T SELL ANY PHILCO PRODUCTS.

In 1962, we built our home in Panaca, which was about half-way between Caliente and Pioche. We had six children, with another on the way. This seemed to us to be a wise move. We had rescued our young daughter VANDA twice, when she had slipped away and rode her tricycle down the steep Main Street in front of our store. It was also a bit concerting when tiny ROXANNE escaped the bathtub and ran down Main Street nude—with her older sister trying to catch her. Then there was the time our young children sought treasure a little beyond their playground—which was also part of Treasure Hill. Without our

A VIEW OF CALIENTE, NEVADA. THE TALL THREE-STORY HOTEL BUILDING ACROSS
THE UNION PACIFIC RAILROAD TRACKS RENTED US THE LOWER FRONT CORNER FOR OUR STORE.
U S 93 TURNED WEST IN FRONT OF OUR STORE. MOST OF THE BUSINESS DISTRICT WAS
THEN ACROSS THE TRACKS FROM OUR DRUGSTORE.

knowledge, our three oldest took a pick and shovel and dug through the cement ceiling and into the bathroom that was built under the dirt as part of the
Masonic Temple around the corner. With dreams of a great buried treasure inside a cement box, their disappointment was huge—but our embarrassment
was perhaps greater, when our kind neighbors informed us about it.

BLUEBEARD PRODUCTION CAST — PIOCHE, ABOUT 1961
LEFT TO RIGHT: *FATIMA*, RUTH BELLINGHERI; *SALIM*, DOMINICK BELLINGHERI;
BLUEBEARD, GROVER SWALLOW; *DIRECTOR*, BROOKIE SWALLOW;
SISTER ANN, BETTY WILKIN; AND OUR *MELODRAMATIC PIANO PLAYER*, JOE WILKIN

In the fall of 1962, when JAMES and JERRY were married, mother was relieved of her duties as the caregiver of JAMES' children. It was hard for her. She had lost her purpose and she sincerely loved those three grandchildren. Her neglected ranch and rangeland called out, and she soon returned to Twin Falls and renewed her old friendships. It was very apparent that JAMES would not be returning to Carey. She had an excellent leaser; but he wanted to buy the property. It took a few years for her to make that decision. With family encouragement, she went to Salt Lake City to study and do genealogy and temple work. She resided in the Kimball Apartments within walking distance of Temple Square and the Genealogical Society and Library—the best in the world.

In Panaca, the architect had designed a large wing on the east side of our Panaca home to include a living room, kitchen, family room, half-bath, and laundry. The surrounding acre was to have a tennis court, a front carport, a playground and an outdoor swimming pool—more than we could afford in 1962, so we limited our home to the remodeling of the bedrooms and baths, and continued to use the old kitchen and laundry with the future library as our living room. We quickly completed the playground with its swings, teeter-totters, slide, monkey bars, and merry-go-round. Our friend, Joe Wilkin, designed and built it of metal.

THE OLD MERRY-GO-ROUND STILL WORKS! SEVERAL OF OUR GRANDCHILDREN TRIED OUT
THEIR PARENTS OLD PLAYGROUND AT A REUNION SEVERAL YEARS AGO—WITH PERMISSION.

I had limited my working hours as pharmacist in the Pioche store to around four hours a day, although the store opened from 9-6. Its soda fountain was a community hub and we carried all kinds of merchandise, including Keepsake Diamond Rings—the only drugstore in the nation that was allowed to sell them. Mildred Adair was willing to stay with the pre-school children during this time, except our infant, EMILY, who I would take with me. EMILY would sleep most of the time in her infant seat. At times I would leave her sleeping in our old home behind the drugstore, as it was unoccupied, but heated by the same drugstore coal furnace. We had an excellent monitoring intercom in the pharmacy. It was better than having our daughter in the next room. The two of us would return home shortly after four o'clock. Mildred was wonderful with the children, and at times would cook a big pot of chili beans and make a large pan of hot rolls for our evening meal. We all loved her. Unfortunately for us, Mildred found the right husband and became Mildred Francis, instead of our helper.

In Salt Lake City, Mother had fallen and broken her wrist. She gave up her apartment, and after extended visits to all of her scattered children and their families, she came to stay in our vacated old home behind the drugstore and helped with our younger children, while I worked. She sold the ranch; but kept and leased the rangeland. Then she sold her home in Twin Falls and her parent's home in Salina, Utah. After a short time, she purchased a double-wide trailer home, which we placed on the lot next to our home in Panaca. She loved Panaca, and once stated that it was like being in paradise. The children all loved her, and GROVER and I were delighted to have her near.

Shortly after we had moved to Panaca a school teacher and an administrator stopped by one evening and asked GROVER if he would file to run for the Lincoln County School Board. The Panaca board member had decided not to run for re-election. GROVER felt he was sufficiently involved already in the county. He was the Chairman of the RAD (Rural Area Development) or as it was later known, the LAD (Lincoln Area Development.) Working with the Agricultural Extension Agent, Clair Christensen, and vice-chairman Lester Mathews, they were able to do many projects, including the Eagle Valley Dam. GROVER was also the stake Sunday school superintendent in our L.D.S. Uvada Stake, which included Enterprise, Utah. He was also involved in the leadership of the Rotary Club in Caliente with its many projects.

Highly concerned for our children's education, I told them I would run for the school board. They agreed. No one filed to run against me, nor in any future elections, which came every two or four years. There were five board members. I was the only woman for many years on the board; later, there were two of us. We later had seven children attending school in our district at the same time.

By the summer of 1966 we began to build the east wing on our home, including all the patios, driveway, fence and tennis court, but the swimming pool and carport building would have to wait. Nelson Bleak of Pioche and his adopted son, Francisco Escobedo, did the building and subcontracting for us. It was a major project, and, as we were warned by our banker, cost twice as much as we projected. Our plans included many custom-built cabinets in the living room, dining room, kitchen, family room, and laundry, plus shelves for our library—all of which we did in walnut and birch. It was the spring of 1967 before it was completed. We loved the fireplace and flagstone from the Star Dust Mine near Baker, Nevada. One large stone was shaped like the State of Nevada. Governor Paul Laxalt was quick to point it out, when he visited our home later.

Lincoln County had Senator Floyd Lamb (D) of Alamo and two assemblymen, Cyril Bastion (D) of Caliente, and Nelson Bleak (R) of Pioche, when we arrived in the county. They were able to get the Nevada Girls Training Center for the delinquent girls of Nevada built in a canyon near Caliente in the early 1960s. With reapportionment forced on the states of our country by the legislation of the Supreme Court in 1964, Lincoln County was combined with White Pine County to the north. White Pine County included Ely, McGill, Ruth, Lund, and some smaller towns. The votes in White Pine County were five times as great as our votes in Lincoln County.

Senator Floyd Lamb quickly moved his residence to Clark County (Las Vegas) when reapportionment came and was reelected from there. Our two assemblymen never even bothered to file. After the 1964 elections, Lincoln County was totally dependent on White Pine legislators, who cared little about Lincoln's economic problems. The people of both counties were mostly registered as Democrats (4 to 1), because of the strong mining labor unions.

By the end of the 1965 legislature, Nevada had approved the shorter highway between Ely and Las Vegas that would totally bypass the three communities of Pioche, Panaca, and Caliente. In addition, the Union Pacific Railroad had closed their roundhouse and depot which cut back considerably on their railroad employees in Caliente. Our only medical doctor in the county was in Caliente, and he was considering retirement. A replacement seemed impossible.

The legislature was planning to move the Nevada Girls Training Center to Henderson, because they claimed our medical facilities were inadequate. The mines in Pioche had been unable to compete with foreign mines and still were mostly closed. Their hard-rock miners were driving to the Nevada Nuclear Test Site where underground testing was proceeding—rocking our homes with their explosions. We had kept our Pioche drugstore open, while over 100 other businesses in Pioche had closed their doors. Without a medical doctor, the Pioche Pharmacy was struggling—in fact, I received no salary and our loss was still over $4,000 the past year. The Secretary of the Nevada State Pharmacy Board wanted a pharmacist on duty every hour we were open, unless we did a major construction that would isolate and secure the whole pharmacy department.

In 1967, with reapportionment having almost destroyed the county economy, GROVER, as rural development chairman, wanted me to write an article decrying the problems this Supreme Court decision was creating in large land areas, like our own, with small populations. We later decided with our ten children, our share of the county by population was forty-five square miles. I started on the project; but always the thought kept nagging at me that no one had even tried to be elected from our county after reapportionment. The White Pine Democrats were not sympathetic to our plight—they held all the offices already. The odds for a Lincoln County Republican to win the election were 20 to 1, but we really didn't know it couldn't be done.

With our home building debt and the county economy escalating on a downward slide, GROVER and I determined that there was no way we could keep the Pioche Pharmacy open—working a nine hours daily schedule. We set the date for closing, but hadn't announced our decision publicly.

Republican Governor Paul Laxalt came to Lincoln County. GROVER attended the meeting. Paul was working for Republican control of the State Senate. He thought that if we could get the Democratic Lincoln County to support White Pine's Republican senate candidate, they would support a Lincoln County Republican for one of the two seats in the State Assembly. GROVER went after our former Republican Assemblyman, Nelson Bleak; he refused. On the day before the filing deadline (in Carson City, because of the late date) Grover had an offer from county commissioner Chet Oxborrow to fly Nelson Bleak to Carson City, if GROVER could talk him into it. Stopping by his home that evening after work, he found only his wife Martha. Her answer was quick and forceful,

> "Listen here, GROVER SWALLOW, if you want someone to run for the legislature that bad, you do it yourself; but leave my husband alone!"

That evening we decided he would do just that, and the next morning he flew to Carson City. The Secretary of State let him file. He was registered "Non-partisan;" but the Secretary said fine; he wasn't registered Democrat. So that was the how and why of his run for the Nevada State Legislature. We were in the process of closing the drugstore in Pioche, and I could then work the Caliente Pharmacy—and be his campaign manager, wife, and mother of our children. It was the middle of July. There would be no primary election for him as only two Republicans had filed. The Democrats had many contenders.

Unfortunately, when the announcement was made locally that we were closing the Pioche Pharmacy, it was the same day that GROVER made his last-minute decision and flew to Carson City to file for the office of assemblyman on the last hour of the last day. Because the two events were announced the same day, many people in Pioche believed that he had decided to close the store so he could run for the assembly. Some resented this.

Our school district was under-funded by our Nevada State allotment and unable to afford the necessary teachers. Our high school gym and auditorium in Panaca had been condemned along with several of our elementary schools. Plans were made by our superintendent to join Lincoln County School District with Clark County School District (Las Vegas). William (Bill) Orr of Pioche and I were chosen to be the new members of the Clark County School Board by our school administrators with the approval of our school board. This would make eleven members on the Clark County board.

Bill and I went with our superintendent to a meeting with their superintendent at a restaurant in the Star Dust Hotel and Casino. The plan at that time was to build us a new large combined school facility (K through 12). Their superintendent showed us a quick drawing he had made. The local elementary schools would be closed, and the children would all be bussed, probably including Alamo—at first. The new facility would include a school swimming pool, where swimming would be taught, and our teachers and administrators would be paid the larger salaries of the Clark County District. Our superintendent would represent Lincoln County and assist their superintendent. Both superintendents were very positive, and in later meetings with their school board, I found them to be very gracious and anxious to help.

The real problem began when the people of the two counties became aware of these plans. The Lincoln County residents were the first to know. The news swept the county faster than a wildfire, and with almost as much heat. Our county commissioners quickly staged an informal ballot poll to give the people a chance to vote on the proposed school consolidation, which was defeated by a landslide. Citizens were highly concerned about a possible future consolidation of the two counties and our loss of independence, among other reasons. Clark County was slower to know about the plan; but when their newspapers became aware of it, the last days of November, they blasted it with words of dynamite. Lincoln County was not going to get any of their money.

During August, GROVER added a new item to his own election platform. The national committee favoring abortions on demand had chosen Nevada as their first line of attack—believing Nevada to be the most likely of all the states in the union to allow legalized abortions. Hundreds of thousands of dollars were being spent in the state. Their literature was flooding the mailboxes, and money was going into the pockets of willing would-be legislators.

GROVER and I never equivocated. Every campaign message he gave included his strong stand against the issue. He also spoke strongly for a medical school in Reno. Both White Pine and Lincoln Counties needed doctors. There wasn't a medical school in the state, and Howard Hughes had volunteered a large sum of money, if they would approve one in Reno during the next session. Las Vegas opposed the Reno location. They wanted the medical school, but weren't ready—nor would HH agree to help them.

In early August we attended a "Republican Skull Session" in Carson City with Governor Paul Laxalt. My heart turned a flip-flop when the group predicted that it would take at least $5,000 to elect an assemblyman. We were then budgeted for $500. Asking for money was not in our game. We got signs, stamps, and postcards. We soon decided door-to-door would be the best way. Grover was ready for that on the 6th of September, after the primaries had ended.

That day I worked the Caliente Pharmacy. Arriving home very tired, I was taking off my jacket when the deputy sheriff rang the doorbell. He carefully told me about the school bus wreck. Our two oldest daughters were in the eastbound bus that was taking the pep band to their first football game of the season. One of the young boys had been killed on impact; our daughters were among the many that had been hospitalized. He suggested I call the high school principal, Neldon Mathews, at the Cedar City Hospital for more details. Afterwards, I tried to call GROVER; but he wasn't at the motel in Ely. He had gone out for a hamburger. I asked our telephone operator to give him a careful message as soon as he returned, and left for Cedar City—there were no cell phones then. Our son, TOM, a student at Brigham Young University, was home until the next Tuesday. He accompanied me on that desolate 80-mile-drive with Faye Lee, whose daughter Nancy was not expected to live until morning and her father-in-law, Elwood Lee.

BUS WRECK

About 12 miles out from Cedar City we passed the bus and the big tanker that lay in the gutter on the side of the highway. In our dusky head lights, the eerie school bus looked like a great giant turtle lying on its shell with its feet in the air. No one was there. At the hospital parking lot, a large group of well-wishers greeted us; but Neldon grabbed Faye in one arm and me in the other and whisked us into the hospital, past the crowded lobby with reporters and lawyers, and into the intensive care unit of the hospital, where Faye's daughter, Nancy, and my younger daughter, BROOKIE CAY, had been placed. My son, TOM, followed; but the sight and sounds in intensive care were worse than my usually steady son was prepared for. He quickly left and found his other sister, DANA, whose less dramatic head scalping had already been treated.

GROVER drove with a companion from Ely at a speed that even Nevada's "no speed limit" might have questioned. They arrived after midnight. The telephone operator had not been kind to him. Instead of softening the blow, she had exaggerated the situation and told him that one of his daughters was not expected to live until morning. The sweet goodness, kindness, and blessings, however, we received from everyone, especially including God, through this period were more numerous than can be told in this history. The hospital had just completed an experimental emergency trial-run just a few days before, and they were prepared and did an excellent job with the 24 students, many quite severely injured. All of the young students pulled through—for which we are eternally grateful. Dr. David Brown later stated that they would have saved the young boy who was killed during the crash, if he had lived to get there.

The Democratic primary election had been quite brutal, and GROVER was able to enlist the help of one of the Ely candidates that had lost out, Burrell Bybee. His support was very helpful. The Ely business district, in general, supported GROVER; his strong stand against abortion gave him support from members of the various churches. There were four candidates on the ballot and each voter could vote for two. In November, GROVER's total votes gave him second place and a seat in the Nevada Assembly.

Election night was very interesting. We found out around 8:30 P.M. that he had won. Alone at home, we watched our Las Vegas television stations— there was nothing about our district. None of our local friends knew or cared enough to call us, or suggest a celebration. Around ten that evening, GROVER got a call from one of his friends from White Pine County who had car trouble and needed help. It was a long drive—over 100 miles away through the desert; but he went. He hadn't returned when Lieutenant Governor Ed Fike called from Carson City around midnight. Ed was very excited and couldn't believe that GROVER had won. This would give the Republicans the majority in the Assembly—something that hadn't happened in the last forty years. The news was electric; but Las Vegas T.V. was not plugged in and was still in the dark.

Shortly after, a reporter from a Reno newspaper called. He wanted verification, also. He started asking me questions. Was I going with him to Carson City? What legislation was he preparing? All at once, I realized that GROVER was expected to do something about all those campaign promises— legislative bills, twenty unknown senators, thirty-nine unknown assemblymen—only weeks away? Where would he stay? What would he do? I had no answers. A heavy burden slithered through my mind, squashing the elation that had been so vibrant before. The Reno paper called GROVER the "sleeper of the election." The Las Vegas papers were too late or too embarrassed to report anything more than statistics. Another assemblyman from Reno was added to the Republican majority before morning—they reported that.

The next seven months were one of the most intensive educations of a lifetime. It began with the Republican caucus at the Dunes Hotel and Casino in Las Vegas. The Republicans would now become the chairmen of all the committees—a first for all of them. Many of the wives of the male assemblymen met to get acquainted in the rather elaborate suite of one of the more established assemblymen. Spouses were not invited to the caucus; neither was the press— nor the Democrats. They needed a speaker, a majority leader, a whip, and all the chairmen, vice-chairmen, and committee members. It was tense—votes were being collected and traded for positions. GROVER wanted to be on the committees for Health and Welfare, and Education. What else?—he wasn't sure. No one particularly wanted the Elections Committee, so he was given Chairman of Elections, Vice-chairman of Health and Welfare, and a member of Education.

He found friends and helps beyond his belief. I arranged to be at the session the first two weeks, as a member of our county school board—we needed money. I met with the dynamic Senate Chairman of Education (Democrat Senator Carl F. Dodge, Churchill-Lyon District) and the State Superintendent of Schools, while GROVER was busy in his own committee meetings. With the help of Assemblyman Frank Young, I was able to meet with the Ways and Means Committee, who finally agreed to charter a bus for the whole nine member committee to Lincoln County, where they visited the schools and spoke with our superintendent of schools and the superintendent of the Nevada Girls Training Center. I prepared, with community help, a buffet luncheon for them at our home, since we had no restaurants in Panaca.

When the session ended, we had increased the per pupil money significantly for our county schools and other small school districts throughout the state; the Nevada Girl's Training Center would stay in Caliente; Reno would get their medical school. Joe Wilkin, who built our playground would later go to the new medical school in Reno and return to Lincoln County as our medical doctor. His brother Bruce also attended and went to Ely to practice. Replacing Dr. Joe Wilkin, after his death, was Dr. Pluncket, one of the first University of Nevada medical students. We still think of the University of Nevada's medical school as ours, as GROVER was the much-fought-for swing-vote in the Nevada Assembly that allowed its original construction and funding. When he announced to the southern caucus that he was voting for the bill that would fund it in Reno, a Clark County assemblyman angrily told him, "Listen here, GROVER SWALLOW, this isn't a Sunday school class." Without his vote, it would not have happened. In his Elections Committee, they lowered the voting-age from 21 to 18-years-old.

As vice-chairman of the Health and Welfare Committee, GROVER had spearheaded the hoped-for defeat of AB 229—the item of greatest interest, nationally and statewide. Had it passed both houses, Nevada would have been the first state in the nation to legalize abortions. GROVER had tried to kill the bill in committee, never letting it reach the floor of the Assembly for vote. Assemblyman Woodrow Wilson was chairman of this committee. Wilson, originally from the deep south of Alabama, was said at that time to be the first African American to be elected to a state legislature in the United States. We knew him quite well, as Frank Young, "Woody," with my husband, had rented a three-bedroom house together for the length of the legislative session. He told

GROVER, as the swing vote, was invited to stand with this group of legislators and University of Nevada administrators for Governor Laxalt's signing to give Nevada a Medical School. Standing behind GROVER is the University of Nevada's Comptroller Neil Humphrey. He was an old friend from our college days at Idaho State. He gave us this (below) photographic memory of our old days as waiters and dishwashers in the Graveley Hall dining area. His wife, Mary Pat Smith is standing next to me with Neil and GROVER on each end. Nearly all the men were veterans of World War II.

us how he had been kicked out of most of the Las Vegas hotels and casinos when, as a member of the NAACP, they had challenged the casino bosses on their rights as black people for equal admission with white people. He laughed as he told us about a time he had been in a restaurant and a young white girl had come up and touched his arm and then looked at her finger to see if the black came off. Some of the more militant from Las Vegas West Side, considered him an "Uncle Tom," and he was under great pressure to allow AB 229 to be voted on by the whole Assembly.

I was present at the committee meeting that day. My nine-year-old son, BRUCE, came with me. The Committee surrounded the long table with Assemblyman Wilson at the head. Two reporters were seated on the chairs next to us. Three women sat behind the Assembly women on the other side. It was a small committee room; but there were still a few vacant chairs.

It was well known that the seven-member committee was divided, half the members would vote strongly in favor of the bill, and half would vote with equal passion to kill it. The deciding vote would be made by the chairman, Woodrow Wilson, who had promised to vote with the dissenters. AB 229 was the only item on the agenda that day. The tension within the group was supercharged as the vote was taken. All had declined discussion. It was tied. The chairman would have to decide.

Wilson stood up. His hand was slightly shaky. With carefully chosen words he stated he had decided, after talking with his people at home, to let the vote proceed to the whole assembly, although at that point, he would vote against it. The committee meeting was quickly closed, and without a word the betrayed assemblymen rushed from the room—their emotions too great to remain seated. The members of the press were equally anxious to leave. The exuberant winners followed close behind—hoping to be interviewed by the press.

Still seated, while Wilson stood silently alone at the head of the table, I decided to introduce my son to him. We had come in late the night before and the assemblymen had left before we awakened. BRUCE solemnly shook his hand, and then to my chagrin, our son turned his hand over and looked at it. GROVER had come back into the room by then. "Woody" broke into a laugh and drawled with his deep southern accent, "What I tell you!" All the strain of the previous moments had evaporated. GROVER gave "Woody" a hug. The conversation changed, and AB 229 would go to the floor of the Assembly.

On the eightieth day of the Fifty-fifth Session of the Nevada Legislature, Carson City, (Wednesday) 9 Apr 1969, AB 229 was called to the floor of the Assembly. It had been delayed two days, because Eileen Brookman, who was one of the sponsors of the bill, was under such great tension that first scheduled day that she fainted and was rushed from the floor. The Assembly extended her the courtesy and delayed action until she could be present.

The following is from the Legislative Journal, April 9th. The gallery was filled.

"Assembly called to order at 8:40 a.m. Mr. Speaker presiding.

"Roll called.

"All present.

"Prayer by the Chaplain, Father Robert G. Pumphrey.

"Pledge of Allegiance to the Flag."

The proceedings on the floor continued with the usual procedures of the day. Assemblymen slipped out to attend committee meetings, etc. — Then

"Mrs. Frazzini moved a call of the Assembly.

"Motion carried.

"Time, 9:56 a.m.

"Mr. Speaker directed the Sergeant at Arms to close the doors.

"Roll called.

"All present except Messrs. [Harry] Reid and Wilson.

"Mr. Speaker directed the Sergeant at Arms to bring in the absent members.

"Roll called.

"All present.

"General File and Third Reading

"Assembly Bill No. 229.

"Bill read third time.

"Remarks by Mr. Torvinen, Mrs. Frazzini, Messrs. Dini, Fry, Frank Young, Bryan Hafen, Schouweiler, and Wood."

The remarks of Mr. Dini, Frank Young, and Wood were requested to be entered in the Journal. Some were quite long; but they were included.

"Miss Foote, Messrs. Bryan, and Lingenfelter moved the previous question.

"Motion lost.

"Remarks by Messrs. Lowman, Homer, SWALLOW, Hilbrecht, and Mrs. Brookman."

The remarks of Mr. Lowman, SWALLOW, and Hilbrecht were requested to be entered in the Journal. Mr. SWALLOW's remarks, who wanted to speak short and near the end, were (partially) recorded as follows:

"The dignity of a human individual has never been based on physical surroundings—never. Most of our great leaders tried to prove this—Ghandi, Christ, Washington, Lincoln and so forth. The worth of an individual has never been based on material wealth. Most of our laws pertaining to abortion have been based upon the material or social desires of the individual or the immediate physical needs of the mother. Now, I know many people through my profession who may not wish they were pregnant, but, a few months later, would give their very lives for that little child. I also know many disabled and older people who wish they had more children when they were younger. I know many people who are mighty glad their mothers did not have an abortion. I am mighty glad my mother did not have an abortion. And, I would like to conclude today by asking you if you aren't just a little happy that your mothers did not have abortions?" . . .

"Messrs. Lingenfelter, Bryan, and Fry moved the previous question.

"Motion carried.

"The question being on the passage of Assembly Bill No. 229.

"Roll call on Assembly Bill No. 229:

"Yeas — 20.

"Nays — Ashworth, Bowler, Branch, Capurro, Close, Dini, Espinoza, Getto, Bryan Hafen, Tim Hafen, Howard, Lowman, May, Prince, SWALLOW, Tyson, Viani, Wilson — 18.

"Absent — None.

"Not voting — Smith, Webb — 2.

"Assembly Bill No. 229 having failed to receive a constitutional majority, Mr. Speaker declared it lost."

The journal does not record that after the first roll call and before the tally was given one assemblyman rose to his feet and changed his vote from yea to nay. He explained that he had promised in his campaign to vote "Yea," but having done so, as promised, he now wanted it to be changed to "Nay." He later told GROVER he changed it because of his speech. Another explained that he had switched his to not voting.

A Reno paper, the following day, printed a *Letter to the Editor*, signed by a nurse of one of their medical facilities who stated (from my memory),

"Mr. SWALLOW said he was glad his mother didn't have an abortion, but I say that it would have been better for the State of Nevada, if she had."

GROVER was pleased with this negative recognition, as well as the many favorable commendations he received.

Of course, there were many other legislative bills: taxation; wages for the state employees; money for the school districts (the teacher's union was the most demanding.) GROVER was able to get the Lincoln County Eagle Valley Dam designated as a State Park and some funds allocated; dog racing was not allowed within the state; a heavy penalty was placed on the vast amounts of pornographic materials that were being sent through the mails, mostly unsolicited; help was given to the Nevada pharmacists and their board to control illicit drugs; a bill was killed that would have allowed chiropractors to prescribe prescription drugs; another patrolman was assigned to the Alamo area; Martin Luther King Day was added to the state holidays, and of the thousands of bills accepted or rejected—Freshmen Democrat Assemblymen Harry Reid and Richard Bryon presented the majority. The small $60 daily salaries the Assemblymen were given ended after the sixtieth day—after that they only received the per-diem expense addition. The biannual session (held only every two years) continued on through the 95th day.

One bill of small interest to anyone but the legislators was a bill for a special license plate for their automobiles that would read ASSEMBLY or SENATE, numbered 1 to 40 in the assembly, starting with the earliest elected legislator. GROVER was going to vote against it; but Woody argued with him and reminded him, "That's all you get!" He got number 38; the second term, it was 28—helpful at times—but the best part—he had been able to aid in the passage or defeat of those bills that gave him 100% on his campaign promises.

At a farewell Republican brunch with Governor Paul Laxalt, Assemblyman Frank Young of Las Vegas, with humor, nominated me [BROOKIE] as the best lobbyist of the session. It was quickly seconded and carried with a strong voice vote. It was great to find so many solid friends—if only for that brief moment.

An exciting honor was his receiving the coveted A. H. Robbins *Bowl of Hygeia Award for Outstanding Community Services in Pharmacy*, on the 26th of September, 1970. One was given each year to a pharmacist from each state—chosen by the various state pharmacy associations. Part of the award included a trip for two to the A. H. Robbins Pharmaceutical Company in Richmond, Virginia, and included a tour of their facilities and a one-day jaunt down to Williamsburg with a reception in the evening at the Valentine Museum in Richmond. The fifty recipients were shown on a page of Time Magazine. Today, 2008, the award is still given, without the trip, by a larger pharmaceutical company that swallowed many of the smaller ones.

One honor (?), which our children laugh at, is a plaque presented to him for being a *Distinguished Visitor of the Nevada Nuclear Test Site*. During World War II, the atom bomb was developed with utmost secrecy in Los Alamos, New Mexico. Then, when it appeared to be successful, the pilot and crew were trained in the desolate, top secret area of the salt flats near Wendover, Utah—on the east border of Nevada. When the bomb was dropped from the *Enola Gay* over Japan, GROVER's brother CHAD was part of her maintenance crew on the island of Tinian, near Guam, that loaded the deadly bomb—first for Hiroshima, and then when the Japanese still didn't surrender, several days later another one for Nagasaki. After the war ended, the hydrogen bomb was tested on Bikini Island in the Pacific Ocean. Additional nuclear testing was continued and the

Nevada Nuclear Test Site was chosen northwest of Las Vegas on the Lincoln/ Nye county border at a site about 100 miles south-southwest of Pioche. The tests above-ground began on 21 Jan 1951, with the supposed last one visually exploded 31 Oct 1958. There were a few later in 1962. Underground explosions that swayed the hanging lamps and clothes in the closets continued many more years.

At first, the danger of the radiation dropping from the cloud was not recognized, and JERRY OLSON (Condie) remembers that her whole school class went outside to watch it pass over our communities. When we bought our original home in Panaca, there were small cracks in the ceiling plaster of the kitchen—said to be from the early shock waves of the first bombs. They learned to nearly control these. When the last underground bomb was exploded in the 1990s, I was awakened by the earthquake it created, which occurred at 6:00 A.M. It felt very similar to the time I was awakened around 4:00 A.M. by the major earthquake that had occurred near the entrance of Zion National Park several months before—also over a 100 miles away.

When we arrived in Pioche in 1957, they were still testing above ground and then concerned about possible radiation. We were required to wear a small metal, clipped to our uniforms. The government agents would collect these every month to test for radiation. There was an old Geiger counter in the drugstore basement. It was used only as a secret toy by our children. If radiation was collected on our metal badges, the agents would never admit it. GROVER and I watched as many of our friends developed cancer and died. Those who worked at the test site appeared to be more numerous. We always felt there was a relationship—long before the lawsuits started.

The above-ground tests were scheduled (in 1957) when the wind was from the south, away from Las Vegas. The cloud remained quite uniform in size and could be traced. It moved north; then it would turn to the east with the westerly winds and move over the desert by Tooele, Utah. Many of their sheep died. Strangely, the cloud would usually turn again and move southward, spreading its radiation fall-out over the cities of southern Utah. The high number of leukemia cases in young "downwind" victims alerted the people and government to the danger.

This deadly mushroom grew in Nevada Monday, the fifth and mightiest of the atom blasts. | AEC officials refused to comment on the line of searing fire running across top.

—Associated Press Wirephoto

Erupts Twin Fireballs

Mightiest Blast of Series
Flares in Nevada Desert

Top Scientists
Report to Ike,
Bomb 'Clean'

WASHINGTON, June 24,

ATOMIC BOMB BLAST IN THE NEVADA DESERT 25 JUNE 1957

While the sun crept over the horizon in the east and silhouetted our older children in our Plymouth station wagon, the bomb blast brought a far greater light in the western sky. Our little Brownie camera missed the details of the NUCLEAR CLOUD; but it was quite visible to the naked eye (with sunglasses) from the upper picnic site of Cathedral Gorge—five highway miles above Panaca, Nevada.

Today, much of the air flight above our county is still restricted. Many days, pilots in their fighters and bombers from Nellis and Hill Field Air Force Bases learn war maneuvers and refueling throughout the day and night. Sonic booms are forbidden; but we still get them at times. Strange looking foreign planes are tested. Some days we feel like a war zone, when the planes dive close. Still in the U.S. Congress is a much-debated bill to make Yucca Mountain (in Lincoln and Nye Counties) a burial ground, as a depository for the nuclear waste of the nation's nuclear power plants. There is Groom Lake, surrounded by armed guards. However, the "Stars at Night, are Deep and Bright," and our air is not polluted by hundreds of thousands of automobiles and trucks, or the continual landings of passenger jet planes.

Throughout the decade of our political involvement in county and state, it became very evident that you can't please all of the people, all of the time—especially when vile lies are deliberately planted by opponents to destroy you, if they can—not only politically, but economically. GROVER and I and our business were audited or inspected by every state agency; and then came a phone call from the IRS regarding a small issue. We, on a few occasions, woke up to find eggs splattered on our front door, or on the windshield of one of our cars. I could be walking down the street and observe former friends turning and walking the other way, or crossing the road to avoid me. The local newspaper printed disparaging letters to the editor—sometimes editorials. Cottage meetings were held in some homes to discourage voters from supporting GROVER in his election. A rattlesnake in his wood box became a threat to a vocal supporter. I visited with our local district attorney on some school board issues in the lower mid-70s, and he commented,

> "BROOKIE, you have a very good case to sue for slander, and, if you will let me, I will take your case and not charge you anything. You could definitely win! I have information that you are totally unaware of."

I wouldn't do that, but I was comforted by his offer.

GROVER was re-elected to the Nevada Assembly in 1970, representing Lincoln/White Pine Counties. The campaign was not as frightening, nor was his winning as unexpected, but the opposition was better organized. The former Democrat Lincoln County Senator Lamb that had moved his residence to Clark County after reapportionment (1964) and had been re-elected as one of their senators, was the chairman of the powerful Senate finance committee. Although he believed GROVER's chance to win in 1968 as very negligible, he still made a trip a few days before the election through the county scaring bank employees in Pioche with the lie that GROVER was planning to close their bank, like he had closed his drugstore. In the Alamo area, he lied saying GROVER was opposed to their forthcoming and desired White River Road, which his committee had already approved and passed the previous term, but on our side of the county he gave the opposite lie—GROVER favored its construction and had sold himself out to the interests of the Ely Republican businessmen. Fortunately, the majority of the people knew GROVER and trusted him. The election in 1970 was meaner and more personal and included personal economic threats. Bribes were not offered to GROVER. His reputation for honesty forewarned them.

Republican Governor Paul Laxalt campaigned for the U. S. Senate through our county, staying at the home of one of our commissioners. He requested that the window blinds be closed. There had been serious threats on the Governor's life. Paul Laxalt became our U.S. Senator from Nevada that year. When Ronald Reagan ran for president of the United States, Senator Laxalt was the Republican National Chairman, and Reagan's right-arm man in the senate. Their close relationship continued through Reagan's administration.

About two weeks before the November election in 1970, our L.D.S. Uvada Stake was reorganized in Enterprise, Utah. Apostle Mark E. Peterson was the presiding authority. In the past, the stake president had always been from Enterprise; this time Caliente's bishop, Wesley Holt, was called as the stake president; Lyle Jones of Enterprise was his first counselor, and GROVER, who had been a high councilman for several years, was called as his second counselor. Elmer Tibbetts was the stake clerk, and Lester Mathews was executive secretary.

When GROVER was set apart by Apostle Peterson, he blessed him in his political travels as well as his church calling—adding a special blessing for his family at home. Winning his second election, GROVER would continue to drive home the four-hundred-and-fifty miles from Carson City every weekend. He had several close calls, including one very scary one on the way to Enterprise with other members of the presidency; but he always arrived safely.

At home with the children, an interesting thing happened. One of our nearby neighbors had a large German shepherd. He was so fierce that GROVER would not deliver prescriptions to the owner's home, unless she would lock-up her dog. Strangely, while GROVER was in Carson City, every night that dog would lay on my partially open cement patio by the sliding doors to our bedroom. The drapes were never pulled shut by this patio, as the view was completely private. He would stretch out his long body in front of those doors and peacefully look at me. By morning he was gone. When GROVER was there on weekends, he never came, and after the legislature ended, he never came back. It was a comfort to me to see him there.

Because of the 1970 census and the Supreme Court's earlier decision, the 1971 legislature was highly involved in a new reapportionment of the legislative districts throughout the state. Our Lincoln/White Pine District would get only one assemblyman, and the senate district would have to be much larger, because of the rapid growth in the size of Las Vegas. The popular Democrat Assemblyman Ross Prince from Ely, had always received more votes than GROVER, and he had no desire to run for the Senate seat. It was obvious that if GROVER stayed in the legislature, he would need to run for the Senate, so the boundaries of that new district were very important to him. Working with Clark County Assemblyman Frank Young, they drew a plan that passed in the Assembly and included the outlaying areas of Clark County in this Senate District—making it a southeastern district; however, the Senate had their own plan, which eventually passed both legislative branches. Clark County added their new Senators to their own boundaries. The Lincoln/White Pine District would include the broad southern expanse of Esmeralda, Lincoln, Mineral, Nye, and White Pine Counties, representing about one-third of the land area of the whole state. Today, Las Vegas has continued its rapid growth. It now controls the whole state of Nevada—the result of majority rule and Supreme Court legislation.

The 1971 abortion bill was again the hottest debated issue in the Assembly. GROVER, in the Health and Welfare Committee, spearheaded the opposition; but this time it barely passed the Assembly. The Senate, however, was prepared by Senator Jim Gibson, Democrat, an L.D.S. stake president and senator from Henderson, Nevada. When the Bill moved into the Senate, it was killed before it went to committee. The twenty senators were not desirous of allowing the same heat the Assembly had experienced into their chambers. Once more the notorious "Sin State" had rejected becoming the first State in the Union to embrace abortions—other states took the dubious honor.

The Republican Convention of 1972 was held in Elko, Nevada. Assembly woman Mary Frazzini of Clark County, who had authored the abortion bills, had been chosen as chairman of the Republican platform committee. Feeling strongly that the abortion issue would be placed on the platform, GROVER tried to get on her committee—total unequivocal rejection. The Lincoln County Republicans were so few in numbers that we had only one delegate that could be appointed; but this appointment could be split—allowing a half-vote for two delegates. GROVER and I managed to be appointed and drove to Elko. During this long five-hour drive, we brainstormed what could be done about the abortion issue—other issues were of small consequence. We knew that a direct attack on the issue would not do. We needed a new approach—but what?

Sitting in our own little delegate group of two and surrounded by the hundreds of unknown delegates, we still wondered, "What?" As we had strongly suspected, the Republican support for allowing abortions within our state was on the platform list to be approved. GROVER was determined to speak on the issue when the time came. He wanted to be the last speaker, so he remained in his seat as the long line quickly formed. We listened to the heart-rending appeals of many of the delegates—both pro and con. As we sat there, a new thought popped into my head. I whispered it to GROVER. He quickly wrote it in his notebook and shortly after rose to his feet to take his place at the end of the much shorter line.

He began with the words I had whispered to him, "Why saddle ourselves with an issue that could defeat some candidates?" He added a few more sentences of his own about letting each candidate decide for himself, not even stating his own position on the issue. The convention chairman took the stand immediately after he left the podium and called for the question. A quick motion was made from the audience to delete the abortion proposal. Nine people immediately stood to second it. A voice vote was called by the chairman. The "Ayes!" far overpowered the "Nays!" The proposal was struck from the platform. It all happened so rapidly that GROVER was still walking toward our bench. As we left the Convention Hall, three women were walking on the sidewalk toward us. Mary Frazzini was in the center. Seeing us approach, the unhappy women deliberately turned as a unit in their tracks and escaped. The following day, small headlines on the lower front page of one Las Vegas newspaper read, "Republicans Reject Abortion Proposal." The article's lead statement quoted Assemblyman SWALLOW's above words.

GROVER had no problem winning the Republican primary election for the Senate. He was given a beautiful front page write-up with his picture in the Ely Times. In Lincoln County, his fund-raising dinner was well attended; and the Nevada Attorney General flew in from Reno in a Lear jet to be our main speaker.

Arriving just shortly before the dinner, I picked him up at our Panaca Airport to take him the 15 miles to Caliente. As I carefully observed the speed-limit, 55 mph, he instructed me to speed up to at least 80 mph. If anyone dared stop us, he felt sure he could handle the situation. Everything appeared positive for GROVER's November election.

GROVER's first hint of a major problem came quite soon. The Ely Times appeared to have turned against him in their write-ups. He quizzed them directly, and he was told it was our Democrat Governor Mike O'Callahan who had issued them the ultimatum. We were surprised. When GROVER's second term as assemblyman had ended; he had stepped into the Governor's office to tell him, "Goodbye." Mike was very friendly. He thanked GROVER for his support on his welfare bill, and further told him that he had been more help to him throughout the session than many of his own party. He extended his hand in friendship, stating that his office would always be open to him, if he needed help. Then additional phone calls were made into Lincoln County, with the subtle suggestion that state positions could be lost. Once more, we were told it was the governor that called. What had happened? And what was happening in the other three counties? We didn't know, but continued on positively with the campaign and GROVER's door-to-door campaign. We later learned that deliberate lies were told to the governor that would not only hurt GROVER and me, but also the economy of our county.

Our pharmacist friend and his wife flew in from Tonopah the evening of the election. They felt sure GROVER would win, and they wanted to be there for the celebration. It was a long night. Lincoln and White Pine Counties were strong in their support and their votes came in early; but GROVER was about 100 votes short when the final votes were tallied for the whole district of around 22,000 voters. Democrat Rick Blakemore of Tonopah would be our new Senator. We liked Rick. He had promised to do about everything GROVER had wanted to accomplish including a negative vote on NOW, but, of course, we were greatly disappointed—it's more fun to win. Many Republicans lost their seats that fall. Watergate had ended with a fury, and the Democrats now controlled the Assembly, as well as the Senate.

I believe it was in February 1974 that Commander Zell Lowman, former

Republican Majority Leader in the Assembly asked GROVER and I to go on a trip to the Naval Academy at Annapolis, Maryland, to make him a Blue and Gold Affiliate. He was to bring the high school principals and district administrator with him. We would tour the facilities and then promote the academy to our exceptional students, especially football stars with high grades. We left Nellis airforce base by Las Vegas in the colonel's four prop troop plane, no chairs, with about 30 others and landed at Andrews Air force Base in Washington D.C.

LCHS principal Elmer Tibbetts, PVHS principal Gerald Wilson, vice-superintendent
Lorell Bleak, Commander Zell Lowman, GROVER, school board president BROOKIE, and
plebe escort Rollins, the son of Commander Jack Rollins who grew up in Pioche, Nevada.
His helicopter with crew was shot down early in the Viet Nam war—his back broken in four places.
The Viet Cong stripped them of all clothing, put them in a metal cage in a public square, where they
were spit on, until they were moved to a damp floorless room with mucky food and water and
no bathroom facilities—no medical attention was given to his back for years.
He was released after the war and was then on a speaking tour across the nation.

Two years later, a group from Ely approached GROVER, again. They wanted him to run for the Assembly—Ross Prince was no longer a candidate. We were both skeptical. With only one assemblyman, would White Pine give up their only legislative representative? GROVER agreed to try. It was close, but he lost.

On my last trip to Carson City in 1975—still the legislative representative of our school board—I sat in the gallery for the first time. [Wives could sit next to their Assemblymen husbands.] One of the Assemblymen recognized me and introduced me from the floor, adding I was the wife of their former Assemblyman GROVER SWALLOW. The whole Assembly rose to their feet and clapped. Going towards the committee room I was first greeted by Democrat Senator Blakemore, who seriously wanted to know if he could do anything more for Lincoln County. A former Lincoln County principal next greeted me graciously and introduced me to his many students from another county, whom he had brought with him to witness the legislature in action. They were going to the same committee meeting I was. Alone, I continued on, and then Democrat Senator Dodge, still the Senate Chairman of Education, stepped into the hall and proceeded towards me. Grabbing my hand, he said it had been awhile since he had seen me. I told him he was doing a good job for our district, or I'd have been there. He looked at me kindly for a moment and then stated,

"I am convinced that if there is anything you want, you will get it."

With a warm smile, he moved on. I had not expected the compliment, but I also knew that he knew I would only want to be fair—no special favors.

~ 49 ~

A GLIMPSE OF ETERNITY—
THE HANDSHAKE

When GROVER and I lived in Preston, Idaho (1951–1953), we had our first new car, a fabulous 1950 fishtail light green Pontiac. The Pontiac had sold for a little over $1,800, and in those days it was necessary to have 1/3 down before a car could be purchased. We had saved carefully for the $600. The Logan Temple was 25 miles from Preston, and we would try to go one evening a week to the temple. We would also use our new mobility to collect genealogy from my mother's sister, aunt PEARL, who lived in Logan, and also from the Logan Genealogy Library, which was the second largest in the State of Utah. On our occasional visits to Salt Lake City, we would spend some time at the Salt Lake City Genealogical Society Library in the large archive room containing their collected handwritten or typed genealogical records of the Church.

My grandfather's youngest brother, PARLEY M. CONDIE, lived across the street in Preston, when we first moved there. He was a great genealogist (also a lawyer). I spent many hours copying by hand his *Book of Remembrance* for my CONDIE ancestors. His tall youngest son, DeLYLE, was in high school, and he would spend hours alone on the corner lot basketball court, also across the street, dribbling and throwing shots at the basket. DeLYLE would become one of the star forwards for the University of Utah's basketball team during his college years, and was chosen for the All-Star-Team. He completed his education as a lawyer, like his father, who was also very tall.

The Salt Lake City Genealogical Society archives had a fat volume which contained only the records that great-grandfather JAMES TUCKER had submitted on the TUCKER line—far more than I could copy by hand—in those days. There were no copy machines, and certainly no computers. I did find out that great-grandfather's personal records had been given to a grandson by the name of VAN ORDEN, who lived in Idaho Falls, Idaho. I wrote to him, and eventually he sent me the TUCKER pedigree chart and family group sheets of my direct ancestors.

Great-grandfather JAMES TUCKER was often mentioned by my CONDIE aunts and uncles during the few days following my father's death, many of them expressed the feeling that he was present in spirit at our ranch home near Carey, Idaho. He had lived at the GIBSON A CONDIE home in Logan with these children before his death. I have never heard a harsh or unkind statement spoken about this humble spiritual man. They knew him very well.

To understand a little more about the spirit world, the following out-of-body event occurred in Carey, Idaho, on the 20 Jan 1920. As a child I had heard the adults mention it from time to time; but this record of the event was given to me by my daughter ROXANNE, who got it from a missionary companion during her mission to the Dominican Republic. Several years prior to this spiritual event, a tragedy had occurred in the CAMERON family of Carey.

My aunt MARGARET CAMERON, who married my father's youngest brother GIBSON CONDIE in the 1930s, was a tiny baby when her father, a drunkard, came home and, with a gun, killed her mother's father and mother, and brother (Adamsons), who had come to help their daughter Isabelle with her anticipated divorce. He then killed (from my memory) three of his older children, at which time her mother ran into the back yard, believing her drunken husband would follow her, thus hoping her remaining children might survive. He did follow her, shot her, and then killed himself. In his inebriated state, he had sworn earlier to others that if he couldn't have her, no one else could. It has always created sadness in my heart to view their tombstones in the Carey cemetery. Aunt MARGARET, the baby, and her older brother were raised by their mother's brother, Blaine stake president Lennox Adamson and his wife Laura Rawson (Adamson)—the daughter of W. R. Rawson, who is mentioned below. Heber Q. Hale ordained my father a Seventy in 1920, before Daddy went on his mission to Arizona.

"The Heavenly Manifestation given to Heber Q. Hale, President of the Boise Stake, as related by him at the General Conference held in the

Auditorium of the Bishops Building, Salt Lake City, Utah, October 1920, requested by the President of the Church of 1920.

"It is with a very humble and grateful spirit that I attempt to relate on this occasion, by request, a personal experience which is very sacred to me. I must of necessity be brief. Furthermore, there were certain things made known to me which I don't feel at liberty to relate here, let me say by way of preface that between the hours of 12 and 7:30 on the night of January 10, 1920, while alone in a room at the home of W R Rawson in Carey, Idaho, this glorious manifestation was vouchsafed to me. I was not conscious of anything that transpired during the hours mentioned except what I experienced in this manifestation. I did not turn over in bed nor was I disturbed by any sound which indeed is unusual for me. Whether it be called a dream, a vision, or a pilgrimage of my spirit into the world of spirits, I know not, I care not. I know that I actually saw and experienced the things related in this heavenly manifestation and they are as real to me as any experience of my life.

"For me at least this is sufficient. Of all the doctrines and practices of the Church the principle of vicarious work for the dead has been the most difficult for me to comprehend and whole-heartedly accept. I consider this vision is the Lord's answer to the prayer of my soul on this and certain other questions.

"I passed but a short distance from my body through a film into the world of spirits; this was my first experience after going to sleep. I seemed to realize that I had passed through the change called death and I so referred to it in my conversation with immortal beings with whom I immediately came in contact. I readily observed their displeasure of the use of the word death and the fear which we attach to it. They use there another word in reference to the transition from mortality to immortality which word I don't recall. . . . My first visual impression was the nearness of the world of spirits to the world of mortality. The vastness of this heavenly sphere was bewildering to the eyes of the spirit-novice. Many enjoyed unrestricted vision and action. The vegetation and landscape were beautiful beyond description, not all green as here, but gold with varying shades of pink, orange, and lavender as the rainbow. A sweet calmness pervaded everything. The people I met there I did not think of as spirits, but as men and women, self thinking and self acting individuals, going about important business in a most orderly manner. There was perfect order there and everybody had something to do and seemed to be about their lives of purity and their subservience to the Father's will was subsequently made apparent. Particularly was it observed that the wicked and unrepented are confined to a certain district by themselves, the confines of which are as definitely determined and impassable as the line marking the division of the physical from the spirit world. A mere film, but impassable until the person himself was changed. The world of spirits is the temporary abode of all spirits pending the resurrection from the dead and the judgment. There was much activity within the different spheres, and appointed ministers of salvation were seen so doing from the highest to the lowest sphere in pursuit of their missionary appointments.

"I had a pronounced desire to meet certain of my kinsfolk and friends but I was at once impressed with the fact that I had entered a tremendously great and extensive world, even greater than our earth and more numerously inhabited. I could only be in one place at once, could do only one thing at a time, could only look in one direction at a time and accordingly it would require many, many years to search out and converse with all those I had known and all those whom I desired to meet unless they especially summoned to receive me.

"All men and women are appointed to special and peculiar service under a well organized plan of action directed principally towards PREACHING THE GOSPEL TO THE UNCONVERTED, TEACHING THOSE WHO SEEK FOR KNOWLEDGE, AND ESTABLISHING FAMILY SURVIVORS OF THEIR RESPECTIVE FAMILIES, that the work of baptism and sealing of ordinances may be vicariously performed for the departed in the temples of God on earth. . . . I was surprised to find there no babies in arms. I met the infant son of Orson W. Rawlings, my first counselor. I immediately recognized him as the baby who died a few years ago, and yet he seemed to have the intelligence, and in certain respects, the appearance of an adult, and was engaged in matters pertaining to his family and its genealogy. . . . I presently beheld a mighty multitude who I immediately recognized as soldiers, the millions who died, who had been slaughtered and rushed to the spirit world during the First World War. Among them moved calmly and majestically a great general in supreme command. As I drew nearer I received the kindly smile and generous welcome of a great loving man, General Richard W Young. Then came the positive conviction to my soul that of all the men living or dead, there is no one who was so perfectly fitted for the great mission unto which he had been called. . . .

"As I passed from this scene forwards I saw my beloved mother. She greeted me most affectionately and expressed surprise at seeing me there

and reminded me that I had not completed my allotted mission on earth.
. . . I presently approached a small group of men standing in a path lined
with spacious stretches of flowers, grasses, and shrubs, all of gold and blue,
marking the approach to a beautiful building. The group was engaged
in earnest conversation. One of their numbers parted from the rest and
came walking down the path. I at once recognized my esteemed President
Joseph F Smith, he embraced me as a father would his son and after a few
words of greeting, quickly remarked 'You have not come to stay.' This remark I understood as a declaration not a question.

"For the first time I became fully conscious of my uncompleted mission on earth and as much as I would have liked to remain, I at once asked
President Smith if I might return . . . 'You have expressed a righteous desire,' he replied, 'and I shall take the matter up with the authorities and let
you know later.'

"We then returned and he led me toward the little group of men from
whom he had just separated. I immediately recognized President Brigham
Young and the Prophet Joseph Smith. I was surprised to find the former
a shorter and heavier built man than I had pictured him in my mind to
be. On the other hand I found the latter to be taller than I expected to
find him. Both they and the President were possessed of a calm and holy
majesty which was at once kind and friendly. We then traced our steps and
President Smith took his leave, saying he would see me again.

"From a certain point of advantage, I was permitted to view the earth
and what was going on there, there was no limitation to my vision and I was
astounded to see my wife and children at home. I saw Heber J Grant at the
head of the great Church and Kingdom of God and felt the divine power
that radiates from God giving it light and truth and guiding its destiny. I
beheld this nation founded as it is upon correct principles and designed to
endure, but beset by evil and sinister forces that seek to lead man to thwart
the purpose of God. I saw towns and cities, the sins and wickedness of men
and women. I saw vessels sailing the oceans and scanned the battle scarred
fields of France and Belgium.

"In a word, I beheld the whole world, as if it were but a panorama passing before my eyes. Then there came to me the unmistakable impression
that this earth and oceans and persons upon it are open to the vision of the
spirits only when special permission is given or when they are assigned
to special service here. This was particularly true of the righteous who are
busily engaged in the fields of activity at the same time, the wicked and un-
repentant have still, like the rest, their free agency and applying themselves

to no useful or wholesome undertaking, seek pleasure, about their old haunts, and exalt in the sin and wickedness of degenerated humanity.

"To this extent they are still tools of Satan. It is these idle, mischievous and deceptive spirits who appear as miserable counterfeits at spiritual séances, table dancing and Ouija board operations. The noble and great ones do not respond to the call of the mediums and to every group of meddlesome enquirers, they would not do it in the world of mortality. These wicked and unrepented spirits are allies of Satan and his host, operating through willing mediums in the flesh. These three forces constitute an unholy trinity upon the earth and are responsible for all the sin, wickedness, distress, and misery among men and nations. . . .

"While standing at a certain vantage point I beheld a short distance away a wonderful beautiful temple, capped with golden domes, from which emerged a small group of men dressed in white robes, who paused for a brief conversation. They were in uniforms, in this group of holy men my eyes centered upon one more splendorous and holy than the rest. While I thus gazed, President Joseph F Smith parted from the others and came to my side. 'Do you know Him?' he inquired. I quickly answered, 'Yes, I know Him.' My eyes beheld my Lord and Saviour. 'It is true' said President Smith and oh how my soul thrilled with rapture and unspeakable joy filled my heart.

"President Smith informed me that I had been given permission to return and complete the mission on the earth which the Lord had appointed me to fulfill, and then with his hand upon my shoulder, uttered these memorable and significant words. 'Brother Heber, you have a great work to do. Go forward with a prayerful heart and thou shall be blessed in thy ministry. From this time never doubt that God lives, that Jesus Christ is the Son, the Saviour of the world that the Holy Ghost is God of spirits and messenger of the Father and the Son; never doubt the resurrection of the dead and immortality of the soul; that the destiny of man is eternal progress. Never again doubt that the mission of the Latter-Day Saints is for all mankind, both the living and the dead, and that the greatest work in the holy Temples for the living and the dead has only begun. Know this that Joseph Smith was sent of God to usher in the gospel dispensation of the fullness of times, which is the last unto mortals upon the earth. His successors have been recognized and ordained as head of the Church of Jesus Christ on earth. Give him your confidence and support. . . . Much you have seen and heard you will not be permitted to repeat when you return. Thus saying he bade me goodbye and 'God Bless You.'

"Quite distraught, through various scenes and passing innumerable people, I traveled before I reached the sphere where I first entered. On my way I was greeted by many friends and relatives, certain of whom sent words of greeting and counsel to their dear ones here, my mother being one of them. One other I will mention. I met Brother John Adamson, his wife, his son James and their daughter Isabelle, all of whom were killed by a foul assassin in their home in Carey, Idaho, on the evening of October 29, 1915. They seemed to discern that I was on my way back to mortality and immediately said, 'Tell the children that we are very happy and very busy and they should not mourn our departing, nor worry their minds over the manner by which we were taken. There is purpose in it, and we have a work to do here which required our collective efforts and which we could not do individually.' I was at once made to know that the work referred to was that of genealogy on which they were working in England and Scotland.

"One of the grandest and most sacred things of heaven is the family relationship. The establishment of the complete chain without any broken links being a fullness of joy. Links wholly bad will be dropped out and either new links put in or the two adjoining links welded together. Men and women everywhere throughout the world are being moved upon by their departed ancestors to gather genealogies. These are the links for the chain. The ordinances of baptism, endowments, and sealings performed in the temples of God, by the living for the dead, are the welding of the links.

"Ordinances are performed in the spirit world effectualising the individual recipient for their receiving the saving principles of the gospel vicariously performed here.

"As I was approaching the place where I entered, my attention was attracted towards a number of small groups of women, preparing what appeared to me wearing apparel. Observing my inquiring countenance one of the women remarked, 'We are preparing to receive Brother Phillip Worthington very soon.' As I gasped his name in petition, I was admonished, 'If you knew the joy and the glorious mission that awaits him here, you would not ask to have him longer detained upon the earth.' Then came flooding my consciousness, this awful truth that the will of the Lord can be done on earth as it is in heaven only when we resign ourselves completely to his will and let his will be done in and through us. On account of the selfishness of many, persons who might have otherwise been taken in innocence and peace, have been permitted to live and have lived to their own perils—man and the assertion of the personal will as against the will of God. Phillip Worthington died January 22, 1920, of which I was advised by telegram on returning to Boise, and preached his funeral sermon on January 25, 1920.

"Men, women and children are often called to missions of great importance on the other side and some respond gladly, while others refuse to go and their loved ones will not give them up. Also many die because they have not the faith to be healed. Others yet live among and pass out of the world of mortals without any special manifestation of action of the divine will. When a man is stricken ill the question of prime importance is not . . . is he going to live? Or is he going to die? What matters is not whether he lives or dies as long as the will of the Father is done.

"Surely we can trust him with God. . . . To the righteous person birth into the world of spirits is a glorious privilege and blessing. The greatest spirits in the family of the Father have not usually been permitted to tarry longer in the flesh than to perform a certain mission then they are called to the world of spirits where the field is greater and workers fewer. This earthly mission may therefore be long or short as the Father wills. I passed quietly out where I had entered the world of spirits—immediately my body was quickened. And I was to ponder over and record the many wonderful things I had seen and heard.

"Let me here and now declare to the world that irrespective of the opinion of others I know of my own positive knowledge and from my own personal experience that God is the Father of the spirits of all men and that He lives. That Jesus Christ is His Son and Saviour of the world. That the spirit of man does not die, but survives the change called death and goes to the world of spirits. The world of spirits is on or near earth. That the principles of salvation are now being taught to the spirits and the great work of saving the Father's family among the living and the dead is now in progress and that but comparatively few will ultimately be lost and spirits will literally take up their bodies again in the resurrection and that the Gospel of Jesus Christ has been established upon the earth with all of its keys, that this is the power that will now only save the world; that the burden of our mission is to save souls unto God. And that the work for the salvation of the dead is no less of importance than the work for the living."

As a child of 10 years of age, I [BROOKIE CONDIE] knew that my father, MARION A. CONDIE hadn't died because of his lack of faith, or that my mother and his parents lacked faith. When my sister IVIE and I had quietly dressed and tip-toed downstairs, not wanting to disturb our father in his bedroom below us, we were greeted by a living room filled with tearful relations on that fateful morning, including my three very young sisters, who had been staying at our grandparents home at Carey. I didn't need my mother to further explain that my father had died that night. I sat on the plush footstool my mother had purchased for my father to use when he came home (we had been told to die) from the Sawtelle Veteran's Hospital in Los Angeles. Neither my mother nor my father would ever admit that death was a possibility, although Dr. Fox from Hailey would come quite often, and when he would leave, my mother with tear-stained eyes would proclaim that she hoped he never came again, because he insisted on telling her that my father's condition was hopeless, and he tried to give him narcotics to relieve the severe pain, which Daddy always declined taking. I don't recall Daddy ever complaining or crying out because of this pain he must have suffered. My faith in his recovery had been so sure that I had asked him only a week earlier when we were going to build our new home in Carey. Our parents had made their plans for it the previous summer. He gave me a big smile and simply said, "Just as soon as I get well." I accepted that.

When I was later told that my patriarch grandfather, GIBSON A CONDIE, had set him apart as a missionary in the spirit world during his blessing the previous evening, I accepted that, too, and believed the Lord needed him, probably more than we did—my patriarch grandfather would know the Lord's will. I was very sad; but my tears were not profuse. Daddy had been strong and courageous. I could do no less. As I listened to my aunts and grandmother say how they felt great-grandfather JAMES TUCKER was present that day, although no one claimed to see him, I accepted as a fact that the two of them, my father and his maternal grandfather, would be missionary companions, working together. They would also take care of us. My mother had told us that in one of my father's many blessings, while he was ill, that he was promised that because of his sacrifice none of his children would be lost. Our father's response was that for that blessing, he would endure even more. I hope that extends to all his posterity.

Present in our living room that morning, in addition to our immediate family, were our grandparents, GIBSON and EMILY CONDIE, uncle JAMES and aunt ADA BAIRD, and aunt HELEN SMITH—of my father's immediate family. There is a spiritual sequel to this event that happened in 1994. It involved my father, MARION A. CONDIE, uncle JAMES A. BAIRD, grandfather GIBSON

A CONDIE, and great-grandfather JAMES TUCKER.

The JAMES A. BAIRD family was very close to our family in my child-hood. They had six children. ELIZABETH, EDITH, and MARGARET were older cousins; their daughter ADA was near my brother MARION ASHER's age; a son JAMES C. "JIMMY" was the age of my sister IVIE; and their young-est daughter HELEN was a week younger than I was. MARION ASHER and JIMMY would pair off at parties, and ADA and IVIE were close companions. We celebrated Christmas at the BAIRDs and Thanksgiving on the ranch. Our CONDIE grandparents were always included.

JIMMY AND HELEN ENTERTAIN OUR COUSIN EDNA SMITH ON A SHEEP AT CAREY, IDAHO

In 1994, JIMMY and his wife EVELYN WHITING BAIRD were living in Manti, Utah. GROVER and I were living in Orem, Utah. They telephoned me and asked if EVELYN could stay at our home in the evenings, while JIMMY had sur-gery at the Utah Valley Hospital in Provo. He had been diagnosed with Hodgkin's disease—a form of cancer that attacks the lymph nodes, especially in the neck. The disease had spread into his facial and chest areas. Of course, EVELYN would be more than welcome in our home.

They were the directors of the Manti Family History Center, includ-ing record extraction. EVELYN would spend her days at the hospital and would only arrive late to sleep at our home. In the mornings, when I arose around 7:00 A.M., I would find her busily engaged in record extraction on my kitchen table. Her work went with her to the hospi-tal—almost an obsession with her.

HELEN BAIRD {later SNOW]

This Twin Falls high school graduation picture was taken in 1947. When the BAIRDs sold their ranch in Carey and later moved to Montana, they sent HELEN to live with her two sisters in Twin Falls. They had an apartment near the high school and we became very close friends once more. Sisters, ADA and EDITH were exceptional secretaries in that area at the time. They would all later marry.

A very thin JIMMY, whose life had been spared as a young child from drowning in the Carey canal (written earlier), had a successful operation. His stapled scar extended from his forehead, past his neck, and into the chest area.

About six months later, he called on the phone and asked us to come to Manti and join with others in helping with baptisms for the dead for the TUCKER family— a quantity much larger than he and his wife could do alone.

When we arrived that Saturday, he asked us to dress properly and wait for him in an instruction room by the baptistry. As I remember it, he told us:

"I awoke and a voice spoke to me saying, 'Pay attention! I've told you once and you didn't listen, so I'll tell you again." He then described his following dream or vision: "There was a large group of people in the distance—in the tens of thousands. They seemed to be on a sea shore and were dressed in various costumes, varying with the different ages of history. As I approached closer, I saw a small group of men assembled in front of them—some of whom I recognized: great-grandfather JAMES TUCKER; (his son-in-law,) grandfather GIBSON A CONDIE; uncle MARION A. CONDIE; my father, JAMES A. BAIRD, and my father-in-law, A. R. WHITING.

"Great-grandfather TUCKER spoke, 'Well we've really done it. These people have been taught and converted. Now they are all dressed up with no place to go and they are holding us responsible for their lack of progress. What is to be done?'

"Grandfather GIBSON CONDIE stated, 'Well, it's obvious, we need to see that the temple ordinances are done for them.'

"Uncle MARION said, 'Well, yes, Father, but you know that we can't do that. Do you have any ideas?'

"Grandfather GIBSON A CONDIE countered, 'Of course. We'll let JIMMY do it.'"

JIMMY then explained that as a child, Grandfather CONDIE used the phrase quite often. He was always having him do things to help him when they lived neighbors in Carey.

"Uncle MARION stated, 'That's a good idea. JIMMY's a good boy. He can handle it,' and turning to my father, 'JIM, is that all right?'

"My father responded, 'Well, right now, JIM's got more than he can handle. He's really discouraged. If you get any help from him you will have to make it easy.'

"Uncle MARION reminded him, 'It can never be easier than now. Brother WHITING, you've seen the records, are they ready?'

"My wife's father replied, 'Yes they are. I'll get EVELYN to help; she can help JIM.' This answer was made as a matter of fact. It seemed as natural as if he was to ask her to feed the cat or do some simple task. With that I went to sleep."

JIMMY told us that within a week records were found at the Manti City Library in an old locked cabinet in the basement. They gave them to the Family History Center. They included volumes of the English parish registers and a book of *Devonshire Wills* by Charles Worth, published 1898. A minister, Dr. Campbell, had prepared an index of Somerset christenings and marriages, arranged alphabetically by surname. Jimmy extracted over 9,000 names.

A few years later in 1996, Jimmy attended a GIBSON A CONDIE reunion in Reno, Nevada. I asked how many names he had then extracted? His response was over 70,000 names.

While many visited the famous *Harold's Club display of Old Cars*, some of us went to the Reno Family History Center, where GROVER's sister THERA and her husband SHELDON ROSS were workers. In addition to the Church records, their Washoe county library had given their stake all of their genealogical records, and the Church had a special room built in their Stake Center to house this marvelous collection. JIMMY remained longer and extracted many of these records, while the rest of us motored up the mountain to Virginia City for dinner and a view of its many historical sites.

JIMMY BAIRD with MARION"s daughter KAREN at the table in 1996, at a GIBSON A CONDIE reunion in Reno, Nevada.

VIEW OF THE RENO VALLEY FROM THE ROAD TO VIRGINIA CITY

My sister CeCELIA completed the 200 endowments and sealings she had requested to take to the Jordan Temple and arranged for another family group to go to the Manti Temple. The night before going, a man in a dream requested, "If you will do my temple work, I will take care of Chuck."

He then told her his name. Her son Chuck had been somewhat lax in keeping the commandments and had lost his testimony. She awoke, but couldn't remember the man's name. Arriving at the Manti Temple, the recorder pulled out the names saying, "I guess you would prefer to do names with the TUCKER surname," and passed over some on the top of the pile.

"Wait! Who do you have on the top?" she asked. "CHILCOTT names," was the reply. "I want those!" That was the name of the man in her dream.

I [BROOKIE CONDIE SWALLOW] have had spiritual experiences while doing research and temple work, as have many others. One a little different happened in the mid-60s. Church president David O. McKay was getting old and feeble. GROVER was the Uvada Stake Sunday school superintendent. I was his secretary. Lynn Campbell of Pioche was one of his counselors. The church Sunday school organization had a church-wide conference for the stakes the afternoon and evening, after General Conference closed in Salt Lake City, Utah.

Being pharmacists in Nevada, our time was quite limited. We arose very early Sunday morning and drove to Salt Lake City—listening on the radio to the morning session. Lynn was with us. We arrived in Salt Lake City around noon just as that session ended. As the crowd exited the dome-shaped tabernacle, we slipped into the seats vacated by the morning audience and missed our lunch in order to obtain a seat for the afternoon session. Then when that session closed, we hurried to different locations for more individual Sunday school instructions.

Prior to becoming an apostle, David O. McKay was the president of Weber College and the general superintendent of the Sunday schools. He always loved the Sunday school and would attend their large evening sessions, which were held in the 3 to 4000-seat tabernacle. The center-seats in the lower main floor level were reserved until five minutes before the session began for the stake Sunday school presidencies that were in attendance. At that time, others were allowed to occupy any vacancies, and it would immediately fill to capacity.

This particular Sunday, we were unable to quickly obtain food in their nearby restaurants and arrived after the 5-minute deadline. Showing our admittance cards, the ushers took compassion on us and allowed us to be seated in some vacant seats above the choir, which was much smaller than the Tabernacle Choir. This was the last General Sunday School Conference that President McKay was able to attend and he entered slowly with the help of his counselors on each side of him, while the congregation sang *We Thank Thee, O God, for a Prophet.*

When the session ended, Lynn Campbell observed the stairway going down from behind the organ that was used by the choir members. Our 250 member Southern Utah Women's Relief Society Choir had used this exit when we had sung in the two October, Friday sessions, of General Conference in 1964, under the capable direction of Florence Madsen. We thought we could leave more rapidly through the choir door, so we descended the stairway. Unfortunately, the crowd was very congested, and we lost our way. Searching for the way out, I ended up at the door where the general authorities exit. Outside was President McKay's limousine and the young children were packed closely together on both sides of the reserved space, hoping to shake his hand. I quickly backed off, and as I tried to find the right way to leave, I looked up and apostles Bruce R. McConkie and his father-in-law Joseph Fielding Smith were standing by me. Joseph Fielding Smith stated flatly,

WOMEN'S CHOIR IN THE SALT LAKE TABERNACLE.

President McKay wrote to Director Florence Madsen in 1964, "They sang like angels."
It was her final performance as a choir director at General Conference.

"I don't know why they do this to him. He's so frail and tired after these long meetings. He hasn't the strength for all of this."

Then GROVER tapped me on the shoulder. "Come quickly. President McKay is coming and Lynn is holding us a place in line. We can shake his hand as he leaves."

After hearing the apostle's remark, I didn't feel I should join the line. GROVER joined Lynn and I climbed halfway up the vacant stairs that lead to the podium above. I could see them, but I wasn't in line. I remembered, I had shaken the hands of Church presidents, Heber J. Grant and George Albert Smith. I had also shaken the hand of David O. McKay on occasions when he was an apostle attending our stake conferences. I wanted to save his strength, too.

I watched as the dear man shook the hands of those in the line. The line ended at the foot of the steps that I was standing on. He raised his wistful eyes and spotted me. He stopped and it appeared to me that if I didn't rush down those stairs, he would climb them to shake my hand. Unwilling to appear ungrateful, I hastened downward and shook his hand.

Never have I experienced a handshake like that one. I thought of the woman who touched the robe of our Savior Jesus Christ and was healed. An actual power had consumed my whole body and total love filled it to overflowing. President McKay continued on at his slow pace to the door and into the waiting hands of the young children beyond. I thought of the New Testament apostles who had tried to keep the children away from Christ, and he had told them,

"Suffer the little children to come unto me and forbid them not, for
of such is the Kingdom of Heaven."

It was like a spiritual journey back to the Holy Land.

I asked Lynn Campbell and GROVER if they had experienced any special feelings. No, it was just a fine handshake. Somehow, I had been given a very special blessing that I have continued to cherish throughout my life. That night we stayed at the home of LYNN and OPAL SWALLOW JONES [GROVER's sister] in Murray. Her children were not at home, so we slept in one of their beds. We told OPAL about the experience.

When OPAL died in 2005, their youngest son FRED rushed to me as I was leaving the cemetery. With his arm around my shoulder, he told me that he couldn't let me leave without telling me that he always thought of me as his

"Eternal Companions"

In Loving Memory of
Opal Swallow Jones

Born – December 21, 1916 – Meadow, Utah
Died – September 11, 2005 – South Jordan, Utah

Daughter of ~
Thomas Charles & Vanda Duncan Swallow
Wife of ~ A. Lynn Jones *(Deceased)*

Interment
Murray City Cemetery – 5600 So. Vine St.
Dedication of the Grave – Gordon Jones, *son*

aunt that shook President McKay's hand, and then proceeded to tell me the story very much like I have told it. His mother had repeated the story to him, and he said it had helped him considerably through the years. He was a young teenager then and a very independent thinker who loved to ski and was excellent in his jumps—working on the ski patrol. At her death, he was a very successful businessman and a member of the high council in his stake. He had served many years as the bishop of his ward in the Murray/Holiday area of Salt Lake County.

How much we need each other. How *Broad are the Branches*—both living and dead. I marvel at the thinness of the veil that separates the two. In JIMMY's vision, the spiritual genealogy worker missionaries were not just the male direct line, but included the lines of mothers, wives, in-laws, children, cousins, and distant relations—all working together for a better kingdom to come that will bring about the final *Peace on Earth for Everyone*—that total peace and joy I felt for a small moment in the tabernacle in Salt Lake City, Utah.

CHRIST IN THE GARDEN OF GETHSEMANE, BY BROOKIE CONDIE SWALLOW

About 1967, the Church Presidency asked the members of the Church to have a picture of Christ hung in their living rooms. We had just completed our new addition, and I wanted it to be very special. I couldn't find any that I wanted, so I decided to paint a large 3' x 5' of my own. I felt the most important event in his life was his struggle in the Garden of Gethsemane, when he atoned for the sins of all mankind. I loved the small classical picture this composition was taken from, but I felt the original artist had been too placid in his painting. I felt the rocks, the sky, and his clothing would even protest, so I used vibrant colors, and the pain he suffered needed to be more poignant. I completed the painting in one afternoon, working until three in the morning. I had planned to refine it the next day; but I loved the feeling it gave me, and I've left it as it was, afraid I might spoil it. I never signed the picture—except on the back. Others like it, too. Who inherits it may be a problem.

It was 1976. Our three oldest children had been married in the temple. They, and our fourth child, VANDA, had all attended B.Y.U. TOM had served a mission in Guatemala/San Salvador. ROXANNE, number five, had graduated from Lincoln County High School and had been student body vice-president that year. She received a four-year full scholarship to UNLV, which she had accepted. All were active in the Church. Our home in Panaca was paid for; our drugstore was doing well. We had a full-time pharmacist in Caliente, but felt that one pharmacist with a vacation relief pharmacist could handle the shorter hours. We began to look for expansion into additional drugstores.

The early 70s were a difficult economic time across the nation, and Walgreens Drug Company was closing their stores in Utah. They had one at the University Mall in Orem that we were interested in. It was a 15,000-square-foot store that included a restaurant. We were able to purchase it for a very reasonable price with an SBA loan and assume their lease. A home in Provo, the B.Y.U. a few blocks away, it all seemed right. Our children could be near us, work in our own drugstore, and help financially with their educations at the university. Our pharmacist, Robert Murdock, in Caliente would manage our Caliente Pharmacy; we would work during his vacations, keeping our home in Panaca. We incorporated the two stores separately to avoid paying Utah income taxes on Nevada profits, which didn't have any state income tax.

Within a few months, the Dean of Music at B.Y.U., Loren Wheelwright, visited with GROVER. He was the stake president of the B.Y.U. Ninth Stake and wanted GROVER to be the branch president (changed later to bishop) of the new B.Y.U. 89th Ward. It encompassed our area and extended west from State Street, south to 5th North and along Colombia Lane to the Provo/Orem border. On the west was I-15. They knew of about 165 students and they asked GROVER to find more, "Digging them out of the woodwork," and to include singles that were working, not attending B.Y.U. The small ward grew rapidly. They created two Relief Societies and two Elders Quorums. The growth continued. With the attendance over 400, the ward was divided; then, it was divided again and again. During the approximately four years GROVER was bishop (or branch president), we counted over 3200 young people that had been members of his ward. His nightstand bulged with wedding invitations.

At first they met in the Grandview Elementary School; then in an elementary school on the corner of 5th North and State Streets. During the summers they were moved to various unused buildings on the B.Y.U. campus; Joseph Smith Memorial; Eyring Science; Harris Fine Arts; and others. When our regular new stake center was completed, GROVER requested to have his ward occupy the unused third bishop and clerk's offices that had been added for possible future expansion. It was the first time they really had a place of their own. Our home had been his office and social center.

I thought it was of interest that we had four active church bishops living in a row on our street. We were on the corner; our family ward bishop lived next to us, with two more B.Y.U. bishops to the south. We might have been called "Bishop's Row;" but we weren't.

With our many young children, I attended our own ward. I felt they needed the association of children their own age. Our youngest child, DIANNA, was only four years old at first. I would take her to work with me at the mall, which opened at 10:00 A.M. My main duty was the daily accounting and banking on the five business days, and I would go home around three o'clock. We never opened on Sundays. We had even included in our lease that if the mall ever started to open on Sundays, we would not be required to do so.

Three more of our children went on L.D.S. missions while we lived in our Grandview home. First, VANDA was called to the Tempe Arizona Mission. Shortly after J. BRUCE was called to the Bogota Colombia Mission; then ROXANNE, who was taking pharmacy at the University of Utah, was called on a Health Service Mission to the Dominican Republic.

The Sunday came when it was announced that our home stake was ready to be divided. The stake had over 9,000 members and held our stake conferences in the Marriott Center at B.Y.U., where the Cougars played their basketball games. We would be part of the newly created stake, which would be known as the Grandview Stake, and it would extend east to include homes in the lower valley located near the Provo River. After Sacrament Meeting ended, I tapped on GROVER's office door, where he was holding his regular bishop's meeting, to tell him the news. He already knew. He left his meeting and took me into his vacant clerk's office. There he told me that he felt strongly he would be called to be a member of this new stake presidency, not the stake president—probably the second counselor. He was quite agitated. Apostle M. Russell Ballard would interview the priesthood leaders within the stake for the new stake presidency, and he was scheduled for Friday evening. After a very short interview that night, he returned home and reported he must have been mistaken. They would choose the presidency on Saturday, the following morning. He was scheduled to work in our Layton Hills Mall store, an hour and half away. He left early.

I was working in our laundry room when GROVER returned. Our regular managing pharmacist, our old college friend Homer Brighten, had greeted him when he arrived in Layton—Homer would work that day. The call had come to our Layton store with the request that GROVER return immediately and bring his wife to the old stake center. Apostle Ballard greeted us and hastened us to the conference room where the others were seated. After the introductions were made, Elder Ballard broke the silence with the following statement.

"I guess you know the Lord called you, no one else knows you."

It was true. We didn't know the new president, or his first counselor, who were close friends and lived in the valley, and were both B.Y.U. professors. GROVER was chosen after much prayer by the three of them. Actually very few people within the whole stake knew GROVER, even within our own ward, because he attended the B.Y.U. 89th Ward. I had been asked sometimes if my husband was inactive, since the family came without him. Elder Ballard asked me if I was willing to sustain and support him as the second counselor in the new stake presidency, then I was soon excused to go home; he would be there most of the day, and they would bring him home.

The following morning, GROVER and I were ushered and seated on the rather large assembled stage on the basketball court of the huge Marriott Center. The thousands of chairs on the south and extending into the east and west were mostly filled, as well as the folding chairs on the court, where our family was invited to sit. It was an awesome congregation, and humbling, at least to me, when the calling was announced and the sustaining vote of raised hands was witnessed. GROVER, of course, was one of the speakers.

A smaller congregation, but a more personal and tearful experience soon followed when stake president Loren F. Wheelwright released GROVER as the bishop of the 89th B.Y.U. Ward. He was replaced by the brother of the Salt Lake

Tabernacle Choir organist. Both of us were asked to address the students this time. It was very difficult to say goodbye to those sweet young people that we had come to love so dearly, and who joined in our tears. In GROVER's patriarchal blessing he had been told he would work with the youth of the Church. This was certainly at least a partial fulfillment of this promised blessing. When Elder Ballard had spoken with us, earlier, he had mentioned that he wanted GROVER to help initiate, as a trial in the Grandview Stake, a possible new church program they would call the "single's ward," and it would be under the stake presidency, not the B.Y.U.—singles not attending the B.Y.U. would be moved into it from the stake area of his former ward.

When we first moved to Provo, our home was within the boundaries of the Provo 26th Ward, until it was divided to form our 30th Ward. Our bishop was SPENCER J. CONDIE. He was the grandson of GIDEON CONDIE, a younger brother of my grandfather GIBSON A CONDIE. Great-uncle GIDEON and his wife CARRIE CLAUSON CONDIE had lived on a farm east of Preston. In 1951, great-uncle GIDEON had been very good to us and would call us early in the morning to come pick some of his peas, when they were at their best, and before they were taken to the canning factory. Two of his sons, SPENCER, and ANGUS with their families, had bordering farms.

Next door, in a much smaller house, lived his bachelor brother great-uncle JOHN. He had strayed from the L.D.S. Church and seemed very lonely. The smell of coffee emanated from his home. He died while we were living in Preston. I played a violin solo at his funeral that was held in a small room at the mortuary. Only a very few people attended—his two brothers, PARLEY and GIDEON, with their wives, a few of their adult children, GROVER and I, our tiny son TOM, and my accompanist.

Young SPENCER J. CONDIE was eleven or twelve. His father SPENCER was an auditor for the I.R.S. in addition to his farm. GROVER's boss was not happy with him at that time, as his income tax records were being audited. When we moved to Provo/Orem, SPENCER and his wife JOSIE lived across the street from their son SPENCER J., his wife DORTHEA and their young children. SPENCER Sr. and JOSIE were ordinance workers in the Provo Temple, where he preformed sealings for the dead. Both families were our good customers.

This picture was taken by a good friend, Fred Anderson, when we lived in Preston, where I was asked to play many solos—also, in Montpelier and Lincoln County, until I had a partial paralysis of my right arm. I learned to control the problem and still play a solo occasionally.

When GROVER was a counselor in the Grandview Stake, SPENCER J. CONDIE was called as one of the high councilmen, until he was called to be the stake president of one of the B.Y.U. stakes. SPENCER J. was a professor at the B.Y.U. in the Sociology Department and the author of several books—always a popular lecturer during Education Week. His wit and humor collected crowds beyond the capacity of his large lecture room and speakers were extended into adjoining classrooms. He became a mission president in Austria before the Iron Curtain was dismantled and President Reagan said, "Mr. Gorbachev, tear down that wall!" Later he became a member of the First Council of Seventies, and our daughter VANDA asked him to perform her marriage to HYRUM HAYNES in the Provo Temple. Recently, 2006, he was assigned to help our good friends, Lorell and Terry Bleak of Panaca, prepare for their new assignment as mission president to the newly created Marshall Islands Mission, over 3,000 miles across. Earlier, SPENCER J. helped two more of our close friends from Panaca, Neldon and Carol Mathews on their administrative mission to the Salt Lake Genealogical Library. I visited him recently in his office in the Church Office Building where he then was in charge of all the Church periodicals and publications.

My mother, LILLIE CONDIE, moved to Provo at the same time we did. We tried to get her to buy or build a home next to ours, or even live in an apartment in our basement. She didn't want to. She said she was tired of being BROOKIE's mother. She wanted to be LILLIE CONDIE and independent. She bought a home about a mile from us—still on the Grandview Hill. She would have dinner with us every Sunday, and bring delicious hot rolls. She had her own Family Home Evening group of ladies and learned ceramics and writing at the Senior Center. She would do at least 25 endowments in the Provo Temple each month, taking other women with her. Several of her 62 grandchildren stayed with her from time to time, while they attended the B.Y.U., working, or on an extended visit. She would remember all of her grandchildren on their birthdays with a book that included several $1.00 bills. Her heart developed an arrhythmia problem and she took Lanoxin. While she was staying with LILLIE and BILL her body became over digitalized and she became very ill. My nurse sister LILLIE helped her discover the problem and nursed her back to health. On another occasion she fell and broke her leg at the Los Angles Airport, returning from Hawaii. ADELIA and JOE rescued her, and she stayed with them, until the bone healed.

Late one evening, when we were living on Driftwood Lane above B.Y.U., we received a phone call. She had fallen in her kitchen and struck her face in the process. Her nose was bleeding and wouldn't stop. Rushing to help her, we found a large amount of blood on her kitchen floor; but the bleeding had stopped. We called her doctor, stopped her daily aspirin, and cleaned everything. The following day it bled again. This time I took her to the emergency room. Her blood pressure was almost nonexistent. They quickly gave her transfusions, cauterized the wound in her nose, and kept her overnight. She never took another aspirin.

Several years later, I was working as the pharmacist at our Orem store when I received a phone call from ADELIA's daughter STEPHANIE, who went daily to Mother's home to clean and do the laundry. She was crying.

"Aunt BROOKIE, Grandma is in bed and I can't wake her up!"

I had them call our relief pharmacist, rushed quickly over to her home, and called her doctor. It was obviously a comatose stroke—whether from a clot or from bleeding in the brain was questionable. I've been told that the symptoms can be the same. She was 93 years old. The doctor felt she would do just as well at home as in a hospital, if we turned her every two hours.

ADELIA and CeCELIA arrived that evening. After one night, without any of the three of us getting any sleep, we called the ambulance and had her admitted to Utah Valley Hospital. LILLIE flew in from Virginia. She was prepared to stay as long as necessary. IVIE and BYRON drove in from Seattle. My sisters took turns on the night shifts at the hospital. I still had to be the pharmacist eight hours a day; but I somehow knew that my mother would not die, unless I was there. Still, it was difficult to sleep at home. My mind would not relax.

Mother would open her eyes and speak with difficulty, at times. She could weakly squeeze our hand, if we held hers; but other movements seemed impossible. One evening her nephew GRANT IVIE and his wife, from the Salt Lake valley, came to visit with her. She seemed to know them and he asked, "Aunt LILLIE, how are you doing." Her slow reply (the last words I heard her speak) was, "I'm doing the best I can." I think she did this all her life.

JAMES and MARION were slower to come. I finally called them and told them that she was only waiting to say, "Goodbye" to them before she died. They arrived. Within 24 hours, she was gone. MARION, LILLIE, and I were at her bedside at the time. REBECCA, LILLIE and BILL's daughter, was a nurse at Utah Valley Hospital. Another nurse had been assigned to mother; but REBECCA quickly took over. She would take care of that final preparation "of my own grandmother."

LILLIE IVIE CONDIE died on the 22 Mar 1989 at the Utah Valley Hospital in Provo, Utah. Her funeral was held in her own ward on the Grandview Hill in Provo, Utah, where the chapel was filled with relatives and friends from Utah, Idaho, and more distant states. She was buried next to her husband, MARION A. CONDIE, in the Carey cemetery, Blaine County, Idaho. Once more it was a cold and windy day. The Carey Ward Relief Society served our large group a delicious meal in the recreational room of their [new and much larger than when I was a child] L.D.S. Church building. My mother's righteous influence and love has been felt through these past years from time-to-time by many of her numerous posterity. She is a choice individual, and we all love her. She was preceded in death by all her siblings and their spouses.

THE SEVEN CHILDREN AND THEIR SPOUSES AT THE FUNERAL OF LILLIE IVIE CONDIE.

(LEFT TO RIGHT) MARION AND SUE CONDIE; BYRON AND IVIE BABBEL; WAYNE AND CeCELIA WILSON; BROOKIE AND GROVER SWALLOW; LILLIE AND BILL CLAY; JERRY AND JAMES CONDIE; ADELIA RILE. (HER HUSBAND JOE WAS UNABLE TO ATTEND.) PICTURE BY RAY IVIE.

WAYNE, ADELIA, AND JOE POSE IN THIS PICTURE TAKEN "UP ON TOP" AT OUR
RANGE LAND IN THE PIONEER MOUNTAINS NORTH OF CAREY, IDAHO. JAMES AND GROVER
ARE FURTHER BACK. IN THE FAR DISTANCE IS THE SAWTOOTH MOUNTAIN RANGE.

LILLIE CONDIE'S YOUNGEST GRANDSON JIM CONDIE WITH HIS PARENTS MARION AND
SUE CONDIE, HIS AUNT BROOKIE, AND UNCLE GROVER CLIMBED THE STEEP TRAIL TO THE
TIMPANAGOS CAVE IN AMERICAN FORK CANYON. WE WENT SLOW AND MADE IT TO THE TOP AND
THROUGH THE CAVE, BUT MY KNEES GAVE OUT HALFWAY DOWN, AND WE WENT MUCH, MUCH SLOWER.

~ 50 ~

LEAD KINDLY LIGHT
"DON'T DIVE! JUST JUMP!"

After my father, MARION ASHER CONDIE, died when I was 10 years old, our mother, LILLIE ALICE IVIE CONDIE, asked my patriarch grandfather, GIBSON A CONDIE, to give her four older children a blessing. The blessings were to have been "Father's Blessings;" but since he gave us our lineage and recorded them in the Church records, they became our "Patriarchal Blessings." Part of my blessing reads as follows:

> "You shall have trials, but for a brief period. It shall [redound] to your good for remember you gain strength by overcoming and by resisting evil."

My mother was quick to tell her young daughter that a "brief period" could be much longer than I might think—maybe as long as two years. As a ten-year-old, two years seemed like a very long time. I was not happy with that part of my blessing. Through the years, I have wondered about which struggling event was my "brief period" and whether it was past, present, or still in the future? I still wonder; but some experiences have been very difficult.

It was late in the spring of 1968, after we had completed the new addition to our lovely home in Panaca and built the tennis court, that GROVER and I had an unexpected visitor. Our young pharmacist friend, Bruce Wilkin, came to see us. He had grown up in Pioche and worked for us for a few months before he took a job as a pharmacist with Mel Cowley in Cedar City. GROVER had spoken with him about our desire to start a cooperative one-man pharmacist drugstore chain in some of the smaller cities, and he bluntly asked us if we were serious and ready to do it. If so, he wanted to be part of it; if not, he would make his plans to become a medical doctor. We were to let him know the following day. Still in debt from our recent building project, we were skeptical about further debt and expansion; but we liked Bruce. That night we offered a very long prayer before we retired. With no immediate answer, we finally gave up and went to sleep.

Just before dawn, I had a dream. In the dream, I was on our bed watching through our patio sliding door while two tiny white swallow birds, with black tips on their wings and tails, built a nest in a small cove in a light cream-colored marble (dream) wall that was near our door. I was fascinated as I watched the nest completed, the egg laid and hatched. The father bird would fly off for periods and then return briefly from time to time. The beautiful little baby swallow grew and learned to fly; but was still much smaller than the parents.

Then the father bird returned again and appeared to talk to the mother bird; tears came into her eyes and I saw the tears fall to the patio cement before the three birds flew off into the vast sky that was covered by millions of larger birds that flew so close together that the sunshine became extinct. The flapping of the wings of this mass of birds was ominous as the tiny birds dutifully flew into the dark mass—first the father bird, followed by the mother bird and the tiny baby swallow followed them with its wings doing double or triple-time to keep up. In my dream I cried out to the heavens,

"Why? Why do they have to go. She doesn't want to go. I see her tears."

The deep echoing voice from the heavens answered,

"Because they don't belong here."

I looked around our backyard to a little hill where we had planted a balsam spruce. Two large robins were playing under it in the bright sunlight.

"But these birds are staying," I called.

"They belong here!" was the answer.

In sorrow I watched the three small birds disappear into the thunderous noise and darkness of the surrounding multitude of flapping black wings.

I awoke with tearful eyes. The dawn was breaking. It was time to get my older children to early morning seminary. Quietly I moved to the kitchen and started their breakfast. My tears wouldn't go away and the words and music of *Lead Kindly Light* came into my mind forcefully—over and over again. It had not been my favorite song; in fact, I was surprised I even remembered the words. Helen O'Connor, with her beautiful deep alto voice, and I had sung it as a duet at a funeral a few years before; but we used the hymn book to remember the words. The most emphatic phrases that kept recurring that morning were:

"Lead Kindly Light, amid encircling gloom;
Keep thou my feet, I do not ask to see the distant scene,
One Step Enough for me,"
and
"I loved the garish day in spite of fears. Pride ruled my will.
Remember not past years."

With the older children on their way to seminary and my husband preparing for his workday, we concluded that our long prayer had been answered. We would remain in Panaca, at least until another child arrived—number ten, DIANNA. She was born on 30 Mar 1972. We also knew we could stay in our lovely home until she was old enough to meet the struggles that awaited her and our other children in a more difficult, highly-populated, and dangerous world.

It was the middle of July, 1968, that GROVER filed for Assemblyman in the Nevada Legislature. After two terms, two defeats and the L.D.S. Temple marriages of our three oldest children, we moved to the Provo/Orem area in November, 1976, when Walgreens decided to sell all their Utah stores, except the one by Temple Square in Salt Lake City. Walgreens subleased us their location in the University Mall in Orem, which lease lasted until 1997. They had negotiated good terms that included our right to sublease, the option that in 1995 we could leave without penalty, and we would be able to close our store on Sundays. We loved our beautiful 4,500 square foot home in the Grandview area. Everything seemed wonderful. My mother moved with us, buying her own home.

Throughout the next five years, GROVER became the President of the University Mall Association, a Councilman for the Orem Chamber of Commerce and a member of their Rotary Club. In our Church, he became the bishop of the B.Y.U. 89th Singles Ward, until he was released to become the second counselor in the newly organized Grandview Stake. We still owned our store in Caliente. The three oldest remaining children, VANDA, ROXANNE and BRUCE, went on L.D.S. missions. EMILY and DORCAS enjoyed Provo

High School, where EMILY excelled in gymnastics—coming in second in the "all-around" Utah County High School gymnast event, which included the beam, floor, vault and uneven parallel bars. After she broke her arm, she successfully ran for cheerleader. That year she was elected Preference Queen by her male classmates. DORCAS excelled in track and was part of their relay team, played on the girl's basketball team and became a member of the Provo High School Supreme Court.

Home from their missions, ROXANNE and MARC PROBST were married in the Salt Lake Temple. MARC was a friend and companion to BRUCE during their Bogota Columbia missions, where MARC was an assistant to the president and BRUCE was their mission clerk. MARC's father was the CEO of the vast mainframe-computer Sperry Corporation with its skyscraper bordering Central Park in New York City. MARC's short visit with his friend BRUCE had quickly resulted in his marriage proposal to ROXANNE. The couple attended the University of Utah after their marriage, where MARC worked for his MBA and ROXANNE graduated in Health Science.

We "loved the garish day in spite of fears. Pride ruled" our wills. It was the years of the Big Malls and double-digit interest rates that spiraled higher and higher to over 20 percent. We had built a gorgeous new store and restaurant in the newly constructed Layton Hills Mall, against the advice of Walgreens, who helped us with our plans, as we still retained their franchise. The debt grew larger and interest rates continued to escalate. Sales were not as rapid in our new venture as we had hoped. After struggling several years and drastically cutting expenses, the profits in Layton finally went from red to black; but the accumulated debt was far too high.

In July 1982, while GROVER was in Caliente relieving Robert Murdock for his vacation, a legal paper was posted early one morning on the outside door of our University Mall drugstore. It was a court order from Walgreens. We were given five days to pay our outstanding debt with them, or they would reclaim their original lease. The bomb had exploded. Without our most profitable store we could never pay our debts; but raising the amount owed in five days was beyond our already over-extended credit level. The darkness of the flapping bird wings choked out all the sunshine. Total despair nearly surfaced. Miraculously, my brother MARION from San Jose, California, had chosen that time to visit us in Provo. His compassion, kindness, and support was deeply needed and appreciated. Pride no longer ruled the day. This "brief period" would extend far beyond the two years my mother had mentioned to me as a child. I remembered the Lord had told Joseph Smith in Liberty Jail, "thine adversity shall be but a small moment." [D&C 121] His small moment lasted many years, and a "brief period" sounded greater than a "small moment."

I called my cousin-once-removed lawyer, former U of U basketball star, and "All American" DeLYLE CONDIE, a partner in the Salt Lake City law firm of McKay, Burton, Thurman, and Condie. He quickly drove to our home in Provo, and before the Federal Court had closed in Salt Lake City that ominous day, Swallows Drugs Corporation–Utah had filed a Reorganization, Chapter 11, which also added personally GROVER and BROOKIE SWALLOW, who had personally guaranteed their loans. That evening I spoke several hours on the telephone with brother-in-law WILLIAM (BILL) CLAY in Virginia.

Several years before, BILL had been the manager of Cabana, a luxury motor home company on the Oregon Pacific Coast, when a huge shortage of gasoline, with a corresponding rapid rise in the price, had brought the motor home production in our nation to its knees. Sales plummeted, especially the luxurious models, and Cabana was forced into bankruptcy. BILL, as manager, had guided them through the process, while they closed their doors—forever.

BILL was very emphatic with me. All our assets could be frozen and we would no longer be able to borrow from anyone. Our creditors would come upon us "like a pack of wolves with blood in their eyes," including even those we believed to be our close friends. We must immediately close our Layton Hills Mall drugstore and restaurant, before other creditors became aware of the Chapter 11. I reminded him, it was now making a profit.

"That's not good enough! If you survive, you will need to convince many lawyers, banks, and businessmen that you *can* succeed. You will need every asset in your possession to do so, for you will get nothing else. Don't tell anyone, including your employees, about your problem; but get everything you can out of Layton, before another court-order takes it away from you."

That Saturday night, after the mall closed at 9 P.M., with the great help of our children and some of their spouses, we boxed up our total inventory and moveable fixtures into huge U-Haul trucks, and transferred them to the large storage room of our University Mall store. It was a tremendous effort, for the Layton venture was 14,000 square feet. I watched my spouse and children with a heavy heart as they struggled under the load. I think I can speak for all of us when I say that we felt much like thieves working at night and attempting to accomplish the task without anyone being aware of it. The "garish world, in spite of fears" had changed overnight. Now those fears would have to be met.

Our largest secured creditor was Bergen Brunswig Drug Company, who was in the first secured position for the inventory of our Utah Corporation. Their lawyer from Los Angeles wanted an immediate exact total of the inventory and gave us only a few days to get it and meet with them in Salt Lake City with our lawyer and a projected plan for payment. Inventories are constantly changing on a daily basis in the drugstore business. Without daily replacement by our suppliers, the business would soon die. Bergen was our main supplier. If we lost their support, others would quickly follow suit, and reorganization would become impossible; yet their immediate demand was huge, as our inventory was thousands of small items totaling into the hundreds of thousands of dollars. The reorganization plan was also difficult. There wasn't much time for planning and projecting. I was the accountant.

The inventory started the next morning. With the expedience of the situation, it was impossible to hire an inventory company. All our family and personnel arrived at daybreak to begin the gigantic task of counting, multiplying, and adding figures. My sister CeCELIA and her husband WAYNE surprisingly arrived from San Jose, California, with several of their children to help. When the day ended and the counting was done, CeCELIA, daughter DANA, and I continued until 4:00 A.M. on our ten-key calculators with multiplying and additions until the job was finished. I had completed our projections and plans earlier.

That morning GROVER and I met in one of the law offices of McKay, Burton, Thurman, and Condie with the multiple lawyers and administrators of Bergen Brunswig Drug that had flown into Salt Lake City from Los Angles. We went armed with our large grocery store paper bag filled with the entire inventory counting booklets and figures. We gave them our projections and plans for repayment. They appeared amazed at the size of our inventory and the huge bag of figures we presented them with to support it. Seeing the effort it would take, to dispute it, they accepted our totals and projections—we could still be their customer, if the inventory remained above our debt level.

DeLYLE CONDIE had wanted us to have the best lawyer possible and had suggested that we change to their bankruptcy lawyer in his firm, William T. Thurman Jr., whom he claimed was the best in the state of Utah. We were not disappointed in Bill Thurman's exceptional ability or his helpfulness in meeting the onslaught of difficult and determined creditors. He was very helpful in preparing and standing by us in our efforts for reorganization, and later congratulated us for being able to stand the pressure, telling us that most of his Chapter 11s, gave up their reorganization plans and changed to Chapter 7s, leaving all their debts behind in oblivion.

After many similar meetings and court appearances with other creditors during the next year-and-one-half, our plan was finally accepted by the court, and we were able to legally retain our business in the University Mall. The bankers, who had our two homes and other real estate as security, foreclosed and sold them at far below what we believed to be a fair market price. This action cleared much of their greater debt, but left us without anything extra. As I was cleaning our personal items out of our bedroom in our Grandview home, I was feeling quite depressed and a few tears were collecting. A male voice from the heavens kindly spoke and comforted me in my mind with the words, *"I never said it would be easy."*

It wasn't; but there were those who stood by us, usually not our former friendly creditors, many of whom "came at us like a pack of wolves, with blood in their eyes," as predicted by my brother-in-law BILL CLAY.

Of course, we were not alone in our troubles. The high interest rates were destroying hundreds of thousands of businesses across the nation. The nation's pharmaceutical manufacturers and other large industries were merging for their survival—the smaller or less fortunate ones totally disappeared. Unemployment was over 8%. The bulging housing market was in deep trouble, especially the more expensive homes, which were entirely unaffordable with their double-digit interest to almost everyone. The foreclosures on homes and automobiles were massive. The savings and loans businesses reached their crisis and created a scandal throughout the nation. The owners of the Layton Hills Mall sold at a loss to new buyers. Vacancies in the University Mall were numerous.

The stock market crash of 1987 was not particularly eventful to those of us who had already experienced similar problems. Perhaps it was even helpful in some ways, for GROVER and I were finally able to purchase a home in Orem at approximately 50% off its original value with a single-digit interest rate from a mortgage company that was fighting for its own existence—it went into bankruptcy about six months later. It was a time of desperation for many businesses and people.

I was consulting our lawyer Bill Thurman one day in his office, probably in 1984. His whole desk was covered with a mass of pink slips—telephone calls he needed to return. "Look at this mess," he stated waving his hands over the endless pink papers. He shook his head and sadly stated, "I've got to get out of this bankruptcy business. There's no way I can keep up with it all!"

It was amazing that through these difficult times, the nation's big businesses continued to replace our local orchards with larger and larger commercial buildings, competing with the already struggling established businesses. Center Street in Provo became a large mall of cruising student automobiles, after the failing businesses had closed their doors each evening, or indefinitely. The vacancies multiplied. The greater part of their business had at first gone to the University Mall, and then expanded into the multiple mini-malls that grew like spider legs across the two neighboring cities.

The established chain stores and mini-malls slowly aged and dwindled and were replaced by the superstores that bargained for minimal taxes, greater privileges, and laws that the independents were not given. Drug manufacturers gave these huge conglomerations special prices that allowed them to undercut our costs. HMOs and Health Insurance Companies bargained against the independents, taking loyal customers into their fold as the ever-increasing need for health insurance increased.

Then it became time for their struggles. The retail pharmacies, at least ours, were left holding thousands of dollars of unpaid debts from those we called third-party insurance receivables, as many of these insurance companies crumbled, merged, or reorganized. Gone were the days of the "fair trade" and meaningful "anti-trust laws." Gone were those days when a doctor's office call was $5, a ton-sillectomy was $25, an appendectomy $50, and the mother's care and birth of her baby was only $75, as it had been when our first children were born. Bigger was not necessarily better; but many believed it was. All the medical profession was being mesmerized by increasing lawsuits and mega-dollar settlements.

Through all of this, we stayed alive and paid our debts. After ten years, all bankruptcies are dismissed. All of our secured creditors and taxes had been paid along with the bulk of the unsecured. With our long-term lease near expiration, we were threatened with a new lease of more than twice the dollars. We sold our inventory and prescription files to Payless Drugs, a very large chain store per-haps 10 blocks north of us on State Street and closed Swallows Drugs–Utah, 31 Dec 1994. Payless Drugs had their problems, too, and soon sold that business to Rite-Aid. Rite-Aid found the space much too large, closed their lease and built a smaller, controllable store nearby with far less employees.

Recently we visited the University Mall. We spoke with an old friend who still managed a store near our old location—mostly vacant through the years. He told us that our nearby anchor department store had been recently sold for the second time. The last leasers, a national department store chain, had told him that their best year's sales, while they occupied the space, were only 50% of the worst sales-year of the previous tenant.

Our children all married, GROVER and I returned to our remaining drug-store in Caliente, Nevada—a separate Nevada Corporation. We rented our home in Orem to our youngest daughter DIANNA, husband DALE, and their children, purchasing a new motor home to stay in at Caliente, while planning to build a new store on a lot we had purchased near the clinic and medical center. The old three-story hotel, where we rented the corner space on the ground floor, was deteriorating rapidly. We were third on our builders list and many months away from the actual construction. Then unexpectedly, a strong wind and long, heavy rain storm hit our usually dry county.

The wind blew off the hotel roof, and the rain spilled quickly into the upper vacated third and second floors above us. At first we placed buckets under the drips and plastic covers over the merchandise under the ever-increasing small streams from our ceiling; then as small became large in the never-ending rain, with water dripping from our light fixtures and chunks of the plastered ceiling preparing to fall, the danger was eminent. We quickly found another place to rent and prepared to move our store. It was an old service station with a two-stall cement-floored car repair unit attached. The landlord could immediately make the necessary structural changes. The rain stopped; but the mites grew, creating coughing and sneezing. It was time to go quickly.

By the second weekend we were ready and moved our merchandise and business to the new location. We had switched to McKesson as our main drug supplier many years before, when Bergen Brunswig had become difficult to deal with. They sent a crew to help with the move, and VANDA, husband HYRUM, daughter JENNI, DIANNA and children TAYLA and JADEN, drove down to help us once more with another undesirable situation.

The prescription room needed a carpenter. Gary Elmore of Caliente took on the challenge. Of course, the drug inspector from the Nevada Board of Pharmacy was also involved. To add to the distress of the burdensome period, our drugstore personnel chose that time to collectively bargain for higher wages. We did have insurance for windstorm. It helped some, but created additional work and time to come up with a figure and collect what they considered to be an exact amount. Part of the expenses were entirely refused. When it ended, building the new beautiful store we had planned on our already purchased lot was put on an undetermined hold.

The computer fears of Y2K were increasing and we decided that we should expand the tiny home on our remaining lot in Panaca by adding a small storage basement, with a bedroom, bathroom and kitchen above in case it was needed. Gary Elmore was willing to do it. DIANNA and DALE missed their former neighborhood and returned to their old home in Pleasant Grove, which had not sold during the buyers market. With that change, we decided to sell the house in Orem and enlarge our home construction in Panaca. I drew the plans to fit our furniture and added an indoor vinyl-lined swimming pool and garages. The little house was moved to another spot as the new construction encompassed that area.

DALE and DIANNA watch the happy grandsons (above)
with VANDA and DANA joining the swimmers (below)

Daughter EMILY

In 1980, our daughter EMILY was given a patriarchal blessing—part reads:

> "Honor thy father and mother. The ties that bind them to thee and to thy brothers and sisters are eternal and will become more precious with the passing of time. Do not take for granted thy ability to speak, to think, to see, hear, and walk. Stand erect, proud yet humble, and make thy decisions listening to the promptings of the spirit."

Whenever EMILY read her blessing, she worried a little about the mention of her ability to speak, walk, and so forth, thinking of diseases like M.S., or a debilitating accident; but it didn't prevent her from enjoying life. Twenty-one years after the blessing was given, she would understand this warning.

EMILY attended B.Y.U. and graduated as a nurse practitioner. She married DEREK during his third year of medical school at Southwestern in Dallas, Texas. DEREK did his residency in Phoenix, Arizona, and then set up his practice in Salt Lake City. They had six children when they came to visit us that Friday, 2 Nov 2001. It was less than two months after the disaster of 11 Sep 2001, and the outrage and horror of that day had created a somber atmosphere in our discussions during breakfast that morning. Swimming was a relief for the children; but as they did flips from the side of our indoor pool, I was worried and called to them to stop. EMILY strongly supported my insistence, and the fancy jumps ceased immediately. All diving was prohibited in our small pool.

I had not joined in the swimming that morning, and when DEREK and EMILY decided, while sitting in our spa, that it was time for lunch, I left the family to get some sandwiches started. It takes awhile for showers, so I decided to finish some accounting on my computer first. Perhaps five minutes later, their oldest daughter, JESSICA, came screaming up the short stairway,

"Grandma! Come quick! My mother is hurt really bad." As I hastened to help, another command came.
"My Dad wants you to call 911 right now; before you come down!"

With the ambulance on its way from Pioche [Panaca's was in use] and a call to GROVER in Caliente, I first saw my daughter lying on her side on the ceramic tile decking by the foot of the pool with blood pouring from her nose and being vomited out her mouth. She was breathing—but appeared unconscious.

DEREK asked me to get a towel to absorb the blood.

I rushed to get the towel; but first grabbed young seven-year-old ALICIA and sat her down with tiny twenty-one-month-old AMANDA on the couch in our den where cartoons were playing on our cable channel. Emphatically, I told ALICIA to watch her young sister and not let her get off that couch. We didn't need another accident. Returning with the towel, I found that EMILY was awake, but not moving. The older children were hugging each other in uncontrollable tears as they watched their mother. I sent MARISSA to watch her two younger sisters—away from this tragic scene. Dr. DEREK looked up at me with the most forlorn look I had ever witnessed, "Mom," he said quietly, "There's nothing I can do."

JESSICA, still hugging her two weeping brothers, cried, "Grandmother, is my mother going to die?" My response was a quick, emphatic, "No!" Something inside had told me that EMILY would be all right, and I never questioned her ability to recover. As the blood continued to flow from her nose and was coughed-up through her mouth, DEREK was telling her to move her right foot, which she was barely able to do, then her left foot, with a similar result. He then asked her to move each of her hands. There was a weak response in both of them. One of the children asked how much blood she had lost.

"About two pints," DEREK answered.

"What happens if she loses three pints?"

"That's very dangerous," DEREK calmly stated.

"What happens if it's four pints?"

"She dies!" There was a new explosion of tears.

DEREK asked me to get a throw-away pillow for her head and then a blanket. Returning, the ambulance siren was screaming, and he asked me to direct them to the nearest entrance. Rushing out the garage door, I saw our good neighbor Barry Isom, who had flown helicopter rescue missions in Viet Nam. He was already directing the ambulance around to our back swimming pool entrance—no fence at that early date. In minutes, an IV was started and EMILY was on the stretcher and transported to the ambulance. With DEREK by her side, EMILY arrived at the Grover C. Dils Medical Center, where they were joined by three additional well-prepared doctors, GROVER, and our bishop, Paul Christensen, who just happened to be there. A Flight-for-Life helicopter was already on its way from the Las Vegas Trauma Center. The heavy bleeding had ended; but severe damage to the brain was the universal diagnosis. How did it happen?

Their oldest son RYAN was the first to see her fighting for breath in the pool. He quickly brought her to the shorter end. MARISSA, who was emerging from the pool, yelled to her dad—upstairs—just out of the shower. Rushing down the stairs, he was able to set EMILY carefully on the side of the pool, where I first saw her. The accident? None of the three remaining children had actually seen it, and EMILY was unable to tell us anything.

GROVER needed some consecrated olive oil for the sick and called our former Caliente bishop, Kurt Lee, who quickly brought it and stood with the group as the blessing was given before EMILY was wheeled to the helicopter. GROVER anointed and DEREK sealed the anointing with a promise that she would be restored to her normal health and strength. All who participated in the blessing expressed their feelings that the spirit was very strong and they believed this promise would be fulfilled.

DEREK was disappointed when they refused to allow him to accompany his wife on the flight, and stood with the others as they somberly watched the flight disappear southward. Returning to our home, DEREK changed his blood-stained clothes and drove to Las Vegas. GROVER, with their son RYAN, went the next morning. Two of DEREK's brothers and their wives joined them in Las Vegas, flying down from the Salt Lake City airport.

At home in Panaca with the children, after the ambulance was on its way, Barry Isom sent me quickly out of the pool area.

"I'll clean this up!" he told me. "You don't need to deal with this scene."

Looking at the profuse blood that had flowed over the tile and into the swimming pool, I gratefully agreed and thanked him. After checking on the children, who had already escaped downstairs to the T.V. family room, I made my telephone calls to our many children, who were scattered from Boston to Los Angeles. VANDA and DIANNA arrived quickly from Orem and Pleasant Grove with their young children and helped me drain the pool and scrub the blood stains that still remained. JESSICA insisted on joining us in this endeavor—against our judgment. The children were taken north to their home on

Sunday by DEREK's brother BRETT and his wife, so the older children could continue their school. DIANNA, VANDA, with their families, and I then went to Las Vegas, and GROVER returned back to our drugstore.

Palace Station was quite near UMC and gave us special medical discounts on our rooms. My memories of Las Vegas through the next week include the feeling of the dark flapping wings of millions of large birds, shutting out the sunlight. VANDA and JENNI flew back to their home on Sunday evening, because DIANNA and car remained longer. They remember the guards with large guns at the airport, and JENNI, age six, was afraid to fly, expecting the plane to crash into some tall building. Our son GROVER and his wife AMBER arrived from Salt Lake City. TROY, DORCAS and baby TRENTON flew in from Boston. DORCAS, and her tiny son stayed on for many weeks. Her great optimism and coaching were always a ray of sunshine.

TOM arrived from Los Angles by bus and walked from the bus station to the trauma center about 4:30 A.M. Only one visitor at a time was allowed into EMILY's room, and since the rest of us were asleep in our rooms, he had a long visit with his sister. EMILY still remembers the overflowing love and appreciation she felt that morning for his sacrifice in coming and can still feel the peace and love that he brought with him that morning. Her appreciation extended to all her siblings and others who visited her. Tears came to her eyes as she tried to express her great love for all of them.

The Trauma Center at UMC had a very cold cement feeling about it. There was an armed guard, equally cold and efficient, at the entrance into their intensive care unit. The waiting area had only stiff cushioned metal chairs and a few limited vending machines. When my turn came to go in and see my daughter, she was stretched out on her back on the thin hospital bed. She was attached by tubes to the surrounding machines that bleeped various colors continually. Part of her hair on the top of her head was shaved off—where they had penetrated her skull with a needle to monitor the cerebral pressure. Her right wrist, with all its needles for meds and nourishment, was taped to the raised metal guard on the bed—they were afraid she would pull out the stomach tube from her mouth. There was oxygen being administered through her nose, and a catheter for her urine. Her eyes would barely open; but she was able to slowly blink them. One blink for "Yes;" two blinks for "No." When the eyelids were lifted by her doctors, her eyes were crossed—everything she saw was double. When I squeezed her right hand, she could weakly return it; her other appendages lay motionless, although her right leg would respond lightly to a doctor's needle prick on the sole of her foot.

We were told that her injury was a broken skull at the lower-back of her head. The cracks extended in many directions—like a windshield crashed by a stone. The impact had also broken a forward part of the lower skull, creating the extensive bleeding from her nose. Internally, the "pons" of the brainstem had been severely injured. This is the center part of the stem—the area where the motor and sensory nerves cross from left to right and right to left—hence, the apparent paralysis and lack of sensations. The upper part of the brainstem that controls the ability to think area of the brain was apparently uninjured. The uninjured lower brain stem controls the breathing, heart, and other automatic functions. Her neurologist, we were told, was the best in Las Vegas—the one who did all the head injuries for Evel Knievel. Since EMILY was unable to speak at this time, there was much speculation and wonder about how such an injury could occur in our swimming pool. Some of us felt she had slipped on the tile surrounding the pool and hit her head on the edge of the side-tile as she slid into the pool. Personally, I felt confident that she would never have dived into the pool, which was not designed properly for this activity.

During one of my turns at EMILY's bedside in the Trauma Center, a teacher with many of her young nursing students came into the room. They brushed past me without a word and went to the machine that was measuring the pressure of the spinal fluid in her brain. As the instructor proceeded to explain how it worked to her students, she seemed to speak of my daughter more like an object than a patient. When I had heard enough, I interrupted and told her,

"Do you realize that my daughter is a nurse practitioner? She is fully awake and can hear and understand everything you're saying."

The teacher's face reddened slightly and she quickly approached EMILY and asked, "How am I doing, nurse?" EMILY gave her one blink, and although the muscles of her face were still mostly immovable, I saw the light of a smile projected when she became recognized as a person.

After a few days in the Trauma Center, the stomach tube was removed and her wrist released, which allowed her to shakily move her right arm. DEREK asked them to bring a large board with the alphabet on it. It was difficult for her to point to the letters, because of her double-vision and slow coordination; but her first communication was "D–O–V–E––S–O–R–R–Y."

She later reported how frustrating it was to listen to all our theories and not be able to tell us what had happened—she was able to speak softly and slowly a few days later—more like a whisper.

As her speech improved, she told us how she had been attempting to clear the toys from the pool. Several were lying on the bottom. EMILY later wrote:

"I asked the children to help clean-up the pool area in preparation for putting the pool cover back on. I asked several times and got no response. Deciding that the best thing to do was to just jump in and work with them, I started for the pool, planning to do a surface dive from the shallow end of the pool, like I had done many times before, [unknown to her mother.] I then planned to swim to the other side of the pool and start to clear out the toys.

"As I approached the pool, a voice as clear as if someone had spoken it came into my head, 'Don't dive.' The instruction was very clear. I responded to it with a thought, 'It's just a surface dive.' I continued toward the side of the pool. 'Don't dive,' the voice came again. I responded with confidence, 'I've done this before.' As I got closer to the pool, a third time I heard the voice, only this time it said, 'Just jump.' The voice was more firm, but it wasn't louder. With mild irritation, I responded as I prepared to take action, 'It's just a surface dive.'

"I was just fine until half way across the pool. I suddenly decided that I wanted to go back to the shallow end of the pool and start clearing the pool toys there first. I had always wanted to do a flip turn just as I had seen the professionals do in swim meets. It hadn't looked that hard. Still moving fast from the inertia of my dive, I tucked my head hard and prepared to flip my legs over my head. It was easy and everything was all right until, smack, I hit my head on the bottom of the pool where it was angling down from the shallow end to the deep end. The water was about five feet deep in that area.

"The impact hurt, but not much more than the other times that I had swam into the side of the pool. I didn't think much about the pain at that time. I just knew that I had to get to the surface. It seemed so far away. I swam for the surface as hard as I could. It seemed to take forever. I was running out of air and was beginning to feel an urgent need to take a breath. I couldn't understand why it was taking so long to get to the surface when in reality, the pool was shallow enough that I could have stood on my tip toes and my head would have been above water. Finally, I broke the surface. The deep breath of air that I took felt so good, but then I immediately went under again. I realized that I was in trouble. My son RYAN was still in the pool, but getting his attention was far from my mind. I just had to get to the surface. As I broke the surface again, and took a refreshing breath, I was greatly relieved that RYAN was there to help me. For all I know, he had helped me get to the surface that second time. As RYAN scooped me into his arms and held me above the water, I knew that I would be safe. 'Now I can relax,' I thought as I closed my eyes.

"The next instant, I was fully conscious and was standing in the southeast corner of the pool room, just inside the sliding door. . . . Immediately, I saw DEREK kneeling over someone with dark hair that was hurt and was lying at the edge of the pool. There was a pool of blood around the person's head. It was clearly an emergent situation, and I was very concerned for the well being of what I was sure was one of my children.

"Filled with worry, I walked, or thought that I was walking, toward them. 'It's not AMANDA,' the person on the pool deck was too big to be her. As I got closer, I thought with relief, 'It's not MARISSA,' because I realized then that the person DEREK was assisting was me. I was no longer in my body! I was just a spirit.

"Immediately, I knew, 'I've got to get back in there!' I advanced toward my body. As I did so, I heard a voice say in a matter of fact tone, 'Okay, let's get to work.' The voice was firm, but kind and loving. I felt sad remembering that I had been warned, but hadn't listened. However, I also knew that I was not alone and took comfort in the presence of the spirit that accompanied me. I am not sure just how I was able to be rejoined with my body. In fact, it was simple and instantaneous. It was painless.

"Immediately, I was nauseated and began to vomit. I had seen the blood when I had been a spirit, and I knew that I must have blood in my stomach. The nausea was horrible! My stomach heaved over and over again and I felt warm liquid on my arm. I opened my eyes for just a moment and looked at my outstretched arm in front of my face. It was covered in bright red blood. 'Breath, just breath,' came the same voice in my head. With the words came the understanding that I should hold still, very still. With what had happened, I didn't hesitate to listen to the spiritual prompting. I felt great comfort and peace as I focused on inhaling deeply and filling my lungs with life-giving air, and careful to be still and 'just breath' deeply and evenly.

"I heard the voice again, 'You will be paralyzed, but you will recover.' I thought to myself, 'It's just a random thought.' I then hoped it wasn't only words just coming from my own worries. But, deep inside, I knew the words were from the same spiritual presence, and they were true. The words had come into my head as strongly as if they were a proven fact read out of a book. Thankfully, the words came with the comfort and assurance that I would be all right. From that moment forward, I never doubted that I would have a future on the earth.

"The words the spiritual presence had spoken to my mind, and the peace that came with the words, often came to mind as I later worked towards recovery. Those words took away my fear and let me focus on doing all I could to recover and return to health and to my family. I felt calm, and I knew that I was not alone. I can't say who was with me for sure during those first minutes after my injury; but...I believe Grandmother CONDIE was the one that was there coaching me and comforting me. I joked with several people later that I was prevented from being able to see her and to speak with her face to face because I would have talked too much.

"As I lay there with my eyes mostly closed, I was aware of the action going on around me. DEREK would ask me to squeeze his hand, move an arm or a leg and even though I felt weak, I was able to follow the commands."

At dinner one evening in Las Vegas with all the visitors, DEREK and his brother GREG were discussing the diving event. GREG, a dentist, made the following observation:

> "If EMILY's skull hadn't fractured in the lower front and caused all that loss of blood, which lowered the pressure, she wouldn't have lasted three seconds. The rapid bleeding saved her life."

It was difficult for DEREK, as a doctor and husband, to stand by and let other physicians determine what should be done for his wife. It became even more difficult when he discovered, from reading her charts and his own observations, that one of her lungs had been punctured accidentally by an inexperienced intern and that a painful infection was developing. Then he arrived one morning to discover that the pain medication that was supposed to go into her vein was detached and running onto the floor. At first, EMILY had not wanted any pain medication; the sensory nerves were not yet reacting. But shortly the pain in her sinuses became severe. She requested and continued to request the pain medication—the nurses inspected the drips, but not the destination of the tube. It was a long painful night and an embarrassed nurse the next day.

When the doctors locked up her charts so DEREK couldn't read them, he wanted to have her placed in Health South, a rehab center in Salt Lake City. One week after her injury, she was transported north with her uncomfortable husband squished beside her in a small ambulance. This change allowed her to be closer to her children and DEREK to his work. He sincerely believed she would receive better care in more pleasant surroundings. I cornered one of her neurologists just before her departure—trying to find out her long-term prognosis. He was very careful in his promises. He finally told me that the next six months would determine how much she would be able to do; after that, her remaining disabilities would be permanent.

DORCAS and tiny TRENTON drove with me to Salt Lake City. Every day, the three of us would arrive early and return home late. ROXANNE supervised or drove EMILY's children to school and coordinated the care of the younger children, who at times stayed with DIANNA, VANDA, or friends and neighbors. Dinners were brought in regularly to her family by the L.D.S. Relief Society of their ward. The outpouring of love and service was abundant.

On the Sunday after her arrival in Health South, the visitors arrived in such profusion that DEREK had them post a limit of two visitors at a time, with a limit of ten minutes. After visiting for their ten minutes, DANA and MIKE quietly told me that EMILY had said that, "Grandma and Grandpa had come to see her that morning." All of her grandparents had died previously. Pointing to a certain place in the room, she continued, "They were standing right there but wouldn't let me see them. They told me I would be able to live and do the things I was sent to do; but I needed to work hard." The next morning, I asked EMILY which grandparents had come to see her. "Your mother and dad," she barely whispered. She didn't elaborate further, nor did I ask. Several years later, EMILY explained:

> "When I arrived at Health South Rehabilitation Center I had a hard time breathing. I wondered if I was going to ever be able to breathe normally again. I questioned if I was having an asthmatic reaction of some kind,

because my breathing just wasn't improving. I was unable to move my left side by myself, and could not yet turn myself. I was being turned in bed every two hours to prevent bed sores. In the early hours of the morning two nurses came into my room. 'Should we turn her?' I heard one of the nurses say, to which the other replied, 'No, she's asleep.' Then, I heard a sweet and gentle chuckle and sensed the presence of both my grandmother and my grandfather CONDIE. Once again, I heard that same inner voice that told me, 'This will be your turning point.' The experience was so touching and real that I told others about it the next day. The most interesting thing to me, however, was that in truth my breathing started improving that night and truly became the turning point in my recovery. My breathing was so difficult I could only speak in a weak whisper. With my head injury, the tears and weeping began occurring suddenly with the slightest provocation and became nearly uncontrollable once started, making the matter even worse . . . completely unable to talk.

"I cannot express one-hundredth of the gratitude I feel for all who showed their love and support for me during this trying time. The love I felt coming from others was truly immeasurable. It did much to increase my confidence and determination on the road to recovery. To this day, April 2007, I feel that love and the great inner strength it gives me."

During the following week in Health South, our son BRUCE and his wife CINDY arrived from Des Moines, Iowa, and stayed about a week. It gave her new courage to keep trying. DEREK's parents, IVAN and JOANN MUSE, came regularly. IVAN had a malignant brain tumor and was not expected to live many more months, but still comforted her with his love. Members of their church ward were regular visitors and helped greatly in keeping normalcy in her children's lives. Cousins, aunts, uncles arrived. Flowers and plush animals abounded.

EMILY had a fair movement in her right leg and a little in her left leg when she left the Trauma Center in Las Vegas, but her left arm and hand had no motor ability—it would lay limp by her side. At Health South three therapists helped on a daily schedule, except Saturdays and Sundays. The speech therapist would work on the facial muscles, eyes, speech, eating and swallowing. The occupational therapist would work with her arms, hands and fingers, and the physical therapist would work on her legs, walking, and lower body movements. Eating in their dining hall was at first very difficult and messy. Later, pool therapy was added.

During that first week of therapy, she was on a heavy dose of Duragesic (patch), and seemed quite lethargic and nauseous. I had accompanied her in her wheelchair to the speech therapist. She seemed to have great difficulty in doing any of her facial muscle movements., and the therapist told her to just relax for awhile. She then quietly said,

> "While you're resting, let me tell you that it's a miracle you are even here. We don't ever get injuries like yours—maybe one other; but quite different. Injuries like yours never survive long enough to come here. We're all struggling to find the best ways to help you."

That afternoon, I suggested to DORCAS, also a pharmacist, that I thought the pain medication was creating the nausea. She agreed and immediately talked with the doctor, who lowered the dose considerably. Our lethargic patient perked up and started doing better.

Her left arm and hand were still totally paralyzed. After the occupational therapist left, I would continue to massage and work with it. EMILY had been taking violin lessons, and I kept trying to move it into the left arm position—moving the various fingers in the proper way—even trying to attempt a vibrato. Then one day during occupational therapy, she was able to get a tiny twitch from her left middle finger. Tears of gratitude immediately flowed from her eyes for she knew that was the first sign, and she would be able to regain the use of her left arm. It was a day of thanksgiving for all of us.

When the Thanksgiving holiday arrived DEREK brought EMILY in her wheelchair to ROXANNE and MARC's home for our large family dinner. Dad (GROVER) had arrived from Caliente and most of our children and grandchildren from the Salt Lake and Utah valleys had joined the group. My brother JAMES and his wife JERRY were there from Washington D.C., and would go into the Mission Training Center during the following week to prepare for their two-year mission to India. My sister CeCELIA and husband WAYNE WILSON with some of their children also joined with us. EMILY was still very weak, and DEREK took her home after the dinner to rest.

The physical therapist started her walking. First it was very slowly with a harness and his support. She continually improved and the harness and support were removed. The many occupants of the gym gave her a loud cheer, "Way to go, EMILY," as she walked several yards toward the therapist without any support. DORCAS continually urged her onward. "You can do it! Come on! Move those feet higher! Climb those steps! Push those weights!" Her physical therapist told me that she was doing in days what it was taking his older patients months to do.

When EMILY was able to sit with strength, the occupational therapist would give her simple things to do with her hands—like large-pieced picture puzzles to put together. This helped to develop the coordination between her eyes and her hands. Her double vision was improving slowly. They had a kitchen, where she was challenged to stand and remove dishes and food items from the cupboard without dropping them and develop the strength to return them back into the cupboard. While eating, the challenge was for her to get the food into her mouth with a spoon without spilling it or smearing it on her face. Straws were used in her liquids. This helped her improve her lung capacity. I was constantly reminded that all of us should be more grateful for the many small things we are able to do daily—mostly without appreciation for our many abilities.

Before Christmas, she was home with her children, and DORCAS and I returned to our homes. She was not then allowed to drive a car, but was still taken to Health South for therapy for awhile. DEREK's fear that their home would need to be restructured with a lift to the various floors had passed completely. Her percentage of recovery kept steadily increasing. It reached 98% before the six months allowed by the Las Vegas doctor had expired, and still improved afterward.

Her bishop had not removed her from her position as Primary President in her ward throughout this ordeal. One day I visited Primary when she was just beginning to take charge of the meetings. Their pianist had not arrived and she attempted to accompany the singing; but the coordination between her eyes and hands was not yet rapid enough to keep up. Another son, JARED, arrived, unexpectedly but truly welcomed, before the end of 2002. Today, no one would know she ever had a problem; but she does not "take for granted [her] ability to speak, to think, to see, hear, and walk," as was admonished in her patriarchal blessing. Of course, there is no more diving in our swimming pool by anyone; but EMILY still swims happily with her family.

EMILY, 2007, WITH HER FATHER

July 2009, EMILY just read a medical study on the internet on brain stem injuries similar to hers. The author claimed he had discovered eight cases that lived. Seven of these had died in the first 35 days. The eighth was in a wheelchair and could write slowly with the right hand.

Much more could be said about GROVER and me, our ten children, spouses, 47 grandchildren, and 32 great-grandchildren. We love them all. Overhead, war planes are training. They are flying quite low today. Sometimes we wonder how often they have us in their bombsights. It is quite a different world than the one we were born into; yet, the need to struggle, learn and grow has not changed that much. Free agency, its use and limitations are similar. I would like to end this chapter with a poem that GROVER memorized and first gave when I became a new member of the Lamba Delta Sigma (L.D.S.) fraternity at Idaho State College. The author is unknown to me. GROVER has used this poem in many of his funeral and church assignments.

"An Angel took me to a mountain top and from its lofty heights
I saw the Earth beneath my feet and stars above.
He showed me kingdoms, principalities, and matter,
Un-endowed with life –
The rocks and vibrant living things, the birds, the bees,
The plants, the trees,
And crowning overall, I saw humanity, with all its creeds.
At first it seemed to me that I beheld a seething,
Boiling mass of fighting things,
Then as I gazed upon this confusing scene and I began to think,
My vision cleared.
Instead of chaos, order and design appeared.
All nature took upon itself a purposeful existence,
Each with parts to play in this great drama of the Earth.
Behind it all, I saw in vision clear,
The Great Designer of the Universe.
The Angel said to me, 'What doest thou here?
What purpose hast thou in this earthly life?'
I stood transfixed.
The vision of my life loomed up before me, as I answered him,
'I—I am a child of God, sent here to live,
To walk the paths of progress and grow into Celestial Life,
Here, upon the Earth.
The things I see before me now
Are the means by which I rise into the realms of Joy.
'Tis given me to choose the course I'll take.
Free Agency is mine from worlds afar.'
The voice within me says,
'Climb up, forever up progression's stairs, beyond the stars.'
So, here I am, progressing toward my goal
Through devious ways of Earth's experience.
God grant that I may choose the proper course,
And find my way into a glorious home."

Special Remembrance

Since completing this book and before its first printing, my husband,

GROVER SWALLOW

passed on into this "glorious home" on 22 Apr 2009.

GROVER AND BROOKIE AT THEIR 50TH WEDDING ANNIVERSARY

About six months after he died, I went to the temple. That night as I was preparing for bed,

I looked at one of GROVER's recent pictures and said out loud,

"Well, I went to the Temple today; but I didn't see you there!"

Just before I awoke the next morning, I dreamed that I was sitting at my computer and turned toward the kitchen and he was standing there by the table. He looked somewhat like he looked in our young wedding pictures —shaven, with a full head of dark hair, but with a dark single-breasted suit, white shirt, and impeccably tied yellow tie. He appeared more mature, but without any wrinkles. His smile was a little broader, and love seemed to emanate from his whole person. I started to move towards him, breathlessly, in my dream, and he quickly disappeared.

I'm so glad our marriage is for "Time and Eternity "and we will be together always.

I awoke with grateful tears in my eyes. As I sat up in my bed thinking about it at 6:00 A.M. my phone rang. It was my sister in Virginia telling me that my brother-in-law BYRON BABBEL had just died in New Mexico in his daughter's home.

Sometime around 1993 my children expressed the feeling that it was unlikely I would get anymore grandchildren. They all seamed to believe they were finished. Surprise! Surprise! Within the following year six babies arrived.

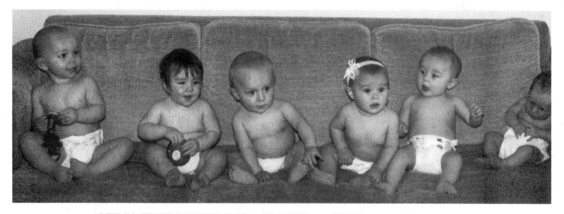

ALEX, MATTHEW, JADEN, ALICIA, BRANDT, and JENNI —from 6 mothers

Five months later a seventh one arrived. She was ROXANNE's HEATHER a tiny down-syndrome baby girl. They are now all teenagers. HEATHER has developed leukemia, and for awhile the chemo put it into remission—then it came back with a furry. Last year, 2010, ROXANNE was with her in the hospital for at least eight months. Nothing was working. They wanted to do a bone marrow transplant, and checked her siblings for the perfect match. All three of them qualified. GREG was chosen to be the donor. This picture was taken after the successful operation. I call it my "Perfect Love" picture. She brings much joy to all our families.

OUR DESCENDANTS AT GROVER'S FUNERAL

We assembled all my descendents and their spouses at GROVER's funeral after the dinner was served in the recreational room of our church building for this photo. Cousin RAY IVIE was there and took the picture with TROY's camera. Two of our granddaughters were expecting babies and were not allowed to fly from Minnesota and Texas, so they and their families are not present. A grandson-in-law from Utah was taking his final and couldn't delay it.

A green beret Special Forces grandson was in Iraq—they wouldn't let him come, but most of us were there. They came from Massachusetts, New Jersey, Michigan, Iowa, Texas, Utah, Nevada, Colorado, and California. We all love him.

OUR SEVEN DAUGHTERS AT BRUCE'S WEDDING

DIANNA, DORCAS, EMILY, ROXANNE, VANDA, BROOKIE, DANA

OUR THREE SONS DANCE AT DORCAS' WEDDING

TOM, BRUCE, AND GROVER

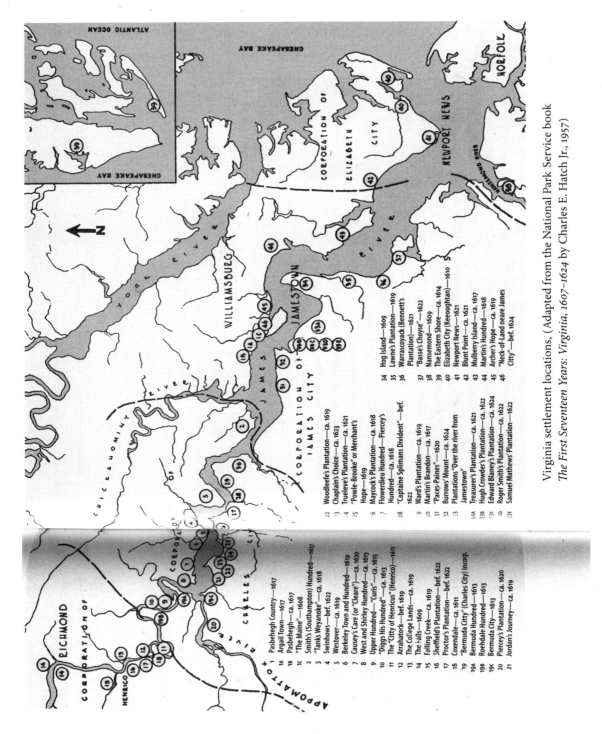

Virginia settlement locations, (Adapted from the National Park Service book
The First Seventeen Years: Virginia, 1607–1624 by Charles E. Hatch Jr., 1957)

1 Pasbehegh Country—1617
1A Argall Town—1617
1B Pasbehegh—ca. 1617
1C "The Maine"—1608
2 Smith's (Southampton) Hundred—1617
3 "Tanks Weyanoke"—ca. 1618
4 Swinhows—bef. 1622
5 Westover—ca. 1619
6 Berkeley Town and Hundred—1619
7 Causey's Care (or "Cleare")—ca. 1620
8 West and Shirley Hundred—ca. 1613
9 Upper Hundred—"Curls"—ca. 1613
10 "Diggs His Hundred"—ca. 1613
11 The "City of Henricus" (Henrico)—1611
12 Arrahatock—bef. 1619
13 The College Lands—ca. 1619
14 The Falls—1609
15 Falling Creek—ca. 1619
16 Sheffield's Plantation—bef. 1622
17 Proctor's Plantation—bef. 1622
18 Coxendale—ca. 1611
19 "Bermuda City" (Charles City) Incorp.
19A Bermuda Hundred—1613
19B Roehdale Hundred—1613
19C Bermuda City—1613
20 Piercey's Plantation—ca. 1620
21 Jordan's Journey—ca. 1619

22 Woodleefe's Plantation—ca. 1619
3 Chaplain's Choice—ca. 1623
4 Truelew's Plantation—ca. 1621
25 "Powle-Brooke" or Merchant's
   Hope—1619
6 Maycock's Plantation—ca. 1618
7 Flowerdieu Hundred—Piercey's
   Hundred—ca. 1618
28 "Captaine Spilmans Divident"—bef.
   1622
9 Ward's Plantation—ca. 1619
30 Martin's Brandon—ca. 1617
31 "Paces-Paines"—1620
32 Burrows' Mount—ca. 1624
33 Plantations "Over the river from
   Jamestown"
34A Treasurer's Plantation—ca. 1621
33B Hugh Crowder's Plantation—ca. 1622
33C Edward Blaney's Plantation—ca. 1624
10 Roger Smith's Plantation—ca. 1622
33H Samuel Mathews' Plantation—1622

34 Hog Island—1609
35 Lawne's Plantation—1619
36 Warrascoyack (Bennett's
   Plantation)—1621
37 "Basse's Choyse"—1622
38 Nansemond—1609
39 The Eastern Shore—ca. 1614
40 Elizabeth City (Keeoughtan)—1610
41 Newport News—1621
42 Blunt Point—ca. 1621
43 Mulberry Island—ca. 1617
44 Martin's Hundred—1618
45 Archer's Hope—ca. 1619
46 "Neck-of-Land neare James
   Citty"—bef. 1624

MAP OF EARLY JAMES RIVER SETTLEMENTS

— 51 —

THE ELUSIVE SHADOWS OF THE
SEVENTEENTH CENTURY VIRGINIA COMPANY

On 4 Apr 1994, archaeologist William M. Kelso placed his shovel in a pre-determined spot near the James River and broke the ground in an attempt to find the old 1607 Jamestown Fort. His friend Noel Hume was there for that first shovelful of lawn and dirt. Hume had thought the coastal fort had washed away into the river until he discovered the glassmaking crucible in the collection of the Association for the Preservation of Virginia Antiquities. Kelso writes:

> "There is no way to describe the elation when that digging almost imme-diately produced fragments of early seventeenth century ceramics. The incredible chain of discoveries that followed literally connecting the dots, unfolded like a mystery novel over the course of eleven electrifying years, 1994 to 2005." [He discovered soil stained archaeological evidence of a palisade wall:] "marks of decayed circular or split timbers once standing side by side and held upright by solid packed clay in a narrow straight sided, flat bottomed trench. Transformed in time into rich loam, the dark stains retained the exact shape of the vanished logs they had replaced."

This was only the beginning, as they unearthed and rediscovered on the peninsula only yards from the wide James River the ancient buried remains of the triangular Jamestown Fort, its people, their homes, eating habits, DNA, Indian arrowheads, and general history.

About this same time in 1994, I was working in our drugstore in the University Mall in Orem, Utah, when I was approached by two women with some fat manila envelopes. They had driven from Logan, Utah, to visit my mother, not knowing that she had died in 1989. Mother had spent many years researching her early American IVIE line. The ladies had their own research and wanted to know which of several theories was correct. I was working in the Orem Park Stake Family History Center as a consultant at that time, but because my mother had worked so hard on this line, I had neglected it in favor of other lines. I promised to get back with them.

ARRIVAL OF THE FIRST PERMANENT ENGLISH SETTLERS OF JAMESTOWN ISLAND.
The *Sarah Constant*, the *Goodspeed*, and the *Discovery* reached what was to be the site of the first permanent English colony in North America on 13 May 1607.

Jamestown and the James River were named after the English King James I, who followed Queen Elizabeth after her death 24 Mar 1603. He was the only child of Mary Stuart, Queen of Scots, and was known, also, as King James VI of Scotland. In January 1604, he was approached in conference by the Puritan Dr. John Reynolds with the suggestion that "things pretended to be amiss in the church." With the king's permission, the group revised the Bible and printed it in 1610 with the title page:

> "To the most high and mighty Prince JAMES by the grace of God, King of Great Britain, France, and Ireland, Defender of the Faith, &c. The Translators of the Bible wish Grace, Mercy and Peace, through JESUS CHRIST our Lord."

It is difficult to assess the magnitude of this event upon the people who came to America in these early colonial days. It combined the scattered pages into one magnificent book, with the help of the previous invention of the printing press, Martin Luther's reforms, and William Tyndale's translation of the New Testament into English. Tyndale was exiled from England, and finally strangled and his body burned near Brussels on 6 Aug 1536. The *King James Version of the Bible* has been the #1 best selling book throughout early colonial America and until our present day.

The London Company was organized by "gentlemen" of that area of England. As men of fortune, they wanted their place in the "New World." Tobacco had been introduced to the European continent by Sir Walter Raleigh, and it was in great demand. The Spanish had St. Augustine, Florida; much of the West Indies, and money was flowing into their coffers. The English would compete. They defeated the Spanish Armada in 1558 and became the "mistress of the seas and the preserver of Protestantism." Virginia had a great harbor, could grow tobacco, and within the Corporation of Elizabeth City they soon established the Elizabeth River Church of England parish, and others, to support their break with the Catholic Church and the Holy Roman Empire.

In those days, ships were the most important method of travel. The highly foliated roads and Indian trails were very dangerous, not only because of unfriendly Indians, but also because of the robbers of the less moral white society. Ships brought the new adventurers, planters, cavaliers, and the prisoners from London's Newgate prison to serve their sentences. They also brought clothing, guns, survival supplies; orders to the governors; and the mail for all these intrepid settlers from the homeland. Ships returned across the Atlantic with Virginian tobacco. It was a cash crop that could not be grown in England. The demand was so great that it was used as a medium of exchange. Tobacco was money in the bank. Early settlements located and increased in population on the coastlines of this densely timbered new country. A boat dock was more important than a carriage entrance to their homes. The Indians respected their large ships, their firearms, and their larger settlements much more than the lone rider on their inland trails through the forests.

The captain of a ship was the master of the crew and passengers until they reached port, but on reaching port, he needed records of cargo and passengers. Among the 1607 Virginia Company Records, we find the name of WILLIAM WILKINSON, surgeon (spelled chirugeon), listed with this first group of arrivals composed only of men and boys. He was not listed later with the survivors. The first women came in 1608.

On 3 May 1609, word was sent that the "goods shipped to Virginia for the use of English planters there are to pass duty free." On the 4 Oct 1609 word went back to London in a "report by John Radcliffe . . . that 100 men have been planted but a further 180 have not yet arrived and are feared lost." This was the "starvation time"—being surrounded by angry Indians. Archaeologist William M. Kelso discovered the butchered bones of horses, rats, and poisonous snakes that they had evidently eaten at that time. The group became discouraged and was on board their ship ready to return to England when the 140 men and women arrived at Virginia on 23 May 1610. The new arrivals had built two boats after their ship was wrecked at Bermuda; all were saved according to a report by Sir George Somers of Jamestown.

On 17 Aug 1610, Sir Thomas Dale reported that the 300 disorderly persons he took with him to Virginia are mutinous and unchristian and are so disordered that only 60 of them are employable.

Courts were soon established in Virginia and many of these early records are very readable. They include land patents and transfers of ownership, debt, criminal records, wills and estate records. At times a list or *muster* was taken of the people and occupations of those who were living in the various communities. It sometimes included a list of those who had died. In 1622, the records show, "29 July, The Virginia Company, having through negligence and the barbarity of the savages lost nearly 400 persons there, it is ordered that some old ordnance (cannon) be sent." In this "1622 massacre" Thomas Kemis, governor, is listed among the dead.

In Captain John Smith's early history, (vol. II p. 93) he gives an account about going ashore in the bitter cold weather. It reads: "riding at Kecoughtan, [later known as Elizabeth City] Master JOHN ARGENT, son to DOCTOR ARGENT, a young gentleman that went with CAPTAINE BUTLER from England to this place, Michael Fuller, WILLIAM GANY et als. . . ." THOMAS IVY's wife was ANN, the daughter of GEORGE ARGENT, gentleman. So, relative ARGENT was in Jamestown and knew Captain John Smith.

According to Ridpath *History of the World (1910)*, after Captain John Smith's escape from his captivity with the Indians, he returned to Jamestown to find only thirty-eight of the settlers alive. After about two years, "on his way down the James, while asleep in a boat, a bag of gunpowder lying near by exploded, burning and tearing his flesh so terribly that in his agony he leaped overboard." Smith was rescued, but was so tortured by his wounds that about the middle of September, 1609, he returned to England and never came back.

Ancestor Lieutenant FRANCIS MASON, approximately 29 years old, arrived in 1613 on the ship *John and Francis*. He was perhaps the son of FRANCISCO MASON de BRAMFELDE and ANNA, daughter of JOH'ES COXDE and MARGARETA (daughter of JOH'IS CLEVERLY de com CESTER) [Vis. Shropshire 1623 p.156]. With him in 1613 was his wife MARY and a daughter ANN. MARY survived the massacre of 1622, but died before the muster roles of 1624 when the Lieutenant's wife is shown as ALICE (believed to be ALICE GANEY). At this time they were living at a settlement called Basse's Choice, across the James River from Jamestown. ALICE, age 26 years, came over on the *Margaret and John* in 1622. The Captain of the *Margaret and John* was JOHN LANGLEY. The five servants of FRANCIS MASON are listed in the muster role.

LT. FRANCIS MASON and WM. GAINYE were granted passes to go to England in 1626 and a "MRS. GENY at the house of FRANCIS MASONS" refused to pay tobacco (on a debt) to Capt. Whittaker until her husband came home.

In 1640, FRANCES MASON was the Church Warden and in 1648 he was the vestryman of the Elizabeth River Parish. In 1646/7 he was High Sheriff and THOMAS IVY was Undersheriff. The Sheriff was appointed by the Governor and had a lot of authority within the early British colonies. FRANCES was one of the Commissioners presiding at the first court held in Lower Norfolk County in 1637 and served until his last appearance at court held 15 Aug 1648. He died 15 Nov 1648, when the relick (or widow), ALICE MASON and her son, LEMUEL MASON, were soon after granted administration of his estate.

LEMUEL MASON was elected to the Vestry of Elizabeth River Parish 14 May 1659. He was a major in the Norfolk County Militia in 1650, a colonel in 1695 and commander in chief of the Norfolk County Militia in 1699. He was Norfolk County Justice of Peace from 1650 until his death (will proved

15 Sep 1702.) He married ANNE SEAWELL. They had eight daughters and three sons. One of their sons was Capt. GEORGE MASON, who was a member of the House of Burgess in 1705. He had a son, GEORGE MASON, who was also a burgess from Norfolk. (This GEORGE MASON was not the George Mason whose estate was near George Washington's Mount Vernon estate.) Williamsburg became the capital city of these settlements in 1699. Prior to that time, Jamestown had moved inland from the peninsula fort and was the center of government.

Ancestor ELIZABETH MASON, a sister of LEMUEL MASON, gentleman, married JAMES THELABALL, a wealthy French Huguenot who was naturalized as a British citizen in 1683. JAMES and ELIZABETH MASON THELABALL were the maternal grandparents of ELIZABETH LANGLEY who married GEORGE IVY (seventh-great-grandparents), as shown by her will dated 3 Apr 1692 and proved 15 Sep 1693.

Another sister, ALICE MASON, married Dr. THOMAS VICESIMUS IVY (Captain), the son of THOMAS IVY and brother of GEORGE IVY (whose son GEORGE married ELIZABETH LANGLEY.) In one of Dr. IVY's return trips from London, she is listed as "his wife, ALICE." Their descendant Mrs. Alice G. Walter of Virginia Beach has done extensive research into wills and land patents in the area. She is a direct descendant of ABIGAIL LANGLEY (Granbery) and also THOMAS V. IVY and his wife ALICE.

ELIZABETH LANGLEY (Ivie) was the daughter of WILLIAM LANGLEY, who was a justice of Norfolk County in 1694, a captain in 1708, and a member of the House of Burgesses in 1715. He held 487 acres of land in Norfolk County in 1704. His will was proved on the 16 May 1718. [Adventures of Purse and Person p. 440] His father WILLIAM may have come on the *Falcon* of London which embarked for the Barbados on 3 Apr 1635. Its roll shows WILLIAM LANGLEY age 14, then the word "deleted." The following first person account is of interest.

> "I, Thomas Harwood, departed from England aboard the 'Margaret and John', 1622, but the ship did not arrive in Virginia until April 1623. . . . we received great wrong and injury through the evil dealings of the late deceased Mr. JOHN LANGLEY, who failed to bring us on a direct course to Virginia . . . and spent much time in the West Indies. . . . Owing to the delay,

we are like to hazard losing the best of our crop.... His [LANGLEY's] successor Master Douglas refuses to let us have our goods ashore."

This was in a petition made to Governor Wyatt. Thomas Harwood was listed in the census of 1623/4 at the Neck of Land at James City. Ancestor ALICE GANEY also came with Captain JOHN LANGLEY on the *Margaret and John* in 1622. One report states that it left London before the news of the massacre reached there. Perhaps either news of the massacre at Barbados or LANGLEY's health delayed their arrival in Virginia.

WILLIAM GAYNE, born about 1588, came to America in 1616 on the *George*, in 1617 in the *Treasurer* at his own cost, in 1620 on the *Bona Nova* bringing his wife ANNA.

THOMAS IVY, born about 1604 (36 years old in 1640), came to America in 1637 on the *Rebecca* with his wife, ANN ARGENT IVY. He was credited with transporting three persons: himself, his wife and William Brown. He bought a parcel of land in Lower Norfolk County from Mr. William Julian. (Lower Norfolk County Court Records, Book A.) In 1641, he was appointed Churchwarden of the Elizabeth River Parish in which capacity he served until at least 1648. In July 1643, he was constable and, as mentioned earlier, 5 Mar 1646/7 FRANCES MASON was sworn High Sheriff and THOMAS IVY was sworn Undersheriff in James City Quarter Court. In 1646, he made a list of the "Tytheables from Daniel Tanners Creek downwards to Captain Willoughby." In 1648 THOMAS IVY is a Member of the Vestry. Shown in April 1649, TRUSTRAM MASON sold THOMAS IVY one-half of "his devident of land, the houses excepted." This was dated 2 Nov 1644.

> 1647—THOMAS IVY was granted a license to "keepe an Ordinary" (B 60), and a record of October, 1649 statd that the Court was held at "THOMAS IVIE's House," and (B 124a, 126, 129) the last day of November 1649, because of the unseasonableness of the weather, and at Mr. IVIE's in December 1649. In February 1649/50 and March 1650, THOMAS IVY was to arbitrate "yee business of Henry Sewell, deed Estate" (B 138), and he was one of four arbitrators to value the Estate of Mrs. Aloe Sewell, deceased. In June 1652 he was to "take lists of Tytheables."

In August 1652, "Mr. LEMUELL MASON, John Hill, THOMAS IVEY and George Kempe" were to appraise the estate of Captain John Sibsey. Then a little over a year later, Mr. THOMAS IVY was to be punished for defaming the name of Mrs. Elizabeth Sibsey (C 16, 62). (My mother told me that when she went to Williamsburg, a THOMAS IVY was portrayed by one of the actors in the process of receiving his punishment at one of the pillories.)

On 13 Mar 1653/4, WILLIAM GAYNEY and THOMAS IVY witnessed this Item: At his death, on 25 Jan 1654/5 the *Letters of Administration of the Estate of THOMAS IVEY* was granted to George Kempe,

> "he beinge a great creditor . . . Mr. LEMUEL MASON being paid in the first place 500 pounds of tobacco yearely untill his debt is paid."

On 15 Feb 1654/5 an inventory of the THOMAS IVY estate was to be taken by: Captain Thomas Willoughby; Thomas Lamber; Mr. Richard Conquest; Mr. LEMUELL MASON; Mr. Wm. Jermy; WILLIAM LANGLEY, and Jasper Hodgkinson . . .

> "in behalfe of the poore distressed orphanats and Creditors to be paid so farre as estate will afford and to dispose of the said orphants as shall seem fitt" (C 125a).

It appears that the orphans were four sons and a daughter, who were taken back to England, until they were of the age to claim their inheritances. ANNE ARGENT (Ivey) had died before her husband died, as proved by her father GEORGE ARGENT's will (in England), dated 16 Aug 1654, in which he makes his bequest to

> "the children of my late daughter, ANN IVEY, deceased, who were borne in Virginia, where she died, to be equally divided betweene them according to the will of JANE BAKER, deceased, their Grandmother."

The early colonists who lived along the lower Virginia coast suffered greatly from the climate. Undoubtedly yellow fever and malaria took their toll. ANNE's father was living in the Hoxton Parish, St. Leonard, Shoreditch, Middlesex County, England. His will was proved 27 Feb 1653/4, about a year before the death of THOMAS IVY. GEORGE ARGENT requested to be buried in the Parish Church of St. Leonard, Shoreditch "as neare unto my late WIFE and sonne WILLIAM ARGENT as may be."

He named "Cousin" WILLIAM ARGENT and Executors: "Cousins" Master JOHN LANGLEY and Master JOHN GLASCOCK, whom he gave

10 pounds. He gives the home in which he lives to his daughter ELIZABETH (husband HENRY POTTER) and since she has no children, it was to go to her brother GEORGE ARGENT upon her death. [This JOHN LANGLEY is not the sea captain mentioned earlier, who had died previously.]

He gives a "Tenement wherein Master Morrel Goulds Gouldsmith dwelleth" to a daughter MARY (HODGES) which will go to son GEORGE ARGENT upon her death.

Daughter JANE (STEWARD) was given "1/3 share of 3/4s of the plate, and 1/2 of the two-thirds residue of my Goods." Her husband THOMAS STEWARD was given the thirty pounds he owes me.

ANNE'S CHILDREN were given "the 1/4 part of all the rest of my plate."

Son GEORGE ARGENT was given "1/3 share of 3/4 of the plate and 1/2 of a 2/3s residue of my Goods."

In the *Caribbeans vol I p. 23* is found a deed between "GEORGE ARGENT of Bermudas in parts beyond the Seas, but then in London, Gentleman, son of GEORGE ARGENT, late of Hoxton in Parish of Shoreditch, Gentleman, (London), and HENRY POTTER, Citizen and Apothecary of London," which relates to land and a very large house in Hoxton called the *White Hart* with the signature of GEORGE ARGENT.

THOMAS and ANNE ARGENT IVY's five children were their daughter ANN and sons, THOMAS VICESIMUS (the eldest son), GEORGE, JOHN and WILLIAM.

There is evidence that their daughter ANN was in England when her Grandfather ARGENT died and was one of the witnesses to his will. This daughter ANN married Colonel JOHN SIDNEY, who was sheriff in Norfolk, Virginia, and chose her brother THOMAS V. IVY as his undersheriff on 15 Apr 1662.

[Note: On 7 Mar 1663/4 there is a court record certifying that "THOMAS and GEORGE IVY are legitimate sons of THOMAS and ANN (ARGENT) IVY and that they were born in Virginia and that THOMAS is the eldest son and has for many years since and yet is troubled with a sore upon his leg and is conceived immoveable and not fit for travel."]

THOMAS's middle name VICESIMUS means twentieth in Latin. This was probably part of his father's name, who was believed to be the twentieth child of Judge THOMAS IVIE and LETTICE CULPEPER of Oxford, England. This line is said to go back to St. Ives of France, whose descendant was a very close friend of William the Conqueror. He came with him to England with the other Norman French. It would appear that the children of THOMAS and ANN ARGENT IVY were probably born from 1637 to 1645 in Virginia.

[Additional note: THOMAS V. IVY and his wife ALICE (MASON) IVY had six daughters and four sons, THOMAS, LUIDFORD, ANTHONY and LEMUEL. THOMAS V. as the oldest son seemed to inherit part of his father's lands in Lower Norfolk County and upon his death (will proved 17 Oct 1684) his oldest son THOMAS inherited these lands, then part of Princess Ann County when Lower Norfolk County was divided in 1691. THOMAS V. and ALICE's youngest daughter ALIFF (ALICE) was born posthumously and married John Cornick, a Justice of Princess Ann County. They are the ancestors of the genealogist Alice Granbery Walter of Virginia Beach. There is a 1668 Deed (Book E p. 36a, 37) it reads: "upon Col. MASON Little Creek and land of Thos. Pulcher, formerly granted to THO. IVY by pat(ent) 22 Aug 1648 and his sons THO. GEO. IVY, sold to Richardson who sold to Thrower." (6 pg 472)]

My ancestor GEORGE IVEY, the second son of the original THOMAS IVEY, was probably named after his grandfather, GEORGE ARGENT. He married HANNAH BLANCH, the daughter of SAMUEL and ELIZABETH BLANCH, also of Norfolk County. The will of ELIZABETH BLANCH was written in August 1680 and proved 15 Jun 1681. It confirms that HANNAH and GEORGE IVEY were her daughter and son-in-law. Thomas Jefferson had ancestors in the area at this time named Samuel and Elizabeth Branch. Do not confuse them.

In order to help with the early settlement of Virginia, land grants were given to those who would pay the transport costs of others. The early patent books contain many of these entries.

It would seem that GEORGE and HANNAH IVEY made at least one trip back to England. Some of their lands may have been acquired by transporting others.

[Note: One of them reads, "DANIELL MACOY, 189 acres, Lower Norfolk County, East side of the South branch of Elizabeth River, 23 Oct 1673, p. 470. On north side of the Little Creek, adjacent . . . for transport of two persons: GEO. IVEY, HANNA IVEY." (Patent Book No.6, p. 131.)

Patent Book No.7, p 283 shows ancestor: "GEORGE IVY, 550 acres, Lower Norfolk County, 21 Oct 1684, p. 411. 50 acres called Julians Neck; adjacent Danniell Tanner, upon North side of said Tanner's Creek; granted to John White, 10 July 1639, & by Josiah Crouch, son & heire of Wm. Crouch, assigned to said IVY, 2 Nov 1682; 500 acres on North side of said Creek; adjacent Col. LEMUELL MASON; bought of said Josiah Crouch, 23 Oct. 1682 & acknowledged in Lower Norfolk County Court, by Mr. Thomas Bridge, Atty. of said Josiah."]

GEORGE IVEY's will was written on 6 Mar 1685/6. It was proved in the Norfolk County Court on 17 Jan 1689. He names his widow HANNAH and the following children: ALEXANDER (his oldest son), GEORGE, SAMUEL, THOMAS, JOSEPH, LEMUEL, JOHN, ELIZABETH and HANNAH. He noted that JOHN was not yet of age. He left to his wife the "plantation whereon I now live, 146 acres, after her decease to ALEXANDER, eldest son." This will was witnessed by WILLIAM and THOMAS LANGLEY.

ALEXANDER settled in Prince George County and died without issue. GEORGE, who married ELIZABETH LANGLEY, was given in his father's will "Couches Old Field, 100 acres." They moved to Surry County, which on division was part of Prince George County. In the 1704 Quit Rent Rolls, he is given 496 acres in Norfolk County, Virginia. [Virginia Humphrey.]

GEORGE (II) died in Weynoke Parish, Prince George County, Virginia. His wife ELIZABETH LANGLEY (Ivey) left a will that was probated in Prince George County on 26 Apr 1718. There were six adult surviving children: GEORGE (III), HENRY, GILBERT, ADAM, ELIZABETH and SUSAN HAYS. My ancestral line has many second sons and HENRY IVEY was my connection. Usually the first son was given the bulk of the original estate, under the laws of primogeniture that existed in England. Second sons needed to go further inland. HENRY, born in the 1690s went south. On 21 Jul 1720, he patented 165 acres in Surry County, Virginia, on the Meherrin River, west of the "Dismal Swamp." He had married ANNE EXETER whose father was THOMAS EXETER of Norfolk County.

[Note: ELIZABETH MASON (Thelaball's) will mentioned a grandson, son of her daughter ELIZABETH, who married GEORGE IVY. This was uncle WILLIAM. He married ANN the widow of James Lowery, and was a sea captain, perhaps the Captain (or father of) WILLIAM IVY who lived on Tanner's Creek and had two plantations and a shipbuilding business that were burned by the British when they destroyed Norfolk shortly after the Revolutionary War began. ["The Navy of Virginia."] To add to the confusion of all the THOMAS IVYs of Norfolk County, GEORGE (I) and HANNAH BLANCH IVY's son THOMAS was bequeathed by his grandmother ELIZABETH BLANCH "140 acres in Daniell Tanners Creek bounded on ye east side with ye land of Rob't Woody as by pat. to Woody and then to ELIZA. BLANCH"(4 DB 100 Lower Norfolk County.) He also owned land adjoining Colonel LEMUEL MASON, 50 acres near the mouth of Broad Nick left to him by his father.

GEORGE and HANNAH'S son JOSEPH was given by his father "50 acres called Cods betwixt Deep Nick & Couches Old Field." SAMUEL was left a "Neck of Land called Cedar Neck, 100 acres."

According to the *Pedigree File no. 1169*, GEORGE and HANNAH's son JOHN married MARY and they had four sons and three daughters: JOHN, WILLIAM, THOMAS (b. 1723), LEMUEL (who "being bound out of the Country" left his brother JOHN all of his estate), CHARITY, PATIENCE and AMY.

JOHN and MARY's son WILLIAM IVY had a son JOHN IVY who married ELIZABETH NASH in Norfolk County, 4 Jun 1760. WILLIAM also had a daughter ELIZABETH IVY who married Captain THOMAS SNALE. In this territory, the title *captain* was very likely to mean a ship's captain.]

A COLONIAL WEDDING

On 27 Feb 1619, the names of THOMAS THRESHER and PHILLIP WILKINSON are listed with the names of "the boys and wenches appointed to go to Virginia." The following year ROBERT THRESHER, age 22, is listed with the passengers on the *Bona Nova* which arrived in Virginia in 1620. WILLIAM GAYNE and his wife ANNA were also on this ship. This was WILLIAM GAYNE's third voyage. ROBERT EARL THRASHER brought with him his wife ELIZABETH and at least one son, an infant, WILLIAM THRASHER, and seven other people, and was granted four-hundred-and-fifty acres of land in or near "Elizabeth Cittie" [Upper Norfolk, north of the James River.]

ROBERT and his wife ELIZABETH were born at Bradford, near Bath and Stone Hedge, Wiltshire, England (now known as Bradford-on-Avon). He was a merchant, known at that time as a draper, as he dealt in cloth. Bradford was granted by the king the exclusive rights to make tweed cloth, which brought prosperity to this area. This also brought many sheep, which hurt the farming landowners. There are many gravestones in the cemetery of the Holy Trinity Church of Bradford, built around 1000 A.D., with the THRASHER surname. There was a major cloth depression during the 1640s, which may have brought the THRASHERs to Virginia.

ROBERT THRESHER's name is included in the muster (or census) taken in 1623 of the Elizabeth City residents; so he survived the Indian massacre of 1622. In "Patent Book No. I—Part I, page 341, William Woolritch was granted

"400 acs. [acres] Eliz. Citty Co., 17 June 1635, p. 309. A ridge of land lying in the woods butting in length westerly upon land of Capt. Christopher Calthroppe, easterly upon Samuell Bennett & ROBERT THRESHER, N. upon Mr. Phettiplace Cloyse & southerly into the maine woods. Transport of 8 persons."

On page 54: "ISSABELL THRESHER, Widdow, 450 acs. upon the back cr. of the new Poquoson river. Northerly upon Thomas Brice, Southerly towards the old Poquoson, Easterly upon the head of a small Cr. upon Thomas Symons and Westerly into the woods. 50 acs. for the per. adv. of her late husband ROBERT THRESHER, 50 acs. for her own per. adv., & 350 acs. for trans. [transporting] of 7 pers: ROBT. THRESHER Jr. ... 16 Feb. 1636, p. 411."

So, ROBERT's first wife, ELIZABETH, had died and he had remarried ISSABELL, who had paid for his son ROBERT's trip back from England after his father's death. Children at this time period returned to England for their education, if possible. The above mentioned land seems to be near Elizabeth City, Virginia. On page 116, Hannah Bennett is granted "450 acres . . . Nov. 1, 1639 . . . upon the New Poquoson River, N. upon the pinye swamp and S. upon ROBERT THRASHER." This must be ROBERT THRASHER Jr. as his father was the late husband of the widow ISSABELL and the land seems to be the same location.

On page 184, WILLIAM THRESHER is transported to Virginia by Richard Vaughan,—dated 15 Sep 1649. If this is the same infant WILLIAM THRASHER who came originally in 1620, then he would be about 30 years old. From *Makers of America* Leonard Wilson:

"WILLIAM THRASHER, the progenitor of the family of this name, who settled in Virginia, sold his house, lands, and his business as a clothier, in Bradford-on-Avon, Wiltshire, England, and with his wife and son, ROBERT, came to America in 1649, settling in Pittsylvania Co., Virginia.

[In the early 1700s] ROBERT married ABBY A. STEVENS, daughter of DANIEL G. STEVENS and his wife, SIBBEL. Their children were: SAMUEL,

JOHN, RICHARD, JOSEPH, PLEASANT and WILLIAM. [no daughters?]

"SAMUEL THRASHER was Justice of Essex County, Virginia from 1695 to 1700 [Essex County is north of Elizabeth City towards Fredericksburg on the west bank of the Rappahannock River.] He is said to have been born about 1673. He was also Justice of the Peace in Essex County again from 1710 until 1753. He died there about 1761. DANIEL, son of SAMUEL, married LYDIA SWIFT in 1724, and their children were: ROBERT, RACHEL, SUSAN, SAMUEL and perhaps others.

"When the Revolutionary War broke out, members of the THRASHER family were not slow to offer their services in defense of their country. MICHAEL THRASHER and SAMUEL THRASHER served with honor throughout the war, MICHAEL rising to the rank of Captain. One branch of the family moved to Rockingham County, Salisbury District, North Carolina, where many of the name are still to be found."

Our Thrasher Heritage p. 6 states:

"At this point in time, the Justice of the Peace was a very powerful individual, and there was a great deal of controversy about the harshness of some of the sentences of this Justice, SAMUEL THRASHER (1673–1761). There had been a great deal of robbery in the outlying areas at the water crossings. There were men who laid in wait to rob the people returning home after selling their crops. Three of these men were caught, and Justice SAMUEL THRASHER sentenced them to be hung, drawn and quartered, and the five parts of their bodies (head and four quarters) be put up on poles with a plaque describing their crime, at fifteen water crossings. After a long exposure they were reassembled and allowed to be buried in holy ground to compensate for the indignities on their bodies, otherwise they would not have been permitted to be buried in holy ground."

Fourth-great-grandmother ELIZABETH THRASHER (Allred) was probably an older daughter of JOHN THRASHER of Rockingham County, North Carolina, a border county to Pittsylvania County, Virginia. She was not mentioned in his will, nor was her sister MARY CLOUD THRASHER. Both were married at the time of his death and JOHN divided his estate between his four sons—some of these sons were with the ALLRED and IVIE ancestors in South Carolina and Georgia after the Revolutionary War.

JENNI AND I POSE FOR A PICTURE NEAR THE GATE OF THE
SHIRLEY PLANTATION IN 2004. THE LOCATION OF THIS PLANTATION IS SHOWN ON
THE OLD MAP AT THE BEGINNING OF THIS CHAPTER.

(PICTURES TAKEN BY HER FATHER HYRUM HAYNES, WHO GREW UP IN COLONIAL HEIGHTS, VIRGINIA.)

52

PILGRIMS, PURITANS, ROYALIST, AND QUAKERS IN NEW ENGLAND

The first Queen Elizabeth of England was highly aware that her rule depended upon the split with the Catholic Church to legalize the marriage of her mother to Henry VIII. This split with the Catholic Church also gave her control of both Church and State. In Europe, most of the kingdoms under the Holy Roman Empire had separated this power and were ruled by Rome as well as their individual monarchy. Elizabeth loved the pageantry and power that existed in the Catholic Church; so she retained as much of this as possible in the Church of England. Scotland was Presbyterian and many of their people hoped that when King James I of England (VI of Scotland), replaced her on the throne that freedom of religion would increase. This did not occur; however, they were indebted to him for the King James Version of the Bible. His son, Charles I, followed him to the throne. He used his power even more capriciously and at times would even disband parliament. The Puritan movement in England was an attempt to purify the Church. They wanted less pageantry and more spirituality and recognition of the individual conscience. The Puritans, however, did not want to break with the Church of England, only purify it.

Some felt this was not enough and they wanted to separate the Church from the control of the king and allow even more religious freedom. This group of Separatists or Pilgrims was not welcome in England, so they went to Holland, where they were tolerated for awhile; but soon found it advantageous to leave. Landing at Cape Cod, instead of New York, as they had planned, they wrote and signed the *Mayflower Compact* during November 1620. It reads as follows:

"In the name of God Amen! We whose names are underwritten, the loyal subjects of our dread sovereign Lord King James, by the grace of God, of

Great Britain, France and Ireland, King, Defender of the Faith, etc., have undertaken for the glory of God and the advancement of the Christian faith, and honor of our King and Country, a voyage to plant the first colony in the northern parts of Virginia; do by these presents, solemnly and mutually, in the presence of God and of one another covenant and combine ourselves together into a civil body politic for our better ordering and preservation, and furthermore of the ends aforesaid; and by virtue thereof to enact, constitute and frame just and equal laws, ordinances, acts, constitutions, and offices from time to time, as shall be thought most mete and convenient for the general good of the colony; unto which we promise all due submission and obedience. In witness whereof we have hereunto subscribed our names, at Cape Cod, the 11th of November, in the year of the reign of our sovereign Lord, King James of England, France and Ireland, the eighteenth, and of Scotland the Fifty-fourth, Anno Domini 1620."

With this agreement they established the first permanent English settlement in New England at Plymouth, Massachusetts, the following spring, and later expanded into Salem. It was a very difficult time. All the extreme difficulties they faced in the miraculous preparation, crossing the angry ocean, surviving an extremely cold winter on the Cape—still living on their ship, while contemplating an area they could settle without arousing the ire of the less than friendly native Indian inhabitants, diseases, death—all of it was a beginning for a new way of life—like a butterfly struggling to escape its cocoon.

THE LAST GROUP OF OUR SWALLOW REUNION ON CAPE COD GATHER FOR A FINAL PHOTO SHOT ON THE BAY BEACH BEFORE PACKING TO GO HOME. IN THE DISTANCE ON THE FAR RIGHT IS THE TINY IMAGE OF THE PROVINCETOWN *PILGRIMS MONUMENT*, SHOWN IN MORE DETAIL IN THE PICTURE OPPOSITE. [I MADE IT TO THE TOP.]

PILGRIM MONUMENT

Back in England the country was becoming more and more divided with the Puritans on one side and the Royalists, or those who upheld the king, on the other side. Roger Williams, who was born about 1607 in Wales, was educated at Pembroke College, Cambridge University, and took his degree in 1626. He soon became a decided opponent of the liturgy and ceremonies of the Church of England, which placed him on the side of the most radical Puritans. He embarked for New England with his young wife and arrived at Nantasket 5 Feb 1631. As a champion of religious liberty, he immediately came in conflict with the church and civil authorities of the colony. He was offered the position of a teacher in a church in Puritanical Boston, which he refused noting that they were an unseparated people with the Church of England. He accepted a position with the Pilgrims of Salem, until the Boston authorities were able to persuade them to get rid of him. He then went to Plymouth where he was accepted with much respect.

During his residence in Plymouth he became well acquainted with many of the Indian chieftains of that area. In 1633 he returned to Salem. Once more he was in constant combat with the civil authorities for maintaining that civil authority should have no control over the absolute liberty of conscience. In January, 1636, he left Salem to escape arrest and to seek a refuge from the tyranny of the church brethren. His five companions were William Harris, JOHN SMITH, Francis Wickers, THOMAS ANGELL, and Joshua Verin. They settled and named their location Providence in gratitude for "God's merciful providence to him in his distress." In March 1638 a large section of land was conveyed to him by deed from the Indians and Rhode Island became a sanctuary for those desiring to worship as they pleased. It would become a refuge for the Quaker movement until the New Jersey and Pennsylvania colonies were established. The Friends (or Quakers) began in England with George Fox, who began his public speaking in England in 1648. [The SMITH and ANGELL names show up in some of my early collateral lines in Rhode Island.]

Thomas Shrouds of the *Salem National Standard* told about the LIPPINCOTT family, 28 Nov 1875:

"The LIPPINCOTTs in America are all descended from RICHARD and ABIGAIL (GOODY) LIPPINCOTT, who moved from Devonshire, England in 1639, and settled at Dorchester, near Boston, New England. Having been excommunicated from the Church for non-conformity (withdrawing from communion), and suffering much from Puritanical oppression, RICHARD LIPPINCOTT returned with his family to England, and resided at Plymouth (England) in 1653, and early thereafter became a member of the religious 'Society of Friends' [Quakers], then emerging from the various sects around them, and in consequence endured much persecution for the testimony of a good conscience. On the 20th of January, 1660, he with other Friends was taken from the meetinghouse at Plymouth [England] and committed to prison by Oliver Crooly, Mayor. How long he remained in Prison we have no account. In 1663 he emigrated to Rhode Island, where he resided for several years, and finally in 1669, established himself at Shrewsbury, Monmouth County, New Jersey, in which place he was the largest landed proprietor among the patentees of the new colony. He was a consistent and exemplary Friend, accompanying George Fox during his religious visit in this country, and a man of character and influence. A short time previous to his death, which occurred 9 month (Nov. Old style) 25 – 1683, he purchased of John Penwich, one thousand acres of land in the Shrewsbury Neck, upon which some of his descendants now live. Previous to the death of ABIGAIL, on the 6 month

2nd 1697, she liberated all of her slaves, which act is sufficient to perpetuate her name to the latest posterity. In the records of the town of Freehold, New Jersey, mention is made of RICHARD LIPPINCOTT as one of the overseers of the town of Shrewsbury in 1670. His book of record is said to be the oldest deed book in New Jersey, it having been commenced 14th of 12th month, 1667. RICHARD and ABIGAIL LIPPINCOTT had six sons and two daughters. They are said to be named after trials, successes, vicissitudes, etc. of parents. REMEMBRANCE [my ancestor]—their oldest son was born at Dorchester, New England, in 1641. He was baptized on the 19th of July 1641, and died 11th of February 1723. He married MARGARET BARBER of Boston. They had issue—Four sons and eight daughters. They resided in New Jersey. [His son, WILLIAM, my ancestor, married HANNAH WILBUR of Newport, Rhode Island 1 May 1710.]

"JOHN—their second son, was born at Boston, New England, September 6th 1644, and died February 16th 1720. He married JANETTE AUSTIN. They had four sons and four daughters. They resided in New Jersey. ABIGAIL—their eldest daughter, born at Plymouth, England, Nov. 17, 1646, died an infant. RESTORE—was born at Plymouth, England . . . . He represented Burlington County in the state legislature in 1703, (the year that east and west New Jersey were invited under government), and continued a member of that body for several years. Thomas Chalkley mentions in his journal that he was present at his funeral. He further stated that he was informed that RESTORE left behind him nearly 200 children, grandchildren, and great-grandchildren. FREEDOM—their fourth son, was born Jan. 1650, at Stone House, England, and died in 1697. He was married Aug. 14th 1680 to MARY CURTIS of Burlington and had three sons and two daughters. INCREASE—their second daughter, was born at Stone House, England, October 5, 1657 and died September 29, 1695. She married SAMUEL DENNIS who came from England and settled at Shrewsbury in 1675. He died June 7th 1723 at the age of 73 years. They had 2 sons and 3 daughters. JACOB—their fifth son was born in England in March 1660 and died Dec. 6th 1696. He married, had 1 son and 1 daughter. Both died in infancy. PRESERVED—their 6th son, was born in Rhode Island Dec. 25th, 1665 and died in 1666."

[Note: Another decendent of RICHARD LIPPINCOTT is U.S President Richard Nixon.]

In England, the Royalist and the Puritans became violent and the great Civil War of 1642 broke out, lead by Oliver Cromwell. The following is taken from FHL US/CAN 974.8 D2c 1978 v.2 which seems to tell the story of ancestor,

LAWRENCE WILKINSON:

"LAWRENCE WILKINSON, born in Lanchester, county Durham, at about the date of the grant of arms to his distinguished grandfather, for whom he was named, was, like his ancestors, for many generations a strong adherent of the English crown.

[Note: The Grant of Arms occurred on 18 Sep 1615, by Richard St. George Norrey, King of Arms, and duly recorded in the College of Arms.]

"He was a lieutenant in the army of Charles I during the Civil war, and was taken prisoner by the Scotch and Parliamentary troops, at the surrender of Newcastle-on-Tyne, October 22, 1644. With the success of the Parliamentary party, and the downfall of the monarchy, in common with thousands of others of the English nobility who were adherents of the House of Stuart, LAWRENCE WILKINSON was deprived of his ancestral estates. On the record of sequestrations in the county of Durham during the years 1645–47, we find the name, 'LAWRENCE WILKINSON Officer in Arms', and after it this entry, 'Went to New England.'"

We also find the following in the above named volume:

"Captain LAWRENCE WILKINSON married, in England, SUSANNAH, daughter of CHRISTOPHER SMITH, who also settled at Providence, Rhode Island. Captain LAWRENCE and SUSANNAH (SMITH) WILKINSON had six children, SAMUEL; JOHN; SUSANNAH, who died young; JOANNA; JOSIAS; SUSANNAH."

LAWRENCE's son SAMUEL married PLAIN WICKENDEN in 1672. They had a daughter RUTH, born in 1685, who married WILLIAM HOPKINS (a descendent of the STEPHEN HOPKINS who arrived in 1620 on the Mayflower). RUTH WILKINSON (Hopkins) was the mother of STEPHEN HOPKINS, who was the Governor of Rhode Island on ten occasions and was one of the signers of the *Declaration of Independence*. RUTH and WILLIAM also had a son ESEK HOPKINS (of New England) who was named commander in chief of the Colonial Navy shortly after George Washington (of Virginia) was declared commander in chief of the Colonial Army. SAMUEL's second son JOHN was my ancestor who moved as a youth to Hunterdon County, New Jersey, where he married MARY. In 1713, he purchased 307 acres of land on the Neshaminy River, just north of Philadelphia—Wrightsville. This became his family home. JOHN was his oldest son—the colonel of the Revolution. He remained in Pennsylvania. His second son, JOSEPH, my ancestor, returned across the Delaware River to their property in Hunterdon County, New Jersey. The Pennsylvania and New Jersey families were both Quakers (Friends).

The Religious Society of Friends, commonly called the Quakers, was started by George Fox, the son of a weaver, born at Drayton, in Leicestershire, England in 1624. He started his preaching in 1649. His teaching differed from the established Christian views in the following ways:

1. Divine revelation for everyone;

"I was commanded to turn people to that inward light, spirit and grace, by which all might know their salvation and their way to God."

2. Worship and Ministry;

"All true and acceptable worship to God is offered in the inward and immediate moving and drawing of his own spirit. All other worship, praises, prayers and preaching, which man sets about in his own will, at his own appointment, and can begin and end at his pleasure are but superstitious will-worship . . . . As our worship consisteth not in words, so neither in silence as silence; but in a holy dependence of the mind upon God; from which dependence silence necessarily follows in the first place, until words can be brought forth which are from God's spirit . . . . No special training or educational qualifications are considered necessary for the ministry, and no consistent 'Quaker' minister accepts pecuniary compensation for services in that capacity . . . . Freely ye have received, freely give."

3. Sacraments. Sacraments require the services of a priest or minister. Friends denied this necessity, rejecting all types and outward ordinances.

4. War, Oaths, etc.

"Friends have always maintained that war and oaths were inconsistent with Christianity, being forbidden by Christ and his apostles in the New Testament. Consistent members refuse to perform military service or partake in war-like preparations. They refuse oaths in civil courts or elsewhere as forbidden by Christ's language, 'Swear not at all'"

[*The Encyclopedia Americana, 1945 Edition*]

From the first imprisonment of Fox in 1649 to 1687, Friends were the objects of almost continuous persecution. In 1656 Fox computed there were seldom less than 1,000 members in prison. Between the years 1661 and 1697, over 13,000 Friends were imprisoned in England; 198 were transported as slaves, and 338 died in prison or of wounds received in assaults while attending meetings.

These persecutions were upon various pretexts, as the refusal to pay tithes, to swear, or to remove the hat [STEPHEN HOPKINS is shown with a hat in the picture portraying the signing of the *Declaration of Independence*]; for preaching in public places; and as Sabbath breakers—for traveling to their meetings on the day called the Sabbath. Many were apprehended for keeping an unlawful assembly under the Conventical Act.

In New England stringent laws were quickly enacted in Boston to keep the Quakers out and prevent the owners of vessels from bringing them into the colony. Regardless of the cruel penalties of these laws, the Quakers continued to arrive and suffer the consequences. It is said that in numerous instances women were "striped naked from the middle up, tied to a cart's tail and whipped through the town", which continued through other towns. Four Quakers were hanged on Boston Common, one of them a woman. Nevertheless they increased in numbers.

When the LIPPINCOTT's returned to America, they chose Rhode Island with its religious tolerance. William Penn, with his experiment in "brotherly love" government for Pennsylvania, was not granted a charter until 11 Mar 1681. The LIPPINCOTTS had left Rhode Island and arrived in New Jersey and their chartered land by 1669. There are pages of LIPPINCOTT names indexed in the Quaker Congregational records of New Jersey, Philadelphia, New York, and other congregations. Another early family name that is very prevalent in these records, especially in Philadelphia is the name PRESTON.

[Note: There are quite a number of PRESTONs listed in the "Emigration Records—1609-1685." Perhaps they are related; but they are not my direct ancestors. Notice how young most of these early settlers were. Living at Jordan's Journey, 1624, ROGER PRESTON, who in 1625, is listed again: "Jordan's Journey [21 January . . . ROGER PRESTON 21 by *Discovery* March 1621"

16 Mar 1635, "the following persons with certificates from St. Mildred, Bread Street, London, and having taken the oaths are to be transported from London to New England in the *Christian of London . . . . EDWARD PRESTON 13 . . . 6-17 April. Passengers embarked in the *Elizabeth* bound from London to New England: RODGER PRESTON 21. On the *Elizabeth & Ann* London to New England . . . DANIELL PRESTON 13 . . . HENRY WILKINSON, tallow chandler 25 . . . JOHN OLDHAM 12, THOMAS OLDHAM 10."

6 Jun 1635: Going from London to Virginia on the *Thomas & John*: .JOHN WILKENSON 28; ANE WILKINSON 20; LAWRENCE PRESTON 21; WILLIAM LACY 18.

10 Aug 1635, London to Virginia by the *Safety*: RICHARD PRESTON 17; JOHN WILKINSON 14. On 21 Aug 1635: London to Virginia by the *Thomas*: JOSEPH PRESTON 20.

19 Sep 1635: London to New England by the *Truelove*: WILLIAM PRESTON 44; MARIA PRESTON 34; ELIZABETH PRESTON 11; SARA PRESTON 8; MARIE PRESTON 6; JOHN PRESTON 3. On

13 Oct 1635, London to St. Christopher's, aboard the *Amity:* .MATHEW PRESTON 22. On 24 Oct 1635: London to Virginia embarked on the *Abraham:* GEORGE PRESTON 20.]

Ancestor, WILLIAM PRESTON, came from Newcastle-on-the-Tyne, Northumberland, England. The Tyne River borders both Northumberland and Durham Counties. He married ELIZABETH OLDHAM in England. Fifth-great-grandfather PAUL PRESTON was their eighth child, and the first to be born in America. He was born 30 Sep 1690 in Shrewsbury, Monmouth, New Jersey. Their three younger daughters were born in Frankford, Philadelphia, Pennsylvania. PAUL's ninth daughter MARY PRESTON married SAMUEL LIPPINCOTT on 7 Apr 1743. Of course, both families were Quakers.

— 53 —

LONG ISLAND IS WHOSE? BARTON? DUTCH? ENGLISH? OR THE INDIANS?

The BARTONs came early to this continent. Various family histories differ as to where they first settled and their reason for coming, but seem to agree that they were highly independent and not a part of the usual established groups. One family history stated that MARMADUKE BARTON was the original parent of this family, who was a descendent of GILBERT de LOTTUN and his wife, EDITH GRELLE, or GREDLE, called "LADY" of BARTON of the Manor of Barton of Lancashire, England. This record also states that he settled in Essex County, Massachusetts in 1632 and had two children they were sure of:

1. SAMUEL BARTON, who married HANNAH, daughter of EDWARD BRIDGES and settled in Oxford Massachusetts. He died 12 Sep 1732. [Other records say he was EDWARD's son, not brother.] 2. EDWARD BARTON, the sea captain who died in 1671 at Cape Porpoise, Maine, and left a widow, ELIZABETH.

According to this record, EDWARD and ELIZABETH had the following children, but not necessarily in this order: EDWARD; WILLIAM, who resided in Cape Porpoise; ROGER, my ancestor, who moved to New Amsterdam and then to Rye, New York, located on the coast near Connecticut; RUFUS, who died in Rhode Island in 1648, and THOMAS of Massachusetts.

Another family record stated that MARMADUKE BARTON had been given a very large estate in the New World by the king of England which included a large part of Long Island. [Of course, the Dutch were claiming it, and buying it from the Indians in the early 1600s.] This record also suggests that the BARTONs were landed Royalists. Other records from the Ancestral File show

ROGER BARTON to be the son of EDWARD BARTON and a grandson of the sea captain EDWARD BARTON. MARMADUKE BARTON is shown in this record as a brother of ROGER BARTON. No great-grandfather is listed. Another Ancestral File record shows RUFUS as the son of SAMUEL BARTON.

The *General Dictionary of First Settlers of New England before May 1682* lists these BARTONS:

"EDWARD BARTON, perhaps of Exeter 1657, was of Cape Porpoise to die June 1671 leaving a widow to administer on his property.

[Note: Exeter was one of four independent city-states that would later become part of New Hampshire. Cape Porpoise is nearby on the coast of Maine.]

"EDWARD BARTON, of Pemaquid [on the Maine sea coast], perhaps a son of the preceding, adm. Freeman of Mass. 1674. RUFUS BARTON, of Providence, had fled from persecution by Dutch of Manhattan, and sat down 1640 at Portsmouth RI. In Winth. II, 323, is a letter from him to the Governor in 1648, and a few months after he died in such a manner, as causing one to be charged with his murder, but without conviction. By the town council of Providence as Judge Brayton assures me, a sort of distribution as testament of his estate was made 20 Mar 1666 to the children. [At this time] his wife, MARGARET, had married WALTER TODD. The children of RUFUS and MARGARET were PHEBE, who married RICHARD CODNER of Swanzey May 1671; ELIZABETH who was under 21, 20 Mar 1666; and BENJAMIN under 21 in 20 Mar 1666. "

Another record states that RUFUS was on the town council 8 Aug 1647 and town magistrate in 1647. ELIZABETH married THOMAS GREENE 30 Jun 1659. THOMAS was born 4 Jun 1628, in Salisbury, Wiltshire, England, and died 5 Jun 1717. He was the son of JOHN and JOAN (TATTERSALL) GREENE. This record also states that RUFUS was a Quaker, which may be the reason for the persecution, as the early Dutch adopted an ordinance in 1640 that prohibited the exercise of all other religions except the "Reformed as it is at present preached and practised by public Authority in the United Netherlands.'" The following year this bigoted mandate was temporarily revoked. However, this period predates the actual establishment of the Religious Society of Friends, or Quakers. Its founder, George Fox, began his preaching in England in 1648, the year RUFUS died. The *General Dictionary of the Early Settlers* continues:

"THOMAS BARTON, of Mass. 1646, (maybe) Brother of RUFUS.

Maybe a son, STEPHEN BARTON of Bristol was representative 1690 at Plymouth Ct. and under new Charter 1692, at Boston.

"MARMADUKE BARTON, of Mass. 1643, condemned to slavery and to be branded. Offence not set out. "

Civil War in England was in progress at this time. In 1642 Charles I had fled London and gone to Nottingham with his court. Battles were being fought. Parliament, which was controlled by the Puritans, had the Courts and financial assets of London to aid them. Charles I had only his Royalist friends. The Puritans of Boston had welcomed many of the revolutionaries that had been exiled by the king. Sir Henry Vane had been elected their Governor for one year, until he returned to England. Sir HUGH PETERS, a dissenting clergyman in exile first at Rotterdam and afterwards in New England, returned to England in 1640 to become an influential leader of the parliamentary party. John Hampden and his cousin Oliver Cromwell had planned to come to the wilds of America to establish a colony when they were out of favor with the King. This venture was stopped when Charles I proclaimed an Edict that forbids shipmasters from carrying English subjects out of the kingdom without a special permit. They were thus prevented from sailing. In 1643 with the "Roundheads" (as the Puritans were called by the followers of the King) in control at Boston, it is possible that they chose to get rid of the old "Cavalier or Malignant" (terms used by the Puritans for the Royalists) MARMADUKE BARTON. The charges were not set out—perhaps because they were trumped up in the first place.

"BENJAMIN BARTON, of Providence, freeman 25 Mar 1669, chosen as Assist. 1674. Married SUSANNAH June 1669 daughter of the celebrated SAMUEL GORTON. Died 1720. Will: 22 Oct 1720, children: RUFUS; ANDREW; PHEBE; NAOMI; SUSANNA; another daughter who had married JABEZ GREENE of Providence was then probably deceased [MARY].

SAMUEL GORTON and JOHN GREENE were the leaders of this third colonial settlement in Rhode Island at Warwick, where BENJAMIN BARTON settled and was Asst. and Dep. many years; Commr. of Bounties, 1699; & Speaker of the House of Deps. 1703-1704. SUSANNAH died May 28, 1734.

[Note: "JAMES BARTON, Newton, had been of Boston where he had a good establishment and was a ropemaker. By his wife MARGARET he had MARGARET; JOHN, born 5 Sept 1686, & others. He died 1720 aged 86 leaving a widow who died 1731 aged 87.

"JACKSON BARTON, will 1720 lists two daughters: MARGARET SIMPKINS and RUTH COOK. Grandson THOMAS STANTON, together with (maybe sons of JOHN) grandsons JAMES, JOHN, SAMUEL and MICHAEL, all remembered."

(Maybe JACKSON was the son of SAMUEL BARTON who went to his home in Barbados when his father MARMADUKE was convicted in Massachusetts.)

"JOHN BARTON, of Salem, son probably of the preceding [JACKSON]. A physician, married 20 Apr 1676 LYDIA ROBERTS, perhaps daughter of Thomas of Boston. They had a son

1. JOHN born 2 Feb 1677, died in 5 days;

2. JOHN born 30 Jan 1678, died young;

3. THOMAS a physician of Salem born 17 Jul 1680, many years town clerk, Colonel of Regiment, married 10 May 1710, Mary, granddaughter of Dept. Gov. Willoughby, died 28 Apr 1751, son JOHN H.C. 1730 had two wives, Mary Butler and Elizabeth Marston, died 13 Mar 1772;

4. ZACCHEUS born 1 Apr 1683;

5. ELIZABETH born Oct 1685;

6. SAMUEL, of Salem, born 30 Aug 1688, he was a sea captain and went home more than once and died on a voyage to Bermuda."]

[Note: The New York or New Jersey BARTONS, of course, would not have been considered part of this dictionary of New England residents. It might be of interest to note that BENJAMIN BARTON named a son ANDREW. There was an ANDREW BARTON who was a Scottish naval commander, who flourished during the reign of James IV of Scotland and who belonged to a family which for two generations had produced able and successful seamen. His father was JOHN BARTON and his three sons were ANDREW, JOHN, and ROBERT (afterwards Lord High Treasurer of Scotland.) In 1506 ANDREW cleared the Scottish coasts of the Flemish pirates with which they were infested, and as a proof of the thoroughness of his work, sent the king three barrels full of their heads. In 1476 letters of marque had been granted by James III to the BARTONs against the Portuguese for plundering the ship of JOHN BARTON, the father. These letters had been repeatedly suspended in the hope of redress. However, in November of 1506 they were renewed to the sons, granting them liberty to seize Portuguese goods until they were repaid 12,000 ducats. ANDREW's daring and skill impressed the King sufficiently that he built him a "great and costly ship" the Lion, which he used in destroying the Flemish pirates. In 1508 he was sent to assist Denmark against Lubeck. The damage he inflicted on Portuguese ships engaged in the English trade aroused such great resentment in England that Henry VIII allowed Sir Thomas and Sir Edward Howard "to fit two ships with the view of effecting his capture." In an engagement between his ship, the Lion, and the two ships specially fitted out against him, a brilliant and desperate battle ensued. BARTON was shot through the heart by an arrow and the resistance of the Scots ended. ANDREW BARTON was killed (2 Aug 1511). BARTON's ship was brought in triumph to the Thames and became the second man-of-war in the English navy. King Henry freed the sailors of BARTON, giving them enough money to return home to Scotland. However, James of Scotland was not satisfied and the resulting dispute was fought out on Flodden Field.

There was an EDWARD BARTON (about 1562–1597) who was the second English Ambassador sent to Constantinople—probably the second son of EDWARD BARTON of Yorkshire, who died in 1610. EDWARD BARTON was popular with the Turks and fought under their flag. In 1597 the plague struck this Turkish capital. BARTON fled to the little island of Halke, but died there on the 15 December. A slab marks his grave by the church attached to the convent of the Virgin on the island. It was believed that he never married or had children.]

The early book of Emigrants lists:

"5 March. [1635] The Providence Island Company receives news that the *William and Anne* has been wrecked on the coast of Brittany. ISAAC

BARTON is appointed sheriff of Providence and is to have six servants. The following are to go to Providence as passengers: a minister and 3 servants; Mr. Lane, his wife, two children, maid and 6 servants; [Could this be a relative of the Methodist minister Lane of New York and Pennsylvania, spoken of in Part I: DRIVEN?] Mr. BARTON and 6 servants . . . 22 January. [1641] Deposition re the voyage of the *Providence*, Mr. Pinkard, to Providence and New England with passengers of whom SAMUEL BARTON . . . came away again in the ship . . . "

[Note: 2 May, [1654] Deposition by William Tapping of London, vintner aged 37, and John Houghton aged wq, servant of THOMAS BLAND of London, scrivener, that William Bannister of Barbados signed a financial obligation to ISAAC BARTON of London, merchant . . . 31 October. [1654] Joshua Draper of Braintree, Essex, gent aged 40, desposes at the request of Edmond Plume of Hawkedon, Suffolk, executor of William Holgate of Shalford, Essex, gent, that on 6 May 1640 John Hawkridge of London, merchant, and James Heron Esq of Rayne, Essex, signed a financial obligation to Holgate. EDWARD BARTON of Barbados, merchant, appointed attorney to recover. 14 January [1656] LAWRENCE BARTON of Lancaster, Lancs, labourer, bound to Thomas Mawson of Bristol, seaman, to serve 4 years in Barbados . . . 17 June. [1656] copy of bond by JOSEPH BARTON of Southampton, merchant, to Armiger Warner of London, merchant, for goods adventured in the Supply of London, Mr. Thomas Flute, to Barbados."]

CLARA BARTON of the American Civil War and Red Cross fame was from North Oxford, Massachusetts. Her father and brother were both named STEPHEN BARTON. Her brother STEPHEN had a son SAMUEL BARTON, who was very helpful to her during the American Civil War. She never married. One history states that her earliest American ancestor was MARMADUKE BARTON, another history claims it was EDWARD BARTON.

ROGER BARTON, my ancestor, in 1642 was on Manhattan Island where he leased some farm land on the North River from Rev. Everardus Bogardus. This was part of the Anneke Jans, or later Trinity Church property—where the first Secretary of the Treasury, ALEXANDER HAMILTON, is buried. This is the only mention of ROGER BARTON's name in the searched New York records until 1664, when he is in Brookhaven, Long Island. ROGER BARTON had moved there and was Deputy of the General Court in March 1665. According to records previously quoted, RUFUS had left New Amsterdam in 1640, fleeing the persecution of the Dutch. Most histories say that ROGER's stay in Manhattan was brief for the same reason that RUFUS had fled to Rhode Island.

ROGER BARTON later settled in Rye, New York, about 25 miles east of Manhattan Island on the coast of Long Island Sound about a mile from the

Connecticut border. Further west along the coast about three miles toward Manhattan Island is Mamaroneck the home of Dutch ancestor, ROBERT COLES, who married an English woman, MERCY WRIGHT, whose father NICHOLAS WRIGHT drowned in Oyster Bay, November 1682. Oyster Bay is just southeast across Long Island Sound. The WRIGHTs came from Bartons Turf in Norfolk, England. ROGER's great-grandson NOAH BARTON would marry ROBERT COLES' great-granddaughter MARY COOLEY, 25 Sep 1791 in Hunterdon County, New Jersey, joining the two lines of these progenitors.

ROGER BARTON's grandson, Captain ELISHA BARTON, one of my ancestors of the Revolutionary War period [the son of above NOAH BARTON] married JEMIMA VAN KIRK. JEMIMA's second-great-grandfather JAN JANSEN VERKERK or VAN KIRK emigrated from Bueer Maetsen, Gelderland, Holland, with his wife, MAYKE GISBERTS and five children. His second son AERD JANSE VERKERK was my ancestor. They came on the ship *Rosetree* in 1663 and settled in New Utrecht, Long Island, the present location of Brooklyn, Kings, New York, where he owned large tracts of land. He was on the assessment rolls of New Utrecht in 1675, in 1683, and 1693. He was magistrate in 1678 and 1684; on Dongan's Patent in 1686; on the census in 1688; and took the *Oath of Allegiance* to the English king in 1687. His will was dated 10 Nov 1688. It would seem that the early history on this contested real estate of Long Island and the continental surrounding settlements is closely tied to the history of many of my 6th, 7th, and 8th great-grandparents. For awhile, the Dutch controlled the western half of the island, and the British inhabited the more desolate eastern half.

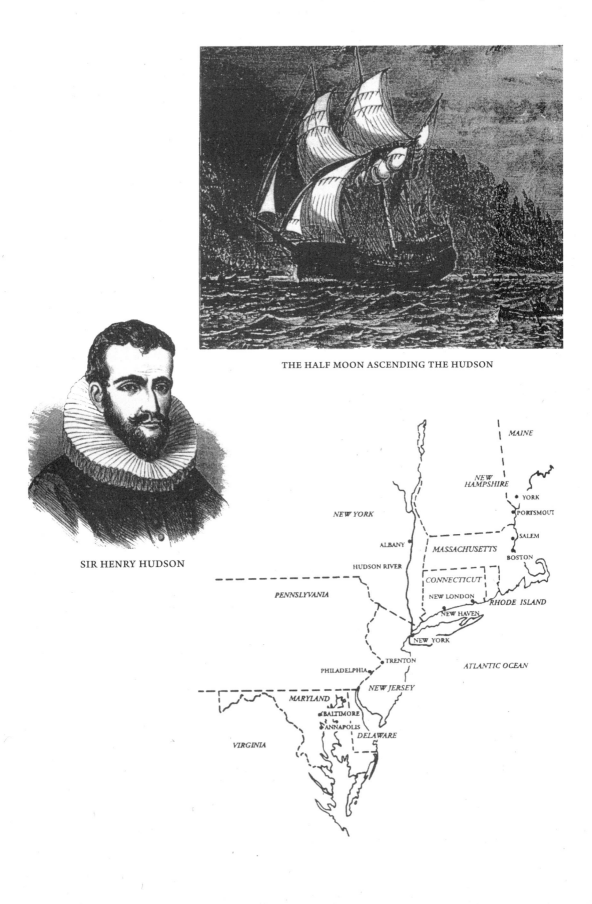

THE HALF MOON ASCENDING THE HUDSON

SIR HENRY HUDSON

MAINE

NEW HAMPSHIRE

YORK

PORTSMOUT

NEW YORK

SALEM

ALBANY

MASSACHUSETTS

BOSTON

HUDSON RIVER

CONNECTICUT

NEW LONDON

PENNSLYVANIA

RHODE ISLAND

NEW HAVEN

NEW YORK

TRENTON

ATLANTIC OCEAN

PHILADELPHIA

NEW JERSEY

MARYLAND

BALTIMORE

ANNAPOLIS

DELAWARE

VIRGINIA

$\sim$ 54 $\sim$

THE NEW NETHERLANDS —
THE DUTCH CLAIM THE HUDSON RIVER

After Columbus claimed much of the West Indies for Spain, and St. Augustine became a permanent settlement in Florida, tobacco plantations flourished in this New World, as the habit-forming desire for nicotine spread across the European Continent. The English established a beachhead at Jamestown in 1607. The Netherlands had a substantial fleet of ships, also. They established the West India Company, backed by some of the wealthier shippers and financiers of Holland, and, in 1623, they sent an expedition to fortify and prepare for their colonists along their claim of the Hudson River. One of the financiers was HERR KILIAEN VAN RENSSALAER who, in 1625, sent two of his nephews to watch over his interests, JAN CORNELIUS COELY (VON ROTTERDAM), age 30, and ARENDT VAN CULER, only 18 years old, with two shiploads of cattle, horses, swine, and sheep, and other colonists.

The Dutch built a fort on the Hudson River near an old French fur trading fort, (now Albany), and called it Fort Orange after the Prince of Orange.

[Note: The Prince of Orange was also the Stadtholder of the Netherlands, another name for their royal king.. WILLIAM I Prince of Orange, Stadtholder, was murdered in 1584. He married LOUISE, the daughter of Casper, who was a cousin of the French General COLIGNI, whose half sister ELEANOR married LOUIS I, Prince of COND'E of France. Their son inherited the title, succeeded by his son WILLIAM II. WILLIAM III added to this title King of England after James II lost his throne, because of his Catholic beliefs. He died in 1702. More will be said in later chapters.]

JAN was at first in charge at Fort Orange; but by 1641, ARENDT was given this command, while JAN took over in the Brooklyn area of Long Island called the Flatlands and across the Hudson River at a settlement they called Achter Cul, presently the location of Newark, New Jersey. The French were to the north, Canada, and the English were to the east where the newly established

Pilgrim Colonies had come to Plymouth in 1620. To stake their claim against this English colony on the east they started another fort on the Fresh River (now Connecticut River) at the present day site of Hartford, Connecticut. They named it the Fort of Good Hope and JANS' brother PETER COLET, my ancestor, was part of this colony. ARENDT was his first cousin.

An island of 22,000 acres (Manhattan Island) near the mouth of the Hudson River was purchased from the Indians for the value of sixty guilders (about $120.00) in beads and finery. The Indians were quite content. They had lots of land, if they could keep it from their warring Indian neighbors. There, the Dutch built another fort for protection and started their farms and orchards. Along the eastern shore, they built a long line of one-story log houses, with bark or straw roofs and wooden chimneys. There were perhaps thirty of them for the approximately 200 new settlers—the beginning of Pearl Street, the oldest street in New York City.

> "The colony 'boomed' from the beginning and the stock of the Dutch West India Company sailed upward. Under the 'Freedoms and Exemptions Act', adopted in 1628, the company gave authority to every person who should send over a colony of 50 souls above the age of 15 years, the title of *Patroon* and the privilege of selecting tracts of land, except on Manhattan Island, eight miles in length along the river and as far inland as he pleased. It was obligatory for the patroon to be a member of the company. He was looked upon as a feudal prince. His possessions were exempt from taxation for 10 years. The colonists were prohibited from manufacturing woolen, linen or cotton cloth. Under authority thus conferred KILIAEN VAN RENSSELAER of Amsterdam, a diamond and pearl polisher, obtained, through Sebastian Jansen Krol, who had come two years before as 'consoler of the sick,' a tract of land 20 miles in length, from Baeren Island to Smacks Island, and 24 miles on either side of the river 'stretching two days journey into the interior,' constituting [most} of the present counties of Albany, Rensselaer and Columbia. . . . The patroons practically became rivals of the West India Company in the fur trade. As the business of the latter diminished, the wealth of the former expanded. [Governor] Minuit, unable to readjust the differences, was recalled." [*Americana, New York*]

Concerned for his people, the Dutch Governor, Minuit, soon stopped work on the Fort of Good Hope and brought most of his colonists from the Fort Orange area back to Manhattan Island. A small garrison was left at Fort Orange with ARENDT VAN CURLER in charge. He was to be a counselor and peace-maker with the Indians who traded there with the Dutch. It was a position of confidence and trust which he held many years.

From the *Encyclopedia International*:

"VAN CORLEAR OR VAN CURLER. Arendt (c. 1600-67). A Dutch colonist, born in Holland. Emigrating to New Amsterdam (New York) about 1630, he became the superintendent of Renssalaerwyck [Albany] in 1642, and as such was called upon to conduct frequent negotiations with the Indians, whom he treated with uniform consideration and justice, and over whom in consequence he exercised a powerful influence, by which he preserved peace for many years between them and the whites. Throughout the Mohawk country and to a certain extent among the Eastern Indians generally the name 'Corlear' soon came into use to designate the English governor (especially of New York) and was so used for more than a century. On several occasions van Corlear rescued French prisoners from the Iroquois or saved them from torture. In 1661 he bought the 'great Flat' of the Mohawk River from the Indians and in 1662 founded Schenectady, the first agricultural settlement in the province in which farmers could hold land in fee simple, free from Feudal annoyances. In 1667 while on his way to Quebec to visit the French governor he was drowned off Split Rock, in Lake Champlain."

From John Fiske's *Dutch and Quaker Colonies in America*: "In the terrible summer of 1675, when the Wampanoags were working such havoc in the Plymouth colony and the Neponinds in the central highlands of Massachusetts—and the frontier settlements of Virginia and Maryland were being goaded into war by wandering Susquehannocks, Governor Andros of New York, understanding the gravity of the Indian situation, felt it was clearly a time for preserving friendly relations with the formidable Long House (the Indian council house of the Five Nations— the Mohawks, Oneidas, Onandagoes, Cayugas and Senecas.)

"He made up his mind to go in person and secure their favor and that of their confederates. His journey took him into the Indian country, and after landing at Albany his party struck into the great Indian trail, a route followed closely in later days by the Erie Canal and the New York Central Railroad. After a march of about 16 miles they came upon the Mohawk River at a fording place where there was a tiny Dutch hamlet founded fourteen years before by ARENDT VAN CORLEAR (CURLER), a man of noble and generous nature. As a commissioner of Rennsalaerwyck he had long been known to the Indians in whose minds his name stood as a synonym of truth and integrity.

"In 1667 this good CORLEAR came to a melancholy end. As he was sailing on Lake Champlain he passed a rock whereon the waves were wont to dash and fly up wildly and the Indian folk-lore told of an ancestral Indian who haunted the spot and controlled the weather, so that passing canoeists always threw a pipe or other small gift to this genius of the lake, and prayed for a favorable wind. But CORLEAR not only neglected this wise precaution but in his contempt for such heathen fancies made an unseemly gesture as he passed the rock; whereat the offended spirit blew a sudden gust which capsized his boat and drowned him."

Fiske quoted from Colden's *History of the Five Nations*, published in London, 1755. "The Indian name of the village founded by CORLEAR was Onoaligone, but the village itself was known to Indians and French simply as 'CORLEAR'S'. The Dutch inhabitants, however, transferred to it the Indian name Schenectady which was originally applied to the country about the site of Albany. It means Beyond-the-openings or Beyond the pine-plains."

From *A Story of Pioneering* by Lura COOLLEY Hamil:

"JAN CORNELIUS COELY (VON ROTTERDAM) and ARENDT VAN CULER (whom the Indians and the French called COLEAR) were nephews of KILLIAEN VAN RENSSALAER, 1580-1646, First Patroon of the Manor of Rensselaer-wyck. He sent his nephews to represent him in the new colony, ARENDT with many directions calculated to control his associations and companions, the young man being 18 when sent in 1625. JAN, the older, was born in 1595, and married in 1615 at Amsterdam, at age of twenty, ANNETJE SWEFFENS, age 21. He made his first voyage January 1624 and in November, on the 14th, was back at Amsterdam. He sailed again in May or June and was commander of Fort Orange for a time later. He lived on a small farm-plantation on Long Island before 1630, and his father and brothers followed him here in 1638."

JAN was the son of CORNELIUS LAMBERTSON COOL and ARENDT was a son of JACOB VAN CURLER (COOL). CORNELIUS and JACOB were brothers whose mother was a sister of KILLIAEN VAN RENSSALAER. The COOLEYs of Hunterdon, New Jersey, are descendants of CORNELIUS and JAN's brother PIETER CORNELISSON COOL (PETER COLET).

Because of the similarity and changes in spelling of these early names, it is sometimes difficult to keep everything straight. The Dutch Reformed Church records of this period are of course written in Dutch, and, as the Dutch or English have Anglicized many of these names, different children choosing for themselves various spellings, it increases the difficulty. But at this time it appears that JAN, the older of the two young (grand) nephews of KILLIAEN, had a daughter HESTER. She evidently was the first wife of a younger brother of Arendt, JACOB VAN CURLER, whom she married in Rotterdam, Holland. We are told that when JACOB came to America in 1628, JAN was his faithful friend and foster father.

The following excerpts are from Fiske's *Dutch and Quaker Colonies in America:*

"It will be remembered that in 1623 the Dutch had started to build Fort Good Hope but soon desisted. Their numbers were too small for the territory they wished to cover. But in 1628 Indian affairs drew their attention eastward. The Mohegans were asking for protection from the Pequota. As allies of the Mohawks, the Dutch could not help them with firearms so in the summer of 1632 the Dutch agents bought of the Mohegans large tracts of land on both sides of the (Connecticut) river and at its mouth [on a large oak tree] they nailed the Arms of the States-General.

"In the next summer Director van TWILLER sent JACOB VAN CURLER to what is now the site of Hartford, Connecticut. There he built Fort Good Hope with yellow brick from Holland. As commander of the garrison he armed it with two cannons. The fort was finished early in June 1633."

After Minuit was recalled by the Dutch of Amsterdam the office remained vacant for two years. Then they sent WOUTER VAN TWILLER as a replacement. According to the Encyclopedia Americana, VAN TWILLER was

"a name synonymous with farce, burlesque, contempt and arrogance. VAN TWILLER had married a niece of VAN RENSSELAER. He was an administrator of fair parts. He began construction of a new fort; be built the first church edifice; a bakery; a brewery; he substituted brick for frame houses and new wind-mills for old. But his plans failed to mature because of his peculiar disposition. Dominie Bogardus, who had accompanied him to this country in the same ship, stigmatized him a 'child of the devil' and threatened to 'shake him from the pulpit as would make him shudder.' VAN TWILLER was removed under charges in 1637 and left office, as did many of his successors, with a fortune he had accumulated in service. His successor was William Kieft."

In my family records we show JOHAN VAN RENSSALEAR married to ELIZABETH VAN TWILLER. JOHAN was KILIAEN's son and therefore a first cousin of my ancestor CORNELIUS LAMBERTSON COOL.

"The Plymouth government that summer bought some land at Windsor [near Hartford, Connecticut] and in September sent a barge loaded with a blockhouse all ready for raising, with a party of Plymouth men and some Mohegan Indians sailing up the Connecticut River. As they passed Fort Good Hope the Dutch commander (JACOB VAN CURLER) shouted to them to turn and go back under the penalty of a volley from the two cannons. Holmes replied that he was under orders from the governor of Plymouth and should go on, volley or no volley. So they passed along and, though the Dutch threatened them hard, they shot not.

"On reaching the site of Windsor, Connecticut, they quickly put up their blockhouse and built a stockade around it. They were not long in hearing that their dealings had given mortal offense to the Pequots, but the Indians' revenge, when it came, did not fall upon these men of Plymouth but upon another party of Englishmen."

The revenge fell upon Captain Stone of Virginia as follows:

"Early in the following January as Captain Stone, a skipper from Virginia, was sailing up the Connecticut River on an errand to Fort Good Hope, he imprudently allowed a dozen Pequots to come aboard his little vessel. At night the Indians murdered them all. VAN CURLER, the commander at Fort Good Hope, captured some of the Indians who were known to have a hand in these murders and had them hanged, turning the wrath of the powerful tribe against the Dutch. In consequence, the Indians sent emissaries to Boston offering (1) to cede more [of their supposed] land on the Connecticut [to the English], (2) to surrender the surviving Indians concerned in the Stone Massacre [this was never done] and (3) to pay a handsome tribute in wampum, besides, [in exchange] for English protection. Meanwhile the English held their ground at Windsor, tore down the Arms of the Dutch States-General from the tree to which it had been nailed when the Mohegans sold their lands to Dutch agents.

"Fort Good Hope was practically cut off from New Amsterdam by Fort Saybrook, built by the English under John Winthrop further down the river, and overland communication [with other Dutch colonies] through the primeval forest was full of difficulty and danger. The Dutch fort, forlorn hope of eastern New Netherlands, was about to be not merely isolated but overwhelmed in a new tide of English migration. In 1636, under their great leader Thomas Hooker, the Cambridge congregation came in a body through the wilderness to the fields which Fort Good Hope vainly aspired to command, and began building Hartford. So wholesale was the removal that only eleven families were left in Cambridge, which but for new arrivals from England would have presented the appearance of a deserted village."

Similarly, Dorchester [Massachusetts] came to Windsor and rapidly swallowed up the little Plymouth settlement. The English population of 800 souls brought into Connecticut far outnumbered all the Dutch. Against such odds "the Dutch remained for some years, unmolested at their Hartford fortress, since the English could so well afford to disregard them."

With this Dorchester group were the Walcotts who later married into the Benjamin Cooley family who settled Springfield, Massachusetts, in 1636. The Walcotts' history describe their arrival in Connecticut as follows:

"That first winter in the new settlement of Windsor was severe. Many returned to Massachusetts. Those who remained suffered extreme hardships. They were forced to subsist on acorns, malt, and grain. Cattle perished.

"Spring brought new hope. . . . One hundred men, women, and children began the arduous journey to their new homes in early May of 1636. Their baggage was sent ahead by boat. They drove their cattle before them as the travelers sought their way through forests and swamps and across streams. Only the young and feeble were given the luxury of riding horseback along Indian trails less than two feet wide. The travelers lived on the milk from their cattle and the prayers in their hearts. Each night they lay wrapped in their cloaks and blankets fearing the attack of wild beasts or unfriendly Indians. They reached their destination in two weeks and fanned out to build the Connecticut communities of Windsor, Hartford, and Wethersfield."

One D.A.R. record claims that my JOHN COOLEY was a descendant of the Walcotts and Benjamin Cooley, but the records claimed do not correspond with the Walcott records.

PETER COLET, who had been trained as a boatswain, was one of the Dutch farmers who tried to save Hartford for the Dutch. The record shows that he, with Evert Duycking and Sybrant Sybolts, had engaged in a heated altercation with the New England settlers on one occasion. *A Story of Pioneering* states:

"Director VAN TWILLER's administration was a time of bickering with the English, but a very brisk trade was carried on meanwhile with the English colonists. Salt and tobacco were carried on Dutch vessels from Manhattan to Boston and Salem, and horses and oxen of the finest breeds were brought over from Holland for use in New England. The voyage from Amsterdam [Holland] to Boston usually took from five to six weeks."

In Manhattan,

"Numbers of yellow brick houses were built, a wooden church and parsonage, three windmills and a brewery. Agriculture made some progress at Manhattan, and tobacco grown near the site of the present City Hall was exported in considerable quantities to Holland where it brought nearly as good prices as tobacco from Virginia."

Tobacco was a cash crop and could be used in lieu of money to pay taxes.

"Large estates were bought by VAN TWILLER and his friends in the expectation of a rise in prices. One of [his] purchases was . . . Governor's Island. Others were on Long Island, comprising the present district of Flatlands. JACOB VAN CURLER bought here as well as JAN COELE 'from Rotterdam,' as he continued to sign his name. His family, father, and brother-in-law made larger purchases in this area later. The Indian occupants of these lands had been paid for them after the usual fashion but in order to get a valid title under the West India Company's regulations it was necessary that such purchases should be formally approved by the Amsterdam chamber. VAN TWILLER foolishly disregarded this ruling and laid himself open to charges of dishonest dealing and was in consequence removed from office.

"Soon after the coming of Kieft to take the place of Director VAN TWILLER another VAN CURLER came over from Holland and purchased a plantation in Brooklyn in 1639. This was CORNELIUS LAMBERTSON COOL, for he chose to change the spelling of the name and so signs his documents. CORNELIUS was the father of JAN (from Rotterdam) who had come earlier with ARENDT who was followed by JACOB.

"GERRITT WOLLPHERTSON, son-in-law of CORNELIUS COOL, husband of his daughter AELTJE, bought land in Brooklyn at this same time, 1639. WOLPHERTSON was speedily made a member of Governor Kieft's Council of Eight, the very first example in New Amsterdam of anything resembling a representative form of government. He was a most able and kindly man."

Kieft was inclined to ignore this "Council of Eight" and so a few years later they wrote to Holland requesting his replacement, which request was granted and Peter Stuyvesant was sent as a replacement—about 1644.

In 1641, an unoffending citizen of Manhattan, Claes Swyts of Smit's V'Iei, was killed by an act of vengeance. This area is near CORLEAR Park, a tiny open spot on CORLEAR's Hook, the most south-easterly point on Manhattan.

"After the murder of Claes, the smith, had thrown the settlers and Indians into conflict, the excited Indians committed grave crimes against the scattered settlers. Achter Cul, the little Dutch settlement in New Jersey, 'back of Newark Bay,' was attacked. This settlement was under the authority of JAN COELE, the oldest son of CORNELISSON COOL—Jonckheer, 'the young master.' he was called. [He] had also been made commissioner of cargoes by the council.

"There is a record of a report to the council where he asked for authority to remove the settlers from Achter Cul and for means to winter the cattle across the bay. This was in February 1642. In the summer of 1643 JAN COELE was killed fighting (the Indians) on Long Island."

Kieft had unwisely tried to demand a tribute in maize from the Indians because they had supported them in defense of their enemies. When they refused, he attempted to stop the sale of guns and ammunition to them. Turbulence broke loose along the New York frontier. For three years the bloody strife continued and the Dutch were driven into the fort at New Amsterdam for protection.

There were the Manhattan Indians to the north of them; the Long Island Indians from the east, and the Delaware Indians from the south and west. Roger Williams helped to bring peace for a short while; but the following year brought greater violence. Kieft solicited the support of Capt. JOHN UNDERHILL, a valiant warrior, under whose skill and energy an able-bodied force was raised, which encountered and defeated the Indians in several pitched battles. In 1645, a peace pact was made with the Algonquin tribes which ended the fighting.

[Note: ROBERT COLES married DEBORAH UNDERHILL of Moskito Cove, Queens, New York about 1713.]

Kieft failed to profit from his lesson. Without the slightest provocation, he crossed to the west coast of the Hudson, with soldiers from the fort composed of mobs from the streets, privateersmen, and sailors from the harbor. Under cover of darkness he fell upon a band of peaceable and unsuspecting Indians at Pavonia and massacred men, women, and children indiscriminately. The act resulted in his recall. Kieft left for home with a fortune. The ship was wrecked off the coast of Wales and governor and fortune went down together. Everardus Bogardus, who had come on the same ship as VAN TWILLER, and had quarreled strongly with him and Kieft, was returning home on this same vessel, also, and he suffered a similar fate.

Indian outbreaks excited the colony for several years, killing at one time in three days 100 Dutch colonists and taking 150 as prisoners. But there was another devastating problem—the English. Stuyvesant claimed for the Dutch the whole coast from Delaware Bay to Cape Cod and

> "his masterful demeanor toward his neighbors at New Haven was a fine exhibition of bluffs. But when he came face to face with the commissioners for settling questions of jurisdiction, he knew when to yield."

In the treaty of Hartford, 17 Sep 1650, he practically gave up New England. His "council of nine" soon found reason to complain about him, and petitions were dispatched across the sea, complaining of his arbitrary and unreasonable exercise of power. As the dissatisfaction of the Dutch burghers increased against him, sympathy for him increased with the English and he was able to expand the Dutch market in New England. In 1652 the city of New Amsterdam was incorporated; a year later the palisades were constructed to the north of the present Wall Street.

With the outbreak of the war between Holland and England, the city was put in a state of defense. When the English entered the harbor with an overpowering force, Stuyvesant recognized the odds were too great and the rule of Holland ended peacefully in 1664. The population amounting to 1600 inhabitants of New Amsterdam was transferred in loyalty to England, and the appointed English William Nichols became governor of a newly named New York City.

> "ARENDT CORLER served English Governors as faithfully as he had served the Council and kept the peace, until his death three years later."

The *Encyclopedia Americana, History of New York* states:

> "ARENDT VAN CURLER, long loved and trusted by the Indians as 'CORLAER,' had purchased the great flats at Schenectady and the colony was spreading forth like a blossoming plant, north, west and southwest of Albany."

After he left Fort Good Hope, JACOB VAN CURLER, its longtime commander, taught school and in 1638 he took up a patent of three flats on the Island of Manhattan known as CORLEAR'S FLATS. It was on 4 Jun 1638, that he sold the most easterly flat of his bouwerie or farm to Claes Swyts, the smith. [Claes Swyts, the smith, was murdered as told previously in 1641.] JACOB signed a document giving power of attorney in the matter of a transfer on CORLEAR'S HOOK in 1640 and in 1652 he obtained the patent for a plantation in Flatlands [on Long Island]. In 1655 he resided in Gravesend, in 1660 on his plantation. He was magistrate in 1659 and 1660, clerk in 1662. On 20 Mar 1662, he bought plantation number 18, in Gravesend, of Eman Benam. He sometimes signed his name as J. V. CURLEY.

JAN CORNELISSON COELE—*Jonckheer, the young master*—had very early occupied the plantation where CORNELIUS, his father, afterward settled. JAN's second wife was AELTJE (Elizabeth) and three children were born to them: JAN, CORNEL, and MARIETJE. The children's baptisms are recorded in the old Dutch Reformed Church of Manhattan records. JAN, the father, was killed in the Indian fighting on Long Island. His widow, AELTJE, gave a lease to the plantation for one year, but in a few months married PETER CORNELISSON COOL (who always signed his name PETER COLET), a brother of JAN [and the direct ancestor of my Hunterdon, New Jersey COOLEY ancestors.] By this marriage she had a son, WILHELM PIETERSON COLET, who was baptized 4 Aug 1644. She was again left a widow [PETER's death circumstances are not yet ascertained.] Her third marriage was to a third brother, CORNELIUS COOL, by whom she had a son, PIETER CORNELISSON COOL, baptized 14 Oct 1646. The young mother died shortly after the birth of this child and in 1647 her household goods were administered by CORNELIS, in New Jersey, where the records of LEENDERT (Lambert), son of WILHELM PIETERSON COLET, were found.

> "Her children were cared for by various relatives. WILHELM (or William), only son of PETER COLET married SUSANNAH and is listed in the Westchester census of 1698 as having sons THOMAS and ABRAHAM, at home, and daughters, SUSANNAH and SARAH. Their sons, LEENDERT and ROBERT, were married at this time and had homes of their own. When SUSANNAH, WILHELM's widow, remarried she gave a quitclaim

deed of property left by her husband and named THOMAS, oldest son of ROBERT COOLEY, which authenticates this connection with this Dutch branch of the COOLEY, COOLLEY, COLLET, COLES, KOOL, COOL, COLE, CULER, CUYLER, (and other variations) family. ROBERT took up land in Mamaroneck in 1731, and then went into New Jersey where some of the family remained and others went on to Pennsylvania."

In 1673, during the war between the Netherlands and England, New York was recaptured by the Dutch and renamed New Orange. Dutch rule was restored. However, as the war ended on 10 Nov 1674, a peace treaty returned New York to the British and Sir Edmund Andros took over his commission as governor. He was an intelligent and wise officer but was directed by the English crown, Charles II, to bring New England and New York under the absolute authority of his majesty. Andros was unable to successfully rule this independent and liberty-loving people.

In 1685, Charles II of England died and his brother James ascended to the throne. James II created certain problems, as he was Catholic and wanted to return England to the doctrines of the Church of Rome. This brought a second revolution in England. In the end, in 1688, James II fled to Paris and the protection of Louis XIV, and William and Mary became the joint rulers. Mary was the daughter of James II and had married William Henry, Prince of Orange, Stadtholder of the Netherlands. He was the political leader of the Protestant cause in Europe, and his wife was in hearty accord with her husband. William's mother, Mary, was the eldest daughter of England's Charles I. In English America the result brought a reason for friendship between Holland and England but with that there was a stronger animosity toward Catholicism and the Catholic French nation under the absolute control of its king, Louis XIV.

Louis XIV was a devout Catholic; or at least, a devout believer in the authority it gave him as a monarch. After the death of Cardinal Mazarin in 1661, Louis adopted his motto *L'Etat c'est Moi*—"The State is Mine." No cardinal was sent to replace Mazarin. Unwilling to allow his colonies in America to become as divided religiously as the English were, he only allowed immigration of strong Catholics and chose his military that came to this Continent in the same way. In Nova Scotia and along the shores of the St. Lawrence River there were only Catholic churches. The Jesuit missionaries were sent to befriend and convert the Indians to the ways of France. France was moving southward and claiming the Ohio and inland territory.

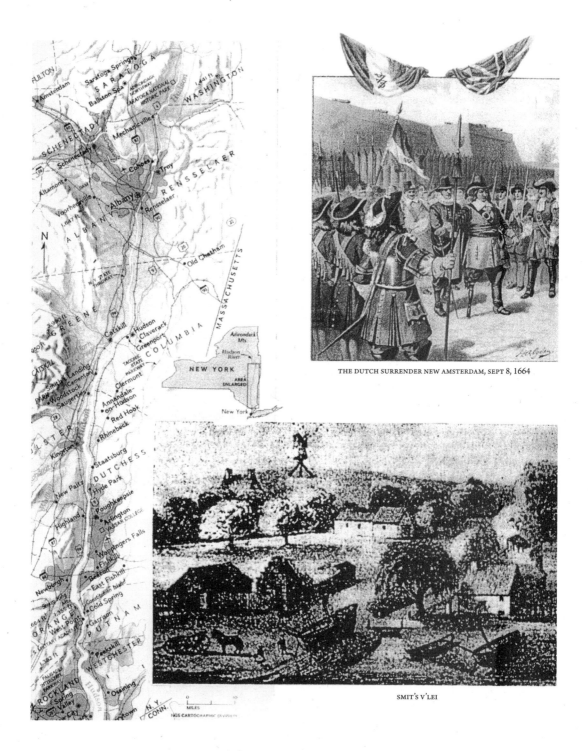

THE DUTCH SURRENDER NEW AMSTERDAM, SEPT 8, 1664

SMIT'S V'LEI

⇥ 55 ⇤

MORGANS AND EATONS OF CONNECTICUT

The following is quoted from the *Genealogy & Family History of Northern New York, p. 83,* capitalization added:

"JAMES MORGAN was born in 1607, in Wales probably in Llandaff, Gllmorganshire, whence the family moved to Bristol on the opposite side of Bristol Channel, prior to 1636. There is a tradition that his father's name was WILLIAM. In March, 1636, he sailed from Bristol, accompanied by two younger brothers, JOHN and MILES, and arrived in Boston, Massachusetts, the following month. His brother JOHN MORGAN was a high churchman, and was parted from the austere Puritans and made his home in Virginia. [In those days, Virginia extended north and included New York and parts of New England.]

"It is supposed that JAMES MORGAN lived for a time at Plymouth, but this cannot be proven. He was in Roxbury [now part of Boston] before 1640, and was made freeman there 1 May 1643. He appears there in 1646, and was a freeholder as late as 1650, the same year in which he removed to Pequot, New London, Connecticut, and had a house and lot assigned to him there. The records of that town show that lands for cultivation were granted him in that year, and soon occupied by him. His homestead was on the 'new street now Ashcroft Street,' and a subsequent entry shows that 'JAMES MORGAN hath given him about six acres of upland, where the wigwams were, in the path that goes from his house toward Culver's, among the rocky hills.'

"These tracts were located near the present third burial ground, in the western suburbs of New London, a sterile and dreary location which was soon abandoned by its occupants, who made their homes in the more promising district east of the river Thames.

"JAMES MORGAN became a large landed proprietor in that district which has ever since been occupied largely by his progeny. He was public spirited, was often employed in surveying lands, establishing highways and boundaries, and as a magistrate in adjusting civil difficulties. For several years he served as selectman, and was one of the first deputies sent by New London plantation to the general court at Hartford (May, 1657), at which time he was fifty years old.

"An active member of the church, his name is prominent in every movement of that body. 'JAMES MORGAN, Mr. Tinker and Obadiah Brown are chose to seat the people in the meeting house, which they are doing; the inhabitants are to rest silent.'

"In 1661 he was one of a committee to lay out the bounds of New London 'on the east side of the great river,' and the next year he was on a committee to contract for building a house for the ministry of New London. He died in 1685, and his estate was soon after divided among his four surviving children. He married August 6, 1640, MARGERY HILL. Children: HANNAH, JAMES, JOHN, JOSEPH, ABRAHAM, and a DAUGHTER who died unnamed.

"His brother, MILES MORGAN, who came with him from Bristol, England, in 1636, to Boston, became one of the founders of Springfield, MA. There was a RICHARD MORGAN who was a pioneer of Portsmouth, New Hampshire, and had many descendants in that state."

MILES MORGAN is the ancestor of the controversial JOHN PIERPONT MORGAN, the American financier, born in Connecticut on 17 Apr 1837, and died in his sleep the morning of 31 Mar 1913. J. P. MORGAN was a contemporary and sixth-cousin of my great-grandmother MARY CATHERINE BARTON, who was also born in 1837. There are many biographers of J. P. MORGAN, and depending on the bias of the various authors, he is depicted as the worst of all the "robber barons" or honored for his "Morgan Dollar" and his financial genius in saving the nation and world economy through a very troubling financial situation.

In the Jean Strouse 1999 epic *MORGAN: American Financier* he was called as a witness in a House hearing in 1912, and at one point was asked the question:

"Is not commercial credit based primarily upon money or property?"

MORGAN answered, "No sir: the first thing is character."

Question: "Before money or Property?'"

MORGAN: "Before money or property or anything else. Money cannot buy it . . . because a man I do not trust could not get money from me on all the bonds in Christendom."

Samuel Untermyer, the questioner, after the long interview told the press,

"Whatever may be one's view of the perils to our financial and economic system of the concentration of the control of credit, the fact remains, and is generally recognized, that Mr. MORGAN was animated by high purpose and that he never knowingly abused his almost incredible power."

After his death in 1913, about a year later, the financial world was shocked to find that his total assets were approximately $85,000,000, much less than they had expected. John D. Rockefeller read the newspaper, shook his head, and said,

"And to think he wasn't even a rich man."

[Note: My ancestor, JAMES MORGAN, the older brother of MILES MORGAN, had a son JOHN, and another son JOSEPH. One record states that son JOHN was my ancestor, another record believes that it was JOSEPH. I have favored JOSEPH, basically, because he moved west to Fairfield, Connecticut, and his wife was DOROTHY PARKE. Great-grandmother MARY CATHERINE BARTON's second-great-grandmother was DOROTHY MORGAN of New Jersey.

Mistress ANNE MORTON (Yale, Eaton) was the second wife of THEOPHILUS EATON. It is claimed by some that *their* daughter ELIZABETH EATON, a widow of a Mr. Williams, was the second wife of JOHN MORGAN, who was born 30 Mar 1645 and died 12 Feb 1712. They had eight children. If genealogist #1 is correct, then ANNE would be my eighth-great-grandmother. If I am descended from JOSEPH, she would be a relative-in-law. The next chapter includes an interesting case study of ANNE MORTON YALE EATON and her court records.]

The following quotes about the EATON family are from *A Genealogical Dictionary of the First Settlers of New England, before May, 1692* microfiche #6019972. Some abbreviated words are completed and capitals and italics added for easier reading.

"EATON, NATHANIEL, Cambridge, brother of Governor THEOPHILUS, was born about 1609, freeman 9 June 1638, the first head of Harvard College, but not dignified with title of President. On censure by the government fled to Virginia and finally went home [England], where he died it is said, in gaol. A very curious confession of his wife showing the unfavorable management of domestic economy at the College in its earliest day, is given in notes to Winth. I 310. His wife with her children, exc. Benoni, before mentioned followed him to Virginia in a ship, never heard of after. Winth. II 22.

"EATON, SAMUEL, New Haven, brother of the preceding, son of Richard, bred at Magdalen College, Cambridge, [England] where he had his degree in 1624 and 1628, came to New England 1637, probably had wife but no children, went home after three years, had a living at Duckenfield,

County Chester, near Manchester, until the great ejection, and died at the neighboring parish of Denton 6 Jan 1665 or 6, aet. [age] 68.

"EATON, SAMUEL, New Haven, son of Governor THEOPHILUS, born probably in London 1630, came with his father 1637, Harvard College 1649, and afterwards a tutor there, chosen 1654, an Assistant of the College. Married 17 Nov 1654, Mabel, widow of Governor John Haynes of Hartford, and with his wife died in July of the year following."

"EATON, THEOPHILUS, New Haven, brother of first SAMUEL and of NATHANIEL, the two ministers, was born at Stony Stratford in County Buckinghamshire, not Oxford, as Mather has it. His father was minister there, and after at Coventry. But an English authority makes him son of Richard, vicar of Great Budworth, in Cheshire. He was Deputy Governor of the East land or Baltic company in London and by King James was employed as his agent at the Court of Denmark. He had a wife and children *who died at London*, and married for second wife ANN, widow of DAVID YALE, daughter of THOMAS MORTON, Bishop of Chester, who had kindness for the Puritans. The family seat was in that shire, and the Governor in his will devises the estate at Great Budworth in the same County.

"He [EATON] came in 1637 to Boston, and in April after went with his fellow passenger Davenport to found the settlement of New Haven, in 1639 was made Governor and so, by annual choice was continued until his death 7 Jan 1658, [age] 67. His will of 12 Aug 1656, names three children only, THEOPHILUS, MARY, wife of VALENTINE HILL of Boston, late of Piscataqua, and HANNAH; but mentions his wife, her son THOMAS YALE, and son-in-law EDWARD HOPKINS, [married to her daughter ANN YALE,] late Governor of Connecticut, then in London, whose death preceded EATON's by 10 months. The Inventory included the estate in England of pounds 1440 15 7, was made February 1658, and the will probated 31 May following, yet the record at New Haven carelessly makes the burial 11 January 1656, near a year before his death. The widow (who had been sadly worried by the church about 1644, then probably insane, when Mary Launce, an inmate of the household, and probably a ward of her husband was called to testify as to her extravagant behavior, of which Dr. Bacon in his charming lectures upon the early history, has furnished adequate detail to illustrate the melancholy history of church discipline in that era) went home [to England], and died 1659. The son and unmarried daughter went with the mother. THEOPHILUS [son] living after at Dublin; but HANNAH married 4 J. 1659, at London, WILLIAM JONES, who next year came to New Haven and spent his days."

[Note: There are a few questions on this line. The MORGAN history states that JOHN MORGAN's second wife was a widow ELIZABETH WILLIAMS, who was the daughter of the Connecticut Governor THEOPHILUS EATON. The English records show the birth of ELIZABETH, 19 Sep 1624, St. Nicole Acona, London, England, and her sister MARY EATON two years later. If his marriage to ANNE was indeed in 1627, then these were the daughters of his first wife, GRACE HILLER. This daughter ELIZABETH, not mentioned in the household problems in the next chapter, would have been about 20 years older than JOHN MORGAN, and it would seem unlikely she could have been the mother of the eight children born to them in the 1670s–80s.There was no daughter ELIZABETH mentioned in THEOPHILUS' will of 1657. Was there a younger, unmarried daughter, another ELIZABETH, born in America to Mistress ANNE EATON nearer the time of JOHN MORGAN's birth in 1645?]

The following story is taken from Mary Beth Norton's recent historical book, *Founding Mothers & Fathers, Gendered Power and the forming of American Society*. Ms. Norton, Professor of American History at Cornell University, used several hundred of her students to research the 1620-1670's New England Court records for the substance of her book. *Mistress Anne Eaton and her Friends:–A Case Study pp. 165-180 is* greatly condensed using the original quotes from the church 1644-45 and court records of 1646, of New Haven, Connecticut, which are centered around possible ancestor or relative-in-law MISTRESS EATON and her husband, THEOPHILUS EATON .

56

THE STORY AND COURT RECORDS OF ANNE EATON AND YALE UNIVERSITY

According to Ms. Norton, ANNE MORTON [Yale Eaton] was the daughter of an English Anglican bishop. She was described as a "prudent and pious" Widow YALE with three children [DAVID, ANN, and THOMAS] when she married in England, in 1627, THEOPHILUS EATON, a widower with two children, ELIZABETH and MARY. Ten years later they emigrated to New England, where in 1638 THEOPHILUS became the first governor of the New Haven colony. They had at least one of *his* children [ELIZABETH is not mentioned in these records], *her* children, *their* children, and *his mother*, Mrs. ELIZABETH SHEAPHEARD EATON, all living in the same household. This, evidently, created a great deal of friction, as attested to in the court records.

It, perhaps, should be noted here that New Haven's Yale University, was established by the efforts of Jeremiah Dummer. In 1711, he contacted ELIHU YALE in London, who was described as a nabob with a "prodigious estate." After some pressure, Drummer wrote the following in a letter:

> "Mr. YALE is . . . more than a little pleas'd with his being Patron of such a Seat of the Muses, saying that he expresst at first some kind of concern, whether it was well in him, being a Church man, to promote an Academy of Dissenters. But when we had discourst that point freely, he appear'd convinc't that the business of good men is to spread religion and learning among mankind without being too fondly attach't to particular Tenets, about which the World never was, nor ever will be agreed."

After THEOPHILUS EATON's death in 1658, ANNE returned to England, where her son, by her first husband, DAVID YALE and his family lived. My research suggests that the wealthy ELIHU YALE of Yale University was ANNE's grandson.

Mistress ANNE EATON started the big problem that led to her trials by questioning the principle of infant baptism and seeking out another high-status Englishwoman in America, Lady Deborah Moody, who had been excommunicated from the church in Lynn, Massachusetts, for being an Anabaptist. Lady Moody gave her a recently published book opposing infant baptism, which Mistress EATON read "secretly." Her husband's good friend Reverend John Davenport said that she then compounded her error

> "for she neither asked her husband at home . . . nor did she seek for any light or help from her pastor . . . nor did she seek for help from the body whereof she is a member, nor from any Member." Instead, "she showed her book "with the "charge of secrecy" only to one or two women, whom she hoped to convert to her beliefs. Basically, she had not consulted men, including her husband, at any time. Davenport cited scripture to prove her error—First Corinthians 14:35 ordered wives to direct their religious questions initially to their husbands. And THEOPHILUS EATON would have "held forth light to her according to God," because he was widely known for his piety and his leadership of religious exercises.

Since Mistress EATON reached her decision through her own personal reflection, the first inkling John Davenport, THEOPHILUS EATON, or the congregation as a whole had of her change of mind was

> "by her departing from the assembly, after the morning sermon, when the Lord's Supper was administered, and the same afternoon, after sermon when baptism was administered, judging herself not to be baptized, nor durst she be present at the latter, imagining that predo baptism is unlawful."

The governor's wife sat in the front row of the meetinghouse, so her departures that Sabbath were observed by all the colony. Within a week the Reverend Davenport convened a meeting of the church, at which ANNE EATON for the first time explained to others her spiritual struggle and her newly acquired Anabaptist beliefs. Mr. Davenport then refuted the contentions in the book, responding to them point by point, first in a sermon and later in writing. Her husband and two church elders went over the book and Davenport's document with her in minute detail, but she refused to change her position. During Davenport's sermon she muttered, "sotto voce (It is not so)," under her breath. She was later openly "contemptuous" of the men's arguments and "neither would object nor yield" during their sessions with her. Moreover, she continued to leave the church whenever infant baptism was being administered, sometimes even "absenting herself from the sermon and from all public worship in the congregation."

This, declared Mr. Davenport, was a "public offence, which she knows is grievous to us . . . divers rumors started through the town." Once these tales had become "common fame," Davenport and the elders, in spite of their friendship with the governor, decided that they were required by scripture to "inquire, make search and diligently ask whether it were true." Although the two families lived next door to each other, Reverend Davenport later claimed he was one of the last to hear the stories by noting that he was "almost continually in my study and family except some public work or private duty called me forth." But it seems more likely he ignored the scandal as long as he could.

Their first approach was to talk to Governor EATON about the rumors; he referred them to his wife, who in turn referred them to her mother-in-law, daughter, and servants.

From these witnesses the investigators not only learned that the tales were true but also discovered "more evils . . . than we had heard of." They concluded that "these evils would by the just judgment of God hinder (her) from receiving light"; in other words, that Mistress EATON's conduct in her household would, unless corrected, prevent her from recognizing her theological errors. So, they decided to "deal with her in a private way" about the familial disorders before attempting to wean her away from Anabaptism.

Puritan doctrine, as expounded by the Reverend William Perkins in 1603, stated, "Such as beare publike callings, must first reforme themselves in private. . . . How shal he order publike matters for the common good, that cannot order his owne private estate?"

So Mistress EATON's conduct reflected not only on her, but also was highly embarrassing to her husband, the governor. Davenport and the elders returned to speak with ANNE EATON, reviewing with her what she had done and the rules she had broken. Then they left her alone after "exhorting her to repent." After a time when no signs of repentance on her part were observed, they informed her that because of "her hardness of heart" they were being forced to go to the church as a whole.

Trying to prevent at least some of the details from becoming public knowledge, they urged her to agree to discuss them "in private, by holding forth her repentance privately for such particulars as were not commonly reported; for we were unwilling to bring forth such things into public."

> Davenport reported that "she refused to give any private satisfaction for any. Told us that these were also common talk, and that she herself had met with reports of them in other houses."
>
> Eventually, Mistress EATON "told us we labored with her in vain and should have no other answer, and wondered that the Church did not proceed." Consequently, Mr. Davenport informed the congregation at the opening of ANNE EATON's first church trial in August 1644, "we are compelled to bring sundry particulars of which she was privately admonished into the public notice of the Church, because she refused to hear us in a private way, according to the rule in Matt. xviii, 17."

In the record of Mistress EATON's 1644 trial, the discussion of infant baptism occupies three pages, less than half the space consumed by the recital of her conflicts with other members of her household. There were confrontations with her servants, her stepdaughter MARY, her mother-in-law ELIZABETH, and her husband. Her own children by either marriage were not part of these conflicts. She was accused in the records of having slapped her mother-in-law in the face twice at the dinner table; of having falsely implied that her unmarried stepdaughter was pregnant; of twice alleging witchcraft on the part of members of the household; of having made numerous unfounded complaints against her male and female servants; and of having told her husband she would be better off if he left the house. All these offenses, the church concluded, violated the Ten Commandments—primarily the Fifth (honoring thy father and mother) and Ninth (bearing false witness).

Author, Ms. Norton, gave her impression, describing ANNE as a:

> "hot-tempered woman who lacked patience with her underlings, clashed repeatedly with her elderly mother-in-law, and detested her adult stepdaughter. But some of the grievances enumerated by the servants—that she had called one maid a liar and a thief, had termed two of them 'wicked wretches,' and had accused the black slave, Anthony, of ruining the beer—would hardly have been unusual in other households. The maids . . . described her 'unquietness with them' and their seeming inability 'to give

her content.' These sorts of commonplace complaints from servants were usually ignored by masters, mistresses, neighbors, and justices of the peace alike. Yet . . . they were solemnly heard without questioning their validity.

"One confrontation with her husband seems particularly significant. One morning . . . she criticized a male servant for not bringing water into the house, and complained to THEOPHILUS about the servant's negligence. But Mr. EATON failed to back up his wife: 'he not seeing cause for it did not reproach the man according to her mind.' With 'much heat of Spirit,' Mistress ANNE then told her husband, 'you and this man may go together,' and (the elders added) 'that desire of getting from her husband she has prosecuted importunately,' which was 'against the Covenant of Marriage.' Behind this homely tale . . . appears to lay Mistress EATON's intense frustration at her husband's failure to support her management of their large household, which at times included as many as thirty people. From the prominence of her mother-in-law in many of the charges, including four of those involving the servants, one suspects that ANNE EATON felt her authority continually undermined by ELIZABETH EATON's presence in her home and that THEOPHILUS often sided with his mother in the event of conflicts."

After the congregation heard all the evidence from the various witnesses, it was their duty to decide whether she should be excommunicated or to merely give her "public admonition." The Reverend Davenport argued strongly for the later. He contended that it was unclear whether the charges "could be proved to proceed from a habitual frame of sinning in her, so as that she may not be counted a visible saint." He also pointed out that some of her misdeeds were minor. The congregation followed his advice, and despite Mistress EATON's last minute request that "there might be no censure passed upon her," she was publicly rebuked and directed "to attend unto the several rules that you have broken, and to judge yourself by them, and to hold forth your repentance according to God."

Mistress ANNE then submitted a written statement to the Elders, who considered it inadequate. They insisted that she acknowledge the truth of the charges against her, repent fully of her sins, and change her behavior to the satisfaction of those "that ordinarily converse with her"--presumably, her husband, mother-in-law and stepdaughter MARY. As the months passed without any noticeable change in her behavior, other churches in Connecticut and Massachusetts began to criticize the New Haven congregation for failure to adopt the "last remedy" available to them.

In November, 1644, the Bay Colony formally banished all known Anabaptists, terming them "incendiaries of common wealths."

So once more the Elders approached her and asked why she failed to repent. She admitted that "she was not convinced of the breach of the Fifth Commandment . . . for she did not acknowledge her husband's Mother to be her Mother."

This "obstinate" response brought a threat of excommunication from the Elders, so she sent them another document that they deemed to be more unsatisfactory than the first, and they once again, in 1645, called her before the church. In two separate meetings the old charges were reviewed and five new charges were added. One charge was for her apparent lack of repentance and the other four were family related. The most important again involved THEOPHILUS and his mother:

> "She charged Mr. EATON, her husband, with breach of promise, in bringing his Mother into the house against her will, but it was proved it was with her consent."

How it was proved was not told in the records. Later in the month at the end of the second meeting, ANNE was excommunicated, which meant that she would be unable to attend the church services and would be forced to stand outside the door if she wished to hear the sermon; however, New Haven did not banish the Anabaptists.

In 1649, Ezekiel Cheever, one of the original leaders of the New Haven church, was excommunicated. His trial adds some additional information about Mistress ANNE's concerns. It was testified that at some point, Mistress EATON became frustrated with her interactions with the Elders and asked to defend herself before the church as a whole. Some members of the congregation, including Cheever, regarded her request as reasonable. So, the Elders decided to let her do it with the provision that only her critics could respond to her in her presence. Not until she left the meeting would her defenders, like Cheever, be able to express their views.

> Cheever recalled that "this did not satisfy Mrs. EATON's desire, and therefore she accepted it not." When the church members upheld the Elders'

decision, Mr. Cheever grumbled afterward to several men, "This I appre-hended, was so to subject the Church to the Elders, that they had nothing to do in this case but to consent with the Elders, or to say Amen."

This remark was one of the charges against him in his trial. Cheever in-sisted in his trial that "I know no order appointed by Christ, that the Church shall require every member to act with them in every vote." The leaders dis-agreed with him and excommunicated him for violation of the Fifth and Ninth Commandments.

In September 1646, Gov. THEOPHILUS EATON presided over a case that brought him further embarrassment. The testimony intended to be included in the deposition revealed that a woman named Susan (perhaps one of the EATON's servants) had disclosed to several people that:

> "Mrs. EATON would not lye with her husband since she was admonished, but caused her bedd to be removed to another roome, . . . (and had) de-nyed conjugall fellowship" to THEOPHILUS. The Governor ruled in fa-vor of the witness.

One afternoon, in early May of 1646, about one year after ANNE's excom-munication, she was visiting with three high-ranking women friends at one of their homes. The conversation ranged widely over a number of topics and inci-dents. They expressed their opinions to each other freely and without reserve, knowing that they (a church member, an excommunicate, and two nonmem-bers) generally concurred in their criticisms of the magistrates and the church. Such gatherings of female friends were commonplace, but this one received a remarkable amount of official attention because of their prominence and the ex-plosive implications of the ideas they expressed. On 2 June, Mistress EATON's three friends were brought to trial, charged with "several miscarriages of a pub-lique nature."

The chief witnesses were Mistress Leache's servants, Elizabeth Smith (vis-ibly pregnant) and Job Hall, who were trying to gain favor with the magistrates, that they might be married. According to their testimonies, Mistress Lucy Brewster had remarked that some recent criminals (adulterers) had been

> "cruelly whipped & that her son said he had rather fall into the hands of Turks, & hath rather be hanged then fall into their (the New Haven mag-istrates') hands." She declared of the magistrates that "they goe two and

two together, & writt down what scandelous persons say & soe hurrey them & compare their writeings, & if they find any contradictions they are chardged for lyes . . . I pray God keep me from them (the magistrates)."

The servants also testified that the three women had denounced the Reverend Davenport's assertions that only members of the New Haven church would be saved, and that clergymen had a special status in God's eyes, indeed that they should properly be regarded as the heirs of the angels.

Mistress Moore had declared "pastours & teachers are but the inventions of men." She compared New Haven to "the wildernesse of Sinai" and commented that "a vayle is before the eyes of ministers and people in this place, & till that be taken away, they cannot be turned to the Lord." On one occasion, she reportedly prayed that no one in her family should "have any fellowshipp with them." Mistress Brewster was accused of having said that Davenport's ideas turned her stomach, making her "sermon sicke," and Mistress Leach with having asserted that she would not try to become a church member because there were too many liars in the church. Only two remarks of Mistress EATON's made it into the official trial record. She defended the congregation's practice of having members come forward publicly to donate money to the church, a custom criticized by Lucy Brewster, who compared it to "going to masse." She also commented that she had confessed her faults, "but not to the churches satisfaction."

At one point the friends discussed Mistress EATON's status. Lucy Brewster told ANNE EATON that "they could not banish her but by a Gennerall Court, & if it came to that shee wished Mrs. EATON to come to her & acquaynt her with her judgment & grownds about baptizing, & she would by them seduce some other weoman, & then she, the said Mrs. Brewster would complayne to the court of Mrs. EATON & the other women should complayne of her as being seduced, and soe they would be banished together & she spake of going to Road Island."

Mistress Brewster, admitting that she had said this, explained that "she spake it in jest & laughing." The magistrates were not amused: "she was told, foolish & uncomely jesting are sinfull, but to harden one agaynst the truth who already lyeth under guilt, may not passe under a pretence of jesting."

The leaders of New Haven were not accustomed to such obstreperous opposition to their authority, especially not from women. Accordingly, they fined the miscreants heavily and this seems to have successfully dissuaded them from subsequent outspokenness, as none of them appeared in court again.

It seems suspect that Mistress ANNE EATON was independently wealthy and contributed greatly to the family's position. She described the home as her home. She was evidently raised by her Anglican Bishop father to think and act independently. Evidently, she was a devoted student of the scriptures and highly valued her own opinions, even if the governing men refused her that right. I do not find any evidence of insanity as indicated by the Dictionary account first given. The Puritans seemed to strongly believe in righteous force.

Ms. Norton's book tells about the dismissal of NATHANIEL EATON, brother of Governor THEOPHILUS, when he was head master of Harvard.

"After a minor disagreement one evening, Mr. NATHANIEL EATON, the head of the new college [Harvard]in Cambridge, ordered his live-in assistant Nathaniel Briscoe to leave the house immediately. Briscoe replied that he would depart in the morning, but that was not soon enough for Mr. EATON. He took what John Winthrop later described as a 'cudgel . . . big enough to have killed a horse,' told two of his servants to hold Briscoe, and then hit him approximately two hundred times, a task which occupied nearly two hours. At one point Briscoe drew a knife, at another [point] he began to pray, which according to Winthrop, only caused EATON to beat him harder 'for taking the name of God in vain.' Briscoe's cries of pain eventually attracted attention from passersby, including the Reverend Thomas Shepard, pastor of the Cambridge church. Mr. Shepard and the other witnesses did not come to the young man's aid, though the arrival of outsiders did cause EATON to stop the beating. Instead Shepard accompanied Mr. EATON as he went to see Governor Winthrop, 'complaining of Briscoe for his insolent speeches, and for crying out murder and drawing his knife.' The two men asked that Briscoe be brought before the Court of Assistants to acknowledge his fault publicly.

"When the magistrates inquired into the circumstances that had led to the beating, they discovered not only that NATHANIEL EATON had over-reacted on this occasion but also that he had mistreated his pupils. The students boarding in the house testified that they had been fed an 'ill and scant diet' consisting primarily of 'porridge and pudding' and that they had been beaten repeatedly for minor failings. Mr. EATON, they declared, would not stop striking them 'till they had confessed what he required.' Asked for his response to these charges, EATON blamed his wife for any problem with the students' food and said that 'he had this rule, that he would not give over correcting till he had subdued the party to his will.' A group of church elders spent hours trying to convince Mr. EATON that his brutality was inappropriate; finally, they thought they had succeeded, and EATON made what Winthrop termed 'a very solid, wise, eloquent, and serious (seeming) confession' of error during a public court session. But when the Assistants nevertheless fined him and barred him from teaching in Massachusetts Bay, Winthrop recorded, EATON 'turned away with a discontented look.'

"He soon fled the colony for Virginia, leaving behind his wife and family and a large number of disgruntled creditors . . . Only when Shepard learned that EATON's justification for his action was inadequate did he 'discern' EATON's sin. The vicious assault by itself did not prove EATON to be an improper family governor. What instead caused Mr. NATHANIEL EATON's disgrace was that the state and community both judged his treatment of Nathaniel Briscoe to be an excessive response to a minor slight. Had Briscoe's offense been more serious, or had EATON not exhibited similarly cruel tendencies in his treatment of his students—at least one of whom was the son of a magistrate—EATON's authority over Briscoe would undoubtedly have been upheld."

In December 1647, Governor THEOPHILUS EATON told the court that he had learned from others that his slave Anthony had been drunk, and "because it was openly knowne, he thought it necessarie the matter should bee heard in the courte, whereas, had it bine keept within the compase of his owne family, he might have given him family correction for it." Mr. EATON's fellow judges heard testimony about the incident, decided that there were mitigating circumstances, and agreed to forgo "any publique corporall punishment." In light of the "governor's zeale and faithfullnes . . . (not conniving at sinn in his owne family,)" they left it up to him to give Anthony "that correction which hee in his wisdome shall judge meete," acknowledging that at least in this case the court trusted his household governance.

The New Englanders viewed the maintenance of proper order as essential to the survival of their society. Governor EATON told one early offender that "drunkenesse is among the fruits of the flesh, both to be witnessed against, both in the church and civill court, and its a brutish sinne." In the Chesapeake region it was rarely punished unless there was injury of persons or property.

THE MONARCHS OF FRANCE.

From Henry IV., 1589, to Louis Phillippe, 1850.

EXPLANATION:

Those who reigned are printed in SMALL CAPITALS and numbered.
The connecting links in Roman.
Names of dynasties in dark-faced type.
The * shows the places where the Bonapartes have reigned.

Robert of Clermont.

LOUIS OF BOURBON.

Jacques.
John.
Louis.
John.
Francis.
Charles.

Anton of Navarre.

27. HENRY IV., 1610.

28. LOUIS XIII., 1643.

29. LOUIS XIV., 1715.

Dauphin.

Duke of Burgundy.

30. LOUIS XV., 1774.

Dauphin.

31. LOUIS XVI., *
1793.

32. LOUIS XVIII.,
1824.

33. CHARLES X.,
1836.

Duke of Berri.

Duke of Bordeaux.

Louis XVII, 1795.

LOUIS OF CONDÉ.

Henry I.

Henry II.

Prince of Condé.

Henry Jules.

Louis III.

Louis Henry.

Louis Joseph.

Louis Henry.

Duke of Enghien.

ARMAND OF CONTI.

**FRANCIS LOUIS
OF POLAND.**

Louis Armand.

Louis Francis.

PHILIP OF ORLEANS.

Regent.

Louis.

Louis Philippe.

Egalité.

34. LOUIS PHILIPPE, 1850.
*

Duke of Orleans.

Count of Paris.

57

THE FRENCH CONNECTIONS—
HUGUENOT, CANADIAN, ACADIAN

The early ancestors of the CONDIEs who came to Utah were descended from a coal mining ancestry in Clackmannon, Scotland, where even young five-year-old boys were virtual slaves to the mines until the middle of the 1790s. The men and boys were taken before dawn into the mines and kept there until after dark, never seeing the light of day. The mine owners could move the families to another mine, but the individual and his posterity were cast as colliers throughout their lives. When I first copied their genealogy by hand, it ended around 1700. In an old list of the origins of various surnames of Scotland, the CONDIE name was said to be of French origin. From my grandfather's old leather-covered set of *Britannica Encyclopedia*:

> "COND'E, a town of France, in the department of Nord, arrondissement of Valeuciennes, is situated at the confluence of the Scheldt and Haine, and at the terminus of the Mons canal, two miles from the Belgian frontier. It contains a hotel de ville and an arsenal, a church and a hospital. Brewing is carried on to a small extent, as well as the manufacture of oil and salt, and there is a large trade of coal. The place is of considerable antiquity, dating at least from the later Roman period. Taken in 1676 by Louis XIV, it definitely passed into the possession of France by the Treaty of Nimeguen two years later, and was afterwards fortified by Vauban. During the [French] revolutionary war it was attacked and taken by the Austrians (1794); and in 1815 it again fell to the Allies. COND'E gives its name to a distinguished branch of the Bourbon family. Population of the town in 1872, 3748; of the commune, 4964."

It was not a very exciting town from that description, but they had coal; however, the Bourbons and the Prince of COND'E interested me. The original LOUIS

I, Prince of COND'E, was quite a hero with the Huguenots, the Protestant followers in France of John Calvin during the Reformation. Scotland and Northern Ireland were also followers of Calvin with their Presbyterian church.

I pictured the possibility that the CONDIE's were Huguenots driven from France and forced into this coalmining servitude as a means of survival. LOUIS of COND'E (b. 1530) was the youngest brother of Anthony of Navarre (b. 1518), who married the Queen of Navarre (land near their Spanish border). The brothers were descendants of Louis of Bourbon, the son of Robert of Clermont, brother of the ninth King Phillip III, 1285, whose descendants kept the title of King until the 26th king, 1589-1594, who died without heirs. The line then shifted to the distant Bourbon line of Anthony and Louis, who were militarily and politically leading the rebel Protestant Huguenots, against the domination of the Catholic Church and the Holy Roman Empire in France. Anthony of Navarre's son Henry was the first king from this much poorer Bourbon line.

From my *Americana Encyclopedias (1945 edition)*, I found: "CONDE— the name of a French family, the younger branch of the Bourbons, who took their name from the town of COND'E, department of Nord. One GODFREY de COND'E about 1200, was in possession of a part of the barony of COND'E. His great-granddaughter, JEANNE de COND'E, married, in 1335, JACQUES de BOURBON, Comte de la Marche, and the barony of COND'E went to their second son, LOUIS de Bourbon, Comte de Vendome, whose great-grandson, LOUIS de Bourbon, Prince of COND'E, in virtue of his blood-relationship to the royal family, assumed the title of Prince, and is regarded as the founder of the new house of this name."

I drove to the new 26-story Church Office Building in Salt Lake City, where the Genealogical Library was located at that time, to find out if any of the people in the lands of COND'E had that surname in the 1600s. At the library, I was informed that these French records were in the tower and it would be several hours before they could have them for me, which meant that interest in them by other people was practically nonexistent.

I soon realized, when they were brought down, that they were old and difficult to read and, of course, written in French. I could, however, read names and dates and copy, as written, other things that might be of interest in their church registers—then burden a French student to translate it for me. I searched all the microfilms. There was no COND'E or variation in the surname records, although the name COND'E was at the beginning of the register. I did notice many with the surname of FAWSETT with other variations. I had FAUSETTs in my mother's early American ancestral line--but they were from Ireland. I passed them by. I copied some of the pedigree charts of the Bourbon kings of France, and went home quite discouraged with the whole idea. (Later, I found that my FAUSETTs were French Huguenots who had escaped to Ireland and came later to America.) The old encyclopedia stated:

"LOUIS de Bourbon, Prince of COND'E (1530-1569) fifth son of Charles de Bourbon, duke of Vend'ome, younger brother of Anthony, king of Navarre, was the first of the famous House of COND'E. Brave though deformed gay but extremely poor for his rank, COND'E was led by his ambition to a military career. He fought with distinction in Pedmont under Marshal de Brissac; in 1552 he forced his way with reinforcements into Metz, then besieged by Charles V; he led several brilliant sorties from that town; in 1554 he commanded the light cavalry on the Meuse against Charles. He then joined the Huguenots, and he was concerned in the conspiracy of Ambroise, which aimed at forcing from the king by aid of arms the recognition of the Reformed religion. He was consequently condemned to death, and was only saved by the decease of Francis II.

"At the accession of the boy-king, Charles IX., the policy of the court was changed, and COND'E received from Catherine de' Medici the government of Picardy. But the struggle between the Catholics and the Huguenots soon recommenced; in 1562, 200 of the latter were massacred at Vassy by Duke Francois of Guise. Upon this COND'E retired from Paris, put himself at the head of 1500 horsemen, and took possession of Orleans. Having raised troops in Germany, and entered into negotiations with Elizabeth of England, he marched on Paris, with 8000 foot and 600 horse. A battle took place at Dreux, in which the leaders on both sides, COND'E and Montmorency, were taken prisoners. COND'E was liberated by the pacification of Amboise in the next year (1563). In 1567 the war broke out again.

"It was strongly suspected by the Huguenots that Catherine was meditating a great and final blow—the revocation of the Edict of Amboise, the perpetual imprisonment of COND'E, and the death of General COLIGNI; and their suspicions were confirmed by the levy of soldiers, including 6000 Swiss, which she was engaged in making. COLIGNI determined to oppose her with a still bolder plan.

"The Huguenots were to rise 'en masse' crush the Swiss before they could join the main army, and take possession of the young king, his brother, and Catherine herself. But both the Swiss and the royal family escaped safely to Paris. Paris was blockaded, and an indecisive battle fought at St Denis. During the next year peace was again made, but soon after Catherine attempted to seize both COND'E and COLIGNI. They had fled to La Rochelle, and troops were collected. At the battle Jarnae, with only 400 horsemen, and without having made himself sufficiently certain of the support of the infantry, COND'E rashly charged the whole Catholic army. Worn out with fighting, he at last gave up his sword, and a Catholic officer named Montesquieu treacherously shot him through the head (15 December 1569)."

[Note: John Calvin, the great religious reformer of the sixteenth century was born in Noyon, Picardy, France, 10 Jul 1509. "Even as a lad, Calvin was deficient in physical vigor, but gave early tokens of more than ordinary intellectual powers." He was sent to the Coll'ege dela Marche at Paris; then to the Coll'ege Montaigu where he was trained in logic. After his father died when he was 22 years old, he returned to Paris, and not long after experienced what he called his "sudden conversion." He wrote: "on a sudden the full knowledge of the truth, like a bright light, disclosed to me the abyss of errors in which I was weltering, and sin and shame with which I was defiled." In a speech he had prepared for his friend Nicholas Cop, elected to the rectorship of the University of Paris , he expressed his reformed doctrine. The Sorbonnists made his life intolerable and he escaped Paris for the countryside. For awhile he was at the residence of the Queen of Navarre, but went from place to place—writing, preaching, driven out, triumphant at times, he continued on. In 1551, he made his permanent home in Geneva, Switzerland. He died 27 May 1565, shortly before LOUIS, Prince of COND'E was shot in the head.]

The B.Y.U. Harold B. Lee Library, History and Genealogy department had 12 volumes on LOUIS, Prince of COND'E. Unfortunately, they were all written in French; but I was able to check-out two fat tomes written in English--one with his history, the other on his Catholic enemy, the Duc of Guise. These were interesting; but the 12 French volumes fascinated me. I needed to learn French. Our drugstore opened at 10:00 A.M. GROVER and I audited 7:00 A.M. French at the B.Y.U.

In 1550, young LOUIS, Prince of COND'E, went to court, fell in love, and obtained the permission of the king to marry ELEONORE de ROYE, a half-sister of COLIGNI. She was described as "a very devoted wife--most noble of the Huguenot women. . . . She yielded to none of her sex in beauty, in grace, in intelligence and in chastity and she surpassed everyone in knowledge, in courage and in magnanimity." During the troubles in Paris, Prince COND'E could be found every Sunday escorting the Huguenot pastors through the howling mob to their meeting place—pistol in hand with 100 gentlemen.

The following is part of one of his speeches to the King in their behalf.

"I speak for a faith which is better in suffering than in avenging wrong; but remember sire, that it is an anvil which has worn out many a hammer."

ELEONORE and LOUIS had a son HENRI de Bourbon, who would be the second Prince of COND'E. He had a Protestant marriage. The King demanded that he be remarried by the Catholic priest. This he refused to do.

"Mad man! Conspirator! Rebel! Son of a Rebel! If in three days you do not change your tone, I will have you strangled!"

He was imprisoned, and brought back to the king three days later. The King shouted,

"Mass! Death! Or the Bastille!"

To this demand HENRI replied quietly,

"God allows me not, my Lord and King, to choose the first--of the others, be it, at your pleasure, whichever God in his providence directs."

With him, at this time, was his first cousin, Henry of Navarre, who had also had a Protestant marriage. This cousin later became Henry IV of France. With the death of the king, both men were finally set at liberty. Still they led and took sides with the Protestant Huguenots.

After the death of LOUIS de Bourbon, Prince of COND'E, 1569, Catherine de Medici of Spanish/Italian birth, regent mother of young King Charles IX of France, plotted to rid France of general COLIGNI and all the Huguenots. In 1571, young Henry of Navarre's Huguenot wife suddenly and strangely died, while she was a guest of the Queen in Paris. Catherine quickly arranged a second marriage for Henry of Navarre, the young Huguenot military leader, with her less-than-willing daughter, who was in love with the Duc de Guise. Catherine invited Protestants throughout the nation to attend this wedding and the following gala events in Paris, August 1572. Of course, general COLIGNI must attend. Four days after the wedding, with masquerades, banquets, and other events still in progress, COLIGNI was fired at and wounded twice by an assassin behind a grated window. The wounds were slight, but the Huguenots were alarmed and gathered around their stricken leader. The king and queen mother tried to allay the fears of his followers and expressed great grief and indignation at this outrage. They told COLIGNI of their deep concern and informed him that they were closing the gates of Paris, so the Huguenots attending the festivities would be protected from additional Catholics entering the city. They procured a list from COLIGNI of the abodes of all the Protestants in Paris with the supposition of protecting them. With this list and with the gates closed (actually, to prevent the escape of the Huguenots), they proceeded with the final phase of their dastardly plot.

It was arranged that the massacre should begin at the sounding of the matin bell, in the Church of St. Germain, on the morning of St. Bartholomew's Day. At that signal the Duc of Guise and the Italian guards of the palace were to rush forth and set the example of butchery, beginning with the murder of COLIGNI. This done, the work was to be carried on by the Catholics throughout Paris until the last Huguenot was exterminated. Orders were secretly issued to all the provincial cities of the kingdom to proceed in the same manner until none should be left to trouble the peace of Catholic France. A few cities declined to follow this inhumane order.

The horrible program proceeded on schedule. Catherine de Medici, the Duc of Guise, and the young King Charles IX had no pity. COLIGNI was stabbed to death in his bed chamber. Paris soon reeked like a butcher's stall. The streets were slippery with blood. The residence of every Huguenot had been marked. Crowds of fugitives surged along the streets, pursued by other crowds with drawn swords dripping with blood. This continued for seven days. In Paris, nearly all the Huguenots were killed. Throughout the kingdom, the massacre continued, until on the third of October in the waters beyond Bordeaux, the drama ended. The exultation of the Catholic French court was unbounded.

It was one of the strange features of the massacre that Prince HENRI of COND'E escaped the massacre—perhaps it was his royal blood and the reaction this might have on the people of France that saved him.

His cousin Prince HENRY of NAVARRE was then married to Catherine's daughter and was next in line for the kingdom. Imprisoned in the Louvre, attempts were made to convert the prisoner to the Catholic faith. At length the captive prince yielded, attended mass, and pretended to be a good son of the Church, but STILL championed the cause of the Huguenots.

PRINCE OF CONDÉ

COLIGNI

CATHARINE DE MEDICI
in her youth

THE CARNINAL OF LORRAINE RECEIVING THE HEAD OF COLIGNI

CATHARINE DE MEDICI AND CHARLES IX
After a contemporary painting

SCENE DURING THE NIGHT OF ST. BARTHOLOMEW
Drawn by A. de Neuville

Prince of Condé, Catharine de Medici, The Cardinal receiving the Head of Coligni,
Scene During the night of St. Bartholomew.

Catherine de Medici's four sons had all become kings. By 1589, all four had died without heirs. The House of Bourbon was now in line. Henry of Navarre was the heir—but a Protestant! A king must be accepted by his people. After much civil strife, in March 1594, Henry entered Paris. He had already been crowned at Chartres and Henry of Navarre became Henry IV of France—but only on the condition that he become Catholic. As king, Henry IV was able to enact the *Edict of Nantes*, April 1598, which allowed "freedom to worship as they pleased" for all the people of France. Unfortunately, as France was blossoming with peace and liberty under Henry IV, he was assassinated in 1610. His young son Louis XIII by his second marriage was but nine years of age.

The assassination of Henry IV was perhaps internationally provoked. The Hapsburg Dynasty with fingers into most the royal families of Europe and the leadership within the Holy Roman Empire and the Catholic Church was the greatest power on the continent. The King of Spain, Charles V, was their emperor. The Protestants were joining forces against them to preserve a large and valuable strip of land above France for the Dutch. Henry IV had been asked to join them, and it was rumored that he was ready to accept when the assassin prevented this alliance. The Bourbons were the greatest power threat to the Hapsburgs, and the surviving government was greatly weakened with Henry's death. Spain arranged a young marriage between seventeen-year-old Louis XIII and the Infanta Anne of Austria, hoping to bring France solidly back into the Holy Roman Empire. With the *Edict of Nantes* still intact, the Huguenots increased rapidly throughout the kingdom.

The main forces of Protestants against the Hapsburgs were the Lutherans, who were exceptionally strong in Germany and northward into Sweden, and the Calvinists, who included the Huguenots, predominated along the coastal regions of France, The Netherlands, Denmark, and into Scotland and Ireland. Austria, Italy and Spain were firmly Hapsburg and stood solidly with the Emperor. The Catholic Church had great landed interests that were not taxable by the Crowns of the various kingdoms.

The British had problems, too. The Puritans were trying to purify their Protestant Church of England. Civil war was beginning to stir. In Continental Europe, the international war that would pit Catholic against Protestant, or perhaps more correctly Hapsburg against Bourbon, was even closer.

HENRY IV, AT IVRY

ASSASSINATION OF HENRY IV

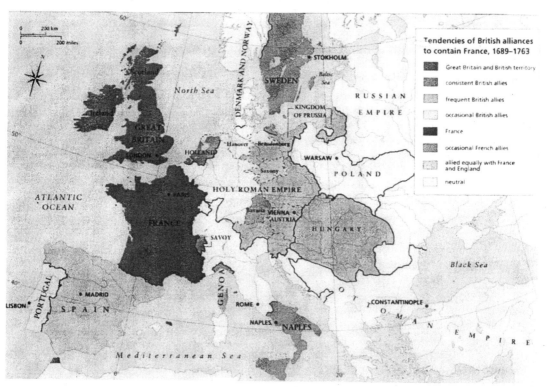

The House of COND'E, members of the Bourbon Dynasty, was no longer the poor cousins from the country—their lands and palaces increased in size. HENRI, son of LOUIS I, Prince of COND'E was known as Duc d'ENGHIEN, Prince of COND'E, in turn;, his son (1621-86) inherited both titles.

Europe, A History [by NORMAN DAVIES] says this young Duc d'ENGHIEN was the finest general in Europe.

"His stunning victory at Rocroi in the Ardennes (1643) ended the Spanish military supremacy which had lasted since Pavia in 1525. From 1644 the diplomats were hard at work, shuttling between the Protestant delegates at Osnabruck and the Catholic delegates at Munster. Whilst they argued, the French and the Swedes ravaged Bavaria. The Treaty of Westphalia . . . set the ground plan of the international order in central Europe for the next century and more. It registered both the ascendancy of France and the subordination of the Hapsburgs to the German princes. On the religious issue, it ended the strife in Germany by granting the same rights to the Calvinists as to Catholics and Lutherans."

The following PRINCES of COND'E are listed in my *Americana*:

Louis I de Bourbon, Duc de Enghien, b. Vendome, 1530; d. 1569.

(his grandson) **Henri II de Bourbon**, Duc de Enghien, b. 1588; d. 1646.

(Son of Henri II) **Louis II de Bourbon**, b, Paris, 1621; d. near Fontainebleau, 1686. also known as the Duc de Enghien. French general during 30 Year War.

Louis Joseph de Bourbon, b. Chantilly 1736; d. Paris 1818. French General in Europe during the Seven Year War (French and Indian War.)

From Ridpath's History of the World, (1894):

"In February 1637, Ferdinand II of Germany died. . . . It has been estimated that this benign Christian sovereign went into the world of spirits with the blood of ten millions of people on his soul. . . . In the whole history of the German race no other sovereign ever contributed so largely to the woes of the people. Not the least of the curses which he inflicted upon the world was a son like unto himself, who, with the title of Ferdinand III, now succeeded to the Imperial dignity."

The Thirty Year War by C. V. Wedgewood states:

"The war between France and Spain progressed fitfully but with an ever-growing balance in favour of France. Richelieu's difficulty to the end was his army; he needed his best men always for Germany, where the danger was greatest, and he did not always trust the noblemen who commanded for him in the Pyrenees, Flanders or Burgundy. He had nevertheless singled out for particular confidence the DUC d'ENGHIEN, eldest son of the PRINCE de COND'E, a man in his early twenties of whom he expected much. . . . [He] was made commander-in-chief of the forces on the Flemish [northern] frontier in the winter of 1642. . . .

"Richelieu did not live to see the crowning of his long political work by the victory of his last important nominee. . . . On November 28th, he was taken seriously ill, and four days later asked permission to resign his office. . . . The King came on December and; on the following night Richelieu received extreme unction and sank slowly into a coma. Towards midday on December 4th he died, and the Parisians, more in curiosity than in sorrow, crowded in to take their last farewell of the man who had never been popular yet always respected, always feared, always in the crisis of their fortunes, called upon and trusted. . . .

"In the ensuing spring, ENGHIEN . . . began operations on the Flemish border . . . in Paris, Louis XIII was ill, and his physicians saw little hope of recovery . . . his successor would be a child of barely five, under the regency of his mother and a council [included Cardinal Mazarin]. . . it was not likely that [the people] would tolerate the rule of the Spanish queen and the Italian Cardinal.

"Under the shadow of these fears, ENGHIEN moved his troops to defend the line of the Meuse. In the Louvre the King lay on his huge bed day after day . . . motionless, sometimes sinking into troubled sleep, sometimes speaking . . . a little before his death the King woke from a short sleep to see COND'E watching him. 'Monsieur COND'E,' he said, 'I dreamt that your son had won a great victory.' Early in the morning of 14 May 1643, Louis XIII died. [HENRI II, Prince of COND'E died in 1646.]

"On the evening of the [May] 17th, (General) ENGHIEN had the news, where he lay with his troops somewhere between Auberton and Rumigny, in the flat country to the west of the Meuse, on his march to the relief of Rocroy, a strong frontier fortress besieged by Melo."

He did not tell his troops of the death of their king—fearing they might panic, but told his officers and plead for their loyalty.

Melo lay with 8,000 horsemen and 18,000 foot soldiers between ENGHIEN and the town, well entrenched. On the following day, not knowing the strength of his enemy, Melo allowed the whole French army, 15,000 foot and 7,000 horsemen, to emerge unmolested from the narrow defiles onto the open ground, hoping to surround them with his superior numbers of better trained troops. ENGHIEN had so arranged it so the advance of his infantry was partly concealed by those of his cavalry, advancing in front and on both sides and confusing the Spanish, who had prepared for traditional battle. Taking the situation at a glance, ENGHIEN

> "rallied his own cavalry and proceeded with the recklessness of genius to cut himself a passage through the Spanish centre."

The Spanish veterans' first line infantry engaged the French infantry pressing them hard. Some of the French gave them a sharp struggle and then gave way to the farther side of the field, in position to attack Melo's rear. Melo's horsemen, caught between two assailants, broke and fled from the field, leaving the Spanish infantry of eight thousand alone. ENGHIEN advanced his infantry, enforcing them with his cavalry, but they were repulsed three times. There was much bloodshed. On his fourth attack, with added cavalry, the Spanish realized they were surrounded on all sides and their leader, Fontaine, had been killed by a chance shot; their officers signaled for a truce.

ENGHIEN was willing and advanced towards the Spanish with a few of his men. Some of the Spanish believed it was a fresh attack and fired on them.

> "With cries of indignation the French forces surged forward to protect their leader, the word that he was in danger spreading fast from line to line, until all sides of infantry and cavalry converged on the Spanish position ... furious on the attack on their leader, they cut down all whom they encountered, and the prince himself with difficulty saved some few of the enemy who clung to his stirrups in the melee and claimed his personal protection."

Of the 18,000 infantry, 7,000 were prisoners, 8,000 had been killed. Twenty-four cannon, innumerable arms and the military treasury fell into ENGHIEN's hands. He entered Rocroy in triumph the next day, and the citizens recorded the story on the gates of their little town. It was the end of the Spanish army. From this time on Europe turned toward peace, which was finally achieved in 1648.

King Louis XIV was five [or four] years old when his father died. COND'E and Turenne had led the French armies to much glory in their war with Spain and the emperor, but at home his country was in the throes of civil war; Cardinal Mazarin's avarice, Anne of Austria's conduct of the regency, and Fouquet's peculations had angered the people. Two attacks were made on the government of

France by the people—the Duc d'ENGHIEN is said to have lead one of them. The king, his mother, and Mazarin fled from Paris.

The Spanish streamed over the northeast boundaries from Holland and were victorious through Champaign and Lorraine. When war broke out between England and the Dutch, Louis XIV joined his strength with Holland and after several sea battles the war ended in 1667. Mazarin had died in 1661, Fouquet was condemned to perpetual imprisonment after being compelled to disgorge his ill-gotten gains, and when the king was asked who was to be referred to in matters of public business he astonished his courtiers by declaring, "L'etat c'est moi," (The state is mine!) He appointed Colbert to take charge of the public exchequer, who instigated a multitude of needed reforms. All of Europe was impressed with the Grand *Monarch.* More is said of him in other chapters.

Barton & Hummell Family Histories p. 398 *Faucett Genealogy* reads:

"Forefathers were French, left France during the time of the banishment of the Huguenots to Ireland. I have a copy of a letter given to FAUCETT by the High Church of Ireland in Donegal County.

"W. T. Faucett
I do hereby certify that the bearer, WILLIAM FAUCETT of ye
County of Donegal, in the Kingdom of Ireland, has lived in ye
parish from his childhood and has always behaved himself with
honesty and industry and belonged to the Church of Ireland as by
law established. Given under my hand this first day of July, 1762.
Adam Harvey, Preacher of ye Parish

. . . a true copy of my grandfather's certificate. GEORGE FAUCETT
The name is spelled Fossett, Faucett, and Fausett in family records."

The following is taken from an address by Honorable Ashton Dovell, at the Ninth Annual Assembly, Richmond, Virginia, in April, 1940:

"The Protestants of France had grown in numbers and in wealth during the period of comparative repose that lasted through the early years of the reign of Louis XIV. They no longer formed a political party in the land, and were now devoting themselves chiefly to enterprises of commerce and manufacture. At least one-third of the tradesmen in the country were of the Reformed religion. In every sea-port there were found wealthy

Huguenot merchants, who by their ability and integrity commanded the confidence even of the Catholics, and who were the trusted agents and correspondents of foreign houses. Many important branches of industry were controlled almost entirely by Protestant artisans. Acquainting themselves with the methods of business pursued in England, Germany and Holland, they adopted very generally the system of combined labor, which enabled them to secure the best workmen, and to carry on extensive business enterprises. The northern provinces of the kingdom possessed a large share of this commercial and industrial wealth. The linen manufacturing of Picardy, Normandy, Maine and Bretagne gave employment to thousands of families in the villages of those provinces, and enriched many a powerful commercial house. . . .

"The increasing harshness of the government toward its Huguenot subjects, at this period, led many of them to remove from the kingdom. As in the case of the earlier emigrations, the greater number of these refugees made their way to Holland; and from Holland not a few, between the years 1658 and 1663, crossed over in America. For the most part, they were natives of the northern provinces."

My ancestor, the wealthy Huguenot, JAMES THELEBALL, who owned large lands in Virginia and married ELIZABETH MASON, came to America about this time. They were the maternal grandparents of ELIZABETH LANGLEY, who married GEORGE IVEY.

"As the violence of the persecution increased in France, other Huguenots sought refuge in the Antilles. Among these, in 1679, came Elie Near, afterwards the heroic confessor of the faith in the French galleys.

"The Huguenots in southern and western France surpassed all others as cultivators of the soil. In many of the seaboard towns Huguenot merchants had long been foremost in commercial enterprise. The foreign trade of the kingdom came to be, very largely, controlled by them.

"Inventive and industrious, they applied themselves with great success to the mechanical arts. The manufactures of woolen cloth, and linen goods, of serge, and silks, and sail-cloth, the iron works and paper mills, the tanneries, that enriched France at this period, were founded or promoted chiefly by Protestants. In every department of labor, they were fitted to excel by their morality, their intelligence, and their thrift. The truthfulness and honesty of the Huguenot became proverbial.

"'They were bad Catholics,' said one of their enemies, 'but excellent men of business.'"

"'All our sea-ports,' complained another, 'are full of heretic captains, pilots and traders, who, inasmuch as their souls are altogether bruised in traffic, make themselves more perfect therein than Catholics can well be.'

"Religiously observing one day in seven as a day of rest, their devotion to trade was not interrupted by the many saints' days of the Roman Catholic calendar. Surrounded by watchful enemies, and schooled to self-restraint, they were prudent and circumspect in their dealing with others, and ready to combine and cooperate among themselves in their business procedures.

"Meanwhile, their loyalty to the government could not be impeached. Even Louis XIV acknowledged at a later day that his Protestant subjects had given him abundant proof of their fidelity. . . . Where the migration was to settled communities, it is interesting to note the readiness of the Huguenot for leadership."

He mentions as French Huguenots, Governor Minuit of New Amsterdam, who was involved in the purchase of Manhattan Island from the Indians, and President James A. Garfield, whose mother was Eliza Ballou. He tells of the little company of Huguenots who settled early in Virginia at Manakin. MARY FAWCETT, a Huguenot, was the mother [or grandmother] of ALEXANDER HAMILTON, the first Treasurer of the United States, whose financial acumen has placed him second only to George Washington in the establishment of this country. ALEXANDER's father was Scotch. MARY's father was a French Huguenot physician who had been driven out of France during the persecution.

"ALEXANDER HAMILTON was born on the island of St. Nevis, in the British West Indies. He was precocious as a child and when he was 12 years-of-age [or 15], then living on the Dutch Isle of St. Croix, the settlers of the whole island pooled their resources to send him to school in New York [histories vary in this regard]. When the Revolutionary War broke out, although still very young, he was first an artillery captain and then became an aide to George Washington.

"HAMILTON is without doubt America's greatest genius in the matter of finance and statesmanship." (FHL 975.5 B2hm)

[Note: In my family records, WILLIAM FAUCETT and MARGARETE had the following children: ROBERT, b. abt 1741; DAVID, b. abt 1743; RICHARD, b. abt 1745; JOHN, b. abt 1749; WILLIAM, b. abt 1753; and ELANE b. abt 1755. (Proofs are not given).

ROBERT's children are GEORGE, ROBERT, THOMAS, EDMUND, FANNY and ELIZABETH.

DAVID and ELEANOR's children are SARAH, b. 1767; RICHARD, b. 1769 (my ancestor); WILLIAM, b. 1771, and ABRAM, b. 1773. (This record did not list any spouse, or any children for RICHARD or ELANE.)

JOHN's children are THOMAS, POLLY, and PHERABA.

WILLIAM married LYDIA HALL and they had eleven children: RALPH; MARY (POLLY); WILLIAM; GEORGE; ELI; JAMES; MARGARET; ANN; ROBERT; ELLEN (ELEANOR), and LUCY (LUCIA.)]

The early French in Canada: It was in 1608 that Samuel de Champlain established a trading post at Quebec and serious French colonization began on the St. Lawrence River. He had been an earlier pioneer of Acadia (Newfoundland). In 1609, Champlain first disturbed the already not so peaceful Iroquois Confederacy of Mohawks, Oneidas, Onondagas, Cayugas and Senecas, which controlled the territory south of the St. Lawrence River and east of Lake Ontario by accompanying a Huron war party up the Richelieu River to the Lake which would bear his name. He introduced the Indians to gunpowder. Indian life would not be the same. The Iroquois lived in permanent villages established on good agricultural land and used the mountainous areas for their hunting grounds. Their greatest enemy was the Huron Indian tribe. The French were then added to the Iroquois list of enemies, which the English and Dutch were quick to befriend. Within 50 years the Hurons had dispersed and the French settlements on the St. Lawrence were nearly destroyed.

Unwilling to give up his vast lands in America, in 1665, King Louis XIV of France declared it a Royal Colony and sent 1,200 of his most loyal soldiers to Canada to make it safe for settlers, missionaries, and the long established fur traders. Four companies of the Carignan-Salieres Regiment were led by a young captain, Jacques des Chambly, who was sent up the Richelieu River at the rapids to build a fort. Eventually both the fort and rapids would be named after him. Other forts were built along the war road and in 1666 were used as bases for two French attacks on Iroquois villages to the south. Among his soldiers was Sergeant JACQUE POYER, perhaps a direct ancestor whose children's births were recorded in the Chambly Catholic church records. When he died, JACQUE was buried in Sorel, at the mouth of the Richelieu River, as it enters the St. Lawrence River.

Relative peace came to Canada for 20 years. M. de Chambly was given the honor of becoming governor of Acadia in 1673. He was also granted a seigneury on the land about Fort Chambly. Here he began a small settlement, which included men disbanded from his old regiment. This was the first permanent settlement on the Richelieu River and the beginning of the town of Chambly.

On 4 Oct 1687, 150 Mohawks attacked. There were about 80 French settlers in the community. They presumably took refuge in the fort and helped the 19-man garrison resist the onslaught. The Indians succeeded in capturing one soldier, his wife and child, but the fort held out. The garrison was expected to curtail the smuggling of French furs to the British at Albany, a practice some local people engaged in even when the countries were at war.

In 1702, a fire, accidentally caused by the chaplain who died in the blaze, destroyed the fort—leaving the settlement unprotected on the route the British would probably take if they were to attack Montreal. When this threat became very real in 1709, Governor Vaudreuil ordered the people of Montreal to carry to Chambly the stone, lime, and timber required for the construction of a new and more massive fort. The invasion prepared by the British never reached Chambly.

Throughout the next 50 years only a small detachment guarded the fort and the civilian population grew and flourished in peace. But with the Seven Years War (French and Indian War), in 1760, a British force advanced north along Lake Champlain and down the Richelieu River. The garrison at Fort Chambly could not expect to hold out and surrendered without a shot. A few days later Montreal fell and Canada soon became British.

~ 58 ~

CONCLUSION OF PART II: STANDING FIRM
Broad are the Branches—an American Saga

The *Edict of Nantes*, April 1598, that allowed the coexistence of the Huguenot Protestants with the Catholics in France, brought peace and prosperity to this war torn nation, but slowly these rights were being taken away by the influence of the Catholic cardinals, Richelieu and Mazarin, until in 1685 Louis XIV revoked it entirely and attempted to imprison, or kill, rather than allow escape from his country. His dragoons were ordered to quarter at will in the houses of those who refused Mass. The Huguenot peasants were hunted into the woods like wild beasts and were shot down or tortured at the caprice of their persecutors. Neither the decrepitude of old age nor the pleading weakness of infancy stirred any remorse in the breasts of the bloody butchers. Many of the Huguenot women were dragged into convents where they were kept from sleep until they had consented to go to Mass. The regions where the Huguenot population predominated were reduced to desolation, and some histories estimate that France by her frightful barbarity to her own people lost fully half a million of her most industrious inhabitants by the folly of her king and the cruelty of his ministers. Louis' attempt to reinstate the Catholic James II, grandson of Mary, Queen of Scots, on the English throne failed, but the *Grand Monarch* continued his foreign wars and kept Europe in poverty.

[Note: Actually Louis XIV and James II were first cousins, both were descended from their grandparents Henry IV and Mary de Medici of France, and came under the strong Catholic influence of the Italian/Spanish Medici line. James II, a brother of Charles II, wanted to return the Church of England to the Catholic religion—resulting in his forced abdication, and his replacement in England with his sister Mary who had married William III, stadtholder of the Netherlands, who had strong Protestant beliefs going back to his grandfather William I, whose wife was related to the House of COND'E and COLIGNI (or spelled COLIGNY). James II's mother was a year old when her father, Henry IV, was assassinated—probably by friends of her mother.]

One historian suggests that the then aging, but still glorious "Sun King" with this revocation of the *Edit of Nantes* brought the beginning of the *age of reason*, which replaced the *age of faith (and the reformation)* that had preceded it in France. If so, then it was because he killed or forced those of faith from his borders—some even across the Atlantic into the West Indies and the American continent.

On 1 Sep 1715, on his death bed, to his heir, a great-grandson (his son and grandson had preceded him in death) Louis XIV admitted his error.

> "You will soon be king of a great kingdom. What I most strongly recommend to you is, never to forget the obligations you are under to God. Remember that to him you owe all that you possess. Endeavor to preserve peace with your neighbors. I have been too fond of war. Do not follow my example in that, or in my too lavish expenditure . . . . Ease your people as soon as you can, and do that which I had the misfortune of not being able to do."

His great-grandson was weak, and the next heir was weaker, even beheaded by the guillotine during the French Revolution (1793). At least two descendants of LOUIS I, PRINCE of COND'E and his wife ELEANORE de Roye, half-sister of COLIGNI, survived the French Revolution, joining with the Allies who opposed the tyranny of the citizens of the republic.

Napoleon was quick to take advantage of the reign of terror, rapidly changing the almost shattered French Republic and declaring 12 Nov 1799 that their badly contrived Constitution was dead. The book *Napoleon Bonaparte* by Alan Schom, quoted the self proclaimed military usurper as saying:

> "Weakness in the supreme power is the worst sort of calamity that might befall a people. . . . Religion is useful for the governments of every country. We must use it to control the people. In Egypt I was a Muhammadan, in France I am a Catholic. . . . Here after, only one sentiment must stir us all, the love of the fatherland."

This statement reminded me of my youth when another bold leader quickly destroyed the German republic and proclaimed himself dictator of Germany. Both men had planned carefully and then acted quickly in their destruction of the governing bodies and their constitutions; their destruction of religious freedom of conscience; their takeover of the educational training of the youth—even to be against their parents—choosing only acceptable textbooks; changing history by writing their own; burning the old traditional books; willing to kill all who opposed them with their military might. I still remember with dread the often used term of *fatherland,* and the goose-stepping arrogance the word represented to me during World War II.

I even cringed, when one of our presidents stated in his State of the Union address in the early 1960s, *"Ask not what your country can do for you, but what you can do for your country."* The populous cheered. In my mind, the semantics of this sentence meant a greater increase in government—the beginning of totalitarian rule. Of course, he probably referred to the land, all of its people, and its God inspired constitution, for which I happily cheer, too. We all need less selfishness, more forgiveness, and much more *"Love thy neighbor as thyself"* in our lives.

Napoleon, at first, made great promises: no more enforced loans from the rich; no more villages destroyed; all religious restrictions were to be lifted at once; no more kings; no special ranks or distinctions, all men would be equal. Not trusting him, the republican/nobility leaders joined forces against this dictator. Immediately his tone changed—to his army, "Surprise your enemies . . . exterminate the wretches. To arms! To arms!"—60,000 troops went west.

The disturbed young Duc d'ENGHIEN (House of COND'E) lamented,

"It takes only a cheap action to become a great man these days, that is, when that man is Bonaparte. Nothing seems to stop him, not even God."

Napoleon closed all the banks, except his own government controlled bank— giving credit only to those who befriended him. He created in a blizzard of legislation a new code of laws, greatly protested by the people, to go into effect in 1804. He tried to placate the people with comedies, but serious entertainment of historical nature was prohibited. The students in his schools were to wear uniforms and march to their approved courses with Napoleon's chosen teachers. He built beautiful school buildings, universities, other state buildings, and ornaments to extol his triumphs. There was no room for the individual thinker or for political disagreement. He moved into the palaces of the former kings, ever bent towards greater and greater power—militarily expanding towards the total control of Europe. Spain gave him new territory in America to obtain a peaceful takeover of their country, but the treaty stated he was not to sell it to the United States. He ignored the treaty and sold it in 1803 to President Jefferson for $15,000,000. He needed the money to build the flatboats to cross the channel and conquer England, believing he would get the land in America back after he had subjugated Europe.

With diplomacy, the English diverted his plans away with subtle suggestions that he become the emperor of Europe, which he could not resist, and afterwards he looked towards Russia while the English built up their military and alliances to defend themselves in his final downfall at Waterloo [1814].

"After the royalist rising had taken place in France, he [Napoleon] committed an arbitrary but effective act of violence against the old dynasty by kidnapping and executing the Duc d'ENGHIEN, last of the COND'E line of Bourbons [1804]. . . . The creation of his own Empire caused the extinction of the centuries-old Holy Roman Empire. . . . One thing was certain, after his career Europe could never be the same."

[*Lines of Succession* by Michael Maclagan and Jir'i Louda]

The total extinction of the House of COND'E in France was shown as 1830 in this same book. Another Prince of COND'E lived after the young Duc. This was LOUIS, Joseph de Bourbon: b. Chantilly, 9 Aug 1736; d. Paris, 13 May 1818. He distinguished himself in the Seven Year War by his courage and skill. At the outbreak of the French Revolution in 1792, at Worms, he formed a little corps of emigrant nobility, which joined the Austrian army; then the Russian service until they separated from the coalition; at which time he joined with the English. After Waterloo he returned to Paris, where he published *Essai sur la Vie du Grand COND'E, par L. J. de Bourbon, son 4me Descendant (1806)*.

It is interesting to me that the author Maclagan chose the incident of the murder of the last Duc d'ENGHIEN of the House of COND'E as the final connection between the death of one long-lasting Empire with the birth of another equally devastating tyrannical Empire—both of which the House of COND'E seemed to oppose—often leading and fight against them. Napoleon's Empire lasted until 1870 with the death of Napoleon III.

From all my studies of the French, I have not found the time or reason for a small branch of CONDIEs to immigrate into Scotland, or their coal mining region. Further research in Scotland goes back several more generations. But

I still suspect their arrival there will eventually be found to be—an escape to retain their individual free agency and personal beliefs in God.

THIS CURIOUS WORLD By FERGUSON

"WHEN PICTURES LOOK ALIVE WITH MOVEMENTS FREE; WHEN SHIPS, LIKE FISHES, SWIM BENEATH THE SEA; WHEN MEN OUT-STRIPPING BIRDS SHALL SCAN THE SKY; THEN HALF THE WORLD, DEEP-DRENCHED IN BLOOD SHALL DIE!"

A PROPHECY MADE OVER 400 YEARS AGO!

TOMBSTONE INSCRIPTION ON STONE OF SAINT FRANCIS OF PAULA, 1416-1508. Kirby Cemetery, Essex, Eng.

A NEWS CLIPPING FROM MY MOTHER'S GENEALOGY RECORDS.
NO DATE, BUT IT WAS YELLOWED WITH AGE.

As I was completing Part II for publication, my sister IVIE paid me a visit, and related a rumor she had heard about two *Mormon* missionaries in England that had contacted a professor at Cambridge University. He had told them that there were courses for credit given on Mormonism in his university. He had studied it quite thoroughly and believed it to be true and the only answer to world peace. They wanted to baptize him, but he said, "No, I've been to America and observed the *Mormon* people. They are not living their religion."

[Note: If this rumor is true, I would like to remind this professor that the two missionaries who offered him baptism were in England at their own expense (or that of parents or friends) for two years, and had the authority to confer the greatest of all gifts personally upon him—the *Gift of the Holy Ghost*. The 14,000,000 active members of the *Mormon Church* pay 10% of their incomes to help build their chapels, temples, and general church needs. In addition they fast from two meals the first Sunday of every month and give the cost of these two meals to their local ward bishop to use to help those in their local area that are in need. All their wards, temples, and stakes are governed by lay members who volunteer their services without any remuneration from the church. This includes stake presidents, bishops, presidents of auxiliary organizations, choir members, organists, choristers, family history consultants, record extraction researchers, all teachers of the many classes, temple workers, clerks, historians, stake and ward missionaries, relief society visiting teachers (women), home teachers (men), boy scout leaders, librarians, and various other callings. The Church Welfare Program is a light to the world.

The L.D.S. church does not become involved as a church in politics. Joseph Smith stated: "We teach them correct principles and let them govern themselves. "

These principles include moral issues, but they do not endorse any candidates. Before any major election they admonish the members to choose good candidates, personally support and vote for them, but none are allowed to campaign within their buildings.

One member of the general authorities told me: "The church belongs to the people. We are only here to help them."]

This above rumor also brought to my mind the following incident that happened near the end of my high school *World History* class.

Our teacher, Ms. Rees, one day opened our class discussion by starting with the front row of students and telling each of us individually our weaknesses. I sat quite smugly waiting. I truly believed she would praise me rather than belittle me, as I always got an "A" and was usually well prepared and raised my hand to answer questions, but she squashed my smugness with one sentence.

"And BROOKIE, you hide your light under a bushel basket."

In 2006, GROVER and I visited our daughter and family near Boston. They drove us across Rhode Island, Connecticut, and crossed the Hudson River on the Tappan Zee Bridge into Hawthorne, New Jersey, where our son GROVER and family live—fifteen minutes from Manhattan Island. Early the next morning, we left New Jersey to cross the Washington Bridge to begin their predetermined agenda to show us the city. It started with the Museum of Modern Art, which had on display the *Starry Night* by Van Gogh—among many other wonderful paintings. Our son drove us through the skyscraper's narrow street maize of Manhattan taxi cabs like a pro—showing us points of interest like Chinatown, crossing the Brooklyn Bridge, Radio City, the Woolworth Building, Ground Zero—Wall Street with the whole financial district was closed to the public. We took a break at Central Park and then hastened to our matinee at the New Amsterdam Theater on 42nd Street—they gave us tickets to the stage play *Lion King.* We had dinner at an expensive Manhattan restaurant, and then in the early evening, we joined the 42nd Street Circle Line Sight-seeing Cruise on a tour of the New York harbor, which took us south to the East River, under the many bridges, turning northward until we reached the United Nations Complex.

GROVER & BROOKIE IN FRONT OF BOAT

Coming back, we crossed the harbor almost to the New Jersey coastline—passing the Statue of Liberty and Ellis Island, while the last rays of sunlight disappeared below the horizon and the cities on both sides lit up in their nighttime splendor.

There she was "STANDING FIRM" in the harbor, holding her arm with its lighted torch of LIBERTY high above her head for the entire world to see, while she cradled in her right hand the laws and constitution of a free nation. Her seven rays of glory welcomed the tired and weary to a land of opportunity—a wonderful gift from the nation of France.

"Ye are the light of the world.
A city that is set on an hill cannot be hid.
Neither do men light a candle, and put it under a bushel,
but on a candlestick;
and it giveth light unto all that are in the house.
Let your light so shine before men,
that they may see your good works,
and glorify your Father which is in heaven."

St. MATTHEW 5:14-16

It would seem that where much is given, much is expected. We Americans have been given much by those who have gone before us. I guess getting an "A" in World History isn't quite good enough, if we want to light up the world.

⟅ EPILOG ⟆
The Last Beatitude
PART I: DRIVEN AND PART II: STANDING FIRM

When I seriously started to research and compile this book over fifteen years ago, I told my daughter and son-in-law it would be the truth to the best of my knowledge. I would not try to spin it, excuse, hide the actions of some (even myself), or spin events to comply with my own factitious bias. I have used the honest journals of many people in this attempt, and expect no less of myself.

As current history is rapidly occurring that is changing the economics, politics, the very lives of our nation's citizens and those throughout the world, I feel impressed to add this personal epilog before these pages are printed. Consider it a small case study on the local level of government of what is expanding into worldwide conflict.

From D&C 121:39-42:

> "We have learned by sad experience that it is the nature and disposition of almost all men, as soon as they get a little authority, as they suppose, they will immediately begin to exercise unrighteous dominion. . . .
>
> "No power or influence can or ought to be maintained . . . only by persuasion, by long-suffering, by gentleness and meekness, and by love unfeigned;
>
> "By kindness, and pure knowledge, which shall greatly enlarge the soul without hypocrisy, and without guile . . ."

It was the late spring of 1972 in Panaca, Nevada. I was greatly confused. Something very different was going on. I didn't understand. I was not a sociologist. The superintendent was. The anger and unjust accusations resounding in his son's voice that I heard on the telephone the night before weren't right. The superintendent had told me himself he was leaving Lincoln County several weeks before.

The Humboldt County school board trustee had called me around noon. He had called the president of our school board first, who was very surprised and knew nothing about it. That surprised me, too. After speaking with me on the phone for a half-hour or more, the trustee seemed satisfied and told me they would offer him the job that afternoon. Their county had a great problem—a social war—they needed a strong leader to pull it all together and restore the peace. As I hung up the phone, I realized that my high school daughter, home for lunch, had heard my half of the conversation. She quizzed me about it. I explained that this was a private conversation and she must not speak about it to any of her friends. The temptation was too great. She told a friend, admonishing her to keep quiet, but the friend told his daughter, which brought on the explosive phone call I had received in the evening—his family knew nothing about it, either. He was out of town.

Why? Why was I told and not the others? What was going on?

As I considered it, I remembered a recent school board meeting. The Pioche member of our board had resigned—he was moving. Surprisingly, a smiling board agreed that I was to choose between the three candidates that the people of Pioche had recommended. I said I wanted to talk to them, and our superintendent quickly volunteered to arrange the times and drive me there. It was during this journey that he had told me he planned to leave the county. I choose the adult newly married son of a former board member. Many Pioche people were unhappy, and one candidate had already filed against him for the fall election.

All this was a dramatic change from my previous experiences. The three community high school was in Panaca and I was often approached by the braver teachers, noncertified personnel, parents, and administrators with their concerns within the district. Defending their interests, I was quite often at odds with the superintendent and a solid majority of his friendly trustees.

One day he had asked me to come to his office. He placed a microphone before me and informed me that our conversation was being recorded. He then bluntly stated that my husband GROVER and I were the only people that stopped him from controlling the whole county. I wished then that I had also brought my recorder. I couldn't understand why he wanted to control the whole county—wasn't the school district enough? I told him that many in the county felt stronger against this control than we did. Rising to his feet and glaring at me from his standing position, he demanded, "Who? Who?"

I had no desire to name anyone who had come privately to me. A recent local newspaper had headlined an angry exchange he had recently had with one of our county commissioners. I mentioned him as an example.

Sitting down he retorted, "Oh him, I can handle him." I gave him no more names, and he gave me the usual cliché, "Well, all right, if that's how little you are concerned about the children."

I gave him my usual answer, "It has nothing to do with the children, and you know it!" and left his office.

In the end, he won. Two more excellent high school teachers were not going to get their contracts renewed. I had asked them to come to the board meeting and tell their stories and had asked a few other concerned parents to come and support them before the board. Only the two soon to be dismissed teachers came besides my husband GROVER. The superintendent packed the room with supporters—even some who had privately spoken against this decision. The vote from the board was 4 to 1 against the teachers.

Still concerned about yesterday's events, I was prompted in my mind to drive up to the Pioche public library and check-out the English translation of Adolph Hitler's *Mein Kumpf*. I had never read any of it before, but I truly believed I would find an answer to my dilemma in it.

In his first chapters Hitler blamed all that was wrong in Germany and Austria on the Jewish people. He told how God had told him that he was to get rid of all of them—genocide. He was to build the Aryan and Nordic populations. From his prison cell, he wrote how he would organize the Nazi party with the support of storm troopers and university students. I skimmed quickly through this part. I was interested in how he became Chancellor and took over the *Reichsrat* government. About 1/3 through the book, I found what I was looking for. Hitler explained why it was important to have dissenters in his political bodies at that time, as long as they were a minority—never a majority. He explained how they become a buffer against the unrest of the people, who could talk to them, air their differences, but always be out-voted in the end. These rebellious people felt represented and relied on their representatives to help them, when, in effect, they could not—always out-voted, but the general public got rid of their objections and steam without their group personally taking further action.

I then understood why they had never had anyone file against me. I was their whipping boy—someone to blame for any discord and unable to stop the abuse. I further recognized that three of his friendly board assenters were up for election that year, and if we didn't get a majority change, there would be another four years of the same. I realized that was why this whole *leaving the county farce* was going on. The unfinished book went back to the library. I was no longer confused. This was confirmed at the next board meeting—it proceeded as usual—no reference to his leaving the county.

The following day, after the store closed in Caliente, I stopped by two homes of friends whom I considered to be highly concerned about the county school district. They were not personally potential board members. I told them what I believed was going on and then added that if I didn't have a majority support on the board in the next election, I was going to resign. I was not going to be a scapegoat any longer. I made a few suggestions as to whom they might ask, but I was not going to ask them or help with their elections. The deadline for filing was less than a week away. I went home.

Five minutes before five o'clock, when the county clerk's office closed on that final day, two people filed for the two Caliente men's seats on the school board. One had told GROVER what they were going to do, so I was somewhat aware. That evening was our regular board meeting. I arrived slightly late. I wanted to avoid any discussion before the meeting started. They were aware of the two that had filed. The superintendent had called the county clerk's office before she went home, and he informed me as I sat down. There was strong anxiety reflected on their faces. The oldest member of the board, who had never faced an opponent, was sitting next to me. He pleadingly asked me if I would give him an endorsement. I couldn't help feeling some sorrow for him, but I answered honestly:

"I'm not going to endorse anyone, I have a state senator I need to get elected, and I need the whole county to support him."

The board election became quite heated before it was over. One of the candidates bought a special headlined front-page spot in the local weekly newspaper stating his strong reasons for running for the school board, and he also paid the paper to have a copy delivered to every post office box in the county—two weeks before Election Day. He explained to GROVER that the extra week was to give his opponent a chance to give his answer. The answer came from the superintendent himself—headlined front page and delivered throughout the county the next week—his strong endorsement of the current board member slammed and belittled the new candidate's intelligence and his education to the delight of the contestant.

"I smoked him out!" he told my husband.

The vitriol of the replied endorsement from the superintendent brought out the voters and the school board would have three new members the first week of 1973.

A few days after the election, word was sent through GROVER that the three newly elected board members wanted to elect me their president in January. They wanted a president who knew more about the board than they did. I wanted to talk to them about it and invited the three to visit with me at my home. There I explained that I would only be their president if they would help me change the school board rules.

At that time, the rules, which were written by our superintendent, put the president at a disadvantage. He (or she) was more like the vice-president of the United States in the senate. He was in charge of the meetings but would only vote in the case of a tie. He was also supposed to arbitrate the meeting without introducing the question or speaking his own views unless a tie existed, and he signed his name to any contracts or documents that the board agreed upon. I had been the president for two years—previously. The rules also stated that no members of the board could discuss issues with other members of the board before the board meeting. Also, the superintendent prepared the agenda for the board without consulting with any board members, and at one time had even declined to add a personal item to the agenda that I had asked him to include. Possessing a full set of the Nevada Revised Statutes, Robert's Rules, Mason's Manuel, the Clark County School Board rules, and my observations of the Nevada Legislature, I realized that as school board members we had the right not only to choose our officers but to change these rules that we would vote to accept after the new members were officially installed—but we needed to be totally prepared at the short installation meeting.

I brought in my copy of the present official rules for them to see. We discussed each one carefully and the group found much to add or take away. I typed up our much shorter set, documented them, and took them to our district attorney to read. He read them, smiled a little at our boldness, but could find nothing illegal in our new rules. We invited our board president, who had not been up for election that year, to come to our final preparatory meeting in December. He was not happy, but promised not to tell anyone about our proposed new rule changes until the meeting began a few days away.

Of course, the short installation meeting became much longer. When seated as president, I stopped lengthy discussions from school personnel. Every new rule was challenged as it was read. The documentation held and the new rules became official with a vote of 4 to 1.

As president of the board, a week before our regular January meeting, I presented the superintendent with the items the board wanted on our agenda. They included a retraction of his letter to the governor to resurrect the old legislative bill that would combine the school districts of Lincoln and Clark counties, and a retraction of the decision of the previous board to bus the kindergarten children from Caliente (25 miles away) and Panaca (11 miles away) to Pioche, where they were taught five days a week in one large classroom by an uncertified teacher's aide (currently his capable wife). They also included a separation of his personal salary contract with the board from those of the other school administrators. Since he had written the proposal, the board thought it was a conflict of interest. That January all the salaries in the district were on the agenda.

Our superintendent was very kind to me and appeared compliant, stating that he would work with the new board and would write a new kindergarten program and salary proposal for the approaching meeting. Believing in his honesty, I relaxed and went home.

The meeting arrived and we were "submarined." The meeting had been moved to a much larger room—all the administrators were there, a large percentage of the teachers and noncertified personnel, the local newspaper manager, the district attorney (who was given a seat at the table with the members of the school board) and many of his supporting citizens. As the meeting progressed, every item on the agenda was challenged—everyone wanted to be heard—with the exception of GROVER they were all representing the opposition to the school board. When the kindergarten change came up, the superintendent denied everything he had told me before and refused any responsibility to write a new proposal on anything. If we wanted something different, we could write it ourselves. The district attorney, when allowed to speak, backed the superintendent. As midnight arrived, one member of the board made a motion that we recess until the following Monday. He was tired. The motion was seconded and passed without discussion. As we were leaving, this board member stopped me and told me, he had enough. He was going to resign. He had been to many controversial county commissioner meetings—but nothing like this meeting.

The next day, the county newspaper headlined the meeting, standing firmly behind the superintendent. That evening I wrote an equally long answer to the article. I never sent it to the paper. GROVER and I discussed it and decided it was too harsh on many school personnel and others that had been wrongly set up by the smoothness of the superintendent—but to say less was ineffective. What should we do?

Friday evening we had an invitation from Frank and Jean Young at their home in Las Vegas. Woody and Nora Wilson would be there. It was a loser's party. All three former assemblymen had lost their elections. As I was preparing everything to drive down and was trying to also decide what to do about the pending school board meeting the next Monday, a male voice spoke to my mind, "You can get rid of him, if you act fast." It might have been my father's voice. GROVER and I brainstormed all the way to Las Vegas.

It was great to see our former legislative friends that evening. Much was said about Watergate, which they believed to be the main reason for their defeat, as well as other Republican legislators—the republicans had become the minority party again. We stayed with Frank and Jean that night, and we had a lovely breakfast in the morning.

GROVER and I had decided to talk to them about our county school board problem. They were highly concerned, and advised us to get rid of him quickly.

How? He had a valid contract, tenure, and our attorney had taken his side.

Frank quickly replied that the last meeting was sufficient grounds to dismiss him, and as for an attorney, I should talk to Helen Cannon, president of the

Clark County School Board. He felt sure they would lend us their attorney—the best school board attorney in the state of Nevada. They had quite recently got a *Letter of Resignation* from their own superintendent. Frank handed me his phone and grabbed his phone book to look up her number. I got the number, but changed my mind. I needed to talk to the other three board members first. I asked permission to make a long distance phone call instead, calling our clerk to set up a meeting of the four of us at her home in Caliente around noon. I would be there.

When I arrived, the Pioche member had not yet arrived, and our clerk was concerned. The superintendent had been talking with him for a long time Friday evening in his car, and he wanted to talk to her personally about it. When he arrived, he was very reluctant to vote for dismissal. He was almost convinced that the former county commissioner and I had a personal vendetta against the superintendent. I mostly let the other two convince him otherwise. When we were finally agreed, I called Helen Cannon, who quizzed me about the number of members who wanted him dismissed. She then told me she would have their attorney call me Monday morning. She did not want to know any more about it and felt confident the other members of their board would agree to it.

Their attorney and I had a long talk on the telephone Monday morning. The board was to get a *Letter of Resignation* from him that evening and be sure it was signed. He didn't want to know anything yet about grounds for dismissal, and we were not to give the superintendent any reason for asking for his resignation. If he wouldn't give the letter to us, I was to talk to him (their attorney) again, and he would meet with the board and the superintendent the following Monday for his dismissal.

The board meeting went very smooth that evening. It was not heavily stacked with supporters, and the superintendent was very kind and helpful. The board public business was all finalized quickly and the time came for the executive session—only the board members with the superintendent discussing personnel matters. The superintendent had only one item to discuss with us. Some of our personnel had taken a 4% raise in their salaries for the past two years in exchange for agreeing to retire after that time. Two of them didn't want to retire and wanted to give back the increase plus interest and stay in their positions. The board decided not to allow it. As president and spokesman for the board, I gave this decision to the waiting principal involved. He was extremely unhappy and slammed the door hard as he left. I then dismissed the superintendent from our session.

The board was so pleased with the competence of the superintendent and how he had acted that evening that it took some discussion and solemn reminding of last week's meeting and the many people that had been forced to leave the county through the years before the board came to an agreement, officially. It was not a question about whether he *could* be a good superintendent, but *would* he be one?

I was spokesman (a job I didn't want) and we had a tape recorder turned on—which I called to his attention when he returned. I asked for his *Letter of Resignation*. He was very calm and asked for a reason. I explained that the letter was to be his, not the board's letter, and if he chose not to submit one to us, we would proceed with our reasons for dismissal the following Monday. He asked who we would use as our attorney. I told him. He said he didn't want to go that way, but would like a little time and secrecy to prepare his letter. No one objected. As we went to our cars, I saw a large group of school administrators with the superintendent and our fifth board member having a great laugh in the superintendent's outer office.

He had asked for our secrecy but was not submitting to any secrecy on his part. I was later told that he had told all of them, "Well, I got the boot." This worried me. I called our attorney in Las Vegas the next morning.

He emphasized the immediate need for a signed *Letter of Resignation* and if we didn't get it he would come next Monday, as he had previously said. Then he went into the details of what we could offer the superintendent as compensation for his unused vacation pay, his unused sick pay, and the cash we could offer for the balance of his contract. He also advised that, after we got his resignation, we should be very careful to speak only as a board—assign one trusted spokesman (that would say nothing additionally) and the rest were to keep totally silent on the subject. We should write our own short announcement for the newspaper and give a copy with written instructions to all the school principals without further comment. This, of course, was to minimize public rumor and place all responsibility on our whole school board, rather than individuals—hopefully stopping a war in the county.

I had the board clerk call a special meeting of the board to get that letter. If we were all present, the delay from notice was not needed. We would meet at the clerk's home. It was a long night and after several animated phone calls by our clerk to the superintendent's home, we got his *Letter of Resignation* delivered in person. The board's statements to the press and school district were delivered the following day personally by the board members with our clerk assigned as public spokeswoman.

My part was to deliver the written message to the Panaca elementary school principal and the two secretaries in the superintendent's office. This principal, who had slammed the door in our faces on Monday evening, was very angry—in fact, his blistering remarks ended by stating that every time he cashed his retirement check he would remember what I had done to him—and all this after he had donated $100 to GROVER's campaign. I kept silent, but I went home, took five twenty dollar bills from our much needed Caliente Pharmacy banking and wrote him a personal letter, after getting my husband's approval.

In it I simply reminded him that as the president of the board, I spoke for the board's decision, which may or may not reflect my own opinions. I further told him that GROVER had accepted the $100 to help get what I believed to be a very good candidate elected, and if it was intended for any other reason, he couldn't accept it—so we were returning it. I handed him the letter, while he was teaching. When school ended, he was at my door apologizing and insisting that I keep the $100. We remained friends until his death a few years ago.

Our superintendent wasn't quite as placid. The local newspaper was owned by a retired multimillionaire former lawyer from California who had moved to our county, bought a large ranch to raise pedigreed horses and the county newspaper in which he weekly expounded his anti-alcohol and usually conservative views every week. He liked GROVER and had written him several personal congratulatory letters for what he had accomplished in the legislature. At this time he was hospitalized with a heart problem. As the local pharmacist, GROVER would fill the hospital prescriptions and deliver them daily. He would often stop in and say hello to various patients. The retired millionaire asked him about his manager's newspaper article. GROVER told him I had written an answer, but had decided not to send it. He asked if I would bring it to him and let him read it, which I did the following morning. He read it and thought it would have been all right to publish, but he would respect my feelings and would additionally tone down his manager. He later told GROVER that he had two more visitors that same day, the superintendent and the high school principal. He told him to tell me not to worry, he could see through them, but they were on their way to Carson City. His newspaper that week had his personal editorial that supported the school board position, along with the headline of the superintendent's resignation and picture—also the superintendent's letter to the editor, which was not complimentary to the school board or me.

I also received a certified letter that day from our resigning superintendent. He mentioned his trip to Carson City and in addition he added that he would act as a consultant to our district for $300 a day. I was disgusted. We were already paying him his salary until the end of June. Talking with our clerk of the board, she was relieved. It gave us a reason to terminate his services immediately, in spite of his many threats that the budget had to be immediately submitted. I called the secretary of the State School Board Association, whom GROVER and I knew quite well during the legislatures. He got permission from the State Superintendent of Schools to come to Lincoln County and act as our superintendent through this tough period, until we appointed a superintendent pro tem. He took our budget back with him, and with the help of the state superintendent of schools, completed the budget at no cost to the district.

The superintendent's trip to Carson City had created additional problems for our county. It was the next morning I got a phone call from our Lincoln County district attorney. He was very apologetic for his past actions at the board meeting. I was so positive in accepting his humble apology that he never told me the whole story, but he did tell me he had been in Carson City on other business that same day and had learned things that he was ashamed to tell.

I would soon learn from another source that the two school administrators had seen him on the street and invited him to accompany them to their appointment with the governor. While they were there, the superintendent took from his briefcase the contract between our school district and the Nevada Girl's Training Center in Caliente. It was several years old and had my signature on it as the president pro tem of the school board. The governor was told that I was out to get him, and I was going to use this document to do it. It was the contract prepared by our superintendent and the superintendent of the training center, which allowed the school district to hire and supervise the teachers that taught these wayward girls so they could graduate from high school.

It was very fat—beyond a careful reading by the school board in a single meeting on a tight agenda. The superintendent had assured us it was fine. None of us had seen it before the meeting or retained a copy to refer to later. I had not even made the motion or second or voted for it. He claimed at his meeting with the governor that the document gave the school district fraudulently $40,000 of state funds, and that I was going to blame this on the governor? I still don't understand that. I also learned that our district attorney was so horrified by that meeting that he had told my informant he was prepared to resign his position as district attorney—rather than be any part of it.

The legislative council auditors came to the training center and did a complete audit. Everything appeared to be in order, but the school board had already met in the superintendent's office, as stated above, and demanded the superintendent's keys and the removal of his personal belongings from the office. We even changed the locks, in case he had another set. The two newly elected male board members were sufficiently worried about me that they asked to change my seating to the far side of the office and they would take more open seats near his desk and watch carefully in case he had a gun in one of his drawers. They believed I might be a target—but he wasn't that foolish.

It was months later that I was driving home alone from Carson City, after attending a school trustee's meeting, that I turned on my radio to hear the news as I came within the broadcast area of the Las Vegas stations. Our former superintendent was being interviewed by one of their news anchors, and he was claiming proudly to all the listeners throughout southern Nevada that he was the reason that GROVER SWALLOW had not been elected to the state senate, (GROVER had lost by a little over 100 votes in the five county district,) and that was why his wife BROOKIE had dismissed him as a superintendent in Lincoln County. The anchor changed the topic to inquire about his strong support of the owner of houses of prostitution in his newly adopted county; I turned off the radio and went back to listening to my recorded music tapes. I didn't need more of that. We had sufficient problems without adding any more, but as I thought further about it, maybe he *was* the reason for GROVER's defeat. Maybe there had been other previous meetings telling other lies to the governor and leaders within the NSEA—the Nevada State Educational Association. I couldn't say, but to claim this as the reason for his writing his own *Letter of Resignation* was not true, and, of course, he was aware of that.

Governor Mike O'Callahan was told the truth of the situation by the superintendent of the Girl's Training Center. The governor came to Panaca that spring and delivered the keynote speech to our graduating class. I gave out the diplomas, so I sat on the stage. I had no problem congratulating him, shaking his hand, and thanking him for coming. I was somewhat amused, though, as I watched him from the stage as he made his way around the auditorium shaking the hands of the students with their parents. GROVER was at the far end near the exit door with our daughter who had graduated. I could see Mike continually turning his head to watch where GROVER was, and when he came close he turned away from the line and spoke with others until he passed by him, then he resumed his congratulations down the other side of the auditorium. I felt his conscience might be bothering him. He was definitely not talking to GROVER.

We moved many administrators around a little but fired no one. One excellent administrator quit. Several have apologized personally to me or to GROVER through the years—deeply sorry.

Our school board would not agree to replace the superintendent with anyone from Lincoln County. We finally gave a contract to a Utah man who had a doctorate in school administration—mostly because his salary demand was lower than the others and no one really impressed us. He had previously been a leader in the UEA teacher's union. In the spring our local chapter of the NSEA forced us into binding arbitration in Las Vegas where each side would have an hour and a half to explain their positions. Our superintendent refused to prepare for it—knowing his own contract would not be renewed. We enlisted the help of our district secretaries, our district attorney, and between all of us, we were able to win our case against the very tough state educational union.

That year, we hired a former highly qualified high school principal as our superintendent, who with persuasion accepted our offer and returned to Lincoln County as our superintendent—much loved by the citizens.

As I continued my journey home alone from Carson City that day in 1974, my thoughts went back to 1971 and the legislative session when GROVER was chairman of the education committee. The NSEA wanted a 15% raise in teachers and administrators salaries that year. This union placed GROVER under great pressure to move this bill out of his committee for passage. He refused to do so until the state employees and other expense items were submitted and the overall total budget could be balanced.

A pharmacist from Las Vegas called and wanted to take GROVER and me to dinner at Williams Ranch on a Saturday night. We went with him. He told us his wife was associated either as a teacher or in some other capacity with the Clark County NSEA, and he was representing their interests. We had a delicious dinner and a pleasant conversation. When we arrived back home, I left his car to be with my children. GROVER remained and shortly told me that he had been threatened—if he didn't get the bill out of committee immediately, bad things would happen—he did not agree to do it.

Not long after that, our original superintendent became part of a frame-up to destroy our pharmacy licenses. This same pharmacist with the drug inspector from Las Vegas came the following day while I was busy filling prescriptions. They looked at my files a few minutes then excused themselves, saying they were going to check the hospital and the doctor's office. It was two to three hours later the drug inspector returned alone. He didn't tell me any details, only that I had been used very badly. After talking to our doctor, he wanted me to know how sorry he was for being any part of it. He was very upset at the pharmacist, who was still very angry and had left earlier.

This same pharmacist managed in the following years to get himself appointed to the state pharmacy board. They went after our only local doctor, and sent the sheriff to get copies of all our Schedule II narcotic prescriptions. First they took away the doctor's right to prescribe them. Another doctor and his nurse wife came into our county. They were young and very efficient, but didn't stay long—they went to Montana, where he was tried on narcotic charges. He asked GROVER to testify in his behalf, which he did. I don't know how the trial ended, but later his wife was caught bringing Schedule II drugs into our country on her person—I believe she was caught coming from Mexico.

The copy of our files of narcotic prescriptions remained in Carson City, and a friend of our son, who was attending law school in California, told our son that while he was hired as a clerk during the summer he with others were required to go through these many prescriptions and look for any pharmacist's errors.

When this was completed, the Nevada Pharmacy Board charged GROVER with unprofessional conduct. He wouldn't let that stand against his name. We were living in Utah at that time, but we hired the most highly recommended lawyer in Las Vegas to defend him. In the end, all that they legally had found wrong was two missing dates and a patient's address that were missing in these hundreds of prescriptions. We paid the board the $300 they wanted for this. The missing address and one of the dates had our pharmacy manager's initials on them, not GROVER's—still GROVER's fault, as he had hired him. The unprofessional conduct charge was removed.

Much more could be added about the "tangled web we weave, when once we practice to deceive" (Sir Walter Scott.). Where does it all end? In the case of this threatening pharmacist, it ended a few years later when he died of a heart attack, after which we personally wrote the new pharmacy board, which then proceeded to have a troublesome Nevada State statute revised.

When we were building our present home here in Panaca around the turn of the century, our neighbor across the street had a small herd of peacocks. At night they would roost on some rather tall locust trees in his yard. During the days, the hens would sometimes visit us, following their male leader who would proudly strut before them with his four or five foot tail feathers displayed to perfection.

One day I returned from church and he was sitting on one of the carpenter's tables all by himself in front of one our six foot sliding doors proudliy admiring his own reflected image with his beautiful feathers draping nearly to the cement patio below. Even my presence did not disturb him.

A year or so later, I was working on my computer when there was the sound of a heavy crash into my front door. When I opened the hollow metal door to discover the cause, I discovered a dent in the metal just above the shining golden kick plate on the bottom of the door. Limping badly with his small head wobbling back and forth and barely able to drag his long tail behind him as he crossed the street to return to his home was our neighbor's usually strutting peacock. It was the mating season. It was obvious. With his small proud mind, he had attacked head first his own golden image in the kick plate of our door with all the power his frame could produce, and he was then straggling home in defeat. To me, it was a lesson in how "pride goeth before a fall."

There are evil forces that work toward the destruction of the truth, the liberty, and the rights of the people who are governed. Our founding fathers and mothers had similar problems creating this nation. We, today, need to stand firm as individuals and try personally to understand, unite, and keep our liberties.

The following quote of President THEODORE ROOSEVELT, a distant relative-in-law on the IVIE line, was sent to GROVER in 1970 by President RICHARD NIXON, a distant cousin on the LIPPENCOTT line of ancestors. It is on fine parchment paper, suitable for framing. I treasure these words. I might add that President NIXON would have been better off months later to have worked harder on the "work worth doing" part. On the negative antonym side of these two impressive "W" words, *work* and *worth*, we might mention *Waterloo* and *Watergate*. Putting honest people and truth on your side is very important. It can't be done in a clandestine society—where the real truth is hidden.

"*Far and away the best prize that life offers is the chance to work hard at work worth doing*."

Theodore Roosevelt

Congratulations on your 1970 victory.

Richard Nixon

When a teenager, we sang courageously at many of our meetings two songs:

1.

"Shall the youth of Zion falter in defending truth and right?
While the enemy assaileth, Shall we shrink or shun the fight?
No!
True to the faith that our parents have cherished.
True to the truth for which martyrs have perished.
To God's command, Soul, heart, and hand,
Faithful and true we will ever stand."

2.

Firm as the mountains around us, Stalwart and brave we stand,
On the rock our fathers planted For us in this goodly land....
For the heritage they left us, not of gold or of worldly wealth,
But a blessing everlasting, Of love and joy and health....
O youth of the noble birthright
Carry on! Carry on! Carry on!

Children of America—and old or young, we are all children of this nation—in this passing parade with its pomp and indulgence, open your eyes and recognize that in this current parade of supposed finery throughout the world—the emperor (of deceit) has no clothes. We must not ignore or fear to speak the truth.

We need to sincerely understand what we are promising when we say:

"I pledge allegiance to the flag of the United States of America
and to the Republic for which it stands—
One nation, under God, with liberty and justice for all."

This nation needs a new birth of freedom, with each of us standing firm on righteous principles and doing something individually about it. We should be as united in purpose as the members of congress appeared to be, when they stood as a unit on the steps of the Capitol building and sang with one voice after 9/11 *God Bless America.*

~ Bibliography for Part II ~
Standing Firm

A Genealogy of a Cooley family of Hunterdon County, New Jersey and a Tillou famly of French Huguenots, presented by Watchung Chapter N.S.D.A.R., 1937 US/CAN, FILM AREA, 0873024 item 5

Adventurers of Purse & Person, FHL, Salt Lake City, Utah, many volumes.

Alder, Douglas D. & Brooks, Karl F., *A History of Washington County,* Orem Park Stake FHC F832.w214 A42x1996

Allred, Colonel Redick N., personal journal

AF, Ancestor File, FHL, Salt Lake City, Utah, and On Line

Anderson. Robert, *Family Record Book, late of Williamsburg, VA., ca. 1737-1846*

Armstrong, Milton G., Chairman, *Early History of Ephraim, First One Hundred Years.*

Arrington, Leonard J., *Great Basin Kingdom,* University of Nebraska Press, 1958

Automated Archive Records, FHC Park Stake, Orem, Utah,

Averett, Walter R., *Through the Rainbow Canyon,* Self, Grand Junction, Colorado, 1995

Bancroft, George, *History of the United States, Vol. 4, pg. 349-353; Vol. 5, pg. 140, 155,*

Barton, Elisha Kember, *personal genealogical records, ca 1840-1890*

Bartholomew's Road Atlas of Great Britain, John Bartholomew & Son LTD., Edinburgh 9, 1963

Bennett, R.N., of Sanpete County, Utah, ca. 1865, journal

Beschloss, Michael R., *Taking Charge, The Johnson White House Tapes, 1963-1964,*Simon & Schuster

Book of Mormon, The Church of Jesus Christ of Latter Day Saints 1829

Borg, Grant, *Federal Writers' Project, Interview with Mrs. Elizabeth Dianthy Allred at Spring City,Utah.* FHL US/CAN 979.2 D3U 9.3 The Genealogical Society, Salt Lake City, Utah, 1946

Brown, Ivan H., *BARTON "All Bartons are Kin",* privately published, 1976

Brown, Jr., Stuart E., *Rev. Thomas Barton (1728-1780,* FHL, US/CAN 929.273 B285kr

Bullock, Alford and others, *FHL film, 0288405,* includes relationship of William Alexander Ivie to Theodore Roosevelt and Martha Bullock (Roosevelt)

Byrd, William, *A Journey to the Land of Eden,* Macy-Masius, Vanguard reprint, 1928

Bucks County, Pennsylvania Birth Records, for Canby, Morgan, Preston, Wilkinson, Lacey

Carter, Kate B., *Our Pioneer Heritage,* DUP, Salt Lake City, Utah, 1971

Cavaliers and Pioneers, Patent Book No. l---Part I., FHL, Salt Lake City, Utah

Census Records, US, Early Colonial Census, various

Charles City, Virginia, court records from 1655, from official county records

Clay, Lillie I. C., (sister) *They Chose to Serve,* B.Y. U. Printing, 1998

Clint, Florence, *Northumberland County, Pennsylvania, AREA KEY,* FHL, 974.831 D25a, SLC 1977

Commemorative Biographical Record, Dutchesss County, New York, J. H. Beers & Co. 1897

Complete book of Emigrants, Vol. 1, 1607-1660 FHL, Salt Lake City, Utah

Condie, Lillie A. I., *journals, books of remembrances, personal genealogical research and records*

Condie, Gibson A, (grandfather), *journals, autobiography, genealogical records.*

Condie, Gibson (brother of great-grandfather Thomas Condie) *his life story autobiography*

Condie, Marion A., ((father) *personal journals, Book of Remembrance, original documents*

Condie, Marion Asher (brother), *personal reading and correction of his history*

Conner, Colonel Pat, *U. S. Army Journal*

Conover, Don W. Grandson., copy, *Journal of Peter Wilson Cownover, Utah Pioneer Biographies,* FHL volume 7, Salt Lake City, Utah, 1946

Contributions to the History of the Ancient Families of New York, 1879

Cook, Fred S. & Deane, Jim, *Historic Legends of White Pine and Lincoln Counties,* The Printery, Pahrump, Nevada

Crane, Malvina, (Longsdorf), journal 1926

Croft, Grace Hildy *With a Song in Her Heart,* Nicholas G. Morgan, Sr. Publisher

DAR Patriot Index, Centennial Edition, Orem Park Stake FHC, Orem, Utah

Day, Sherman, *Sherman Day's 1843 History, Northumberland County, Pennsylvania*

Day, Stella H., and Ekins, Sebrina C., *100 Years of History of Millard County,* D.U. P. of Millard County, Art City Publishing Co., Orem City Library, 979.245 D333

Deseret News Weekly, ca July 1872, 1867, 1872,

Doctrine and Covenants. The Church of Jesus Christ of Latter Day Saints

Dovell, Ashton, *The Contribution of the French Huguenots to the Cultural Life of America,* Ninth Annual

Assembly, Richmond, Virginia, April, 1940

Drake, G. Samuel G. , *The New England Historical & Genealogical Register, Volume V.,* A Heritage Classic, Boston, Samuel G. Drake, Publisher, 1851

Edwards, Tryon, Catrevas, C.N., & Edwards, Jonathan, *The New Dictionary of Thoughts,* Standard Book

Co, New York, 1955

Elizabeth Cittie, Virginia, Musters, (ship, 1618-1623 pp 66,67), Orem Park Stake FHC, Orem, Utah

Ephraim, Sanpete, Utah, Cemetery Records, 27 September 1887 – February 1941, FHL 979.256/E 1 V3e

Fawcett, Edward Charles, *The Fawcett family: 1736 (of Fawcett Gap, Virginia & heir descendants.*

Fawcett, Thomas Hayes, *the Fawcett family of Frederick County, Virginia,* FHL US/CAN 929.273 A1 no.. 990

Dew, Sheri L., *Ezra Taft Benson, A Biography,* Deseret Book Co., Salt Lake City, Utah

Emmison, F.G., *Catalogue of Essex Parish Records 1240-1894,and Guide to the Essex Record Office,* The

Essex County Council, Chelmsford, England 1966 and 1968

Farmer, John, Drake, Samuel G., *The Genealogical Register of the First Settlers of New England,* Genealogical Publilshing Co., Inc. 1851

Fillmore County Court Records, 1866

Firmage, Richard A., *History of Grand County (Utah),* Utah Centennial County History Series, F832.665 F57x 1996 Orem Park Stake FHC

Fish, Joseph, *History of Enterprise,* FHL US/CAN 979.248/E1 H2f, Salt Lake City, Utah

Franklin County, Idaho, *Official Program , Idaho Day, 14-15 Jun 1910*

French. Ellen Cochran, *Barton & Hummell Family Histories,*Tribune Printing Company, Fairfield, Iowa

1967; *Part Three, Faucett Genealogy Ireland to Orange Co., North Carolina pg. 398-421*

Genealogical and Biographical Annals of Northumberland County Pennsylvania, J. L. Floyd & Co., Chicago, 1911, FHL US/CAN 974.S31 D2go

Gibbs, Josiah F., *Black Hawk's last raid---1866,* Utah Historical Quarterly, State Capitol, Salt Lake City, October 1931

Ghost Town Gazette, Fall, 1996, Pioche, Nevada---Nation's Liveliest Ghost Town

Gledhill (Christensen, Buchannan) Ida Belle, (first-cousin-once-removed) *History of Lillie Belle Ivie Gledhill,* ca 1930 or after

Grant, Heber J. Grant, *Conference Report,* April 1932; p. 123, Oct 1994 p. 4

Gottfredson, H. J., *Ute and Piute Traditions,* ca. 1880

Gottfredson, Peter, *Indian Depredations in Utah, Utah Indian War Veterans,* Skelton Publishing Co. Salt Lake City, Utah, 1919; *The First Fire in Pioche*

Greenwood, Val D., *The Researcher's Guide to American Genealogy,* Genealogical Publishing Co., Inc., Baltimore, 1977

Hamil, Mrs. Lura Coolley, *A Story of Pioneering,* Illinois Printing Company, June 1955

Harwood, Thomas, early journal, *Adventurers of Purse and Person, p. 361-3, FHL* Salt Lake City, Utah

Hale, Heber Q., *A Marvelous Heavenly Manifestation, copy of speech in the Bishops' Building, Salt Lake City, Utah, Oct. 1920*

Hamilton, Dr. Alexander, journal, *Colonial American Travel Narratives,* Penguin Classics

Hamming, A., *Roosevelt's thrilling experiences in the Wilds of Africa,* J. H. Moss, 1909

Hart, Newell, *The Bear River Massacre,* Cashe Valley Newsletter Publishing Company, Preston, Idaho 1982, Orem Public Library 979.601 H251

Hawke, David Freeman, *Everyday Life in Early America,* Harper & Row, 1988

Helligso, Martha Stuart, *George Mason including one line of descent,* US/CAN 929.272 M38/h FHL, Salt Lake City, Utah 1983, also, *The Five George Masons*

Historical records of The Church of Jesus Christ of Latter Day Saints, Church Office Building, Salt Lake City, Utah

History of Provo, Provo Public Library, Special Collection 979.2 M172u

History of Relief Society 1842-1966, The General Board of Relief Society, Salt Lake City, Utah 1966

Holy Bible, King James Version

Hoes, Roswell Randall, *Baptismal and Marriage Registers of the OLD DUTCH CHURCH OF KINGSTON, Ulster County, New York, 1660-1809,* Baltimore Genealogical Publishing Co., Inc., 1980

Hoover, Herbert, *The Challenge to Liberty,* Charles Scribner's Sons, New York, London, 1934

*Huguenot Emigration to Virginia, . . . A partial list of the descendants of Bartholomew Dupuy.*ca 1113-1745

Hymns, Corporation of the President of the Church of Jesus Christ of Latter-day Saints, Deseret Book Co, Salt Lake City, Utah, 1985

Ivey, George Franks, *The Ivey Family in he United States,* The Southern Publishing Co., Hickory, N.C.

Ivie, Annie Catherine Mortensen, (grandmother) journals

Ivie, Evan, *Records of wills County of Monroe,* Paris, Missouri, *1833-1845 deed,* also Jasper County, Geoorgia *Will of Lot Ivie and other papers.*

Ivie, Hyrum Smith, ca. 1867, journal

Ivie, James Oscar, (grandfather) journals

Ivie, Lloyd Oscar, (uncle) journals and other records in possession of his son, Grant Ivie

Johnson, Dora Day, (Anderson, Valentine L.) Longsdorf, 1924

Johnston, Eliza Ann Ivie, (granddaughter of William Franklin Ivie of Scipio, Utah) *Life Sketch (of Grandfather).*

Judd, Denis, *Empire,* HarperCollins Publishers, London, 1996

Kearl, J.R., Pope, Clayne L., & Wimmer, Larry T., *Index to the 1850, 1860 & 1870 Censuses of Utah,* Genealogical Publishing Co., Inc. 1981

Kelso, William M., *Jamestown, the Buried Truth,* University of Virginia Press, Charlottesville and London 2006

Kennedy, David M., *Freedom from Fear,* Oxford University Press, Madison Ave., New York, New York

Klett, Joseph R., *Genealogies of New Jersey Families, From the Genealogical Magazine of New Jersey Volume I, Pre-American Notes on Old New Netherland Families, A-Z,* Orem Park Stake FHC, 044-119A

Larsen, Gustive O., *Outline History of Territorial Utah,* Deseret Book Co., Salt Lake City, Utah 1958

L.D.S. Church records of baptisms and other ordinances: Temple Index Records, Computer, extraction.

LDS Collectors Library '97, 1996 Infobases, Inc, 8/04/97

Lippincott, Abigail, *Complete Pedigree Chart, four generations, 28 Oct 1753 to 1642*

Louda, Jir'I & Maclagan, Michael, *Lines of Succession*, Barnes & Noble, 2002

Longsdorf, Hilda Madsen, *Mount Pleasant 1850-1939*, Stevens & Wallis, Inc., Salt Lake City, Utah

Love, Terry Marvin, (1944), *The descendants of Thomas Love of Orange County, North Carolina*, Lakeville, Minn., 1991 FHL 929.273 L941ev (Faucett)

Lund, Marinus (of Spring City) journal

Lytle, Carolyn , short history

Madsen, Andrew, of Sanpete County, Utah, journal

Martineau, Colonel J. H., *Military History of Cache Valley*, ca 1863

Mackeys and Allied Families, New York, New Hampshire, Delaware, Pennsylvania, New Jersey, Virginia, South Carolina, North Carolina, British Isles, FHL, Salt Lake City

McQueen, James Broom, *personal story about how he got his name*, Preston, Idaho, 1953

Millard Milestones, Fillmore City Library, Fillmore, Utah

Miller, Donald C., *Ghost Towns of Idaho*

Moffitt, John Clifton, *The Story of Provo, Utah*, Provo Public Library, Provo, Utah, 1975

Morgan, Joy Elmer, *The American Citizens Handbook<* The National Education Association of the United States, Washington, D. C. 1941

Mortensen, Jens Fredrick, *Personal Missionary Journal* 1880, (died 1886)

Mortensen, Christian J. (great-uncle) journal ca 1866

Muse, Emily G. S., *personal story* 2001

National Archives of Canada: Library, Agen: Chez la Veuve Nouabel er Fils, 1791. Broadside.

Nelson, Lee, *The Black Hawk Journey*, Cedar Fort Inc., Springville, Utah, 1999

Nelson, William, *Franklin County Citizen* , 1Feb 1917

Nevada Legislature, fifty-fifth Session, Assembly Journal, 1969

Nevada "The Silver State", Volume One, Western States Historical Publishers, Inc., Carson City, Nevada 1970

New Jersey, FHC Park Stake, Orem, Utah, *Lippincott*, pp., 74-77, 46-47, 60-61, 190-195

Nicholson, John, *The Martyrdom of Joseph Standing, or Murder of a "Mormon" Missionary*, The Deseret Book Co., Salt Lake City, Utah, 1886

Nielsen, Emil, of Salina, Utah, journal ca. 1866

Norton, Mary Beth, *Founding Mothers & Fathers*, Alford A Knopf, New York, 1996

One Hundred Years, Centennial Celebration of The Church of Jesus Christ of Latter Day Saints, 1930

Palmer, Wm. R., *The Pahute Fire Legend*, The Utah Historical Quarterly, State Capitol, Salt Lake City, October, 1931

Paullin, Charles O., *Mark Twain's Virginia Kin*, ca. 1935

Peterson, John Alton, *Utah's Black Hawk War*, The University of Utah Press, Salt Lake City, 1998

Porter, Larry C., *B.Y.U. Studies, Vol. 9, No. 3. p. 330 (about the Rev. Lane,)*

Pratt, Parley P., *Autobiography of*, The Deseret Book Co.. Salt Lake City, Utah

Pruett, Dorothy Sturgis, *Our Thrasher Heritage*, FHL US/CAN 929.273 T412p, Salt Lake City, Utah

Quate, Boyd E., *Pioneers of Snake Valley*, 8 Nov 1894

Reay. Lee, *Lambs In The Meadow*, Meadow Lane Publications, Provo, Utah, 1980

Richman, Larry L., Editor, *Prominent Men and Women of Provo, 1983*, Orem Public Library, Orem, Utah

Ridpath, John Clark, *Ridpath's History of the World, Volume V*, The Jones Brothers Publishing Company, Cincinnati, Ohio 1910

Robins, Nettie M., of Scipio, Utah, *History of James Russell Ivie and Eliza McKee Fausett Ivie*

Robison, Russell M. & Gloria J., *Our Swallow Heritage, Volume I*, Image Pro, Cedar City, Utah, 2004

Roberts. Cokie, *Founding Mothers*, HarperCollins Publishers Inc, New York, New York, 2004.

Russell, Thomas H., *America's War for Humanity*, L. H. Walter, 1919

Sanders, Mrs. Ellen Lucinda Lee, of Beaver County, Utah, and Nacozari, Sonora, Mexico, *Indians at the J. P. Lee's Ranch* ca 1866

Stanford, I. Pearl Ivie, *Personal Life History (short),*from the records of Melvin Stanford

Sanpete County, Utah, Court House records, Manti, Utah, 1852-1870

Scholl, B. Frank, edited by, *Library of Health,* Historical Publishing Co. Philadelphia, PA, 1923 Ediion

Schwantes, Carlos A., *In Mountain Shadows, A History of Idaho,* Orem Public Library, 979.6 Sch94

Seeley, Major William S. of Mount Pleasant, Utah, ca 1866

Sever, W. H., *History, Sanpete and Emery Counties, Utah,* Ogden, 1898

Shannon, David A., *The Great Depression,* A Spectrum Book, Prentice-Hall, Inc. Englewood Cliffs, N.J.

Shaw, Russell, *Abortion On Trial,* ,Pflaum Press, Dayton Ohio, 1968

Stone, Conway B., *Ships, Saints, and Mariners, 1830-1890,* Orem Park Stake FHC, BX 8673.4 So59sh 1987

Strouse, Jean, *MORGAN, American Financier,* Perennial, HarperCollinsPublisher,l 2000

Smith, Helen Condie, (aunt) *personal pictures, stories, and records, ca. 1990*

Swallow, Grover, *journals, personal documents, Book of Remembrance,*

Swallow, Thomas Charles, (Grover's father) *personal records and stories*

Swallow, Brookie Condie, *journals, personal knowledge, personal research papers*

The New York Genealogical and Biographical Records, 1879

The State Records of North Carolina, The journal of the convention of North Carolina, 1788

The Story of Samuel Cooley and his descendants, FHL, US/CAN 929.273 C7764

The Virginia Genealogist, Includes land grants, tax lists, and various genealogy of families FHL

Tucker, James (great-grandfather), *Life Story* ca 1923

Twin Falls Times News, Twin Falls, Idaho, 17 Oct 1960

Virginia Company Records, 1622,1624, 1625,1628,1635, 1637,1638,1639, 1640, 1645, 1646, 1649, 1652, 1653, 1654, 1655, 1656,1657, 1659, 1660, Complete Book of Emigrants 1661-1699.

Walter, Alice Granbery, *The Journal of Abigail Langley of Nansemond County, Virginia,* "the Langley, Mason and Thelaball families of Virginia . . . were the progenitors of Abigail Langley. . . 1695, 1723; *General Ped File no. 1122, 1154, 1166-7, 1169,* FHL, Salt Lake City, Utah,

Warnock, President and Mrs. Irvin L., *Memories of Sevier Stake, 1874-1949,* Art City Publishing Co., Springville, Utah, FHL 979.255 K2w, Salt Lake City, Utah, 1965

Wedgwood, C.V., *The Thirty Years War,* Book of the Month Club, New York

Weibye, Jens C. A.,journal, voyage from Hamburg, Germany, 1862

Wheelwright, Lorin F., *Valborg, An Autobiography,* Pioneer Music Press, Salt Lake City, Utah , 1978

William and Mary Quarterly, collected by James Oscar Ivie, Williamsburg, Virginia, 1891

Young, Mrs. Jewel Waller, *Lineages and Genealogical Notes, A Compilation of Some of The Lineages And Family Lines In The Genealogy of CLOUD THRASHER BARTON,* B&W Printing & Letter Service, Dallas, Texas, 1973

Youings, Joyce, *Tuckers Hall,* The University of Exeter and The Incorporation of Weavers, Fullers and Shearmen, 1968

Your Ancient Canadian Family Ties, FHL, #971D2o, Salt Lake City, Utah

Young, Levi Edgar, *The Founding of Utah,*

Index for Part II
Standing Firm

[NOTE: MAIDEN NAMES ARE USED FOR WOMEN, IF KNOWN.]